Robin Vallacher offers an exceptional guide to social psychology. The book directs and escorts the reader by laying the psychological foundations of intrapersonal experiences, on which he builds the interpersonal and collective extensions that are necessary to understand social behavior. The book not only explains the basic findings and insights of the field; it also embeds them into a broader framework that extends the boundaries of social psychology. Last but not least, it is exceptionally well-written and fun to read.

    – Fritz Strack, Emeritus Professor, University of Würzburg, Germany

Probably the clearest, most coherent, and engaging presentation of social psychology that I have seen. Rather than providing a laundry list of topics, or exhaustively reciting the available research, Vallacher focuses on presenting a core set of ideas and findings, with the aim of ensuring that students understand key concepts. The book is clearly organized around a set of key principles for understanding human social behavior, and the presentation of topics nicely progresses in line with those principles.

    – Stephen Read, Mendel B. Silberberg Professor of Social Psychology, University of Southern California, USA

One of my favorite books in our field, *The Self in Social Psychology*, was co-written by Dan Wegner and Robin Vallacher. It is of no surprise then, that Robin Vallacher has written a highly accessible summary of research and theory in this introductory social psychology textbook. Notably, Vallacher provides enough detail on methods so that students can understand why the researchers came up with their conclusions, and also so that students may practice being good consumers of research by having enough information to evaluate the validity of the claims.

    – Kip Williams, Distinguished Professor of Social Psychology, Purdue University, USA

SOCIAL PSYCHOLOGY

This textbook provides a thorough insight into the discipline of social psychology, creating an integrative and cumulative framework to present students with a rich and engaging account of the human social experience.

From a person's momentary impulses to a society's values and norms, the diversity of social psychology makes for a fascinating discipline, but it also presents a formidable challenge for presentation in a manner that is coherent and cumulative rather than fragmented and disordered. Using an accessible and readable style, the author shows how the field's dizzying and highly fragmented array of topics, models, theories, and paradigms can best be understood through a coherent conceptual narrative in which topics are presented in careful sequence, with each chapter building on what has already been learned while providing the groundwork for understanding what follows in the next chapter. The text also examines recent developments such as how computer simulations and big data supplement the traditional methods of experiment and correlation.

Also containing a wide range of features, including key term glossaries and compact "summing up and looking ahead" overviews, and covering an enormous range of topics from self-concept to social change, this comprehensive textbook is essential reading for any student of social psychology.

Robin R. Vallacher is Professor of Psychology at Florida Atlantic University, USA, and Research Associate in the Center for Complex Systems, Warsaw University, Poland. He has authored or edited eight professional books and published over 150 journal articles and book chapters on topics ranging from intrapersonal processes (e.g., self-concept) to societal phenomena (e.g., conflict, social change).

SOCIAL PSYCHOLOGY

Exploring the Dynamics of Human Experience

Robin R. Vallacher

Routledge
Taylor & Francis Group

NEW YORK AND LONDON

First published 2020
by Routledge
52 Vanderbilt Avenue, New York, NY 10017

and by Routledge
2 Park Square, Milton Park, Abingdon, Oxon, OX14 4RN

Routledge is an imprint of the Taylor & Francis Group, an informa business

© 2020 Taylor & Francis

Library of Congress Cataloging-in-Publication Data
A catalog record for this title has been requested

ISBN: 978-0-8153-8289-8 (hbk)
ISBN: 978-0-8153-8290-4 (pbk)
ISBN: 978-1-351-20739-3 (ebk)

Typeset Interstate
by Apex CoVantage, LLC

Visit the companion website: www.routledge.com/cw/vallacher

CONTENTS

DETAILED CONTENTS

ACKNOWLEDGMENTS

Silly me. I assumed that writing a textbook would simply be a matter of, well, writing a textbook. I've been a social psychologist for quite a while, and I have acquired a pretty solid grasp on what the field is all about. So, what could be more straightforward than sitting down at my computer and describing what the field's leading scholars—myself included—have discovered about the nature of human experience in social contexts? What I learned—and in retrospect, what I should have anticipated—is that writing a textbook involves far more than describing the various principles and insights, supported by empirical findings, that define the ways in which people think about and interact with one another. Not that such a task is easy; I knew it would be a challenge to provide an overview of a field that both did justice to what has been learned and yet did so in a way that had a chance of standing out in a crowded field of other such attempts.

What I soon discovered after undertaking this task is that the creation of a textbook involves much more than writing a set of chapters. To convey what social psychology is all about, and to do so in a manner that is engaging and likely to generate and maintain interest in students with little or no prior exposure to the field, it is necessary to supplement and amplify the text with real-world examples, graphical displays of research findings, and photos that illustrate the material that is presented. And then there are the relatively mundane tasks of assembling the references, creating a useful subject index, and obtaining permissions to present material and photos from other books, chapters, and articles. Fortunately, I was able to do all this—but only because of the able and willing assistance of many other people.

To begin with, I want to acknowledge the consistently constructive and often surprising feedback I received from undergraduate students who worked in my lab at Florida Atlantic University while I was toiling on the book. The book's primary audience is, after all, undergraduates, so I wanted to hear what they had to say about the material I selected and how I presented it. They took on this task eagerly and were not shy in letting me know when they thought I could improve the presentation of ideas and research findings. I am grateful in particular for the feedback provided by the following students, several of whom have since moved on to professional pursuits or graduate schools in psychology: Robert Boswell, Victor Capellan, Emilee Constantakos, Savannah Cuddy (who also graciously posed for the facial feedback photos in Chapter 4), Selina Cuevas, Jane Fletcher, Sevonte Miller, Sean Mohammed, Krystel Orjales, and Michael Still.

I also sought feedback from graduate students who are preparing to join the professional and academic ranks in psychology and thus have a vested interest in the subject matter of the field and a keen eye for noting the good, bad, and ugly in the way it is presented. The following students at Florida Atlantic did not disappoint in this regard: Will Blackmon, Michele Stoehr, Emily Stark, and Joseph Williams. Joe also helped compile the references for the text into a coherent list. Emily played an especially useful role in translating my rather "basic" figures and graphs into professional quality images through her mastery of R. Much of the text was written while I was on sabbatical leave at Claremont Graduate University in the fall of 2017. While there, I met on a regular basis with very sharp and motivated graduate students: Leslie Acuna, Blake Beckmann, Noah Boyd, Sejal Desai, Shannon Feil, Krista Jensen, Jiing Jung, Minii Kim, Cara Phillips, Briana Pisauro, Rowan Pockat, Amelia Rodriguez, and Alison Young. In light of my focus on the text at that time, their feedback on various chapters could not have been more timely. Many of these students were preparing for careers in organizational psychology, so they routinely provided a novel perspective on many of the topics I was attempting to cover in the text, often with an emphasis on applications to real-world settings.

The assistance and feedback provided by several colleagues proved invaluable at various points. Judy Langlois, Todd Shackelford, Jennifer Vonk, and Lisa Welling directed me to sources of certain photos I wished to include; Jennifer and Lisa graciously made some of these photos available to me. Ryne Sherman, Melvin Lerner, and Andrzej Nowak provided constructive—and often pointed—commentaries on initial drafts of several chapters. I also sought feedback from family members, who I knew would be supportive but also would have no hesitation in pointing out where I needed improvement. My thanks are extended to my sister Catherine Wills, my niece Pauline Pardiwalla, my daughter Camille Fontanella, and my unbelievably tolerant wife Phyllis. Phyllis should receive a medal for her special blend of support, encouragement, and no-nonsense efforts to keep me focused when I offered lame excuses for doing something completely different.

Last, but certainly not least, I want to acknowledge the encouragement, patience, and efforts of the editorial team at Taylor & Francis. Paul Dukes was instrumental in getting me to undertake this task and putting together the contract. Eleanor Reedy took over the task midstream when Paul moved on to a different role at Taylor & Francis, and she didn't miss a beat in bringing the project to fruition. Alex Howard proved to be invaluable in advising me on the creation of figures and in securing permissions for such material and for the photos I wanted to include.

Creating a text that attempts to provide a faithful and coherent overview of a decade's worth of social psychological theory and research, yet does so in a novel manner, is not a task for the fainthearted—nor one that could be accomplished on one's own. If this text is judged to have met these criteria, you now know who to credit. Any shortcomings, of course, signal that I didn't listen to them as much as I could and should have.

Robin R. Vallacher
Boca Raton, Florida
March 2019

MAPPING THE BOOK

Chapters	Topics	What the book has to offer	Extras
1: The Scope of Social Psychology	The rationale/goals of social psychology; social psychology and other human sciences; the road ahead (rationale for sequence of subsequent chapters).	This chapter provides an extensive overview of social psychology. It opens with a focus on four reasons for the field's existence: explaining mysteries of human experience, understanding social problems, resolving philosophical issues, and providing theoretical integration for the diversity of human social experience.	Overview of classic and contemporary attempts to integrate social psychology: psychodynamics, social learning, cybernetics/control theory, evolutionary psychology, cultural psychology, and dynamical systems theory.
		The chapter then places social psychology in the context of other human sciences, from genetics and brain science to economics and political science.	An examination of how social psychology has translated enduring philosophical issues (good vs. evil in human nature, free will, human uniqueness, utopia) into topics that are open to research-based answers.
		The concluding section provides the roadmap for the subsequent chapters. Part II consists of four chapters devoted to intrapersonal processes (beliefs, attitudes, and values; emotion; self-concept; and personal control), which set the stage for Part III, which consists of four chapters devoted to interpersonal processes (social judgment; social interaction; close relationships; and social influence). Part IV consists of four chapters devoted to collective processes (antisocial and prosocial behavior; group dynamics; prejudice, stereotypes, and discrimination; and dilemmas of social life). In this way, the ideas and principles reflected in each chapter build upon the ideas and principles conveyed in preceding chapters. Important intrapersonal processes (e.g., attitudes, emotion, self-concept) play significant roles in interpersonal processes (e.g., social interaction, relationships), and both intrapersonal and interpersonal processes play significant roles in collective processes (e.g., group dynamics, prejudice).	A consideration of why social psychology, given its relevance to human experience, is the youngest science. The chapter concludes by providing a rationale for the unique sequence of subsequent chapters, emphasizing expanding levels of human experience from intrapersonal to interpersonal and collective processes.
		The concluding chapter of the text develops the implications of the preceding chapters for understanding and resolving important personal, interpersonal, and collective issues.	

(Continued)

Chapters	Topics	What the book has to offer	Extras
2: The Approach of Social Psychology	The scientific method; research strategies; social psychology and other human sciences; social psychology and biology.	An overview of the scientific method, with emphasis on its added value over other modes of understanding human social experience. The chapter then considers how science is adapted to explore the unique subject matter of social psychology, with an overview of computer simulation and big data in addition to a description of the traditional approaches of correlation and experiment. The advantages and disadvantages of each research strategy are presented. The chapter considers the relevance of biology, especially methods of genetics and neuroscience, for understanding social psychological processes.	The chapter provides a consideration of why people in today's world reject certain scientific conclusions regarding human nature and are suspicious of science generally. This discussion foreshadows concepts and principles in subsequent chapters (e.g., social cognition biases, opinion conformity, need for closure, in-group versus out-group relations). An embedded "box" that points out the non-representativeness of participants in social psychology research and discusses the implications of this for the validity and generalizability of research findings.
3: Beliefs, Attitudes, and Values	The function and organization of attitudes and values; the evolutionary, cultural, and psychological foundations of values; the relation between attitudes and social behavior; conscious and unconscious attitudes; mental control.	This chapter provides an overview of theory and research on how and why people develop broad generalizations about the world, from attitudes toward specific topics and individuals to broad values about what is important in social life. The chapter also focuses on the relation between attitudes and action, with attention given to the insights of cognitive dissonance theory. The chapter then considers two aspects of mental control: whether people are consciously aware of their attitudes, and whether they can control how and what they think.	Discussion of conscious versus unconscious thinking, noting the advantages and disadvantages of both. Overview of implicit attitudes and the Implicit Association Test (IAT), with a novel IAT test for sexism included. An overview of the dynamical systems perspective on the organization of attitudes and the tendency to impose coherence on complex information. There are several extras, embedded as boxes in the chapter: 1. The genetic basis for attitudes. 2. Selected items from the Need for Closure Scale. 3. A comparison of the ironic nature of thought suppression and ego depletion in their respective explanations of apparent lapses in self-control, using an incident involving Mel Gibson several years ago.
4: Emotion	Varieties of emotion; universal and cultural aspects of emotional expression; mind, body, and emotion; the role of emotion in thought and action; the means by which people control their emotions; emotional intelligence.	This chapter begins by discussing the varieties of emotional experience, the universality versus cultural variability of emotion, and the link between mind and body in producing emotion. It then discusses the role of emotion in attention, thinking, and action. The final section discusses how people attempt to control their emotions and the relative effectiveness of these methods.	Discussion of the evolutionary and cultural bases of emotional experience and expression. Discussion of the mental dynamics of emotion, emphasizing the relation between mental speed and anxiety and depression. Discussion of perceptual fluency and the concept of "flow" in emotional experience. Discussion of personal happiness, noting the adaptive value of individual variation in happiness. Discussion of emotional variability, emphasizing the temporal patterns of emotional experience rather than simply the "average" value of an emotional experience.

Chapter	Key Concepts	Overview	Detailed Description
			Discussion of the role of emotion in shaping thinking (e.g., judgment, reasoning) and action (e.g., optimal level of arousal).
			Discussion of self-regulation of emotion, with focus on behavior versus cognitive control, gender differences, and emotional intelligence.
5: Self-Concept	Self-awareness; sources of self-knowledge; self-concept formation; self-esteem; self-concept defense and change; self-handicapping.	This chapter begins by developing the fundamental features of self-knowledge, beginning with the (fairly) unique human potential for self-awareness.	The research on self-recognition in animals is presented to highlight the mental thresholds for self-awareness. An embedded box identifies the other species that demonstrate self-recognition with a mirror and thus pass the minimal threshold for self-awareness.
		The chapter then discusses different means by which the abundance and diversity of self-relevant information is organized into a coherent self-concept and a relatively stable level of self-esteem.	The chapter distinguishes among general processes of self-knowledge, including self-perception, social feedback, and social comparison.
			There is an extended discussion of cultural variation in self-concept generally and self-esteem in particular.
			The chapter distinguishes among how self-relevant information achieves coherent organization by means of introspection and the emergence scenario of dynamical systems (demonstrated with a computer simulation of progressive integration and differentiation of self-relevant information).
		The chapter then focuses on various modes of self-defense, including self-verification, threatened egotism, and self-handicapping.	The chapter discusses individual variation in the degree to which self-concepts achieve coherence, noting the relevance of action identification principles. An embedded box presents the Behavior Identification Form, a measure of individual differences in the level at which people think about and control their actions.
			An embedded box presents the Rosenberg self-esteem test.
			The distinction between explicit and implicit self-esteem is presented (with implications for narcissism).
			An embedded box presents the dimensions associated with the positivity bias in self-esteem.
			The chapter discusses individual variation in self-concept certainty and the role of such variation in promoting threatened egotism and self-handicapping.
		The final discussion centers on how and why, despite these defensive processes, people's self-concept can undergo dramatic change.	The chapter discusses how the emergence scenario of dynamical systems is relevant to change in self-concepts that are otherwise well defended and impervious to change.

(Continued)

Chapters	Topics	What the book has to offer	Extras
6: Personal Control	Personal agency; intrinsic motivation; self-regulation; self-conscious emotions; performance impairment; self-regulation failure; illusions in personal control; free will.	This chapter brings together two different topics in contemporary psychology that have in common the notion of "personal control." *Personal agency* reflects people's self-perception of competence and subsumes issues and phenomena, such as internal vs. external locus of control, learned helplessness, perceived stress, achievement motivation, high vs. low level control of action, and intrinsic motivation. *Self-regulation* reflects people's ability to transcend immediate self-gain in accord with personal standards of appropriate conduct. It subsumes such issues and phenomena as impulse control, delay of gratification, honesty, cheating, and regulatory focus. These two aspects of personal control are typically presented independently of one another and in separate chapters. But they both represent a counterweight to the field's assumption of the "power of the situation." And together they reflect two major dimensions of social judgment: competence (personal agency) and morality (self-regulation).	This chapter emphasizes two aspects of personal control: whether a person feels he or she can do something (personal agency) and whether a person feels he or she *should* do something (self-regulation). The specific phenomena discussed include self-perception of control and stress, subjective well-being, intrinsic motivation, self-awareness, conflict among standards, and self-conscious emotions. The final section discusses the problems associated with both forms of personal control. It focuses on performance impairment (e.g., non-optimal level of action identification), breakdowns in self-regulation (e.g., ego depletion), and illusions in self-control (e.g., free will belief, illusion of external agency). Embedded boxes present the internal vs. external locus of control scale (selected items), the Hohmes-Rahe Life Stress Inventory (selected items), and a discussion of "blushing" in humans.
7: Social Judgment	Personality inference; evaluation; attribution of responsibility; mental effort; priming; culture; biases in social judgment.	The chapter integrates the enormous literature on social judgment with respect to three issues: the function of social judgment, the factors that influence social judgment, and the factors that promote maintenance vs. change in social judgment.	The chapter begins by identifying the evolutionary foundations of social judgment and distinguishing among three functions of social judgment: knowing others (personality inference), evaluation (distinguishing good and bad), and attribution (assessing responsibility). The chapter then organizes the factors that influence social judgment in terms of mental effort, accessibility and priming, and culture. The chapter then focuses on the biases that maintain social judgment, including biases in thinking (e.g., confirmation bias, selective attention) and biases in action (e.g., self-fulfilling prophecy, autistic hostility). The chapter then discusses how social judgment can be modified or changed despite these biases by engaging perspective-taking and by means of the emergence scenario in dynamical systems. Embedded in the chapter are boxes concerning the reasons for liking cuteness and the tendency for political judgments to be based on nonverbal behavior, an effect that is apparent in so-called political debates.
8: Social Interaction	Function and goals of social interaction; self-verification; self-presentation; nonverbal	This chapter emphasizes social interaction, a feature that is central to human experience but which is rarely highlighted in a separate chapter in social text.	The chapter discusses the motivation for interaction with respect to evolutionary adaptations and the anticipated goals of engaging other people.

	communication; mimicry; behavior confirmation.	This important topic is organized with respect to three general issues: the motivation for social interaction, the expression of self-concept in social interaction, and the dynamics of social interaction.	Attention is given to several topics, including cognitive clarity; the need to belong; the distinction among acceptance, liking, and respect; loneliness; social rejection; Maslow's hierarchy of needs; and social networks.
			The expression of self-concept in social interaction is discussed in terms of the distinction (and potential conflict) between the desire for self-verification and the tendency toward self-presentation.
			The dynamics of social interaction are discussed with respect to nonverbal communication, behavioral mimicry, emotional synchrony, and interpersonal expectations (e.g., behavior confirmation).
			Embedded in the chapter are four boxes: the Loneliness Quiz (selected items); a discussion of the causal link between social rejection and obesity; the relation between the size of social networks and the size of the amygdala (brain structure associated with basic emotions); and the Self-Monitoring scale (selected items).
9: Close Relationships	Physical attraction; similarity; propinquity; social exchange; dimensions of love; evolutionary bases of close relationships; exchange versus communal orientation; attachment; sex-ratio dynamics; male and female agendas; dissolution of relationships; jealousy; cheating.	This chapter attempts to organize a large and diverse topic in terms of a basic set of issues: What determines attraction? Why do people go beyond attraction to form close relationships? Why do close relationships succeed or fail?	The chapter begins by noting the obsession with love throughout history and represented in literature, music, and movies, and points out the double-edged sword of close relationships (e.g., the loss of autonomy and the potential for violence in such relationships).
		Each issue subsumes a wide variety of principles, including evolutionary mandates, cultural norms, social exchange dynamics, and gender differences.	The chapter then discusses attraction, with emphasis on universal features of physical attraction (e.g., symmetry, culture averages), gender differences in attractiveness (e.g., waist-hip ratio in females, masculine vs. femininized male faces), similarity, propinquity, perceptual fluency, complementarity in immune systems (MHC complex), interpretation of arousal, and social exchange dynamics (e.g., reciprocity, comparison levels).
			The chapter then focuses on romantic relationships, including love. The topics include the triangulation of love, the biological bases of love (e.g., oxytocin), cultural differences and historical changes, the distinction between exchange and communal orientations, attachment theory, male vs. female agendas, the role of sex ratios, and homosexuality.
			The chapter then focuses on the factors that can promote the dissolution of a close relationship. Attention is given to perceptions of fairness, infidelity, and jealousy (including gender differences).
			Embedded boxes include a discussion of the language of flirtation, the ironic staying power of secret relationships, and gender differences in sexual regret.

(Continued)

Chapters	Topics	What the book has to offer	Extras
10: Social Influence	Behavior control; obedience to authority; persuasion; controlled vs. automatic processing; emotional appeals; manipulation strategies; norms; priming.	This chapter organizes the vast literature on social influence in terms of three basic means by which people change how others think and act: behavior control (external rewards and punishment; legitimate authority); persuasion (e.g., communicator and message characteristics), and manipulation (e.g., liking, norms, mood, priming).	The chapter begins by noting the role of reward and punishment in controlling behavior in animals and humans. Obedience to authority is discussed in this context, with a detailed discussion of the Milgram experiments. The limitations of heavy-handed influence are discussed (e.g., reactance).

The chapter then discusses persuasion, with a focus on characteristics of the communicator (e.g., credibility, vested interests), characteristics of the message (e.g., one-sided vs. two-sided, speech rate, primacy vs. recency, gain vs. loss, fear), central versus peripheral processing, and the relevance of the emergence scenario (e.g., disrupt-then-reframe) derived from dynamical systems, and temporal effects (e.g., sleeper effect, decay of emotion).

The chapter then discusses the variety of ways in which people can be influenced by manipulating their desires and feelings of obligation. The techniques include liking, scarcity, and appeals to norms, certain compliance strategies identified by Cialdini), mood manipulation, and priming.

Embedded boxes include a discussion of the effectiveness of torture to extract confessions and information and a discussion of how people detect lies by influence agents. |
| 11: Antisocial and Prosocial Behavior | Good vs. evil in human nature; evolutionary foundations; genetic bases; social learning of aggression; media and video game violence; culture and aggression; income inequality; threatened egotism; social rejection; norms and prosocial behavior; empathy; diffusion of responsibility; free will. | This chapter differs markedly from other texts by considering antisocial and prosocial behavior together rather than in separate chapters. The rationale is to show the duality of human nature, with the potential for positive and negative social behavior ready for expression in daily life (as well as in unusual circumstances). For both expressions of human nature, the chapter discusses the evolutionary, biological (e.g., genetic, hormonal), and cultural factors that are relevant.

Although antisocial and prosocial behavior both characterize human psychology, prosocial expressions are more fragile and more easily derailed. This idea is developed in the context of classic research in social psychology (e.g., bystander intervention, suspicion and distrust, self-protection). | The chapter begins by discussing whether people are basically good or evil, altruistic or selfish, in their approach to social life. Different forms of hurting and helping are distinguished. The evolutionary foundations of both tendencies are then developed, as are hormonal causes and gender differences.

The chapter then discusses the factors that bring out the aggressive potential in people. Emphasis is placed on social learning generally, with attention devoted to media and video game violence. Discussion also centers on societal factors, including income inequality, cultures that devalue and suppress women, culture of honor, and urban vs. rural regions.

The chapter then identifies triggers of aggression, including frustration and discomfort, revenge, loss of self-control, threatened egotism, social isolation and rejection, and the availability of weapons. Included here is a discussion of the factors that combine to increase the likelihood of school shootings.

The chapter then focuses on the bases of prosocial behavior. Emphasis is given to universal social norms, especially reciprocity and social responsibility, and urban versus rural regions. |

		The chapter then notes that despite the normative and geographical factors that support prosocial action, people often fail to act accordingly if these factors are overwhelmed by psychological factors such as informational influence, diffusion of responsibility, anonymity, and information that undermines belief in free will.
		An embedded box highlights research on the fragility of the "Good Samaritan" tendency.
12: Group Dynamics	Defining features of groups; evolutionary foundations; social identity; group mind; group polarization; individuality in groups; deindividuation; roles; leadership; individual versus group performance; social networks; social relations in modern society.	This chapter identifies principles of group dynamics that are common to classic theory and research and to contemporary perspectives. The voluminous literature on groups is organized into four sections.
		The chapter begins by asking the simple question, "What are groups and why do people form them?" Four factors are discussed that turn a gathering of people into a group. The attraction to groups is discussed in terms of evolutionary mandates, some of which are less relevant today than in our ancestral past, and in terms of personal motives such as social identity.
		The chapter highlights several perspectives, including evolutionary psychology, social exchange, and dynamical systems, that have been shown in earlier chapters to characterize intrapersonal and interpersonal processes. So although people think and behave differently in groups than as individuals, the underlying principles are remarkably similar.
		A computer simulation model is presented, for example, that shows how the emergence of social structure follows the same dynamical scenario as the emergence of self-concept structure discussed in the chapter on self-concept (Chapter 5).
		The chapter then addresses how groups alter the way individuals think. The classic work on group mind is discussed in terms of coherence processes and integrated with contemporary perspectives on conformity, groupthink, group polarization, and the emergence of norms and attitudes.
		The positive versus negative manifestations of deindividuation capture the central theme throughout the book that good and bad behavior often are traceable to the same underlying dynamics.
		The chapter then addresses how individuals' actions are altered in group contexts. This provides a context for discussion of several topics, including deindividuation (with both positive and negative manifestations), behavioral contagion, the emergence of social roles, leadership, social loafing, and performance facilitation versus impairment.
		A key feature of this chapter is the extended discussion of social networks in modern society. Basic properties of networks are discussed, including scale-free networks, small-world phenomenon, social capital, and clustering within networks. This section concludes with a discussion of the implications of networks for social processes in contemporary society, including the rise of echo chambers and changes in the nature of social interaction.
		The chapter then focuses on social networks, a topic that is rarely addressed in texts despite its emergence as a widespread phenomenon in recent years.
		An embedded box discusses the pros and cons of brainstorming in groups.

(Continued)

Chapters	Topics	What the book has to offer	Extras
13: Prejudice, Stereotypes, and Discrimination	Social identity; in-group versus out-group relations; mind perception; discrimination; intergroup conflict; personality and prejudice; cognitive biases; self-fulfilling prophecy; modern racism; implicit prejudice; reduction of intergroup conflict.	This chapter organizes the classic and contemporary work on this central topic in terms of three issues: the nature of in-group and out-group relations; the factors that maintain prejudice and stereotypes; and possible means by which intergroup conflict can be overcome in today's world.	This chapter shows how phenomena at a collective level are built on processes at the intrapersonal and interpersonal level. The tendency to derogate out-group members, for example, is discussed in terms of basic processes of social judgment identified in Chapter 7 (e.g., confirmation bias), concerns with self-esteem discussed in Chapter 5 (e.g., threatened egotism), the nature of attitudes discussed in Chapter 3 (e.g., implicit attitudes), and dynamics of social interaction discussed in Chapter 8 (e.g., self-fulfilling prophecy).
		The nature of intergroup relations is discussed in terms of the positive feedback loop among thought (stereotypes), emotion (prejudice), and action (discrimination) that was emphasized in Chapters 3 and 4.	But judgments of out-groups also have unique qualities, including dehumanization (denial of mental complexity and self-conscious emotions) and suppression of individual differences.
		The maintenance of negative intergroup relations is also traced to factors introduced in earlier chapters	The discussion of classic theory and research on discrimination is expanded to include recent work on the dynamics of inter-group conflict and violence, including dynamical models of these phenomena, and processes of system justification at the societal level.
		on intrapersonal processes (e.g., personality, social judgment biases, implicit attitudes) and interpersonal dynamics (e.g., self-fulfilling prophecy, cognitive clarity, and conformity).	An embedded box discusses recent research showing that the hormone oxytocin facilitates bonding within groups but increases the tendency for out-group derogation.
		The potential for reducing intergroup conflict is discussed from several perspectives. Attempts to simply suppress negative thoughts and feelings is discussed as ineffective, in line with the discussion in Chapter 3 on the ironic effects of thought suppression. More viable strategies include the creation of superordinate goals and cross-cutting social identities–both of which are features of modern society.	An embedded box discusses the double-edged sword of religion with respect to out-group antagonism.
			An embedded box discusses research on the genetic basis for prejudice.
			An embedded box discusses whether stereotype threat exists for female scientists and has the effect of discouraging females from pursuing science as a career.
14: Dilemmas of Social Life	Social dilemmas; tragedy of the commons; prisoner's dilemma; public goods game; defection vs. cooperation; justice and human nature; just world belief; system justification; political orientation; morality; religion; moral hypocrisy.	This chapter is unique in integrating topics that are usually treated as separate in texts: social dilemmas, social justice, and morality. The common thread is that these topics all represent dilemmas for how the individual accommodates his/her personal concerns and motives with the demands and expectations of life in an increasingly interdependent world.	The chapter tackles what is arguably the fundamental concern of social psychology: how do people balance their personal needs and desires with those of others in order to promote a function-ing social system?
		The chapter begins by defining the nature of social inter-dependence, with a focus on social dilemmas and the tension between cooperation and defection investigated in social dilemma scenarios (e.g., tragedy of the commons) and games (e.g., prisoner's dilemma).	This issue is tackled from three perspectives that are typically treated as separate topics in social psychology. The chapter shows how the "individual vs. society" dilemma has roots in social interdependence, social justice, and morality. In so doing, a wide variety of perspectives is brought to bear on a common topic.

Chapter	Topics		
		The next section investigates the nature of social justice and its manifestation in social life. The discussion focuses on the extent to which justice is inherent in human nature, the tendency for system justification (an extension of belief in a just world) in the face of inequality, and how different political orientations interpret fairness and approach issues of social justice.	The chapter shows how social dilemmas are investigated with several mixed-motive games: the prisoner's dilemma, public goods, and the trust game.
		The next section looks at the role of morality in shaping how people think about the dilemmas of social life. Discussion centers on the relative roles played by rationality (e.g., moral reasoning) and emotion (e.g., feelings rooted in evolutionary mandates) in judgments of morality. The role of religion is also discussed, emphasizing its role in both promoting suspension of self-interest for the sake of the group and justifying antagonism toward those who don't share the group's religious convictions.	An embedded box discusses research on the neurochemistry of cooperation, showing that cooperation can activate the reward centers of the brain.
		The final section discusses recent research on moral hypocrisy and its relation to power and status in modern society.	An embedded box discusses recent findings regarding the effect of oxytocin on people's willingness to suspend their self-interest for the sake of a group.
15: The Relevance of Social Psychology	Stress and modern life; happiness; criminal justice; social change; what the future holds; concluding comment.	This chapter discusses how the theories and research findings presented in the text are useful for understanding contemporary life and for solving pressing social problems.	This concluding chapter is unique. Rather than restating the ideas and principles developed in the preceding chapters, the chapter focuses on the implications of these ideas and principles for issues in contemporary life. These implications, in turn, have potential for practical application to confront such issues as stress, personal well-being, criminal justice, and preserving the environment.
		The chapter begins by showing how social psychology can go beyond implications to applications. Four issues in particular are discussed: the experience of stress, happiness and well-being, law and criminal justice, and environmental damage. The points raised in the earlier chapters are brought to bear on these issues.	A defining feature of contemporary life is the rapidity of social change—both positive changes and undesirable changes. A computer simulation based on principles of dynamical systems is presented to highlight the nature and consequences of rapid social change.
		The chapter then discusses the nature of social change and the consequences of change for social life as we proceed through the 21st century. A computer simulation of rapid social change is presented to illustrate these consequences.	Despite the knowledge generated by social change, the future of social relations is uncertain and can follow scenarios that are pessimistic or optimistic. Certain factors, however, can tip the balance in favor of one scenario or the other. With these ideas in mind, the reader is challenged to consider how the future will unfold.
		With these considerations in mind, the chapter presents both a pessimistic and an optimistic scenario for the future of social relations, pointing out the factors that could make one or the other scenario manifest.	

PART I

SCIENCE AND SOCIAL PSYCHOLOGY

1 The Scope of Social Psychology

You obviously have begun reading this book, and I hope you will continue doing so. But before you go any further, ask yourself a simple question: *Why* are you reading this book? Really, what has prompted you to do this instead of, say, reading your chemistry or history text, or doing something entirely different, like going to the gym or surfing the internet? There are no right or wrong answers to this question. Indeed, there are many possible (and reasonable) answers, some that are unique to you and some that are shared with students (and other classes of humanity) everywhere. You may be sticking to an academic schedule or, conversely, you may be acting on impulse with no clear goal in mind. You may be concerned about getting a good grade on an exam, or you may be curious what social psychology is all about. You may want to become enlightened about personal relations, to understand pressing social issues, or to gain new insight into your own psychological makeup. For that matter, your reasons could reflect all of these considerations or others that aren't mentioned.

The wide variety of plausible reasons for this simple act says something fundamental about what it means to be a human being—and why science has been adapted to investigate the nature of human experience. Unlike our animal brethren, we can choose what to do from an enormous range of possible courses of action, and we are often inclined to think about our reasons for making these choices. Every day, we interact with many different people, form relationships with a subset of them, come into conflict with yet another (hopefully smaller) subset, and sometimes do things by ourselves (like reading a book). In each case, any of a wide variety of motives may be propelling the action, and these motives in turn could reflect a wide variety of factors, from those in the immediate context to those that are carried over from childhood. All this makes human thought and behavior highly complex and variable. Our personal and interpersonal worlds are rich in possibilities and awash in possible causes and consequences.

This is where science enters the picture. Events in the physical world can be complex and variable, with hidden mechanisms and forces that cry out for explanation. Science has evolved as the primary way of exposing these mechanisms and forces, allowing us to recognize and understand regularities and patterns in the world around us. Having proved its utility in understanding the physical world, science over the past few decades has been adapted to tackle the complexity and variability of human experience. Rather than simply marvel at the nuance and diversity of human thought and behavior, scientists attempt to identify the basic forces and tendencies that give rise to our complexity. Social psychology is the field of science that focuses on the forces and tendencies in people's interpersonal thought and behavior. This book—regardless of the reason that propelled you to begin reading a couple of minutes ago—is an attempt to show you how social psychologists go about this task and to convey what they have learned so far. Keep in mind, though, that science is a never-ending quest, often generating new questions as soon as old ones are answered. This book is intended to illustrate this feature of science as well, stimulating you to reflect on new questions even as familiar ones are addressed.

CHAPTER OVERVIEW

What Are You Going to Learn?

Understanding the complexity and variability of human social experience is a lofty goal, but too abstract to have much meaning for students who wonder what social psychology is really all about. To provide a more concrete and useful depiction of the field, I have organized this introductory chapter in terms of a few basic questions, each addressed in a separate section.

- **What is the point of social psychology?** What does social psychology attempt to do? What are the basic questions this discipline tries to answer? Does it clarify patterns of social behavior that are hard to square with intuition and common sense? Is it relevant to understanding and resolving persistent social problems in contemporary life? Can the discipline bring new insight to age-old philosophical issues concerning human nature and the meaning of life? Is it possible to identify common themes and principles underlying the enormous diversity in how we think and behave in different contexts?
- **How is social psychology related to other human sciences?** Social psychology is one of many areas of scientific psychology, which in turn is one of many disciplines of social science. How does social psychology intersect with the other fields of psychology, and with the other social science disciplines? What does social psychology bring to the table that is unique? If social psychology is so important, why has it emerged as a scientific discipline only recently, centuries after the development of other areas of science?
- **What is the plan for describing what social psychology has to say?** Social psychology covers a lot of ground, from private thoughts and nonverbal gestures to intergroup conflict and social change. How are the principles describing experience at one level (e.g., the formation of attitudes) relevant to the principles describing experience at other levels (e.g., the formation of groups)? Is it possible to present the subject matter of social psychology in a progressive way, with each new topic building upon the ideas presented in the discussion of earlier topics?

The Rationale of Social Psychology

Why Do We Need a Science of Human Experience?

Social psychologists, rumors notwithstanding, are human beings—not just in their personal lives but in their professional lives as well. The motivation for their professional activity is remarkably similar to some of your likely motives for reading this book. True, they are not concerned with passing exams and getting a grade in a course. But that motive cuts across all the courses you take. When it comes to social psychology in particular, the concerns that compel scientists to conduct research and develop theories reflect concerns that occupy a fair portion of your mental and social life—not just when preparing for an exam but when going about your everyday life. As an intellectually curious human being, your thoughts (and discussions with others) often center on four general topics that occupy center stage in social psychology.

Explaining Mysteries of Human Experience

Social psychology is unlike other scientific disciplines—geology, astronomy, chemistry, and so on—in that people have a privileged relationship with the field's subject matter. We don't know what it's like to be a rock, a star, or a molecule, but we have a pretty good feel for how people think, feel, and interact with one another. Having interpersonal experiences, however, is no guarantee that these experiences are accurately interpreted, and it certainly does not guarantee that we have "deep" insight into the basic processes shaping how we think and behave—or into the process of interpretation, for that matter.

Personal observation, experience, and intuition may be suspect, but surely there are some obvious principles that provide a backdrop for all of our social experiences. Two principles in particular seem undeniable. The first is that people are motivated to seek rewarding states of affairs and to avoid those that are punishing or costly. Thus, we prefer pleasant activities over painful ones, we want to be liked rather than despised, and we would rather win than lose when competing with others. The second, equally straightforward principle is that people's thoughts shape and control how they behave. Humans have impressive minds, know how to use them, and put them to use before doing things. Thus, we weigh the pros and cons of different courses of action, we formulate plans, and we consider the implications of acting in a certain fashion. The results of these mental processes then set the stage for what we actually do.

Individually, each of these principles is very sensible; taken together, they would seem to account for just about everything we do. Thus, the typical human act involves a person exercising his or her mental capacities in service of maximizing his or her personal gain in some setting. With these fundamental features of human behavior in hand, understanding any specific topic—from making online purchases to forming romantic relations—should amount to little more than filling in the blanks. This should make social psychology easy.

Social psychology, as we shall see, is not that easy. The two intuitions noted earlier—that people seek positive outcomes and operate with mental control—have been repeatedly called into question over the last several decades as clear exemptions to them have been demonstrated in psychological research. In fact, these intuitively sensible notions are commonly relegated to the role of a straw man in relation to some less obvious and "deeper" principle that is advanced to explain how people *really* operate. Social psychologists have become especially adept at framing a wide variety of social processes as counterintuitive and then coming up with insightful explanations for them.

To get a feel for the various mysteries identified by social psychologists, consider the following ideas. Each is well documented and has changed how we think about the nature of human social experience. I do not want to spoil the surprise by describing how these mysteries are resolved—this chapter is designed to whet your appetite, not satisfy it—but I do indicate the chapters that explore them in detail in case you wish to take a peek.

- Trying not to think about something can cause people to think about nothing else. (Chapter 3)
- An intense emotional state, whether positive or negative, tends to dissipate more quickly than does a less intense emotional state. (Chapter 4)
- People sometimes will choose a course of action that is destined to result in failure, even when a more reasonable course of action with a higher probability of success is available. (Chapter 5)
- People sometimes come to dislike actions for which they are handsomely rewarded. (Chapter 6)
- The more abundant and complex the information concerning a topic, the greater the likelihood that people will form a simple judgment about the topic. (Chapter 7)
- Some people prefer to hear critical rather than flattering feedback about themselves and seek out others who are likely to provide such feedback. (Chapter 8)
- The past relationships people remember most vividly are not the most passionate or long-lasting ones, but rather the ones they tried to keep secret. (Chapter 9)
- People are more influenced by someone who exercises little or no control than by someone who exercises strong and obvious control over them. (Chapter 10)

- Having very high self-esteem is sometimes a greater risk factor for antisocial behavior than is having low self-esteem. (Chapter 11)
- The same factors that promote horrific acts of violence can promote heroism and acts of compassion. (Chapter 12)
- The less certain a person is about a personally important topic, the more likely he or she will demonstrate intolerance toward others with a dissimilar opinion. (Chapter 13)
- The stronger a person's belief in justice, the greater the potential for derogating victims of crime and misfortune. (Chapter 14)
- Paying close attention to the details of an event make people vulnerable to arbitrary interpretations of the event's meaning. (Chapter 15)

These strange features of human thought and behavior, as well as many others, will be demystified in the succeeding chapters. In each case, what looks mysterious on the surface becomes quite understandable when couched in terms of basic principles that are quite sensible.

Understanding Problems in Social Life

Understanding the problems associated with social life has been a priority for social psychology from its beginning in the early 20th century. This focus is front and center in contemporary social psychology, with theorists and researchers exploring four categories of problems that pervade our lives: (1) the tensions and conflicts between different groups; (2) the forces within groups that can transform the way individuals think and behave; (3) the potential for discord (and worse) in interpersonal relations; and (4) the factors that promote individuals' self-defeating (and sometimes self-destructive) behavior patterns.

Intergroup Conflict

Social psychology came of age in the aftermath of World War II. Entire countries had lined up against one another and engaged in military campaigns that led to the death of over 10 million people. This was not the first time that nations had engaged in warfare—human history is littered with violent conflicts that erupt with disturbing regularity—but social psychology had recently emerged as a scientific discipline with theories and tools to identify factors responsible for such events. Psychology labs were established at Columbia University, Massachusetts Institute of Technology, University of California--Berkeley and other institutions with the goal of shedding light on the horrendous events that took place during the war.

Many theories were advanced during this period, some of which are still around today. Some theories held that intergroup conflict stemmed from personality characteristics that exacerbated the tensions that exist when groups compete for resources or hold different religions or ideologies (e.g., Adorno, Frenkel-Brunswick, Levinson,& Sanford, 1950; Rokeach, 1960). The assumption was that intergroup conflict carried to the extreme of warfare was an expression of individual pathologies (e.g., intolerance, belief in the superiority vs. inferiority of different ethnic groups) that could in principle be minimized, if not eliminated, with enlightened child-rearing strategies. Other psychologists turned their attention instead to social forces—such as economic stress within a society or competition over resources between groups and nations—that can provoke intense antagonism in anyone toward other groups and nations (e.g., Deutsch, 1973; Lewin, 1948; Pruitt, 1998; Sherif et al., 1961/1988). The assumption was that intergroup conflict could be held in check without escalating to warfare and genocide if the destructive social forces could be avoided or dealt with in an enlightened fashion.

Intergroup conflict remains a lively topic in social psychology, and for good reason. There are currently over 30 wars and violent conflicts being waged around the world, and for every one of these there are an untold number of less visible conflicts between groups at smaller scales (e.g., drug cartels, gangs in urban areas, feuds between neighboring population centers and tribes). In investigating the roots of such conflicts, contemporary social psychology emphasizes the nature of *in-group/out-group relations*. In the modern world, contact with people from different countries with different ethnicities, ideologies, values, and religions is impossible to avoid. There are good reasons for contact between different slices of humanity. But to avoid or at least minimize violent conflict when contact occurs, it is vital that we understand the conditions and forces that shape the relations between groups. Such understanding can then be recruited to prevent conflicts or resolve them once they occur.

The "Group Mind"

Humans are a highly social species, and our inherent sociality is a big part of our success and preeminence in the animal kingdom. We would not have survived in prehistoric times without a natural tendency to form social bonds and work together to defend against predators, acquire food, nurture offspring, share experiences, and build communities that address common needs and distribute resources. Sociality is vitally important in the modern world as well. We could not build metropolitan areas without collective action, and we certainly couldn't live in them were it not for our willingness to suspend our individual self-interest for the sake of the common good—from obeying traffic signs to paying taxes.

But there are some downsides to human sociality, some of which represent persistent and pressing social problems. Perhaps the more serious of these is the tendency for people in a group to sacrifice their personal decision-making and code of appropriate conduct in favor of the decisions and conduct of other group members. There is a readiness, described eloquently if somewhat cynically early on by Gustav Le Bon (1895), for people in groups to develop a coordinated mindset that is referred to as the *group mind*. The group mind is somewhat analogous to a horse stampede or the synchronized flashing of fireflies (Strogatz, 2003). Individuals may be as different as day and night when acting individually, but they spontaneously get on the same wavelength emotionally, mentally, and behaviorally under certain conditions.

Although getting in sync with people can feel great (e.g., at a party or a music festival) and can lead to practical group action (e.g., a political rally, assistance in a community emergency), the group mind is more often noted for its undesired consequences. In a large unstructured crowd, it can lead to mob violence, rioting, even murder and gang rape. Even in a formal group charged with making decisions with important consequences, the tendency for group members to adopt the same mindset can result in recommendations and actions that do not meet the standard of common sense, let alone rationality (Janis, 1982). These effects are not always observed, so identifying the factors responsible provides a major focus of contemporary social psychology.

Interpersonal Discord

Despite the tendency for people to adopt a common mindset under some circumstances, interpersonal relations are often characterized by tension, mistrust, conflict, and violence. People are motivated to get along, but they are also motivated to promote their self-interest and to avoid being taken advantage of in their one-on-one encounters. The greatest danger is when people have first learned to like and trust one another and then feel betrayed in some fashion. People are likely to feel greater anger toward a friend who has taken advantage of them than they are toward a stranger who has done the same thing. Homicides, apart from those committed during a crime, often involve people who know each other quite well, even intimately. Assaults also occur more frequently among people who are close than among strangers or those who are casually acquainted. Bullying in schools, too, is typically directed toward people with whom the bully has sustained contact (e.g., classmates) rather than toward strangers.

Interpersonal discord has taken on new forms in modern society with the rise of the internet and social media. People may feel mistrustful or vengeful toward someone, but having to confront the person face-to-face can prevent aggressive actions based on these feelings. The internet removes this constraint, enabling people to blast their enemies without fear of immediate (or even delayed) retaliation. The internet also makes it easy to damage someone in the eyes of others by spreading negative thoughts—not to mention unsubstantiated rumors—to a large network of other people. Cyberbullying, too, has become relatively common in recent years (Hinduja & Patchin, 2009), especially among young people who have grown up with social media and are able to use this outlet in a way that is often lost on older generations.

In light of these new means for acting on hostile impulses and feelings, social psychologists today are broadening their theories and developing new tools for understanding antagonistic interpersonal relations. The insights forthcoming from these efforts may provide clues about how to channel interpersonal relations—whether face-to-face or electronic—in more appropriate or at least more benign directions.

Personal Dysfunction

The next time you go to a party and meet someone new, tell the person you are taking psychology courses and note how he or she reacts. Although the majority of psychological theory and research centers on normal functioning, the new acquaintance is likely to make comments reflecting an assumption that you are learning about personality disorders, strange motives, and other forms of abnormal functioning. The focus on personal dysfunction does in fact have a long history in certain fields of psychology, most notably in the study of personality. The best-known theory in personality—in all of psychology, for that matter—is Freud's (1933) psychoanalytic theory, which has a great deal to say about psychological problems. But until relatively recently, social psychology has stuck to basic processes that capture how perfectly normal people think, feel, and act. Theory and research have always been devoted to problematic functioning, but the focus has typically been problems at the level of interpersonal relations, group dynamics, and conflict between groups.

Things have changed a great deal in the past few decades, with social psychology turning its attention to the various forms of personal dysfunction. Rather than viewing problematic behavior as an aberration better left to abnormal and clinical psychology, social psychology tends to view such behavior as manifestations of basic and largely adaptive principles that work well most of the time. A desire to think well of oneself, for example, is perfectly reasonable, but psychologists have shown how people's concern with achieving and protecting a positive self-concept can lead to problems of various kinds (e.g., Baumeister, Smart, & Boden, 1996; Jones & Berglas, 1978). Conversely, research has shown that some people prefer to think about themselves in negative rather than positive terms (Swann, 1990). This way of thinking sounds anything but reasonable, but it too reflects processes that are adaptive in other contexts.

Resolving Philosophical Issues

Social psychology has strong roots in philosophy. Basic questions of human existence that have preoccupied philosophers for centuries provide the focus of theory and research in modern social psychology. Four questions in particular have been transformed from long-standing philosophical debates into topics that are investigated in psychology labs: (1) Are people basically good or evil? (2) Do people have free will? (3) Are humans unique in the animal kingdom? (4) Is it possible to achieve a utopian society in which everyone is happy, productive, and morally responsible? As brilliant as philosophical treatises often are, it is difficult to declare any one of them a convincing winner in the absence of some objective means of evaluating them. Social psychology provides such means and thus is in a position to declare winners.

Good and Evil

It is hard to resist the temptation to make sweeping statements about human nature. For some people, human nature is considered basically good. People are assumed to be empathic, socially sensitive, cooperative, and well intended in their everyday interactions. Bad behavior is attributed to the corruptive influence of bad environments, tough childhoods, or extreme social conditions. The opposite point of view is held by others who feel that human nature cannot be counted on to produce socially desirable behavior. People are assumed to act selfishly when they can get away with it and to have a natural inclination toward aggression rather than helpfulness. From this vantage point, were it not for clear and strict forms of social control, people would pursue their own goals without considerations of morality, fairness, and the welfare of others. Yet others recognize both good and evil in human nature but divide people into one of these two camps. We admire and want to be around those who are naturally good, but we despise and wish to punish those who are naturally bad. Mother Teresa and Abraham Lincoln are in the "good" camp, whereas Adolf Hitler and Osama bin Laden are exemplars of "evil."

Psychology tends to avoid descriptions of human nature as either good or evil, and it has also avoided dividing humanity on this basis. Many psychologists assume instead that human nature is a tabula rasa—a *blank slate* that can take on different tendencies depending on the quality of one's experience, especially during childhood (e.g., Skinner, 1938). Anyone can become a saint or a sinner—a Lincoln or a Bin Laden—if they grow up under conditions that foster one of these orientations. And even if a person follows one path or the other, there is always room for change, with a fall from grace for the saint and redemption for the sinner.

While acknowledging the role of environmental influences in shaping good and bad behavior, contemporary psychology has begun to question the assumption that humans are blank slates (Harris, 1998; Pinker, 2003). This challenge comes from two sources. *Evolutionary psychology* holds that there is a human nature that shapes the way every member of our species thinks and acts. Just as our physical features have evolved over the millennia as adaptations to environmental conditions, so too have our mental processes and basic motives adapted to solve the demands of social living (Buss, 2015). Both revenge (commonly viewed as bad) and forgiveness (commonly considered good), for example, are inherent in human nature because each orientation serves an important function that enables group living (McCullough, 2008).

The second challenge to the blank slate assumption comes from research on *behavior genetics* (Bouchard et al., 1990). This approach maintains that individual differences are not solely a product of environmental influences but rather reflect in part the genes people inherit. No one goes so far to say that some humans are "good" and others "evil" because of their genetic makeup, but some suggest that there are genetic bases for things like impulsiveness and the threshold for aggression, and that these predispositions are risk factors for behavior that society might deem undesirable and deserving of strong condemnation.

Social psychology, in short, does not ascribe inherent good or evil to people, but it does recognize the role of both "nature" (evolution, genetics) and "nurture" (childhood, social forces) in promoting behavior that is exemplary and admirable or antisocial and discouraged.

Free Will

I opened this chapter by asking you to reflect on your reasons for reading this book. Did you do this? If so, did you feel compelled to reflect on your reasons, or did you choose to do so, fully confident of your ability to have ignored the request? Your answer to this question (assuming you chose to answer it!) is directly relevant to the age-old controversy surrounding the concept of *free will*. One side of the debate argues that people's actions are a direct response to social and biological forces, with conscious control limited to the means by which the action is implemented. The other side argues that people's actions reflect an inner faculty that makes choices between alternative courses of action and that can override outside forces and resist strong inner impulses. If you responded to the opening request without contemplating whether to ignore it, or if you complied because you felt compelled to do so, your behavior does not count as an act of free will. But if you deliberated before responding, your action comes closer to representing free will. It doesn't matter what you did—whether you ignored the question or took it seriously. What counts is whether you exercised personal choice in behaving as you did.

People like to think of themselves as having free will. After all, we make choices all the time and are capable of resisting courses of action that might lead to more rewarding outcomes. A person on a diet, for example, may feel a strong urge to visit the cookie jar before going to bed, but decide to forgo that action in favor of sticking to the eating regimen. Social psychologists, however, are uncomfortable with the notion of free will and tend to focus their attention on forces that induce pretty much the same behavior in everyone. There are two aspects to their reservations. First, free will does not make sense from a scientific perspective (Bargh & Chartrand, 1999; Skinner, 1971). Every action has a cause, even if the causes are hard to identify (e.g., subtle influence, a hormonal surge). Even if the person makes a conscious choice, it can be traced to a variety of influences, from genetics and neurotransmitters to family size and cultural expectations. In this perspective, the feeling of free will is due to people's lack of insight into the causes of their behavior (Nisbett & Wilson, 1977; Wegner & Wheatley, 1999).

The second reason reflects social psychologists' belief in the *power of the situation*. In reading this text, you will encounter persuasive demonstrations of this power, both in the real world and in laboratory studies. Slight changes in the nature of social settings tend to induce corresponding changes in people's thoughts, feelings, and actions. People may feel as though they are acting freely, but the fact that most people in the same situation make the same choice suggests that the feeling of freedom is an illusion.

Social psychologists over the past 30 years have begun to question the assumption of overarching situational power. People are still considered responsive to social forces and expectations, but they are also seen as capable of engaging in *self-regulation* (e.g., Baumeister & Heatherton, 1996; Carver & Scheier, 1999; Higgins, 1998; Vallacher & Wegner, 1987). This means that people sometimes act in accordance with personal goals or standards, even if doing so means resisting the influence of other people, the promise of rewards, or the threat of punishment. Self-regulation can take different forms, from resisting a cookie that would break one's diet to resisting the order of a legitimate authority to shock someone else because such behavior runs counter to one's personal values. When framed in terms of self-regulation, the tricky concept of free will becomes amenable to scientific investigation (e.g., Baumeister, 2008).

Human Uniqueness

There has been an ebb and flow over the years in the way people view their connection with other members of the animal kingdom. We have always acknowledged our animal status, of course, and no one denies that we are primates, similar in many respects to gorillas, orangutans, and especially chimpanzees. But philosophers and laypeople alike have held different views on the ways in which humans are distinct from other species and the extent to which humans have a privileged status in the animal kingdom. Rene Descartes, perhaps the most influential philosopher of the 17th century, argued that people are alone in having conscious minds, self-awareness, and a spiritual essence. In his view, which was widely embraced by people through much of the 19th century, animals were somewhat machine-like, operating in accordance with basic instincts and simple rules of reward and punishment. Apart from sharing basic biological needs, humans were presumed to have a qualitatively different psychology.

That view changed dramatically in the mid-19th century, especially in response to the publication of Charles Darwin's *On the Origin of Species* in 1859. This book, based on Darwin's meticulous observation of various animal species, argued that species are not static but rather constantly evolve in response to pressures from the environment. Evolution by means of natural selection—colloquially known as "survival of the fittest"—was offered as an explanation for the emergence of modern human beings, which first appeared between 100,000 and 200,000 years ago in southern Africa. Prior to that development, there were several transitional species (e.g., *Homo habilis, Homo erectus*) that bridged the gap between a common ancestor with chimpanzees about six million years ago and who we are today.

The connection with other species has been confirmed since Darwin's time by scientific breakthroughs in several areas. Paleontology, which focuses on the fossil record, has revealed successive changes in our ape ancestry leading to modern humans. Genetics has established the degree to which we are similar to, versus different from, other species. For example, we are more similar to chimpanzees, with whom we share 95%–99% of our genes, than we are to gorillas, with whom we share 90%–95% of our genes. And research on animal behavior has questioned long-held assumptions about human uniqueness. The more we come to know chimpanzees (and other species), the less unique we seem. We assumed that only humans had language, but chimps can learn to communicate with sign language (Gardner & Gardner, 1969). We assumed that only humans could fashion tools, but chimps make tools as well, although they are considerably more basic (Goodall, 1986). We assumed that only humans were self-aware, but chimps (and a few other species) pass certain tests that signal some level of self-awareness (Gallup, 1977). And studies of chimpanzee social behavior have revealed striking parallels to human social behavior, from mating to the formation of political alliances (de Waal, 1998).

The issue for many, however, is far from settled. Some argue that the emergence of culture has created a gulf between human psychology and the psychology governing the behavior of lesser organisms—even that of our great ape cousins (e.g., Nisbett, 2003; Shweder, 1991; Triandis, 1989). Beyond that, large brains enable us to acquire new ways of thinking and behaving that are not tethered to innate behavior patterns and instincts. Even the expression of our most basic biological needs—food preference and eating habits—varies in important respects across individuals and from one society to another. Social psychology has yet to settle definitively the question of human uniqueness, and this issue will surface throughout the text.

Utopia

> *Imagine there's no Heaven, it's easy if you try. No hell below us, above us only sky. Imagine all the people living for today.... You may say I'm a dreamer, but I'm not the only one. I hope someday you'll join us and the world will be as one.*
> —John Lennon, "Imagine"

Philosophers since Socrates in the 5th century BC have attempted to define the good life, and throughout human history there have been repeated attempts to create social systems reflecting these utopian ideals. Utopian visions vary, but most place emphasis on people living in harmony, experiencing joy and contentment, and having an enlightened view of themselves and their place in the cosmos. Utopian communities were relatively common in Europe and America during the *Second Great Awakening* of the 19th century, and many hippies of the 1960s flirted with communes in which the ugliness and pettiness of bourgeois life (as they saw it) were replaced with a lifestyle reflecting peace, brotherhood, and communal sharing—not unlike the vision expressed by John Lennon. Interpersonal harmony and enlightenment are lofty goals, but are they truly attainable? Social psychologists do not address utopian visions directly, but they do attempt to identify people's basic motives and the means by which they are satisfied, and to investigate the conditions that foster positive relations between individuals and between groups.

In recent years, a movement called *positive psychology* (Fredrickson & Losada, 2005; Gable & Haidt, 2005; Seligman & Csíkszentmihályi, 2000) has undertaken the challenge of specifying what it takes for people to be happy and get along with one another. The key idea is that in order to have harmonious social relations and cultivate one's potential, there must be more good experiences than bad ones. This sounds simple enough, except that research has shown that "bad is stronger than good" (Baumeister, Bratslavsky, Finkenauer, & Vohs, 2001). Bad events are more readily noticed and have greater impact than good events, and people are more sensitive to negative characteristics in one another than to positive characteristics. This means that in order for people to be happy and have harmonious relations with one another, the positive-to-negative ratio in their experiences must be at least 3 to 1 (Fredrickson & Losada, 2005). Achieving utopian ideals is clearly a tall order given the realities of human nature.

Positive psychology is part of a larger trend in contemporary social psychology that focuses on subjective well-being (e.g., Diener, 1984; Haidt, 2006; Myers, 2000), human potential (e.g., Csíkszentmihályi, 1996), positive interpersonal relations (e.g., Gottman et al., 2007), social justice (e.g., Deutsch, 1985; Lerner, 1980; Thibaut & Walker, 1975), and constructive means of conflict resolution (e.g., Vallacher, Coleman, Nowak, & Bui-Wrzosinska, 2010). So although utopia per se is not an area of theory and research, social psychology investigates each domain of human experience—from private thoughts and feelings to the relations between groups—with an eye toward identifying factors and principles that promote desirable functioning.

Integrating Human Experience

Explanations of specific phenomena are certainly important and the results of such efforts can have enormous utility. But the larger goal of science is to integrate different phenomena in a more comprehensive account. One line of research may demonstrate the forces that promote social conformity, another might come up with an explanation for heroic behavior, and a third might identify the factors that are necessary and sufficient for social change. This is all well and good, but the goal of social psychology, shared with the goals of every other science, is to find a common set of principles that integrate these seemingly quite distinct phenomena. Are conformity, heroism, and social change all manifestations of a more general process?

There have been many attempts over the years to identify a basic model of human behavior that can account for virtually everything we do. Not all models have held up well when subjected to scientific scrutiny. Here are a few that have done fairly well.

The Psychodynamic Perspective

Everyone has heard of Sigmund Freud, the early 20th-century psychologist who gave us such memorable notions as the Oedipus complex, castration anxiety, penis envy, the anal stage, and repression. Many of his ideas (including four of those listed above) have long since fallen out of favor (or are outright discredited), but the basic thrust of his theory—*psychodynamics*—continues to influence many areas of psychology. The basic idea is that people operate much like a pressure cooker. People are born with basic desires of a physical nature and seek to gratify them at all costs. As babies, this is not too much of a problem. When hungry, they cry and get fed in short order. When uncomfortable, they cry again and receive comfort from a caregiver.

As people develop, however, they discover that they cannot get everything they want, at least not when they want it. A teenager who craves food may have to go without satisfying this need until a regularly scheduled mealtime, and even then, the meal he or she gets (e.g., a healthful salad) may not be what he or she had in mind (pizza). Beyond that, some desires that come online with age (e.g., sex, physical aggression) are not supposed to be satisfied on demand and may in fact be frowned upon by others. Such desires may not even be acceptable to the person, in which case they are not consciously acknowledged but rather are locked up in the unconscious. This works up to a point, but in true pressure cooker fashion, the suppressed wishes and impulses behave like hot steam, forcing its way out through the gaskets that seal the lid to the pot. Because they are unacceptable, however, the suppressed thoughts and feelings that escape are not acknowledged for what they are, but rather they are disguised, reinterpreted in more acceptable terms, rationalized as justifiable, or simply denied altogether. These means of dealing with hard-to-suppress thoughts are the *defense mechanisms* that Freud (1936) outlined.

For years, scholars dismissed psychodynamic theory as untestable, if not just plain wrong. How can we gain insight into thoughts that are, by definition, not open to conscious inspection? And why should we believe in the unconscious anyway? Things have changed over the past couple of decades, largely because of new tools for exploring brain dynamics and exposing unconscious attitudes. Psychologists now realize that much of mental processing occurs without conscious awareness (Gazzaniga, 1992; Mandler, 1975; Nisbett & Wilson, 1977), and that people have unconscious attitudes that may be in conflict with the attitudes they freely express (Greenwald, McGhee, & Schwartz, 1998). Research has also confirmed that people attempt to suppress their thoughts, and that suppressed thoughts rebound back into consciousness under certain conditions (Wegner, 1994). And when people behave in a way that is socially unacceptable or conflicts with their personal values, they are remarkably adept at rationalizing the action, blaming others for it, or discounting its importance (Tesser, Martin, & Cornell, 1996).

The Social Learning Perspective

Psychodynamics is rich in concepts and deep in its implications for human experience. Indeed, this perspective proved to be a bit too rich and far too deep for scientists, who wished to keep hypothetical constructs (unobservable factors and forces) and untestable assumptions to a minimum. Partly in reaction to psychodynamics, psychologists in the early 20th century advanced an approach that came to be known as *behaviorism*, which claimed that human behavior can be explained in terms of rudimentary principles of learning. Just as a dog salivates when it hears a bell that has been associated with the smell of food (Pavlov, 1927), or just as a rat learns to press a lever that has produced pellets of rat chow (Skinner, 1938), people acquire new behaviors that become habitual because of the association between these behaviors and some noteworthy events and consequences. This simple idea was extended to the acquisition of social behaviors and became a dominant point of view for several decades, well into the 1960s.

Of course, even a committed behaviorist would admit, off duty, that people are more than rats without a tail. Once human social behavior became the focus of theory and research, the behaviorist approach morphed into *social learning theory* (Bandura, 1971). This perspective goes beyond behaviorism in maintaining that people can learn by observing the actions of other people. A person may not have been rewarded for telling jokes, for example, but he or she may nonetheless adopt this behavior in informal social situations if he or she observes other people acting in this manner—particularly if the behavior resulted in winning friends and charming potential dates. Learning through imitation and modeling is especially likely if the model is admired by the person or at least similar to him or her in important respects.

The social learning perspective continues to inform social psychology. In fact, the tendency for people to observe and model the behavior of others is more pronounced than originally realized. Even without intending to do so, people mimic one another's movements and facial expressions, even when there is no obvious benefit for doing so and the individuals do not have a relationship (e.g., Chartrand & Bargh, 1999). In a conversation between unacquainted people, for example, if one person rubs his or her face, the other person is likely to follow suit, usually without awareness that he or she is doing so and without a concern with immediate or long-term benefits. People are highly social animals and have an inherent tendency to achieve *behavioral coordination* with one another (e.g., Dijksterhuis & Bargh, 2001; Marsh, Richardson, Baron, & Schmidt, 2006; Newtson, 1994). Coordination, which includes imitation and mimicry, facilitates social bonding and is critical for performing actions that cannot be done by one person alone.

The Control Systems Perspective

The social learning perspective does not pay the mind a great deal of respect. It assumes that thought processes are designed primarily to notice and remember what other people do and what consequences follow from these behaviors. In essence, thinking is a means for learning without having to stumble through life in a trial-and-error fashion. Not a great deal of intellect is required for this function, and in fact social learning is fairly widespread among mammalian species with far less brain power than that of humans. A somewhat more flattering view, informed by *cybernetics* (Weiner, 1948), is provided by theories emphasizing *self-control* mechanisms (e.g., Carver & Scheier, 2002; Miller, Galanter, & Pribram, 1960; Powers, 1973).

The goal of cybernetics is to understand the function of systems that have goals and means of assessing whether there is progress in achieving these goals. The thermostat that controls room temperature provides a useful metaphor. In a thermostat system, there is a continuous sampling of the current air temperature. This input information goes to a device that compares the sensed value to the thermostat's setting. If the two values are the same, nothing happens—the system is at an equilibrium. But if the device detects a difference between the values, it sends a message that activates another device that begins to dump warm or cold air into the room. Eventually this process eliminates the discrepancy between the thermostat's setting and the room temperature. In this way, the system regulates itself and maintains a state of equilibrium (desired room temperature) despite factors (sunlight, an open window, large number of people in the room) that move the room temperature away from the equilibrium value.

Clearly people are a lot more complex than a thermostat. But the basic process has intuitive appeal and resonates well with everyday notions of goal-directed behavior. Some goals are specific and short term, such as getting to class on time, maintaining a low-calorie diet, or finishing a chapter in a social psychology text. Other goals are broader and long term: graduating from college, mastering a new sport, winning someone's affection. In each case, the person assesses the degree to which his or her current behavior or situation is discrepant from the goal. When a discrepancy is perceived, the person engages in mental and behavioral processes intended to eliminate the discrepancy and thereby achieve the goal. Psychological models based on this idea add emotion to the mix (e.g., Carver & Scheier, 2002; Higgins, 1987). *Positive emotions* signal that a discrepancy has been reduced. People feel excited or relieved when they have acted in a way that has achieved a goal or at least made progress in reducing a discrepancy. *Negative emotions* are associated with discrepancies between a goal and the current state: the larger the discrepancy, the more negative (e.g., anxious or depressed) the person feels.

The control systems perspective thus provides a simple and elegant way of thinking about the relationship between mental processes, goals and values, emotion, and action. It also provides a counterpoint to the assumption that people's actions are dictated solely by situational factors. People operating as self-control systems can resist temptations, postpone gratification, help others in need without expectation of reward, and defy legitimate authority—assuming they have the relevant goals or values in place to keep their behavior on track.

The Evolutionary Perspective

The suggestion that species evolved by means of natural selection was highly controversial when first introduced by Darwin in the mid-19th century. People balked at the prospect that they were closer to monkeys than to God. They found it hard to accept the idea that if they could somehow trace their ancestry back to the beginning of life on earth, there would be no Adam or Eve in a Garden of Eden, but rather bacteria-like organisms confined to swamps. No one was remotely aware that the earth was 4.5 billion years old, there was no understanding of genetics, and no one suspected that the ground in certain parts of the world was littered with fossils of extinct species—including species that were transitional between primitive apes and modern humans. For that matter, most people had never seen a monkey.

All that has changed, of course, since Darwin's time. We have made amazing strides in our knowledge of the earth, genetics, the fossil record, and the diversity of species that have lived on this planet. In every instance, these strides have provided confirmatory evidence for Darwin's theory. For the most part, people who are familiar with science have no problem with the idea that species evolve over time, and that humans are no exception. But in recent years, evolutionary principles have been applied to human psychology (e.g., Buss, 2015; Dunbar & Barrett, 2007), and once again some people feel a bit edgy and skeptical.

The central idea of *evolutionary psychology* is that the human mind evolved many millennia ago under conditions that are dramatically different than the conditions in which we now live. The world was dangerous, unpredictable, and no doubt quite mysterious for the first modern humans, who first appeared in southern Africa about 150,000 years ago. There was no medical care, advanced technology, sophisticated weaponry, agricultural systems, governments, laws, emergency warning systems, history books, or anger management courses. The selection pressures were intense, and mortality rates were very high, with relatively few people living into their thirties or even surviving childhood. On top of this, human ancestors were frail compared to other species and thus defenseless as individuals against predators. Against this backdrop, certain adaptations were critical to ensure survival of the species. Evolution requires uneven mortality; only those individuals who display the "right" characteristics have a chance of reaching adulthood, securing a mate, and passing on their genes to their offspring. The differential survival rates of human ancestors effectively eliminated traits that were not adaptive, while reinforcing traits that were useful.

Some general traits were selected for, including big and powerful brains, a strong desire to form social bonds, and attachment to offspring. But evolutionary psychologists go further than this. They argue that a large number of specific preferences and motives were selected for and these became ingrained as information-processing "modules" in the human brain. These mental modules include kin selection (preferential helping and sacrifice for close relatives), reciprocal altruism (exchanging help and favors with other people), selective sexual preference (attraction to opposite-sex people with specific facial and bodily features signaling reproductive fitness and fertility), pair bonding (monogamous male-female sexual relations), sexual jealousy (expressed differently in males and females), sensitivity to injustice (expressed as revenge), and an astute ability to perceive the intentions of other people (including deceptive intent).

The evolutionary perspective is prominent in social psychology today, in part because it offers insight into behavior patterns that do not seem personally adaptive or socially useful. Risky behavior by adolescent males is unnecessary and often dangerous in today's world, for example, but those males who were more willing to take on difficult and risky challenges may have had an advantage in establishing dominance in the group, thereby gaining access to young women for mating opportunities. Physical aggression, revenge, prejudice, and hostility toward people with different beliefs and values, and unthinking conformity in group settings all pose problems in the modern world, but these tendencies represent the lingering legacy of adaptations to far different circumstances thousands of years ago.

The Cultural Perspective

People readily adapt to the norms, values, customs, and lifestyles of the societies in which they live. This tendency distinguishes humans from other species, which behave pretty much the same way regardless of their environment. The malleability of human thought and behavior is central to the *cultural perspective* in social psychology (e.g., Markus & Kitayama, 1991; Triandis, 1989). Social psychologists have always been aware of cultural differences, but for the most part they assumed that such differences did not go to the core of basic processes of mind and action. If two cultures differed in their food preferences or in the degree to which men and women conformed to different expectations, that said little or nothing about the essence of eating or social roles. Just as people from England and Saudi Arabia speak different languages while operating within the same linguistic constraints, perhaps the greater separation of roles for men and women in these countries are simply different expressions of a more general tendency to structure interpersonal relations in a group.

In recent years, cultural variation has been accorded greater significance. There is growing recognition that basic processes of mind and action are fundamentally different in different parts of the world. Even perception of the physical world is shaped by cultural norms and values. Masuda and Nisbett (2001), for example, showed animated cartoons of underwater scenes to university students from Japan and the United States, and asked them to report what they saw. The US students tended to report something about the most salient, rapidly moving, or brightly colored objects in the scene—the fish that were swimming back and forth, for instance. In contrast, the first thing the Japanese students noticed and commented on was information about the context—the rocks and plants, for instance (see Figure 1.1).

FIGURE 1.1 What do You See?
Source: Masuda & Nisbett (2001)

This difference in perception is said to reflect a basic difference between cultures in their sensitivity to context generally (Nisbett, 2003). Some cultures, such as the Japanese, emphasize the context in which events occur, whereas other cultures, such as Americans, emphasize instead the events themselves, particularly if they stand out from the context. The emphasis on context reflects a cultural orientation that stresses *social interdependence* or the ways in which people are connected to each other by virtue of occupation, family, social class, or national identity. People in interdependent cultures explain an individual's behavior in terms of roles and expectations that provide a backdrop for everyone's actions (e.g., Choi & Nisbett, 1998; Kitayama & Masuda, 1997; Miyamoto & Kitayama, 2002). The emphasis on features that stand out from the context reflects a cultural orientation that stresses *social independence* rather than interdependence. People in independent cultures (e.g., the United States) are inclined to explain an individual's behavior in terms of the person's unique personality traits or motives rather than in terms of social roles and expectations that provide a common frame of reference for everyone.

In an ironic twist, the evolutionary perspective provides a rationale for the cultural perspective (Schaller, Simpson, & Kenrick, 2006). Culture is a unique human adaptation that enables survival in very different circumstances. Rather than being constrained by inflexible ways of thinking and acting, humans can adjust to the challenges and uncertainties associated with different parts of the world. This flexibility, though, reflects a very deep universal tendency to develop social bonds and achieve coordination with the members of one's group.

The Dynamical Systems Perspective

The most recent entry into the unification game is based on insights developed in the study of *nonlinear dynamical systems* (e.g., Gleick, 1987; Holland, 1995; Strogatz, 2003). This approach achieved prominence in the natural sciences in the 1970s and 1980s because it showed how very complex processes in all areas of science could be understood in terms of a few basic principles. It might seem that the rules of the natural world have little relevance to the principles underlying human minds and social processes. But because dynamical systems proved so advantageous in providing integration for the natural sciences, psychologists began to wonder whether this approach could be adapted to serve the same function in understanding human thought and behavior (e.g., Kelso, 1995; Nowak, Szamrej, & Latané, 1990; Vallacher & Nowak, 1994). Could the formation, maintenance, and change of personal attitudes, for example, be understood in terms of the same principles that promote the formation, maintenance, and change of norms and customs in a society?

The basic idea is that any phenomenon can be understood as a complex system consisting of parts—referred to as *elements*—that influence each other to produce higher-order structure for the system. The mind, for example, can be viewed as a mental system in which thoughts and feelings interact to produce such higher-order states such as beliefs, attitudes, and values. A social relationship can be viewed as an interpersonal system in which the interactions among individuals generate such higher-order states as expectations, rules of behavior, and global feelings about one another. An entire society can be viewed in a similar fashion, with the interactions among individuals and groups generating shared beliefs, ideologies, norms, and customs. In each case, order emerges by means of *self-organization* among the elements rather than being imposed on the system by external forces.

The dynamical systems perspective captures the tension between stability and change in human experience. Even a highly disorganized set of elements tends to generate a coordinated higher-order state—in effect, "order emerges from chaos." A person may experience a sequence of seemingly random thoughts about someone, for example, but in time the thoughts tend to converge on a global judgment of him or her. Once a higher-order state emerges, it functions as an *equilibrium* and resists change despite new elements that contradict the higher-order state. Having formed an opinion of someone, a person is unlikely to change his or her mind in the face of contradictory information. In like manner, once a structure emerges in a small group, it is difficult for a low-ranking member to change where he or she fits in the hierarchy. Attempts to change a mental or social structure may have a temporary impact but are met with resistance so as to maintain equilibrium in the mental or social system.

When change does occur in the higher-order state of a psychological system, it is because the organization of elements has been disrupted. From this disassembled state, however, the self-organizing tendency of system elements promotes the emergence of a new equilibrium. If a person's judgment of someone becomes destabilized, for example, his or her thoughts will become organized in a new, and perhaps quite different, manner. Respect can turn to disdain, for example, and vice versa. This scenario of assembly, disassembly, and reassembly of elements may characterize systems at all levels of psychological reality, from mental processes to societal stability and change. Because this scenario unfolds in time, research in *dynamical social psychology* (Nowak & Vallacher, 1998) tracks how people's thoughts, feelings, and actions stabilize and change on different time scales (e.g., seconds and minutes for mental processes, months and years for societal processes) (Vallacher, Van Geert, & Nowak, 2015).

Social Psychology and Other Human Sciences

How is Social Psychology Related to Other Topics of Human Behavior?

Long before social psychology was a blip on the scientific radar screen, several other human sciences had come into their own. Social psychology adds something new to the mix, but it also has emerged as a "hub" discipline that provides a bridge between other disciplines that are not directly connected (Cacioppo, 2007). Sociology has relatively little in common with economics, for example, but both build upon principles identified in social psychological research. It is also a hub in the sense that its methods and findings are directly relevant to a wide range of concerns, including education, health, sports, business, politics, criminal justice, and international relations.

Other Areas of Psychology

The "hub" status of social psychology is clear within the field of psychology. Its principles are informed by theory and research in other areas of psychological research, and the findings it generates informs these fields in turn (Van Lange, 2006).

Personality Psychology

Personality psychology focuses on people's inner processes as well as on differences among individuals in the expression of these processes. All people have goals that direct their behavior, for example, but individuals differ in their specific goals as well in their persistence in working to attain these goals. Social psychology also appreciates basic inner processes but tends to emphasize how these motives and concerns are made salient in different social contexts. Although the two disciplines are complementary, historically they have had somewhat of a competitive relationship, with personality focusing on individual differences that operate across situations and social psychology focusing on situational forces that overwhelm differences among people. In recent years, this distinction has blurred a great deal. Personality psychologists appreciate the importance of social context, and social psychologists recognize the importance of variation among people in the strength and mode of expression of inner processes.

Cognitive Psychology

Cognitive psychology focuses on basic processes of thought and memory. Social psychology has borrowed heavily from this discipline in recent years, utilizing its methods for measuring processes such as attention and memory. Perhaps the most investigated topic in social psychology is *social cognition*, which investigates how people think about their social worlds, including other people and personally relevant events. The relationship between social psychology and cognitive psychology is a two-way street. Social psychology has borrowed much from cognitive psychology, but it has also shown how a person's behavior, and the context in which it occurs, influence thought and memory. It has also exposed the role of emotions in shaping the process as well as the content of thinking.

Biological Psychology

Biological psychology focuses on the bodily processes that underlie psychological processes. It investigates the nervous system and the effects of hormones on thinking, emotion, and overt behavior. A subfield called *neuroscience* uses modern technology to investigate the structure and function of the brain. Social psychologists employ neuroscience methods to identify regions of the brain, and the connections among them, that are associated with various aspects of social experience, including face recognition, self-awareness, and social judgment.

Developmental Psychology

Developmental psychology focuses on how people develop across the life span, with special emphasis on the childhood years because of their presumed importance in shaping personality, adjustment, and values. It borrows heavily from social psychology, investigating the development of social thinking and social interaction patterns that have been identified in social psychological research. In turn, developmental psychology informs social psychology, by showing how such basic social topics as gender identification, self-awareness, self-control, cooperation, justice, and aggression emerge during the course of development.

Clinical Psychology

Clinical psychology focuses on mental illness and behavior disorders, and the means by which these conditions can be treated. Although social psychology focuses on "normal" behavior, many of the principles it has identified are relevant to the dysfunctions people experience in their personal and interpersonal lives. Clinical psychology, in turn, informs social psychology by showing the wide variation in people's thoughts, feelings, and actions.

Other Social Sciences

One cannot discuss the other social sciences without taking into account key issues and topics in social psychology. Even if these fields do not explicitly address these concerns, their theories make assumptions about social processes. The principles uncovered in social psychological research can therefore inform and perhaps refine sociology, anthropology, political science, and economics. But the relationship is a two-way street. These disciplines provide new insights and findings that inform theory construction in social psychology.

Sociology

Social psychology is closely related to *sociology*. Both disciplines study human societies and the groups that form these societies. They differ in their unit of analysis, however. Sociologists focus on the group as a single unit. Their concern is with how collectives—whether small groups or entire societies—affect the way people think and act. This concern orients them to broad group-level variables such as culture, social class, and ethnicity. For example, they might investigate why the homicide rate is so much higher in some nations (e.g., the United States) than in other nations (e.g., France).

The unit of analysis in social psychology is the individual members that make up a group. This concern orients them to variables of a psychological nature such as the degree of contact among group members, personal accountability versus anonymity, and the rewards and costs associated with different behaviors. The goal is to identify principles that apply to everyone, regardless of social class, ethnicity, and other group-level variables. In investigating homicide, for example, a social psychologist might home in on such variables as psychological stress, the influence of role models in the media, and the anticipated consequences of aggressive behavior.

Sociology and social psychology can provide complementary insight regarding behavior patterns and social issues. A sociologist might find that homicide rates are higher in low-income communities, and a social psychologist might identify the responsible psychological processes—for example, greater social or psychological stress in such communities.

Anthropology

Anthropology is the study of human culture—the values, beliefs, and practices shared by a group of people that are passed down from one generation to another. An anthropologist might study the social significance of various eating habits and food preferences in different cultures, for example, or the ways in which gender is implicated in rights, responsibilities, and social interactions. To gain such insight, the anthropologist observes the culture firsthand, becoming acquainted with the people and noting how their activities and interactions unfold on different time scales, from daily routines to seasonal rituals.

As noted earlier, social psychology has embraced the idea that culture shapes the way people think, behave, and interact with one another. But instead of embedding themselves in a culture, social psychologists focus on a feature of culture that can be isolated and examined under controlled circumstances. To compare how Japanese and American students see the world, for example, Masuda and Nisbett (2001) had their participants view the same objects in the same (experimental) situation. In this way, they could make precise statements about the Japanese and American differences that were not influenced by differences in their social environments.

This may strike you as somewhat ironic from a cultural perspective—after all, the context is precisely what matters more to Japanese than to American students. But without controlling for the cultural context, Masuda and Nisbett could not have been certain that the differences they found were due to perceptual tendencies per se, or whether the differences were due instead to the context in which the study was conducted. The concerns of anthropology and social psychology may be the same, but their differences in methodology provide unique and complementary perspectives. Anthropology can provide a feel for what it is like to be a member of a particular culture, whereas social psychology is better suited to identify and analyze the cognitive, motivational, and behavior processes that underlie cultural differences.

Political Science

Political science is the study of political organizations and parties, political institutions, and forms of local and national governments. Social psychologists have contributed to this field by extending principles of social judgment, values, social conformity, social influence, group dynamics, in-group/out-group relations, and decision-making to political behavior (Forgas, Fiedler, & Crano, 2015; Tetlock, 2007). This concern with *political psychology* focuses on a wide range of topics including voting, party identification, liberal versus conservative political philosophy, public opinion, and political advertising. Social psychologists also are beginning to explore social change, including dramatic societal transformations, such as the sudden transition from state socialism to democracy and free-market capitalism in Eastern Europe after the collapse of communism in the late 1980s (e.g., Nowak & Vallacher, 2019).

Economics

Economics is the study of the production, distribution, and consumption of goods and services. It compares different economic systems such as socialism and capitalism. Economics often focuses on large-scale social systems, such as the labor market or the monetary system, and the findings from this work have proven useful to social psychologists who study the influence of social systems on individual decision-making and behavior. Some social psychological theories are based on economic principles. Social exchange theory (Thibaut & Kelley, 1959), for example, predicts commitment to relationships by considering factors such as each person's rewards and costs, investments, and available alternative relationships.

Social psychology also informs the study of economics. Indeed, economics can be looked upon as applied social psychology. It is noteworthy that two Nobel Prizes in Economics have been awarded to psychologists (Herbert Simon and Daniel Kahneman). The emerging field of *behavioral economics* uses research on social, cognitive, and emotional biases to understand how people make economic decisions (Ariely & Norton, 2007; Thaler, 1980). Daniel Kahneman, for example, received his Nobel Prize for showing how well-documented biases and errors in social decision-making shape the way people view economic matters, including fairness and self-interest in making economic decisions (Kahneman, Knetsch, & Thaler, 1986, 1991).

The Youngest Science

The issues addressed in social psychology are important and thus would seem to have been the subject of intense investigation for as long as any other set of issues investigated by science. Yet the first social psychology experiment was conducted just over 100 years ago, and the first laboratories devoted to social psychology were established in the mid-20th century. If social psychology is so important, why did it take so long for it to become an area of scientific inquiry? There are three good reasons for the recent emergence of scientific social psychology. In an ironic twist, each provides an insight into the subject matter of social psychology itself.

"Common Sense" and Social Psychology

People are not shy about commenting on one another's motives and personality traits, nor do they seem to be at a loss when posed questions about human nature in general. The seeming transparency of interpersonal processes generates a complaint among some observers that social psychology is little more than "common sense" (Furnham, 1983). Why turn to science to explain what we already know? Common sense notions are certainly useful in decoding the nature of social experience, but there are two reasons to be cautious about giving a great deal of credence to ideas and principles based solely on personal observations and intuition.

First, common sense can lead to very different conclusions. Consider the following pearls of wisdom: "Absence makes the heart grow fonder" and "Out of sight, out of mind." Both have a "how true!" feel to them, but they are clearly contradictory. Knowing which one is correct is obviously important if you plan to spend a considerable period of time separated from your relationship partner. Or how about this pair of well-known adages: "Birds of a feather flock together" and "Opposites attract." The first suggests that people are drawn to each other if they are similar, but the second suggests instead that people are drawn to each other if they are different. Getting this straight is clearly important in deciding whether to establish a relationship with someone in the first place. Many other contradictions abound in everyday discourse (e.g., "The definition of insanity is doing the same thing over and over again and expecting a different result" vs. "If at first you don't succeed, try, try again"; "He who hesitates is lost" vs. "Look before you leap"; "You can't teach an old dog new tricks" vs. "You're never too old to learn").

The second problem is that many ideas seem obvious and predictable only *after* something has occurred. This *hindsight bias*—also called the *I-knew-it-all-along phenomenon*—has actually been documented in research (Slovic & Fischhoff, 1977). When an experiment is described along with possible outcomes, people express uncertainty over which one is most likely to occur. But if the experiment is described with a particular outcome, that outcome strikes people as unsurprising. So if someone were to learn that a study provided evidence for "absence makes the heart grow fonder," the person might claim (and feel) that he or she knew that was the case. But if the same person were to learn instead that the experiment provided evidence for "out of sight, out of mind," that too would strike him or her as obvious. Of course, once the results of research on the hindsight bias are known, people might be inclined to shrug their shoulders and say they knew it all along. Social psychology is not without its ironies.

Spotlight of Scientific Attention

When the scientific method was developed, it was used to solve concrete problems of a practical nature in the physical world. For the vast majority of human existence, people's primary concerns have centered on survival and mastering the environment—how to predict the weather, how to defend against predators, how to grow crops and hunt animals, how to stay warm in the winter and cool in the summer, how to deal with disease, how to create tools for agriculture, and how to fashion tools for fighting enemies. These issues, quite understandably, were the first to grab the spotlight of scientific attention. Science in its early days was synonymous with chemistry, physics, biology, botany, and medicine.

Only when the issues of physical survival were at least partially satisfied did people have the time and luxury to explore matters of human motivation and behavior. Even today, of course, many parts of the world experience enormous hardships in living, including famine, drought, tropical storms, pestilence, and disease. But in countries that have experienced some success in overcoming these concerns, people can afford to turn the spotlight of scientific attention on the nature of social relations, personal fulfillment, and other issues of a psychological nature.

This is not to suggest that social psychology is frivolous, an enterprise that people undertake when they have nothing more pressing to do. Quite the contrary, social psychology is becoming increasingly practical as we face difficult challenges of a social nature that hold potential for diminishing the quality of life, if not the odds for long-term survival of the species. The world is racked with violent conflicts, and these are likely to become more frequent and intense in the face of population pressures and competition over diminishing resources such as water, oil, and croplands. Understanding the roots of violence as well as the means by which conflicts can be resolved peacefully has never been more critical. This requires developing insight not only into the factors that call forth the "evil" side of human nature, but also into the factors that elicit cooperation, shared sacrifice, and altruism toward those who experience the greatest suffering.

Cultural Relativity

The contemporary world is not considered modern only because we have developed advanced technologies and gained knowledge about the universe and our place in it. The modern world is also increasingly interconnected. You can hop on a plane in Boston or Miami and land in Dubai or Warsaw in a matter of hours. For that matter, without even leaving your room, you can make contact with someone in these countries (or anywhere else) in few seconds by hitting a few keys or clicking a computer mouse.

The connectedness of the world has happened in an eyeblink of human history. Cultures located on different landmasses were isolated from one another for thousands of years before the first explorers set out to visit (and often attempt to conquer) new lands. This tended to insulate cultures from challenges to their respective worldviews, as expressed in their customs, religions, philosophy, and shared notions of reality. When people from different cultures did come into contact, there was often an asymmetry in power, so that the worldview of the more powerful party tended to prevail. Lacking opposing points of view, there was little need to seek scientific verification for the view of human nature and social order expressed by one's culture.

That has changed forever. Today, even people in the most isolated regions of the world are exposed to a broad spectrum of different beliefs, values, and social relations. And this exposure is taking place on an increasingly level playing field, in which countries exchange goods and services with one another instead of trying to dominate one another. This is certainly preferable to living in ignorance of other cultures, let alone attempting to conquer them. But contact has exposed the relativity associated with different ideologies, religions, values, and norms of social relations. We have come to realize that culture plays a vital role in shaping virtually every aspect of human experience, from food preferences and hobbies to relations between the sexes and assumptions about the meaning of life. In becoming exposed to other ways of seeing the world, people today are inclined to look "at" their assumptions rather than look "through" them. Our intuitions and beliefs have become increasingly explicit and subject to examination.

As the preferred (and modern) tool for achieving insight, science has become a primary means by which we attempt to discover what is truly universal about human experience. Because there is much in common among people in very different cultures, however, the focus on culture in contemporary social psychology is informative about the relative contributions of, and interactions between, our biological blueprints (e.g., genetics) and our social and cultural experiences (e.g., parenting, socialization).

The Road Ahead

How Will we Proceed?

Human experience covers a lot of territory. If social psychology hopes to do justice to this diversity, it must tackle an enormous range of topics, from facial expressions to social revolution. Imposing order on this complex array of topics is a daunting task. Our starting point is the recognition that these topics can to some extent be mapped onto different levels of experience—*intrapersonal, interpersonal*, and *collective*. This means we can talk about mental states, emotions, self-representations, and internal bases of thought and action as processes within the individual. Other processes characterize what goes on between individuals—social judgment, social interaction, social influence, and close relationships. Yet other processes characterize processes at the collective level—what happens within and between groups. This level of psychological experience encompasses group dynamics, prejudice and discrimination, conflict and aggression, and cooperation and altruism.

The plan for this text is to depict these expanding levels of experience, from the intrapersonal to the interpersonal to the collective. This sequence is intended to show the progressive integration of processes, from micro-level (intrapersonal) phenomena to macro-level (interpersonal and collective) phenomena. It is impossible to discuss social interaction without understanding the basics of social judgment, for example, and a discussion of group dynamics requires an understanding of basic social interaction principles. So rather than abandoning each topic after its preliminary discussion, further aspects of the topic and its relevance for interpersonal and collective experience will be developed in subsequent chapters. This should have the effect of providing a cumulative sense of social psychology to counter the disconnected sense you might have if you simply read the chapters on their own without the benefit of the chapters that preceded them.

The Approach of Social Psychology

Before embarking on this journey, it is important to clarify how social psychological wisdom is acquired and confirmed. Chapter 2, therefore, describes in detail the approach that social psychology uses to generate ideas, test them, and express them as basic principles. This will enable you to appreciate the ideas and findings in the subsequent chapters, which are presented in the following sequence.

Intrapersonal Experience

We begin by describing theory and research on the basic processes that occur in our mind and body. This may seem strange since this book is ultimately concerned with how people relate to other people. But to appreciate how we do this, we need to understand what goes on inside the person. How does the mind work? What are the fundamental concerns and motives that preoccupy people privately and that become manifest in their social lives? The relevant intrapersonal processes can be unpacked in terms of the following specific topics, each of which warrants a chapter all its own.

- Chapter 3 focuses on the *beliefs, attitudes, and values* that people inevitably develop as they think about their encounters with people and events. What are the fundamental features of mental experience? How and why do people develop generalizations about social reality? How and why do people develop views about the meaning of life? Can people control what they think?
- Chapter 4 adds to the account of mental life by describing what social psychologists have learned about *emotions*. What does it mean to feel an emotion? Why do people have emotions? How do people control their experience and expression of emotion? What makes people happy?
- Chapter 5 focuses on what can be considered the most personal aspect of social psychology of all—people's concept of themselves. What does it mean to think about oneself? How do people develop a *self-concept*? How do people protect their self-concept? Can self-concepts change?
- Chapter 6 describes theory and research on the capacity and desire for *personal control*. Why do people desire control, and why is this desire largely adaptive? When do people feel in charge of their behavior? How and why do people transcend the motivation to seek pleasure and avoid pain? When is personal control illusory or ineffective?

Interpersonal Experience

The next section of the book gets to the heart of the matter—how people relate to other people. The fundamentals of intrapersonal experience described in the previous chapters are on full display in our interpersonal lives. But these fundamentals take on different looks depending on which aspect of interpersonal experience is considered. And there are many aspects indeed, as evident in the chapters comprising this section.

- Chapter 7 focuses on *social judgment*—how people think about and evaluate one another. Why do people try to understand other people? How do people form judgments of one another? How and why do people resist change in their judgments of other people? How and why do people change their judgments?
- Chapter 8 describes the essential features of *social interaction*. Why do people interact with each other? How do people choose with whom to affiliate? What are the basic rules and processes shaping how people interact? Why and how do people try to control how they are seen by others?
- Chapter 9 examines *close relationships*. What determines whether people are attracted to one another? How and why do people form intimate relationships? Why do close relationships sometimes fail?
- Chapter 10 reviews what psychologists have learned about *social influence*. How do people exert direct control over others? How do people manipulate others' preferences and decisions? How do people change other people's opinions, beliefs, and values?

Collective Experience

Intrapersonal processes and interpersonal relations take on different qualities in the context of social forces that people experience as members of society. Many of the principles developed in the preceding section are relevant, of course, but behavior in a societal context has emergent properties that cannot be reduced to the principles of interaction between two people in isolation. An understanding of how people's psychology changes in such contexts sets the stage for exploring the potential for antisocial and prosocial behavior, the dynamics of thought and behavior in groups, the tension associated with intergroup relations, and the conflict between personal self-interest and sensitivity to the interests of other people.

- Chapter 11 reviews what research has revealed about *antisocial and prosocial behavior*. Are good and evil equally represented in human nature? To what extent are both tendencies shaped by one's personal experiences and one's shared experiences in a culture? What personal and situational factors trigger antagonistic behavior and altruistic action? Why is the tendency to behave in a prosocial manner so easily derailed?

- Chapter 12 focuses on *group dynamics*. What are groups and why do people form them? How do people think in groups? What do groups do? Do individuals perform better in groups or by themselves? What are social networks, and how do they work to connect people in society and around the world?

- Chapter 13 describes theory and research on *prejudice, stereotypes, and discrimination*. When and why do people judge members of other groups negatively? Why are broad generalizations about other people resistant to change? How are prejudicial attitudes manifest in modern society? How can stereotypes and prejudicial thoughts be eliminated or brought under control?

- Chapter 14 explores the *dilemmas of social life* that individuals experience as members of society. How do people balance their personal interests with the interests of others with whom they are interdependent? What are the foundations for personal morality, and why do people sometimes act in ways that contradict their moral code? What is the basis for social justice, and how is the belief in justice expressed in people's worldviews and interactions with others?

Social Psychology in Perspective

Chapter 15 revisits the major ideas developed in the preceding chapters. This concluding chapter, however, goes beyond summarizing what social psychologists have learned to outline how this knowledge is relevant to the many difficult issues that we face in contemporary life. The chapter also looks to the future. Do established social processes predict the nature of social change? What can we expect social relations to look like as we progress through the 21st century? The chapter concludes with the potential personal benefits of learning about the foundations of your intrapersonal, interpersonal, and collective experiences. The lessons learned in this text could be confined to your storehouse of knowledge or they could affect your conduct as you move forward in life. This choice, of course, is yours.

Key Terms

Intergroup conflict	Psychodynamics	Cognitive psychology
In-group/out-group relations	Social learning theory	Biological psychology
"Group mind"	Behavioral coordination	Neuroscience
Interpersonal discord	Control systems perspective	Developmental psychology
Personal dysfunction	Cybernetics	Clinical psychology
Good and evil	Goal-directed behavior	Sociology
Human uniqueness	Evolutionary psychology	Anthropology
Behavior genetics	Cultural psychology	Political psychology
Nature versus nurture	Social interdependence versus	Behavioral economics
Free will	independence	Cultural relativity
Power of the situation	Dynamical systems theory	Hindsight bias
Self-regulation	Self-organization	I-knew-it-all-along phenomenon
Utopia	Emergent properties	Levels of psychological
Positive psychology	Dynamical social psychology	experience
Subjective well-being	Personality psychology	

2 The Approach of Social Psychology

You will be exposed to a dizzying array of generalizations about social life in this text. Many of these ideas will strike you as reasonable and you may accept them without protest. Others may strike you as surprising, or perhaps as counterintuitive or even bizarre, and you may be less inclined to accept them without reflecting on them or checking other sources. In either case, you should be asking yourself, "How did they come up with this idea?" How do social psychologists generate the conclusions that get published and find their way into textbooks? This chapter is intended to help you answer this question. The focus is on the approach that social psychologists employ as they go about their job of investigating and explaining what you do in your interactions with other people.

There is a very broad answer to the question of how social psychologists resolve big issues and gain insight into important topics. They employ the scientific method. Science has served humanity well, providing understanding of the physical world that was unimaginable before the advent of this method in the 16th and 17th centuries. But it may not be obvious to you that science can solve the riddles of human experience. After all, people are not atoms, rocks, or weather fronts. The application of the scientific method to how people think, feel, and interact requires some explanation, if not justification. As we shall see, how to investigate human experience from a scientific vantage point is not always obvious, nor is it an easy exercise. But there are enormous advantages to doing so. Just as our understanding of the physical world has advanced tremendously because of science, so too has our understanding of the social world benefited a great deal from the adaptation of science to people's encounters with one another.

CHAPTER OVERVIEW

What Are You Going to Learn?

This chapter is not intended to provide insight into how people think and behave in social settings. We are not going to tackle the social problems described in the first chapter, nor will we describe the success of social psychology in resolving philosophical issues, explaining the mysteries of human experience, or identifying common principles underlying everything we do. The goal instead is to describe *how* social psychology attempts to address these basic concerns. Insight into the methods of social psychology will prove invaluable as the subject matter of the field comes into focus in the subsequent chapters. Before you can understand, let alone critically evaluate, what social psychology claims to have shown about the dynamics of human experience, you need to learn the ground rules for making important claims. The chapter is organized with respect to the following questions concerning these ground rules.

- **How is science relevant to social psychology?** Science is not the only way to understand what it is like to be a human being. And it certainly is not the easiest way. What are the advantages of science over other ways of understanding how and why people do what they do? What exactly is the scientific method anyway?
- **What methods are used to investigate social psychological processes?** Science was not developed to address the sorts of issues considered in this book. As noted in Chapter 1, the spotlight of scientific attention for centuries was on the physical world. How has the scientific method been adapted to tackle the subject matter of social psychology? What are the basic strategies for doing so? What are the advantages and disadvantages of each strategy?
- **What is the relationship between social psychology and biology?** The defining features of human experience—thoughts, feelings, desires, hopes, and so forth—seem independent of physical properties. A mental state does not have mass and its force is metaphorical in nature, not measurable like gravity or electromagnetism. When asked where thoughts come from, a person doesn't respond by naming regions of the brain or discussing how genes are expressed. But the disconnect between mind and matter is more illusory than real. Research at the interface of biology and psychology is finding common ground between mind and body. What research strategies are employed in the search for biological bases of psychological experience?

Scientific Social Psychology

How Is Science Used to Understand Human Experience?

Have you ever wondered whether you perform better or worse when trying to do something in the presence of other people? Can you run faster, solve word puzzles more quickly, or write a more effective essay if there are other people around? What if they are doing the same thing? For that matter, what if you are competing against them in a race, puzzle challenge, or writing contest? As it happens, this simple issue provided the source for what is commonly considered the first scientific study in social psychology. A little over 100 years ago, Norman Triplett (1898) examined bicycle racing records. He discovered that cyclists who competed against each other had faster times than did those who competed against the clock, and considerably better than did those who did not compete against either other cyclists or the clock (but who presumably were trying hard anyway). Triplett hypothesized that the presence of the other riders facilitated performance because it released what he termed the "competitive instinct."

To test this idea, Triplett recruited 40 children to wind up a fishing reel as quickly as they could. They alternated between working alone and working side by side. The results confirmed what Triplett had observed with the cyclists: the children had faster winding times when they worked side by side than when they worked alone. The results may not seem all that remarkable. But they do have implications. It suggests, for example, that you might run faster, solve puzzles quicker, or write a stronger essay if you do these things when competing against others.

By today's standards, Triplett's approach was rather primitive. Still, it qualified as science and provided an answer to the narrowly defined issue he was addressing. But more importantly, it helped to establish a new way of thinking about human action in social contexts. Since that time, this approach has taken hold in social psychology with thousands of studies conducted on every conceivable aspect of human experience—from the formation of private opinions to the political and economic transformation of societies. What are the essential features of the scientific method that enable psychologists to understand this enormous range of topics?

The Scientific Method

Science sounds technical and sophisticated, far removed from people's normal way of thinking about things. But in fact, the scientific method parallels in important respects the way all of us think. Without any formal training, people approach questions about social life in a manner that captures the essence of what scientists do when tackling such questions (Nisbett & Ross, 1980; Wegner & Vallacher, 1977). In both cases, understanding is achieved through a progression of stages. And in both cases, it is not uncommon for different conclusions to be reached through the application of these stages. In this section, we first describe the stages of the scientific method. Then we describe the criteria by which different conclusions—different theories—are evaluated to determine which one is better.

Stages of the Scientific Method

The path to scientific understanding often begins with a hunch or an intuition based on personal experience or observation. Perhaps you notice, for example, that one of your friends has a 12-year-old brother who spends hours playing video games revolving around violence (e.g., *Grand Theft Auto*) and watching TV shows in which fights routinely break out, often with one of the characters experiencing his or her demise. Perhaps you also get the impression that the boy has an aggressive streak and is easily provoked into physical encounters with others (playmates, siblings, unsuspecting pets). You begin to wonder whether there is a link between these two sets of observations—is the boy's exposure to video violence related to his aggressive tendencies?

You could let these observations stand and move on to other concerns. But if you approach this issue as a scientist, you would attempt to explain the apparent connection between video exposure and aggressive behavior. This second step—constructing an explanation that makes sense of one's observations—is the foundation of *theory construction*. A theory consists of unobservable constructs that are linked together in some logical manner. The concern is no longer with the specific observations, but with a relationship that applies to many observations that have yet to be made. Rather than saying that playing *Grand Theft Auto* is linked to altercations with classmates at school, you make a far more ambitious claim—that children who witness aggressive behavior by others tend to display aggressive behavior of their own.

A theory does more than provide a generalization of some observations. It also specifies the reasons for the relationship. The reasons are usually expressed in terms of a causal connection or mechanism. At this point, you go beyond observations entirely to propose some process that characterizes how people think and behave. In the case of video exposure and aggressive behavior, you might theorize that children learn how to behave by observing, and then internalizing, the actions of other people (Bandura, Ross, & Ross, 1963; Mischel, 1973). In developing this theory, you have left the real world of observations and entered the virtual world of abstract concepts and mechanisms.

Science does not stop with the construction of a theory. For a theory to be taken seriously, one must assess its validity. This brings us to the third stage of the scientific method—*hypothesis generation*. One cannot test a theory directly. But one can make predictions of what should happen under certain conditions if the theory is valid. This prediction—the hypothesis—is what one tests in science. If your theory regarding the effect of media violence on aggression is that children learn how to act by observing how others act, a wide variety of hypotheses could be generated. You might predict, for example, that children who witness violence firsthand (e.g., in their neighborhood) rather than on TV or other media should show greater even aggression in their relations with other children. Or, since the theory specifies that modeling of behavior is the critical factor, you might hypothesize that children who are exposed to friendly or helpful behavior should display friendly and helpful behavior in their social relationships.

With a hypothesis in hand, the scientist moves on to the fourth stage—*verification*. This is where the actual research takes place. There are various ways of conducting research, which will be discussed in a bit. For the time being, assume that an appropriate study is performed. If the hypothesis is confirmed, this provides support for the theory. But what if the hypothesis is not confirmed? For example, what if children who watch violent content are not necessarily all that aggressive? Does that mean the theory about children modeling the behavior of other people is wrong? Perhaps. But a good scientist might dig deeper and consider whether the theory needs to be revised in order to accommodate the new observations. One possibility is that children model the actions of others, but that they are selective in whose behavior they find worth modeling. Maybe the model has to be admirable or likable, for example, or someone of the same gender. If the theory is revised to take into account such subtleties, a relevant hypothesis is generated and then tested to see if it is confirmed.

The point is that the scientific method is not a simple one-shot process that ends with the verification stage. Rather, science is an ongoing process in which the results produced by research provide new input for theory construction, which provides the basis for new hypotheses to be verified (or not), and so on, in a cycle that holds potential for producing increasingly valid and precise understanding of the topic in question. Nor does the scientific method always begin at the observation stage. A researcher may be interested in a theory and get involved in the process by generating new hypotheses that follow from the theory. For that matter, a researcher might begin at the verification stage, testing a hypothesis generated by someone else. This actually describes a common role played by graduate students working in a scientist's lab.

This graphic visualizes the feedback among the stages of the scientific method. The process can start at any stage and progress through the others. If the verification stage produces results that do not confirm the hypothesis, these results are combined with the original observations and a revised theory is constructed, which sets the stage for new hypotheses, new research, and so on.

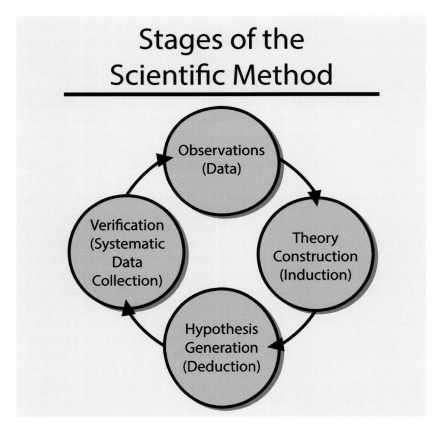

Evaluating Theories

Recall the study by Triplett (1898), which seemed to show that an individual's performance is enhanced when he or she is in the presence of others who are doing the same thing. Around the same time, another study seemed to show precisely the opposite—that people exert *less* effort when performing a task with other people present (Ringelmann, 1913). Ringlemann was curious whether men expend more effort in pulling a rope if they do so individually or do so as a member of a rope-pulling team. Ringelmann found that individual effort was less rather than greater in the group task. So who was right—Triplett or Ringelmann? Does the presence of other people enhance individual performance, or does it lead to performance decrements?

There are three general ways of deciding what to make of an apparent conflict between different theories. The first is to determine if the support for one of the theories is weak. Perhaps the study showing one effect is flawed, so that the researchers' interpretation should not be accepted. A critical examination of the research supporting a theory is always the first order of business when evaluating the merits of a theory. But what happens when the research is not flawed? Both Triplett and Ringelmann were very careful and systematic in their respective studies, and no one has challenged the results they produced.

The second approach is to look for important factors that distinguish between the theories. In Triplett's study, each individual was trying to distinguish himself as a top performer and tried harder when he could see how well others were doing. In Ringelmann's study, each individual was part of a team and had no reason to think that his personal performance would be measured, let alone evaluated. An individual could relax a bit without worrying about the quality of his performance. These are noteworthy differences. When the conflicting results are considered in light of these differences, one can envision a more comprehensive theory that specifies when individual effort is enhanced versus diminished in a group context. When individual performance is the center of attention, people *try harder* in group contexts, but when individual performance is masked by the overall group performance, people *try less hard* in group contexts.

This scenario is actually quite common in research. Several researchers tackle what appears to be the same issue, but using somewhat different procedures and looking at different measures. By comparing the pattern of results generated by these studies, one is in a position to identify factors that determine when one set of processes or another (e.g., enhanced vs. diminished individual performance) is likely to be operative. This enhanced understanding might have gone unappreciated had it not been for the results that seemed conflicting at the outset.

Sometimes, though, there is a direct conflict between theories that explain the same topics or issues. Assuming the research in support of the rival theories is equally solid, it can be hard to declare a winner. In such instances, scientists evaluate the respective merits of the theories in terms of their parsimony. *Parsimony* is achieved when one can "explain the most with the least." If two theories both explain a topic (e.g., formation of romantic relationships) equally well, but Theory A does so with fewer assumptions and principles than does Theory B, Theory A is more parsimonious and preferred in the scientific community. The preference for Theory A over Theory B is even greater if Theory A explains more topics than does Theory B. Perhaps Theory A explains not only the formation of romantic relationships, but also the formation of social groups and the transformation of societies, while Theory B is confined only to romance.

Parsimony is something of a holy grail in all areas of science. Physics, for example, has valiantly strived for decades to find a "theory of everything" that can unite the four fundamental forces (gravity, electromagnetism, the strong nuclear force, the weak nuclear force) in terms of a single set of principles that could be "worn on a T-shirt" (Green, 2004). Not to be outdone, many social psychologists aspire to find the fundamental laws of mind and action that give rise to the entire range of human experience, from personal processes to societal phenomena.

Parsimony as a general guideline is fine, but there can be a trade-off between "explaining the most" and "explaining with the least." A complex theory may explain many topics, for example, while a simple theory might explain a single topic. In this case, scientists must judge the trade-off: is the increase in a theory's complexity worthwhile because of its application to several topics? There is no simple rule for calculating this trade-off. For this reason, battle lines are sometimes drawn between different theoretical camps, with scientists fueling their respective sides by generating and publishing supportive studies. You will get a flavor of this when we discuss several controversial topics in subsequent chapters.

The Scientific Advantage

Science involves a lot of effort, ingenuity, patience, and tolerance for setbacks. The research studies that get published in scientific journals and make their way into textbooks are a small fraction of the studies that are performed.

A scientist might spend years, filled with long days and short nights, trying to find a way to test a hypothesis that supports a particular theory. Even if the hypothesis is confirmed, the scientist must contend with the razor-sharp critiques of his or her peers, who decide whether the research strategy was appropriate and whether the results can be interpreted in a different way.

Is it necessary to go to all this trouble if there are other, far less strenuous means of understanding social behavior? The answer, of course, is "yes"—if it weren't, this text would not have been written and you would be reading (or doing) something quite different right now. To understand the advantage of the scientific method, it is helpful to compare this approach with other means by which people gain insight into the nature of social life. After making this case for scientific psychology, we will point out some of the limitations of science. Interestingly, the imperfect nature of science is itself informative about the way people think and behave.

Implicit Psychology

Most people have never had the benefit of taking a psychology course, yet they feel they know how their minds work. Nor are people shy about coming up with explanations for one another's behavior. If people have confidence in their understanding of themselves and others, they may not feel a great deal of urgency in turning to social psychology to provide further clarification. As noted earlier, the way laypeople try to understand their social worlds parallels the scientific method employed by psychologists in understanding personal and social processes.

There are four key differences, however, between psychologists and laypeople in their approach to understanding how the social world operates. First, lay understanding is rarely expressed in formal terms. Instead, people's understanding is typically *implicit* rather than *explicit* (Wegner & Vallacher, 1977). People look "through" their theories rather than "at" them. They may not be able to express in words the criteria by which they evaluate one another, for example, but by looking at the specific things people say about those they like versus dislike, psychologists can identify the more general criteria that underlie people's judgments. Nonetheless, laypeople's implicit view of their social world may satisfy their need to predict whether someone is good or bad—no scientific psychologist needed.

Second, people's inferences about their personal qualities and those of other people are tainted with biases that mostly go unnoticed (Ross, 1977). These biases affect the things that people notice and consider relevant, their interpretations and explanations of these things, their predictions about the future based on their explanations, and how they test these predictions. One bias of laypeople, by the way, is their belief that they do not have biases!

A third difference is that laypeople often do not test their predictions. Sometimes it is enough to reach a strong conclusion, then move on to other matters without bothering to see if the conclusion holds water. This is likely when a person has formed a negative judgment about someone else, especially if that person belongs to a different group. Why bother interacting with such a person to see if he or she is really as boring or unpleasant as one thinks? Such *autistic hostility* (Newcomb, 1947) can clearly leave people with unfounded attitudes and unchecked prejudices, but the conclusions nonetheless satisfy their concerns with knowing others.

Finally, even if people did not see the world through distorted lenses, they still would come up short in their understanding. People simply do not have very good introspective skills (Nisbett & Wilson, 1977). Research has established that much of what goes on when making inferences and passing judgment happens at a nonconscious level (Dijksterhuis & Aarts, 2010). Perhaps that is just as well, at least under some circumstances. There is evidence that when people try to take conscious control of their judgments and decisions, they run the risk of undermining their judgment and reaching an entirely different conclusion (e.g., Wilson & Stone, 1985). Although this might be a good way at changing a personally dysfunctional or socially destructive attitude (as we shall see in Chapters 10 and 13), it could also lead a person to generate a judgment or decision that is less accurate or beneficial than the one that would have been generated if the person had let his or her nonconscious thought take care of things.

Implicit psychology, in short, may obviate the personal need to take guidance from science in understanding one's personal makeup and social experiences. However, this approach to understanding is not self-correcting in the way that science is, and it is prone to errors and biases that go unnoticed and unchecked. By studying these pitfalls in implicit psychology, one can learn a great deal about how people think and form judgments about themselves and others—as we shall see in subsequent chapters. Indeed, were it not for the pitfalls of implicit psychology, there would be little need for a science of social psychology in the first place!

Social Wisdom

Sometimes implicit psychology falls short in satisfying people's desire to understand features of social life. People can feel stumped by an event they witness or read about, or have a difficult time making sense of a personal experience that does not line up with expectations. A natural disaster that kills hundreds, a strange behavior by an acquaintance, a run of bad luck, or an unanticipated change in one's mood calls for explanation. When lacking an obvious explanation, people turn to other people who are presumed to have relevant expert and insight. Much of the time, people simply look to friends, family, or lovers to provide a meaningful explanation of events when introspection and intuition come up short. But people also turn to others who are charged by society with providing explanations. Religion has historically played an important role, informing people about good and evil, offering guidance on how best to live one's life, and providing understanding (and comfort) when bad or seemingly unfair events happen. In a more secular environment, people may turn instead to politicians, writers, and news commentators to help make sense of the actions of other people, groups, and countries.

So why, then, has scientific social psychology become a source of understanding, at least for some people, in recent times? In today's world, reliance on politicians, writers, and columnists to provide unequivocal understanding of one's experiences and observations can prove highly problematic. We no longer live in homogeneous societies where everyone feels the same way and turns to the same sources. From the roots of terrorism to the best way to conduct one's personal life, there is a wide range of authorities available to clarify matters, and there is often outright conflict in what they say. In response to this lack of social consensus, many people have begun turning to science—or sometimes to pseudo-science—to obtain understanding that is less subjective and more authoritative. "Self-help" books are increasingly popular, and interest in psychology as a college major and professional career is at an all-time high.

Science in Perspective

Science clearly has the upper hand when trying to untangle the complexity, and resolve the ambiguity, of human thought and behavior in social contexts. It parallels implicit psychology, but it has built-in safeguards against the generation and maintenance of unwarranted ideas that characterize both implicit psychology and social wisdom. Using the scientific method, one can eliminate or at least control personal biases, so that the conclusions obtained in a study cannot easily be dismissed if they do not conform to people's intuitions or preferred way of thinking about the topic. And science, unlike implicit psychology and social wisdom, is self-correcting. No matter how sensible and well supported a theory is, it is always open to challenge from alternative theories with their own base of support. Science is a constant battle of ideas. Just as species evolve through natural selection, theories are continually refined, revised, or even discarded in the face of challenges from competing theories and new findings.

All of this is true—in principle. In reality, the conduct of science is far from perfect. This is because science is a human endeavor and cannot completely escape the influence of human motives, biases, and shortcomings. Thomas Kuhn (1970), a prominent philosopher of science, suggested that a scientific theory operates as much like a blinder as an eye-opener. Scientists, like laypeople, look "through" their theories. When these theories are challenged, scientists mount vigorous defenses and resist new findings that might otherwise be considered. Even a bad theory is preferred to having no theory at all, in much the same way that the layperson prefers an unflattering view of the world over a feeling of being baffled by events.

This does not mean that bad theories are never abandoned. The history of science is littered with blatantly false ideas that seemed like a good idea at the time, but were replaced by new theories that provide better explanations. Every area of science is punctuated with such wholesale transitions in scientific thinking—a point that is also central in Kuhn's insightful analysis.

Science is clearly not perfect, then, because it is performed by humans, not by heartless automatons. But it is far and away the best way we have for understanding our physical and psychological worlds. Until a new way of understanding human experience comes along, psychologists will vigorously defend this approach, all the while being on guard for false starts and theories about whose time it is to go.

Why Don't People Believe the Results of Science?

The public has a love-hate relationship with science. When asked which professions they trust, people put science at the top of the list, right up there with the military and the clergy—and far ahead of business and politics. But their respect for the results of science is less firm, with certain conclusions rejected out of hand by many people. Prominent examples today include evolution by natural selection (especially human evolution), climate change as a result of the use of fossil fuels, and the biological bases of homosexuality.

In part, the rejection of certain conclusions is due to the alternative sources of understanding we have discussed—implicit psychology and social sources of wisdom. People's implicit theories cannot easily incorporate the idea that humans are descended from primitive life forms, that erratic and extreme weather patterns are caused by filling up our gas tanks, or that genetics influence sexual orientation. And none of these conclusions has a long history of support by clergy, politicians, or grandparents. Science faces an uphill battle in these matters.

Scientific conclusions also run the risk of rejection when they conflict with the beliefs and attitudes that members of a social system take on faith. Attitudes serve important psychological functions (to be described in Chapter 3), and many attitudes are rooted in basic values that provide a shared reality for members of a society. In most cultures, for example, it is assumed that humans are distinct from all other animals and that homosexuality is a perversion of normal sexual desire. The idea that fossil fuel consumption contributes to climate change, meanwhile, is at odds with contemporary society's long-term reliance on petroleum as an all-purpose energy source. The commitment to social values and personal lifestyle can prove more important than objective evidence in deciding what (and whom) to believe.

Yet another reason why scientific conclusions are sometimes questioned, if not outright rejected, centers on what is arguably the strongest reason to *believe* what scientists say. Science, when done well, is open to revision and even dramatic overhauls. The scientific method is a cyclic process, with new research findings sometimes prompting reconsideration of the results of prior research. This means that a theory, even a well-established one, is always subject to change. Laypeople look for stability in their understanding, however, and tend to become suspect when "truth" loses this quality.

Consider the science of climate change. In the 1970s, a popular view among scientists was that the concentration of greenhouse gases in the atmosphere would block sunlight from reaching the earth and thus would produce global cooling. By the 1990s, however, the conventional wisdom in science was precisely the opposite—that the predominant effect of greenhouse gases was to trap heat in a layer around the earth and thus promote global warming and disrupt weather patterns. This shift in scientific consensus reflects the accumulation of new (and better) data, the development of sophisticated models, and more nuanced understanding of how factors in a complex system interact to produce global patterns. But to the layperson, such a reversal might seem more like waffling and uncertainty than progressive scientific understanding. When "truth" changes, the method that produced it may be called into question. When the topic is personally important but complex—and the need for updated scientific understanding is therefore greatest—people are especially prone to favor theories that provide a stable equilibrium over those that admit to change. Dogma and received wisdom fit this bill better than science.

Research Strategies

What Are the Methods Used in Social Psychology Research?

Research in social psychology has the same goals and follows the same rules as research in other fields. To understand a feature of the physical world, scientists try to identify the relevant factors concerning the feature in question and investigate how they are related to one another. A physicist, for example, might attempt to understand momentum by investigating how it is related to the mass of an object and the object's speed. In like manner, a social psychologist attempts to understand a class of behavior (e.g., love, aggression) by investigating how the behavior is related to people's characteristics and relevant features of the context in which the behavior is observed. Social psychologists employ three strategies to generate such enlightenment.

Correlation

The simplest type of relationship between variables is a *correlation*. Two variables are correlated if changes in the value of one of them are reliably associated with changes in the value of the other one. Correlations are all around us and are usually easy to detect. The appearance of dark clouds is associated with rainfall, the pounding of a hammer is associated with a loud sound, and physical exertion is associated with sweating. The association does not have to be perfect to produce a reliable (and meaningful) correlation. Dark clouds sometimes occur without rainfall, a hammer is associated with little sound if it is pounded into a pillow, and it may take a great deal of physical exercise to make a top athlete sweat. The issue is how strongly two variables are associated with one another. Some variables may be only weakly correlated and go unnoticed without careful observation and mathematical computation. There is a reliable association, for example, between cigarette smoking and lung cancer, but this is far from a perfect correlation, and it certainly is not obvious on a day-to-day basis.

Identifying Relationships

Like correlations in the physical world, associations involving mind and action can go unnoticed or prove difficult to assess. Frustration, for example, seems to be associated with aggressive action, but people do not turn hostile every time their goal-directed behavior is derailed. When driving, you do not always pound the dashboard or threaten other drivers if you miss a green light or get cut off by another driver. It can prove challenging to determine whether people's thoughts, feelings, and actions are associated with other aspects of their experience.

Consider the possibility of an association between children's exposure to violence in the mass media and their threshold for aggression in their interactions with peers. There is good reason to suspect that such an association exists. Children learn how to act by observing and modeling what other people do, and they spend a great deal of time watching people do things on TV, in the movies, and in video games. If they watch media depictions of violent behavior, perhaps they will learn to behave in a similar fashion in their non-media portions of the day (e.g., at school, playing with friends). Beyond its theoretical relevance, an answer to this question has important practical implications. If children learn to be aggressive by watching actors pretending to beat up each other, then parents might be well advised to monitor their children's viewing habits, and perhaps government regulations regarding video content should be considered as well.

The correlational method in this case makes sense because there is considerable variability in both variables. Children differ in what they watch and in what video games they play, and they also differ in their frequency of acting aggressively toward one another. The question is whether these two variables are co-related: do children who view more media violence also display more aggressive behavior? If so, the correlation is far from perfect. Children can spend hours watching episodes of *CSI: Miami* and call it a night, after first giving Mom and Dad a big hug. Conversely, they may watch reruns of *The Brady Bunch* one night and get into a fight the next day at school. If the association between viewing video violence and aggressive behavior was direct and unequivocal, psychologists would not need to spend time trying to document it.

There are different ways to quantify the association between children's viewing habits and their aggressive tendencies. For example, a researcher might ask parents to report on their children's media habits and their frequency of altercations at school or in social situations. For both variables, the answers need to be converted into numerical scores. Every TV program or video game could be given a value between 1 and 7 to indicate the level of violence it portrays, with 1 signifying virtually no violence (e.g., *Sesame Street*) and 7 signifying virtually no peaceful interactions (e.g., *Grand Theft Auto*). The children's social interactions could similarly be given a value between 1 (friendly contact) and 7 (physical conflict). For both variables, the researcher could compute an average score for each child and then compare these scores across the sample of children. The comparison value is the *correlation coefficient*.

To show a correlation, one variable (amount of televised violence viewed) is plotted on the *x*-axis, from low values to high values, and the other variable (aggressive behavior) is plotted on the *y*-axis, from low values to high values. If the two variables are related, a line (shown in red) is drawn to indicate the direction of the relationship (positive or negative). The stronger the relationship, the closer the points are to the line. If the two variables are unrelated, a line cannot be drawn and the points do not produce a visual pattern. Three categories of correlation are possible (Figure 2.1):

1. *Positive correlation*. As the value of one variable increases or decreases, the value of the other variable also increases or decreases.
   EXAMPLE: As the amount of televised violence viewed by children increases, so does their frequency of aggressive behavior.
2. *No correlation*. Changes in the values of the two variables are unrelated to one another.
   EXAMPLE: There is no relationship between the amount of televised violence viewed by children and their frequency of aggressive behavior.

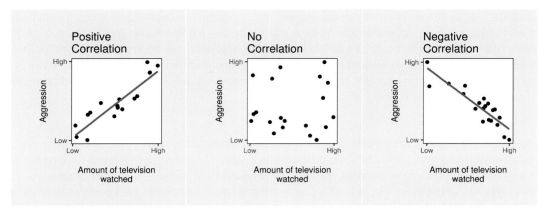

FIGURE 2.1 The Three Types of Correlation between Variables. Correlation Coefficients can vary from -1.0 (Perfect Negative Correlation) to +1.0 (Perfect Positive Correlation).

3. *Negative correlation.* As the value of one variable increases or decreases, the value of the other variable changes in the opposite direction.
    EXAMPLE: As the amount of televised violence viewed by children increases, their frequency of aggressive behavior decreases.

Archival Research

Correlational data can be obtained from surveys, as in the example just described, or from fresh observations of people in real-world settings. Yet another technique is *archival analysis* (e.g., Mullen, Rozell, & Johnson, 2001). In this approach, the data are derived from the accumulated documents—the archives—of a culture. The archives can include diaries, novels, popular music lyrics, television shows, newspaper articles, and even suicide notes.

By identifying patterns in archival data, the researcher can gain insight into a society's belief and values, but also into the relationships between certain societal practices and consequences. For example, one could look at the content of television programming and the crime statistics concerning assault to get a sense of what the society likes to watch and the society's tendency for aggressive behavior. By comparing these two measures across different societies, one can gain insight into how the two phenomena are related. Perhaps societies in which violent media content is common are also the societies in which aggressive behavior is relatively frequent.

Mining archival data can be a very useful way of assessing the relationships among social conditions and provide support for some theories of social processes at the expense of others. Keep in mind, though, that archival data are available for many features of a society, and some of these factors could influence the correlation between the variables of interest. It may be, for example, that the relationship between video portrayals of violence and societal indices of aggression is observed only in societies experiencing tough economic conditions, or in those characterized by a great deal of income inequality.

Limitations of Correlation

Explaining patterns can be great fun and can fuel great debates. Consider the link between exposure to violence in mass media and aggressive behavior by children. You may get the ball rolling by arguing that viewing video violence causes children to act aggressively in their interactions with peers. But the person listening to you may ask a follow-up question: *why* does video violence have this effect? There is hardly a shortage of possible explanations—some of them even plausible. One could argue, as suggested above, that viewing video violence teaches children that aggression is an effective (and exciting) way to deal with conflict. In a related vein, perhaps viewing violence lowers the threshold for aggressive "solutions" to frustrating events or interpersonal discord. Yet another possibility is that viewing video violence desensitizes children to the upsetting consequences of violence—pain, suffering, trauma, and so forth—and that this desensitization removes the constraints against hurting someone else.

Note that these explanations all assume that exposure to video violence is a cause of aggressive behavior. But stop and think about this for a second. Couldn't one just as reasonably argue for the opposite causal link—that aggressive behavior enhances the interest in violent video content? Children with a low threshold for hostile and violent behavior may be drawn to such behavior in their spare time and find the right TV channel or acquire the right video game that provides the opportunity to watch such behavior performed by other people. After all, people who enjoy football or tennis may prefer watching football games or tennis matches over other types of video content. Aggressive children may simply enjoy being a spectator as much as being a participant in physical conflict.

Yet another possibility is that both viewing video violence and aggressive behavior are caused by some other factor that was not measured in the study. The two behaviors (watching video violence and acting aggressively) may be highly correlated, but both behaviors may be independently caused by some other experience. There is no shortage of possibilities. Perhaps tough economic circumstances, a troubled family life, or an emotional trauma at an early age creates both a desire for TV content emphasizing dramatic solutions to problems and a tendency for poorly regulated interpersonal behavior characterized by aggression rather than compromise, empathy, or concern over consequences. Negligent or indulgent parents, too, may produce children who cannot control their aggressive impulses and who also have free rein in deciding what to view on television, at the movies, or on the internet.

Deciding among the interpretations of a correlation can be difficult. It is tempting to settle on one and dismiss the others, but this hardly settles the matter. This inherent limitation of correlational research can be summarized in a basic adage: "correlation is not causation." When a correlation is observed, there are three plausible causal interpretations (see Table 2.1).

The ambiguous nature of causality in a correlation is common in psychology (and in other sciences as well). Consider, for example, the finding that people with high self-esteem tend to be more extraverted and have more friends than do people with low self-esteem (Leary, Tambor, Terdal, & Downs, 1995). Perhaps your immediate response is to assume that having high self-esteem makes a person confident and outgoing in social settings and therefore likely to attract friends. But one could just as plausibly infer the opposite causal relation: perhaps an extensive social network promotes high self-esteem. In this interpretation, extraverted people may experience greater satisfaction of their social needs, and this fulfillment may make them feel good about themselves (Baumeister & Leary, 1995). Alternatively, a different factor may independently promote high self-esteem and generate heightened interest in forming relations with others. Having a secure attachment with one's parents (Bowlby, 1969), for example, may both prevent self-doubt later in life and also make one trusting and accepting of other people.

There is actually a fourth possibility regarding the causal foundations of a correlation. Two variables may be directly linked by causation, but the causation may work in both directions. Consider the link between video violence and aggressive behavior. Perhaps a child watches a violent TV show and the next day acts out aggressively at school. This captures one direction of causality: video violence creates the potential for aggressive behavior. But that is not the end of the story. After his aggressive encounters at school, the child goes home and may seek out a TV show (or choose a video game) with content that matches his or her mood—a show or game loaded with fights, battles, and other forms of physical conflict. Now the causal direction is reversed: aggressive behavior increases the likelihood of viewing video violence. This experience in turn may increase his or her willingness to use aggression to settle conflicts on the playground, and so on, in a self-reinforcing pattern. Over time, in other words, the causal influence between

Table 2.1 Three Causal Interpretations of a Reliable Correlation between Two Variables

*1. **Variable A causes Variable B***
Exposure to video violence causes children to respond to frustration with aggression.
*2. **Variable B causes Variable A***
Aggressive behavior causes children to seek out and prefer violent video content.
*3. **Variable X causes Variable A and B***
An unmeasured factor (*Variable X*) independently causes both exposure to violent video content and aggressive behavior. For example, poor parenting can promote poor self-control in children, leading them to seek out violent video content and to respond aggressively when frustrated by their peers.

video violence and aggression works in both directions. This state of affairs is known as *bidirectional causality*—also referred to as *reciprocal causality* (Bandura, 1986).

The lesson here is to be wary when you hear a scientific finding establishing a correlation between different psychological and behavioral factors. With this in mind, consider the various correlations presented in Table 2.2. What is your immediate interpretation of each one? Now consider how the correlation could be turned around and interpreted in very different ways.

Experiment

Knowing that two variables are related is useful, but until the ambiguity regarding causality is eliminated, the relationship does not qualify as a theory with clear implications. Far different recommendations follow from a causal relation beginning with video violence ("watching violence promotes aggression") and one beginning with aggression ("aggression promotes watching violence"). To decide between these causal scenarios, or to determine if causality is bidirectional, social psychologists create simulations of the relationship in a controlled setting that reframes the relationship in cause-effect terms. This is the essence of an *experiment*.

Identifying Causes

An experiment essentially consists of two kinds of variables—one serving as a stand-in for a suspected "cause," the other as a stand-in for the anticipated "effect." These are referred to, respectively, as independent and dependent variables. An *independent variable* is any observable event that causes the person to do something. It is "independent" in the sense that its values are created by the researcher and are not affected by anything else that happens in the experiment. It is a "variable" because it has at least two levels, categories, types, or groups. For example, in a study testing the effects of video violence on aggression, the independent variable is the level of video violence, which is presented at two (or more) values: (a) violent content, and (b) nonviolent content. The *dependent variable* is any observable behavior produced by the person. It is "dependent" in the sense that its values are assumed to depend upon the values of the independent variable. In studying the effect of video violence on aggression, the dependent variable is a response that reflects the intensity of aggression (very low to very high).

In an experiment, each construct under investigation must be given an *operational definition*—a definition in terms of observable procedures and measurements. Creating valid operational definitions can be tricky business (Cook & Campbell, 1979). A social psychologist might have a compelling theory about the nature of love, for example, but this concept can prove elusive when searching for an appropriate operational definition that can capture the essence and intensity of this special internal state. Despite these problems, social psychology has proven to be remarkably adept and downright clever in translating abstract concepts into concrete operations and testing theories about virtually every aspect of personal and social experience.

Specifying independent and dependent variables, and translating them into operational definitions, are critical to isolating cause-effect relations, but two other features are just as critical. First, every feature of the experiment apart from the independent variables must be identical. This means that every participant is treated the same, except for the level of the independent variable he or she experiences. By exercising this form of control, the researcher ensures

Table 2.2 What Do These Correlations Mean?

- Generosity is associated with happiness (Chapter 4)
- People with high self-esteem have more friends (Chapter 5)
- People who drink alcohol in excess have poor impulse control (Chapter 6)
- People who are physically attractive have better social skills than do people who are less attractive (Chapter 8)
- Teenagers who use smartphones the most tend to be depressed and anxious (Chapter 8)
- People with similar attitudes are attracted to one another (Chapter 9)
- Resistance to social influence is associated with a desire to maintain one's sense of personal freedom (Chapter 10)
- Powerful people are more likely than less powerful people to disregard rules that they feel others should obey (Chapter 14)
- Liberal and conservative political orientations are associated with different fundamental values (Chapter 14)

that any difference observed in the dependent variable for different levels of the independent variable was caused by the independent variable, not by other factors.

The second critical feature might seem strange in a scientific context, where the name of the game is strict control. But for unequivocal causality to be established, there must be *random assignment* of participants to each level of the independent variable. If the independent variable has two levels (e.g., violent vs. nonviolent video content), the researcher could flip a coin for each assignment, with "heads" participants assigned to the violent video and "tails" participants assigned to the nonviolent video. If the independent variable has more than two levels (e.g., very violent, moderately violent, nonviolent), the research might roll a die, draw a number from a hat, or use a chart of random numbers to assign participants to their conditions.

When randomly assigned to conditions, the participants in one group should be no different—no angrier, no more short-fused, no smarter, no more liberal or conservative, no more willing to do what is expected—than the participants in any other group. If there are still differences between conditions in the dependent measure (e.g., greater aggression after viewing the violent video), these differences can reasonably be attributed to the independent variable rather than to any differences in the personal characteristics of the participants in each condition.

Sometimes random assignment is not feasible, or even desirable. A researcher might be interested, for example, whether boys or girls are more influenced in their aggressiveness by violent video. When a researcher incorporates preexisting differences among individuals, the study is called a *quasi-experiment*. Within each group of participants (e.g., boys and girls), the researcher will use random assignment to determine who experiences which level of the independent variable (violent vs. nonviolent video). The results of such an experiment might indicate that gender does not matter (i.e., boys and girls were equally affected by the violent video), or the results might reveal an *interaction* between the two variables—it may be, for example, that video violence promotes violence among boys but not among girls.

Limitations of Experimental Research

Taking part in an experiment may clarify the cause-effect issue but this experience is not exactly representative of behavior in everyday life. How can we be sure that what a person does in a 20-minute laboratory session, which is quite a bit different from any other circumstance in his or her daily life, tells us anything about how the person behaves in their interactions with other people? This concern with *psychological realism* is well recognized in social psychology (Aronson, Wilson, & Brewer, 1998). Psychological realism is heightened if participants feel like they are involved in a real as opposed to a manufactured event.

To make the event seem real, researchers commonly provide a *cover story*, which is a disguised version of the experiment's true purpose. A classic example is provided by a set of famous (and infamous) experiments designed to determine the extent to which people would follow the orders of a legitimate authority figure, even if doing so might lead to the injury of another person (Milgram, 1974). Participants were told that the researcher wanted to see if punishing someone (with electric shocks) for incorrect responses would eliminate the errors and promote better learning. Can you imagine how participants would have responded if they were told what the *true* purpose of the study ("We want to see if you will deliver painful electric shocks to a 50-year-old man with a heart problem because we tell you to do it")?

Psychologists are quite adept in concocting credible cover stories ensuring the psychological realism of experimental settings. Participants in a study of social judgment, for example, may be told that an individual they are evaluating is real and that they will interact with him or her later, even though the target person is fictitious (and thus no interaction is about to take place). The researcher is not being candid with participants, but this deception is justified as necessary to test something interesting and important about people's mental machinery.

Box 2.1   Is Social Psychology WEIRD?

Social psychology claims to identify processes that are universal, reflecting how people everywhere experience their social worlds. But this claim has come under close scrutiny in recent years. The concern is not the level of mundane and psychological realism in social psychology experiments—that issue has pretty much been settled (although there is still some dissent). The issue instead is the population from which research participants are drawn. A recent survey of leading psychology journals found that 96% of research participants come from Western industrialized nations, with 68% coming from the United States alone (Henreich, Heine, & Norenzayan, 2010). Of the American participants, moreover, 67% were undergraduate psychology majors. This means that a randomly selected American undergraduate is 4,000 times more likely to be a participant in research than is a random non-Westerner.

This might not be a problem were it not for the lessons social scientists (including social psychologists) have learned from comparing and contrasting how people in different cultures think and act. In most respects, the differences are slight and do not preclude establishing universals of psychological functioning. But some differences are not so easily dismissed, reflecting instead the impact of culture on how people experience events, relate to other people, and even view themselves (e.g., Haidt & Keltner, 1999; Markus & Kitayama, 1991; Shweder, 1991). For one, American participants assign greater value to choice and individualism than do citizens of most other countries. In a survey of six Western societies, for example, only Americans preferred to have a choice among 50 ice cream flavors rather than 10 flavors. Americans (and other Westerners), moreover, tend to define themselves in terms of psychological traits (e.g., "I'm outgoing, stubborn, and energetic"), whereas many non-Westerners define themselves in terms of their social relationships (e.g., "I'm the oldest of four brothers and sisters," "I belong to a soccer club"). Perhaps, as Henreich et al. (2010) suggest, the presumed universals of social psychological research really apply only to a group of WEIRD outliers–those from *Westernized, Educated, Industrialized, Rich, and Democratic* nations.

Not all psychologists are so concerned. They recognize cultural variation, but they contend that the differences between, say, American and Chinese individuals are simply superficially different manifestations of underlying universals, and that psychologists are on the right track in focusing on what unites rather than divides people around the globe. Yet others (e.g., Rozin, 2010) argue that extrapolating from Americans is acceptable because the world is becoming Americanized anyway, so that understanding the psychology of Americans provides a glimpse into the future.

What may seem like a problem with social psychology has actually provided a new perspective on personal, interpersonal, and collective experience. Indeed, the nature and significance of cultural variation in psychological processes has emerged as a primary focus of research attention in the United States and elsewhere (e.g., Kashima & Kashima, 2003; Markus & Kitayama, 1991; Nisbett, 2003; Triandis, 1994). This research has documented that cultures differ in certain features of their psychology, but more important (and somewhat ironically), it has identified a small set of universal dimensions along which all cultures can be located. You got a taste of these dimensions in Chapter 1; they will be brought into sharper relief in the chapters that follow as we explore the various domains of social psychology. Of course, if people like Rozin are right, these chapters may someday have to be trimmed a great deal to accommodate the increasing homogenization (i.e., Americanization) of the world.

Ethics of Experimental Research

In solving the issue of psychological realism, social psychologists have created another problem that is even trickier and harder to solve in a clear-cut fashion. If the situation created in an experiment is truly realistic for participants, it has the potential to alter, at least temporarily, the state of mind that the participant had before coming to the experimental session. An individual who participates in an experiment is exposing him or herself to information or forces that are hypothesized to change the way he or she thinks, feels, or behaves.

Some experiments, in fact, are designed to make participants uncomfortable or to get them to behave in ways they might not otherwise consider. Consider again the Milgram (1974) experiments. Psychologists were alarmed by the results of this research, which showed that a majority of participants obediently delivered up to 450 volts of electricity to a middle-aged man when he provided incorrect answers to a series of questions. But psychologists–and other scholars, including those professionally concerned with ethics–were also concerned about the potentially harmful effects experienced by participants. Imagine how you would feel if you delivered what you felt were painful shocks to someone else, only to learn afterward that your behavior had nothing to do with learning, but everything to do with blind obedience to authority.

Most experiments are not as extreme as Milgram's. In fact, that kind of research is rarely performed these days. But sometimes it is hard to draw the line between an experiment with benign consequences and one that has the potential to affect participants in a more consequential manner. Social psychologists are interested in a variety of personally sensitive topics, such as self-esteem and impulse control, and highly charged social issues, such as racial prejudice, aggression, and hypocrisy. To explore the factors that increase or decrease individuals' self-esteem, for example, a researcher might provide false feedback regarding participants' performance on a test or perhaps lead them to think that someone they just met has a positive or a negative impression of their personality. Participants are randomly assigned to receive either the positive or the negative feedback, after which they are asked to indicate how they feel about their personal characteristics or even their overall self-worth. This line of research may provide insight into the bases for self-evaluation, but is it worth the risk that participants—especially those in the negative feedback conditions—might begin to think differently about themselves than they did prior to their participation in the experiment?

For this reason, research conducted at universities has to be evaluated by an *institutional review board* (IRB), a panel of people charged with weighing the scientific benefit of the research against the risk the research poses to participants. IRBs include at least one scientist who can evaluate the scientific merit of the research. But if only scientists were involved, critics could argue that this would be like putting a fox in charge of guarding the henhouse. So in addition to scientists, IRBs must include at least one nonscientist and one person who is not affiliated with the university. Without vested interests in promoting a colleague's research agenda, the nonscientists and non-university people can focus on the potential risk to participants' well-being and balance this risk against the scientific value of the research.

This so-called *risk-benefit ratio* is not always obvious, and consensus on the part of IRB members can be difficult to reach. To the extent possible, IRBs insist that the researcher obtain *informed consent* from research participants. To do so, the researcher explains the nature of the experiment before it begins and asks for participants' agreement to take part. If participants are made fully aware of what they are going to experience and state they are willing to participate, there is no ethical dilemma. This is feasible in some research studies, but not in all of them. As noted above, researchers commonly mislead participants about the true purpose of the experiment, providing them instead a cover story about the events they will experience. When a study involving deception is approved, the researcher is obligated to conduct a *debriefing* session, in which the true purpose of the study is explained and the deceptions are described. If a participant experienced discomfort, the researcher must attempt to alleviate it.

In the vast majority of experiments, participants understand and appreciate the need for deception, provided the researcher takes sufficient time in the debriefing session to review the purpose of the study and to explain why alternative procedures could not be used. In an interesting twist, several studies have investigated the impact on people of participating in experiments involving deception (e.g., Chistensen, 1988; Epley & Huff, 1998; Finney, 1987; Gerdes, 1979; Sharpe, Adair, & Roese, 1992). These studies have found that people do not object to the mild discomforts and deceptions they experienced. In fact, participants who participated in deception studies feel they learned more and enjoyed the experiment more than do those who participated in studies that did not employ deception (Smith & Richardson, 1983).

Computer Simulation

It may seem strange, but human experience can be investigated in a way that does not even require the participation of humans. In this approach, a psychological process is expressed in terms of a few simple rules, which are then implemented in a computer program to simulate how the process unfolds over time. The *computer simulation* approach has emerged as a popular research paradigm in recent years (Epstein, 2008; Jackson et al., 2017; Liebrand, Nowak, & Hegselman, 1998; Read & Miller, 1998; Smith & Conrey, 2007; Vallacher, Read, & Nowak, 2017). The enormous advances in computer science and technology over the last couple of decades have made this approach feasible and relatively easy to implement. The rise in popularity is also due to the increasing recognition that human psychology can be investigated from the perspective of complexity science and nonlinear dynamical systems, a set of ideas and methods introduced in Chapter 1 that holds promise for identifying the common features linking different topics in social psychology. Computer simulation is the primary method for developing and testing ideas inspired by the dynamical systems perspective (Nowak, 2004).

Computer simulations come in many forms, each with pluses and minuses for capturing something basic about how people behave individually, interpersonally, and collectively. If you intend to pursue social psychology in college (and beyond), you will no doubt learn about the various ways of simulating a social process. But that is getting ahead of ourselves. The point to take away right now is that this approach provides a way to identify the basic rules underlying human experience and to observe how these rules shape the way people think, feel, and behave.

The Advantages of Computer Simulation

The experimental approach is well suited to establish causal relations and has rightly become the preferred means of gaining insight into social processes. But it has two noteworthy limitations that can be overcome with the computer simulation approach. First, experiments usually focus on the immediate impact of a suspected cause (the independent variable) on a variable of interest (the dependent variable), without tracking how this effect plays out over time. Imagine, for example, that someone soundly criticizes you for something you did. Your immediate reaction might be defensive ("that's wrong!") or accepting ("you're right, what was I thinking!"). It is useful to know the immediate reaction, of course, and experiments are well suited to reveal such cause-effect relations. But that is hardly the end of the story. Within minutes, your reaction might change in a variety of ways. For example, the reaction might become stronger—an initial defensive reaction could turn into a desire for revenge against the critic, whereas an initial acceptance could lead to increasing self-criticism. Alternatively, the reaction might show a sharp reversal—an initial defensive reaction might give way to serious self-evaluation, whereas an initial acceptance might ultimately be rejected as one downplays the credibility of the critic or the criticism. Knowing the temporal pattern associated with a psychological process provides greater insight into the nature of human experience than does knowing only the first step in the process (Vallacher et al., 2015).

It is possible to track changes in a psychological process with the experimental approach (e.g., Gilbert & Wilson, 2007; Pratkanis, Greenwald, Leippe, & Baumgardner, 1988; Swann, Hixon, Stein-Seroussi, & Gilbert, 1990; Tesser, 1978). But this is not feasible if the process changes on a very fast time scale (e.g., moment to moment or minute to minute). Nor is the experimental approach useful if the process takes place over a very long period of time (e.g., days, weeks, years). Social change, for example, may be set in motion by events this week, but the change itself might not become manifest for several months or years. For that matter, the researcher may not know in advance what time scale is the right one for capturing the process. He or she might examine how a person feels once a day, for example, but the person may be experiencing important changes on an hourly basis or not until a week has passed.

Computer simulations get around this limitation by repeating the operation of the process (i.e., the rule being investigated) over and over again, with each repetition providing an update of the previous state of the system. By observing how many simulation steps are necessary for the system to stabilize on a single state (e.g., a stable opinion held by a person) or on a stable pattern of changes (e.g., continual oscillation between conflicting opinions), one can determine the time scale associated with the process in question.

The second advantage of the computer simulation approach is that it allows researchers to investigate topics that are simply off limits because of ethical considerations. As discussed in Chapter 1, social psychology is concerned with a variety of very troublesome features of human thought and behavior. At the intrapersonal level, there are important issues concerning self-defeating behavior, impulse control, anxiety, and depression. At the interpersonal level, there is hardly a shortage of troublesome issues: relationship difficulties ranging from mistrust and tension to abuse and homicide, and antisocial behavior ranging from harassment and bullying to hatred and physical violence. At the level of collective dynamics, many important topics are especially troublesome: racism and other forms of prejudice, intergroup and international conflict, and in the extreme, genocide perpetrated by one group on another group.

There is only so much one can do to human participants in the name of science. All the informed consent and debriefing in the world would not justify testing the conditions under which people experience personal humiliation or engage in armed conflict with people from different social groups. The limits to the questions that experimental research can address became the focus of spirited debate in the aftermath of Stanley Milgram's (1974) studies of obedience to legitimate authority. Because of the ethical issues associated with the research, certain topics in social psychology have been declared off limits since that time. This is ironic since, as noted in Chapter 1, the dark side of human nature is a primary agenda of social psychology and is what inspired many to learn the techniques of the field in the first place.

Because computer simulations do not involve humans, the ethical issues that hamper the experimental approach are moot. Rules can be implemented in a simulation that promote the mutual destruction of (virtual) individuals or groups, and no one looks aghast in horror at the cruelty of scientists. Although computer simulations are employed to investigate mundane processes such as attitude formation, they have proven especially useful in illustrating processes with potentially harmful consequences, including intergroup conflict (Vallacher et al., 2010), mistrust in close relationships (Nowak, Vallacher, & Zochowski, 2005), and the formation and maintenance of group stereotypes (Queller, 2002).

Limitations of Computer Simulation

The computer simulation approach is appealing and is becoming an established way to investigate topics in social psychology (Vallacher et al., 2017). But we should not get carried away—at least, not yet. The reality simulated in a computer program is a far cry from the reality that people experience in their everyday lives. People are not interchangeable "elements" that blindly conform to simple rules. Each individual has his or her own idiosyncrasies, hopes, fears, and values. It is possible to program elements to represent individual differences, but that misses a larger point. No matter how much one pins down what a person is like, he or she can choose among alternative courses of action and resist forces that are presumed to dictate these choices. From momentary impulses to the expression of self-defining values, a person's behavior can depart from the rules specified in a computer program and therefore defy prediction.

These tendencies are not exceptions, but rather represent central features of human psychology that are incorporated into theories and research agendas—as you will see in the subsequent chapters. One of the basic rules of human functioning, in fact, is people's capacity for reflecting on their operating rules and attempting to override them. This does not necessarily mean that people have free will—perhaps social psychology can one day identify the external factors and internal dynamics that determine people's seemingly unconstrained choices and decisions. A central and distinguishing task of social psychology is to identify lawful regularities regarding people's tendency to behave independently of lawful regularities! See Table 2.3 for a summary of the pros and cons of Correlation, Experiment, and Computer Simulation.

The Promise of "Big Data"

The amount of information in today's world is almost beyond comprehension. There has always been an abundance of information, but in recent years the amount available for research purposes has increased dramatically. This increase is due in part to the new technologies available for personal, government, and commercial information gathering, including smartphones, GPS tracking, satellite monitoring, cameras (often unobtrusive) in public places, websites such as Google and Amazon, and software for building databases on every conceivable topic or interest. Beyond the

Table 2.3 The Pros and Cons of Social Psychology Research Strategies

	Advantages	Disadvantages
Correlation	Identification of subtle relationships between factors and processes	Cannot specify causal relationships among variables
	Relatively easy to perform	Requires large number of participants
Experiment	Unambiguous identification of cause and effect	Can overlook bidirectional causality
	Control over other potential causes and influences	Emphasizes the immediate impact of a "cause"
	Recreate the "realism" of psychological processes	Troublesome ethical issues
Computer simulation	Identification of patterns in large number of potential causes and factors	Artificiality of "elements"
	Identification of most important factors	Potential for neglect of "human" qualities
	Identification of long-term consequences of a process	Requires considerable technical expertise
	Harmful processes can be investigated without ethical issues	The true "human" impact of psychological processes may be missed

information yield per se, new means of storing this information on computer servers, websites, and the "cloud" have emerged, as have new means of finding and characterizing the relationships embedded in this vast amount of information. *Big data* has emerged as the term to describe these large interconnected data sets—so large and interconnected that traditional statistical methods are inadequate to investigate them (Kosinski, Wang, Lakkaraju, & Leskovec, 2016; Snijders, Matzat, & Reips, 2012; Silver, 2012). In response, sophisticated methods have been developed to identify patterns that might otherwise be overlooked or dismissed as noise.

Big data has provided new and often unanticipated insights into a wide variety of topics and issues, from consumer preferences and the geographical distribution of hobbies to economic forecasting and signs of impending political upheaval. The rapid ascendance and widespread use of social media (e.g., Facebook, Twitter, Instagram), meanwhile, has generated research into how information and rumors are transmitted through social networks. But does big data have implications for how theories are generated and tested in social psychology? It is too soon to know whether this approach will become a new paradigm for the field, complementing—or perhaps even replacing—the laboratory and survey-based approaches that have served as the standard in the past (e.g., Mast et al., 2015). The value of big data comes from the patterns one can derive by connecting different sources of data, whether about an individual, relations between individuals, or groups and large-scale social systems. Analysis of big data might reveal, for example, a connection between an uptick in the number of Twitter feeds devoted to an event and various aspects of the event—its economic or political relevance, its short- versus long-term impact on public opinion, or its potential for producing harmony versus conflict between segments of society. These questions are considerably different from the sorts of questions one can address in a standard study in social psychology.

Although big data is becoming an important means for gaining insight and building models of social processes, its value needs to be put into perspective. For one thing, in framing new questions (e.g., how ideas and information percolate in social networks), this approach may neglect other questions that are better addressed in a laboratory experiment (e.g., how affect is communicated nonverbally in a face-to-face social interaction). Big data, moreover, cannot directly test the causal factors responsible for the patterns that are discovered in large data sets. Knowing that a high volume of Twitter feeds devoted to a topic promotes a change in public opinion concerning the topic does not tell us *why* this change occurs. Perhaps awareness of the high volume creates a bandwagon effect, with everyone wanting to be part of the conversation or feel solidarity with others, or perhaps the content of the tweets has information value that clarifies the meaning of the topic for those who previously did not know what to think.

Another issue concerns the advantage of big data: uncovering patterns in large data sets. With enough information, one can always find patterns—the trick is to distinguish the "signal" from the "noise" (Silver, 2012). This problem is analogous to the persistent popularity of conspiracy theories. If one believes the terrorist attacks on September 11, 2001, were really an "inside job" coordinated by the Bush administration, for example, the information relevant to that event is so enormous that one can find a way to "connect the dots" and maintain that belief. The advanced statistical methods employed in big data research get around this problem for the most part, but there is always a risk of identifying a pattern that is illusory rather than real.

Finally, the mining of big data raises ethical concerns regarding personal privacy (Kosinski et al., 2015). Facebook posts, for example, reveal a great deal of information about people's personal lives and their social relationships, and such information can obviously be traced to all the individuals involved. The use of cameras in public places, meanwhile, can generate interesting insight into social interaction and the synchronization of movement among large numbers of people, but cameras can also be used to identify individuals—and do so without their permission. The privacy issues are not easily resolved but must be addressed, as big data continues its ascendance as a new approach to exploring the social dynamics of everyday life. In combination with correlation, experiments, and computer simulations, big data has an important role to play in 21st-century social psychology—whether we feel comfortable with it or not.

Social Psychology and Biology

How Is Biology Relevant to Social Psychology Research?

Most people today acknowledge our membership in the animal kingdom. We are a bundle of biological processes and no one would argue that these processes are irrelevant to the way we think, feel, and act. But the relationship between psychology and biology is far from settled. Some scholars (and many laypeople) argue that biology simply provides constraints on how we operate, leaving it to a disembodied mind to make the final decision on how to proceed. Others go one step further, arguing that psychology is primary, with biology providing the mechanisms by which thoughts, feelings, and actions are expressed. In this view, a person gets angry as his or her mind contemplates an unpleasant experience, and it is this mental state that gets the neural circuits humming and the blood coursing through his or her arteries and veins.

These ideas may be satisfying and provide a boost to our collective ego, suggesting that we are a transcendent species, but they have not held up too well in the face of increasingly sophisticated and detailed understanding of our biological selves. This onslaught on human dignity is manifest in two areas: the role of genetics in shaping how humans think and act, and the direct links between our subjective experience and brain function.

Nature Versus Nurture

According to *evolutionary psychology* (Buss, 2015), the way humans think and behave today reflects cognitive and behavioral tendencies that helped our ancestors survive under very different and far more difficult conditions thousands of generations ago. These tendencies—referred to as *adaptations*—are encoded in our common genetic makeup. Natural selection favored genetic profiles associated with patterns of thinking and acting that enabled early humans to live long enough to mate and pass on their genes to their offspring. Less adaptive genetic profiles were weeded out in the struggle for survival and mating opportunities.

This does not mean that everyone alive today has an identical genetic makeup. Our species would not have survived if we were simply clones of one another. The challenges of group living require a broad repertoire of physical attributes, skill sets, interests, and social orientations. If everyone had the same capacity for and interest in planting crops, there would be no one to take on the challenge of hunting prey animals or taking care of the sick and injured. And if everyone was socially outgoing or motivated to take risks, no one would take on the role of security guard and attend to dangers and things that could go wrong. Even variation among people in emotional stability, aggressive tendencies, and risk for depression makes sense from the point of view of adaptive diversity in social group living (Figueredo et al., 2005).

There is variation among humans in their genetic makeup and in their psychological characteristics. What is less clear is whether these two sources of variability are linked. Do genetic differences account for psychological differences? Or is genetic variation confined to physical dimensions such as bone structure, skin pigmentation, and height? Social experiences impact the way people think and behave—this is a working assumption of social psychology, after all. Perhaps some experiences, particularly those during childhood, establish patterns of thought and behavior that last a lifetime. The question, then, is whether psychological characteristics reflect genetic differences or experiential differences among people.

Psychologists are keenly aware of both sides of the *nature versus nurture* debate. One commonly employed strategy in this debate is to investigate monozygotic ("identical") twins—siblings who have an identical genetic makeup. Researchers compare the psychological characteristics of monozygotic twins who are reared together (as is most often the case) versus those who are reared in different families in different geographical regions (because of adoption at an early age) (Bouchard et al., 1990; Plomin, DeFries, McClearn, & McGuffin, 2008). This line of research is correlational in nature—a researcher obviously cannot randomly assign children to either the same family or different families. Nonetheless, the results of dozens of studies converge on very similar findings. Virtually every psychological characteristic reflects the influence of both genes (nature) and childhood social experiences (nurture). But the relative contribution of nature and nurture is different for different characteristics.

The major personality traits generally have a considerable genetic component. Extraversion (socially outgoing, talkative) and neuroticism (emotional instability) are especially similar among monozygotic twins, even when they are raised in different homes (and thus experience different environmental influences). Across various measures of these traits, the average correlation for identical twins reared apart is +0.5. Genetic influence has been established for other cognitive and behavioral characteristics as well, including subjective well-being, achievement motivation, sense of alienation, risk-taking, religiosity, and sexual orientation (e.g., Bailey, Pillard, Neale, & Agyei, 1993; Johnson, 2007; Plomin et al., 2008; Tellegen et al., 1988).

Keep in mind that even a correlation of +0.5 leaves a great deal of variability in a characteristic unexplained, and this variability can be traced to a wide range of experiential factors. For one thing, all humans internalize the values and norms of the culture in which they were raised, and these features of culture provide guidelines and constraints for how people think and act. Within a culture, people's patterns of thought and behavior are shaped by a wide variety of social factors, from childhood experiences to their social class and geographical location within the larger society. The diversity of these social factors creates the potential for considerable variability among people in their characteristic patterns of thinking and acting.

The nature-nurture issue has become more complex in recent years due to developments in *epigenetics*, the study of changes in gene activity that do not involve alterations to the genetic code but still get passed down to successive generations (Youngson & Whitelaw, 2008). This work has shown that genes and environmental influences are not merely separate factors that combine in various proportions to shape human characteristics. Rather, genes are malleable, capable of turning on or off, or becoming expressed in different ways, depending on environmental influences. This impact, moreover, can be preserved during reproduction, so that offspring are predisposed to exhibit the same gene expression. Among mice (and perhaps people) that become obese, for example, genes for obesity express themselves more strongly, with the next generation predisposed to gain excessive weight as well. Epigenetic effects can be preserved for several generations. This suggests that people with poor eating habits may be unwittingly condemning their great-great-great grandchildren to obesity.

It is not known yet whether epigenetics play a role in shaping psychological characteristics. But if experience can influence the expression of genes responsible for psychological tendencies, how a person conducts his or her life can influence the characteristics of successive generations. Perhaps people who emphasize active social relations and pursue intellectually challenging activities, for example, can provide a head start for their children—and their children's children—in their inclination toward extraversion and intellectual curiosity.

Brains and Minds

People are remarkably adept at reading one another's minds. But they do so in a very indirect manner. As we shall see in the discussion of social judgment (Chapter 7), people infer what other people are thinking by monitoring their gestures and other nonverbal behaviors and by taking into account the context surrounding their actions. But what if you could read a person's mind directly, and did not have to settle for inferences and interpretations? In recent years, psychologists have begun to do just that—by watching the brain in action as a person thinks about another person, looks at a familiar face, makes a decision, reflects on a past act, or experiences an emotion. This approach to psychology is known as *neuroscience*; when issues of concern to social psychologists are investigated, the approach is referred to as *social neuroscience* (Cacioppo, Berntson, Sheridan, & McClintock, 2000; Harmon-Jones & Winkielman, 2007; Lieberman, 2007; Ochsner, 2007). Using several advanced technologies, neuroscientists have made headway (so to speak) in mapping areas of the brain responsible for—or at least associated with—a host of important processes, from face recognition and imagination to decision-making, empathy, action planning, social judgment, and self-awareness.

Perhaps the most popular technique for watching the brain in action makes use of *magnetic resonance imaging* (MRI). This involves applying brief but powerful magnetic pulses to the head and recording how these pulses are absorbed throughout the brain. For very short periods, these magnetic pulses cause molecules in the brain tissue to twist slightly and then relax, an action that releases a small amount of energy. Differently charged molecules respond differently to the magnetic pulse, so the energy signals reveal brain structures with different molecular compositions. To study the function of brain structures, psychologists use *functional magnetic resonance imaging* (fMRI), which focuses on the twisting of hemoglobin molecules in the blood when they are exposed to magnetic impulses. Hemoglobin is the molecule that carries oxygen to our tissues, including the brain. Because active neurons require more energy and blood flow, oxygenated hemoglobin concentrates in the active areas of the brain. By tracking changes in these concentrations on a fast time scale, fMRI not only localizes the brain structures responsible for psychological functions, but it also tracks psychological processes that occur very quickly.

This approach has proven useful in identifying the brain processes underlying a wide variety of mental processes, including self-awareness, action planning, revenge motivation, loneliness, attraction, and moral reasoning. In linking social psychological processes to the workings of brain structures, social neuroscience raises the possibility that such processes can be decoupled from their customary moral foundations. Consider, for example, the "seven deadly sins"— acts that philosophers and theologians single out as signs of human weakness that must be overcome by force of will and virtue. Brain imaging has revealed that each of these excesses—gluttony, envy, pride, lust, and the like—can be described in terms of the activation or inhibition of distinct neural circuits or brain regions. These patterns of activation and inhibition, moreover, occur automatically upon perception of the relevant stimulus (e.g., the sight and scent of food that elicits gluttony), and it is these patterns that promote the corresponding "sin."

At the same time, social neuroscience has also identified brain structures (e.g., the prefrontal cortex) that become active (i.e., consume oxygenated hemoglobin at a rapid clip) when people exercise willpower and resist temptations—including the seven deadly sins (e.g., Harmon-Jones & Winkielman, 2007). When framed in terms of neuroscience, then, the issue of "sin" becomes less an issue of morality and more an issue of competing brain functions. The implications of this perspective—and of social neuroscience more generally—for such time-honored concepts as personal responsibility, good versus evil, and free will have yet to be worked out.

SUMMING UP AND LOOKING AHEAD

- **Science conjures up images of flasks, test tubes, microscopes, or perhaps a particle accelerator or weather balloon. None of these is particularly useful in trying to understand human experience. Social psychologists are interested in people's thoughts, feelings, and behaviors, but these phenomena are not concrete in the same way that chemicals, charged particles, or wind currents are. The adaptation of the scientific method to social psychology thus entails a different set of tools. People's internal states and action tendencies are commonly assessed by indirect means, including self-report questionnaires, response latencies to stimuli presented on a computer screen, and verbal expressions.**

- **The scientific method has advantages over other means of understanding how people function. People can introspect into their own operating rules and can gain insight into human nature by drawing lessons from their observations of other people. But people's access to their own processes is limited and subject to bias, and their observations of other people can be non-representative, misinterpreted, or wildly distorted. People can also gain insight by turning to "experts" or an assortment of self-proclaimed authorities, from talk show hosts and news commentators to theologians, politicians, and writers. These sources often provide inconsistent points of view, however, and they are subject to their own biases and limitations.**

- **Science is conducted by humans and thus cannot completely escape many of the biases and limitations associated with these nonscientific ways of understanding social processes. The scientific approach to social psychology should be viewed as an ongoing competition between competing perspectives, with agreed-upon rules such as parsimony deciding the victor in any given match-up. Because science is a continuous venture, a theory that wins the battle one day may relinquish its crown in the future. The new champion must account for what has been established by previous champions, however, which provides for progressive understanding rather than simple reversals of fortune in the search for knowledge.**

- **The scientific method is defined as a sequence of stages—observation, theory construction, hypothesis generation, and verification—that selects for some ideas while discarding others. The implementation of this general method can take one of three forms, each with its own set of advantages and limitations. Correlations are very useful in identifying patterns among different classes of events, but this approach cannot establish the causal link between correlated variables.**

- **Experiments are designed to take correlations to this next crucial step in explanation, and they have become the backbone of social psychological research for this reason. However, experiments are unnatural events for participants, raising concerns whether they really capture the essence of the psychological process in question. Researchers have become quite adept at dealing with this issue, but three other limitations have proven a bit trickier. First, experiments are not designed to assess bidirectional or reciprocal causality—whether an effect at Time 1 might function as the cause at Time 2. Second, the usual focus in experimentation is the immediate impact of a causal factor, leaving unaddressed how the process that is launched plays out over time. Third, some important topics are off limits to experiment research because of ethical issues. Humiliation, prejudice, and genocide exist in the real world, but they cannot be realistically replicated in the laboratory out of respect for the well-being of research participants.**

- **Social psychology has begun to embrace computer simulation, an approach that allows researchers to get around these issues. By framing psychological processes as simple rules, psychologists can observe these processes unfold in time. This approach can explore and visualize processes that occur on vastly different time scales, from seconds to centuries. And because actual humans are not involved, the computer** simulation approach sidesteps thorny ethical issues that would prevent some issues from being explored in experiments. But the very artificiality of this approach can cause researchers to neglect or dismiss human idiosyncrasies and the random influences that characterize everyday life. The elements in a computer program are nice and tidy, but real humans are not so easily pegged and certainly not so interchangeable.

* Each approach to exploring the dynamics of human experience is a unique mix of advantages and limitations. By employing a multidisciplinary strategy that taps the strength of each approach, scientists are able to cross check their results and hone in on the true nature of human experience. In identifying patterns, correlational studies suggest where one should look for cause-effect relations in experimental studies. To reveal how causal forces unfold in time, and to identify bidirectional causality, computer simulations can be designed to capture the nature of psychological processes. The complementarity of these methods is gaining recognition in social psychology and may become the dominant approach in the years to come.

* The insights generated in social psychology have been enhanced by ideas and methods employed in two areas of biology. The study of behavior genetics has provided insight into the genetic causes of behavior and the interplay of these causes with the social processes that traditionally garner attention in social psychology. Recent work has shown that experiential factors can influence how genes are expressed—not just for the individual, but for his or her offspring as well. Social neuroscience, meanwhile, has exposed the brain dynamics at work that underlie mental processes. In linking mind to brain, neuroscience is reframing issues of central concern to social psychology, including the meaning of personal responsibility and free will.

This chapter began by noting that you should not expect to learn much about the subject matter of social psychology in reading the chapter. I was wrong about this, or at least I overstated the point. In describing how researchers approach the dynamics of interpersonal experience, I have presented some basic insights into how people attempt to understand themselves and others, and into how these attempts are related to people's interactions with one another. These simple lessons are the tip of the iceberg, however, showing in broad outline some important features of social thought and behavior that merit deeper examination. The rest of the text is intended to follow up on the leads presented. Chapter 3 begins this venture by describing what social psychologists have discovered (using the scientific method) about how people think and form beliefs, attitudes, and values.

Key Terms

Scientific method	Dependent variable	Institutional review board (IRB)
Theory construction	Operational definition	Debriefing
Hypothesis	Random assignment	Computer simulation
Parsimony	Quasi-experiment	Big data
Implicit psychology	Interaction effect	Multi-method strategies
Autistic hostility	Observational research	Nature versus nurture
Introspection	Archival research	Evolutionary psychology
Social wisdom	Psychological realism	Adaptation
Correlation	Cover story	Twin studies
Causation	Deception	Epigenetics
Reciprocal causation	Ethics of experimentation	Social neuroscience
Bidirectional causality	Risk-benefit ratio	Human uniqueness
Independent variable	Informed consent	

PART II

INTRAPERSONAL EXPERIENCE

3 Beliefs, Attitudes, and Values

Humans take great pride in their ability to think. We may not be as strong or physically gifted as other animals, but we can outwit them without breaking a sweat. Our mental life is what defines us. *Homo sapiens*, after all, means "wise man." We don't simply react to events—most of the time, anyway—as do other creatures. Instead, we consider the relevant factors in a given context, withholding behavior while doing so, and then act on the basis of our decisions.

At least, that's what we like to think. We certainly have the potential for rational thought, but this potential is not always manifest. Sometimes our thoughts are stunningly shallow and devoid of rational content. And sometimes they are not all that instrumental in doing things. We may act first, and *then* think about what we've done—and such thoughts may be in service of rationalization rather than pure understanding. And even if we develop an opinion for more or less rational reasons, there is a tendency for the opinion to become rigid, unbending in the face of new considerations that our mind is perfectly capable of processing but resists doing.

The mind is clearly a complex thing. To understand how we function as social animals, we need a clear sense of how we function as thinking animals. Our journey into the complexities of human social experience begins with a journey into the complexity of the human mind.

CHAPTER OVERVIEW

What Are You Going to Learn?

- **How and why do people develop beliefs, attitudes, and values?** People are not content to live in a world of disconnected facts and events. We integrate facts and events into beliefs and attitudes that shape our reaction to subsequent facts and events. How do we do this and what are the benefits of doing so? How do attitudes withstand challenges to their validity that are encountered in daily life? People go beyond forming specific attitudes and beliefs to develop basic values concerning personal, interpersonal, and societal conduct. How and why do people do this? What are the evolutionary and cultural bases for these values? Is there a set of universal values that transcend culture?

- **What role do attitudes play in people's everyday social experience?** Attitudes hold potential for shaping the way we evaluate our experiences, make decisions, and interact with others. But so do a wide variety of other factors, and these can propel people to think and act in ways that are independent from—or inconsistent with—their private attitudes. How strong a role do attitudes play in daily life? When do attitudes shape behavior, and when instead does behavior shape or transform attitudes? How do people deal with inconsistencies between their attitudes and their overt behavior?

- **Do we control how our minds work?** We assume, or at least like to believe, that we are in control of our own thoughts. But do our minds have a mind of their own? Is it possible for people to suppress their thoughts? Do people have insight into how they think? Can thinking occur in the unconscious? Can people's conscious thoughts get in the way of sound judgment and decision-making? Do people have attitudes of which they are unaware?

The Nature of Beliefs, Attitudes, and Values

How and Why Do People Develop Generalizations About Social Reality?

People are not detached observers in their everyday life. They attach meaning to the events and topics they encounter, and these meanings provide a frame of reference for understanding events and topics they encounter later on. These meanings are experienced as *beliefs*—general ideas concerning the causes, consequences, and characteristics of the event or topic in question. We do not need to know a great deal about something to form a belief about it. No one knows what it is like to be dead, for example, but most people nonetheless have beliefs regarding this topic. The same can be said about the existence of life elsewhere in the universe, the reasons for a bad economy, the trustworthiness of politicians, or the power of electricity.

Beliefs are rarely neutral in their personal meaning, but rather are associated with positive or negative feelings toward the event or topic at issue. We do not simply know (or think we know) things; we also feel things are right or wrong, good or bad. Your (limited) knowledge about economics may coalesce into a belief about liberal versus conservative economic policies, and this belief carries with it an evaluation—that one economic policy is good and the other bad. The concept of *attitude* subsumes both belief and evaluation concerning a topic of thought. Because attitudes provide the interface between the world and people's beliefs and feelings about the world, they also provide ready-made ways of acting. An attitude, in sum, has three related components: *cognition* (belief), *affect* (evaluation), and *connation* (action).

The Functions of Attitudes

Why not keep our thoughts confined to the facts we encounter on a daily basis? Forming a global assessment of something runs the risk of being mistaken and of coming into conflict with others with a different way of seeing things. Psychologists, however, have identified four functions of attitudes, summarized in Table 3.1, that make the trade-off worthwhile, even beneficial (Eagly & Chaiken, 1998; Pratkanis, Breckler, & Greenwald, 1989).

Utilitarian Function

Attitudes are useful because they alert us to pleasant or rewarding objects and situations that we should approach and to unpleasant or costly objects and situations that we should avoid. Consider sunny skies. If you, like most people, have a good feeling about such days, you will be tempted to spend time outdoors when the clouds have parted.

Table 3.1 The Functions of Attitudes

Type of Attitude	Function Served by Attitude
Utilitarian	*Helps the individual achieve rewards and gain approval from others*
Ego-Defense	*Helps the individual protect him or herself from acknowledging basic self-truths*
Value-Expressive	*Helps the individual express important aspects of his or her self-concept*
Knowledge	*Helps the individual structure the world so that it makes sense*

But if you, like a sizable portion of yet other people, feel sunny skies cause bad things—skin cancer, perhaps, or eye cataracts—you will spend as little time as possible outdoors when the sky is clear.

Some attitudes have a utilitarian function that reflects an evolutionary foundation. For example, people everywhere tend to prefer certain landscapes over others, and to do so without a great deal of learning (e.g., Orians & Heerwagen, 1992). Landscapes comprised of water, lush trees and bushes, semi-open space, ground cover, and distant views of the horizon are viewed in positive terms because such environments signaled to our ancestors important features: reliable sources of water, the potential for hunting animals and gathering food, shelter, predator detection, and the means of hiding from predators. Those ancestors who did not have a positive attitude toward such landscapes, preferring instead dry places and limited views, may not have fared as well in obtaining food or avoiding becoming food for predators. Their genes would have diminished in frequency, leaving it to those who valued semi-open places and the like to pass on their genes to subsequent generations, including yours.

But more often than not, the utilitarian function of attitudes is based on learning and experience and thus can produce quite different approach-avoid patterns in different people. Attitudes toward fairly neutral objects become positive or negative when the object is paired with something else that generates a strong positive or negative reaction (Petty & Wegener, 1998). This idea is exploited in politics and consumer advertising. In politics, an audience's attitude toward a political slogan or even a political figure can be changed by pairing these objects with emotionally arousing stimuli—pleasant odors or pictures on the one hand, and electric shock or harsh sounds on the other hand (Janis, Kaye, & Kirschner, 1965; Razran, 1940; Zanna, Kiesler, & Pilkonis, 1970). In advertising, positive attitudes can be generated for a product about which the audience knows absolutely nothing by simply pairing the product with adorable babies, cute puppies, sexy women and men—not to mention desirable landscapes (Gresham & Shimp, 1985).

Sometimes the evolutionary and learning foundations of attitudes can promote conflicting attitudes. Consider food preferences. Foods loaded with fats and carbohydrates provide bursts of energy, and consuming such food enables people to maintain sufficient body mass to survive periods of limited food supplies. Because variable food resources (poor harvests, unsuccessful hunts) were the rule for much of our evolutionary history, natural selection favored those ancestors who took advantage of food that could be stored as extra weight (fatty foods) and that could provide the energy needed to survive (foods high in sugar and other carbohydrates). Our ancestors did not know the first thing about fats and carbohydrates. They were drawn to such food simply because it tasted good. In much of the contemporary world, food availability is nowhere near the issue it was during prehistoric times, so there is no longer a need to consume massive amounts of fatty and sugary foods. Quite the contrary, the consumption of such foods poses serious health risks, as witnessed in the alarming rates of obesity, diabetes, and heart problems in the richer countries of the world such as the United States. The problem is, these foods still taste good—probably a lot better than they did before the rise of corporations that make billions of dollars by preparing foods that appeal to our evolutionarily based attitudes.

Ego-Defensive Function

Everyday life provides a wide variety of information, and not all of it is pleasant or comforting to think about. Such information can go beyond being merely unpleasant (e.g., a news story about a tragic event) to suggest ideas that one does not wish to acknowledge or accept. Attitudes that are formed to protect oneself from the threatening implications of such information perform the *ego-defensive function*. An adolescent boy who doesn't make the cut on a football team might develop a negative attitude toward football, or perhaps toward sports in general. An adult who cannot find a job in his or her chosen field might display the ego-defensive function in different ways—by deciding the

Magazine ad linking menthol cigarettes with young couple in a beautiful outdoor setting
Source: Alamy.com

field is not all that great or by concluding that unfair hiring practices put him or her at a disadvantage (e.g., preferential consideration based on diversity). And a person who discovers that he or she is not particularly good at chess may dismiss the game as a waste of time if he or she views himself or herself as a strategic thinker.

The ego-defensive function can also reflect deep personal insecurities rooted in childhood experiences (Baumeister, Dale, & Sommer, 1998). This function captures the rationale of the *defense mechanisms* identified by Sigmund Freud (1936), who argued that much of mental life represents attempts to defend against conscious awareness of unresolved conflicts and unwanted impulses and desires. A person with unresolved hostility issues, for example, may develop a fascination with contact sports or gun ownership, because these activities provide culturally sanctioned expression of his or her unacceptable impulses. Alternatively, he or she may defend against these impulses by developing *negative* attitudes toward anything that conveys hostility—guns and contact sports, but perhaps blunt criticism or vigorous debate as well. People with negative attitudes toward homosexuality, meanwhile, may have unresolved concerns about their own sexual orientation and cannot accept that they could be homosexuals (Adams, Wright, & Lohr, 1996).

It can be hard to tell whether an attitude is a defense against deep-seated insecurities or a more or less rational consideration of relevant information. The likelihood that insecurity rather than rationality is at work is increased if the attitude is extreme, held with intense emotion, and seemingly impossible to change (Baumeister et al., 1998; Katz, McClintock, & Sarnoff, 1957).

Value-Expressive Function

Certain attitudes are developed and maintained because they help people express their most cherished values. If you value social justice, for example, you are primed to embrace attitudes on social policy that express this value, regardless of other considerations. You might adopt a positive attitude toward affirmative action, collective bargaining by unions, federal regulations of banking practices, or child labor laws. But if you place greater value on personal responsibility, you might feel at best ambivalent toward such policies, adopting a positive attitude instead toward college admission policies based only on grades and SAT scores, salaries and benefits that are allocated on the basis of personal performance rather than union contracts, deregulation of banking practices, and the non-intervention of the government in hiring by businesses.

The value-expressive function is associated with membership in groups. People have considerable latitude in choosing which groups they join, and these choices are often dictated by the values espoused by the potential groups. If you place greater value on social justice than on personal responsibility, for example, you might join Young Democrats in college. If personal responsibility is a more important personal value, you might opt instead for Young Republicans.

But the relationship between the value-expressive function and group membership can work in the other direction. Sometimes we join a group first for reasons totally devoid of basic values, then adopt attitudes that express the values of the group. In choosing which college or university to attend, for example, students (and their parents) consider a variety of factors including tuition costs, entrance requirements, student body size, and geographical location. Once in the college setting, the values to which students are exposed can shape their attitudes toward a wide variety of topics—even if these attitudes reflect values they did not have before attending college.

This effect was documented several decades ago by Theodore Newcomb (1952). Newcomb studied attitudes of the 600 students who attended Bennington College in the mid-1930s. Bennington, an experimental liberal arts college in rural Vermont, was known at the time for its left-leaning political views, often expressed by charismatic liberal professors. The students who entered Bennington, however, were primarily from upper-class Republican families. Newcomb was interested in whether students' conservative background or the liberal context of the college would have greater influence on students' attitudes while at Bennington. To find out, he tracked students' attitudes throughout their academic careers at Bennington.

The answer turned out to be straightforward: immersion in the Bennington environment for 4 years proved to be a stronger influence on students' attitudes than their immersion in a conservative family for the preceding 18 years. Most students' initial political conservatism gave way to politically liberal values that were expressed in specific attitudes. For example, first-year students tended to prefer Republican candidates, but by the fourth year, students showed a marked preference for Democratic candidates. These attitudes were not simply a temporary reprieve from students' pre-Bennington background, but tended to persist throughout their adult lives, long after leaving Bennington. In the 1960 election, for example, 60% of a sample of these students voted for John F. Kennedy, the liberal candidate for President, over the considerably more conservative candidate, Richard Nixon.

Knowledge Function

Attitudes help organize people's understanding of the world, influencing how they attend to, store, and retrieve relevant information. This provides for efficiency in processing the complex social information encountered in daily life. This function is expressed in the tendency to pay attention to and recall information that is consistent with their preexisting attitudes (Eagly & Chaiken, 1998). The trade-off is that such information processing is likely to be driven more by one's preconceptions than by an objective assessment of the facts. This efficiency-bias trade-off is easy to see in how people respond to political debates. Undecided voters may be influenced by what they hear—although the nonverbal qualities of the two candidates seem to carry more weight than their actual statements (Olivola & Todorov, 2010; Patterson, Churchill, Burger, & Powell, 1992)—but this is hardly the case for voters who support one of the candidates at the outset (e.g., Lepper, Ross, Vallone, & Keavney, 1981).

Box 3.1 Are Attitudes Inherited?

A person's attitude toward an object or topic presumably reflects his or her experiences with the object or topic. Some attitudes can be traced to experiences during childhood, reflecting the person's interactions with (or indoctrination by) parents, teachers, peers, and other influence agents. But it appears that the source of attitudes can go even deeper, back to the person's ancestry—that is, to the genes that he or she has inherited. In a study of twins, James Olson and his colleagues (Olson, Vernon, Harris, & Jang, 2001) found that as much as 35% of the variability in people's attitudes is attributable to genetic factors. This means that the genes a person inherits from his or her parents are more important in shaping many of his or her attitudes than are his or her experiences with Mom and Dad. Even more surprising, the attitudes one inherits are psychologically *stronger* than the attitudes that are not inheritable (Tesser, 1993). Specifically, inherited attitudes are reported more quickly, are less influenced by conformity pressures, and play a greater role in shaping interpersonal preferences.

To some extent, the inheritance of attitudes is mediated by personality traits—some of which are themselves highly genetic in nature. Sociability has a strong genetic component, for example, and it is associated with a variety of attitudes, including preferences for intense sensory experiences (e.g., loud music, roller coaster rides), desire for equality (e.g., making discrimination illegal, getting along well with others), and concern with outward appearance (e.g., looking one's best, preference for attention-getting clothes).

This does mean that biology is destiny. Even for strong attitudes, the largest source of variability is a person's experiences after birth. But the experiences that give rise to a person's attitudes are not necessarily those that occur at home with the person's parents and siblings. Instead, the largest contribution to a person's attitudes are *nonshared environmental experiences*—the experiences that are unique to him or her (e.g., with peers). The environmental factors that shape attitudes, in other words, differ for members of the same family—even twins. This conclusion is consistent with research on important personality traits such as extraversion, openness to experience, and emotional stability (Dunn & Plomin, 1990; Plomin, DeFries, & Loehlin, 1977; Plomin & Rende, 1991; Scarr & McCartney, 1983). Parents certainly shape the way their offspring think and act, but this influence is often due more to their shared genes than to their shared experiences.

Perseverance of Beliefs and Attitudes

Because of these functions, an attitude or belief once formed is very difficult to change. Even if the basis for the attitude or belief is discredited—for example, the facts that generated the belief turn out to be wrong—people are inclined to maintain the point of view anyway. This effect is called *belief perseverance* (Ross, Lepper, & Hubbard, 1975). This effect was nicely demonstrated in a study by Anderson, Lepper, and Ross (1980). Some participants were led to believe that risk-takers made better firefighters than did cautious people and some were led to believe the opposite—that cautious people were better firefighters. The beliefs were instilled in participants by having them read cases that suggested one of these mutually contradictory conclusions, and then asking them to generate theories that made sense of these conclusions. After participants developed these supportive theories, they were informed that the cases they had read were bogus, written by the experimenters. Undermining the validity of the evidence for the theories participants had generated did little to undermine their belief in these theories. Those who believed that risk-takers were better firefighters continued to believe this idea, just as those who believed that good firefighters were caution continued to embrace this idea.

Belief perseverance is hardly a ringing endorsement of people's rationality and objectivity, but it is understandable in light of the functions that attitudes and beliefs serve. In a sense, facts are simply a means by which we can reach a conclusion—once a conclusion is reached, the specific information upon which it is based cannot match the certainty or personal conviction provided by the attitude or belief. With its job done, the information no longer matters. It is great to feel certain, but consider the implications of this tendency. In criminal justice, for example, once a juror has decided that a defendant is guilty, it is very difficult to convince him or her otherwise, even if the evidence that prompted the guilty belief is discredited (Davies, 1997). Conspiracy theories, too, have a strong element of belief perseverance. After the election of Barack Obama as president in 2008, for example, the belief that he was not born in the United States, and thus not eligible to be president, gained fairly widespread support among those who did not support him (e.g., 45% of Republicans). The "facts" supporting this belief were never strong, but all doubt should have been laid to rest when Obama's original birth certificate from Hawaii was made public in April 2011. Yet despite this ironclad evidence—not to mention the discrediting of whatever shaky information led to the "birther" belief in the first place—over half of the people who held this belief (e.g., 25% of Republicans) continued to maintain that Obama was an alien. Some of these people, in fact, had become convinced that Obama was the "anti-Christ"—imagine trying to discredit that belief!

The Organization of Attitudes

The functions of attitudes help understand why we are predisposed to form coherent and stable patterns of thinking. The trickier question is *how* people manage to achieve coherence and stability in their mental lives despite the complexity and ambiguity encountered in everyday life.

The Press for Coherence

Tremendous advances have been made over the last several decades in understanding how complex systems in nature function and evolve over time (Haken, 1978; Holland, 1995; Strogatz, 2003; Waldrop, 1992). This approach to science—known as *complexity science* or the study of *nonlinear dynamical systems*—has shown that in a system composed of many "elements" that are connected to one another, there is a tendency for the elements to become coordinated and produce a higher-order pattern. Because the emergence of higher-order states is due to the mutual adjustments of the connected elements, the process is referred to as *self-organization*.

This idea has extended to the formation of higher-order mental states, like beliefs and attitudes (Port & Van Gelder, 1995; Read & Miller, 1998; Vallacher & Nowak, 1994). The elements of mind are the specific thoughts and feelings that arise together in the stream of thought. In thinking about a social issue like gun control, for example, you might experience a variety of thoughts—for example, protection against burglars, the potential for serious harm, the right to own guns, the feelings of one's friends regarding gun control, and so forth. Some of these thoughts are likely to reinforce each other, but others are likely to conflict.

As you continue to think, the mind tries to eliminate the conflict and increase the consistency among the thoughts. If most of the thoughts are biased toward the conclusion that "gun control is necessary," for example, the inconsistent thoughts (e.g., protection, personal freedom) might be downplayed in importance or even change their meaning to make them fit the emerging attitude. The protection provided by owning a gun, for example, might be seen as illusory because the likelihood of needing this extreme form of protection is remote and there is a greater likelihood of shooting someone you know by accident. These new considerations arise spontaneously in the stream of thought as the mind strives to achieve coherence among the relevant thoughts and feelings. The result of this self-organization is a higher-order mental state—an attitude—that makes sense of all the individual thoughts.

The mind's *press for coherence* provides for global understanding despite the wide range of thoughts that set the process in motion. Of course, other people's opinions can influence the attitude that is formed from the basic thoughts and feelings. But even in the absence of persuasion, conformity, and other forms of social influence, there is a tendency for the mind to achieve a coherent state on its own. The press for coherence is a basic feature of mind that can trump other motives and concerns, such as optimism or feeling good (Abelson et al., 1968). Even a decidedly pessimistic and dour attitude may be forged and maintained if it provides a more coherent view of things than would a more upbeat way of seeing things.

The tendency of the mind to seek evaluative coherence can be observed when people are simply asked to think about something, and to do so without any outside influence. Under these conditions, people demonstrate what Abraham Tesser (1976) called *thought-induced attitude polarization* (see also Wilson, Hodges, & LaFleur, 1995). When considering a topic—a friend, an enemy, a public policy, or a sports team—people typically have an attitude that is either primarily positive or primarily negative. But as they continue to think about the topic, some thoughts, memories, and concerns are likely to surface that do not quite fit the initial attitude. In thinking about a friend, for example, the person may recall some events that have the potential to undermine his or her general positive feelings about the friend.

At this point, you might assume that the person would adjust his or her overall feelings somewhat to accommodate the inconsistency. This may indeed happen if the topic is not particularly important. Positive thoughts about a casual friend can soften a bit as unflattering considerations enter the stream of consciousness. But if the topic has a great deal of personal importance—as when thinking about a very close friend—the inconsistent thoughts pose a threat to the person's global evaluation (Latané & Nowak, 1994). As these considerations arise in the stream of thought, they come into contact with the many other considerations that paint a favorable picture of the friend. In this process, the inconsistent thoughts are reinterpreted or perhaps discounted in importance so that they come into alignment with the majority of positive thoughts (Vallacher, Nowak, & Kaufman, 1994). Remembering a time when the friend was critical, for example, the person might decide that the criticism was constructive rather than mean-spirited. As inconsistencies are ironed out as people think about an important person or topic, a slight bias toward positive or negative evaluation can become a highly polarized attitude (see Figure 3.1). The press for coherence is stronger in some contexts than in others. In a busy day filled with lots of things to think about, we may not be bothered by inconsistencies concerning any one of them. But sometimes coherence is a very pressing matter, overwhelming all other principles of mental process.

Need for Closure

Attitudes also tend to become very global and polarized under conditions that activate people's *need for closure* (Kruglanski & Webster, 1996). Need for closure reflects an aversion to ambiguity and uncertainty as well as a preference towards firm, definitive answers to questions. Our social and material worlds are highly complex, filled with contradictory information, and open to interpretation. This is particularly true with regard to issues such as politics,

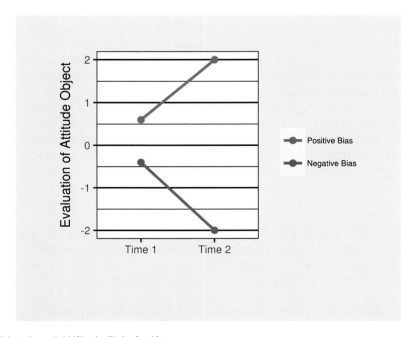

FIGURE 3.1 Thought-Induced Attitude Polarization

economics, or controversial social issues, where very different points of view can all be reasonably defended. If detached, people can entertain these diverse viewpoints and recognize the nuance and ambiguity associated with each one. But such open-mindedness is difficult to maintain when people experience stress, are exposed to an over-load of information, or feel time pressure to adopt one point of view or the other (Kruglanski & Freund, 1983). A noisy environment (Kruglanski & Webster, 1991) can also enhance people's need for closure, as can fatigue (Nelson, Klein, & Irvin, 2003) and intoxication (Kruglanski, Pierro, & De Grada, 2006). Under such conditions, people tend to *seize* and *freeze*: they quickly adopt a point of view (seize) and are unwilling to consider other points of view (freeze).

Everyone is vulnerable to these mental tendencies, but some people are especially likely to demonstrate need for closure even when stress, information load, and time pressure are not all that strong (Webster & Kruglanski, 1994). People with high need for closure cannot tolerate uncertainty and nuance, they ignore conflicting facts, they are rigid in their attitudes, and they are defensive when exposed to different interpretations. They achieve closure by relying on early sources of information and seizing the first answer they come across (Chirumbolo et al., 2004).

High need for closure is associated with other mental characteristics, including dogmatism, simplistic black-or-white thinking, and low intellectual curiosity. Because they prefer definitive answers and seek clarity, they are inclined to follow rules and accept authoritarian leaders, but are reluctant to embrace diversity. People with low need for closure score higher on measures of creativity and are better able to tolerate ambiguity and uncertainty. Such people may be open-minded but they are not necessarily more intelligent than people with high need for closure.

You can get a sense of where you fall on this dimension by completing items from the *Need for Cognitive Closure Scale* (see Box 3.2). I would prefer you wait until you have read this chapter, but then you may find it hard to put off knowing what you are like for another moment.

Box 3.2   The Need for Closure Scale (Selected Items)

1. I dislike it when a person's statement could mean many different things.
2. I feel uncomfortable when someone's meaning or intention is unclear to me.
3. I feel uncomfortable when I don't understand the reason why an event occurred in my life.
4. When I am confused about an important issue, I feel very upset.
5. In most social conflicts, I can easily see which side is right and which is wrong.
6. I'd rather know bad news than stay in a state of uncertainty.
7. When thinking about a problem, I consider as many different opinions on the issue as possible. *
8. I always see many possible solutions to problems I face. *
9. Even after I've made up my mind about something, I am always eager to consider a different opinion. *
10. I dislike questions which could be answered in many different ways.

Note: The full scale consists of 42 items, so your response to these items does not necessarily represent how you score on the full scale. The items with asterisks are worded to express *low* need for closure.
Source: Webster & Kruglanski (1994)

Attitude Dimensions

The tendency for specific thoughts, feelings, and information regarding a topic to become progressively integrated does not mean that attitudes are simply global generalizations devoid of any complexity. You may have a strong feeling about a particular social issue, lifestyle, or occupation, but you can still think about these topics in terms of more specific criteria. Although the mind is programmed to achieve coherence, it can do so with respect to distinct dimensions of meaning. Two occupations may be perceived as equally worthwhile, for example, but one may be seen as more challenging, exciting, or fun than the other.

To some extent, the dimensions along which people integrate information depend on the topic in question. People do not think about political figures in the same specific terms that they think about hobbies, for example. But to a surprising degree, there are common dimensions that enable people to compare and contrast very different topics—including politicians and hobbies. Research going back to the 1950s has shown that people think about most every topic in terms of three basic dimensions: *evaluation, activity*, and *potency/strength* (Osgood, Suci, & Tannenbaum, 1957). Each dimension provides integration for a range of specific thoughts, feelings, and information (see Table 3.2).

These dimensions are largely independent of each other. A politician, for example, may be seen as good (honest, attractive), but not particularly active (delegates responsibility, develops few new policies), and not at all strong (indecisive, avoids confrontation). The generality of these dimensions means that very different topics can be judged by common standards. Abraham Lincoln, hurricanes, and a broken arm, for example, are clearly different topics, but they can be compared and contrasted with respect to the same basic criteria: Lincoln is good, active, and strong; hurricanes are bad, active, and strong; a broken arm is bad, passive, and weak.

The three dimensions are independent, but they are not equally important. Of the three, evaluation provides the best characterization of an attitude (Eagly & Chaiken, 1998; Osgood et al., 1957; Rosenberg, Nelson, & Vivekananthan, 1968). In fact, the other dimensions are commonly used to bolster people's evaluation of a topic (Kim & Rosenberg, 1980). They are independent across different topics, however, because high activity or potency might be considered good when evaluating some topics but considered bad when evaluating other topics. A political figure who is honest and well-motivated, for example, may be evaluated even more positively if he or she is also highly active and effective in getting policies implemented. But a political figure who is distrusted and has a worrisome agenda may be evaluated especially negatively if he or she is highly active and effective. The bottom line in thinking about most anything, in other words, is whether people have a favorable or unfavorable attitude.

Values

The press for coherence does not stop with the formation of beliefs and attitudes. People are concerned with larger meanings that provide guidelines for deciding whether events and courses of action are good (e.g., desirable, moral) or bad (e.g., undesirable, immoral, or even evil). One person, for example, might consider achieving material well-being to be a highly desirable and admirable life theme, but someone else might look upon this perspective on life as shallow, self-centered, greedy, or worse. Global perspectives on what constitutes good versus bad serve to integrate people's specific beliefs and attitudes, and they provide the basis for forming beliefs and attitudes about new events and information. Psychologists and social scientists have identified a relatively small number of such perspectives or *values*.

Values, by their very definition, are subjective. This would seem to suggest that virtually *any* global perspective could function as a value and that people could pick and choose among them to create their own idiosyncratic way of evaluating life's experiences. In principle, a person might find purpose and meaning in avoiding all social contact,

Table 3.2 The Structure of Attitudes

Dimension	Specific Quality
Evaluation	Honest vs. Dishonest
	Warm vs. Cold
	Enjoyable vs. Unenjoyable
	Happy vs. Sad
Activity	Changeable vs. Stable
	Exciting vs. Boring
	Agitated vs. Calm
	Energetic vs. Relaxed
	Methodical vs. Impulsive
Potency	Strong vs. Weak
	Dominant vs. Submissive
	Threatening vs. Reassuring
	Independent vs. Dependent
	In Control vs. Helpless

abusing others who suffer misfortune, seeking out unsanitary conditions, glorifying people or groups with different religions or political systems, or showing disrespect for anyone in a position of authority. In reality, the values that people embrace are far more constrained and tend to converge on a few basic themes. The constraints on value have been traced to three sources: human *evolution, culture*, and the *awareness of personal mortality*.

Evolutionary Foundations

A common misunderstanding of evolution is that the hostile forces of nature thousands of years ago selected only for strength, cunning, and other qualities that gave individuals an edge over one another. In this view, only the selfish survived and passed on their genes—including genes for selfishness—to future generations. Those who were inclined to suspend their self-interest in order to help others or who worried about how everyone in the group fared lost out to those who worried only about themselves. The people living today are presumably the descendants of the latter rather than the former.

Actually evolution works in a far different manner, at least for highly social species such as human beings (M. Nowak & Sigmund, 1998; E. O. Wilson, 2012). In our ancestral environment, humans were not equipped to deal with the forces of nature (predators, disease, food scarcity, disasters) as lone individuals. The strongest male wouldn't stand a chance in a fight with a lion or hyena, nor could he catch or overpower large prey such as an antelope or a buffalo. And if injured or sick, an ancestral human left to him or herself might be hard-pressed to fix the injury or recover from the illness. To survive, our ancestors needed to live in groups, cooperate to get things done, and take care of one another when injured or ill (Caporael, 2005). Only those individuals who thought in these terms lived long enough to pass on their genes.

So despite the potential idiosyncrasy of personal values, the human mind has evolved a tendency to converge on a set of basic concerns that enables people to survive hardships and live harmoniously with one another. Anthropological and experimental research suggest that five basic concerns fulfill these functions and provide the basis for the value systems of people throughout history and around the world today (Haidt & Joseph, 2007; Shweder, Much, Hahapatra, & Park, 1997):

- *Harm/Care* reflects our ability to feel the pain of others. This value is reflected in empathy, kindness, gentleness, and nurturance.
- *Fairness/Reciprocity* is related to reciprocal altruism, a basic feature of social life that enables people to build trust, bond with one another, and engage in cooperative activities. This value is the basis for concerns about justice, rights, and autonomy.
- *In-group/Loyalty* reflects our long history as tribal creatures with the capacity and motivation to form shifting coalitions. This value is the basis for patriotism, the individual's willingness to sacrifice for the group, and vigilance for traitors and enemies.
- *Authority/Respect* is shaped by our primate history of hierarchical social interactions and relationships. This value is the basis for leadership, deference to legitimate authority, and respect for traditions.
- *Purity/Sanctity* reflects the danger posed by pathogens (bacteria, viruses, fungi, etc.) and contamination (e.g., spoiled food, poor sanitation) throughout our evolutionary history. This value is reflected in disease vigilance and disgust regarding contamination, and it underlies religious notions of striving to live in a manner that transcends carnal desires.

Cultural Foundations

Evolution provides a broad blueprint for our survival as a species, so people everywhere share the same fundamental values. Within these broad constraints, however, different cultures throughout history have developed their own notions of right and wrong, good and evil, commendable and intolerable, to deal with the specific issues they face. Every culture is unique, but social scientists and psychologists have identified some basic dimensions along which different cultures can be compared. The most popular dimension, described in Chapter 1, is *social independence versus interdependence* (Markus & Kitayama, 1991; Nisbett, 2003; Triandis, 1989). In interdependent cultures—prominent in parts of Asia, Africa, and Latin America—people are sensitive to how they are connected by virtue of family, occupation, social class, or national identity. In independent cultures, which are more prevalent in Western Europe and North America, people place greater emphasis on personal characteristics and achievement.

Independent and interdependent cultures differ in the relative importance they attach to fundamental values (Schwartz & Bilsky, 1990; Triandis et al., 1988). Compared to cultures characterized by high interdependence, those with an independent orientation place greater emphasis on competition (and less on cooperation), have weaker in-group loyalty, and are less concerned with maintaining respect for authority. These differences are manifest in many aspects of social life, including the following:

Interdependent	*Independent*
Obligation to others	*Individual rights*
Rely on the group	*Self-sufficiency*
Fulfill roles with the group	*Pursue individual goals/interests*
Group achievement	*Individual achievement*
Competition between groups	*Competition between individuals*
Group or hierarchical decision-making	*Self-determination, individual choice*
Shame/guilt due to failing the group	*Shame/guilt due to individual failure*
Property shared within group	*Individual property rights*
Objects valued for social uses	*Objects valued for technological uses*

These differences represent more than people's acceptance of the norms and traditions in their respective cultures. People in independent and interdependent cultures process nonsocial as well as social information in fundamentally different ways (Nisbett & Miyamoto, 2005; Nisbett, Peng, Choi, & Norenzayan, 2001). Interdependent cultures foster a *holistic perceptual style* that is characterized by attention to relationships among objects and to the context in which the objects are embedded. Independent cultures foster an *analytic perceptual style* characterized by attention to salient objects and to people's goals with respect to those objects, with less attention given to the surrounding context. What is the link between the way one processes information and the emphasis in one's culture on interdependence versus independence?

The answer lies in the different social functions associated with the two perceptual styles. Compared with analytic perceptual processing, holistic perceptual processing is tied to social concerns (Kim & Markman, 2006) and is biased toward facilitating behavioral alignment with other people (Van Baaren, Horgan, Chartrand, & Dijkmans, 2004). Holistic perceptual processing helps people attend to others' needs and fit into social contexts. Analytic perceptual processing helps people pursue their own goals without being overly influenced by social relations and the context for their goal-directed behavior.

These differences in perceptual styles can be assessed with the *framed-line task* (FLT), shown in Figure 3.2, developed by Kitayama, Duffy, Kawamura, and Larsen (2003). Participants are first shown a square frame containing a vertical line (the frame on the left). In a second square of a different size, they are asked to draw a line that is identical to the first line in either *absolute length* (the absolute task, top frame on the right) or *relative length* (the relative task, bottom frame on the right). The absolute task requires participants to focus on the first line while ignoring the contextual frame, whereas the relative task requires participants to attend to the relationship between the first line and the contextual frame. Participants who engage in more analytic perceptual processing ignore the contextual frame and thus make fewer errors on the absolute task and more errors on the relative task. Participants who engage in more holistic processing attend to the relationship between the line and the contextual frame and thus make more errors on the absolute tasks than on the relative task.

Miyamoto and Wilken (2010) employed the FLT to assess the processing styles of people from interdependent and independent cultural backgrounds. As suspected, independent participants made relatively few errors on the absolute task but many errors on the relative task. The opposite pattern was observed for interdependent participants: they made more errors on the absolute task and fewer errors on the relative task. Cultural values apparently go beyond influencing how one relates to others to shape our perception of the physical world.

Terror Management

Evolutionary adaptations and cultural experience are useful for understanding the origin of basic values. But one can also ask where *any* value comes from. Is there some fundamental reason why we develop and maintain

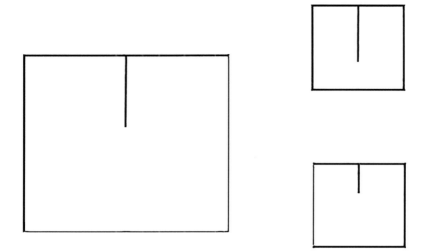

FIGURE 3.2 The Framed-Line Task (FLT)
Source: Adapted from Kitayama et al. (2003)

strongly held beliefs and values? An intriguing perspective on this question is provided by *terror management theory* (TMT), developed by Jeff Greenberg, Tom Pyszczynski, and Sheldon Solomon (1986). This theory is based on the fact that humans are unique in the animal kingdom in being aware that they will die someday. Other species certainly recognize danger and fear things that could do them harm, but lacking self-awareness they cannot comprehend their nonexistence. According to TMT, thinking about the inevitability of one's own death produces a level of anxiety that can be debilitating. The most common way of dealing with this problem is simply to deny it—to convince oneself that one will go on living after one's physical life on earth has ended (Becker, 1973).

But that is not the only way to deal with the terror of death, according to TMT researchers. People can derive some comfort from believing that although they will personally cease to exist, many of the things they value will continue to live on. Having children and focusing on one's role as a parent is one way of maintaining this belief (Wisman & Goldenberg, 2005). But another way of managing the terror of death is to think of oneself as connected to a broader culture, complete with a comprehensive worldview and set of valued institutions that will live on after one has died—indeed, after one's great-great-grandchildren have died. Thus, people embrace basic values—whether it is freedom and democracy, a religious tradition prevalent in the culture, or a means of self-expression—that transcends an individual lifespan.

TMT predicts that people will embrace their cultural values most vigorously when they are reminded of their own death, or even death in general. To test this prediction, researchers employ various manipulations of mortality awareness. For example, participants are asked to write responses to two directions: (1) "Briefly describe the emotions that the thought of your own death arouses in you," and (2) "Jot down, as specifically as you can, what you think will happen to *you* as you physically die." Participants may also complete surveys in front of a funeral home or view pictures of fatal car accidents.

There is impressive support for TMT. When participants are made mindful of death, they become more hostile to people who criticize their country (Greenberg et al., 1990), more committed to their in-group and more hostile to out-groups (Dechesne, Greenberg, Arndt, & Schimel, 2000), more punitive toward those who challenge established laws and procedures (Rosenblatt et al., 1989), and more reluctant to use cultural artifacts such as the US flag for a mundane purpose such as a table covering (Greenberg et al., 1995). When death is made salient, people want to defend the values of the institutions that will live on after their personal demise.

Attitudes and Behavior

How Are People's Private Attitudes Related to Their Public Behavior?

The idea that people strive to achieve and maintain psychological coherence is fine as far as it goes, but by itself it does not tell us much about how people behave in specific situations, each with its own set of forces. People are sensitive to the promise of rewards and the threat of punishment, for example, and these influences may lead people to act as if their personal attitudes were entirely irrelevant. The same could be said of the expectations of other people, social norms for appropriate conduct, and random thoughts and momentary impulses.

To some extent, these other forces are simply independent of personal attitudes, so that the role played by attitudes in deciding how to act can be framed in relative terms—attitudes have a major influence in some contexts and a minor influence in others. But the relationship between attitudes and behavior can take on more complex forms, with other factors and overt behavior transforming—or even creating—attitudes rather than simply muting their influence. These perspectives on the attitude-behavior relationship are discussed in turn below.

Attitudes in Action

Understanding how attitudes are formed is interesting, but psychologists—not to mention politicians, advertisers, and other influence agents—consider attitudes important because of their link to actual behavior. Presumably, if we know how people feel about a certain topic or issue, we can predict how they will act when they confront the topic or issue. What could be a better predictor of voting, car purchase, or vacation plans than a person's attitude toward different political candidates, automobile brands, or forms of recreation? Political campaigns, car manufacturers, and travel bureaus spend enormous amounts of time and money trying to discern people's attitudes in an attempt to predict and possibly influence people's behavior.

The link between attitudes and action is not that straightforward, however. Sometimes, in fact, there is no link at all between a person's attitude and his or her attitude-relevant behavior (Wicker, 1969). Consider, for example, a classic study on the relation between prejudicial attitudes and discriminatory behavior reported by Richard LaPiere (1934). Prejudice against Asians was fairly common in the United States in the early 1930s, and LaPiere was curious (and concerned) whether people who held this negative attitude would act on it in a real-world setting. He embarked on a cross-country trip with a young Chinese couple, expecting that they would be refused service at the hotels and restaurants they visited. To his surprise (and relief), only one establishment out of the 251 they visited refused to serve the Chinese couple. After the trip, LaPiere wrote a letter to each of the establishments, asking if it would serve a Chinese visitor. More than 90% said they definitely would not; the remaining 10% were undecided. In fact, only *one* establishment said they would serve anyone of Chinese ancestry. Clearly, the attitude expressed in writing by the hotels and restaurants was not consistent with their actual behavior.

This study is hardly a controlled psychological experiment, and one can envision several reasons for the discrepancy between attitudes and behavior that have little to do with inconsistency per se. Perhaps the people at the various establishments developed their negative attitudes in the months between the visit and LaPiere's letter. Or perhaps they were not the same people who responded to LaPiere's letter. Still, the lack of correspondence between expressed attitudes and actual behavior highlights the possibility that people's attitudes are not always predictive of how they will behave in concrete settings. Research since LaPiere's study has focused on the factors that dictate whether attitudes predict behavior (Ajzen, 1985; De Bono & Snyder, 1995; Eagly & Chaiken, 1998; Fazio, 1990; Wicker, 1969).

The lack of consistency between attitudes and behavior is testament to the complex and often conflicting set of forces underlying human behavior. Sure, attitudes are important, but so are social norms that prescribe allowable versus frowned-upon behavior, the anticipated consequences of different courses of action, and the ease versus difficulty of enacting attitude-consistent actions (Ajzen & Fishbein, 2005; Armitage & Conner, 2001; Cooke & Sheeran, 2004; Trafimow & Finlay, 1996). A person may have an attitude (e.g., anti-Asian prejudice) that predisposes him or her to behave a certain way (refuse service to an Asian couple), but inhibit that response if such behavior is considered inappropriate (discriminatory and illegal), is likely to produce unpleasant consequences (retaliation or perhaps legal action), or is difficult or awkward to enact (saying "no" to someone who has done nothing to warrant such treatment).

The *theory of planned behavior* (Ajzen & Fishbein, 2005) provides an account of when and why attitudes are predictive of behavior. In addition to the factors noted above (social norms, anticipated consequences, the difficulty of enacting attitude-relevant behavior), the theory emphasizes the degree to which an attitude is general versus specific. A very general attitude provides a broad guideline for action but lacks the specificity required to direct action in particular contexts where more pressing considerations and forces are at work. An attitude that is more specific provides a tighter link between thought and behavior.

This difference was demonstrated in a study of attitudes toward birth control (Davidson & Jaccard, 1979). Married women were asked questions that probed for very general attitudes (e.g., what they thought about birth control) to very specific attitudes (e.g., what they thought about using birth control pills during the next 2 years). Two years later, the women were contacted again and asked whether they had used birth control pills at any point since the initial survey. As Figure 3.3 shows, women's general attitudes toward birth control were essentially unrelated to their use of birth control pills, but their more specific attitudes were highly predictive of whether they actually used birth control pills.

Cognitive Dissonance Theory

Acknowledging that attitudes are but one force in shaping overt behavior implies that the press for coherence in attitude formation and maintenance is minimized when there are other forces operating on people. But there is another way to think about the relation between attitudes and behavior. In this view, it is precisely *because* people are concerned with maintaining a coherent point of view that their attitudes can appear to be irrelevant to their decisions and actions! This ironic idea is at the core of *cognitive dissonance theory* (Festinger, 1957)—widely considered to be the best known theory in social psychology. There is nothing surprising about the theory but it has been a source of counterintuitive predictions since its inception.

Festinger argued that the mind strives for consonance (coherence), such that the thoughts that co-occur at any point in time are mutually consistent and suggest the same course of action. *Cognitive dissonance* is the lack of consistency, with different thoughts suggesting mutually contradictory courses of action. This inconsistency is psychologically uncomfortable and experienced as tension. This tension motivates people to think or act differently in order

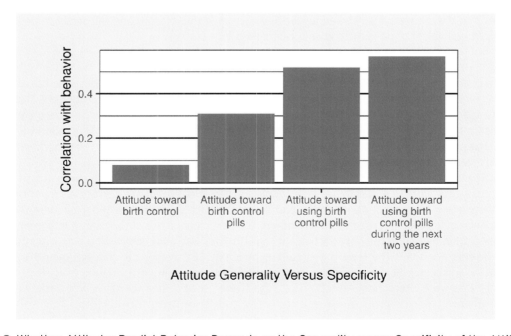

FIGURE 3.3 Whether Attitudes Predict Behavior Depends on the Generality versus Specificity of the Attitude
Source: Adapted from Davidson & Jaccard (1979)

to restore consistency—and thereby reduce the aversive tension. This simple idea has been the source of more than 2,000 published experiments over the past half century.

Attitude-Behavior Consistency

Most forms of inconsistency are not particularly painful and can be managed without much trouble. If you think that vanilla ice cream tastes good but is bad for your waistline, you might be conflicted about whether to indulge, but this conflict is not likely to create mental havoc. You might simply decide to have a small portion or perhaps find a substitute snack. We experience minor episodes of inconsistency every day without feeling particularly tense.

A particular form of cognitive inconsistency, however, can promote considerable tension and lead to dramatic changes in the way you think. This occurs when one of the thoughts is awareness of something you have done or have agreed to do, and the other thought is a negative evaluation of that behavior. Imagine you feel that vanilla ice cream is a bad dietary choice but you nonetheless give into impulse and eat a month's supply in a 10-minute frenzy. This can be tough to swallow, particularly if no one coerced you into eating the ice cream and if several friends witnessed your meltdown. The dissonance here is simple: "Eating vanilla ice cream is bad" and "I just ate like there's no tomorrow." This form of dissonance—inconsistency between one's attitude and one's overt behavior—is what has preoccupied researchers for half a century.

The counterintuitive consequences of cognitive dissonance center on what people do when they have behaved in a counter-attitudinal fashion. Because the behavior is a matter of public record, you cannot rewrite history and pretend it didn't happen. But the attitude is in your head, and assuming you didn't verbalize it in advance of your action, it can undergo revision to make it consistent with the action. You might decide, for example, that consuming large quantities of ice cream isn't such a bad idea—in fact, its wonderful taste more than makes up for its questionable nutritional value. For that matter, there's no proof that ice cream is really unhealthful. The upshot is that you have changed your attitude to reduce the tension you experienced from engaging in the counter-attitudinal action.

Examples abound of attitude change in service of reducing cognitive dissonance. People who smoke cigarettes despite hard-to-ignore health warnings tend to believe that smoking is not all that harmful (Saad, 2002), even if they didn't feel that way before taking up the habit. A consumer may have a tough time deciding whether to purchase a Prius (out of a concern for energy conservation) or a Mercedes (out of a concern for luxury or prestige), but once the decision is made, the choice can reshape the consumer's thoughts. If the Prius is chosen, the person's belief in human-induced climate change may become stronger, but if the Mercedes is chosen, he or she may become a climate change skeptic. And the chosen car will be enhanced in value, while the rejected one will be derogated—even though they were seen as equivalent prior to the choice (Brehm, 1956).

Reverse Incentive Effect

Under the right conditions, a concern for restoring consistency can produce what can be described as a *reverse incentive effect*. This effect was demonstrated in the first cognitive dissonance experiment (Festinger & Carlsmith, 1959). All participants spent an hour repeatedly loading spools on a tray and turning pegs on a pegboard one-quarter turn at a time—tasks that most anyone would consider boring at best. Participants in a control condition were interviewed by someone in the psychology department to see how they felt about their experience in the experiment. Not surprisingly, they didn't rate the tasks as enjoyable.

Other participants were asked to help out the experimenters by talking to the next person to show up for the study. The purpose, they were told, was to see how people's expectations influence performance on the sort of tasks the participants had just completed. Although the participants themselves were in a "no expectation" condition, the next participant was in a "positive expectation" condition. The participants' role, if they chose to accept it, was to help create this expectation by telling the next participant that the task was quite interesting. Participants were offered money for doing this. For some, the reward was quite substantial: $20 (remember this was over 50 years ago); for others, the reward was small: $1 (fairly trivial even then). All participants in both conditions agreed to tell the next person that the tasks were interesting. After doing so, they were asked to rate the tasks on a variety of dimensions, including "enjoyment."

The issue was how participants in the $1 and $20 conditions rated their enjoyment of turning pegs for an hour after telling someone that it was an interesting experience. Presumably, both sets of participants did something that was inconsistent with their attitude—describing boring tasks as interesting. Festinger and Carlsmith reasoned that participants who received $20 could justify expressing this counter-attitudinal view—who wouldn't take some liberty with the truth in exchange for a substantial reward? But those who received a paltry $1 would find it difficult to justify conning someone into performing tasks that they personally felt to be boring. To reduce their cognitive dissonance, the $1 participants should change the way they viewed the tasks—maybe they weren't that boring after all. This would eliminate the inconsistency between their attitude and behavior and thereby reduce the aversive arousal associated with acting in a counter-attitudinal manner. As depicted in Figure 3.4, participants' enjoyment ratings followed this reasoning. The only participants to rate the task above the neutral point were those who received an amount of money that was insufficient to justify their dishonest behavior.

Note the upshot here: the *smaller* the contingent reward, the *more positive* one's resultant attitude toward the behavior, or conversely, the *larger* the contingent reward, the *more negative* one's attitude toward the rewarded behavior. This represents a rather stunning reversal of the conventional wisdom regarding the use of rewards to influence people's behavior. To be sure, large rewards are useful—often necessary—to get a person to perform an otherwise undesirable activity or to express an unpopular attitude. But the effect is likely to be transitory, lasting only as long as the reward contingency is in place. To influence the person's underlying thoughts and feelings regarding the action, and thereby bring about a lasting change in his or her behavioral orientation, it is best to employ the minimal amount of reward.

Choice and Consequences

Everyday life is filled with actions and decisions that are inconsistent with one's personal attitudes. You meet someone at a party who is remarkably unappealing, yet you behave in a pleasant manner when talking with him or her; you know that junk food is bad for your health, yet you will wait in line at the mall for a 500-calorie cheeseburger; you feel it is the duty of citizens to check the qualifications of political candidates before voting, yet you often make your decision based on the candidates' respective political party affiliation or physical attractiveness. What determines whether inconsistency is experienced as sufficiently unpleasant to promote changes in one's attitudes?

This question has been addressed numerous times in experimental research, with the results isolating a small set of factors as critically important (Wicklund & Brehm, 1976). As we have seen, *justification* is a huge factor. A large

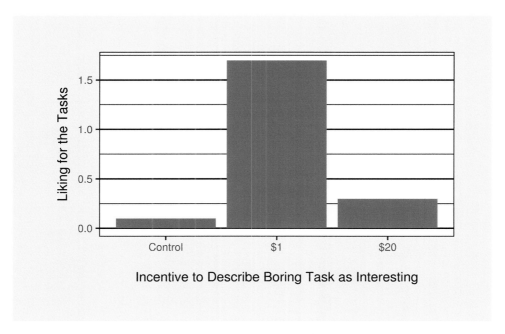

FIGURE 3.4 Liking for a Boring Task after Telling Someone it is Interesting
Source: Adapted from Festinger & Carlsmith (1959)

reward can justify most anything we do, but so can social norms or temptations that anyone would give into. You are nice to the unappealing person, for example, because there are rules of politeness or social etiquette that prevent you from hurting other people's feelings by expressing our unflattering opinions about them. You give into the cheeseburger because no one can resist the chemically enhanced odor of grilled beef presented in a nice, fluffy bun. When the external justification is sufficient, there is no need to change one's attitude about the action in question.

Even if there is little justification for acting in an inconsistent manner, people can avoid cognitive dissonance if they feel that the action was not freely chosen. The critical role of *choice* has been recognized from the beginning of cognitive dissonance research. Linder, Cooper, and Jones (1967), for instance, offered college students either $0.50 or $2.50 (about $4.00 and $20.00, respectively, when controlling for inflation) to write an essay in favor of a state law banning Communists from speaking on college campuses. At that time (the notorious 1960s), most students opposed that law because it seemed to violate the freedom of speech guaranteed by the US Constitution. So in writing the pro-law essay, the participants did something that conflicted with their true attitudes. In a *high-choice* condition, the experimenters emphasized participants' freedom to accept or decline the offer to write the essay. In a *low-choice* condition, participants' freedom was not emphasized; they were simply expected to write the essay.

Figure 3.5 illustrates the role of choice in promoting cognitive dissonance. Among participants in the high-choice condition, the standard reverse incentive effect was observed: those offered the small incentive showed greater attitude change than did those offered the large incentive. But in the low-choice condition, participants offered the large reward actually showed greater attitude change than did those offered the small reward—perhaps because the good feelings associated with a large amount of money rubbed off on their feelings about the essay. The perception of free choice makes people feel responsible for their behavior and thus creates dissonance when they behave in an inconsistent manner.

Acting in a manner that conflicts with ones' personal attitudes can be dismissed if nothing comes of it. Your decision to vote for a political candidate based on his or her appearance rather than qualifications is no big deal if he or she loses the election, or if he or she is elected and does a great job. But when inconsistent behavior has *negative consequences*, it promotes a heightened sense of cognitive dissonance (Wicklund & Brehm, 1976). Imagine how you would feel if you voted for the candidate on superficial grounds and he or she wins the election narrowly, and then

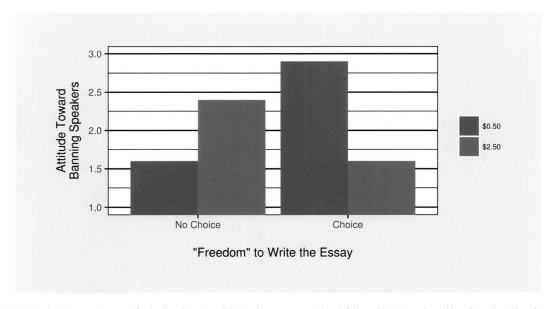

FIGURE 3.5 The Importance of Choice in Cognitive Dissonance. The Higher the Number, the Greater the Support for the Proposed Law Banning Speakers from University Campus.
Source: Adapted from Linder et al. (1967)

proceeds to drive the country into a foreign policy crisis or a deep economic recession. Now your counter-attitudinal behavior is likely to become a big deal for you. You can't take back the vote, but you can change your attitude about how to make voting decisions. After all, there are plenty of facts to support any voting preference, so why not employ gut feelings based on the candidates' relative attractiveness to make the decision.

By the same reasoning, cognitive dissonance is minimized if negative consequences fail to materialize. In the Festinger-Carlsmith paradigm, for example, the experience of dissonance is muted for the $1 participants if the person they are trying to convince of the tasks' interest value acts if he or she is unconvinced (Cooper & Worchel, 1970; Nel, Helmreich, & Aronson, 1969). These participants had freedom to con the person and little external justification to do so, but if the person responds by saying "I have never enjoyed an experiment and I don't think I will find this one much fun," he or she did not suffer the indignity of taking part in boring activities under false pretenses. On the other hand, if the person acts as if he or she is convinced by the $1 participants' description of the tasks ("great, I can't wait to get started!"), participants' dissonance is enhanced and they change their attitude toward the tasks all that much more.

The effect of negative consequences is particularly strong if the consequences were *foreseeable* (Wicklund & Brehm, 1976). It's one thing to freely choose to act in counter-attitudinal fashion that produces negative consequences. It's quite another to do so knowing the negative consequences in advance. If you knew the presidential election was likely to be extremely close and that one of the candidates was likely to do bad things, dissonance is maximized if that candidate wins and you neglected to vote. In this case, you may convince yourself that the candidate's positions and policies are not that bad after all.

Mind and Body

Cognitive dissonance is not all in the mind. The theory assumes that dissonance is felt as unpleasant arousal, and that it is the reduction of this physical tension—not the cognitive inconsistency—that motivates attitude change. Despite the centrality of this idea, almost two decades passed before it was directly tested. But these tests, designed by Mark Zanna, Joel Cooper, and their colleagues (Zanna & Cooper, 1976), were ingenious and well worth the wait.

The approach is based on the idea that people are not always clear about why they feel the way they do. Such *misattribution of arousal* occurs when people experience physical sensations of arousal—a rapid heart rate, shoulder tension, or stomach churning, for example—and think this state is due to something that really had nothing to do with it. A young male walking across a wobbly bridge, for example, may feel a bit tense because of the 100-foot drop to the water below but attribute his heightened heart rate instead to an attractive female he encounters on the bridge (Dutton & Aron, 1974). Zanna and Cooper reasoned that if the source of arousal can be misperceived this easily, then perhaps the arousal stemming from cognitive dissonance could be misattributed to a source that had nothing to do with acting contrary to one's attitudes. If so, changing one's attitude to match one's behavior would do little to reduce one's tension, and thus there would be little motivation to do so.

In an early test of this idea, Zanna and Cooper (1974) gave participants a drug in pill form (which was really a placebo) and told them the pill would have one of three effects: it would make them feel tense, it would make them feel relaxed, or it would have no physical effects (the truth). The participants then wrote an essay arguing that inflammatory speakers should be barred from college campuses, a position with which most students at the time strongly disagreed. As is common in cognitive dissonance research, some participants were induced to think they had free choice to write the essay, while others felt they had no choice in doing so. For participants who were told the pill would have no effect, Zanna and Cooper expected to find standard dissonance reduction—a change in attitude to match the view expressed in the essay—in the free-choice condition. As illustrated by the middle bars in Figure 3.6, this prediction was confirmed. Participants presumably felt uncomfortable expressing an opinion they didn't believe, so they changed their belief about banning speakers to match what they wrote.

The predictions were quite different for participants who were led to believe the drug would affect how they felt. Those who thought the pill would make them feel tense were expected to attribute the discomfort generated by writing the counter-attitudinal essay to the pill rather than to their inconsistency. Feeling that their tension had nothing to do with the essay, they should feel little need to change their attitude about inflammatory speakers on campus. The left bars in Figure 3.6 show that this prediction was confirmed. In contrast, those who thought the pill would make them feel relaxed were expected to experience heightened distress over having written the counter-attitudinal essay. After all, they were feeling tense *in spite of* the relaxing drug, so they must feel especially bad about expressing an opinion they didn't believe. These participants, then, were expected to show even greater attitude change than were

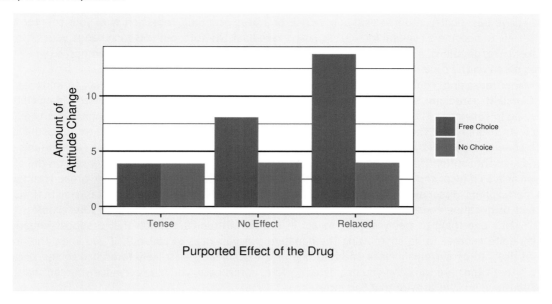

FIGURE 3.6 Amount of Change in One's Prior Attitude When Different Interpretations of Arousal Are Provided
Source: Adapted from Zanna & Cooper (1974)

participants who were told the drug would have no effect. The right bars in Figure 3.6 show that this prediction was confirmed. The biggest dissonance effect—the biggest difference between the free-choice and no-choice participants— occurred when the drug was said to produce relaxation.

Conscious and Unconscious Attitudes

Can People Control What They Think?

We normally don't look upon thinking as work or effort in the same sense as lifting weights, throwing a ball, or running. Physical activity involves muscle exertion and produces sweat, whereas mental activity involves the manipulation of symbols and images, virtual activities that produce few if any physical manifestations—a headache or eyestrain, maybe, but nothing like mental perspiration. But this assumption does not do justice to mental energy and work. The brain, even at rest, consumes calories far out of proportion to its mass and volume. Although the human brain represents a mere 2% of body weight (among normal weight people), it consumes up to 20% of the energy used by the human body (Swaminathan, 2008). It takes energy to think.

Automatic Versus Controlled Processing

Everyone recognizes the difference between spontaneous thought that just "happens"—the immediate recall of someone's name when hearing his or her voice or knowing the answer to 2 + 2—and deliberate thought that requires concentration, as in understanding what one is reading in a textbook. The distinction between these two types of mental experience—referred to as *automatic versus controlled processing*—surfaces fairly regularly in a wide variety of theories and research programs (e.g., Bargh, 1996; Devine, 1989; Eagly & Chaiken, 1998; Greenwald & Banaji, 1995; Petty & Cacioppo, 1986; Shah, 2003; Smith & DeCoster, 1999; Wegner, 1994).

Automatic processing is *unconscious, unintentional, involuntary*, and *effortless* (Bargh, 1994; Schneider & Shiffrin, 1977). Because it does not occupy conscious attention or consume limited mental resources, automatic processing can proceed in parallel on several fronts. Consider, for example, all the mental activities you can perform simultaneously while driving a car. You're watching oncoming cars, attending to the traffic pattern, changing lanes, noticing the scenery, monitoring your speed, estimating distances between your car and the one in front, communicating with a friend in the passenger seat, responding to what he or she says, and listening to music on the radio. Because these acts are inherently easy (e.g., listening to music, noticing scenery) or have become fairly easy and routine through practice (e.g., changing lanes, estimating the distance to the next car), they are not particularly demanding and you have little trouble in performing each one without experiencing interference with the others. You can drive, talk, look, and listen all at the same time.

In marked contrast, controlled processing is *conscious, intended, under voluntary control*, and *effortful*. Imagine that you're driving a car on a slippery road with a difficult-to-manage steering wheel, or that the person in the passenger seat is engaging you in a deep discussion of metaphysics or financial portfolio management. Driving and communicating would each become challenging and require greater deliberation and conscious control on your part—and you might have a tough time trying to do both at the same time.

These two forms of thinking exist on a continuum, with some mental activities requiring greater conscious effort than others. And one form of thinking can transform into the other. If a mental task becomes habitual or mastered, for example, it can change from controlled to automatic, freeing up mental resources for other tasks. Automatic processing, in turn, can give way to controlled processing when the mental task in question becomes disrupted or more difficult. Automatic, parallel processing may be sufficient for driving a well-traveled route on a sunny day, but your thinking can transform to controlled, serial processing when trying to read street signs in an unfamiliar part of town on a rainy day. You can no longer hold a conversation with a passenger and you will probably even turn down the volume on the radio so that you can devote all your mental energy to finding your way.

Cognitive Load

Controlled processes require mental energy, but the brain has a finite store of resources available at a given time. If other mental tasks, even relatively easy ones, must be managed at the same time, there may be insufficient resources to fuel an effortful controlled process. The other tasks can prevent a person from exerting conscious control over the primary task at hand. Imagine if you couldn't turn down the volume or stop the passenger from asking you challenging questions while you're trying to figure out the street signs on the dark and rainy road.

This state of affairs—trying to think about something that requires controlled processes while also trying to manage peripheral tasks that deplete mental resources—has been investigated in terms of *cognitive load* (e.g., Gilbert, Pelham, & Krull, 1988; Miller, 1956; Sweller, 1988). It is difficult to understand the points made in a lecture, for instance, if one is distracted by sounds in the hallway, preoccupied with activities later in the day, or worried that the lecture is too complex to follow. Everyday life is filled with distractions and parallel activities, and these can diffuse the mental resources necessary to engage in challenging mental tasks. In trying to understand the reasons for someone's behavior, for example, trying to hold a 7-digit number (e.g., a phone number) in mind at the same time can promote simplistic rather than nuanced explanations for the behavior (Gilbert et al., 1988).

Even without distractions and other sources of cognitive load, conscious thinking can use up the mental energy required to sustain itself. In effect, the brain needs to become refueled after a period of controlled processing, in the same way that muscles need to regain their strength after strenuous exercise. Such *ego depletion* (Baumeister, Bratslavsky, Muraven, & Tice, 1998) can undermine the capacity for rational decision-making and impulse control, as we shall see in Chapter 6 ("Personal Control"), and promote stereotypical thinking, as we shall see in Chapter 13 ("Prejudice, Stereotypes, and Discrimination").

Thought Suppression

Imagine that someone brings up the topic of white bears, but then tells you, "never mind, don't think about that, it's not important." The person is no doubt right: unless you're from the North Pole and its environs, white bears probably don't hold a great deal of importance for you. So not thinking about them should be no big deal, right? Actually, it can be quite a big deal, according to research on *thought suppression* by Daniel Wegner (Wegner, 1994). This research shows that attempts to suppress thoughts may be successful in the short run, but such success can actually promote a rebound of the suppressed items later on.

It is understandable that people would have a hard time suppressing thoughts about desirable but unattainable goals (e.g., winning the lottery), pleasurable but frowned-upon activities (e.g., romantic liaisons with a co-worker), or other forbidden fruits. But why is it so difficult to suppress thoughts about white bears and other inconsequential topics? Wegner's (1994) *ironic process theory* provides an interesting explanation. Building on the distinction between controlled and automatic processing, the theory holds that the effort to keep thoughts out of consciousness involves two components, one of them controlled and effortful, the other automatic and relatively effortless.

The automatic component is a *monitoring process* that searches for evidence that unwanted thoughts (e.g., white bears) are about to intrude. When this process detects an unwanted thought, the controlled component—called the *operating process*—is engaged. The goal of the operating process is to distract oneself by finding something else to think about ("look, there's a lovely door in this lab!"). The monitoring process, which is unconscious and proceeds with minimal mental resources, is always on call as an early warning system to watch for the suppressed thought. The operating process, which is conscious and cannot do anything without using up mental resources, keeps the unwanted thoughts from making deep inroads into consciousness.

Much of the time the two processes work together to keep unwanted thoughts at bay. But sometimes people's mental resources are deployed elsewhere and not available to engage the operating process. Fatigue, stress, or distraction can divert the resources necessary to keep the operating process viable. Because the monitoring process is automatic and doesn't consume mental resources, however, these experiences of cognitive load do not impair its operation. With only the monitoring process activated, an unwanted thought is detected but nonetheless enters consciousness while the operating process is looking the other way or taking a rest.

This reasoning has paradoxical implications for self-control. Dieting, for example, can be a struggle because it requires the suppression of thoughts about desirable but forbidden food supplies within walking distance from virtually anywhere. A dieter can successfully suppress these thoughts with effort, but if he or she experiences stress or is unduly distracted, there may a sudden preoccupation with Big Macs, cheese fries, and Pop-Tarts.

Thought suppression can wreak havoc on interpersonal relations as well. As we shall see in Chapter 13, for example, the attempt to suppress stereotypical thoughts about people belonging to different categories (e.g., race, gender, political orientation) can backfire if one is under cognitive load (e.g., because of stress or a parallel activity). In interacting with an African American, a White male may blurt out an inappropriate racial comment precisely because he is on guard against doing so, if he happens to be preoccupied by other concerns at the moment. Note that failure to suppress an unwanted thought does not necessarily reflect a deep-seated belief in the validity of the thought. Simply not wanting to think something, perhaps because one knows that it is a patently untrue idea, can keep the thought rebounding into consciousness when one does not have the mental resources available to fuel one's operating process.

Box 3.3   Is Mel Gibson Anti-Semitic? Or Did His Tirade Reflect the Irony of Thought Suppression?

In 2006, the actor and director Mel Gibson was stopped for driving under the influence of alcohol in Malibu, California. During the incident, Mel blurted out a string of anti-Semitic comments, some of them directed at the police officers. None of the comments was remotely relevant to the incident, nor were they particularly helpful to his cause (quite the opposite, actually). The conventional wisdom in the aftermath of this incident was that Mel really harbored anti-Semitic attitudes and that the alcohol caused him to let down his guard, allowing his "real" (or perhaps implicit) attitudes to come out. After all, he had recently directed a movie, *The Passion of the Christ*, which had been criticized for what many people felt was an anti-Jewish undertone. Prior to that, his father had apparently said some inflammatory things about the reality of the Holocaust. Both pieces of information led some people to think that Mel didn't like the Jewish faith or perhaps Jewish people.

But think about the situation from a thought suppression perspective. Because of the readiness of many to see Mel as anti-Semitic, he may have been on guard not to think or say anything remotely anti-Semitic. And with both his monitoring and operating processes intact, he was quite successful in doing so. But because alcohol depletes mental resources, his encounter with the police officers may have left only his monitoring process intact, promoting a rebound of the unsavory thoughts he could otherwise suppress. Just like the college student who has no particular attitudes about white bears but nonetheless becomes preoccupied with them when under cognitive load, perhaps Mel Gibson was caught in the mental trap of thought suppression.

Unconscious Thought

The research on automatic processing challenges the way most people view the mind. We like to think that controlled processing is the default mode of thinking, with automatic processing representing the exemption. Psychologists have discovered instead that the automatic mode predominates over the controlled mode much of the time (Hassin, Uleman, & Bargh, 2005; Wilson, 2002). What does this say about human intelligence and our ability to think logically and effectively? Can we truly understand ourselves, judge others fairly and accurately, or make sound decisions if the mental processes at work routinely occur without conscious control? These issues have become a focus of research attention in recent years. A surprising lesson from this research agenda is that there are advantages to thinking automatically much of the time.

The Advantages of Unconscious Thinking

To appreciate how unconscious thinking can be advantageous, it is helpful to consider why we have conscious thought at all (Baars, 2005; Crick & Koch, 2003; Mandler, 2002; Marcel, 1983; Tononi & Edelman, 1998). Most cognitive processes (e.g., perception, motor control) are unconscious in their operation and do fine without conscious intervention or even conscious awareness. Visual images become spontaneously integrated to generate perceptions of objects and people, and specific muscle movements achieve integration to maintain balance and generate action. Such integration is achieved by means of self-organization—the mutual influence among basic elements (images, muscle movements) to promote a higher-order mental state (a coherent perception, a coordinated action). Unconscious thinking is an extension of autonomous mental activity to attitude formation and decision-making. You experience unconscious self-organization when you have a sudden flash of insight—the "Aha!" phenomenon—or when you "sleep on" a decision rather than trying to settle the issue consciously.

Conscious thinking, in fact, can get in the way of effective and efficient behavior. Attempts to bring a mental process under conscious control can disrupt the spontaneous emergence of order that would otherwise occur. Trying to consciously control each muscle movement in a skilled action, for example, can prove disruptive rather than helpful, introducing awkwardness into an otherwise synchronized flow of movement (Csikzentmihalyi, 1990; Kelso, 1995; Vallacher & Wegner, 1987). Mental elements, too, tend to achieve integration if left unattended and allowed to flow unimpeded by top-down (controlled) processing. In this view, the judgment that becomes accessible to consciousness is an emergent product of self-organization dynamics.

The disruptive nature of conscious thinking has interesting implications for social relations. Have you ever pondered, for example, why you feel so positively about certain people—a close friend, a lover, or a public figure? If not, it is probably just as well. Digging deep to find reasons for feelings runs the risk of undermining the feelings that were doing just fine by themselves. Introspection regarding a well-entrenched attitude tends to bring to mind what is easiest to identify, justify, or capture in words—and these insights may miss the mark entirely.

An intriguing study by Timothy Wilson and his colleagues made this point (Wilson et al., 1984). Participants currently in a relationship were simply asked about the person with whom they were involved. Half the participants were asked only for an overall evaluation of the relationship. The other participants, however, were first asked to list why they felt the way they did and *then* to provide their overall evaluation of the relationship. Wilson and his colleagues then contacted all the participants 9 months later to check on the status of their relationships. Results showed that the group who did not attempt to provide the reasons for their relationship maintained their evaluation over the 9-month period to a greater extent than did the group that was initially asked to introspect into the nature of their relationship. Thinking about why we like someone can promote confusion about what our true feelings are.

This effect is not limited to our attitudes about romantic partners. In later research, Wilson and others have found that introspecting about the reasons for our attitudes concerning a wide variety of topics can undermine how well those attitudes guide our behavior. The reason (established empirically, not through introspection!) is that conscious thinking can lead people to focus on the easiest-to-identify reasons for liking or disliking something instead of the *real* reasons for their likes and dislikes. For example, when people are asked to think carefully about the reasons they prefer one product over another, their choices are less likely to correspond to the "true" value of the product as determined by experts (Wilson & Schooler, 1991). People who merely state a preference come closer to matching the experts' judgments. Research has also shown that when people reflect on their reasons before making a choice, as opposed to simply making the choice, they are more likely to regret their choice later on (Wilson et al., 1993).

Conscious thought not only can undermine an existing judgment, it can interfere with the generation of a good judgment in the first place (Dijksterhuis & Nordgren, 2006). Ap Dijksterhuis (2004) demonstrated the superiority of unconscious thinking with respect to a familiar task: shopping for an apartment. He gave participants a great deal of information about four apartments in a short period of time, which made it difficult for them to determine which one was the better choice. The information was such that one of the apartments had the highest ratio of good to bad attributes (e.g., cost, location, size, appliances). Participants were then randomly assigned to one of three conditions. Those in the *immediate choice* condition were asked to choose the apartment they thought was best right away. Those in the *conscious thought* condition were asked to think carefully about the apartments for 3 minutes and then indicate their choice. Those in the *unconscious thought* condition performed a distracting task for 3 minutes so that they could not think about the apartments consciously.

Strange as it may seem, the unconscious thinkers made the best choice—they were more likely to pick the apartment that was objectively the best buy (i.e., the one that had the most favorable ratio of good to bad attributes). This did not reflect a lack of thought on their part, however. The participants *least* likely to make the best choice were those in the immediate choice condition, who were denied time to think about the apartments. Rather, it was the mode of thought that counted—unconscious thinking proved superior to conscious thinking. Other research has shown that unconscious thinkers choose alternatives with more positive and fewer negative characteristics, choose alternatives that lead to more satisfaction, choose more creative solutions to problems, and make more accurate future predictions (Strick et al., 2009).

The Benefits of Conscious Thinking

This does not mean that conscious thinking is a waste of time and mental energy. Conscious thinking may get in the way of mental processes that can run without executive supervision and control, but it is crucial to getting the relevant mental processes up and running in the first place. In forming judgments (e.g., assessing the quality of someone's performance) or making a decision (e.g., choosing among apartments), a person must first know something about the topic in question—the criteria of good performance or the factors that are relevant to decision-making. This knowledge is acquired through conscious attention to the topic in question. Only after some expertise is established can unconscious thinking take over and allow self-organization to finish the job (Mudrik, Breska, Lamy, & Deouell, 2011; Wojnowicz, Ferguson, Dale, & Spivey, 2009).

A study by Dijksterhuis, Bos, Van der Leij, and Van Baaren (2009) demonstrated the role of relevant knowledge in conscious thinking. Participants viewed 20-second segments of four soccer matches (presented on a computer monitor) and then were asked to predict the winner of each match. Some participants were experts at soccer themselves, but others had little or no soccer expertise. In both groups, participants were asked to make their predictions either immediately (before they had time to think); after 2 minutes, during which they could evaluate what they had seen (conscious thinking); or after 2 minutes, during which they were distracted with a task that required conscious attention and thus could not engage in conscious thinking (but could still engage in unconscious thinking).

If unconscious thinking were always advantageous, one would expect to observe better predictions by participants who were restricted to unconscious thinking. But if the benefit of unconscious thinking shows up only among people who are familiar with the topic in question, one would expect to see an interaction between expertise and mode of thinking. Actually, the interaction would look like the one observed by Dijksterhuis and his colleagues, illustrated in Figure 3.7. Whereas the predictions made by the experts were better when they engaged in unconscious thinking, the opposite was true for the nonexperts—for them, conscious consideration of the soccer teams' respective performance was necessary for them to make a sensible prediction about winners and losers.

Implicit Attitudes

Unconscious thinking may seem strange, but most people can accept the idea that a great deal of mental processing goes on beneath the level of awareness. No one is shocked when a thought seems to pop into consciousness in an "Aha!" manner. It is as though the thought had been assembled by mental functions that run continually in the background until it was ready to burst into conscious awareness. But what about the possibility that people have fully formed thoughts—even important attitudes—that are outside of conscious awareness? That sounds downright

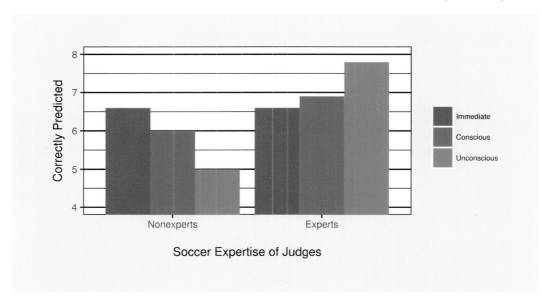

FIGURE 3.7 The Proportion of Correctly Predicted Games as a Function of Expertise and Thought Condition
Source: Adapted from Dijksterhuis et al. (2009)

paradoxical. It's one thing to acknowledge that lower-level processing takes place without conscious attention. But how can we have an attitude—the output of mental processing—and not know that we have it?

Yet that is precisely the conclusion that many psychologists have drawn on the basis of the *Implicit Association Test* (IAT), developed by Anthony Greenwald, Mazarin Banaji, Brian Nosek, and their colleagues (Greenwald & Banaji, 1995; Greenwald et al., 1998; Nosek, Banaji, & Greenwald, 2002). The technique measures how quickly one can associate different concepts. Presumably, if two concepts are related, a person can respond to them very quickly. "Fresh" and "clean," for example, are easy to associate because they both have a positive connotation and we can think of how they occur together—for example, *clean* clothes are *fresh*. The same is true of "smelly" and "dirty" because they both have a negative connotation and we can think of how they go together (e.g., *dirty* clothes are *smelly*). But what happens when two concepts have different connotations—one is positive, the other is negative—and they do not occur together? "Fresh" and "dirty," for example, are evaluated differently and it is hard to imagine how they occur together. The same is true of "clean" and "smelly."

The IAT takes advantage of this difference to assess whether people have unconscious attitudes. A series of words or pictures is presented on a computer screen, and respondents are asked to classify them into categories as quickly as possible by hitting one of two keys. Consider the words listed in Figure 3.8. In the first round of the test, respondents press "d" (with their left hand) if the word signifies "weak" or a female name, but they press "k" (with their right hand) if the word signifies "strong" or a male name (first panel). If people view females as weak and males as strong, they should respond quickly to each word as it appears on the screen.

The rules are then changed in the second round of the test (second panel): the person presses "d" (with their left hand) if the word signifies "weak" or a male name, and presses "k" (with their right hand) if the word signifies "strong" or a female name. If people view males as strong and females as weak, deciding which key to press for each word is not easy. If they see a "strong" word, they are torn between pressing "k" (signifying "strong") and pressing "d" (signifying a male name). Because "strong" and "female" are not strongly associated, it takes longer to press the correct key. The greater the difference in response time between the first and second rounds of the test, the greater the tendency to see males as strong and females as weak.

Some attitudes measured in this way match the attitudes that are revealed in self-report tests, in which people indicate their conscious feelings about various concepts (categories of people, political views, etc.). But this is not

Round 1

Press the "d" key with your left hand for "weak" words and female names.

Press the "k" key with your right hand for "strong" words and male names.

Frank
Tough
Jane
Soft
John
Delicate
Heather
Mighty
David
Energetic
Marie
Dominant
Mike
Powerful
Susan
Shy
Tom
Lazy
Sarah
Forceful
Eric

Round 2

Press the "d" key with your left hand for "weak" words and male names.

Press the "k" key with your right hand for "strong" words and female names.

Frank
Tough
Jane
Soft
John
Delicate
Heather
Mighty
David
Energetic
Marie
Dominant
Mike
Powerful
Susan
Shy
Tom
Lazy
Sarah
Forceful
Eric

FIGURE 3.8 The Implicit Association Test (IAT)

always the case. As we shall see in Chapter 13, most people today report that they are not prejudiced toward African Americans, Latinos, Muslims, Jews, or other racial, ethnic, and religious groups. The attitudes measured in this way are *explicit*, in that people are aware of them and can report them directly. But when people's automatic associations are assessed with the IAT technique, quite different attitudes are often revealed. These attitudes are *implicit*, in that they are revealed in people's reaction times and are not under conscious control. A person might report that he or she is not prejudiced against Muslims, for example, but if he or she takes a long time to respond when Muslim names and pleasant words are associated, this suggests that he or she harbors an unconscious bias against such people.

Since its development in the 1990s, the IAT has emerged as perhaps the most widely employed psychological test on the planet. Over a million people have taken the Web version of the IAT, which has been modified to assess implicit attitudes toward just about everything imaginable—the elderly, racial and ethnic groups, religions, demographic groups, countries, occupations, and various stigma (including tattoos!). Although there is some controversy about what the IAT really measures, the evidence suggests that it taps feelings that are normally not expressed (Lane, Banaji, Nosek, & Greenwald, 2007; Rudman & Ashmore, 2007). People who appear non-prejudiced toward African Americans on self-report tests but score as prejudiced on the IAT, for example, show heightened neural activity in the amygdala (a brain region associated with negative emotions) when presented with faces of African Americans (Phelps et al., 2000).

The existence of an implicit attitude that contradicts a person's explicit attitude may seem strange but it actually makes a great deal of sense. As emphasized earlier, an attitude represents an integration of separate thoughts and feelings that provides a coherent evaluation of the attitude target. That's fine, except that sometimes all the relevant information cannot be integrated with respect to a single attitude. Particularly if there is a great deal of information available concerning the target, there are likely to be thoughts and feelings that cannot be made to fit the dominant or preferred attitude. People go to great lengths to dismiss or ignore inconsistent information, but this does not remove these thoughts and feelings from the mental system.

What happens to thoughts and feelings that cannot be integrated in terms of the preferred attitude? There is reason to think that this information becomes the basis for the emergence of an alternative (and competing) attitude. Timothy Wilson and his colleagues provide evidence that *dual attitudes* may be the rule rather than the exception in people's understanding of events and people (Wilson, Lindsey, & Schooler, 2000). In this view, the diverse facts, memories, and concerns concerning an attitude topic can often be integrated in mutually inconsistent ways. And as noted earlier, the integration of information can take place out of awareness. From this vantage point, the IAT procedure bypasses executive control to allow the mental system's alternative integration scheme to be expressed.

SUMMING UP AND LOOKING AHEAD

- **The mind is always in motion, taking in and making sense of new information on a continual basis. Yet, people manage to integrate this wealth of information into reasonably coherent beliefs and attitudes that provide a stable frame of reference and serve several important functions in daily life. The press for coherence occurs spontaneously as people think about topics or events that hold personal importance, even when there is no external pressure to do so.**
- **People develop basic values that integrate their attitudes and provide a frame of reference for action and judging the actions of other people. There are a few fundamental values that represent evolutionary considerations from our ancestral past, but the relative importance attached to each reflects the influence of culture and personal experience within a culture.**
- **Attitudes and values compete with other forces in influencing behavior in specific situations. Because very general attitudes lack specificity, they tend to be poor predictors of how people behave when faced with more immediate considerations. Attitudes that are framed in specific terms, however, tend to be very good predictors of actions representing these attitudes.**
- **Inconsistency between an attitude and an attitude-relevant behavior can generate an unpleasant state of physiological arousal referred to as cognitive dissonance. Cognitive dissonance is especially intense when the counter-attitudinal action is hard to justify with external incentives and constraints, is freely chosen, and has negative consequences that could have been foreseen. Under these conditions, people change their attitude to make it come in line with their behavior—unless they think the arousal is due to something else and has nothing to do with being inconsistent.**
- **People have limited insight into how their minds work and often make decisions and form attitudes that reflect unconscious processes over which they have no control. Automatic as opposed to controlled mental processes occur when mental resources are diluted or overwhelmed. The suppression of thoughts and attitudes requires mental resources, so when such resources are drained the suppressed material can become expressed. Unconscious thinking is advantageous under circumstances in which consciousness would undermine well-learned means of processing complex information.**
- **Some thoughts are unconscious because they are suppressed, but they remain in the mental system in latent form and can provide the seeds for an attitude at odds with a person's explicit attitude. Such implicit attitudes can be revealed with methods that tap automatic associations.**

  The mind is clearly a powerful tool, but quite often its power is reflected in its capacity for making sense of what one has done for very different reasons. To understand the role that thinking plays in our social lives, it is necessary to broaden the focus to incorporate emotional processes that are intimately linked to features of experience that go beyond the purely rational. This linkage is front and center in the next chapter.

Key Terms

Belief
Attitude
Cognition, affect, connation
Attitude
Utilitarian function
Ego-defensive function
Value-expressive function
Knowledge function
Belief perseverance
Attitude organization
Self-organization
Press for coherence
Evaluation, activity, potency

Thought-induced attitude
  polarization
Need for closure
Theory of planned behavior
General versus specific attitudes
Cognitive dissonance
Attitude-behavior consistency
Reverse incentive effect
Misattribution of arousal
Evolutionary bases of values
Social independence versus
  interdependence
Terror management theory

Automatic versus controlled
  processing
Mental resources
Cognitive load
Ego depletion
Thought suppression
Ironic process theory
Unconscious thinking
Implicit attitudes
Implicit Association Test
Dual attitudes

4 Emotion

Humans may be distinct in the animal kingdom by virtue of their ability to think and develop abstract views of themselves and their place in the world. But human experience would be sorely lacking if we simply thought about things, and did so without registering emotions. The meaning we ascribe to an experience is intimately linked to our feelings about the experience. Acquiring a million dollars or winning an athletic or academic award sounds great, but these events are valued because they elicit positive emotions (e.g., excitement, pride, joy). By the same token, losing one's money or failing to achieve a goal is undesirable to the extent that it makes the person experience a negative emotional state (e.g., frustration, annoyance, despair). Emotions are not restricted to big events like acquiring or losing large sums of money, but arise on a continuous basis in everyday life, providing some level of meaning to virtually every observation, thought, or action. To understand how and why people do what they do clearly requires adding emotional experience to the nature of cognitive experience discussed in Chapter 3 ("Beliefs, Attitudes, and Values").

Despite the importance of emotions and their nonstop experience in daily life, a widely agreed-upon theory of emotion has proven elusive. Some scholars consider emotion a purely subjective experience, but others define it in terms of biological processes—with disagreement about which processes are the crucial ones. Nor is there agreement whether an emotion is a conscious reaction to an event or an automatic response that occurs without conscious awareness. And there is debate regarding the purpose of emotions and the extent to which people can take charge of them or inhibit their expression. Emotion may reside at the core of our being, but penetrating the nature of this core is an ongoing challenge for psychological science.

CHAPTER OVERVIEW

What Are You Going to Learn?

Although an integrative and agreed-upon theory of emotion has yet to be achieved, psychologists have identified the key issues that need to be addressed in such a theory and have made considerable progress in resolving them. This chapter highlights these issues and the tentative conclusions that have been reached for each.

- **What is an emotion?** People recognize that their emotional reactions are different from, and sometimes in conflict with, their logical conclusions. Yet thinking and feeling are intimately connected. What is the relationship between our rational mind and our emotional mind? Our emotional reactions are very diverse, but science has shown that they all reflect a few basic feelings. What are they? Different emotions are expressed in different ways. Are the forms of emotional expression universal, or do they differ from one culture to another? Emotions are felt physically and thus involve the body, not just the mind. What is the link between mind and body that gives rise to emotion? Emotions are typically short-lived responses to events, yet people feel some events can promote long-term changes in the way they feel. Why are emotions transient rather than enduring and why do people fail to recognize this feature of mental life?
- **What purposes do emotions serve?** Are emotions necessary, or are they relics of our animal ancestry that have been rendered irrelevant by higher mental capacities? What role does emotion play in other processes, such as attention, reasoning, and decision-making? Does emotion enhance thinking and facilitate performance, or does it impair thought and behavior?
- **How and why do people control their emotions?** People embrace and savor some emotions but are bothered by others and try to keep them in check. Are emotions, whether wanted or unwanted, open to the same degree of control as other mental states? What strategies do people employ to control their feelings? Do males and females employ the same strategies? Are there downsides to controlling one's emotions? People differ in how well they understand their emotional life and in how well they can bring their emotions under control. What are the consequences of this ability for thinking, action, and social relations?

The Experience of Emotion

What Does It Mean to Feel an Emotion?

Emotional experience is somewhat of a mystery but science has made considerable progress in identifying the varieties of emotional experience, the causes and consequences of emotional expression, and the interplay between mind and body that gives rise to emotion.

The Varieties of Emotional Experience

Your emotional life is complex. On any given day, you may feel such diverse emotions as happiness, frustration, relief, annoyance, boredom, fear, delight, and astonishment. These emotions seem to have little in common, each reflecting a somewhat unique mental state. Faced with such complexity, how can one hope to develop a theory that encompasses them all? Does each emotion require a different explanation?

The Structure of Emotions

To appreciate how the wide variety of specific emotions can be understood within a common framework, recall an important lesson from the discussion of attitudes (Chapter 3). You have many specific attitudes, but they all reflect three underlying dimensions (evaluation, activity, potency)—and they can be reduced further to one of them (evaluation). The same logic holds for your emotional life. The wide variety of emotions you experience can be mapped onto two underlying dimensions (see Figure 4.1) that are similar to those associated with the structure of attitudes (Diener, Smith, & Fujita, 1995; Larsen & Diener, 1985; Watson & Tellegen, 1985).

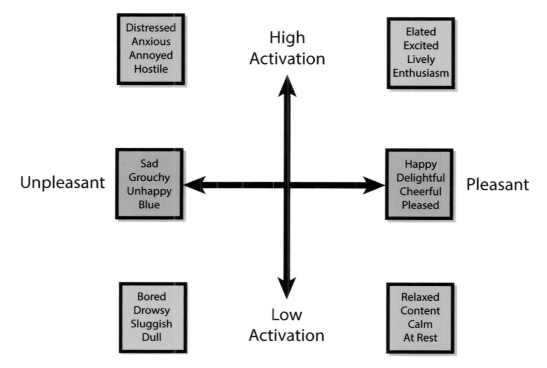

FIGURE 4.1 Taxonomy of Emotions

The most basic dimension is *evaluation*. Just as attitudes are evaluative, so too are emotions positive (pleasant, desirable) or negative (unpleasant, undesirable). Independent of evaluation, emotions differ in the degree to which they represent *high versus low level of activation*. Note the similarity between this dimension and the secondary dimensions of attitude structure: activity and potency. Activation represents the extent to which an emotion is associated with heightened physiological arousal (e.g., heart rate, blood pressure) and heightened potential for taking action in some way.

Look at the emotions in the bottom half of Figure 4.1—the ones representing low levels of activation. Whether these are positive (right quadrant) or negative (left quadrant), they convey a passive response to events (e.g., relaxed, sadness). Now look at the emotions in the top half—the ones representing high activation. Both the positive (right quadrant) and negative emotions (left quadrant) convey an energized response to events (e.g., excited, distressed).

Looking at the structure of emotions, you might get the impression that positive and negative emotions are equally balanced, and perhaps experienced equally often as well. If there *were* an imbalance, you would no doubt prefer to see the scale tipped in favor of positive states like happiness and relaxed at the expense of negative states like sad or distressed. People want to feel good rather than bad, and presumably they do things that bring about the preferred state. However, the scale is actually tipped in the other direction: there are more negative emotions than positive emotions, and the negative ones are experienced more easily as well.

Consider first the number of positive and negative emotions. James Averill (1980) found a whopping total of 558 words for emotion in English-language dictionaries. When he asked participants to rate each one as good or bad, he found a striking imbalance: 62% of the emotion words were rated negative, leaving just 38% rated as positive. People apparently need more words to describe unpleasant than pleasant feelings. Averill found a similar imbalance in the ratings of the 555 words used to describe individual differences in personality (Anderson, 1968). The majority of personality traits devoid of emotion (e.g., honest, hardworking) were rated as positive as opposed to negative (57% to 43%). But for the traits conveying emotion (e.g., happy, angry), most rated as negative (74%) rather than as positive (26%).

Negative emotions may be more frequent, but are they experienced more readily as well? To address this question, Van Goozen and Frijda (1993) asked people in seven countries to write down as many emotion words they could think of in 5 minutes, and noted the 12 that were most commonly mentioned. The most common emotions in six of the countries (Netherlands was the exception) were stacked in favor of bad rather than good. And across all the countries, the emotions that came to mind most readily were anger, sadness, fear, and joy—three bad to one good. People may prefer to feel good rather than bad, but things do not work out that way.

Affect Intensity

Everyone experiences the same basic emotions, but people differ in *how* they experience these emotions. An event might promote the same positive (e.g., happiness) or negative emotion (e.g., anger) in two people, but one of them may feel the emotion more intensely. This feature of emotional experience—*affect intensity*—differs among people (Larsen, Diener, & Emmons, 1986). People with a higher degree of affect intensity not only react more strongly to events, but they also have a higher need for social stimulation, have greater sensitivity to sensory stimulation (e.g., sights and sounds), and tend to be more physically arousable (Larsen & Diener, 1987).

Variation in affect intensity has implications for the effectiveness of social influence tactics that rely on emotional appeals. Moore and Homer (2000), for example, created two versions of a radio ad for a new burglar alarm. The content and length of both versions was the same, but one was decidedly more emotional in its pitch. Here is the script for the non-emotional version:

> Protect your home and your loved ones. Burglars can commit violent crimes. Get the Sentry Alarm from Honeywell. Safety Sentry is affordable, easy to install, and can be turned on and off by remote control. Safety Sentry comes with a loud built-in power horn alarm and senses intruders by detecting body heat and motion. Safety Sentry is available at all major hardware stores.

The emotional version was the same, except that the ad was introduced by an 8-year-old boy who was home alone when a burglar attempted to break in. Appropriate sound effects depicting a break-in and the cries for help by the child could be heard in the background.

Participants with high affect intensity had a stronger reaction to the emotional version (with the frightened home-alone boy) than did the low affect intensity participants. But this did not mean that the emotional version was more effective in selling the burglar alarm to the high intensity participants. The high intensity participants found it more painful to listen to this ad and did not enjoy it as much. Attempts to influence people should take into account the degree to which the audience tends to experience intense emotions in daily life. An emotional appeal may backfire if the audience is predisposed to react strongly to such an appeal because it creates an emotional state that is too intense for the message to be processed and embraced.

Emotional Expression

Charles Darwin did not set out to do so, but not long after his circumnavigation of the globe to understand the origin of species, he contributed a great deal to our understanding of the link between the experience and expression of emotion (Darwin, 1872/1998). At the time, it was generally believed that humans had special facial muscles that enabled them to express uniquely human—and God-given—sentiments such as compassion, love, and spiritual rapture. The idea that human emotional expression is qualitatively distinct from the emotional expression of "lower" species represented a direct challenge to Darwin's proposition that all species—including humans—have a common ancestor, and that traits that proved adaptive for earlier species were preserved and are reflected in present-day species—again, including humans.

Universality in Emotional Expression

Darwin was up to the challenge. His *principle of serviceable habits* maintains that expressions of human emotion can be traced to habitual patterns of behavior that were adaptive over the course of evolution for our primate and mammalian ancestors. He noted, for example, that human expressions of anger are vestiges of threat displays and attack behavior that were useful to our ancestors in aggressive encounters and conflicts. When angry, people—like other primate species—furrow their brows, expose their teeth, tighten their posture, clench their fists, and may even growl a bit. To display warmth and kindness, humans—again, like other primates—open their arms and show their palms to one another. Not limiting himself to primates, Darwin identified a number of parallels between human emotion displays and the displays of the same emotions by his dogs and by animals in the London Zoo. Darwin also pointed out that blind individuals, who lack the visual input provided by culture regarding emotional expression, nonetheless had the same repertoire of emotional displays as did sighted humans and other mammalian species.

Darwin's work was duly noted but did not change many minds at the time about the uniqueness of human emotions and emotional displays. But it did provide the inspiration for a series of studies a century later that investigated whether emotions are displayed in the same way by people in cultures around the world who had no contact with one another (Ekman, Sorenson, & Friezen, 1969; Tomkins, 1962, 1963). If people everywhere express emotions in the same way, this would suggest that a biological basis for emotional expression that might, in turn, reflect evolutionary, as opposed to cultural, origins. In the initial study exploring this idea, Ekman et al. (1969) presented 3,000 photos of actors portraying six emotions—*anger, surprise, disgust, happiness* (or *joy*), *fear*, and *sadness*—to people in Japan, Brazil, Argentina, Chile, and the United States. Their task was to select from six emotion terms the one that best matched the feeling the person was displaying in each photo. The accuracy in matching emotions to faces was extremely high—close to 90%—in all five cultures.

Subsequent research has established that people from 37 countries on six continents (all except Antarctica) can reliably recognize these six emotions (Ekman, 1993; Elfenbein & Ambady, 2002; Izard, 1994). Accuracy is observed even when the photo is of a person from an unfamiliar culture—for example, a photo of a Swede observed by a Papua New Guinean.

Culture and Emotional Expression

Culture is not entirely irrelevant to emotional expression (Ellsworth, 1994; Mesquita & Frijda, 1992; Russell, 1994; Scherer & Wallbott, 1994). Although cultures do not differ a great deal in the facial expressions associated with different emotions, they do differ in the extent to which they teach their members to conceal their emotional reactions (Russell, 1995). Adults who show all their feelings risk being taken advantage of by others, not to mention being mocked or disliked. If a culture teaches people not to reveal their emotions, the facial expressions of these people may be hard to read—especially by people in a different culture.

Restraint and concealment of emotions is emphasized more in collectivist cultures than in individualistic cultures (e.g., Mesquita & Leu, 2007). For example, compared to European Americans (representing greater individualism), Asian Americans (representing greater collectivism) are less likely to display smiles indicating politeness (so-called non-Duchenne smiles), although the two groups do not differ in their expression of smiles indicating inner joy (Duchenne smiles) (Tsai, Chentsova-Dutton, Freire-Bebeau, & Przymus, 2002). At the same time, however, Japanese people are more likely than European and European American people to mask anger with a polite smile. An angry outburst in Japan is considered a shameful loss of control, so it is better to "grin and bear it"—at least in public (Matsumoto & Ekman, 1989). European and European American cultures also readily express joy and excitement, whereas East Asian cultures are more restrained in the expression of these positive emotions (Mesquita & Leu, 2007; Schimmack, Oishi, & Diener, 2002).

Lest you think that Europeans and European Americans are especially unconstrained in expressing their feelings, consider the Yanomami, a group of people who have lived in the Amazon jungle for centuries, most of the time with no contact with people of European or Asian descent. In their culture, public displays of anger are common and far from discouraged. Anthropologists have observed angry Yanomami scream at the top of their lungs and deliver a barrage of imaginative insults (Good & Chanoff, 1991). Imagine being on the receiving end of this candid assessment: "You scaly ass, you bucktooth, you protruding fang, you caiman skin!" One wonders how they really feel.

Mind, Body, and Emotion

Emotions are sort of like thoughts. If you feel angry toward someone, for example, you are likely to experience (and perhaps express) unflattering thoughts about him or her. If you feel warm and trusting toward someone else, your thoughts are likely to be considerably different. But emotions are more than simple outputs of mental process. We *feel* emotions in a way that goes beyond the way we experience a list of facts or an idea. To feel something means that the body, not just the mind, is actively involved. When you are angry, for example, your heart beats at a faster rate and your neck muscles become tense. Your heart rate also picks up a bit when you feel warm and friendly, but your muscles are relaxed and your pupils dilate. The experience of emotion, in other words, provides a link between mind and body.

Facial Feedback

The link between emotional experience and facial expression is not a one-way street, with the face simply providing a visible display of how one feels. Just the opposite causal relationship, in fact, has been observed: adopting a facial expression can bring about the emotional experience associated with that expression. According to the *facial feedback hypothesis* (Tomkins, 1962; Izard, 1990), feedback from muscles in the face magnify existing emotions and can even evoke emotions. This suggests that putting on a "happy face" can generate happiness, while contorting one's face into an angry pose can generate hostile feelings.

One could argue that the effect of facial expressions on emotional experience is due to the thoughts that are generated. If you are told to put on a happy face, for example, you might think of happy events while curling up your lips and widening your eyes. If so, the facial feedback effect is not really all that biological, but rather a psychological phenomenon. To clarify the issue, Fritz Strack and his colleagues (Strack, Martin, & Stepper, 1988; see also Noah, Schul, & Mayo, 2018) developed a clever way of inducing facial displays of emotion without also inducing their corresponding mental states. They simply asked participants to hold a pen in one of two ways: in their lips with the pen pointing out or between their teeth with the pen pointing from side to side. Take a look at the picture below. Better yet, try it yourself (preferably with a clean pen and a blank mind).

Can you distinguish the emotions expressed in the two pen positions? The "pen in lips" pose looks like a frown—representing sadness—whereas the "pen in teeth" pose looks like a smile—representing happiness. To test whether these expressions actually produce the corresponding emotions, participants were asked to rate the funniness of cartoons while holding the pen in one of the two positions. True to the facial feedback hypothesis, participants who held the pen in their teeth—and thus were "smiling"—rated the cartoons as funnier than did participants who held the pen in their lips (and thus were frowning). The two poses, by the way, did not differ in their difficulty or annoyance (as indicated in participants' ratings), so the lack of funniness expressed by participants in the "frown" condition was not due to the hassle of keeping the pen positioned between their teeth.

This effect extends beyond the face. The physical movements we engage in while evaluating things can have an impact on how we feel about these things (Niedenthal, 2007). Movements associated with positive feelings lead us to evaluate stimuli more favorably, even if they are not particularly desirable. Conversely, movements that accompany negative feelings can promote unfavorable feelings to stimuli that might otherwise be viewed in positive terms.

Gary Wells and Richard Petty (1980) demonstrated this effect with head movements. They asked students to test a set of headphones by moving their heads up and down or side to side while listening to music and radio editorials. Later, they asked the students whether they agreed with the viewpoint expressed in the editorials. The students expressed greater agreement with the editorials they heard while nodding their heads up and down (a movement that signals agreement in conversation) than with the editorials they heard while shaking their heads from side to side (a movement that signals disagreement in conversation).

The same effect has been demonstrated for arm movements (Cacioppo, Priester, & Bernston, 1993). Participants observed 24 Chinese ideographs as they were either pressing down on a table (arm extension) or lifting up on a table from below (arm flexion). These movements represent the tendencies to push away things we don't like (arm extension) and pull things we like toward us (arm flexion). As expected, participants evaluated the ideographs more favorably when they were lifting up than when they were pushing down (see also Chen & Bargh, 1999).

Bodily Arousal

Facial expressions and bodily movements can convey, and even cause, emotional states. But emotions involve another bodily connection that can exist independently of what your face and limbs are doing. You can be excited, for example, while remaining motionless, but you cannot feel this way without some degree of *bodily arousal*—a speeding up of your physiological state, such as increased heart rate, breathing rate, or muscle tension. To *feel* an emotion is to experience physical sensations that go beyond expressions and movements. The question is how these sensations are related to emotional experience.

Which Person Is More Likely to Think a Cartoon Is Funny?
Source: Photos by R. Vallacher

The classic account of the role of arousal in emotion was provided by William James and Carl Lange (James, 1884; Lange & James, 1922). They argued that survival depends on very fast and efficient responses to environmental events, particularly those that represent potential danger. Imagine, for example, taking a pleasant stroll in the forest. You come to a fork in the path, pause briefly, choose one direction to proceed—and then suddenly notice a large bear a few yards ahead. How would you react? Would you think, "my god, that's a bear, a member of a species that is fairly carnivorous. Maybe it will look upon me as lunch, which is a really scary idea, so I had better run like the wind. And by the way, why didn't I follow the other path?"

In that scenario, you see the bear, have an appropriate thought, feel scared, and then run away. James suggested that scenario does not capture the reality of your experience—if it did, you might very well wind up as Bruno's lunch because of the time required to think about the situation and experience the emotion before taking action. Thinking about the situation and having an intense emotional experience is testament to our brainpower, but it is not a feature of human psychology that enables us to act quickly in an emergency.

As an alternative, James suggested that there is a direct and immediate link between the perception of a threatening event (the nearby bear) and the bodily arousal necessary for appropriate action. Specifically, the *James-Lange theory* of emotion holds that *stimuli trigger activity in the autonomic nervous system, which in turn produces an emotional experience in the brain*. First you see the bear, then your heart starts pounding and your leg muscles contract, and *then* you experience fear—which is just your experience of your body's activity. Without the heart pounding and muscle tension, you would not have the emotional experience. Emotional experience is the *consequence*, not the cause, of your body's reaction to objects and events.

The James-Lange theory implies that specific emotions are linked to specific types of bodily arousal. There is some evidence for this idea. Indeed, the causal link between physiological activity and emotion may be partly responsible for the facial feedback hypothesis. Levenson, Ekman, and Friesen (1990) showed that moving facial muscles to represent emotional displays produces corresponding patterns of physiological activity. College student participants configured their faces into the six basic emotions that were studied in the cross-cultural studies described earlier. To generate the anger expression, for example, participants were instructed to (1) pull their eyebrows down and together, (2) raise their upper eyelid, and (3) push their lower lip up and press their lips together. They held each expression for 10 seconds, during which several aspects of their physiological activity were compared against a neutral baseline.

The results provided some support for the link between facial expressions of emotion and physiological arousal, primarily for negative emotions. The facial expression of disgust, for example, produced a lower heart rate than did the other negative emotions. Both disgust and fear, meanwhile, produced the highest skin conductance (i.e., sweating on the palms), whereas anger produced the highest finger temperature. These expression-physiological activity links have since been confirmed in other populations, including elderly adults (Levenson, Carstensen, Friesen, & Ekman, 1991) and a Muslim population in Indonesia (Levenson, Ekman, Heider, & Friesen, 1992). For these emotions at least, the relation between facial expressions and patterns of physiological activity appears to be universal.

Interpretation of Bodily Arousal

James' theory attracted the attention of many scholars, but it soon generated some criticisms that suggested a need for an even better theory. Walter Cannon (1927), a former student of James, pointed out several problems, three of which set the stage for revised formulations, including his own *Cannon-Bard theory* of emotion (Bard, 1934; Cannon, 1927). First, people often have difficulty in detecting changes in their autonomic activity. Slight changes in their heart rate, for example, may go unnoticed. Second, nonemotional stimuli can cause the same pattern of autonomic activity as do emotional stimuli, yet they do not produce emotions. A hot day can produce an increased heart rate, but people typically don't panic and run for their lives when the temperature hits 90 degrees. Third, there are not enough unique patterns of autonomic activity to account for all the unique emotional experiences that people are capable of. Think back to the wide variety of emotions generated by the combination of valence and activation displayed in Figure 4.1. It is unlikely that each one of these represents a unique combination of heart rate, muscle tension, sweat production, pupil dilation, and so on.

Stanley Schachter and Jerome Singer (1962) picked up on the points noted by Cannon and offered the additional insight that objects and events do not always have a single unambiguous meaning—with respect to good versus bad or with respect to more specific meanings (safe vs. threatening, exciting vs. risky). As emphasized in earlier discussions, much of everyday life is open to interpretation. In such circumstances, the mind can prove highly useful, even crucial. In the Schachter-Singer model, a noteworthy (e.g., unexpected, consequential) event promotes physiological arousal—in line with the James-Lange theory. And if the event has unambiguous meaning—like stumbling upon a bear—the arousal promotes immediate action without bringing in the mind for a second opinion. But if the event has less clear meaning—stumbling upon a mountain goat—the mind attempts to clarify the significance of the event and direct action on one path rather than others (approach, freeze, or run away).

To test their model, Schachter and Singer (1962) created a situation in which participants were physiologically aroused and then either *informed, uninformed*, or *misinformed* about the source of this arousal. Those who were uninformed or misinformed were expected to engage their mind to determine why they were experiencing heightened physiological arousal. Those who were informed about the source of arousal, however, were not expected to look for other sources or be influenced by cues in the situation that provided reasons for their arousal.

Participants (all males) were told that the experiment concerned the effects of a new vitamin compound—*Suproxin*—on vision. A physician injected them with what they thought was Suproxin, but which was actually one of two drugs: (1) *epinephrine* (adrenaline), which stimulates the *sympathetic nervous system* (SANS) in preparation for fight or flight by increasing heart rate and blood pressure; or (2) a *placebo*, which has no effects on the SANS and thus does not increase heart rate and blood pressure. Some participants who were injected with epinephrine were told what physical symptoms to expect (*informed*)—shaky hands, slight heart-pounding, and a flushed, warm face. Other epinephrine participants were told that there were no side effects (*uninformed*). Yet other epinephrine participants were told to expect symptoms that would *not* occur (*misinformed*), such as shoulder tension or a mild headache.

The experimenters then gave participants something to think about if they were looking for an explanation of their physical symptoms. After the injection of Suproxin (either epinephrine or the placebo), the experimenter returned with another male participant—actually an experimental accomplice playing a role—who allegedly had also received the Suproxin injection. The real and the bogus participants were asked to wait together for 20 minutes before beginning the vision task. During this time, the bogus participant behaved in one of two very different ways, each representing an emotional reaction to the experiment and to the waiting period in particular.

In the *euphoria* condition, the accomplice seemed to enjoy the experience. He crumpled up sheets of paper and launched them into a trash can as if shooting jump shots, shot pieces of paper with a rubber-band slingshot, built a tower out of manila folders, and played with hula hoops that happened to be lying around. In the *anger* condition, the experimenter asked the accomplice and the participant to complete a five-page questionnaire consisting of some seemingly pointless questions (e.g., "Do you ever hear bells?"), as well as some decidedly personal questions (e.g., "How often do you have sexual intercourse each week?"). The accomplice complained about the questionnaire and eventually erupted in anger and stomped out of the lab room.

The question was whether participants would show emotional responses that mirrored those of the accomplice under each combination of conditions. To answer this question, Schachter and Singer watched the participants' behavior and coded the extent to which they displayed euphoric or angry behaviors like those of the accomplice. They also asked participants to complete a post-experimental questionnaire assessing how happy and angry they felt during the 20-minute waiting period. Both measures yielded similar results and largely confirmed the model.

When the accomplice behaved in a euphoric manner, participants felt especially happy if they were physiologically aroused (because of the epinephrine) but did not expect to be (i.e., when they were uninformed or misinformed). But when the accomplice behaved in an angry fashion, the participants felt especially angry if they were aroused but did not expect to be. In both cases, not knowing why they were aroused apparently engaged their mental processes so as to come up with a reason. In their search for an explanation for their unexpected arousal, participants took their cue from the accomplice and assumed that they were having the same emotional reaction as he displayed. Figure 4.2 displays this pattern for the euphoric accomplice.

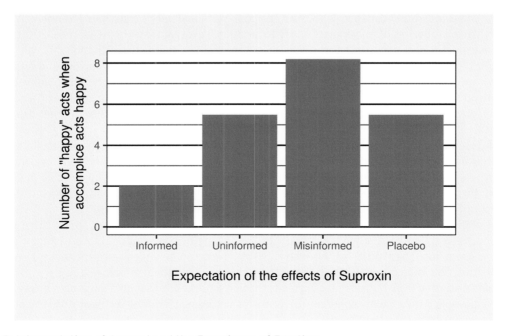

FIGURE 4.2 Interpretation of Arousal and the Experience of Emotion
Source: Adapted from Schachter & Singer (1962)

Misattribution of Arousal

The role of interpretation in generating emotion stimulated a lively interest in what came to be known as the *misattribution of arousal*. Dozens of experiments and field studies explored how arousal from one source (e.g., caffeine, a flickering light, a tough day at work) can be overlooked and attributed instead to some other noticeable source in the immediate environment (e.g., the person sitting next to you, a headline in the newspaper, music on the radio). People who have engaged in vigorous physical exercise, for example, later find cartoons funnier and erotic pictures sexier than do people who have not experienced the exercise-induced arousal (Zillman, 1988, 1989). This occurs because the effect of exercise (e.g., accelerated heart rate) can linger for quite a while, but people are often not aware of this and attribute their leftover arousal instead to something else that could conceivably make them feel this way.

In a variation on this idea, participants are told that something (e.g., a pill or injection) will make them feel aroused, when it is actually a placebo with no arousal-inducing properties. This has the effect of *downplaying* their emotional response to a subsequent experience that actually does produce heightened arousal! For example, people can tolerate keeping their arm submerged in ice water for a longer period of time if they have been given a pill (a placebo) that allegedly accelerates their heart rate and makes them feel uncomfortable (Nisbett & Schachter, 1966). Thinking that the pill is causing their discomfort, they do not attribute this state to the ice water. In an intriguing demonstration of this effect, people who complain of insomnia fall asleep more quickly if they are given a pill before bedtime that is described as a stimulant but which is really a placebo (Storms & Nisbett, 1970). Thinking their agitated state is due to the pill, they stop interpreting any heart rate acceleration as a sign of insomnia. Thus relieved, they drift into sleep.

Mental Dynamics

This discussion so far suggests that conscious mental processes play a somewhat secondary role in generating emotions. Only when a person experiences a diffuse or unexplained pattern of autonomic arousal does conscious mental processing enter the picture. But conscious processes can clearly play a more primary role in emotional experience. Generating a happy thought can create a happy feeling and thinking about a sad event can make one feel sad. Researchers, in fact, often induce emotional states and moods in this way. But this can be an uphill battle. It is difficult to generate a happy thought when one is feeling bad, and even this thought is generated, it might be overwhelmed by the bad feeling in short order.

However, thoughts can play another role in emotional experience that may be more reliable. As discussed in Chapter 3, the mind is inherently dynamic, with thoughts popping in and out of conscious attention on different timescales. Two dynamic properties of thinking are linked to emotional experience (Pronin & Jacobs, 2008): the *speed of thought*—how quickly thoughts occur—and the *variability of thought*—the degree to which thoughts vary widely versus have a common theme. People experience positive affect when their thoughts flow rapidly and are wide-ranging rather than narrowly defined. But thought speed and variability are independent, and one can imagine different combinations. A person may experience a rapid sequence of thoughts (high speed) that all converge on a common theme (low variability), or alternatively, the person's thoughts may occur at a slow rate but show a great deal of variability in content.

Pronin and Jacobs found that different combinations of thought speed and thought variability are associated with two negative emotions: *depression* and *anxiety* (see Figure 4.3). When people's thoughts are slow and repetitive, their emotional state tends to be one of depression or dejection. When people's thoughts are fast and repetitive, on the other hand, their emotional state is characterized by anxiety. These effects, by the way, are independent of the specific content of thought. *How* you think may be more important than *what* you think.

The process of thinking is related to one's emotional state in another way. Recall from Chapter 3 that people experience distress—cognitive dissonance—when their thoughts about something are mutually inconsistent in their meaning and implications for action. The flip side of this idea is that thinking can be a pleasant experience, even enjoyable, if all the thoughts that pop into consciousness point in the same direction about a topic (e.g., a person) or a course of action (e.g., going on a road trip). Consider, for example, reading a book. The thoughts generated by reading are likely to be far more enjoyable if they paint a coherent rather than a confusing picture of a character (if the book is a novel) or generate a sensible rather than a contradictory interpretation of the facts and ideas presented (if the book is a text).

The notion that cognitive consistency is an enjoyable mental experience is a special case of a more general phenomenon referred to as *perceptual fluency* (Reber et al., 1998; Winkielman & Cacioppo, 2001). People like sources of

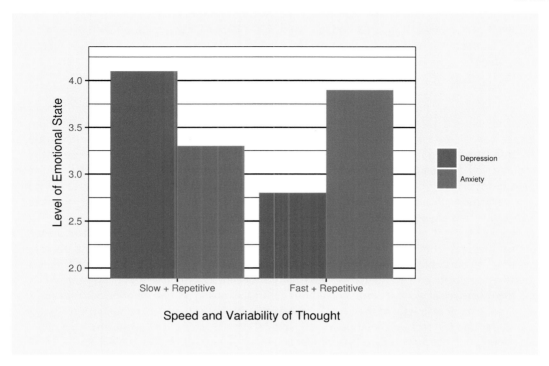

FIGURE 4.3 The Consequences of Mental Speed for Anxiety and Depression
Source: Adapted from Pronin & Jacobs (2008)

information (images, sounds, ideas, events) that are easy to understand and do not tax mental resources. A familiar song is preferred over a new song, even if the new song is more interesting, and a familiar political philosophy is preferred over a new way of thinking about public policy and economics.

But there are limits to the perceptual fluency effect. When images, ideas, stories, and events are *too* easy to process, the experience can prove to be downright boring. After all, you could read stories intended for first grade children, or stare at a painting that provides a perfect rendition of a cow, but you are unlikely to be joyful in doing so. People have an *optimal* mental experience—a state referred to as *flow*—when they are engaged in a task that is neither too easy nor too difficult, but rather matches the capacity to make the activity understandable and doable (Csíkszentmihályi, 1996). Whether making sense of a story, learning a new theory, or solving a jigsaw puzzle, thinking is enjoyable if it utilizes one's mental resources but doesn't overwhelm them. A moderately challenging puzzle is preferable to one that is mind-numbingly easy or one that is too difficult to complete. The same can be said for thinking about most everything—a new topic in college, the meaning of a story or poem, or the character of a recent acquaintance.

It is the process of *achieving* coherence through mental activity that is enjoyable, not merely having a nice and tidy conclusion handed to you. Think back to the example of reading. You could go to *CliffsNotes* to learn the ending of the story or to the end of a textbook to find the answer to a math problem, but thinking about the story or the problem and uncovering its meaning or solution is a lot more interesting and enjoyable. Thinking is a dynamic process that unfolds over time, and this process is enjoyable to the extent that it follows a path from uncertainty or ambiguity to clarity and coherence.

Emotional Adaptation

You have no doubt sat through movies that end on an unmistakable and intense emotional note—usually a happy or an optimistic one. Romantic comedies are notorious for this. A man and woman start out rubbing each other the wrong way, but by the time the closing credits are ready to roll, the two have exchanged a meaningful and sexy look, smiled widely, and fallen into each other's arms, ready to stroll through life in a state of oneness, fulfillment, and snappy repartee. Have you ever wondered, though, what would happen if you followed the couple around for a few weeks? Would their bliss be sustained, or would the glow start to fade a bit—or a lot, with the two rubbing each other the wrong way again?

The Hedonic Treadmill

Of course, everyone realizes that life is not like a Hollywood movie. Happiness cannot last indefinitely, and negative emotions like sadness and anger eventually run their course. The recognition that emotional reactions dissipate is captured by the *hedonic treadmill* metaphor (Brickman & Campbell, 1971; Diener, Lucas, & Scollon, 2006; Kahneman et al., 1991). On a treadmill, no matter how big your steps are or how fast you run, you wind up in the same place (unless, of course, you catapult off the back and end up facedown onto the floor). In analogous fashion, no matter how big your gains or losses are, your emotional state quickly recovers and settles on the same value. It is thought that people have a personal equilibrium for emotion, and deviations from this equilibrium are quickly corrected in order to maintain a coherent view of yourself and your relation to the world.

Think of this in terms of a household thermostat that functions to maintain a constant room temperature. If the temperature departs from the thermostat's setting—becoming too warm or too cool—the air-handling system engages processes to reestablish the setting. In like manner, when your emotional state departs from your emotional "setting"—getting too positive or too negative—your mental system kicks into action to reestablish the setting. To some extent, the processes at work are under conscious control, involving reinterpretation of the event that provoked the emotional reaction, or dismissal of the event's importance. But as we learned in Chapter 3, mental processes are largely unconscious and can restore equilibrium to the mental system without conscious attention or control. All you know is that the emotion has subsided and you are feeling much like you did before the event.

The equilibrium notion helps to make sense of the fate of people who win enormous sums of money in state lotteries and those who have experienced very negative events, such as becoming paralyzed in an accident (Brickman, Coates, & Janoff-Bulman, 1978). In both cases, the initial emotional reaction to the event is very strong—jubilation among lottery winners, anger and depression among accident victims. Over time—usually a shorter period than the people expected—the emotional reaction subsides and their emotional state prior to the event is more or less restored. It takes longer to recover from a negative event (a serious accident) than from a positive event (winning the lottery), but emotional equilibrium is usually restored in both cases.

Of course, extreme events such as these are very rare and clearly unique, and they may set in motion other actions and experiences that reduce the initial emotional reaction. A lottery winner, for example, may encounter tax problems or acquire "friends" whose insincerity is open to question. The accident victim, meanwhile, may gain insight into his or her resilience and capacity for dealing with life-altering events. But even in the absence of these new events and insights, there is a tendency for the initial emotional reaction to subside over time.

Why do people adapt to positive and negative events, returning to an equilibrium state no matter how wildly happy or distressed they were at first? As emphasized at several points in this text, psychological processes are designed to achieve stability and coherence, and to resist forces that threaten to undermine this equilibrium (Festinger, 1957; Thagard & Nerb, 2002). Once you form a stable attitude, for example, it is difficult to think about events in ways that contradict the attitude. Your general emotional tone, too, tends to stabilize and provide a frame of reference for experiencing events (Millgram, Joormann, Huppert, & Tamir, 2015; Parrott, 1993). If the mind did not have an equilibrium for accommodating the range of good and bad events we encounter in daily life, our mental life would be destabilized, and this instability would be like careening off the back of the treadmill.

Personal Happiness

Emotional adaptation is common to everyone. But people vary a great deal in the emotional tone to which they have adapted (Chow et al., 2005; Kuppens et al., 2007; Larsen, 2000). Across circumstances, some people are relatively happy, while others tend toward unhappiness and other negative emotions. Two people experiencing the same event may have very different emotional reactions—one person may feel relaxed and pleased after a nice meal, but another person may remain unimpressed and find things to criticize. Even if they have the same initial reaction to the event (e.g., it was clearly a great meal), over time each will return to his or her baseline level of happiness. One person may wake up the next day feeling relaxed or enthusiastic, while the other may roll out of bed in his or her customary grouchy or gloomy mood.

You might think that one's emotional equilibrium is established by the quality of one's life experiences. Bad experiences (e.g., trauma, illness, poverty), particularly in childhood, should create a predisposition to experience negative emotions, whereas good experiences (warmth and affection, good health, financial security) should promote a positive bias in one's emotional life. But actually, only about 10% of the variation in personal happiness is due to the quality of one's experiences—one's childhood neighborhood, whether one's country is at war or not, and the rights, freedoms, and opportunities one enjoys (Lyubomirsky, Sheldon, & Schkade, 2005). A far larger portion of the variation in personal happiness—about 40%—is shaped by the activities one chooses, the patterns of thought one develops, the ways one handles stress, and the way in which one develops interpersonal relationships. But the largest contributor to individual differences in happiness—a whopping 50%—has nothing to do with environmental factors, but everything to do with genetics (Lykken, 1999; Lyubomirsky et al., 2005)—the DNA inherited from one's parents! For example, monozygotic (identical) twins are twice as similar in their overall level of happiness than are dizygotic (fraternal) twins.

An individual's personal equilibrium for happiness is associated with other personal dispositions. Traits such as optimism and neuroticism tend to shape emotional reactions to events in everyday life (Costa & McCrae, 1980; Lyubomirsky & Tucker, 1998; Scheier & Carver, 1992). Individual differences in happiness are also reflected in reactions to major life events. For example, although people adapt to marriage after about two years on average, some people stay happily married for a lifetime, whereas for others the joys of marriage fade after a few months (Lucas, Clark, Georgellis, & Diener, 2003). Of course, many factors contribute to the success versus failure of a marriage, but individual differences in dispositions related to happiness play an important role (Gottman, Swanson, & Swanson, 2002).

Why would evolution promote variation in happiness? Wouldn't it be adaptive for everyone to feel good and be optimistic? Recall from our earlier discussion that positive and negative emotional states have somewhat different functions. Positive emotions promote goal striving and can establish trust and affection in social relationships. Negative emotions promote vigilance regarding surprises and sensitivity to potential dangers, and can set the stage for defensive responding if a dangerous situation is encountered. Both orientations are adaptive. Sensitivity to goals and friendly relations is great, but imagine if everyone were happy and saw the world this way. No one would be looking out for dangers and everyone might be a bit too agreeable with those who have hidden motives for being nice. Just as diversity in skills and interests are adaptive for a social group, so too is diversity in general happiness.

Affective Forecasting

Imagine how you would feel in response to the following events, and estimate how long you would feel this way: (a) you win an essay contest at your college and receive a nice award; (b) you are accused (falsely) of cheating on an exam and are expelled from the college; (c) you win a million dollars in the state lottery; (d) you discover that your significant other has had an affair with someone. Predicting your immediate reactions is a no-brainer: (a) thrilled and proud; (b) angry and despondent; (c) wildly excited and optimistic; (d) hurt and vengeful. But how long would you feel this way? Research on *affective forecasting* suggests that you would greatly overestimate how long your emotional reaction would persist (Gilbert, Lieberman, Morewedge, & Wilson, 2004). Whether the event promotes positive feelings (e.g., earning prizes or winning lotteries) or negative feelings (e.g., getting expelled, being cheated on), people return to their normal emotional state far sooner than they think they will (e.g., Wilson et al., 2000).

You might think that particularly intense emotions would last longer, or take more time to dissipate, than would milder emotions. A truly wonderful event (e.g., winning a million-dollar lottery) promotes a stronger emotional response than a pretty good event (e.g., getting a thousand-dollar raise), and one would think that the emotional high of the former would persist far longer than that of the latter. Similarly, a really bad event (e.g., losing a friend) is felt more strongly than a less aversive event (e.g., arguing with a friend), and one would think that the negative emotional reaction would dissipate more rapidly for the milder event.

Actually, just the opposite is true most of the time: intense emotional states tend to dissipate more quickly than do milder states (Gilbert et al., 2004). This is because intense emotions engage regulatory processes to correct for the disequilibrium associated with the unusually strong feelings. The lesson from other mental processes, discussed in Chapter 3, is useful in understanding why. When a person's normal way of thinking is strongly challenged, he or she engages in thought processes to counter the disturbance and preserve the attitude. A person who strongly believes in capital punishment, for example, will mount a vigorous defense of this belief when it is challenged by opposing points of view. A far less vigorous defense is mounted by a person whose belief in the superiority of vanilla ice cream is challenged by those who favor chocolate. In similar fashion, the mind works especially hard to restore emotional equilibrium when a very intense emotional reaction is experienced. Winning lotteries or barely surviving a car crash represent a greater threat to one's emotional equilibrium than do getting raises or a sunburn, and more mental effort is expended for the former experiences in an attempt to restore the equilibrium.

Emotional Variability

People differ in the strength of their equilibrium for regulating their emotional experience (Eaton & Funder, 2001; Eid & Diener, 1999; Kuppens, Oravecz, & Tuerlinckz, 2010; Kuppens et al., 2007; Larsen, 1987; Penner, Shiffman, Paty, & Fritzsche, 1994). Those who have a relatively weak equilibrium experience a wider range of emotions over time. This difference is depicted in Figure 4.4, which displays the temporal patterns of emotion for two individuals (Kuppens et al., 2010). Person A displays a fairly restricted range of emotions with respect to both positivity (pleasant vs. unpleasant) and activation (active vs. calm), with most of his or her emotions reflecting positive emotions with high activation. Person B displays an unrestricted range of emotions over time. His or her emotions vary widely in positivity and activation.

A weak emotional equilibrium is also associated with greater errors in affective forecasting. Neurotic people, in particular, are emotionally unstable and lack a clear and stable standard for predicting how they will feel in the future. When anticipating an unpleasant event, they are more likely to predict continued sadness or anxiety after the event than are emotionally stable people. By the same token, neurotic people are more likely to forecast long-term feelings of pleasure when anticipating a positive event.

A study involving the 2008 United States presidential election illustrates this point (Quoidbach & Dunn, 2010). One month before the election, residents of Belgium were asked to predict how they would feel the day following the election if Barack Obama won and if John McCain won. The day following the election, the participants reported how they actually felt. The participants had earlier completed a well-established scale measuring neuroticism, so the researchers could compare the forecasting accuracy of neurotic versus emotionally stable people. Virtually everyone in the sample (98%) supported Obama, so his election was a positive event. To assess forecasting accuracy, then, the researchers simply computed the difference between participants' forecasted emotion and their actual emotion. They found that the neurotic participants showed a stronger tendency to overestimate their happiness after Obama's victory. So although emotional adaptation is unforeseen by everyone to some extent, people who lack a stable frame of reference for their emotional life are particularly prone to predict that their emotional reaction to an event will go unchecked rather than return to an equilibrium state.

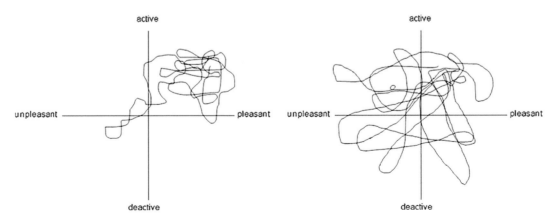

FIGURE 4.4 The Emotional Trajectories of Two People
Source: Kuppens et al. (2010)

The Purpose of Emotion

Why Do People Have Emotions?

Wouldn't life be simpler if we didn't get so worked up over things? Wouldn't the issues of everyday life be easier to manage if people were more like Spock or Data, the emotion-free *Star Trek* characters? After all, emotion can get in the way of rational thinking and lead to intense conflicts. We often speak of emotions as if they were the antithesis of clear thinking and sound judgment (e.g., "he was blinded by love," "she was too angry to admit her mistakes"). This dour view of emotion has strong intellectual roots. For centuries, philosophers have maintained that emotions are primitive ways of perceiving the world and are, or at least should be, subordinate to higher-level processes such as inductive and deductive reasoning (Haidt, 2006; Oatley, 2004).

Psychologists now recognize that it is difficult to decouple feeling and thinking, and more important, that the effects of emotions on attitudes and beliefs are often not all that undesirable (Clore, Gasper, & Garvin, 2001; Forgas, 1995; Isen, 1987; Loewenstein & Lerner, 2003). Emotions play a crucial role in *attention, thinking*, and *goal-directed action*. Lacking emotion, these higher-level processes might flounder or even prove impossible (Damaissio, 2009).

Attention

There is no shortage of things to which we could direct our attention. Right now, you are presumably attending to the words spilling across the page or perhaps to the various headings and subheadings. But you could also attend to nearby objects, the sights outside the window, or the sensations in your legs, arms, and forehead. Many factors (e.g., sudden sounds or sights, unusual objects or movements) can capture our attention and focus it on specific features of the environment. In recent years, emotion has been added to the list. The effect of emotion on attention is manifest in two ways: it makes us vigilant to changes in the environment, and it directs our attention to events that are congruent with the emotion currently being experienced.

People naturally notice changes in the environment, particularly if they are sudden and unclear in meaning. An unexpected loud noise, a bright light, or a blast of cold air can trigger an *orienting reflex* (Sokolov, 1963). When startled in this way, people's eyes widen, their eyebrows raise, their muscles tighten, their heart beats faster, their skin resistance drops, and their brain-wave patterns indicate a heightened level of physiological arousal. When feeling threatened or uncertain, people become especially vigilant to potential dangers in their environment (LeDoux, 1996). Note the potential for reciprocal causation here: sudden changes in the environment (e.g., a loud noise) can make people fearful, and the experience of fear and uncertainty can sensitize people to unexpected changes in the environment. Positive emotions tend to make people less vigilant to sudden changes and potential threats in the environment. When feeling happy or relaxed, people tend to focus on goals and desires without looking over their shoulders to make sure there is no danger lurking nearby (Isen, 1987).

Emotion has an influence on attention even in a perfectly stable and safe environment. In accordance with the *mood congruence principle* (Bower, 1981; Mayer, Gaschke, Braverman, & Evans, 1992), people direct their attention to stimuli that are congruent with their current mood or emotional state (Sedikides, 1992). A happy person is likely to notice positive events—those that are exciting, relaxing, or pleasurable. But a person in a negative mood—sad, depressed, or anxious—tends to notice threatening or disturbing events. The effect of positive and negative emotion extends to memory as well (Blaney, 1986; Mayer, McCormick, & Strong, 1995; Ucros, 1989). When happy, people are inclined to recall good times they have had in the past. When people are in a negative mood, their minds become flooded with negative events in their past.

Thinking

The human mind is a powerful tool—perhaps too powerful. It is capable of generating an almost limitless number of thoughts about any event, topic, or object. Faced with complexity, ambiguity, and a wide variety of interpretations, humans rely on their emotions to make decisions and judgments. The role of emotion in thinking is manifest in two ways: forming value-based judgments about actions and people, and reasoning about events.

Judgment

Imagine being asked how satisfied you are with your life. You clearly have a lot of information to work with in generating an answer. Your progress in preparing for a career, your romantic experiences, your health, your finances, your assessment of your intelligence and other important attributes, your housing situation—all these and many more considerations are relevant to assessing how satisfied you are. You could sit down and make a chart with all the relevant factors listed and a checkmark indicating "fine" or "not so great" for each one, and then calculate an average to determine how good your life is. But do you really consider all these things in generating an answer to this question? Not really. When faced with complexity, people rely on a much simpler strategy that is based on their global feelings. This account of how people reason is known as the *feelings-as-information perspective* (Clore et al., 2001). This perspective holds that emotions provide rapid and reliable information about events and conditions, and these "gut feelings" shape our most important judgments.

Norbert Schwarz and Gerald Clore (1983) provided evidence that people base their judgments about important matters on their current feelings—but only if they aren't aware of the reason for their feelings. The researchers made phone calls to people on either a nice sunny day or a gloomy cloudy day or and asked them, "All things considered, how satisfied or dissatisfied are you with your life as a whole these days?" The participants responded using a 10-point scale, with 10 representing "completely satisfied with my life." They were also asked to use a 10-point scale to indicate how happy they were with their life, with 10 signifying "very happy."

Half the participants were first asked a seemingly trivial, conversation-starter question: "How's the weather down there?" Schwarz and Clore assumed that people are generally happier on sunny days than on overcast, gray days. So, if people use feelings as a basis for making judgments, sunny-day participants should be happier with their life and rate it as more satisfying than should cloudy-day participants. However, this result was predicted only for participants who were *not* consciously thinking about the weather, not for those who were made mindful of sunny versus gray skies by the innocuous "weather" question. These participants were expected to see the connection between the weather and their current mood, and thus be less likely to use the sky conditions as a barometer of their happiness and life satisfaction.

The results, presented in Figure 4.5, confirmed these predictions. Without the "weather" question, participants reported being less happy and less satisfied with life on overcast days, in line with the feelings-as-information per-

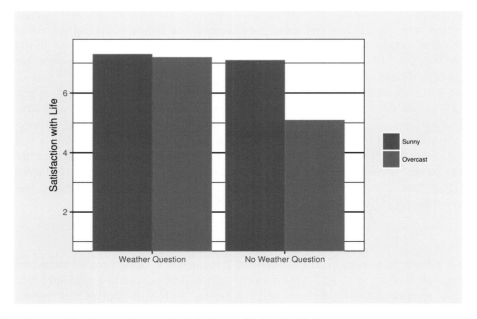

FIGURE 4.5 Can Today's Weather Influence Satisfaction with One's Life?
Source: Adapted from Schwarz & Clore (1983)

spective. But if asked about the weather, participants' reports about their happiness and life satisfaction were not influenced by the sky conditions. This suggests that how one feels in the moment can influence how one feels about life in the long run—as long as one is not fully aware of why he or she is currently feeling good or bad.

The feelings-as-information perspective is not limited to weather conditions. People in a bad mood, for example, are more likely to form negative judgments about consumer products, political figures, and economic policies (Forgas & Moylan, 1987). Some studies have focused on specific emotions. Anger, for example, can influence a wide variety of judgments that are unrelated to the source of anger. Simply asking a person to recall an anger-inducing event (e.g., a bad day at work) can prompt the person to blame other people for his or her problems or to assume that unfair things will happen to him or her in the future (DeSteno, Petty, Wegener, & Rucker, 2000; Feigenson, Park, & Salovey, 2001; Keltner, Ellsworth, & Edwards, 1993).

Fear, meanwhile, prompts people to perceive greater risk in their environment, pay more attention to such threats, and offer more pessimistic estimates about bad things happening in the future (Lerner & Keltner, 2001). Right after the 9/11 terrorist attacks, for example, people who were induced to feel fear about the attacks perceived greater risk, not just concerning future terrorist attacks, but also concerning unrelated matters such as the possibility of a flu epidemic (Lerner & Gonzales, 2005; Lerner, Gonzales, Small, & Fischhoff, 2003).

Emotions tend to shape judgments when the issue is complex or ambiguous (Forgas, 1995)—precisely when a rational rather than an emotional assessment would seem appropriate. In today's increasingly complex world loaded with difficult problems that are open to different interpretations and solutions, there is cause for concern that public opinion on these matters is often shaped more by people's guts than by their brains. Climate change and its impact on the American economy is clearly a complex issue, for example, but because of this very complexity people are inclined to render an opinion based on how they are feeling at the time.

Reasoning

A person's emotional state can affect judgment directly, but it can also affect how the person processes relevant information on the way to judgment. Research on this topic, known as the *processing style perspective*, suggests that positive moods facilitate the use of existing knowledge structures, such as stereotypes and heuristics, while negative moods promote greater attention to details, even those that do not necessarily conform to existing beliefs (Bless et al., 1996; Bless, Mackie, & Schwarz, 1992; Bodenhausen, Kramer, & Susser, 1994; Forgas, 1998a, 1998b, 1998c; Lambert, Khan, Lickel, & Fricke, 1997). Mood-induced reliance on existing knowledge structures is great when one is fairly secure that there are no dangers to worry about. But when in a negative mood, one does not feel all that secure that prior understanding is adequate. Instead, a negative mood (e.g., sadness) can disrupt assumptions and stereotypical thinking and motivate attention to details that may prove useful in reaching a "safe" conclusion (e.g., Bodenhausen, Sheppard, & Kramer, 1994).

This does not mean that positive moods are associated with lazy or effortless thinking. To the contrary, Alice Isen (1987) has shown that positive moods—especially happiness—can prompt people to think in ways that are creative and flexible. To induce positive moods, Isen employs seemingly trivial events: participants are given little bags of candy, they find a dime, or they watch an amusing film clip. These little events have big consequences on participants' reasoning. When given a word and asked to generate a related word, for example, happy participants tend to come up with more novel associations than do unhappy participants, who typically generate obvious associations. In response to the word "chair," a happy person might say "leader" (as in chair of a department), whereas an unhappy person might say "table" or "seat."

Action

One can act on the basis of a thought without experiencing emotion, but the action will lack urgency and commitment. You might decide that someone is in need of help, for example, but unless an emotional reaction accompanies this thought—distress, empathy, or perhaps guilt—you won't be particularly enthusiastic about coming to his or her aid. Even in banal everyday situations, emotion and its corresponding state of bodily arousal can make the difference between action and inaction, and can decide between different courses of action. Neuroscience has verified the importance of emotion to action: every decision or intention that leads to behavior is associated with centers of the brain that register emotions (Damaissio, 2009). Patients who cannot process emotions because of brain damage (e.g., due to stroke or injury) cannot make even simple decisions about what to do (e.g., whether to stand up or stay seated).

The motivational function of emotion arises in social contexts, promoting behavior that changes the tenor of an interaction or even a long-term relationship (Keltner & Haidt, 1999; Oatley & Jenkins, 1992; Salovey & Rodin, 1989). Feelings of anger arise in response to perceived injustice, for example, and are intended to make the unjust person make amends in some fashion. Guilt, in contrast, is a response to a person's own misdeeds and motivates him or her to make amends to the victim of the misdeed (Baumeister, Stillwell, & Heatherton, 1994). Happiness, meanwhile, is experienced in response to positive behavior by someone, and serves to make the other person feel good as well. There is no guarantee, of course, that an emotion will have the intended consequence. Anger could promote retaliation rather than an apology from the offensive party, and guilt could result in a clever rationalization rather than an attempt to make things right with the victim of one's behavior.

There are two aspects to the connection between emotion and action. First, emotion can dictate *what* people do—which course of action they take when faced with options. Second, emotion can impact *how well* an action is performed—whether an emotional state enhances versus impairs the quality of behavior.

Choice of Action

Life is filled with choices between different courses of action. Sometimes the choice is monumental—deciding whether to get married, choosing which college to attend, or opting for one career path over another. But choice among different actions is also a feature of everyday life. Right now, you are reading this text, but at any moment you could decide to stop and do something else—and that something else could be any number of things, from checking e-mail to preparing a nice sandwich. Sometimes the choice between different actions, whether monumental or banal, reflects a rational assessment of the pros and cons of each action. Is getting married more beneficial than putting off that life-changing event? Does College A have better facilities or a preferable curriculum than College B? Which career path—psychology or engineering, for example—makes more sense in the current economy? Would you benefit more from continued reading or from catching up with friends or getting a late-night snack?

As reasonable as this approach to making choices sounds, much of the time our choices are dictated by feelings rather than by thoughtful consideration (Zajonc, 1980). Thinking is useful for framing the alternatives, but emotions are what count when one must choose among the alternatives. Even a rational assessment favoring one action can be overruled by one's emotional reaction. Getting married may make little financial sense, for example, but that may make little difference if it "feels" right to tie the knot. College A may look better on paper, but College B may be chosen instead because you have a good feeling about it. And checking e-mail may derail what you are learning in a text, but you might do it anyway if the prospect generates a positive emotional reaction.

Choosing what to do on the basis of emotion can get us in trouble, but there are good reasons why it is part of our psychological makeup. Everyday life is filled with events that require quick and unequivocal responses, allowing little time to consider all the options. Think back to the James-Lange theory of emotion. Imagine stopping to weigh the alternatives before responding to a threatening event—like the proverbial bear in the woods. True, bears are not encountered all that frequently in today's world, but we do encounter cars cutting us off in traffic, sudden and unexpected noises, and nasty comments in confrontational encounters.

The role of emotion is particularly noticeable in situations involving a stressful event. People, like other animals, respond to stress with *fight-or-flight* behavior. When an animal is threatened by a rival, it experiences intense emotion which is quickly translated into one of two very different courses of action: attack the opponent (fight) or turn tail and run away (flight). Too much deliberation can be very costly, even deadly, in such a situation. Instead, the animal's emotional reaction is manifest in heightened bodily arousal and readiness to take a definitive course of action (Sapolsky, 1994). In similar fashion, when people are under stress, they become mobilized to act in accordance with their emotional reaction. Only later are they likely to think through the sequence of events and reconsider how they responded.

Sometimes emotions do not provide a clear-cut basis for action. The same circumstance can generate conflicting emotions—fight versus flight, for example, or approach versus avoid. The experience of emotional conflict—*ambivalence*—can make it difficult to act, leaving you in state of limbo. It is easy to generate examples of this emotional experience. You feel positive about eating ice cream after a hard night of studying, but you also feel negative about the consequences for weight control of doing so. You are strongly attracted to a stranger, a feeling that compels you to approach him or her, but the possibility of being rejected is associated with strong negative emotion. You anticipate a positive emotional response to acing tomorrow's exam, but the thought of pulling an all-nighter produces a decidedly negative emotion.

Research regarding the *approach-avoid conflict* has a long history, going back to Kurt Lewin (1935), who is widely considered to be the father of social psychology. Insight into this struggle was provided by a famous experiment with rats (Brown, 1948). Rats were equipped with a harness that measured how hard they would pull to reach a location with food. Their pull was measured again, but this time the location that had been associated with food was now associated with electric shock, so the question was how much effort they would exert to get away when placed there. Brown compared the relative strength of the two pulls—one to approach the location (to get food), the other to escape the location (to avoid shock). The resultant gradients of approach and avoid are presented in Figure 4.6. The *blue line* shows the change in force exerted by a rat as it approaches a location associated with food. The *red line* shows the change in force exerted by a rat as it escapes a location associated with electric shock.

Note that the approach gradient is relatively flat: the positive emotional response to the food did not increase a great deal as the rat approached the food location. The avoid gradient, in contrast, was quite steep: the motivation to avoid the shock was very intense near the location, but dropped off dramatically as the rat increased its distance from the location. Because the two gradients are different, they cross each other at some point. This point represents an equilibrium or a balance between the competing emotion-based motives. When *both* food and shock were in the same location, a rat ran toward the goal, then stopped at the balance point and turned around. But in moving away from the location, the approach tendency became greater than the avoid tendency, so the rat reversed its path again and headed toward the location. This back and forth movement could continue indefinitely, although the rat often simply froze at the balance point. By altering the intensity of hunger or shock, Brown (1948) was able to adjust the slopes of the approach and avoid gradients and hence the balance point—extreme hunger promoted a balance point closer to the goal, and intense shock promoted a balance point farther from the goal.

Consider the emotional ambivalence you experience in your own life in these terms. If you desire late-night ice cream, for example, you might move from your room to the kitchen, only to become focused on the downsides of following your desires just short of the freezer. But as you head back to your room, you may slow down and reverse course as the negative consequences lose their punch and the prospect of gratification gains the upper hand. As

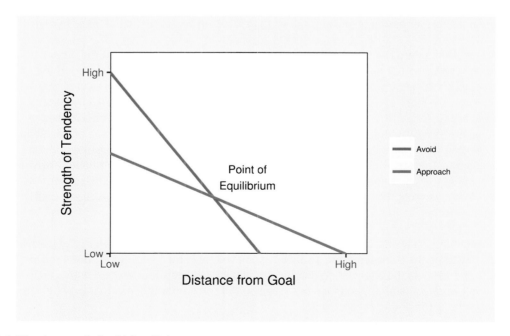

FIGURE 4.6 The Approach-Avoid Conflict

with Brown's conflicted rats, the battle between approach and avoid can persist and become a source of emotional upheaval. Emotion may drive us to do things, but it can also drive us a bit crazy.

Quality of Action Performance

If emotional arousal prepares us for action, you might assume that the greater the arousal, the more effective the action. "Getting psyched up" or "getting the juices flowing" before undertaking a challenging activity is age-old folk wisdom and sounds like good advice. But one could argue for the opposite effect of emotional arousal on performance: to take on a challenging activity, a person should maintain a clear head and not act in a highly emotional manner. So which point of view is the right one? Is it advisable to get psyched up or is it better to keep your head and look upon the behavior in rational terms? As so often is the case in psychology, the answer is "it depends." Both perspectives are correct, but under different conditions.

As noted in Chapter 1, the first social psychology experiment, performed in 1898 by Triplett, was concerned with the effect of arousal on performance (although there is some dissent whether Triplett deserves this credit; Stroebe, 2012). Triplett's findings supported a linear relation: the greater the arousal, the better the performance. But this conclusion soon came under attack, as researchers found that heightened arousal can *impair* rather than *enhance* performance on certain actions. Over the years, a consensus has emerged regarding the apparent conflict between these two proposed effects of arousal (e.g., Yerkes & Dodson, 1908; Zajonc, 1965).

The idea is that for any action there is an *optimal level of arousal* for maximally effective performance. For actions that are familiar, simple, or easy to enact, higher levels of arousal tend to facilitate performance. An experienced sprinter, for example, can run faster when he or she is highly aroused by the promise of reward or the presence of onlookers. But for actions that are novel, complex, or difficult to enact, a high level of arousal can impair performance. Someone attempting tennis or basketball for the first time, for example, is likely to perform terribly if he or she is highly aroused by rewards or the presence of onlookers. The optimal level of arousal, in other words, is lower for difficult or complex acts than it is for easy or simple acts.

To understand why the optimal level of arousal is lower for difficult or complex acts, recall the distinction between low- and high-level action identification (Vallacher & Wegner, 1987). When an action is familiar and easy to perform, focusing on the details of the action (low-level identification) is not necessary and can get in the way of smooth performance. Imagine the experienced sprinter consciously thinking about how to move his or legs. However, when an action is unfamiliar and difficult to perform, conscious attention to the details of the action are critical for effective performance. Imagine a novice tennis player focusing only on the higher-level goals and consequences of the action (e.g., making great shots, impressing onlookers) rather than focusing on how to adjust his or her body and swing the racket.

This is where arousal enters the picture. It is difficult to think clearly and focus on the details of one's behavior when one is too aroused, whether positively (intense excitement) or negatively (intense fear). If the action is familiar and easy to enact, such thinking is not necessary or even helpful. So a relatively high level of arousal is optimal for actions that have become more or less automatic. But if the action is unfamiliar and difficult to enact, a low degree of arousal is optimal because clear thinking and attention to detail are critical to effective performance.

The optimal levels of arousal for easy and familiar versus difficult and novel actions are depicted in Figure 4.7. Note that the relation between arousal and effective performance looks like an inverted "U." Up to a point, the more aroused a person, the better he or she is likely to do. But beyond that point, the relation reverses—the greater the arousal, the worse the performance. This point—the optimal level of arousal—is different for easy and familiar versus difficult and novel acts. For *simple and personally easy actions*, arousal can reach relatively high levels before it begins to hurt performance. For *complex and personally difficult actions*, lower levels of arousal can hurt performance.

So, should you get intensely energized about taking an exam? It depends on how well you've learned the material. If you have truly mastered the subject matter, go ahead and have that extra cup of coffee. But if the material is elusive and requires attention to specific information and details, you should keep your arousal within limits—be motivated, obviously, but don't work yourself up too much because you will come up with ideas that may be automatic for you, but a sign of poor understanding to the instructor.

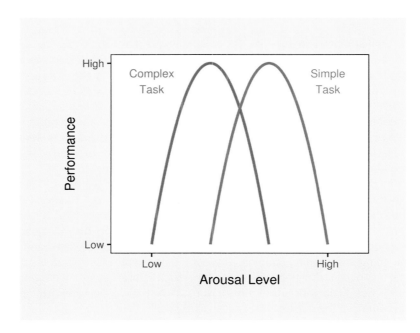

FIGURE 4.7 The Relationship between Emotional Arousal and Performance

The Control of Emotion

How Do People Control Their Emotions in Daily Life?

People prefer to feel good rather than bad. Shouldn't that be enough? If you are in a lousy mood or feel frustrated, why can't you simply decide to feel differently? We can control our bodily movements and our choice of words, after all, so you might think that emotions could also be turned on or off at will. But of course, emotions are not that easy to control. Sometimes, in fact, the control works in the other direction: our emotions control our thoughts—and our bodily movements, for that matter. In this section we dig deeper into this issue—how people attempt to control their emotional experience, and their success in doing so.

Emotional Regulation

Positive emotions (e.g., happiness, contentment) are preferable to negative emotions (e.g., sadness, disappointment), so you might think that people are always motivated to maintain the former and change the latter. In some contexts, though, a positive mood might be inappropriate or even counterproductive (Gruber & Tamir, 2011). Imagine having to present bad news to a friend while experiencing contentment—this would be awkward at best, not to mention highly insensitive. Or imagine making a persuasive argument about the need for action to deal with economic or social injustice. Feelings of anger would clearly be more appropriate, and no doubt would be far more effective in making your case, than would feelings of joy or giddiness. Particularly when future benefits outweigh immediate benefits, people try to adopt the most useful emotions, even if they are unpleasant (Tamir, 2009).

Seeing the need to regulate emotions is one thing; bringing unwanted emotions under control is a quite different matter. Research has shown that people employ three strategies to regulate their emotions—each with varying degrees of success.

Mental Control of Emotion

"Mind over matter" is a familiar mantra in daily life. The assumption is that people can control their emotional reaction or change their mood by controlling their thoughts. This can take the form of thinking about something other than the object or event that generated the unwanted emotion. If you are sad about a recent disappointment, for example, you might try to think instead about puppies and rainbows. This may well prove advantageous in the short run. Why dwell on an event that only makes you anxious or sad, particularly if nothing can be done about it? But the suppression of unwanted emotions can prove maladaptive over time. For one thing, it might not work. Recall from Chapter 3 that suppressed thoughts and emotions tend to burst into consciousness when mental energy is not exerted to keep them suppressed (Wegner, 1994). Not wanting to feel angry, for example, can make you angrier than ever if you cannot marshal the mental resources necessary to get the job done.

Apart from having this ironic effect, the attempt to suppress unwanted (e.g., painful) feelings can have health consequences, especially if the suppression goes on for a long time (Pennebaker & Francis, 1996). Petrie, Booth, and Pennebaker (1998), for example, asked medical students to write about a personal topic once a day for 3 days. After each writing exercise, half the students were asked to suppress all the thoughts they had just written for 5 minutes, while the other half were not asked to do so. The students who suppressed their thoughts and feelings experienced a notable decrease in their immune system functioning, whereas the non-suppressing students did not. In an even more telling study, women who had had an abortion were asked how much effort they exerted trying to suppress thoughts about their abortion experience (Major & Gramzow, 1999). Women who reported greater attempts at suppressing their thoughts and feelings experienced the most psychological distress.

Bodily Control of Emotion

Remember that emotions are linked to the body as much as the mind. By changing one's bodily state, one can change one's emotional state. This can be accomplished with no more mental energy than is required to change the configu-

Putting on a Happy Face.
Note: Some firms in China train their customer service staff members to smile with a chopstick. They do this by keeping it between their teeth and not touching it with their lips. Assuming this training works, customers no doubt see the staff members as happy and positive. But how do the staff members truly feel? Happy—or simply silly?

ration of one's facial muscles (Strack et al., 1988). Standing upright rather than slouching, too, can induce a positive mood, as can pulling one's arms toward the body rather than pushing them away from the body. There are limits to this strategy, of course. It would no doubt take more than straightening up and holding one's head high to snap out of a depressed state. But then, it wouldn't hurt to try.

Behavioral Control of Emotion

Emotions are difficult to control directly, but people can control what they do, and these behavioral strategies can prove effective in changing an emotional state. Much of the time, the goal is to bring about a more positive emotion, and research has identified various means of doing this (e.g., Thayer, Newman, & McClain, 1994). The most straight-forward strategy is to do things that produce good feelings. To make themselves feel better, people can eat a favorite food, listen to music, have sex, engage in exercise, or go shopping—especially if they are beneficiaries of the purchase (Cohen & Andrade, 2004). In a related vein, people can do things that take their minds off the problem. People in an unpleasant mood may distract themselves by watching television, surfing the internet, or taking a shower.

People also control their emotions by seeking social support. Some people call their friends or family members when feeling bad, with the expectation that they will at least get empathy, if not a solution to their problems. Particularly if one is experiencing emotional distress, it helps to reveal this to another person (Pennebaker, 1997). Interacting with people can promote striking mood changes, often for the better, even if the nature of the interaction is banal and not particularly informative, empathic, or memorable.

In both cases—engaging in a different behavior and seeking social interaction—the source of the negative emotion is not necessarily addressed. The goal instead is to replace the unwanted emotional state with a different and more desirable state. But people can attempt to deal with the source of their unpleasant state directly. For example, they may adopt a new course of action intended to avoid the problem in the future. Religious activities and rituals can be a useful way of dealing with unpleasant feelings stemming from difficult circumstances (Rippere, 1977). Or a person might simply vent his or her feelings—whether screaming, crying, or pounding a pillow.

Yet another behavioral strategy is to use alcohol to alter one's feelings. People drink, for example, when they feel socially anxious or uncertain about their ability to cope with challenges (Berglas & Jones, 1978; Hull, 1981). Alcohol, of course, doesn't resolve the issues that led to the negative feelings. To the contrary, alcohol reduces the quality of the higher-order mental functions that are most useful for solving problems. To put it bluntly, alcohol has its effect by making the drinker dumber. Beyond that, using alcohol to feel better is hardly an advisable strategy because it can affect judgment and motor coordination, and long-term use can promote alcohol dependence and serious health problems (e.g., liver damage, fat accumulation).

Drugs, whether prescribed or illegal, are also used to alter one's mood—in some cases, to reduce anxiety or depression, and in other cases to achieve relaxation or exhilaration. There are approved medications for anxiety (e.g., Xanax) and depression (e.g., Prozac). In both cases, the drug works by altering the uptake or balance of neural transmitters—dopamine in the case of anti-anxiety drugs and serotonin or norepinephrine in the case of anti-depressive drugs. And of course, there is a wide variety of illegal drugs that are used recreationally to alter one's mood and bring about a very different one. Marijuana, ecstasy, LSD, and heroin are very different from each other, but they all represent strategies to change one's emotional state. Like alcohol, this strategy doesn't solve the problem that produced the unwanted emotion, but rather blunts that emotional state and substitutes a very different mood. And like long-term alcohol use, prolonged drug use can have harmful health consequences.

Affect regulation, however, is not always in service of trying to feel better. There are situations in which it is advantageous or appropriate to dampen a positive emotional state in favor of a neutral or perhaps even a negative emotional state. Emotion regulation of this type is basic to social interaction. When anticipating an interaction with someone facing a difficult situation, you would probably want to avoid feeling too cheerful or enthusiastic about things. To show respect and feel empathy, you would instead try to maintain a sober mood as you interact with the person. When people do not know in advance the mood of someone they will interact with, they try to adjust their mood to a neutral state, even if they are feeling good at the time (Erber, Wegner, & Therriault, 1996). Interestingly, when people anticipate interacting with someone they feel close to (e.g., a relationship partner), they do not go out of their way to change their mood—they stick with the mood they have, whether it is highly positive or highly negative (Erber & Erber, 2000). People feel comfortable sharing their feelings with those close to them, and they may want the other person to help them feel differently if they are in a bad mood.

Gender Differences in Emotion Regulation

Men and women are equally likely to experience bad moods, but they differ somewhat in how they cope with such feelings. When feeling depressed, women frequently respond with rumination—obsessively thinking about the problem—whereas men are more likely to distract themselves with other thoughts and activities (Nolen-Hoeksema, 1991). This may help explain why women suffer higher rates of depression—focusing on why one is depressed is likely to prolong the bad feelings, whereas shifting one's attention to something more cheerful (e.g., a sports event) is likely to terminate them. Becoming involved in another task not only gets men's minds off their troubles, it can also furnish positive feelings of success and competence.

Men and women also differ in what they consume when they are in a bad mood. Women are more likely to turn to food when feeling bad about something (Forster & Jeffery, 1986; Grunberg & Straub, 1992). For their part, men are more likely to use alcohol and drugs to cope with bad feelings (Engs & Hanson, 1990). Yet another gender difference concerns the use of humor. Men are more likely to make wry comments or make light of the problem, whereas women fail to find the humor in their problems (Thayer et al., 1994). Men also tend to look upon sexual activity as a good way to improve their mood, whereas women prefer to call someone to talk to or go shopping as a way of getting out of an emotional slump (Thayer et al., 1994). These differences are worth noting, but you should keep in mind that the similarities between men and women in their means of emotional regulation are far greater than the differences (Hyde, 2005).

Emotional Intelligence

Far from getting in the way of effective thinking and appropriate conduct, emotions can enhance the quality of thought and behavior—provided they are recognized and exercised intelligently. This idea provides the rationale for theory and research on *emotional intelligence* (Salovey & Mayer, 1990). Emotional intelligence is defined as "the ability to perceive emotions, to access and generate emotions so as to assist thought, to understand emotions and emotional knowledge, and to reflectively regulate emotions so as to promote emotional and intellectual growth" (Mayer & Salovey, 1997). People differ in their emotional intelligence. Some people tend to misread the emotional states of other people, whereas others seem to excel at perceiving and understanding how other people feel. And although emotion facilitates effective decision-making for some people, it can prove disastrous for others.

With this in mind, John Mayer, Peter Salovey, and David Caruso (2002) developed the *Mayer-Salovey-Caruso Emotional Intelligence Test* (MSCEIT) to assess individual differences in *EQ*—the emotional equivalent of IQ. The test measures four aspects of EQ. *Perceiving emotions* is the ability to recognize how other people are feeling. People who score high on this aspect also excel at perceiving emotions in physical stimuli, such as objects, art, music, stories. *Facilitating thought* is the ability to generate an emotion and then use this emotion to facilitate reasoning. People who score high on this aspect know what emotions are appropriate for different mental tasks—for example, they know that tension is more helpful than joy when checking a spreadsheet for mathematical errors. *Understanding emotions* is the ability to understand complex emotions (e.g., admiration tinged with envy) and appreciate how emotions can transition from one stage to another (e.g., how anger can explode or joy can dissipate). *Managing emotions* is the capacity to be open to feelings and the ability to regulate one's emotions in a way that promotes personal understanding and growth. This captures the notion of emotional regulation discussed above.

Emotional intelligence is associated with success in people's interpersonal and professional lives (Brackett & Salovey, 2004; Goleman, 1995). College students in the United States and Germany with a higher EQ, for example, were shown to have better quality friendships than their counterparts with a lower EQ (Lopes et al., 2004). With respect to professional success, employees from a Fortune 400 insurance company with a high EQ received larger merit increases, attained higher company rank, and received higher ratings from both peers and supervisors than did employees with a lower EQ (Lopes et al., 2004). The ability to understand and regulate one's emotional reactions allows for smoother interactions and easier resolution of the conflicts that inevitably arise in one's interpersonal and professional lives.

SUMMING UP AND LOOKING AHEAD

- **Emotional experience is very diverse, but all emotions can be mapped onto two basic dimensions: valence (positive vs. negative) and activation (arousal). Emotions are experienced physically as well as mentally and their physical manifestations (e.g., facial expressions) are largely universal.**

- Theories of emotion differ in the proposed interaction between body and mind. The James-Lange theory holds that emotion is a direct result of specific configurations of bodily arousal (e.g., heart rate, blood pressure), whereas the Schachter-Singer theory holds that it is the cognitive interpretation of arousal that produces emotion. Because of the role of interpretation, people can misattribute the source of their arousal and have a strong emotional reaction to an event or person that would otherwise have little impact. Independent of bodily arousal, the dynamics of thinking—the speed at which thoughts occur and the variability in these thoughts—can promote emotional reactions.

- Emotions are essential to decision-making, reasoning, motivation, and action. Negative emotion promotes vigilance to changes and potential dangers, whereas positive emotion undermines attention to detail, while promoting attention to potential rewards. Emotion also directs attention to events that are congruent in valence (positive or negative), and biases recall of events in the same fashion. Positive or negative feelings due to aspects of the environment (e.g., the weather) can influence how people reason about entirely different events (e.g., life satisfaction), but this effect is weakened if people are mindful of the environmental influence.

- Emotional arousal is necessary for engaging in action, but the relation between arousal and performance quality is curvilinear, with the optimal level of arousal lower for complex and difficult actions than for simple and easy actions. Emotional ambivalence occurs when positive and negative features are associated with the same action, often resulting in a failure to implement the action in an unequivocal manner.

- Emotional regulation is important in everyday life and is attempted in different ways. The mental suppression of emotion is often ineffective and can have negative health consequences. Because of the feedback between the experience and expression of emotion, bodily and behavioral regulation of emotion can prove successful, although some forms of behavior control do not address the source of the regulated emotion. Males and females differ somewhat in their predominant means of emotional regulation.

- People's happiness is relatively stable, determined in part by genetic inheritance, and returns to a personal equilibrium more rapidly than people expect after an event that is highly positive or negative. But individuals vary in their emotional variability, with some people showing weak equilibrium tendencies. Emotional intelligence (e.g., the ability to perceive others' emotions and regulate one's own) is associated with positive outcomes in many spheres of life.

Emotion clearly adds a component to intrapersonal experience beyond that provided by the mind's tendency to develop beliefs, attitudes, and values. But to fully appreciate what goes on in people's minds, we need to consider the human capacity to develop thoughts and feelings about one's self. The lessons learned about mental processes—the processes of thinking and feeling—are directly relevant to the nature of self-awareness and self-understanding. But there are aspects of self-concept that cannot be reduced to the features of mind and emotion discussed so far. The next chapter thus builds on the processes of thinking and feeling, but also introduces new processes to provide insight into the basic features of self-concept.

Key Terms

Emotion taxonomy	Misattribution of arousal	Broaden-and-build hypothesis
Affect intensity	Hedonic treadmill	Fight or flight
Principle of serviceable habits	Affective forecasting	Approach-avoid conflict
Universality in emotion expression	Emotional variability	Optimal level of arousal
Culture and emotion expression	Mental speed	Inverted-U function
Facial feedback	Orienting reflex	Emotion regulation
Bodily arousal	Vigilance	Emotion suppression
Principle of serviceable habits	Mood congruence principle	Bodily control of emotion
James-Lange theory	Feeling-as-information perspective	Behavioral control of emotion
Schachter-Singer theory	Processing style perspective	Emotional intelligence

5 Self-Concept

You think about yourself a great deal. I can assert this without knowing anything else about you, other than the fact that you're almost certainly a human being. Even when you're engaged in an intense activity—talking with friends, running around a track, or reading a chapter in a social psychology text—you're never far from becoming the spotlight of your attention. Your self-directed thought might center on concerns that are profound and enduring ("am I good student?") or those that are trivial and fleeting ("my nose itches"), on events in the past ("I should have studied instead of partying last night") and on those yet to transpire ("I hope I ace the exam next week"). You are also likely to reflect fairly frequently on a wide assortment of personal characteristics that run the gamut from those that are highly specific ("my ears are huge") to those that are considerably more abstract and comprehensive ("I'm likable but not really a crowd pleaser"). And on each of these occasions, your self-directed thought carries with it at least the hint of self-evaluation. Thoughts that are very different by any other criteria (e.g., "big ears" and "not a crowd pleaser") are rarely neutral but rather are experienced as good, desirable, and worthy of advertising or as bad, unwanted, and embarrassing.

The penchant for self-reflection and self-evaluation is more than an unavoidable, often annoying, feature of daily life. People are firmly anchored in the animal kingdom, but their ability to reflect on their existence, operating rules, and idiosyncrasies makes human psychology different in critical respects from the 50 million other species on earth. But the self does not make us different in every respect—having a sense of self has little to do with hunger, pain avoidance, and many other processes that we share with other animals. Why, when, and how is your "self" relevant to what you think, feel, and do? And what is the self, anyway?

CHAPTER OVERVIEW

What Are You Going to Learn?

Interest in the self has exploded over the past two decades, resulting in thousands of studies and dozens of conclusions. To make this vast literature comprehensible, I have organized the chapter around three deceptively simple questions. The answers to these questions about intrapersonal experience are interesting in their own right, but they also provide insight into important features of interpersonal behavior, social relations, group dynamics, and even societal processes—insights that we will pursue in later chapters devoted to these topics.

- **What does it mean to think about oneself?** When do people do focus on themselves and when instead do they think about other people and things? What special mental capacities or motives are necessary for self-directed attention? What comes to mind when people turn the spotlight of attention on themselves? What sources of self-knowledge are especially important in shaping a person's self-concept? Do the answers to these questions vary from culture to another?
- **How do people develop a self-concept?** How do people manage to organize all their self-relevant thoughts into a stable and coherent view of what they are like? Does the self-concept represent a unified sense of what one is like, or is it more like an ensemble of somewhat distinct self-views? How do people extract a global self-evaluation from the complex and continually updated array of self-relevant information? Are there downsides to having high self-esteem?
- **How do people protect their self-concept?** Are people motivated simply to maintain a positive view of themselves or do other concerns come into play? How do people defend their sense of self against contradictory information? When do people change the way the think about themselves to accommodate new information?

Fundamentals of the Self

What Does It Mean to Think About Oneself?

The Capacity for Self-Awareness

The tendency to think about oneself is very rare in the animal kingdom. Other types of mental process are shared with many of our animal brethren. Dogs, elephants, and squirrels all notice other animals, particularly members of their own species, and are quite adept at forming judgments about them—although such judgments center on rather basic "good" (safe, approachable) versus "bad" (dangerous, avoid at all costs) concerns. But these species don't turn the spotlight of attention inward on their own behavior, thoughts, or characteristics. Dogs don't wonder why their noses are wet, elephants don't take pride in their sizable tusks, and squirrels don't marvel at their scampering ability or fuzzy tail. Why not? Or, to turn the question around, why do we think about ourselves if other animals get by just fine without doing so?

Mental Thresholds

The simple answer is that we think about ourselves because we can. Thinking about and evaluating one's characteristics and operating rules, or even becoming aware that one exists as an object in the world, entails a set of sophisticated cognitive abilities. A fairly substantial cognitive threshold must be met before any animal can put its moment-to-moment orientation to the environment on hold and look back at itself. When people focus on themselves, they don't literally see themselves in the same way they see other people—unless, of course, they're standing in front of a mirror or looking at a family photo album. Rather, self-focused attention requires the ability to imagine oneself as another being that can be subjected to scrutiny and inference in the same way one scrutinizes and evaluates other beings. This requires suspending one's usual mode of operation and adopting an outsider's perspective on oneself.

Crossing the cognitive threshold for self-awareness is manifest in two related mental processes: *metacognition* and *theory of mind. Metacognition* means "thinking about thinking" (Flavell, 1979; Dunlosky & Metcalfe, 2009). It's one thing to have a thought; it's another to know that one has had the thought, and yet another to evaluate the thought. This tendency can be annoying at times because it can amount to second-guessing one's immediate thoughts and judgments. But it is also testament to our sophisticated mental machinery. In principle, one could think about one's meta-thoughts—and then think about these meta-meta-thoughts—in an attempt to understand the operation of one's own mind. Such an enterprise would be endless and ultimately fruitless—the mental equivalent of trying to catch one's shadow. Fortunately, people don't seem to get caught in this infinite regress most of the time. Nonetheless, metacognition is a capacity unique to humans that provides the potential for self-understanding.

Theory of mind represents an extension of metacognition to the minds of other people (Papaleontiou-Louca, 2008). When we observe a person do something, we typically go beyond noting the behavior and its consequences. We attribute a mind to the person, complete with thoughts, feelings, and goals that underlie his or her conduct and set the stage for future actions. We cannot see these internal states directly, but we imagine what he or she is thinking and feeling, or what his or her underlying motives might be.

Theory of mind is critical to the experience of self-awareness. This may seem strange—why would thinking about someone else's mind promote thinking about oneself? This circuitous link exists because the other person's thoughts might involve us. In effect, the other person's mind provides the outside perspective through which we can focus on ourselves. In the words of C. H. Cooley (1902), other people provide a "looking glass" that enables a person to reflect on himself or herself. So by adopting their perspective, the person's attention is focused on his or her own behavior, characteristics, and internal states. But this looking glass function would not be available if you did not have the cognitive skills to get inside other people's heads and imagine how you looked to them. All this involves mental capacities such as imagination, abstraction, and inference that require considerable brainpower. So although it might be useful and strategic for any non-human social animal—a dog, goat, or fish—to imagine how it is viewed by others in the pack, herd, or school, such a creature isn't up to the task mentally.

Self-Recognition

But how do we know this? Theories of relative mental ability aside, is there compelling evidence that other animals cannot contemplate themselves? True, animals show little evidence of modesty or other behaviors that suggest a great deal of self-awareness, and no one would argue that they reflect on their mental machinery. But can we deny them the simple recognition of their own existence? They may not be very "deep" or have an appreciation for *what* they are, but perhaps they know *that* they are.

The issue of self-awareness in other species was taken up in the 1970s by Gordon Gallup in an ingenious but straightforward fashion (Gallup, 1977; Gallup & Suarez, 1986). He reasoned that the most rudimentary aspect of self-awareness is *self-recognition*. And what better way to assess self-recognition than to place an animal in front of a mirror and look for signs that the animal sees the image as its own. People certainly pass this test. Even when we catch our reflection in a funhouse mirror that distorts our shape, we know who we're looking at. Gallup, a primatologist, wondered whether other primate species—animals remarkably similar to us genetically and considerably brighter than other members of the animal kingdom—might have the mental capacity to pass the mirror test, surpassing the minimal threshold of self-awareness.

Primates cannot tell us whether they recognize themselves in a mirror, so Gallup had to rely on non-verbal signs of self-recognition. He anesthetized each animal, and while it was unconscious, he applied a colored dye to one of its ears (e.g., left) and to the eyebrow ridge on the opposite side of its face (right). He then noted what the animal did upon wakening when it saw its reflection in a mirror that had been conveniently placed in the animal's cage. If the animal simply looked at the reflection and moved on, or if it shrieked at the image as if it were a new, potentially threatening cage mate, or even if it tried to touch the dyed areas on the reflected image (i.e., the mirror), this would hardly qualify as self-recognition.

But if the animal looked in the mirror, noticed the dyed areas, and then touched itself in those areas, that would be hard to explain as anything other than recognition of the image as itself. Although the dye was non-irritating, Gallup wanted to be sure that any mark-directed touches did not represent a response to a tactile sensation (like scratching an itch). So Gallup compared the number of mark-directed touches exhibited by animals in the presence of a mirror with the number of touches exhibited by animals that simply woke up without a nearby mirror.

Gallup performed this comparison with several primate species, including spider monkeys, macaques, baboons, and chimpanzees. Of these, chimps are the clear mental champs by a wide margin, and thus they represented the best chance to provide evidence of self-recognition. The results of this comparison, illustrated in Figure 5.1, are quite clear: the marked chimps confronted with their mirror image demonstrated far more mark-directed touches than did the marked chimps that did not see their reflected image. No other species tested by Gallup at that time demonstrated

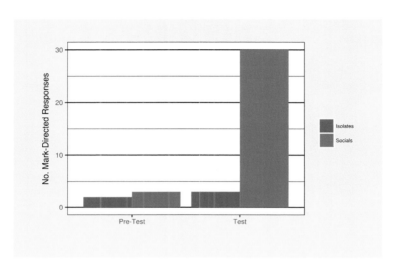

FIGURE 5.1 Evidence of Self-Recognition in Chimpanzees Reared in Isolation or with Other Chimps
Source: Adapted from Gallup (1977)

Looking Good!

Humans less than 18 months do not show self-recognition in a mirror. Tell that to this baby!
Source: R. Vallacher

self-recognition by using the mirror to gain visual access to a dyed ear or eyebrow. It's not that they failed to comprehend what mirrors do. If a piece of food was placed behind a monkey and yet was visible in the mirror, the monkey would turn around to retrieve the morsel. So monkeys and other lesser primates tacitly understand that mirrors reflect the image of objects, but they don't grasp the fact that they are one of those objects.

We noted earlier that people develop self-awareness by taking the perspective of other people in their environment. Gallup tested this notion as well. Some of his chimp participants were raised in a social environment that allowed for interactions with fellow chimps. These chimps tended to pass the self-recognition test, touching the dyed areas of their face when confronted with their image in a mirror. Other chimps were raised in a nonsocial environment, devoid of contact with other chimps. If taking the perspective of others is critical to self-awareness, then these chimps should draw a blank when confronted with their reflected image. And by and large, they did just that (Figure 5.1). Like the monkeys, these chimps responded to the reflected image as if it were another animal (with questionable taste in makeup).

We should note that even humans don't pass the mirror test until they're about 18 months old (Johnson, 1983; Lewis, 1986). This is when they show rapid intellectual gains, most notably an explosion in spoken vocabulary, other markers of linguistic competence, and symbolic play.

Box 5.1   What About Self-Recognition in Other Intelligent Species?

You may be wondering about other animals reputed to have high intelligence. Orangutans and gorillas, for example, are considered by many to be on the same intellectual plane as chimps, and then there are dolphins and porpoises, animals that are revered by some as intellectual giants, right up there with humans in their mental and emotional makeup. Self-recognition studies have in fact been conducted with these species, and the results are illuminating (Reiss & Marino, 2001; Swartz, Sarauw, & Evans, 1999). Orangutans definitely pass and dolphins appear to pass as well, although as you can imagine, the procedure had to be modified quite a bit for them (flippers are a poor substitute for hands).

But what about gorillas? The evidence is at best mixed for this species. With rare exceptions, gorillas fail the mirror test and thus seem to lack this rudimentary form of self-recognition. Interestingly, recent comparative analyses of various primate species have shown that orangutans are every bit as bright as chimps—maybe brighter—but gorillas are a cut below both these species, scoring lower even than spider monkeys (Deaner, van Schaik, & Johnson, 2006). So the fact that gorillas don't show self-recognition is consistent with the cognitive threshold assumption underlying self-awareness.

We should note that self-recognition has recently been observed in two species quite different from primates and dolphins—the Asian elephant (Plotnik, de Waal, & Reiss, 2006) and the magpie, a crow-like bird (Prior, Schwarz, & Gunturkun, 2008). This complicates the picture somewhat. OK, elephants are very bright mammals with enormous brains, so maybe their mental capacities put them in the same league as the great apes. But magpies are not mammals and do not even have a neocortex, the brain structure associated with higher mental functions. Maybe calling someone a "bird brain" is really not that much of a putdown after all.

The Content of Self-Awareness

Self-awareness in humans goes well beyond mere self-recognition. When we direct attention to ourselves, we are sensitive to far more than our ears and eyebrows. In large part, people think about themselves with respect to the same qualities they use to think about other people. This makes sense in light of the role other people play in fostering self-awareness. If we view ourselves from other people's perspective, and if we assume that other people share our judgmental concerns, then we should attempt to identify what we are like with respect to these concerns. Accordingly, people think about and evaluate themselves with respect to basic action tendencies such as extraversion, agreeableness, conscientiousness, intellect, and emotional stability (McCrae & John, 1992), and with respect to basic values such as competence and morality (Aronson, 1992; Vallacher & Solodky, 1979). In the same way that a person might evaluate an acquaintance as highly extraverted, moderately competent, and unbelievably immoral, the person uses these same criteria to evaluate his or her own behavioral tendencies.

Broad personal qualities vary in their personal significance for different people (Kelly, 1955). People develop broad generalizations about the self with respect to some traits but not with respect to other traits. A trait that plays an important role in self-understanding is termed a *self-schema* (Markus, 1977). Someone might have a self-schema with respect to "social sensitivity" and think about his or her behaviors in terms of this dimension, while another person might have a self-schema centering on gender and focus on the masculinity or femininity of his or her actions. For a trait to qualify as a self-schema, a person's self-rating on this dimension must be relatively extreme (e.g., very independent as opposed to equally independent and dependent) and the person must rate the dimension as important to his or her self-understanding.

In her research, Markus (1977) presented participants with specific behaviors representing a broad dimension of self-knowledge (e.g., "assertive" to represent independence) and asked them to indicate whether the behavior was a valid self-description. Participants were able to make this decision more quickly if it represented a self-schema not schematic for them. Participants who rated themselves as extremely independent and who considered independence to be important to their self-definition, for example, displayed very short response latencies (less than 2 seconds) when asked to press a "me" or "not me" button in response to words like assertive or individualistic. Participants who were aschematic with respect to independence (i.e., they rated themselves as moderately independent and didn't consider this dimension to be crucial to self-understanding), meanwhile, displayed significantly longer response latencies (e.g., 3 or 4 seconds) when making "me" or "not me" judgments about behaviors signifying independence.

Sources of Self-Knowledge

In principle, every personal experience is relevant to one's self-concept. In reality, some experiences are more relevant than others. Most people don't build a self-concept based on their encounters with the weather, for example, even if the weather is relevant to their health, comfort, or happiness. What sorts of experiences are pivotal in shaping a person's sense of what he or she is like? This question has fueled considerable theory and research over the years. A variety of answers have been documented, but to a large extent they reflect one of three general processes: *self-perception*, *social feedback*, and *social comparison*.

Self-Perception

Intuitively, the best source of self-relevant information is self-observation. It is certainly the most readily available and convenient source. Observation of your behavior in social settings, for example, could provide self-knowledge concerning your social strengths and weaknesses, as well as your likes and dislikes regarding other people. The role of self-observation of one's behavior in promoting self-knowledge is central to *self-perception theory* (Bem, 1967).

Bem noted that people sometimes do things without having a clear attitude about the behavior. Imagine you find yourself, for example, visiting the salad bar at the cafeteria instead of ordering a double-decker burger at the next concession area. If you have a taste for salads (or have just finished reading *Fast Food Nation*), there's nothing to explain and no reason to think about yourself in a new way (Andersen, 1984). But if the action is somewhat new for you—for example, this is your first trip to the cafeteria—you are likely to think about your reasons for the salad bar choice. If you conclude there were strong factors in the situation, there would be no reason to make inferences about your personal preferences in making this choice. Perhaps the double-decker burger line was too long, or maybe the prices have just been raised so that the purchase didn't make economic sense. The salad bar choice in this case would say nothing fundamental about your food preferences.

But imagine that the burger and salad lines were equally long and that the prices were comparable as well. Or to make it more interesting, imagine the salad bar line was *longer* and the salad prices were *higher*. Now the external factors are seen as relevant to your choice, but they would have promoted a different choice. In reality, your choice may have been simply a momentary impulse or a response to the first option you noticed. But randomness is usually not considered a satisfactory motive for our behavior; people prefer to identify what they do in terms of meaningful consequences and reasons (Vallacher & Wegner, 1987). When plausible reasons for an action are not provided by specific contextual cues (or by cultural scripts or values), people assume that the action represents some personal tendency for behaving that way. So rather than seeing your behavior as simply a sequence of lower-level acts (e.g., looking right rather than left, heading toward the light), you infer that you really enjoy lettuce, cucumbers, and the like, or that you've suddenly realized the health consequences of eating flavored meat paste made in a factory. You are now the proud possessor of a new property of the self—one which you are likely to display frequently and perhaps enthusiastically on subsequent excursions to the cafeteria and other eating establishments (Albarracín & Wyer, 2000; Dolinsky, 2000).

Self-perception applies to situations in which you find yourself doing something unusual, or at least unusual for you, and there aren't obvious forces dictating your behavior. But such conditions are rare. In a typical day, you spend the majority of the time doing familiar things for which you already have a meaningful understanding. And when you do engage in novel actions, the reasons for doing so are often clear rather than obscure, so you don't feel a need to dig deeper and make inferences about your mental and motivational makeup. The self-perception route to self-knowledge, in other words, is probably the exception rather than the rule.

Social Feedback

If self-observation isn't the primary source of self-knowledge, what is? Recall that self-awareness is fundamentally a social rather than a private experience. People look at themselves through the eyes of other people. Even if self-understanding is not part of the agenda for striking up a conversation with someone, we are nonetheless highly sensitive to how we are perceived by him or her. This source of self-relevant information is called *social feedback* or *reflected self-appraisal*. We are especially sensitive to the social feedback provided by "significant others"—people with whom we have special relationships or who are otherwise important to us (Cooley, 1902; Felson, 1989; Mead, 1934). Parents certainly qualify when we're children, but so do siblings, peers, and teachers. As adults, these people continue to matter but we expand the list of significant others to include friends, colleagues, and relationship partners. Such expansion throughout development would seem to increase our vulnerability to new and conflicting information, promoting instability in our self-concept. But with development, the lessons from social feedback begin to crystallize and form a relatively stable core in our sense of self. The reflected self-appraisals become consolidated into what Mead (1934) called a *generalized other*.

But even among adults, the sensitivity to social feedback is never completely extinguished. Of course, people don't always tell us what they think of us in straightforward terms, particularly if their appraisal is negative. But although people can control what they say, they have a far more difficult time controlling their nonverbal behavior to disguise their true feelings (Archer & Akert, 1977). Someone may have a strong aversion to a new acquaintance, for example, but restrain himself or herself from voicing this opinion out of a concern for appearing rude—or risking retaliation. However, the evaluator is likely to "leak" his or her appraisal through a variety of nonverbal channels, including body positions and movement, facial expressions, tone of voice, gestures, and eye gaze (Ambady & Rosenthal, 1992; Argyle, 1975; De Paulo & Friedman, 1998; Gifford, 1991; Knapp & Hall, 1997). Nonverbal displays of emotion are fairly universal, reflecting our common evolutionary heritage rather than different cultural experiences (Darwin, 1872; Ekman & Friesen, 1971). The ability to decode such information is also universal (e.g., Haidt & Keltner, 1999; Izard, 1994), which means that nonverbal displays provide meaningful feedback regarding people's feelings about one another.

The decoding of nonverbal behavior is far from perfect, however (Salovey & Mayer, 1990). Some people are quite adept at "reading others," but others show poor ability to distinguish true feelings from feigned ones (De Paulo & Friedman, 1998). Because the appraisals provided by others through nonverbal channels may be misperceived, people may develop assessments of themselves that do not correspond to objective reality.

Even if people are accurate in decoding social feedback, the reliance on social feedback does not mean that their self-concept will correspond to objective reality. If other people see you through distorted glasses, then you are destined to do the same. A perfectly fine human being with an assortment of assets (intelligence, athletic prowess, a strong moral compass) may nonetheless feel inadequate if the "significant others" in his life (parents, important peers, teachers, and so forth) have dwelled upon his or her relatively few weaknesses and overlooked his or her strengths. By the same token, someone with very little to brag about in objective terms might have a very glowing assessment of him or herself if the important observers in his or her life have viewed him or her through rose-colored glasses. There is considerable evidence, in fact, that people's global evaluation of themselves is only weakly correlated with objective assessments of their IQ, talents, skills, education, and physical health (e.g., Coopersmith, 1967).

Social Comparison

It is not necessary to see ourselves through the eyes of others for them to serve as a source of self-relevant information. They may not even know we exist, yet influence our self-assessments through *social comparison*. We evaluate our physical appearance, athletic abilities, social skills, competencies, and our intelligence by seeing how well we stack up against others. This simple idea is at the core of *social comparison theory*, first articulated by Leon Festinger in 1954. Since then, dozens of studies verified that social comparison is a source of self-knowledge and have yielded insights into how this process works (Suls & Wheeler, 2000; Wood, 1996).

People use social standards of comparison when they are uncertain about themselves but lack objective bases for reducing the uncertainty (Suls & Fletcher, 1983). This answer rules out the use of social comparison to determine one's height, hair color, and number of teeth. There are yardsticks and mirrors available for these areas of self-knowledge. You might think social comparison would be unnecessary in other areas as well, such as one's knowledge of psychology (look at the test results!), one's intelligence (check out the IQ score!), or one's physical ability (count the pull-ups!). But if you are uncertain about such things, you are motivated to see how your performance compares to other people's performance. Earning a "B" on a psychology exam, for example, could denote very good or simply OK knowledge, depending on how others performed. If most people earned a "C" or less, the "B" might signify a budding career in the field; if everyone earned a "B," on the other hand, you are unlikely to feel all that special in this area. The same reasoning holds for intelligence, physical abilities, attractiveness, social charm, and other important areas of self-concept. People assess their strengths and weaknesses in these areas by comparing their performance with that of other people.

But who are these other people? Perhaps we compare ourselves with whoever happens to be available. Or perhaps we compare ourselves with people picked at random, or with those we admire the most, or with national averages. None of these answers is correct. If we used people who happen to be nearby or picked at random, our self-knowledge would fluctuate wildly across circumstances ("Today I feel good about my education because I'm at the bus stop surrounded by schoolchildren") or sampling opportunities ("I feel great today about my health because I happened to think about drought victims in the 19th century"). If we used admired people, we would feel woefully inadequate ("Bill Gates has way more money than I ever will"). And national averages are abstract and often hard to come by ("I guess I'm doing OK financially because I'm above the median—whatever that means").

So with whom do we compare ourselves? The general answer is that we restrict comparison to those who are similar to us with respect to a factor that is relevant to the comparison (Festinger, 1954; Gilbert, Giesler, & Morris, 1995; Thornton & Arrowood, 1966). If you want to find out whether you are a good psychology student, you might avoid comparing yourself to a psychology professor, on the one hand, or to someone who's never taken a psychology course, on the other hand. For that matter, you might avoid comparing yourself to students at another university. Instead, your choice for social comparison is likely to be other students in your psychology classes. And even there, you're likely to restrict the comparison to those who have had about the same amount of exposure to psychology.

But the choice of comparison others is a bit more nuanced than simple similarity. There are two comparison standards, each employed for different reasons. Sometimes we engage in *upward social comparison*: the choice of other people who are better than we are with respect to a particular ability (Blanton, Buunk, Gibbons, & Kuyper, 1999; Wheeler, Koestner, & Driver, 1982; Zanna, Goethals, & Hill, 1975). This happens when we wish to improve or attain goals. The psychology student still might not compare him or herself to a psychology professor, but advanced undergraduates or graduate students at the university could well be fair game.

The other standard—which you may have guessed by now—represents *downward social comparison*: the choice of others who are worse than you on the trait or ability in question (Aspinwall & Taylor, 1993; Buunk, Oldersma, & de Dreu, 2001; Gibbons et al., 2002; Helgeson & Mickelson, 1995; Lockwood, 2002; Wills, 1981). This has the benefit of making one feel good about one's abilities or traits (Taylor & Lobel, 1989). A psychology student, licking his or her wounds after a poor showing on a psychology exam, might compare his or her competence to students who have dropped out of psychology or perhaps never have taken a psychology course.

To sum up, the choice of comparison others is influenced by one's goals. If the point is to gain an accurate assessment of one's abilities, traits, and opinions, one is likely to restrict social comparison to others who are similar. In effect, similarity provides a level playing field and hence a fair test of one's competence. But if one is striving toward greater competence, upward social comparison is the more likely scenario. Finally, if one's primary concern is simply feeling good about oneself, one is likely to demonstrate downward social comparison by focusing on others who are less fortunate or competent in the relevant area of comparison.

Culture and the Self

If the opinions of specific individuals are central to people's sense of self, imagine the significance of the opinions shared by *everyone* in a society. You might be able to ignore or discount the perspective on yourself held by a single individual, or even the perspective conveyed by an assortment of acquaintances and detractors, but ignoring or discounting the thoughts and values of the entire citizenry is a far more daunting, if not impossible, task. Theory and research in recent years have revealed just how pervasive cultural perspectives are in shaping the way members of a culture think about and evaluate themselves.

Every culture is distinct in terms of its language, customs, religious beliefs, economic practices, and political system. Thus, there may be a Canadian flavor to self-concept, a Japanese flavor, an Icelandic flavor, and so on, for each of the 300+ societies in the world. There is certainly some truth to this. But there are basic dimensions underlying the differences among specific cultures that enable some broad generalizations about culture and the self.

Perhaps the best-known work in this area is that of Hazel Markus and Shinobu Kitayama (1991), who expanded on a dimension of cultural variation articulated in the 1970s by Harry Triandis (Triandis, Malpass, & Davidson, 1973). This dimension, *individualism versus collectivism*, refers to the idea that people can think of themselves primarily as autonomous individuals with attributes that distinguish them from other people, even members of their own reference group (e.g., family, neighborhood, occupation), or they can emphasize instead their commonality with, and connection to, other people in their reference group or larger society. As Figure 5.2 shows, cultures differ in the relative strength of these two orientations toward self-definition (Cross & Gore, 2003; Kanagawa, Cross, & Markus, 2001; Kashima & Kashima, 2003; Ma & Schoeneman, 1997; Markus & Kitayama, 1991; Nisbett, 2003; Triandis, 1989).

In individualistic societies, such as the United States and countries in much of Europe, autonomy is given greater emphasis. People in such societies develop an *independent self* and focus on themselves as unique individuals with particular traits and abilities. In collectivist societies, such as those in Asia, Africa, and certain regions of Latin America, personal identities are strongly linked with one's social identities. People in such societies develop an *interdependent self* and focus on themselves as members of a family, village, religion, occupation, and culture. So while a college

FIGURE 5.2 Individualistic and Collectivistic Cultures Around the World
Source: Hofstede (2001)

student in, say, Boston might define herself in terms of qualities that make her unique relative to others (e.g., "I'm outgoing and do well in math"), a student in Beijing might define who she is in terms of attributes that characterize her connection to others (e.g., "I am a Buddhist and the oldest of three children in my family").

Individualistic and collectivist cultures also differ in the flexibility of people's self-concept. Unlike people in collectivist societies, those in individualistic societies have a self-concept that remains relatively stable across different contexts. Tafarodi et al. (2004), for example, found that most of Canadian college students (80%) agreed that "the beliefs that you hold about who you are (your inner self) remain the same across different activity domains," while only a minority (33%) of Chinese and Japanese students endorsed this idea. So while the student in Boston is likely to focus on her outgoing tendencies and unique abilities regardless of whom she is with or where she happens to be, the Beijing student might emphasize her religion in one context but her university or family relations in another.

Characterizing cultures in this fashion comes precariously close to stereotyping and can provide a rationale (or rationalization) for differential expectations and treatment of individuals from different societies. Such broad brushstrokes clearly oversimplify the experience of selfhood in individualistic and collectivist cultures. Within any culture—whether it is the United States or China, France or Argentina, Canada or Kenya—there is considerable variation in the degree to which people have an independent versus an interdependent self. This dimension also varies across a country's regions and political views (Nisbett, 2003; Vandello & Cohen, 1999). And with increasing cross-cultural contact, the differences between East and West in their experience of the self are showing signs of diminishing. For example, after spending 7 months at the University of British Columbia—located in Canada, one of the most individualistic societies on earth—Japanese exchange students displayed signs of self-concept that matched those of their Canadian counterparts (Heine, Lehman, Markus, & Kitayama, 1999).

Still, it is instructive to note cultural differences in the self. For one thing, this line of research identifies a primary source of selfhood and illustrates the malleability of people in developing a sense of who they are. The cultural perspective thus provides a counterpoint to the biological and cognitive factors we outlined earlier. Brain complexity, metacognition, and theory of mind are necessary for a sense of self, but they are not sufficient to specify just how the self takes shape. Experiential factors, including culture, provide the missing ingredients.

Beyond this academic rationale, appreciating cultural differences in the self is critical for understanding cultural differences in communication that all too often promote conflict when people from different parts of the world come into contact. Without such insight, someone from the United States might interpret the deference and humility of a person from Japan as a sign of weakness or self-perceived inferiority. The Japanese citizen, meanwhile, might interpret the American's self-reference and boasting as poor manners, arrogance, and a dominance display along the lines of the "ugly American" syndrome. Armed with the insight of background differences in how the self is experienced in individualistic and collectivist cultures, the potential trigger for conflict stemming from this misinterpretation has a better chance of being defused.

Self-Organization

How Do People Develop a Self-Concept?

William James (1890) suggested that "a man has as many social selves as there are individuals who recognize him and carry an image of him in their mind" (p.179). This is consistent with the "looking glass self" perspective (Cooley, 1902), but it also conveys an image of people devoid of any unity or stability in their sense of self. Imagine attending a party and adopting a different self-view every time you ended one conversation and started another. OK, this is probably hard to imagine. You no doubt maintain a firmly anchored sense of what you're like regardless of the variability among the partygoers' impression of you. Even in collectivist cultures that emphasize context specificity in self-definition, people have a pretty good sense of who they are when they wake up each morning and when they go to bed each night.

But how is a coherent self-concept achieved? Integrating the vast amount of social feedback and social comparison information you experience every day is hardly a trivial task. The sheer amount of such information is challenging enough, and much of this information is open to interpretation, inconsistent with other information encountered at the same time or the next day, and at odds with whatever generalizations about the self have already been generated. Even at the party alluded to earlier, you may encounter wildly different perspectives on yourself as the evening progresses. How do you manage to find your way home with the same view of the self that you entered the party with? And how did you get that self-view in the first place?

Introspection

At various points in life, it is natural and appropriate—even helpful—to sit back and take stock of what one has done and what one is capable of. Such episodes of *introspection* are especially likely for teenagers who are experiencing physical changes, new thoughts and desires, and who are contemplating what sort of person they want or hope to be. Middle age, too, is a time when men and women reflect on themselves and try to put all the pieces together about themselves and discern how they fit into the bigger scheme of things. And at any age, a person engaged in an unfamiliar action in a context that provides weak or ambiguous cues to the action's rationale may attempt to infer personal tendencies for behaving in this fashion, in line with self-perception theory (Bem, 1967).

But the motive for introspection does not guarantee the accuracy of consciously looking inward. Conscious efforts to develop a sense of what one is like are limited in what they can accomplish, often producing answers that are systematically biased (Kihlstrom, 1987; Nisbett & Wilson, 1977). People's attempts at introspection, in fact, can prove to be too much of a good thing. People sometimes overthink the reasons for past, present, and future courses of action, and can wind up totally off the mark, promoting a self-view that is based on a narrow and biased sample of memories, social comparisons, and reflected appraisals (Wilson et al., 1993).

Emergence

Contemporary research suggests that the power of conscious ("executive") thought is overrated, while the functional role of unconscious thought is commonly underrated. Complex decisions are sometimes more accurate or otherwise better (as assessed by objective criteria) when a person engages in unconscious thinking (Dijksterhuis & Nordgren, 2006). The solutions to scientific problems, for example, commonly occur as "Aha!" insights when the scientist is thinking about something entirely different. But how can one possibly forge a coherent self-concept without calling on effortful conscious processes? Without thinking, how is it possible to integrate an untold number of "bits" of self-relevant information into a sensible structure that provides a coherent sense of who he or she is? What makes the unconscious mind so much smarter than the conscious mind?

The Emergence Process

The answer, anticipated in Chapter 3 ("Beliefs, Attitudes, and Values"), centers on the concept of *emergence* (e.g., Holland, 1995; Johnson, 2001; Kelso, 1995) and the extension of this concept to social psychology (e.g., Marks-Tarlow, 1999; Vallacher & Nowak, 1997). The essence of emergence is captured in the familiar phrase "the whole is greater than the sum of its parts." This simply means that, without outside guidance, individual elements influence each other to create a new property that did not exist before.

Consider, for example, certain species of fireflies. On warm summer nights, these insects can be observed producing flashes in a constant rhythm that varies from one firefly to the next. When the number of fireflies in a location reaches a critical threshold, however, they begin to flash in perfect synchrony with one another. This beautiful sight has puzzled scientists for decades. No one would accuse fireflies of being particularly smart, and they are certainly not sophisticated enough to decide as a group what flashing rhythm they should adopt. And there is no conductor with a magic wand who makes this happen. Rather, synchronized flashing at the group level results from local influences between nearby fireflies (Strogatz, 2003). A given firefly has no concept of the larger group but rather adjusts its flashing rhythm to match that of the rhythm exhibited by its immediate neighbors. The sudden emergence of behavior at a group level reflects *self-organization* among the individuals in the group.

Something similar occurs in the human mind when individual thoughts, images, and memories are experienced at the same time (Vallacher & Nowak, 2007). These "mental elements" influence each other to take on a shared meaning, even if the meaning did not exist before. Imagine yourself daydreaming (after reading this chapter, perhaps) and the following elements pop up in your stream of thought: "I aced an exam"; "I worked my tail off studying"; "I haven't left the dorm for two days." None of these thoughts says anything about your interpersonal skills or needs, but their co-occurrence in your mind might nonetheless lead you to conclude something about this feature of self. You might emerge with the insight that you are a social isolate, perhaps, or conversely that you have enough confidence in such matters that you can relinquish social opportunities when other needs assume priority.

The emergence of global thoughts from the self-organization of more basic thoughts need not occur consciously. Sometimes, in fact, a clearer and more reliable pattern emerges when we don't try to force the issue. Just as the scientist faced with a difficult problem will take a walk in the woods and, without warning, experience a sudden insight ("Eureka!") into the problem's solution, people can experience unexpected insights into themselves while doing something totally unrelated to self-examination (e.g., exercising, playing the flute, daydreaming). Keep in mind that the mind is never totally quiescent and that much of our mental process occurs beneath the level of conscious awareness. It's as though our mental elements are constantly interacting with one another, and this interaction prompts the emergence of higher-order conclusions and insights that pop into conscious awareness, often without warning and in unlikely circumstances.

The Emergence of Self-Structure

Computer simulations have proven useful in demonstrating emergence in self-concept (Nowak, Vallacher, Tesser, & Borkowski, 2000; Nowak et al., 2005). In this approach, the self is conceptualized as a large and complex system composed of distinct mental elements, as illustrated in Figure 5.3. These elements can be highly diverse, representing specific memories, self-perceived skills, physical features, hopes and fears, and virtually anything else that is potentially relevant to self-understanding. But despite their diversity, all the elements can be scaled in terms of evaluation—each thought can be viewed as reflecting well or poorly on one's sense of self. In the figure, the light gray cells represent positive elements and the dark gray cells represent negative elements.

All that's required for a coherent self-concept to form is that the elements interact with and influence one another. In this process, each element can change its evaluation, depending on the evaluation of other elements that it comes in contact with. "I'm clumsy," for example, may seem like a negative quality, but if it arises in the context of more positive thoughts—"I'm a deep thinker"; "People find me funny and adorable"; "I'm too busy with important things to worry about physical grace"—this quality could be viewed in benign or even self-flattering terms. At each moment in time, the elements adjust their evaluation so as to achieve a shared evaluation with nearby elements. In Figure 5.3, each element exerts greatest influence on, and is influenced most strongly by, the eight other elements it contacts directly. This reflects the co-occurrence in time of the conscious thoughts that arise in the stream of consciousness, or in the succession of unconscious thoughts that takes place beneath the level of conscious awareness.

Note that the cells differ in how tall they are. This feature represents an element's stability and resistance to change in evaluation. The taller the cell, the more influence from other elements it takes to change its evaluation. A short element might be something like "I like to talk a lot" (which could be either good or bad), whereas a tall element would be a quality with a more stable evaluation, such as "I'm sociable" (positive) or "I'm anxious" (negative). So when the elements interact with one another, the taller elements have greater influence in shaping the shared evaluation of neighboring elements than do the shorter elements. In effect, it takes many little thoughts to counter the influence of one big thought.

As a result of this process, subsets of self-relevant information become increasingly similar in evaluation. Once these areas of the self are formed, they too become integrated into even larger subsets of elements that share the same evaluation. This process of *progressive integration* is illustrated in Figure 5.3. The top figure represents a self-structure that is unintegrated, with each element's evaluation totally independent of its neighbor's evaluation. Note what happens, though, as the elements influence each other to achieve a shared evaluation. As illustrated in the bottom figure, large areas of the self begin to emerge, each composed of many elements that share an evaluation.

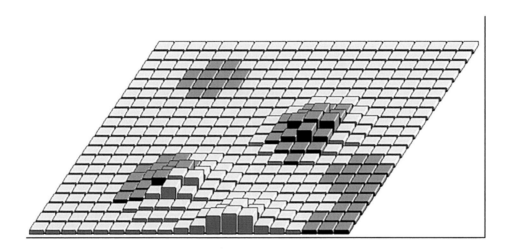

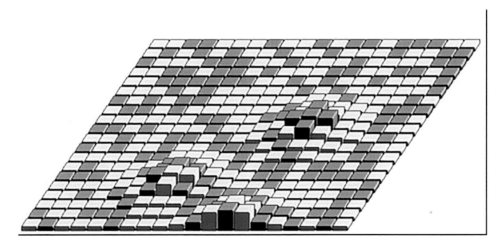

FIGURE 5.3 Self-Organization and the Emergence of Self-Structure. (a) Random Organization of Self-Relevant Information and (b) Emergence of Coherent Areas of Self-Structure Due to Self-Organization
Source: Nowak et al. (2000). Copyright © 2000 by the American Psychological Association.

Each area represents an integrated and relatively global feature of the self, such as a social role (e.g., student, employee), an area of competence (e.g., piano, racquetball), or a broad personality trait (e.g., social sensitivity, honesty). Because specific thoughts about the self have become integrated in this fashion, the person can think about him or herself in terms of global properties rather than in terms of highly specific events and features. Thus, a person might think of him or herself as "a racquetball player" or even as "an athlete," rather than in terms of his or her arm movements or how he or she did in a particular match.

Multiple Selves

In principle, the progressive integration of personal thoughts and feelings could go beyond generating separate regions of the self and result in a self-concept that is totally integrated and uniform in its evaluation. This is analogous to what happens when self-organization takes place with fireflies—they progress from individual flashing patterns to small clusters of fireflies with the same pattern and finally to one big swarm flashing in unison. Could this happen with self-concept? Could the emergence process give you a single view of what you are like that subsumes all the things you know and feel about yourself?

This is highly unlikely. Despite the tendency toward progressive integration, the emergence process eventually stalls at a level of integration far below that of unification. This limit reflects the fact that we have to do many different things and interact with many different people. Each role we occupy or activity we perform calls for an assessment of one's relevant traits and skills that may be specific to the role or activity. In your role as "student," your sense of self probably revolves, in part, around concentration, intellectual curiosity, and at least a bit of self-control (e.g., "study, not party"). In your role as "dating partner," a somewhat different constellation of personal tendencies come to the fore, some of which may be inconsistent with your "student" identity. Intellectual curiosity and self-control, for example, may take a back seat to witty banter, impulsive expression of feelings, and spontaneous action.

So instead of having a single, unified self-concept, people have *multiple selves* (Gergen, 1971; Markus & Nurius, 1986). Viewing the self in a differentiated rather than globally integrated manner has benefits that go beyond handling the conflicting demands of different roles, relationships, and activities. A *multifaceted self* enables people to absorb setbacks and failures without falling into despair about their self-worth (Linville, 1987; Showers, 1992). A setback in one area—say, an athletic competition—is confined to that aspect of the self and does not color the person's self-view in other areas (career, friendship, etc.). If a person had only a global view of the self, the setback might have an equally global impact on the person. Seeing yourself as having distinct competencies and occupying separate social roles allows you to feel good about yourself in regions that aren't tarnished when you experience failure in one region.

People differ in the extent to which they think about themselves in relatively global versus specific terms. For some people, the tendency toward progressive integration promotes a highly unified sense of self that transcends many different roles and contexts. For other people, the integration tendency stalls at a relatively low level, leaving them with a set of very specific self-views, each limited to narrowly defined circumstances. Vallacher and Wegner (1989) developed a self-report instrument, the *Behavior Identification Form* (BIF), that is relevant to this difference (see Box 5.2). Some people—termed *low-level agents*—tend to think about their behavior in concrete, low-level terms, whereas other people—*high-level agents*—tend instead to identify what they do in higher-level terms, focusing on the goals, implications, and larger meaning of their actions. Both a low-level and a high-level agent may take a psychology exam, for example, but the low-level agent may think about this action in concrete terms ("answering questions"), whereas the high-level agent may think instead about the implications of what he or she is doing ("showing what I know").

Box 5.2   The Behavior Identification Form

Any behavior can be described in many ways. For example, one person might describe a behavior as "writing a paper," while another person might describe the same behavior as "pushing keys on the keyboard." Yet another person might describe it as "expressing thoughts." This form focuses on your personal preferences for how a number of different behaviors should be described. Below you will find several behaviors listed. After each behavior will be two different ways in which the behavior might be identified. For example:

1. Attending class
   a. sitting in a chair
   b. looking at a teacher

Your task is to choose the identification, *a* or *b*, that best describes the behavior for you. Simply place a checkmark next to the option you prefer. Be sure to respond to every item. Please mark only one alternative for each pair. Remember, mark the description that *you personally believe* is more appropriate for each pair.

1. Making a list
   a. Getting organized[a]
   b. Writing things down
2. Reading
   a. Following lines of print
   b. Gaining knowledge[a]
3. Joining the army
   a. Helping the nation's defense
   b. Signing up[a]
4. Washing clothes
   a. Removing odors from clothes[a]
   b. Putting clothes into the machine
5. Picking an apple
   a. Getting something to eat[a]
   b. Pulling an apple off a branch
6. Chopping down a tree
   a. Wielding an axe
   b. Getting firewood[a]
7. Measuring a room for carpeting
   a. Getting ready to remodel[a]
   b. Using a yardstick
8. Cleaning the house
   a. Showing one's cleanliness[a]
   b. Vacuuming the floor
9. Painting a room
   a. Applying brush strokes
   b. Making the room look fresh[a]
10. Paying the rent
    a. Maintaining a place to live[a]
    b. Writing a check
11. Caring for houseplants
    a. Watering plants
    b. Making the room look nice[a]
12. Locking a door
    a. Putting a key in the lock
    b. Securing the house[a]
13. Voting
    a. Influencing the election[a]
    b. Marking a ballot

14. Climbing a tree
    a. Getting a good view[a]
    b. Holding on to branches
15. Filling out a personality test
    a. Answering questions
    b. Revealing what you're like[a]
16. Toothbrushing
    a. Preventing tooth decay[a]
    b. Moving a brush around in one's mouth
17. Taking a test
    a. Answering questions
    b. Showing one's knowledge[a]
18. Greeting someone
    a. Saying hello
    b. Showing friendliness[a]
19. Resisting temptation
    a. Saying "no"
    b. Showing moral courage[a]
20. Eating
    a. Getting nutrition[a]
    b. Chewing and swallowing
21. Growing a garden
    a. Planting seeds
    b. Getting fresh vegetables[a]
22. Traveling by car
    a. Following a map
    b. Seeing countryside[a]
23. Having a cavity filled
    a. Protecting your teeth[a]
    b. Going to the dentist
24. Talking to a child
    a. Teaching a child something[a]
    b. Using simple words
25. Pushing a doorbell
    a. Moving a finger
    b. Seeing if someone's home[a]

[a] Higher level alternative. Total score is the sum of higher level alternative choices.
Source: Vallacher & Wegner (1989)

High-level agents are quite adept at describing themselves with respect to broad personality traits—which are, after all, fairly high-level descriptions of behavior. But those who are inclined to identify what they do in lower-level terms—low-level agents—are less certain of what they are like with respect to personality traits. Their self-descriptions tend to center on far more basic and concrete qualities (e.g., mannerisms, appearance). So while a high-level agent might be preoccupied with his or her self-perceived extraversion, a low-level agent's spontaneous thoughts about him or herself might focus on his or her speech rate and frequency of smiling.

As noted above, there are advantages to having a multifaceted view of oneself. But too much specificity in thinking about the self can be just as problematic. A fragmented view of the self provides a poor basis for planning and decision-making. Knowing only that one can tell jokes (a specific social skill) but not whether one has a more general set of social skills, for example, can make it tough anticipating how one will come across at a party and can call into question one's decision to mix it up socially. More generally, an unintegrated sense of self promotes low *self-concept clarity* (Campbell et al., 1996), experienced as low *self-concept certainty* (Baumgardner, 1990; Pelham, 1991; Vallacher, Nowak, Froehlich, & Rockloff, 2002). When asked to indicate what they are like on trait dimensions (e.g., sociable vs. unsociable, energetic vs. lazy), people lacking integration can provide an answer (e.g., moderately sociable, fairly energetic) but they express uncertainty concerning these answers. Individuals with low clarity and certainty may express a particular level of global self-regard ("all in all, I think I'm a good person"), but when then asked to talk about themselves, their expressed self-evaluation tends to vary a great deal between positive and negative assessments, even over the course of just a few minutes (Vallacher et al., 2002; Wong, Vallacher, & Nowak, 2016). In contrast, people with a more integrated self-concept tend to express thoughts about themselves that are fairly stable in evaluation over time (Kernis & Waschull, 1995).

Ironically, people who think about their actions in lower-level terms and thus lack clarity and certainty regarding their broader behavioral tendencies tend to be *more* sensitive to information regarding these tendencies than are high-level agents. Lacking a clear and stable sense of what they are like with respect to broad behavioral tendencies (i.e., personality traits), low-level agents are sensitive to social feedback, social comparison, and other sources of self-relevant information that can provide an avenue of emergence toward greater integration and clarity in their understanding of themselves (Vallacher & Wegner, 1989). The higher-level self-understanding achieved in this way, however, is hard to sustain over time for low-level agents.

The upshot is that there is an optimal level of self-concept integration. Too little integration undermines action planning and decision-making, promotes self-concept uncertainty, and can make one vulnerable to outside sources of information that can create greater (temporary) clarity about one's self. But too much integration is also problematic. Having a single way of thinking about the self may provide a sense of coherence, but it comes at the price of flexibility and openness to changing social roles and activities. It also means that a failure or setback in one area may have implications for one's sense of self as a whole. The trick is to establish sufficient integration to enable effective decision-making and a clear sense of self, but also enough diversity to avoid overgeneralizing from one's successes and failures in specific contexts.

Self-Esteem

Despite the tendency to develop a differentiated self-concept, people nonetheless can be characterized with respect to their global self-evaluation or *self-esteem* (Coopersmith, 1967; Leary et al., 1995; Rosenberg, 1979; Tesser, 1988; Zeigler-Hill, 2013; Wylie, 1979). Different tests have been developed to measure self-esteem (see Box 5.3 for the most popular test), each showing that people can be reliably scored on this trait (although most people consider themselves "better than average").

Box 5.3   The Rosenberg Self-Esteem Test

Please indicate your level of agreement with each of the following statements by choosing the number on the rating scale that best describes the way you feel about yourself.

Strongly . . . . Strongly
Disagree . . . . Disagree . . . . Agree . . . . Agree
    0 . . . . 1 . . . . .2 3

1. I feel that I am a person of worth, at least on an equal basis with others.
2. I feel that I have a number of good qualities.
3. All in all, I am inclined to feel that I am a failure. *(reverse scored)*
4. I am able to do things as well as most other people.
5. I feel I do not have much to be proud of. *(reverse scored)*
6. I take a positive attitude toward myself.

7. On the whole, I am satisfied with myself.
8. I wish I could have more respect for myself. *(reverse scored)*
9. I certainly feel useless at times. *(reverse scored)*
10. At times I think I am no good at all. *(reverse scored)*

To compute your score, first reverse your answers to items 3, 5, 8, 9, and 10 (0 = 3, 1 = 2, 2 = 1, 3 = 0). Then compute the average of your answers (sum of the scores on the 10 items, divided by 10). The higher your score, the higher your self-esteem. In American samples, the average score is 2.2.

Source: Adapted from Rosenberg (1965)

Bases of Self-Esteem

But how is this possible in light of people's multiple selves? If people see themselves differently in different roles and activity domains, how do they manage to maintain a global self-evaluation that cuts across these self-views? There are two ways to think about this issue.

Perhaps people simply average the self-evaluations associated with specific regions of the self to come up with a global sense of self-worth. A person might feel great about his or her intellectual ability, pretty good about his or her social skills, and have a negative assessment of his or her athletic competence. If he or she simply averaged these self-assessments (excellent, good, and bad), his or her self-esteem would be moderately positive. Of course, some self-aspects are more important than others, so perhaps the person's global self-evaluation should give greater weight to the more important regions (Anderson, 1974; Coopersmith, 1967; Harter, 1986). Let's say the person is firmly committed to academics and thus attaches the greatest importance to this aspect of self. In this case, the person's self-esteem might be highly positive, tempered only by a slight concern with his or her social skills and athleticism.

A variation on this possibility assumes that people have *contingencies of self-worth* (Crocker & Wolfe, 2001). Consider two people who have identical self-assessments with respect to each of several self-aspects—academic competence (very good), physical attractiveness (average), and social sensitivity (less than average). Despite their shared self-assessments, they may differ a great deal in their self-esteem depending on which self-aspect their self-worth is most contingent. One person might have very high self-esteem because he or she considers academic competence to be all-important, whereas the other person might have low self-esteem because his or her self-worth is contingent on his or her attractiveness or social sensitivity.

The second way to think about this issue is to assume that self-esteem is independent of specific self-views (e.g., Brown, 1993; Deci & Ryan, 1995; Kernis, 2003). Perhaps self-esteem is more "primitive" or basic than cognitive appraisals of oneself, representing instead the degree of *attachment* to one's parents and caregivers during childhood (Ainsworth, 1979; Bowlby, 1980; Hazan & Shaver, 1994; Orth & Robins, 2014; Simpson, Rholes, & Phillips, 1996). In this view, a tough childhood, associated with neglect and parental inconsistency, can create a foundation for self-doubt that persists throughout one's life. On the other hand, a secure attachment during childhood establishes an unquestioned view of oneself as accepted, desirable, and generally worthwhile, regardless of one's specific self-views. Even if the secure child never achieves excellence in any area of endeavor and the insecure child goes on to win a Nobel Prize, the secure child may have a more positive feeling about him or herself.

A variation on this perspective finds expression in the *sociometer hypothesis* (Leary et al., 1995). This model rests on the non-controversial idea that humans have a fundamental need to belong to social groups and to have meaningful social relations (Baumeister & Leary, 1995). Everyone wants to feel that he or she is plugged into a social network and that he or she has friends. The extent to which a person's social belongingness needs are met can be calibrated in a manner analogous to the way in which a person determines whether there is an adequate supply of gas in his or her car. The *sociometer*, in other words, measures how "full" our social relations tank is, just like a gas gauge tells us how full our gas tank is. The greater one's belongingness needs are met (i.e., the fuller the tank), the higher one's self-esteem.

The emphasis on social foundations of self-esteem (beginning in childhood) certainly makes sense in light of the social origins of self-awareness and the importance of social relations in providing the content for people's self-concept. High self-esteem people do indeed have more friends than low self-esteem people, and they typically score higher on traits suggestive of interpersonal skills (e.g., extraversion) that are useful in attracting and maintaining social contacts (Baumeister & Twenge, 2003; Swann, 1996). But note what the sociometer hypothesis implies: even if they lack skills and accomplishments, people can still have high self-esteem if they feel part of social groups and have a circle of friends they can count on.

The jury is still out regarding which of these perspectives best accounts for the relation between people's overall self-esteem and their multiple selves. In line with the sociometer hypothesis, high and low self-esteem people do not differ in many ways other than their social skills and social relations. High self-esteem people are not necessarily brighter, more athletic, more skilled, more physically attractive, or even healthier than are people with lower self-esteem (Baumeister, 1998; Coopersmith, 1967). However, these findings represent generalizations across large samples of people. For any one individual, one or more of these dimensions could be vital to the person's self-esteem. But if these self-defining dimensions differ across people (as the contingent self-worth perspective suggests), one would not expect to find a connection in the population between any single self-view and people's level of self-esteem.

Both perspectives may have merit, and their respective insights can perhaps be meaningfully integrated. A secure social foundation in childhood, for instance, could promote high self-esteem, which could set the stage for acquiring skills, fostering talents, nurturing interests, and learning social roles as one develops. An insecure social foundation, on other hand, may promote low self-esteem and inhibit children from developing competencies and seeking out new roles. Later in life, these differences in the number and quality of specific self-views provide the foundation for differences in global self-assessment in accordance with the contingent self-worth view. Perhaps global self-evaluation and multiple selves are both the cause and effect of one another in an interplay that begins in childhood and unfolds throughout life.

Explicit and Implicit Self-Esteem

The discussion of self-concept formation noted that much of mental processing devoted to self-understanding takes place below the level of consciousness. This raises the intriguing possibility that people can form two somewhat independent self-views—one reflecting conscious considerations and one reflecting the integration of unconscious information. This rather strange (perhaps disturbing?) idea has in fact generated a major line of theory and research in recent years suggesting that although people have a conscious global self-evaluation, they may also have an unconscious and implicit sense of their self-worth. The primary research tool used to investigate the potential for *implicit self-esteem* is the *Implicit Association Test* (IAT; Greenwald et al., 1998), introduced in Chapter 3.

The IAT exposes unconscious attitudes that go undetected by traditional procedures that ask people to provide explicit reports of their attitudes. A White person might indicate positive attitudes toward members of a minority group, for example, but harbor a stereotyped view of the group that is latent and unexpressed most of the time. The IAT has been employed in recent years to expose implicit self-esteem (Bosson, Swann, & Pennebaker, 2000; Farnham, Greenwald, & Banaji, 1999; Greenwald & Banaji, 1995; Greenwald & Farnham, 2000)—people's latent and unexpressed evaluation of themselves. When asked to evaluate themselves on self-report measures, most people express a relatively positive self-image, in line with the "better than average" tendency. Despite having moderate or high explicit self-esteem, however, some people harbor a negative self-view that is kept under wraps most of the time.

A person's implicit self-esteem is revealed in the IAT procedure by assessing how long it takes him or her to associate "self" words (I, my, me, mine) with pleasant words (e.g., kind, wonderful) versus unpleasant words (e.g., filthy, stinky). If the person takes considerably longer to associate the self words with unpleasant than with pleasant words, his or her implicit self-esteem is high. But if the person takes relatively little time to associate the self words with the unpleasant words, he or she is said to have low implicit self-esteem. Explicit and implicit self-esteem are correlated but not very strongly (Greenwald, Nosek, & Banaji, 2003), so some people can be characterized as having high explicit self-esteem and low implicit self-esteem.

Narcissism and Self-Esteem

It is one thing to have high self-esteem. It is quite another to feel that one is superior to everyone on the planet—and to let these lesser beings know it. These two attitudes do not necessarily go together. Some people with high self-esteem—perhaps many of your acquaintances (or yourself)—are self-assured, but do not feel the need to brag about themselves or look down upon others. But other people with high self-esteem are caught up in their personal

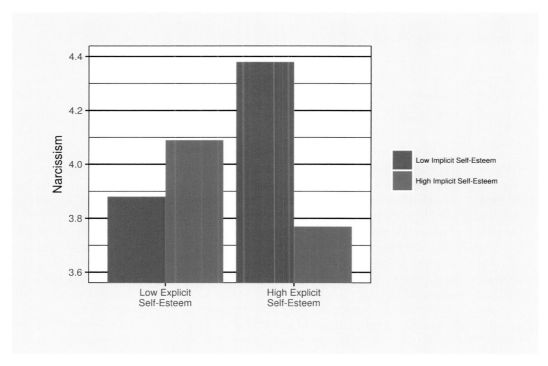

FIGURE 5.4 Narcissism Is the Combination of High Explicit and Low Implicit Self-Esteem
Source: Adapted from Jordan et al. (2003)

wonderfulness and want—or demand—similar adulation from others. They do not take kindly to criticism and their inflated self-view is always evident in their social relations. Although they are clearly arrogant, they constantly seek out reassurance from others that they are truly superior. This type of self-view is associated with the personality trait of *narcissism* (Brummelman, Thomaes, & Sedikides, 2016; Konrath, Bushman, & Campbell, 2006).

What distinguishes the narcissist from others with high self-esteem who are not so obsessed with their greatness? The link between explicit and implicit self-esteem seems to be the key. Jordan et al. (2003) found that whereas narcissists have very high explicit self-esteem, their implicit self-view is considerably more negative. People whose self-view was highly positive on both explicit and implicit measures are considerably less self-absorbed and more tolerant of others (see Figure 5.4).

Note the link here between self-concept uncertainty, self-evaluation, and narcissism. Putting these separate elements together gives rise to an intriguing yet plausible picture of self-esteem. Knowing only a person's explicit self-esteem (as assessed by standard measure such as the Rosenberg test) does not afford unequivocal predictions about how the person conducts himself or herself or relates to other people. A high self-esteem person could behave in diametrically opposed ways: as resilient in the face of setbacks and warm and thoughtful in his or her social relations, or as unable to tolerate setbacks and dismissive of the needs of other people.

The difference centers on the level of the person's implicit self-esteem. If the person's unconscious self-view matches his conscious self-view, his or her self-esteem is likely to be highly certain and should give rise to stability in his or her self-evaluative thoughts. But if there is a conflict between the person's explicit and implicit self-views, he or she is likely to have an uncertain conception of what he or she is really like—a configuration that promotes instability in thinking about him or herself and a corresponding need to solicit praise from other people to prop up the positive side of the conflict. In short, a narcissist is someone who expends considerable effort attempting to shore up a positive self-view because of a negative self-view lurking in the shadows that calls the former into question.

Self-Defense

How Do People Protect Their Self-Concept?

Everyday life provides an endless barrage of self-relevant information, and not all of it is favorable. Some information can provide a direct challenge to a specific self-view (e.g., one's social charm) or to one's global self-regard. Yet people usually recover from such hits and maintain their self-view in specific areas as well as in their overall self-esteem. How do people manage this in light of their reliance on social sources of information to define who they are?

Self-Evaluation Maintenance

Self-relevant information is often open to interpretation. Behaving in a critical fashion, for example, could be seen as negative (as harmful or insensitive), but it could also be viewed in positive terms (as constructive criticism or "tough love"). The flexibility of self-relevant information is critical to the formation of a self-concept (as we saw in the discussion of emergence), but it is also critical to the defense of one's self-concept.

There are a variety of means by which people can change the implications of self-relevant information for purposes of self-protection. Imagine how you might respond, for example, if someone at a party were to call you a crashing bore. It might sting a bit at first, but in fairly short order you would no doubt mount one (or more) of several spirited defenses that would restore your self-view as the highly interesting person that you no doubt are. You might challenge the critic's credibility, noting that he or she is simply a negative person or perhaps a bad judge of character. Alternatively, you might note how unrepresentative the behavior was that prompted the critique. Then again, you might justify your low-key behavior as appropriate in light of the uninteresting people at the party. Yet another line of defense is to question the critic's motive for blasting you. Perhaps he or she is envious of you and wants to bring you down. Or better yet, perhaps he or she really likes you but fears the feeling isn't reciprocated, so he or she engages in a "reject before you're rejected" strategy to protect his or her own self-esteem.

Abraham Tesser and his colleagues have likened the wide variety of means available for self-concept protection to a *self-defense zoo* (Tesser et al., 1996). An especially well-researched strategy is the *self-serving bias*. This simply means that people accept credit for their successes, but blame their failures on external factors or bad luck (Arkin, Cooper, & Kolditz, 1980; Campbell & Sedikides, 1999; Mullen & Riordan, 1988; Ross, Amabile, & Steinmetz, 1977). Students are notorious in this regard. When they perform well on an exam, they see the grade as a reflection of their intellect, their knowledge of the material, or their preparation. When they do poorly, they see things far differently: the exam was unfair and not a valid measure of their competence (Arkin & Maruyama, 1979; Davis & Stephan, 1980; Gilmour & Reid, 1979; Griffin, Combs, Land, & Combs, 1983).

One might think that the most vigorous defenses of the self would occur when dealing with potential enemies or people with whom we have little in common. If a stranger criticizes you at a party, you would probably mount a particularly strong defense. This is undoubtedly true. But under some circumstances, the greatest threat to self-esteem comes from those who are closest to us and with whom we have a great deal in common. Insight into this state of affairs is provided by Tesser's (1988) model of *self-evaluation maintenance* (SEM). The SEM model is primarily concerned with social comparison information. Tesser suggests that two factors are critical in determining how we respond to such information: the *closeness of the comparison person* and the *personal relevance of the behavior* in question. Normally, we hope that people we're close to will excel at the activities in which they engage. Who wouldn't want one's spouse, sibling, or best friend to succeed? You would be proud if your brother or sister won a state tennis championship, for example, or if he or she earned straight As in college.

The problem for the self arises when that person excels at something that you also aspire to be good at. Imagine, for example, that you are also a budding tennis star or trying to stand out in college. Now your sibling's tennis championship or straight As can be a little unsettling because it represents a direct comparison with your success in that area. According to SEM reasoning, you might go out of your way to find other ways to maintain your self-evaluation, or perhaps change your pursuits in order to avoid the inevitable comparisons. Just such a scenario can be observed among friends, whose success in a personally relevant area can prove to be highly threatening (Zuckerman & Jost, 2001). Marital partners, too, can experience this sort of difficulty if they have identical career goals (Clark & Bennett, 1992). It's unlikely that their respective careers will proceed in lockstep with one another. The first one to receive recognition in the career can pose a serious self-concept threat to the partner whose time has yet to come.

People have three choices when someone close succeeds in an area that is personally relevant: they can rethink the importance of that area, distance themselves from the person, or sabotage the person's performance. Marriage partners, for example, can decide to follow different career paths ("Fine, go ahead and cure cancer; I've decided to take a shot at line dancing!"). Or they could become less close ("Perhaps we should move on"), which is hardly a desirable solution for a married couple. Or the threatened partner could try to hinder the loved one's success in various ways ("Say, why don't you try playing tennis with your left hand?").

Perhaps it's fortunate that people have a self-defense zoo to turn to when social comparisons prove uncomfortable. Brothers and sisters, husbands and wives, and close friends do not have to denigrate one another, sabotage their success, or change their aspirations when one outperforms the other. Instead, they can invoke a self-serving bias or come up with a clever rationalization to make sense of their successes and failures. If their partners are truly close, they'll play along and help draft an interpretation that keeps both parties happy.

Self-Verification

Negative social feedback and unfavorable social comparisons engage a host of self-defense strategies, which makes sense if one assumes that people are motivated to develop and maintain high self-esteem. Most people do have relatively high self-esteem and feel that they are better than average on almost every dimension (Allison, Messick, & Goethals, 1989; Dunning & Hayes, 1996; Dunning, Meyerowitz, & Holzberg, 1989; Van Lange, 1991). But not everyone has a flattering view of him or herself in every area, nor does everyone have high self-esteem. When such people protect their self-concept, what are they protecting? A positive self-view or the view they actually have of themselves? Imagine a young man with serious doubts about his social charm being told by a young female that he is the most exciting person she has met in years. Would he buy it? If self-esteem were the issue, he might enthusiastically embrace the feedback. If, however, the real issue centered on maintaining a self-concept, he might discount or even reject the feedback as inconsistent with the way he sees himself.

Box 5.4   Dimensions on which most people feel they are better than average

- *Intelligence*: Most people feel they are brighter than their average peer (*Public Opinion*, 1984; Wylie, 1979). This says something about people's intelligence regarding statistics.
- *Attractiveness*: Most people feel they are better-looking than their peers (Wylie, 1979). Beauty is literally in the eye of the beholder.
- *Insight*: People think highly of their mental lives. Not surprisingly, most people believe they understand themselves better than they are understood by other people. But people also believe they know themselves better than others know themselves (Pronin, Kruger, Savitsky, & Ross, 2001). College students feel they are less naïve and gullible than their peers (Levine, 2003)—or at least that's what they've been led to believe.
- *Health*: Most college students believe they will outlive the age of death predicted by actuarial tables by about 10 years (Larwood, 1978; C.R. Snyder, 1978). Maybe they know something about fast food and high fructose corn syrup that's lost on the medical community.
- Morality: When asked, "How would you rate your own morals and values on a scale of 1 to 100?" 50% of a nationwide sample rated themselves 90 or above and only 11% rated themselves 74 or less. This assumes, of course, that they were being truthful.
- *Competence*: 86% of the people in an Australian sample rated their job performance as above average; only 1% rated themselves below average. Maybe the pollsters didn't do their job right.
- *Driving*: Most drivers believe they are safer and more skilled than the average driver (Guerin, 1994; McKenna & Myers, 1997; Svenson, 1981). This was even true for drivers who have been hospitalized for accidents. It must have been the other guy's fault.

- *Tolerance*: A 1997 Gallup poll found that only 14% of White Americans rated their prejudice against African Americans as 5 or higher on a 0–10 scale. But they perceived high prejudice (5 or above) by 44% of *other* White Americans. People feel they're too good to be prejudiced.
- *Freedom from bias*: People think they are less vulnerable to biases—including the "I'm better than average" bias—than are most of their peers (Pronin et al., 2001). Maybe the information in this box applies to every-one else.

So, is it more important to feel good about oneself or to feel coherent in one's self-knowledge? Insight into this issue is a focus of *self-verification theory*, a model of self-concept developed by William Swann and his colleagues. Swann's answer is that coherence trumps evaluation—but not without a struggle (Swann, 1990). Having a coherent view of the self, even if it is not all that positive, enables one to predict how one will fare in social settings and thus allows one to decide what to do, what contexts to seek out or avoid, and which people to trust. People choose, like, and retain partners (e.g., roommates, friends) who perceive and evaluate them in a way that matches their own self-view (Swann, Griffin, Predmore, & Gaines, 1987). People prefer romantic partners who see them as they see themselves, even if the self-view has some glaring weaknesses (Swann, Hixon, & La Ronde, 1992; Swann & Predmore, 1985).

The tendency to react based on feelings as well as on thinking complicates the picture. Positive feedback feels better than negative feedback, and because feelings occur more quickly and automatically than thoughts (Zajonc, 1980), the first reaction of a low self-esteem person to compliments and flattery is acceptance. And if the person is distracted and unable to marshal his or her cognitive resources to mount a defense against the flattery, he or she may continue to prefer hearing things that are positive but inconsistent with his or her self-view (Swann et al., 1990). Over time, though, people's thoughts tend to overtake their feelings. For the low self-esteem person, this means that the bubble eventually bursts and he or she will engage in a variety of actions to reestablish coherence in his or her self-concept—even if this means sabotaging a relationship with someone who considers the person wonderful.

Threatened Egotism

Imagine someone informs you that you have three eyes and a prominent tattoo of a walrus on your forehead. Now imagine someone else tells you that you are not as bright as you think, that you have questionable social skills, and that you would probably buckle under stress. Which instance of social feedback is the more negative? That's a tough call—buckling under stress isn't exactly a wonderful quality, but then neither is going through life with three eyes.

Now consider your reaction to these two instances of social feedback. Which one would prompt a more negative reaction from you? Would it really bother you if someone attributed those bizarre physical traits to you? Probably not, because you're certain you don't have these features. Besides, you can always check yourself in a mirror to make sure. But what about the comments concerning your intelligence, social skill, and stress tolerance? You might feel that these are inaccurate assessments as well, but can you be truly sure? There is no equivalent of a mirror that can provide an objective assessment with which to discount negative social feedback.

The subjective nature of psychological (as opposed to physical) qualities makes everyone vulnerable to the opinions of other people. This sensitivity to social feedback can be a precursor to aggressive contact between people. Kids get into fights over name-calling, marital partners break up over heated exchanges tinged with unkind character depictions, and nations sever relations and even go to war over derogatory public comments and newspaper editorials. But not every kid gets angry enough to fight, not every couple calls it quits because of adjectives hurled during a spat, and not every country is drawn into conflict because of the demeaning opinions expressed by another country. What makes some people so sensitive that they feel compelled to attack the source of negative feedback?

The intuition here is that low self-esteem is the likely culprit. The last thing someone with low self-esteem needs to hear is that he or she is deficient in yet another way. With a weak grasp on self-respect already, they are likely to push back when their flaws are pointed out by other people. It may come as a surprise, then, to hear that people with *high*, not low, self-esteem are at greater risk for retaliating against others who speak about them in unflattering terms. At least that's the contention derived from work on *threatened egotism* (Baumeister, Smart, & Boden, 1996).

For a low self-esteem person, negative feedback may not feel wonderful, but it is perceived as credible and ultimately embraced. But for the high self-esteem person, negative feedback not only feels bad, but it is also inconsistent with his or her self-concept. If self-verification is a primary motive for self-defense, one would expect the high self-esteem person to react more strongly to criticism and negative social feedback. It is noteworthy that teen gang leaders, terrorists, and even maximum security prisoners—people who hardly "turn the other cheek" when criticized—tend to have *higher* than average self-esteem (Baumeister et al., 1996).

Experiments with normal samples have also provided support for the threatened egotism hypothesis. Brad Bushman and Roy Baumeister (1998), for example, asked undergraduate participants to write a short essay, which they thought was to be evaluated by another student in a different room. In fact, there was not another student—the evaluations were written by the experimenters. They either praised the participant's essay ("this is great!") or panned it ("this is one of the worst ones I've read!"). After this exchange, the two students (the real participant and the bogus evaluator) played a reaction time game. When the evaluator lost, the participant could blast him or her with noise that varied in intensity and duration. Participants who in an earlier battery of tests had endorsed items suggesting that they felt superior to others (e.g., "I am more capable than other people") turned out to be the most aggressive to the evaluator in response to negative appraisals of their essays. Compared to participants with normal self-esteem, these participants delivered three times the auditory torture. Other studies with college students have produced similar findings: when high self-esteem people feel threatened by others, they tend to exhibit greater arrogance, rudeness, and antagonism (e.g., Heatherton & Vohs, 2000).

Self-esteem per se, however, is not the real issue. To the contrary, high self-esteem can promote tolerance and acceptance of different points of view, as long as the positive self-image is grounded in reality and based on competence and meaningful social relationships (Deci & Ryan, 1995; Kernis, 2003). This "true" self-esteem provides a secure foundation for openness rather than defensiveness, and for warm rather than antagonistic social relations (Tangney, Baumeister, & Boone, 2004). Threatened egotism becomes an issue when a person's positive self-view rests on a shaky foundation. False praise for modest accomplishments, for example, can create an inflated sense of self-worth in children that cannot be sustained when real challenges arise. Fragile self-esteem is vulnerable to disconfirmation when the person is confronted with the inevitable setbacks of everyday life (Crocker & Park, 2004; Kernis, 2003).

The *uncertainty* in the person's self-concept is probably what makes him or her a threatened egotist (Jordan et al., 2003; Tracy & Robbins, 2003). Uncertainty signals a poorly integrated self-view, making the person vulnerable to any contradictory information. Alternatively, the uncertain person may have an implicit (non-conscious) self-view (Greenwald et al., 2003) that represents a possible (and threatening) way of thinking about the self. To maintain his or her inflated self-view, the person must censor the unwanted perspective or, failing that, react strongly to the source of the unwanted feedback (Kernis & Waschull, 1995).

Self-Handicapping

Going on the attack is one way of dealing with threats to one's shaky self-concept. But a person who is uncertain about his or her self-worth can also be proactive and prevent threats in the first place. Particularly if the person is unsure of how well he or she would measure up when tested in some way, he or she can avoid the challenge altogether. If the challenge is unavoidable, the person might engage in a different strategy—creating obstacles to successful performance so that if he or she comes up short, it doesn't really reflect on him or her. This strategy is at the heart of *self-handicapping* (Arkin, Lake, & Baumgardner, 1986; Berglas & Baumeister, 1993; Berglas & Jones, 1978; Hirt, Deppe, & Gordon, 1991). This tendency is one of the more ironic aspects of human nature. Why would a person who is concerned with appearing competent sabotage his or her own performance and run the risk of almost certain failure?

People display this tendency when they want to be seen as competent but are not particularly confident that they can live up to that image. Imagine someone—not yourself, of course—who has spent the better part of a party bragging about his or her tennis skills, not expecting to have his or her bluff called by someone who challenges the person to a match the next day. If the person's bragging reflected an honest and secure assessment of his or her skills, he or she might respond to the challenge, even if that meant heading home early from the party to get a good night's sleep and getting mentally prepared for the match.

But what if the bragging was not grounded in reality, but was simply an attempt to appear competent and impress his or her fellow partygoers? In this case, the person might make a point of hanging around the party until the bitter end, then show up for the tennis match the next morning with blurry eyes and other not-so-subtle signs of having "post-party effects" (i.e., a hangover). This would certainly undermine his or her chances of playing well–but it would also provide a convenient excuse for poor performance. If, however, the person managed to win the match, he or she could double down on his bragging–after all, he won the match in spite of having a handicap. In other words, the person could make an *external attribution for failure* ("the party last night hindered my performance today") but an *internal attribution for success* ("I'm obviously quite talented").

Self-handicapping can take a variety of forms. Here are some noteworthy examples:

- Reducing one's preparation for an important athletic event (Rhodewalt, Saltzman, & Wittmer, 1984);
- Listening to loud and distracting music during a difficult task (Shepperd & Arkin, 1991);
- Taking drugs that impair thinking before or during a difficult task (Berglas & Jones, 1978; Kolditz & Arkin, 1982);
- Drinking alcohol before performing a difficult task (Higgins & Harris, 1988);
- Performing poorly early in a task in order to avoid creating high expectations (Baumgardner & Bownlee, 1987);
- Taking on a goal that is impossible to attain (Greenberg, 1985);
- Not trying very hard on a difficult, ego-involving task (Hormuth, 1986; Turner & Pratkanis, 1993);
- Giving an advantage to one's opponent in a contest (Shepperd & Arkin, 1991);
- Not taking advantage of practice time before a difficult test (Alter & Forgas, 2007; Tice & Baumeister, 1990).

Under the right conditions, everyone is tempted to engage in self-handicapping. But some people are more tempted than others and under a wider variety of conditions (Harris & Snyder, 1986; Rhodewalt, 1994; Tice, 1991). Those most likely to give in to this temptation have *high self-esteem* coupled with *low self-concept certainty* (Higgins, Snyder, & Berglas, 1990; Tice, 1991). A person who thinks highly of himself or herself but lacks confidence in this self-assessment has a low threshold for feeling threatened by negative feedback generally (Baumeister et al., 1996) and is more willing than most to sabotage his or her performance to avoid being seen as less competent than advertised. People with *low self-esteem and low self-concept certainty* are also prone to self-handicapping, but their primary concern is protecting their unfavorable self-image from further damage rather than promoting a favorable self-image (Tice, 1991).

Males and females both attempt to protect a shaky sense of competence, but they do so in somewhat different ways (Ferrari, 1991; McCrea, Hirt, & Milner, 2008; Rhodewalt & Hill, 1995). Men are more likely to create actual obstacles to successful performance. Before an important exam or an athletic contest, males who are uncertain of their ability protect their fragile egos by staying up too late, getting drunk, or making a point of not being prepared. Females are less likely to go to these lengths, but they are quite adept at claiming obstacles following failure–although males, not to be outdone, do this too.

Self-handicapping is a risky strategy that can have heavy long-term costs. When people create an obstacle for their performance, they are reducing the chance that they will succeed (Zuckerman, Kieffer, & Knee, 1998). Beyond this immediate impact, people who chronically self-handicap experience long-term problems, including poor health and increased use of alcohol and illegal drugs (Jones & Berglas, 1978; Zuckerman & Tsai, 2005). That people are willing to sabotage their likelihood of success and risk long-term problems is testament to the importance of maintaining a self-image of competence in the eyes of others. Quite a paradox: the desire to appear competent can result in behavior that is lacking in competence.

Self-Concept Change

Self-defense can't be the end of story. If people's efforts were directed solely at maintaining an existing sense of self, they would never display growth or the potential for benefiting from experience. For that matter, people would never develop a meaningful self-concept in the first place if their only concern was protecting what they already believed about themselves in childhood. Clearly, the strategies devoted to self-defense must be overcome in some fashion by forces that prompt a reconsideration of what one is like.

Changing a self-concept is not easy. A person can certainly learn from his or her experiences and update his or her self-assessments. But for the most part, such changes are largely confined to fairly peripheral as opposed to central aspects of the self (Markus & Wurf, 1987). If a person thinks of him or herself in terms of intellectual ability but is less invested in his or her athletic prowess, for example, social comparison information is unlikely to have much impact on the former quality but can promote substantial change in the latter. Thus, the person might rationalize receiving a bad grade in a course (e.g., "The tests were unfair") but view a poor showing on the racquetball court as credible information regarding his or her ability.

With this in mind, one might think it would take a really substantial and hard-to-rationalize experience to induce change in a central aspect of a person's self-concept. To attack someone's intellectual ability, for example, one must present a strong argument that cannot be easily refuted ("My God, look at these grades!"). Such an approach might work if done with sufficient force and without allowing the person much time to launch a counteroffensive (Nowak et al., 2000)—but then again it might only promote strong resistance and aggression (Baumeister et al., 1996).

A far different strategy follows from our earlier discussion of the emergence process (pp. 111–113). When a person thinks about the self in fairly specific or detailed terms, he or she is open to new information that could tie together the low-level information in a meaningful fashion (Vallacher & Wegner, 1987). This can set the stage for self-concept change. Rather than focusing attention directly on a person's integrated self-view, successful agents of influence (e.g., clinical psychologists, friends, or con artists) are likely to experience greater success by going in the opposite direction: inducing the person to focus on the details of what he or she has done. The strategy is to disassemble the person's integrated structure into lower-level elements and then provide clues about how to put the pieces together again.

A study by Wegner, Vallacher, Kiersted, and Dizadji (1986) demonstrates this strategy. The participants were told that the study's purpose was to determine the usefulness of a new computer program for diagnosing people's personalities. As input to this program, participants thought about a recent interaction with a same-sex person and generated five descriptions of what they did in the interaction. Half the participants were asked to describe their behavior in low-level, detailed terms (e.g., specific comments, questions, or gestures). The other participants were asked to describe their behavior in higher-level terms (e.g., the opinions, values, or goals that were expressed). In both cases, the descriptions were recorded by the computer and ostensibly provided the basis for personality assessment by the new computer program.

The program then went to work and, after about 45 seconds, presented the personality diagnosis on the computer monitor. The diagnosis began by informing all participants that they were psychologically healthy and had a nice set of traits. But the program then provided one of two diametrically opposed trait judgments for the participants. Half were informed that they were basically *cooperative* and liked to work with others on a common task and share rewards when the work was completed. The other participants were informed that they were basically *competitive* and liked opportunities where they could attempt to outperform others and claim the biggest share of the reward. After examining this diagnosis (i.e., cooperative or competitive), participants were asked to judge the validity of the feedback and the program that produced it. They also completed a questionnaire assessing their self-concept with respect to 20 trait dimensions, including cooperativeness and competitiveness.

In line with the emergence process, participants who were led to think about their behavior in low-level terms expressed greater belief in the bogus feedback and greater confidence in the computer program than did participants who described their behavior in more integrated (higher-level) terms. Participants in the low-level condition also rated themselves in accordance with the personality feedback they received: those who received cooperative feedback rated themselves as highly cooperative, whereas those who received competitive feedback rated themselves as highly competitive (see Figure 5.5). Participants in the high-level condition did not describe themselves in accordance with the feedback. In fact, they displayed a slight tendency to describe themselves in *opposite* terms: those who received the cooperative feedback tended to describe themselves as competitive and those who received the competitive feedback tended to describe themselves as cooperative.

The emergence process clarifies when people's self-concept is likely to be stable, resisting efforts to change it, and when it is likely to be malleable, open to change in response to social influence or other experiences. In the familiar contexts of everyday life, self-concept change is rare because people have an integrated sense of what their behavior represents. Such high-level understanding provides an effective "shield" against new ways of thinking about the self.

For self-concept to change, a crucial precondition for emergence must occur—the disassembly of integrated understanding of one's action into more specific ways of thinking about the behavior. People are occasionally asked to recount the details of what they have done (as in the Wegner et al., 1986, study) and in this way experience a lower level of identification than would otherwise be the case. Interruption of ongoing action is also a possibility in everyday life, and this too can promote relatively low-level identification of one's behavior. Such events, and many others that

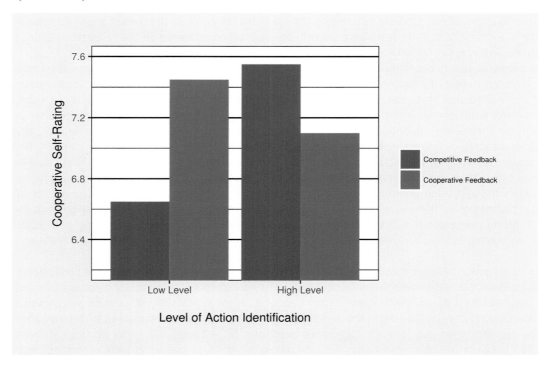

FIGURE 5.5 Self-Rating of Cooperativeness
Source: Adapted from Wegner et al. (1986)

make people sensitive to the details of what they are doing (Vallacher & Wegner, 1987), can make people vulnerable to new ways of thinking about the behavior and its implications for what they are like.

SUMMING UP AND LOOKING AHEAD

- Why do we need a self? Other species seem to get by just fine without dwelling on their characteristics or second guessing their thoughts, feelings, and actions. For that matter, people function most of the time without being self-aware. And when people do focus on themselves, this experience is more often a source of discomfort and negative emotion than a cause for relaxation or pleasure. What's the point of having a process that isn't necessary for survival and that makes us feel bad more often than good?

- The simple answer is that we are self-aware because we can be. Just as the property of opposable thumbs leads inevitably to the manipulation of objects, our highly evolved brain is destined to exercise its power by reflecting on its own operations and the experiences of the person in whom it is embedded. Self-awareness, however, is dependent on social interactions. Only by learning to see ourselves through the eyes of others do we develop a perspective on what we are like. People evaluate themselves in terms of the same qualities they use to evaluate others, although the specific qualities that are most important to self-evaluation differ across individuals. Cultures vary in the degree to which they foster social interdependence in people. In interdependent as opposed to in independent cultures, a person's self-concept is anchored in social identities rather than personal attributes and varies from one social context to another.

- Tracking the constant input of self-relevant information and organizing it into a stable and coherent structure is a daunting task. Introspection can help but the task demands of self-concept formation far exceed the limits of conscious information processing. Self-concept formation can be accomplished with minimal conscious awareness, however, through self-organization, which results in the emergence of higher-level structures (traits, roles, competencies) from lower-level elements (concrete actions, thoughts, and memories).

- Despite the multiple selves that result from self-organization, people develop a level of global self-regard (self-esteem), which is more likely to be positive than negative. It is not clear whether self-esteem represents some combination of people's more specific selves or instead reflects the quality of childhood experiences and the degree to which social needs have been met. The certainty of a person's self-concept shapes how his or her level of self-esteem is manifest. People with low self-concept certainty experience unstable and conflicting levels of self-regard.

- People are quite adept at defending their self-concept against contradictory information. Because the underlying goal of self-defense revolves around coherence rather than positive evaluation, people with low self-esteem are often more comfortable with others who provide unflattering assessments of them. The self-defense of a person with a positive but uncertain view of themselves takes one of two forms: attacking those who challenge his or her self-view (threatened egotism) or creating obstacles to successful behavior so that he or she can maintain positive self-regard in case of failure (self-handicapping).

- To diffuse self-defense and bring about change, the higher-level aspects of a person's self-concept can be disassembled into lower-level identities for his or her behavior. Cues to alternative higher-level meanings can then be provided to promote the emergence of new integrations of his or her behavior that provide new ways of thinking about him or herself.

  The goal in this chapter was to introduce key properties of the self; the subsequent chapters will develop these properties in the context of other central topics in social psychology. Keep reading and you will encounter your self in the following pages almost as frequently as you think about yourself in everyday life.

Key Terms

Self-awareness	Possible selves	Contingencies of self-worth
Metacognition	Introspection	Attachment theory
Theory of mind	Self-perception theory	Sociometer hypothesis
Looking glass self	Self-organization	Implicit self-esteem
Self-recognition	Emergence	Narcissism
Self-schema	Progressive integration	Self-evaluation maintenance
Social feedback	Multiple selves	Self-defense zoo
Social comparison	Multifaceted self	Self-serving bias
Reflected self-appraisal	Levels of personal agency	Self-verification theory
Upward and downward social comparison	Behavior Identification Form	Threatened egotism
Individualism and collectivism	Self-concept clarity	Self-handicapping
Independent and interdependent self	Self-concept certainty	Self-concept change
	Self-esteem	

6 Personal Control

It should come as no surprise that people like to do things that are fun. But if that was the only motive for action, psychology would be a boring discipline—and this would be a very short text. Fortunately for psychologists, other motives have been identified that go beyond simple concerns with achieving pleasure and avoiding pain. Many of these motives center on social relations, as we shall see in Parts III ("Interpersonal Experience") and IV ("Collective Experience"). But to round out the dynamics of intrapersonal experience, we need to focus on a basic feature of human nature—the desire to take charge of one's own destiny—which is manifest whether or not other people are in the picture. Indeed, a concern with social approval, intimacy, and social influence can sometimes work at cross-purposes with taking matters into one's own hands and feeling in control of one's experiences.

There are two aspects to the self-perception of control. First, people like to feel they are competent at the actions they undertake. This feature of self-control, commonly referred to as *personal agency*, is associated with intellectual curiosity, the desire to take on and master new activities, working toward goals and implementing plans, or simply knowing how to do things ranging from operating light switches to managing bank accounts. Sometimes, however, the issue of personal control is not whether one *can* do something, but rather whether one *should* do something. Anyone can eat a Twinkie or tell a lie—neither requires a great deal of skill—but people often feel as though these are not the right things to do. This second aspect of personal control, commonly referred to as *self-regulation*, is associated with resistance to temptation, impulse control, and acting in accordance with standards of right and wrong.

Personal agency and self-regulation are hallmarks of human psychology that prove very beneficial in our interactions with the world. But both aspects of personal control are built on mental processes that can be derailed by conflicting processes and circumstances. So after providing the key insights established in research exploring both forms of personal control, we will discuss what psychologists have discovered regarding the problematic nature of personal control—how it can be undermined and rendered moot in the conduct of behavior.

CHAPTER OVERVIEW

What Are You Going to Learn?

- **When do people feel in charge of their behavior?** People desire to control the nature and intensity of their encounters with the world. What basic motives underlie this desire? What factors influence people's assessment of their personal agency? What are the consequences of feeling that one does not have personal agency? How does the concern with personal agency influence other motives, such as curiosity and enjoyment?

- **How and why do people transcend pleasure and pain?** Sometimes the issue is not whether people feel they are in control and *can* make things happen, but whether they *should* exercise this control in contexts where such action is inappropriate or conflicts with personal standards. Self-regulation can be tough if the inappropriate action would feel good or in some way prove beneficial to oneself. What circumstances amplify versus minimize self-regulation concerns?

- **When is personal control ineffective or illusory?** Despite the desire for personal control and its functional value, it can prove elusive for everyone in some contexts, and for some people in many contexts. What factors undermine people's control efforts, despite their ability to exercise such control? Why do people have lapses in their self-regulation efforts? What factors promote inaccurate perceptions of personal control in everyday life?

Personal Agency

When Do People Feel in Charge of Their Behavior?

Everyone wants to be the master of his or her own destiny. Good luck, pleasant surprises, and support by friends are all valued, but these experiences occur against a backdrop of feeling in charge. Personal agency, however, is not simply an assessment of objective reality. It is a psychological process, and a rather fragile one at that, and thus open to a wide variety of influences. Whether these influences amplify or undermine personal agency has implications for subjective well-being generally, and for the enjoyment of specific actions. These points—the factors influencing personal agency, the consequences of personal agency for well-being, and the link between personal agency and action enjoyment—are taken up in turn below.

The Self-Perception of Control

There are two components to the self-perception of control. First, a person must feel that he or she has the ability to take on activities and challenges. The desire to achieve *competence* and become masterful at various actions is a core feature of human nature (Atkinson, 1964; Bandura, 1986; Maslow, 1954; White, 1959). Whether the action is cooking a meal, playing tennis, climbing a rock wall, selling clothes, or painting a portrait, the person's motivation is rooted in large part in his or her desire to excel and become increasingly proficient at the action.

A person may have the capacity to make things happen but not appreciate his or her agency, feeling instead that he or she is powerless to control the outcomes of his or her behavior (e.g., Seligman, 1975). But a person may also grossly overestimate his or her degree of agency with respect to some activity, overlooking the role that chance or the actions of others play in making things happen (e.g., Alloy & Abramson, 1979). The question, then, is what determines whether or not people *feel* in charge of their behavior in everyday life.

The self-perception of personal agency is based in part on a second subjective assessment—the extent to which a person feels his or her actions reflect his or her personal decisions or desires, or instead are dictated by external forces or other people. This concern is central to *self-determination theory* (Ryan & Deci, 2000). The theory holds that people have an innate need for *autonomy*, with their actions motivated by personal desires and choices rather than dictated by external forces. If a person feels like a pawn of external forces rather than a causal agent, his or her self-perception of control is undermined (deCharms, 1968; Rotter, 1966). So although the feeling that one is competent is important, this basis for personal agency can be overwhelmed by the feeling that one does not have personal choice in whether to engage in the action.

Agency and Subjective Well-Being

People who act as if they have control and freedom derive greater satisfaction from their behavior, have greater self-confidence, perform more effectively, display greater persistence, and tend to be more creative (Amabile, 1996; Deci, Koestner, & Ryan, 1999). Beyond these action benefits, people who feel autonomous and in control of their own destiny have higher self-esteem and general well-being, and are less likely to experience passivity, alienation, and psychopathology (e.g., deCharms, 1968; Langer & Rodin, 1976; Reeve, 2006; Sheldon & Kasser, 1998). Even the mere *anticipation* of choice activates brain regions associated with motivational and positive emotional processes (Leotti & Delgado, 2011).

Internal Versus External Control

Not everyone feels like the master of his or her own destiny. Some people feel that powers beyond their control, or simply fate, luck, or chance, play a greater role in determining what outcomes they experience than does their own ability and effort. The issue once again is not whether this assessment is correct or misguided. Two people in the same situation and possessing the same skill set may have diametrically opposed feelings about their degree of personal control. The *Internal versus External Locus of Control Scale*, developed by Julian Rotter (1966), is a reliable measure of individual differences in this way of seeing the world. Selected items from this scale are presented in Box 6.1.

Box 6.1   The Internal Versus External Locus of Control Scale (Selected Items)

This scale measures generalized expectancies for internal versus external control of reinforcement. People with an internal locus of control believe that their own actions determine the rewards that they obtain, while those with an external locus of control believe that their own behavior doesn't matter much and that rewards in life are generally outside of their control.

For each pair of statements, choose the one that you believe to be the most accurate, not the one you wish was most true. Remember, there are no right or wrong answers.

1. (a) Many of the unhappy things in people's lives are partly due to bad luck.
   (b) People's misfortunes result from the mistakes they make.*
2. (a) One of the major reasons why we have wars is because people don't take enough interest in politics.*
   (b) There will always be wars, no matter how hard people try to prevent them.
3. (a) In the long run, people get the respect they deserve in this world.*
   (b) Unfortunately, an individual's worth often passes unrecognized no matter how hard he tries.
4. (a) The idea that teachers are unfair to students is nonsense.*
   (b) Most students don't realize the extent to which their grades are influenced by accidental happenings.
5. (a) Without the right breaks, one cannot be an effective leader.
   (b) Capable people who fail to became leaders have not taken advantage of their opportunities.*
6. (a) No matter how hard you try, some people just don't like you.
   (b) People who can't get others to like them don't understand how to get along with others.*
7. (a) I have often found that what is going to happen will happen.
   (b) Trusting fate has never turned out as well for me as making a decision to take a definite course of action.*

8. (a) In the case of the well-prepared student, there is rarely, if ever, such a thing as an unfair test.*
    (b) Many times exam questions tend to be so unrelated to course work that studying is really useless.
9. (a) Becoming a success is a matter of hard work; luck has little or nothing to do with it.*
    (b) Getting a good job depends mainly on being in the right place at the right time.
10. (a) The average citizen can have an influence in government decisions.*
    (b) This world is run by the few people in power, and there is not much the little guy can do about it.
11. (a) When I make plans, I am almost certain that I can make them work.*
    (b) It is not always wise to plan too far ahead because many things turn out to be a matter of luck anyway.
12. (a) In my case, getting what I want has little or nothing to do with luck.*
    (b) Many times we might just as well decide what to do by flipping a coin.
13. (a) What happens to me is my own doing.*
    (b) Sometimes I feel that I don't have enough control over the direction my life is taking.

Choice marked with an asterisk represents an internal locus of control.

Source: Adapted from Rotter, J.B. (1966). Generalized expectancies for internal versus external control of reinforcement. *Psychological Monographs, 80* (1, Whole No. 609).

A person's generalized view about internal versus external control has implications for many aspects of personal and interpersonal life, including motivation, resistance to social influence, social relations, self-control, and self-concept (Lefcourt, 1976; Phares, 1976; Rotter, 1990). Compared to people who see the world in external terms, those who have an internal locus of control take on more difficult tasks, persist on tasks in the face of setbacks, maintain their personal attitudes in the face of social pressure to change them, are more dependable in social relations, focus on the consequences and implications of what they do, and have a clearer and more stable sense of their defining personal characteristics.

Carried to the extreme, people who do not perceive a connection between their actions and the outcomes they experience demonstrate *learned helplessness* (Maier & Seligman, 1976; Seligman, 1975). This tendency was first observed in animals (often dogs) that are placed in a situation where they are unable to terminate aversive stimuli (e.g., electric shocks delivered through the floor of their cage) no matter what behaviors they enact (e.g., barking, whimpering). After experiencing helplessness in this manner, the animals generalize this feeling to a wider variety of settings—including those in which their actions *would* affect their outcomes.

The human counterpart to learned helplessness in animals is passivity, dependence on others, and depression (Abramson, Seligman, & Teasdale, 1978; Hiroto, 1974). The issue is not the experience of negative events (e.g., bad grades, social disapproval), but rather the lack of a perceived link between one's actions and subsequent events. Indeed, the experience of very positive events (e.g., good grades, social praise) can promote an external locus of control and helplessness if the person feels these events have no connection to what he or she has done.

Stress

Even if the sense of personal control is not entirely rooted in reality, it can help people cope with unpleasant events. The adaptive value of self-perceived control was demonstrated in research by David Glass, Jerome Singer, and their colleagues (Glass & Singer, 1972; Glass, Singer, & Friedman, 1969). In one of their experiments, participants were exposed to blasts of loud noise that were delivered at random (hence unpredictable) intervals for irregular lengths of time while they were trying to solve a series of moderately difficult puzzles. The noise stress had been shown in earlier trials to undermine concentration on the puzzle task, resulting in poor performance, and to lower participants' frustration tolerance.

To demonstrate the importance of self-perceived control, the experimenters positioned a button on the table at which participants were working. The button was not connected to anything, so pressing it would have no effect. Half the participants, however, were told that pressing the button would turn off the noise when it occurred. But they were discouraged from making use of this option ("press it only if absolutely necessary"), and none of them did so. Participants who had this "panic button" performed considerably better on the puzzle tasks and experienced less stress than did participants who were told that pressing the button would have no effect. Just believing—incorrectly—that they had the power to terminate the aversive noise enabled the panic button participants to perform the task with better concentration and reduced psychological effects. It was the *perception* of control that enabled them to tolerate aversive stimuli that would otherwise have undermined their performance and well-being.

This idea has implications for handling the inevitable stresses and frustrations of everyday life. You are likely to experience setbacks of various kinds in your personal and professional life. You might be rejected by a potential romantic partner, hit a rough patch in college, or get outflanked by a devious co-worker who sabotages your efforts and makes you look inept. For that matter, you may simply be exposed to loud noises while trying to do homework. In each case, whether you are seriously disrupted or bounce back will depend on whether you feel you can do something about the potential stress. If you feel in control, it may not even be necessary to exercise the control in order to maintain your focus and persist in spite of the unsettling event.

Stress is not associated exclusively with aversive events (e.g., loud noises, social rejection). Stress can just as readily be associated with positive outcomes (e.g., pleasant sounds, social acceptance) if a person feels these actions are independent of anything he or she does. Compliments, good grades, and money are wonderful, but if you don't see how they are connected to your behavior (e.g., socially skilled interaction, mastery of course material, solid contribution to a task), they can create the potential for personal stress in the long run.

The recognition that stress is not defined by content (pleasant versus unpleasant events) but rather by perceived control was incorporated into a scale designed to measure the stresses people feel in everyday life (Holmes & Rahe, 1967). The *Life Stress Scale* (see Box 6.2) rank orders 43 life experiences in terms of their potential for making people feel stressed. Some of these events are extremely negative (e.g., divorce, getting fired), but others are very positive and represent goals most people share (e.g., getting married, starting a new career). In both cases, the issue is whether one feels in control of how the event in question unfolds. Marriage, for example, involves many details, not to mention coordination issues with family members and soon-to-be in-laws, and thus can call into question one's ability to control all the pieces.

Box 6.2   The Holmes-Rahe Life Stress Inventory

The Social Readjustment Rating Scale (Selected Items)

In the past 24 months, which of these have happened to you? Read each of the events listed below, and check the box next to any event which has occurred in your life in the last 2 years. There are no right or wrong answers. The aim is just to identify which of these events you have experienced lately. (You may want to consider extending the timeline (e.g., 5 years, 10 years), if you believe it might be more relevant to your current situation.)

Life Event	Mean Value
• Death of spouse	100
• Divorce	73
• Marital separation from mate	65
• Death of a close family member	63
• Major personal injury or illness	53
• Marriage	50
• Being fired at work	47
• Marital reconciliation with mate	45
• Major change in the health or behavior of a family member	44
• Pregnancy	40
• Sexual difficulties	39

• Death of a close friend	37
• Changing to a different line of work	36
• Major change in responsibilities at work (promotion, demotion, etc.)	29
• Outstanding personal achievement	28
• Spouse beginning or ceasing work outside the home	26
• Beginning or ceasing formal schooling	26
• Revision of personal habits (dress, manners, associations, quitting smoking)	24
• Changes in residence	20
• Changing to a new school	20
• Major change in usual type and/or amount of recreation	19
• Major change in social activities (clubs, movies, visiting, etc.)	18
• Major change in sleeping habits (a lot more or a lot less than usual)	16
• Major change in eating habits (a lot more or less food intake, or very different meal hours or surroundings)	15
• Vacation	13
• Major holidays	12
• Minor violations of the law (traffic tickets, jaywalking, disturbing the peace, etc.)	11

INSTRUCTIONS: Mark down the point value of each of these life events that has happened to you during the previous year. Total these associated points. Now, add up all the points you have to find your Life Stress score.

Source: Adapted from Holmes & Rahe (1967)

Resilience

You might think that major life stresses, such as those associated with intense life events, would contribute to severe and chronic emotional problems, such as clinical depression. But this does not seem to be the case (Munroe & Reid, 2009). As long as the stress is not too intense or prolonged, it can build resilience and enable one to handle subsequent stresses (Seery, 2011; Seery et al., 2013). The effect is analogous to that of inoculations against diseases such as measles and polio. A vaccination consists of a weakened form of the disease agent (e.g., the measles or polio virus), which activates the immune system to build antibodies that defend against the invasive agent. If the disease agent is presented in too strong a form, the body cannot fight it. But if the disease agent is too weak or not presented at all, the body does not mount a defense, leaving the person vulnerable when the real disease is encountered.

Does stress work in a similar fashion? Is there an "optimal" level of stress early in one's life that promotes psychological antibodies—resilience—that can counter the effects of stress encountered later? A study by Seery, Holman, and Silver (2010) suggest that the answer is yes. In a multiyear longitudinal study of a national sample, people with a history of frequent and intense adversity did not fare well psychologically, as one might expect. But compared to those with *no* history of adversity, those who experienced a *moderate amount* of adversity also fared better psychologically— they reported the *lowest global distress*, the *least self-rated functional impairment*, the *fewest posttraumatic stress symptoms*, and the *highest life satisfaction* (see Figure 6.1). The study also revealed that people with some prior lifetime adversity were the least affected by recent adverse events. These results suggest that, in moderation, "what doesn't kill you makes you stronger."

People's resilience in the aftermath of stress was demonstrated in the months following the 9/11 terrorist attacks (Eisenberg & Silver, 2011). At the time, psychologists anticipated traumatic effects (e.g., anxiety, depression) that would persist for years, if not a lifetime, on the part of those who were close to the World Trade Center or who knew people who lost their lives during the attack. But for the most part, these effects have not materialized. This has led psychologists to rethink how people handle traumatic effects in general.

It is interesting to consider this issue in terms of the research on *affective forecasting*, introduced in Chapter 4 ("Emotion"). Contrary to intuition, the more intense one's immediate reaction to an event, the more quickly the reaction dissipates (Gilbert et al., 2004). When something big happens, mental resources are recruited to deal with the

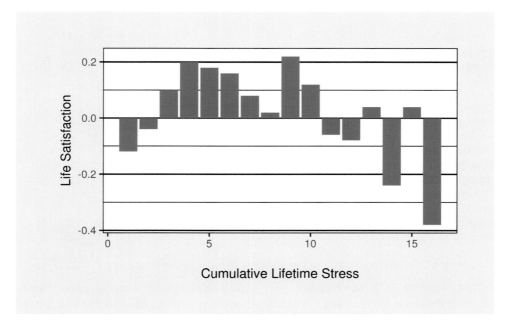

FIGURE 6.1 Life Satisfaction is Associated With Moderate Levels of Lifetime Adversity
Source: Adapted from Seery et al. (2010)

disturbance, so that the emotional system returns to its equilibrium fairly quickly. Less intense events do not generate the same repair function, so they may have longer-lasting effects.

Intrinsic Motivation

Some activities seem more enjoyable than others. Playing with crayons or magic markers, for example, is probably a lot more fun for children than is studying arithmetic or cleaning up their room. Receiving a reward for doing something, in turn, is clearly preferable to doing something for "free." Logically, then, if a fun activity (e.g., drawing with magic markers) is paired with a reward (e.g., money or a prize), the person should enjoy the activity all the more. Asking Johnnie to play with magic markers and promising to give him a nice prize when he is finished should make playing with markers a truly wonderful experience for him.

It doesn't seem to work that way. Sometimes, in fact, just the opposite occurs when rewards are paired with an interesting activity—the enjoyment of the activity is diminished rather than enhanced. This phenomenon, which has provided a major focus of attention in psychological research since the 1970s, is often described in terms of the *over-justification effect* (Lepper & Greene, 1978). The idea is that when people feel that their behavior is in response to the promise of a reward (e.g., money) or to some other external factor (e.g., social norms, pressures, or expectations), they downplay the extent to which the behavior reflects personal desires (e.g., enjoyment) or motives (e.g., mastery, curiosity). The reward or external reason, in other words, provides clear justification for engaging in the behavior, so that the behavior's pure enjoyment value is no longer front and center in the person's mind (Bem, 1967; Deci et al., 1999; Harackiewicz, 1979; Lepper, Greene, & Nisbett, 1973; Ryan & Deci, 2000).

The overjustification effect is based on three assumptions. The first is that the motivation to do something comes in two forms: *intrinsic* and *extrinsic*. When people are *intrinsically motivated*, they engage in an activity because it is enjoyable, interesting, challenging, or personally fulfilling. When people are *extrinsically motivated*, they engage in an activity because it is a means by which they can obtain a reward (e.g., money) or avoid an undesirable outcome (e.g., punishment, negative social feedback). By itself, this assumption does not rule out the possibility that rewards can make an enjoyable activity all the more enjoyable.

This is where the other two assumptions come into play: first, there is often a zero-sum relation between intrinsic and extrinsic motivation, and second, extrinsic motives are more concrete and vivid and thus more powerful than intrinsic motives. Taken together, these assumptions predict that when there are both intrinsic and extrinsic motives to do something, people are inclined to embrace the latter and disregard the former. An activity that would otherwise be engaged because of its enjoyment value (e.g., play) essentially becomes something that must be endured (e.g., work). Because rewards are experienced as controlling, they thwart the person's need for autonomy and self-perception of control (deCharms, 1968; Deci & Ryan, 2000; Harackiewicz, 1979; Sheldon & Kasser, 1998).

Numerous studies have confirmed the potential of rewards to undermine the intrinsic motivation to engage in otherwise enjoyable activities. One of the first (Lepper et al., 1973) makes the point nicely. Children at a preschool were observed as they played with different games, toys, and art materials. Those children who displayed the greatest interest in drawing with magic markers were asked 2 weeks later if they would use markers to draw pictures for a visitor. Children in an *expected reward* condition were told they would receive a "Good Player Award," complete with a nice gold star and red ribbon, for drawing the pictures. As promised, the children received the reward. Children in an *unexpected reward* condition were told nothing about the Good Player Award in advance, but they were given the reward anyway after they drew the pictures. Children in a *no-reward* condition were also told nothing about the Good Player Award, and they didn't receive one.

Between 1 and 2 weeks later, the observers returned to the school to note how much time the children spent playing with the magic markers. Of the three groups of children, those in the expected reward condition showed the least interest in the magic markers (see Figure 6.2). Apparently, they came to view drawing pictures with magic markers to be a task for which they were compensated (or controlled). The children in the unexpected reward condition also received compensation for their drawings, but because they did not expect to be rewarded, they did not see the Good Player Award as the reason for their picture drawing. They drew pictures out of intrinsic interest, but were lucky enough to get a nice prize in addition at the end.

This does not mean that the promise of rewards should be avoided at all costs when attempting to foster intrinsic motivation. Rewards are often necessary to get a person to do something for the first time, particularly if the activity is not personally interesting (Calder & Staw, 1975; Hamner & Foster, 1975; McGraw, 1978). And rewards are less likely to

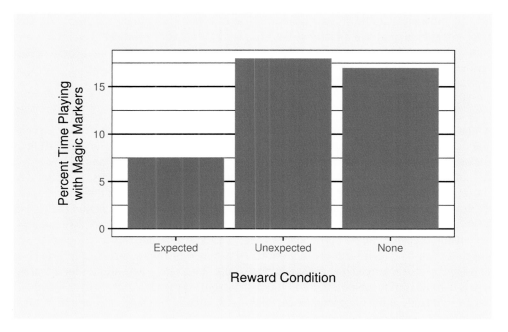

FIGURE 6.2 The Amount of Time Children Played with Magic Markers in a Free-Play Period
Source: Adapted from Lepper et al. (1973)

undermine intrinsic interest if they are *performance contingent* rather than *task contingent* (Enzle & Ross, 1978; Harackiewicz, Manderlink, & Sansone, 1984). Rewarding a person for mere completion of a task (task contingent) emphasizes the controlling function of the reward, but rewarding a person for how well the task is performed (performance contingent) signifies the person's competence at the activity and can reinforce his or her concern with achievement and mastery.

Research inspired by the overjustification effect has implications for many aspects of life. Consider the common practice of rewarding children for doing their homework, practicing the piano, or reading books. If they show little intrinsic interest in doing these things, the use of rewards makes sense and may even be necessary to get them engaged. But if they display interest on their own, attaching the promise of rewards to the activity runs the risk of undermining their motivation. They will continue to study, practice, or read as long as the reward contingency is in place, but their interest may fade once the rewards are withdrawn.

The same concerns can be raised regarding academics, work, and sports participation. What might otherwise be intrinsically motivating for someone (e.g., learning math in school, repairing cars for a living, playing professional basketball) can become a chore if rewards become the reason for engaging in the activity. If the reward contingency is suddenly terminated, the person's interest may come to an abrupt end as well.

Even close relationships—arguably the most intrinsically motivated of all activities—can fall prey to the reward contingency effect. This was demonstrated in a study by Seligman, Fazio, and Zanna (1980), in which romantic partners were asked think about their relationship and provide answers to one of two sentence stems: "I'm with my partner *because* . . ." or "I'm with my partner *in order to* . . ." The *because* stem calls attention to factors that are intrinsic to the relationship (e.g., "because I love him/her," "because he/she is wonderful"), whereas the *in order to* stem calls attention to the instrumental functions of the relationship (e.g., "in order to expand my social circle," "in order to be happy"). In focusing on the external benefits of the relationship, the *in order to* couples subsequently showed a decrease in their feelings of love, unlike the *because* couples who maintained their intimate feelings toward one another. Imagine what would have happened if a third set of couples had been offered money to stay together!

Self-Regulation

How and Why Do People Transcend Pleasure and Pain?

Most people eventually do the right thing. This does not mean that people always do the most enjoyable thing. All too often, in fact, the most pleasurable or least painful course of action runs afoul of appropriate, allowable, or even legal things to do. A person might have an intense urge to consume a box of candy bars, point out an annoying person's character flaws, or roar down a near-empty highway at 80 miles per hour, but inhibit these actions in favor of a healthy diet, norms of appropriate interpersonal behavior, and a clean driving record.

Enlightened Self-Interest

That people behave in ways that do not reflect their private desires is not too surprising. The social sciences are unanimous in their contention that people act in accord with social norms, traditions, criminal statutes, and reinforcement contingencies. These guidelines make it likely that people will take note of how their behavior will be evaluated when deciding what to do. Presumably, in the absence of social rules and constraints, personal desires would go unchecked and people would quickly come into conflict with others who are following their own impulses.

The simplest explanation for why people suspend their own interests in favor of action that is less enjoyable is *enlightened self-interest*. Humans are the smartest species on earth and can recognize consequences of action that are lost on their animal brethren. Some consequences are not immediate but rather are destined to occur in the future. To assure that rewarding long-term consequences are attained or that aversive long-term consequences are avoided, people will incur short-term pain and losses if necessary. The student who studies for a test instead of heading off to a party is demonstrating enlightened self-interest (assuming the short-term cost of studying pays off in a good test grade). Everyday life is full of consequences that are at odds with simple calculations of pleasure and pain. Growing up as members of a family, a neighborhood, and a society, children learn the trade-offs between simple self-interest (immediate gratification) and enlightened self-interest (Mischel, Shoda, & Rodriguez, 1989).

As you probably know from personal observation, self-regulation varies widely across people (e.g., Baumeister, Heatherton, & Tice, 1994; Trope & Fishbach, 2000). Some people are remarkable in their willingness to suspend immediate self-interest in service of saving money, losing weight, earning good grades, and building a career. Others are equally remarkable for precisely the opposite reason. They may experience immediate pleasures and become quite adept at avoiding doing anything unpleasant, but their lack of self-regulation does not bode well for success in life or for their personal adjustment (Tangney et al., 2004).

Individual differences in rudimentary self-regulation (e.g., delay of gratification in order to achieve a better reward in the future) can be reliably measured in children as young as four years (Mischel, Shoda, & Peake, 1988). Those children who demonstrate effective self-regulation as preschoolers have better behavioral adjustment and attain better scholastic performance as adolescents than do their counterparts who could not resist the lure of immediate pleasures (e.g., one yummy marshmallow right now) despite the promise of even greater pleasures in the near future (e.g., two equally yummy marshmallows in a few minutes).

The Self in Self-Regulation

The emphasis on enlightened self-interest implies that if people could get away with it, they would take the money and run. Of course, some people do act selfishly without regard for anyone else when they don't expect to get caught or to have future contact with others they have exploited (Axelrod, Riolo, & Cohen, 2002; Messick & Liebrand, 1995). But not everyone does this, and no one does it all the time.

To some extent, instances of self-regulation when there are no penalties for acting selfishly could be chalked up to learning, habit formation, resistance to extinction, and other principles of conditioning that apply across the animal kingdom (Skinner, 1953). But psychology in recent years has come to emphasize an alternative basis for people's tendency to do the right thing. This basis is *you*—or more precisely, another side of you that keeps the spontaneous, pleasure-seeking you in check. This internal basis for behavior is referred to variously as *self-regulation*, *self-control*, and *willpower*. Social psychological research on this topic has exploded since the 1980s—although the foundation for this work has deep roots, going back to Sigmund Freud (1920) and others in the early 20th century—and now is a major focus of scholarly attention.

Self-Awareness and Human Nature

As we saw in Chapter 5 ("Self-Concept"), only those species with the highest levels of cognitive capacity—chimps, orangutans, occasionally gorillas, probably dolphins, maybe even elephants—are capable of simple self-recognition in a mirror. In humans, self-awareness goes far beyond simple self-recognition of one's body to include awareness of one's internal state (thoughts, emotions) and one's traits, goals, and values. The potential for self-regulation takes a giant leap forward once children develop this form of self-awareness. Rather than focusing on long-term consequences ("more marshmallows in 5 minutes!") or finding ways of distracting themselves ("this chair goes way back!"), children at a relatively young age begin to judge what they do, or consider doing, against internalized notions of who they are or desire to be (e.g., Lewis, 1990). The self-concept, in other words, functions as a regulatory structure for initiating, monitoring, suppressing, and terminating action.

Research has identified several factors that redirect attention from the outside world to one's self (Carver, 2003; Duval & Wicklund, 1972):

- People experience themselves as an object when they are, in fact, the object of other people's attention. Standing in front of a group of people can induce self-awareness, particularly if these people are in a position to evaluate what one is doing. Even a reminder that one *could* be the object of attention is sufficient to induce self-awareness. Mirrors and video cameras are associated with becoming an object of observation, for example, and are commonly employed to manipulate self-awareness in experimental research (e.g., Duval & Wicklund, 1972; Gibbons, 1978; Scheier, Fenigstein, & Buss, 1974; Vallacher & Solodky, 1979).
- Simply being a member of a group, even if one is ignored by the other members, can induce self-focused attention if one has *minority status* in the group (Cota & Dion, 1986; McGuire & Padawer-Singer, 1978). A male college student might feel a twinge of self-awareness and sensitivity to his gender, for example, if everyone else in a class is female—even if the other students are not attending to him at all, but rather focusing on the professor.

Distinctiveness with regard to a wide variety of characteristics can make one mindful of the self. In schoolchildren, for example, the minority status effect has been demonstrated with respect to such identity markers as age, gender, ethnicity, place of birth, parental occupation, and hair color.

- Self-focused attention also results from disruptions to ongoing behavior (Duval & Wicklund, 1972). Singing off-key, tripping on a pebble in full view of spectators, experiencing a computer crash in a lab course, and getting the key jammed in a lock when opening the door for guests can get a person to focus on him or herself. Although this can happen even if other people aren't paying that much attention, the self-focusing effect of such disruptions is intensified when one is in a social setting as opposed to being alone. Humans are highly social animals, and their survival depends on how well they can coordinate their actions with one another (Brewer & Caporael, 2006; Sedikides & Skowronski, 1997). The disruption of a person's behavior in a social context singles the person out and threatens to break this coordination. Of course, if everyone in a group were to trip on a pebble at the same time, this might enhance social coordination and generate a good laugh and a round of exaggerated storytelling later that night.

Consequences of Self-Awareness

A person experiencing self-awareness compares what he or she is doing with *internal standards* for that type of behavior (Carver & Scheier, 1999; Duval & Wicklund, 1972). Under some circumstances, one might act callously toward someone else, or even tell the person a lie, and not give the act a second thought. If one were to become self-aware while behaving in an insensitive or dishonest manner, however, the discrepancy between the action and one's standards for sensitive or honest behavior would be front and center in one's mind.

A discrepancy between one's behavior and a salient internal standard is psychologically uncomfortable and sets in motion thoughts and actions to restore one's psychological equilibrium. You can look upon self-focused attention as a *repair tool*, somewhat analogous to looking under the hood of one's car when the car stalls out or doesn't start in the first place. In thinking about one's characteristics, behavioral tendencies, and mental processes, one is in a position to modify them and enact corrective procedures. The larger the discrepancy is, the greater one's motivation to fix things. A slight insensitivity or a trivial lie can be overlooked more readily than can a heavy-handed jab at the person or a lie with big consequences.

The most straightforward means of reducing a discrepancy is to change one's behavior so that it matches the standard. If the action has already taken place, one might make amends for the action by apologizing to the "victim" or resolving not to behave that way in the future. Or better yet, one can inhibit acting in a way that would create a discrepancy in the first place. One could simply avoid being insensitive or dishonest and dodge psychological discomfort.

This point was made in a clever set of studies trading on the childhood ritual of "trick or treat" on Halloween (Beaman, Klentz, Diener, & Svanum, 1979). These investigators arranged a situation in which unsuspecting kids dressed as goblins and the like were faced with a moral dilemma: whether to take only a prescribed amount of candy from a bowl or ignore this norm and stuff their pockets before slinking back into the darkness. As trick-or-treaters arrived at the entrapment house (one of 18), an adult female invited them into the foyer, where there was a large bowl brimming with bite-size candy bars. She told some groups (or lone children in some cases) that each child could take one candy bar, but told other groups to "help themselves." In both conditions, she then said, "I have to go back to my work in another room," at which point she left the foyer. The children were thus left alone with a large bowl brimming with candy bars. Would the children in the "one candy" rule condition obey this standard, or would they take advantage of the adult's absence and grab all the candy bars they could?

To see whether self-focused attention would influence the children's behavior, Beaman et al. (1979) made use of a mirror, which is a common device for inducing self-awareness in social psychology experiments. For half the groups, the mirror was positioned directly behind the bowl, so that each child could watch him or herself plunge his or her hand in the bowl. For the other visitors, there was no mirror to focus children's attention on themselves. Because self-focused attention elevates internal standards from background features of the self to explicit frames of reference for evaluating actual or potential behavior, Beaman et al. (1979) expected stronger adherence to the "one candy" rule among the children who experienced the mirror.

This is what the researchers found (see Figure 6.3). As you might expect, the majority of children who were not given a standard ("help yourself to the candy!") took more than one candy bar, whether or not they were confronted

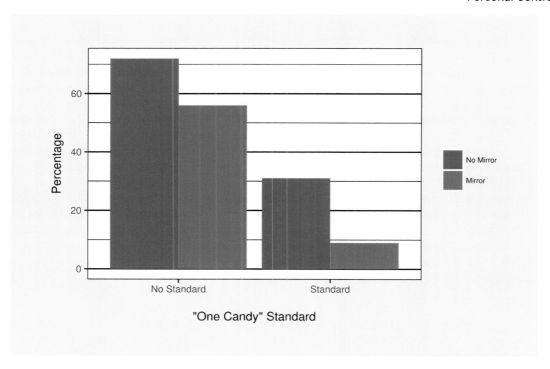

FIGURE 6.3 Percentage of Trick-or-Treaters Who Violated the "One Piece of Candy" Standard
Source: Adapted from Beaman et al. (1979)

with a self-focusing device (the mirror). Halloween is, after all, a license for acquiring as much pleasure food as possible. Providing a "one candy" standard tended to promote self-control among the children, but as Figure 6.3 illustrates, the standard was most effective for children who were confronted with a mirror and thus were made self-aware. Simply having a standard for behavior (the "one candy" rule) may not be sufficient to resist the temptation to do something pleasurable that violates the standard. But when attention is focused on the self, this standard provides a firm basis for self-control.

Changing one's behavior or making amends are certainly viable options and occur commonly in social life, but these hardly exhaust the means by which a discrepancy between one's behavior and a standard can be reduced (e.g., Carver & Scheier, 1999). Under some conditions, in fact, one might change the standard rather than the behavior. Particularly if it is difficult or costly to repair what one has done, one might instead rethink one's notions of appropriate conduct. Interpersonal sensitivity, for example, could be reconsidered as showing weakness and thus lose its status as a personal standard. For its part, honesty could be looked upon as an impediment to pragmatic strategies for influencing other people and thus be abandoned as a standard when a situation calls for other bases for dealing with people. So rather than changing one's behavior or making amends, one could rationalize how one has treated the other person and thereafter approach social relations with a revised set of standards in mind.

When does discrepancy reduction involve a change in behavior versus a change in standard? Behavior is usually more malleable than standards and one can always choose to behave differently in the future. This suggests that discrepancies are reduced most often by making one's behavior conform to the standard in question. But there are important caveats, some of which follow from the discussion of *cognitive dissonance theory* in Chapter 3 ("Beliefs, Attitudes, and Values"). It is psychologically difficult to disavow a behavior that is freely chosen, observed by others, or has produced significant consequences. Instead, one might justify the action, even if this means changing one's previous thoughts about behaving in this manner.

Escaping the Self

But what happens when *both* the behavior and the standard are strong? Imagine a person who has a deep commitment to standards of honesty but who has just lied to someone without being forced to do so and in full view of an audience (e.g., at a party, in a psychology class). Such a combination of circumstances may be rare but they're not unimaginable. A momentary impulse fueled by anger, for example, can promote actions that are inconsistent with one's typical and preferred behavior. How would the person deal with such a conflict? Changing his or her strongly held values may be unthinkable, but backing off from one's public and freely chosen behavior is psychologically unrealistic.

There is an option, though. Recall that discrepancies only arise as a problem when one is in a state of self-focused attention. So rather than changing either the behavior or the standard, the person may find ways to reduce self-awareness and thereby "escape" the discrepancy. There is evidence that *escaping the self* is indeed an option when people experience intense and seemingly intractable conflict between standards and conduct (Baumeister, 1991; Hull & Young, 1983). The person might go home and watch mindless television (Moskalenko & Heine, 2003), for example, or play an intense game of racquetball. Or the person could drown his discrepancies in alcohol, a self-medication strategy that does wonders for reducing self-awareness (Hull, Young, & Jouriles, 1986). The ultimate means of escaping the self—suicide—might be undertaken when the burden of self-awareness exceeds the person's tolerance for unwanted, uncontrollable, and chronic self-awareness (Baumeister, 1990).

Conflict Among Standards

You might assume that the internal standards directing behavior when people are self-focused all revolve around morality (e.g., honesty, concern for the welfare of others, justice and fair play). To be sure, self-awareness does provide restraints against self-interest and often brings people's behavior in line with values and norms that society holds dear (Diener & Wallbom, 1976; Wicklund & Frey, 1980). But moral values hardly exhaust the possible standards that people embrace and internalize as guiding forces in their lives. Most people have standards concerning achievement (Atkinson, 1964) and mastery (Bandura, 1986), for example, and presumably will forgo immediate pleasures in service of performance goals when they are self-aware. Even aggression is embraced as a value by some people (Carver, 1975) and endorsed as a means of punishment more enthusiastically when such people are self-aware.

What happens when two conflicting standards are plausible for deciding what to do? Suppose that a person is asked to take a test that assesses an important mental skill and there is an opportunity to cheat on this test without being detected? There are two standards operating here: personal competence (do well on the test) and personal honesty (don't cheat). Which standard is likely to provide the basis for self-regulation when the person is made self-aware? Vallacher and Solodky (1979) addressed this question in a study with college students—a population concerned with personal competence but sensitive as well to honesty.

The participants attempted to solve a series of tasks, some of which had no solution. The task involved tracing the lines of a geometric form without retracing a line and without lifting the pencil from the paper. This is easy for triangles—one simply starts at one point and draws a continuous line around the triangle back to the starting point. But this task can be made impossible by adding a couple of other well-placed lines (a solvable and an unsolvable puzzle are presented below). There is no way to trace every line in these figures without retracing a line or lifting the pencil to avoid doing so. But the students performed the task in private, so there was no way—from their point of view—that the experimenter would know whether they lifted the pencil or retraced a line to solve the problem. They could therefore claim credit for solving a problem that was insolvable—in effect, they could cheat without being detected.

Half the students were led to believe that success on this task was associated with various mental abilities. The other students were told that there was a strong element of chance in performing the task, so that luck played a big role in how well people did. Students in the ability condition were expected to be concerned with internal standards of competence and achievement. In the chance condition, however, competence and ability were far less relevant. If students cheated in this condition, they would not be demonstrating competence, but only immoral behavior (cheating). In effect, then, the investigators manipulated the salience of two standards: achievement and morality.

Half the students in each of these conditions were made self-aware by seating them at a desk facing a small mirror propped against the wall. This arrangement meant that they could see themselves as they worked on the problems. The other students sat at a desk as well, but instead of a mirror there was a poster of the Grand Canyon—an unlikely

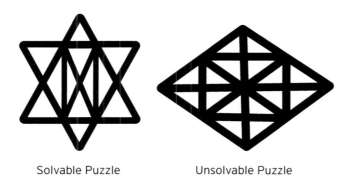

Solvable Puzzle   Unsolvable Puzzle

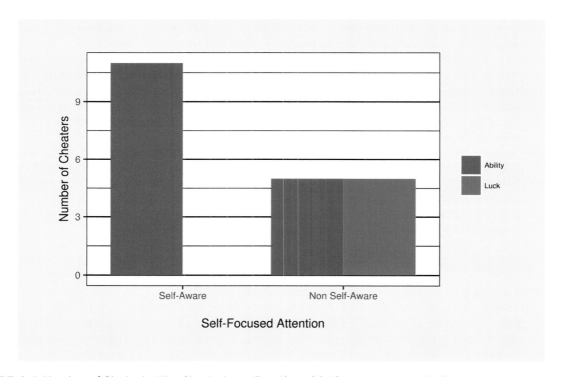

FIGURE 6.4 Number of Students Who Cheated as a Function of Self-Awareness and Self-Concept Standard
Source: Adapted from Vallacher & Solodky (1979)

self-focusing stimulus. To determine whether students cheated, the experimenter simply noted whether they claimed success on the insolvable problems.

Figure 6.4 shows the number of students in each condition who cheated on at least one of the insolvable problems. In the absence of self-awareness (the Grand Canyon poster), half the students in both the ability and luck conditions cheated. Apparently, neither standard provided a clear and compelling basis for deciding whether to claim credit for solving an insolvable problem. But among students who were made self-aware (by means of the mirror), the salience of the achievement and morality standards had a striking effect on students' behavior. *None* of the students in the chance condition cheated on any of the problems, even though they felt they could do so without being detected. However, *almost every* student in the ability condition took advantage of the situation to claim success on one or more of the insolvable problems.

These results are a bit sobering, for they suggest that when achievement is the operating standard for people, the likelihood of cheating may be enhanced rather than inhibited if they are in a state of heightened self-awareness. Self-focused attention promotes self-control, but this does not always translate into moral self-control.

Regulatory Focus

Imagine that everything goes smoothly for you today and that nothing out of the ordinary happens. You go to classes, talk briefly with some friends, have lunch with another friend, head back to your residence, have a quick dinner, hit the books for a while, listen to some music or surf the internet, then go to sleep. How would you evaluate the day? Was this a satisfying day because nothing bad happened, or was it an unsatisfying day because nothing exciting happened?

According to a model of self-regulation developed by Tory Higgins (1997, 2000), your answer to this question depends on your *regulatory focus*. If you feel that today was great because everything went smoothly, you are displaying a *prevention focus*. In this approach to life, events are evaluated with a concern over costly or aversive outcomes. If bad things happen, you feel distressed and are motivated to ensure they don't happen again. If bad or costly things don't happen and everything goes smoothly, you feel content and are satisfied with life.

In contrast, if you feel today was boring and unfulfilling, you are displaying a *promotion focus* in self-regulation. In this orientation toward life, events are evaluated in terms of their potential for enhancing the rewarding and stimulating aspects of one's experience. If bad or costly things don't happen and everything goes smoothly, you feel bored and dissatisfied. Events are not judged to be good unless they are exciting, interesting, or new. Whereas someone with a prevention focus scales his or her experience from negative to neutral, someone with a promotion focus scales his or her experience with from neutral to positive.

The promotion-prevention distinction applies to the standards of self-regulation discussed above. Morality can be expressed in a promotion-focused manner as seeking out ways to help others or making the world a better place. From a prevention focus, morality might be expressed as a concern with not harming others or cheating on one's taxes. Achievement, too, can be experienced in both modes. A promotion-focus might induce a person to achieve status in his or her field of expertise or excel at a new activity. A prevention-focus might induce a concern with avoiding failure or being careful not to embarrass oneself when attempting a new activity.

Emotion and Self-Regulation

Self-regulation clearly goes beyond the notion of enlightened self-interest, but it is not totally independent of pleasure and pain considerations. When a person's behavior deviates from an internal standard, this discrepancy is experienced as an unpleasant emotion. The larger the discrepancy between conduct and standard, the greater the negative emotion (Carver & Scheier, 1999). The particular emotion depends on whether the discrepancy is with respect to an achievement standard or a morality standard (Higgins, 1987). When people experience a personal shortcoming with respect to achievement, their emotional state reflects dejection or, if extreme, despondency and depression. It's easy to see how failing to win a race or achieve one's aspirations in a college course can make one feel dejected. Perceived shortcomings with respect to moral standards center on agitation or, if particularly troublesome, anxiety. Letting someone down who needs your help can certainly promote this type of feeling, as can doing things that reflect poorly on your sense of honesty and morality (e.g., cheating on an exam, hurting someone's feelings without a good reason).

Self-Conscious Emotions

Anxiety and depression may be activated because of self-awareness, but they are basic emotions that people can experience for a variety of reasons. Even lower animals show signs of anxiety and depression under the right circumstances (Seligman, 1975). There is a special class of emotions, however, that are experienced only as consequence of self-awareness. They represent the tendency to view oneself from the perspective of other people and thus are uniquely human in their experience. Keep in mind, though, that the perspectives of other people often become internalized, so these emotions can arise even when one is alone—the observers are present in our mind if not in our line of sight.

The most common *self-conscious emotions* are *embarrassment, shame*, and *guilt*—emotions that rank among the most unpleasant that people can experience (Tangney & Fischer, 1995). *Embarrassment* is the uncomfortable feeling experienced when one does something, usually unintentionally, that makes one look silly, inappropriate, or otherwise inconsistent with one's preferred image in the eyes of others (Edelmann, 1987; Goffman, 1959; Lewis, 1995; Parrott, Sabini, & Silver, 1988). Tripping over a trash can in the front of the classroom just before giving a presentation would probably be embarrassing for most students. Other examples include discovering that one has spinach from a recent meal firmly planted between one's teeth while trying to impress a date, making bodily noises that cause an awkward silence and suppressed giggles in a small group, discovering that one's pants are unzipped while trying to impress someone with your social skill and charisma, and breaking into laughter at a joke that falls flat for everyone else. In each case, the person feels like he or she is the center of attention and is projecting an image of him or herself that is incompatible with his or her own self-view.

Box 6.3   Why Do People Blush?

Mark Twain, a very astute observer of the human condition, once observed, "Humans are the only species who blushes, and the only one that needs to." That may be overstating things a bit—there is evidence that some nonhuman primates show reddening of the face to indicate to another primate that it has higher status and power (Hauser, 1996). But Twain's larger point is well taken: blushing is associated with embarrassment, a self-conscious emotion that is experienced routinely in human social interaction (Leary, Britt, Cutlip, & Templeton, 1992). Blushing is a universal phenomenon in human societies, an observation made by Charles Darwin during his circumnavigation of the globe while investigating the origin of species. Darwin was intrigued by blushing and devoted an entire chapter to its adaptive significance in his 1872 book on emotional expression.

Since Darwin's time, psychologists have been fiendishly clever in investigating the social sources of blushing. They typically create a situation in which participants experience negative, self-focused attention. For example, they may be led to think they have knocked over a can of Coke, which spills into a confederate's backpack, or they may be asked to suck on a pacifier (Buck & Parke, 1972). In a particularly intense blush-inducing study, participants sang "The Star-Spangled Banner" while being videotaped (Shearn et al., 1990). They then watched the videotape with a group of people. In a control group, other participants expected to deliver a prepared speech—an event that produces anxiety but not embarrassment. The researchers then compared the physiological activity of participants in both groups. There were some similarities (e.g., accelerated heart rate and blood pressure), but participants in the embarrassment condition displayed a unique pattern of physiological activity: heightened vasodilation and blood flow to the cheeks. In other words, they blushed.

Other lines of research have confirmed that blushing is a special state, distinct from anxiety, with its own biological causes (e.g., Gross, Fredrickson, & Levenson, 1994; Levenson, 2003; Porges, 1995; Schwartz, Weinberger, & Singer, 1981; Stemmler, 1989). We blush because we are unique in our ability to see ourselves through the eyes of others, and this expression of human uniqueness has its very own set of biological underpinnings. That realization, of course, can be looked upon as a source of pride—or as a source of embarrassment.

Embarrassment may be unpleasant but people get over it pretty quickly. Indeed, in retrospect the embarrassing episode can make for a good story ("remember the time you stepped out of the shower and the door was open and everyone started laughing and …"). *Shame* is a different story. People experience shame when they act in a dishonorable way, say something deplorable, or display a personal characteristic that is disgraceful or flawed, and others witness the action, statement, or characteristic (Buss, 1980; Tangney & Fischer, 1995). Shame comes in many forms: bodily functions (e.g., a child who wets his or her pants), loss of emotional control (e.g., breaking down in public), disappointing other people (e.g., giving up in the face of adversity), hurting others (e.g., humiliating an acquaintance in public), even mental exposure (e.g., having others learn about one's private obsessions). Shame is not funny, even in retrospect many years later. The person who feels ashamed tries to hide or escape observation and judgment by others and can become preoccupied with the incident.

Shame is similar to *guilt*. Both states involve a feeling of personal responsibility for something negative and inconsistent with how one wishes to be perceived and evaluated. But there are important differences as well (Baumeister et al., 1994; Lindsay-Hartz, 1984; Tangney & Fischer, 1995). Shame involves a failure to live up to standards of honor or worth in the eyes of others. Guilt is the emotional reaction to wrongdoings with respect to standards of right and wrong. And although shame and guilt can be generated by the same event (e.g., making fun of a less fortunate person), shame involves a focus on one's unworthiness in the eyes of others, whereas guilt involves a more limited focus on the act itself. Guilt means that one has done something wrong, but shame means that one is an unworthy person.

If a person feels shame over making fun of someone, he or she is likely to feel "small" and attempt to avoid contact with others. If the same act promotes guilt, however, the person may try to make amends by apologizing for the transgression or vowing not to behave that way in the future. Guilt is an important foundation for cooperative living because it motivates people to acknowledge and atone for wrongdoing, and it can prevent people from behaving badly toward others in the first place (Baumeister et al., 1994).

Self-consciousness is not always a negative experience. Imagine how you might feel after finishing at the top of your class on a psychology exam. This experience feels good (unless you cheated, in which case you should feel ashamed!), all the more so when you are the center of attention, basking in other people's adulation (or perhaps envy). OK, you might be a bit embarrassed, but there is almost certainly a fair degree of *pride* when you excel at something.

But even here, the potential for negative affect looms large, ready to displace the positive glow of having distinguished oneself from other people. We are expected to suppress overt expressions of pride and people who fail to do so are often disparaged as conceited, arrogant, and egotistical. No one likes someone who is too full of him or herself, and we are taught from childhood that excessive pride is unwarranted, even sinful. Pride is valued and tolerated only up to a point, then, and only if it isn't perceived as conveying an attitude of superiority. Indeed, pride can morph into shame when it is excessive and viewed negatively by others. So even when self-awareness gives rise to a positive self-conscious emotion—pride—our meta-cognitive machinery can rain on the parade and make us feel bad about having this emotion. But then, you can always feel proud about overcoming your pride. At this point, of course, you'd be well advised to quit while you're ahead and think about something entirely different.

Culture and Self-Conscious Emotions

The intensity and function of the self-conscious emotions differ somewhat across cultures. Because people in collectivist cultures (e.g., Japan, China, Mozambique) have a self that is firmly anchored in social roles and interpersonal relationships, there is a heightened potential for embarrassment, shame, and guilt (Markus & Kitayama, 1991). An act that might simply feel good from an individualistic perspective might distance the person from his or her reference group—or worse, make other members of the group look bad by comparison. This can promote embarrassment and perhaps even guilt and shame if he or she has an interdependent self. People in collectivist societies are less likely than their counterparts in individualistic societies to seek competitive advantage with members of their reference group or to boast about their individual accomplishments. As the Japanese proverb has it, "the nail that stands out gets pounded down."

Problems in Personal Control

When Is Personal Control Ineffective or Illusory?

Everyone has had the experience of failing at an activity, even if he or she has the skill to perform the action effectively. "Choking under pressure" is a common expression of this breakdown in personal agency. Self-regulation, too, can become a problem at times. People break diets, lose their temper, deceive others, and even engage in unambiguously bad behaviors that fly in the face of their internal standards. Beyond experiencing breakdowns in personal agency and self-regulation, people sometimes do not accurately recognize the degree to which they can make things happen, and they may fail to appreciate the degree to which they or external forces are responsible for their behavior.

Performance Impairment

To do something well, you should think about what you are doing. No one would quibble with this assertion. The problem is, people can think about what they are doing in many different ways, and some of these provide better bases for performing the action than do others. To complicate things further, the best way to think about an action depends on the actor, the action, and the context in which the actor is acting. Sometimes it is beneficial to concentrate on the details of what one is doing, but at other times this approach can be disastrous for performance. On the other hand, sometimes thinking about the actions' goals, consequences, and implications can enhance action performance, but this orientation too can prove wholly inappropriate for some actors, actions, and circumstances.

The complications make sense when viewed in the context of *action identification theory* (Vallacher & Wegner, 1987), introduced in Chapter 5. We noted that people can think about their action at different levels, from *low-level act identities* that emphasize the concrete details of what they are doing to increasingly *higher-level act identities* that emphasize the consequences, effects, and implications of the action. In general, the more complex, difficult, or unfamiliar an action is, the more likely people are to identify it in lower-level terms. Something novel and time-consuming (like solving a math problem or a jigsaw puzzle) requires greater attention to detail than does something routine and easy (like talking or riding a bicycle). When an action is easy to do or has become familiar and habitual, however, people tend to gloss over the details and focus instead on their reasons for the action or on the action's consequences and implications. Talking and riding a bike both entail a coordinated sequence of concrete movements, but people normally don't monitor these actions at that level. Instead, they think about the purpose of talking (e.g., exchanging information, making a point, getting to know someone) or bike riding (e.g., getting exercise, going to school, enjoying a nice day).

By and large, people are quite adept at finding the *optimal level of action identification* for performing an action (Vallacher & Wegner, 1987). People who are skilled at a particular activity (e.g., video games, karate, writing, playing a piano), for example, tend to identify the action in higher-level terms than do people who have less expertise (Vallacher & Wegner, 1985). But people don't always follow this rule. There are two forms of *non-optimal action identification*, and both can undermine personal control (Vallacher, Wegner, & Somoza, 1989).

First, a person might identify a difficult or complex action in high-level terms. Imagine thinking that the fate of the free world depends on how well you perform a difficult jigsaw puzzle or solve a math problem. These actions require attention to lower-level details but it might prove impossible for you to think about anything other than the action's implications for planetary survival while attempting them. Students sometimes get derailed in this fashion (e.g., Mange, Senemeaud, & Michinov, 2013). The optimal level of identification for taking a difficult exam is clearly low-level (read the questions carefully, recall the appropriate information, etc.), but it is hard to think clearly about such things if one is focusing instead on the consequences of the action (maintaining a grade point average (GPA), getting admitted to college, etc.). This form of non-optimal identification captures the essence of "choking under pressure" (e.g., Baumeister, 1984).

The second prototype of non-optimal identification is just the opposite: identifying a relatively easy or familiar action in low-level terms. Imagine focusing on the way your knuckles flex, elbows bend, and knees move up and down as you ride your bike. These low-level identities are appropriate when first learning to ride a bicycle, but once these basic features are mastered and occur automatically, attention to them can make for an awkward ride. This form of non-optimal identification is at work when highly trained athletes (e.g., members of professional sports teams and Olympic athletes) "choke" during an important competition (Beilock & Gray, 2007; DeCaro & Beilock, 2010). To ensure that they don't make a mistake, they focus on the specific movements involved in the action—features of the action that have long since become fairly automatic (Beilock, 2007; Nieuwenhuys & Oudejans, 2011; Oudejans & Pijpers, 2010). Skilled golfers, for example, are less effective when they take extra time and concentrate on the details of their golf swing rather than simply focusing on making a good shot and letting the specific movements unfold automatically without conscious control (Beilock & Gonso, 2008).

In both cases of non-optimal action identification, one is likely to experience disruption of the action's performance, as well as heightened nervousness and self-consciousness (e.g., Vallacher et al., 1989). High-level identification of a complex or novel action prevents one from focusing on the details necessary to get the action done. Low-level identification of a simple or routine action, meanwhile, robs the action of its normal automaticity and fluidity.

Self-Regulation Failure

Controlling one's impulses, resisting temptation, or delaying immediate gratification in favor of a later reward can be difficult. A person might believe strongly in personal dignity, for example, but who can blame him or her for making a fool of him or herself on a reality TV show in exchange for 15 minutes of fame and a big paycheck? And when someone is provoked by an antagonist, it's hard to fault the person for retaliating in some fashion, even if he or she believes strongly in tolerance and non-violence. If self-regulation were easy, psychology would be a pretty boring discipline, limited to admonitions like "avoid temptations," "be careful!" or "count to 10 when you're angry." Fortunately for psychologists (perhaps less so for everyone else), people experience difficulties in their attempts at self-regulation.

Mental Control

As noted earlier, thinking about one's behavior in relatively low- versus high-level terms has important implications for how well an action is performed. The distinction between high- versus low-level action understanding has implications as well for people's success at self-regulation. Higher-level thinking is associated with impulse control, resistance to temptation, and other forms of successful self-regulation (Fujita & Carnevale, 2012; Fujita & Roberts, 2010; Fujita, Trope, Liberman, & Levin-Sagi, 2006; Vallacher & Wegner, 1989). The reasoning behind this generalization is straightforward. Because high-level action identification represents a focus on an action's consequences and its consistency with one's goals, plans, and values, this mental state keeps one mindful of what the action means in broad terms, not simply what the action entails in terms of movements and moment-to-moment experiences. So when people think about a behavioral opportunity in high-level terms, they are likely to evaluate the action in terms of its larger meaning and to inhibit pursuing the opportunity if the action is inconsistent with this meaning—even if it would feel good for the moment.

Imagine the dilemma of someone attempting to maintain a diet but who has an opportunity to consume a bowl of macadamia nut ice cream just before going to bed. The person could identify eating the ice cream in low-level terms (e.g., scooping the ice cream into a dish, taking a bite, experiencing the taste, going in for another bite, and so on) or remain mindful of the higher-level identities of this act (e.g., breaking a diet, giving in to impulse, disappointing myself). It can prove difficult to resist temptations such as this, but the person is in a position to do so if he or she remains mindful of what the ice cream experience entails in terms of consequences (calories, fat cells) and implications for his or her self-evaluation ("there I go again!").

People who routinely think about their actions in high-level terms, as assessed by the *Behavior Identification Form* (described in Chapter 5), have an advantage in self-regulation across many circumstances (Vallacher & Wegner, 1989). Compared to those who identify what they do in low-level terms, those who focus on the consequences and implications of their behavior have a greater sense of internal as opposed to external control, display greater self-motivation, have a clearer sense of their personal traits and values, and are less sensitive to immediate social pressures when deciding what to do. People who generally think about their behavior in high-level terms are also better at adhering to a schedule in their daily routine in college (Vallacher & Wegner, 1985). If a student has decided that Wednesday nights are devoted to studying, he or she is likely to follow through with this agenda even if distracted by the promise of fun and libation at a party down the street.

Mental Energy

Self-regulation with respect to an action's consequences and implications for self-evaluation is simple in principle, but it can prove quite difficult in practice. To understand why, recall the distinction between *controlled and automatic cognitive processes* introduced in Chapter 3. Automatic thinking is associated with impulsive action and well-learned behavior patterns—hardly the type of thinking necessary to focus on the implications of what one is doing and to inhibit the action if these implications conflict with one's personal goals and values. Effective self-control—resisting temptations, inhibiting impulses, acting in accordance with internal standards, and the like—requires the exercise of controlled processes, with conscious attention focused on the action's larger meaning. But controlled processes are effortful and consume a person's limited mental energy. Just as physical exertion can wear one out and promote prolonged sitting or a nice nap, mental exertion can deplete one's cognitive resources and make it difficult to maintain an action that requires sustained conscious monitoring and control.

Self-regulation can especially drain mental resources when the goal is *not* to do something, as anyone on a diet can attest. You've gone several hours without comfort food, the smell of Krispy Kremes comes wafting down the hallway from someone's room, and you're not supposed to consume anything other than twigs and berries until the sun sets. Trying not to follow the Krispy Kremes trail requires a lot of mental energy in the form of admonitions ("resist, don't give in, I can do this,...."), attempts at distraction ("look, wallpaper!"), and promises to the self of better things to come ("one day people will walk around me instead of jumping over").

Research on *ego depletion* by Roy Baumeister and his colleagues has made this point (Muraven & Baumeister, 2000). Resistance to temptation—one of the most difficult (and investigated) forms of self-regulation (Mischel et al.,

1989)—is a prime candidate for ego depletion, as shown in a study by Baumeister et al. (1998). College students took part in an experiment that included a taste test. When they arrived for the session, they saw two plates of food: one filled with freshly baked chocolate chip cookies (this is the tempting one) and one filled with radishes (this is the "you've got to be kidding" one). Some of the participants (selected randomly) were told they could eat the cookies, but not the radishes. Other participants were told the opposite: eat the radishes, but leave the cookies alone. After a 5-minute taste test of the assigned food, both groups of participants worked on a challenging set of puzzles. A third (control) group who skipped the taste test also worked on the puzzles.

If self-regulation depletes one's resources, participants who had to exercise the most self-control in the taste test should have the least resources available for exercising self-control on the puzzle task. The relative self-control called for in the two food conditions is obvious: participants who ate the radishes had a greater battle on their hands (and in their minds) than did those who had license to eat the cookies (assuming that none of them were diehard vegans who truly relished radishes). If so, those in the radish-eating condition should be more depleted and consequently have less self-control left over for the puzzle task than should their cookie-eating (and control group) counterparts.

To test this prediction, the experimenters simply recorded how long participants in the three groups persisted at the puzzle task. As Figure 6.5 makes clear, participants in the cookie-eating and control conditions persisted at the puzzle task over twice as long as did those who spent their mental resources resisting the temptation to eat the cookies.

Mental resources can be strained in many ways (Vohs & Heatherton, 2000). People find it hard to exert mental effort when they are under stress, feel tired, or are sad (Tice, Bratslavsky, & Baumeister, 2001). A diet or new exercise regimen that seems doable when exams are finished and you've had a good night's sleep can seem out of the question when new stresses and sleepless nights are experienced. Making a series of choices, even among desirable alternatives, can drain mental resource and undermine subsequent self-control (Vohs et al., 2008). And, of course, alcohol consumption is practically *designed* to undermine self-control, promoting behavior that reflects immediate desires at the expense of long-term self-interest. The effect of strained mental resources applies as well for actions that reflect internal standards and social norms. Being polite to someone who rubs you the wrong way may be easy (not fun, but manageable) when you're relaxed and can concentrate on what to say. But the threshold for expressing blunt and

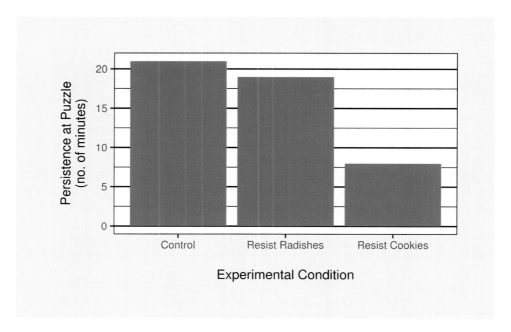

FIGURE 6.5 Persistence at a Difficult Puzzle after Resisting Temptation
Source: Adapted from Baumeister et al. (1998)

critical comments drops dramatically when you're stressed, thinking about more pleasant company, or intoxicated (Vohs, Baumeister, & Ciarocco, 2005).

Is mental effort a metaphor, or is it biological in the same way that physical effort consumes energy resources? Does the mind function like a muscle that gets fatigued with extensive use? The brain is not a muscle, of course, but rather a vast interconnected network of neurons. But some researchers have suggested that the brain burns a special form of glucose, called glycogen, when it performs controlled processes requiring executive resources (Gailliot et al., 2007). Compared to participants who are given a natural sweetener that provides glycogen to the brain, for example, those who are given an artificial sweetener that lacks glycogen-producing properties are more likely to demonstrate subsequent lapses in self-regulation.

This model of self-regulation failure has not gone unchallenged. Some researchers take issue with the assertion that self-regulation is fueled directly by glycogen. They argue instead that the effect of glycogen (like that of other natural forms of sugar) is to activate brain regions associated with reward, and that this enhancement in motivation promotes enthusiasm and persistence on difficult tasks—whether solving a challenging puzzle or inhibiting an impulse (e.g., Molden et al., 2012). Others downplay the role of biology altogether, arguing that the mind trumps the body when demonstrating restraint and behaving in accordance with personal standards. In this view, ego depletion takes place only when people *believe* that willpower is a limited resource (Job, Dweck, & Walton, 2010; Job, Walton, Bernecker, & Dweck, 2015). People who don't share this belief do not demonstrate a breakdown in self-regulation after resisting an impulse or delaying an impulse.

Regardless of the mechanism involved, self-regulation clearly involves mental effort, and there is reason to think that putting forth this effort can train the mind to persist in the face of challenges, delay gratification, and inhibit impulses. Self-regulation may be exhausting in the short run, but it is well worth the effort in the long run.

Illusions in Personal Control

The mind is not an infallible guide for finding truth (Gilovich, 1991; Nisbett & Ross, 1980). As we saw in Chapter 3, when people introspect on the reasons for their beliefs, judgments, feelings, and actions, they may come up with quite reasonable conclusions that completely miss the mark (Bem, 1967; Nisbett & Wilson, 1977; Wegner & Vallacher, 1977; Wilson, Dunn, Kraft, & Lisle, 1989). The limits to introspection apply as well to people's assessment of their personal agency. Sometimes people overestimate the degree to which they have control over their actions, and sometimes they make precisely the opposite mistake, attributing the source of their experiences to external forces when their own desires and actions are the true cause.

Illusions of Personal Agency

People like to feel they have control over their experiences. Whether it's wiggling one's fingers or building a career, there is a natural preference for people to feel like they are the prime movers in making things happen. The self-perception of control is apparent in childhood (Bjorklund, 2007; Stipek, 1984) and continues unabated in adulthood (deCharms, 1968; Taylor & Brown, 1988). Feeling in control doesn't make it true, however. People routinely overestimate their sense of personal agency and take credit for experiences that are really due to external forces, chance, or luck (Bargh, 1999; Langer, 1975; Wegner & Wheatley, 1999).

Ellen Langer (1975) demonstrated some of the conditions under which people experience the *illusion of control*. Langer argued that people sometimes feel responsible for their outcomes even when the outcomes are due solely to luck or chance. This happens whenever features that are normally associated with personal control are made salient in situations for which such features are totally irrelevant. In one study, office workers took part in a lottery for which the prize was $50. The cost of a lottery ticket was $1. Just prior to the lottery drawing several days later, they were given an opportunity to sell back their ticket. Each worker was asked what price they deemed reasonable in exchange for forgoing the lottery.

Here's the interesting part. Some of the workers had simply been handed a lottery ticket but others had to reach into a container and choose a ticket. In many situations, choice is strongly linked to one's assessment of success in a task. One can choose what courses to take at college, what roads to take when going to work, or whom to ask out for a date. In each case, making the choice promotes a feeling that one is in control of the outcome (success in the course, getting to work on time, or securing the date). In the lottery situation, however, choosing among a set of

were remarkably accurate in judging observers' agreeableness, conscientiousness, emotional stability, openness, lik-ability, loneliness, religiosity, and political orientation.

But maybe forming impressions based on photographs has an advantage. After all, you can stare at a photograph without being rude, scanning it for telltale bits of information in a way that might be downright creepy when the target is staring back at you. It turns out, however, that the accuracy of impressions based on photographs is not due to the potential for intense scrutiny. Impressions formed within one-tenth of a second of looking at a photograph tend to be just as reliable as impressions that are formed after a more extensive exposure (Willis & Todorov, 2006).

It is easier to form an accurate impression of an attractive person than of someone who is less so. Lorenzo, Biesanz, and Human (2010) recruited several male and female participants to interact in a group setting to get to know one another, after which they met individually with every other participant for three minutes. After each meet-ing, participants rated each other on five major personality dimensions (extraversion, agreeableness, dominance, conscientiousness, emotional stability). To assess the accuracy of these ratings, they were compared to the target's self-ratings. Participants also rated one another's physical attractiveness. The average attractiveness rating of each participant provided the measure of his or her attractiveness.

After just 3 minutes of interaction, participants provided highly accurate ratings of one another. But participants were especially accurate in rating the personality of good-looking interaction partners. Attractive partners were also perceived more favorably on the personality dimensions. Perhaps physically attractive people provide better informa-tion about themselves than do unattractive people. But we also pay more attention to good-looking people and are more motivated to understand them. So although people tend to judge a book by its cover, it is also the case, as noted by the authors, "that a beautiful cover promotes a closer reading."

Cognitive Heuristics

It is not necessary to observe another person, or even look at a photograph of him or her, to make confident infer-ences about the person's characteristics. Sometimes it is sufficient to know only the most superficial information about the person in order to claim knowledge about what he or she is like. This may seem unfair and error-prone, but taking cognitive shortcuts in assessing someone's characteristics is useful when decisions must be made on the basis of limited information. These shortcuts are referred to as *cognitive heuristics*—simple rules of thumb that allow judgments to be made on the basis of very limited information (Tversky & Khaneman, 1974). Let's take a look at the most popular of these shortcuts.

Imagine you are given a list of 100 male college students, 30 of whom are members of a popular fraternity, *Theta Theta Theta*, and 70 of whom are members of a campus society, *Future Accountants of America*. Then one person from the list, Jack, is picked at random and described as someone who has a taste for beer, likes parties, and prefers watching Steven Colbert to getting his news from NBC. Now you are asked, "Is this person a member of the fraternity or the accountants society?" If you based your answer on simple probability, you would say that Jack is most likely a member of the accountant society—after all, the odds are for that choice are over twice as high (70 to 30) as the odds for the other choice. But if you are like most people presented with this task, you would probably venture that Jack is one of the fraternity people. If so, you would be using the *representativeness heuristic* (Kahneman & Tversky, 1972). Your judgment of Jack is not based on the base rate probability of his membership in the fraternity (only 30%), but rather on how well a few pieces of information about him (beer drinking comes to mind here!) fit your image of fraternity guys. This heuristic represents a well-documented shortcut that people routinely use to classify something (e.g., a person) to a certain category (e.g., a group) to the extent that it is similar to a typical case from that category.

Now imagine that you are given the same information about Jack (party guy, beer drinker, sardonic news con-sumer), but that you have no knowledge of fraternities (e.g., there are none on your campus) and plenty of knowledge about accountants (e.g., you know a lot of accountant wannabes). In this case, the representativeness heuristic isn't particularly helpful—unless, of course, your accountant friends behave like Jack. Instead, your judgment of Jack would be based on the information that comes to mind most readily: the accounting students you have met. This is the essence of the *availability heuristic* (Tversky & Khaneman, 1973). In thinking about students, accounting enthusiasts are more cognitively available than are fraternity members, so the former provides the template for predicting which camp Jack falls into. Even if you switched the percentages, so that 70% of the list consisted of fraternity members, the greater availability of accounting students would likely carry the day in your inference about Jack.

When we make a judgment, we rarely start from scratch. We may have a rough idea what to expect or we may be advised how to think about the person or event. If there is little else to base our impression on, we may employ the *anchoring and adjustment* heuristic (Epley & Gilovich, 2001; Tversky & Khaneman, 1974). The initial idea establishes the anchor, with subsequent thoughts providing the adjustment. If we select a good anchor and adjust it in a reasonable fashion, this strategy is efficient and can result in accurate assessments (Krueger & Clement, 1997). But people usually start with a poor anchor and fail to make sufficient adjustments.

Consider again the case of Jack. Imagine that you believe that Jack is a member of a fraternity (perhaps because of the representativeness heuristic), and that your notion of fraternities involves heavy drinking, light studying, and disinterest in important matters of the day. None of this is necessarily true of fraternities, let alone of Jack. But this is your anchor. Now imagine you are provided with samples of Jack's behavior that include acting as a designated driver when visiting a local bar, pulling an all-nighter to prepare for a midterm exam, and scouring the *New York Times* to learn the positions of political candidates on raising tuition at his college. By themselves, these actions might suggest that Jack doesn't drink, is studious, and attends to important news of the day. But anchored by your preconceived notion of fraternity men, each behavior might prompt only a modest adjustment in your inferences about Jack. He's still hedonistic and shallow, just not as much as most fraternity guys.

Mind Perception

Learning about a person goes beyond inferring his or her behavioral tendencies. To truly understand the person involves knowing how he or she thinks and feels. As noted in Chapter 5 ("Self-Concept"), humans are distinct among animals in their capacity for *theory of mind*—the recognition that other people have thoughts of their own. We attribute a mind to other people, complete with thoughts, concerns, and goals that provide a foundation for their actions (Carruthers & Smith, 1996; Epley & Waytz, 2009; Idson & Mischel, 2001). But theory of mind is just that: a theory about the minds of other people. We cannot peer into other people's brains to see what they are thinking. Instead, we make *inferences* about what they are thinking.

There are biases in perceiving people's minds. If we like someone, we tend to infer that he or she has complex cognitive processes and acts on the basis of high-level identities for his or her action (e.g., goals, plans) rather than on the basis of simple impulses (Kozak, Marsh, & Wegner, 2006). This assumes that the person has acted in a desirable manner, or at least in a neutral manner. But sometimes the people we like do bad things and the people we don't like do good things. For *disliked* target persons, we infer that negative actions reflect goals and plans, while dismissing positive actions as impulsive and lacking in higher-level intent. Because plans and goals are linked to personal responsibility, these results express the tendency to credit liked others (e.g., friends) for good behavior and to blame disliked others (enemies) for bad behavior.

Evaluation: Distinguishing Good and Bad

It is important to know many things about the people we know or come into contact with. But one quality stands out from all the others in its importance: whether a person is good or bad. If a person is considered bad, all the talents and wonderful behavioral tendencies in the world do not make up for that glaring quality and we are likely to keep our distance from him or her. But if a person is considered good, we can overlook his or her shortcomings and maintain contact with him or her. Evaluation is basic to judgments of everything—from automobile brands and fast-food chains to academic topics and political ideologies—and it is the bottom line in social judgment as well. How do people go about making such a basic determination about others?

The Halo Effect

Some models propose that judging whether someone is good or bad is basically a math exercise (Anderson, 1974). The assumption is that the various attributes that are used to characterize people have a fixed meaning with an equally fixed evaluation. A trait like "smart" is very positive, for example, while a trait like "critical" is negative. So if you come across someone who is both smart and critical, this approach to evaluation suggests that you would have a neutral view of him or her—the average of the good trait (smart) and the negative trait (critical). The same *cognitive algebra* is said to hold for people about whom we know a great deal. So if someone is judged to have 10 positive qualities (smart, dependable, energetic, etc.) and 10 negative qualities (deceptive, self-serving, impatient, etc.), people would presumably feel neutral about him or her because of the averaging process.

Nice theory, but social judgment does not work that way. We integrate information about the people we think about, but this process does not simply average away conflicting information. The mind is endlessly constructive, ready and able to create different interpretations of the same basic information, or to generate new information that supports an existing impression. A seemingly positive trait like "smart," for instance, could be viewed as negative if the person in question is perceived as "untrustworthy" and "deceptive." After all, if someone is deceptive, his or her intelligence just makes his or her actions all that more suspicious and deserving of a harsh assessment. By the same token, a seemingly negative trait like "critical" could be viewed as positive and support a flattering assessment of someone who is seen as sincere, helpful, and insightful. Criticism, after all, could be considered constructive and useful in social relations, rather than destructive and counterproductive.

The role of evaluative consistency in social judgment was recognized a century ago by the prominent psychologist and education theorist, Edward Thorndike (1920). He noted that once we see someone as possessing one trait (e.g., friendliness), for example, we tend to attribute a host of other traits to the person (e.g., honesty, trustworthiness, sincerity), even if there is no evidence to back up these inferences. Note that although these traits refer to very different behaviors—one can be friendly without being particularly honest, for example—they all share the same (positive) evaluation. Thorndike coined the term *halo effect* to capture the idea that once people infer one positive quality in a target, they are likely to see the person in a favorable light on many other dimensions. Halos can be negative as well as positive. So when someone is judged to possess a negative trait (e.g., dishonest), he or she is judged to have a range of other distinct traits that have in common a negative evaluation (e.g., lazy, irresponsible, unfriendly).

Some traits are especially influential in creating halos. Solomon Asch (1946) was a pioneer in exploring this idea. He asked participants to read a list of words describing a person. After reading the list, they wrote a paragraph describing their impressions and then selected from a long list of pairs of opposing traits the ones that best described the person. Participants were randomly assigned to read one of two lists of initial traits. For one group, the person was described as *intelligent, skillful, industrious, cold, determined, practical*, and *cautious*. For the other group, the person was described as *intelligent, skillful, industrious, warm, determined, practical*, and *cautious*. The two lists are identical with one exception—*cold* in the first list was replaced by *warm* in the second. If participants in the two conditions differed in their subsequent impressions of the person, the *warm-cold* difference had to be responsible.

In fact, participants in the two groups had very different impressions of the person. The "warm" person was perceived as more generous, good-natured, popular, wise, happy, and imaginative than the "cold" person. Some of these differences make sense—*warm* is similar in meaning to *good-natured*, for example. But other differences, such as imaginativeness and wisdom, do not reflect similarity in meaning to warm versus cold. The participants in the two conditions clearly were thinking about very different people.

When Asch substituted *polite* and *blunt* for *warm* and *cold* in the two lists, participants in the two conditions did not differ in their impressions. Asch concluded that some traits—*warm* and *cold* in this case—are *central* to impression formation, whereas other traits (such as *polite* and *blunt*) are *peripheral* (less important) in forming impressions. People make more extreme and far-ranging inferences on the basis of central as opposed to peripheral traits. Note that these inferences (generous, imaginative, wise, etc.) are evaluative rather than simply descriptive in nature. Central traits create the halo that is used to make inferences about a person's personality. Knowing one glowing and important quality about someone enables people to fill in the blanks with other glowing qualities. By the same token, knowing one damning quality about someone enables people to infer many other undesirable qualities about him or her—even if there is no direct evidence for these traits.

Physical attractiveness qualifies as a central trait in impression formation (Dion, Berscheid, & Walster, 1972; Eagly, Ashmore, Makhijani, & Longo, 1991; Jackson, Hunter, & Hodge, 1995). Good-looking people are judged more positively on a variety of seemingly unrelated traits (e.g., emotional stability, happiness, trustworthiness, dominance) than are those with average appearance or those who are unattractive. Research suggests that the differential evaluation of attractive and unattractive people reflects the disadvantage of being unattractive rather than the advantage of being attractive (Griffin & Langlois, 2006).

Karen Dion (1972) provided an unsettling demonstration of the attractiveness bias. Teachers read a brief report of misconduct by a male student (e.g., throwing rocks at a sleeping dog). The depiction of the act was the same in all cases. What varied, however, was a photograph of the boy that was paper-clipped to the report. For half the teachers, the boy in the photo was very good-looking, but for the other half the boy was plain in appearance. Teachers were asked to rate the severity of the crime and suggest how the case should be handled. It's hard to see how a child's attractiveness is relevant to judging the severity of the child's misconduct or to deciding how the case should be handled. But compared to the unattractive boy, the attractive boy was viewed in lenient terms. The teachers did not consider the act as all that serious and they recommended that he be spoken to about the incident but not punished. The unattractive kid, in contrast, was judged to have acted very badly and was seen as deserving of punishment rather than a heart-to-heart talk. Clearly, the halo effect in this case had unholy consequences.

Box 7.2   In Politics, it's Not *What* You Say, It's *How* You Say it

Social judgment is based in large part on nonverbal behavior. A person's posture, arm and hand gestures, bodily movement, eye contact, and tone of voice carry greater weight in impression formation than do the ideas and opinions expressed by the person (Ekman & Friesen, 1969; Mehrabian & Williams, 1969). This is true not only in everyday social interaction, but even when forming impressions of political candidates (Noller, Gallois, Hayes, & Bohle, 1988). The impressions formed on the basis of nonverbal cues go beyond liking versus not liking of candidates to influence whether people will vote for one candidate or the other. In an analysis of 19 nationally televised American presidential debates, for example, Gregory and Gallagher (2002) found that the voice quality of each candidate conveyed not only his relative social dominance, but also his vote share in the election.

The video quality of television has improved greatly in recent years (think of all the camera angles and close-up shots of people as they spout opinions and express emotions), and this increasing prevalence of visual cues relative to auditory cues is apparent in political campaigns (Bucy & Grabe, 2007). Does this translate into political decision-making? The answer is a clear "yes." In watching a debate, for instance, audience members are more likely to imitate the nonverbal behaviors of highly charismatic political candidates—who smile more and look more often at the audience—than the nonverbal behavior of their less charismatic opponents (Cherulnik, Donley, Wiewel, & Miller, 2001). Presumably, this emotional contagion translates into increased liking and political preference for the charismatic candidate. Even politicians' nonverbal reactions to news events can impact how voters perceive them (Bucy, 2000).

Nonverbal visual cues can also have an indirect impact on voters' preference for political candidates. During the 1976 presidential election campaign, Friedman, Mertz, and DiMatteo (1980) analyzed the facial expressions of news broadcasters as they uttered the names of different candidates (most notably, Ronald Reagan and Jimmy Carter). There were clear differences in the perceived positivity of broadcaster broadcasters' preferences based on their expressions. This effect was replicated in the 1984 presidential election campaign and was found to be associated with voters' political preferences (Mullen et al., 1986). Voters tended to favor the candidate for whom the biased broadcaster exhibited more positive facial expressions.

Similar effects have been observed for political interviews. Interviewers sometimes exhibit different levels of positive and negative nonverbal behaviors toward the politicians being interviewed (Babad, 1999), and this nonverbal expression of affect has an impact on how viewers perceived the politicians (Babad, 2005). A politician's image takes a hit when the interviewer is hostile rather than friendly. What the politician actually says is often forgotten quickly and plays a lesser role in shaping the viewers' judgment regarding his or her suitability for public office. A smile, it seems, can go a long way in shaping a country's political direction.

Implicit Personality Theory

The halo effect allows people to generate a full-blown impression of someone based on minimal information, with inferences about a person's specific traits guided by an overall evaluation of him or her. A person can be good versus bad in two fundamentally different ways, however. As demonstrated in Asch's research, the most basic dimension of evaluation centers on a person's *warmth*. A person is awarded a halo to the extent that he or she is perceived as friendly, sincere, helpful, trustworthy, honest, and moral—traits that suggest one can interact with the person in a comfortable manner. But we also evaluate one another in terms of *competence*. So even if a person is not particularly warm, he or she can be awarded a halo if he or she is perceived as intelligent, talented, skillful, creative, industrious, and effective in getting things done. Within each dimension, specific traits are inferred that are mutually consistent in their evaluation—friendly and sincere are consistent with respect to warmth, for example, while talented and creative are consistent with respect to competence.

Because warmth and competence are independent dimensions of evaluation, people can judge people in purely evaluative terms, yet still form impressions that are more complex than the simple good-bad dichotomy suggests. Someone could be viewed as good by one criterion (e.g., warm) but not so great by another criterion (incompetent). This two-dimensional structure of social judgment represents people's *implicit personality theory* (Bruner & Taguiri, 1954; Judd, James-Hawkins, Yzerbyt, & Kashima, 2005; Rosenberg & Sedlak, 1972; Schneider, 1973; Sedikides & Anderson, 1994; Wegner & Vallacher, 1977). Thus, one person (Jack) may be judged to be highly sociable (warm) and smart (competent), another person (Andy) might be judged as aloof (cold) and efficient (competent), another person (Sam) might be judged as uncaring (cold) and unimaginative (incompetent), and yet another person (Franklin) might be judged as happy (warm) and devoid of talent (incompetent). The structure of implicit personality underlying these impressions is illustrated in Figure 7.1.

There is remarkable consensus among people worldwide in their implicit personality theories (Hamilton, 1970; Kuusinen, 1969). But there are some notable differences across cultures as well. Implicit theories of personality, like other cultural beliefs that link specific ideas, are transmitted from one generation to the next (Chiu, Morris, Hong, & Menon, 2000; Cousins, 1989). In American society, for example, knowing only that a person is artistic, people are likely to assume that the person is creative, intense, temperamental, and unconventional in his or her interests and lifestyle. In Chinese society, however, there is not a well-defined implicit personality theory centered on artistic interests (Hoffman, Lau, & Johnsons, 1986). When an artistic person is encountered, people in China do not assume much else about him or her. On the other hand, the Chinese do have an implicit personality theory concerning someone who is devoted to his or her family—such a person is assumed to be worldly, socially skilled, and somewhat reserved (Hoffman et al., 1986). In American society, people are far less likely to make these inferences about a person who puts family above personal ambition.

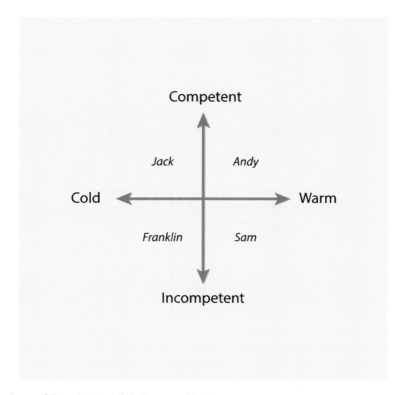

FIGURE 7.1 The Structure of People's Implicit Personality Theory

Because warmth and competence are both evaluative, one might expect a straightforward relationship between assessments on these dimensions and global (overall) evaluation. The rank order of evaluation, from lowest to highest, should look like this:

* *Negative evaluation*: low competence/low morality
* *Moderate evaluation*: low competence/high morality
* *Moderate evaluation*: high competence/low morality
* *Positive evaluation*: high competence/high morality.

This simple order may miss the mark. To be sure, someone who is judged to be neither competent nor moral is unlikely to occupy a top spot among anyone's Facebook friends, whereas someone who is considered both competent and moral is likely to have many such friends. But the mixed combinations are not so obvious. We are especially sensitive to signs of deception and exploitation by others–attributes reflecting the warmth dimension. We don't hate people who are clumsy and clueless, but we can be very harsh on those who are deceitful and hurt others. In fact, the judgment that an immoral person is incompetent might soften the negative evaluation of him or her because of his or her diminished threat. We reserve our harshest judgments for those who cannot be trusted but who may be smart enough to convince us otherwise. Indeed, this is the very combination of traits that can promote a condemnation of someone as "evil." Think of Adolf Hitler, for example, or of sociopaths who use their intelligence to deceive, exploit, or harm others.

Attribution: Assessing Responsibility

When things happen, we like to know who or what was responsible for making them happen. Particularly when events have good or bad consequences, there is a natural concern to identify the factors responsible, so that praise can be given or blame assigned. The action by itself is not always informative about responsibility. A person may do something with undesirable results (e.g., driving his or her car into a ditch), for example, but this may say more about the road conditions than about the person's driving ability. Assessing responsibility for events, and holding people accountable when praise and blame are deemed appropriate, is a basic focus of social thinking and an important area of theory and research.

Internal Versus External Attribution

Theory and research concerning this issue commonly emphasize processes of *causal attribution* (Heider, 1958; Jones & Davis, 1965; Kelley, 1967). In this view, to assess responsibility is to attribute the action to a likely causal factor. The most popular distinction concerning behavior causation is between attribution to causes that are *internal* to a person and attribution to causes that are *external* to the person. An *internal attribution* identifies the actions' cause within the person–his or her personality traits, values, chronic motives, and other internal states that propel him or her to behave in a certain fashion across circumstances. An *external attribution* identifies forces experienced by the person that would cause most anyone to do the same thing. External attributions are an implicit recognition of the power of the situation to induce people to behave in a certain fashion. The promise of reward, the threat of punishment, social rules, pressure from other people, expectations associated with membership in various groups, features of the physical environment–these all constitute external causes that can promote behavior that may not correspond to the actor's usual way of acting.

This distinction can be seen everywhere. Someone slips and falls down–is he or she clumsy (an internal cause) or is the pavement slippery (an external cause)? A person yells at someone with whom he or she is talking–is this the yeller's fault (internal attribution) or did he or she respond appropriately to an insulting comment by the other person (external attribution)? Beyond its relevance to everyday events, the internal-external distinction is operative in the criminal justice system. A young man breaks into a convenience store to steal food. This is clearly a crime, but there is considerable discretion in the sentence that is meted out. If the jury feels that the man has no regard for the law or was acting out of greed (an internal attribution), he is likely to receive a harsh sentence. But if he is seen as responding to dire economic circumstances–he has been laid off from work, has a family to support, and saw no way out of his predicament–the jury might take these mitigating circumstances into account (an external attribution) and go lighter on the sentencing.

So how do people determine whether someone's behavior is internally or externally caused? The optimistic view is that people are like naïve scientists, approaching the task of attribution in the same way that a scientist does (Heider, 1958; Kelley, 1967; Wegner & Vallacher, 1977). Laypeople, of course, do not conduct an experiment every time they observe an event, but perhaps their mode of thinking about the event has key parallels to the way a scientist might approach the matter. Harold Kelley (1967) took this analogy seriously and proposed a model that involves a more or less rational integration of information. Imagine, for example, that Shirley is observed acting nervously at a party. Does Shirley's behavior reveal something about her personality (she is an anxious person), or is her nervousness a reaction to this particular occasion?

In Kelley's model, an internal attribution (Shirley is an anxious person) is made if no one else seems particularly nervous at the party, if Shirley appears nervous in many other situations, and if Shirley always seems nervous at social occasions like this one. However, an external attribution (e.g., this party is awkward and uncomfortable) is made if everyone else seems tense at the party, Shirley does not seem nervous in other social situations, and Shirley always gets nervous in this particular type of social situation.

The Fundamental Attribution Error

As reasonable as Kelley's model seems, it has not received a great deal of research support (Jones & Harris, 1967; Nisbett & Ross, 1980; Ross, 1977). So even if Shirley is not alone in getting nervous at a party and does not get nervous at other social occasions, an observer is nonetheless likely to make an internal attribution for her behavior. The naïve scientist perspective is appealing because it assumes rationality in attribution, but apparently it doesn't capture how people assess responsibility for the actions they observe.

A far simpler depiction of attribution holds simply that people are more like personality psychologists than like social psychologists. Rather than taking into account the power of the situation to elicit behavior, laypeople infer that someone's behavior in a particular situation indicates what he or she is like as a person. This tendency is called the *correspondence bias* (Gilbert & Malone, 1995; Jones, 1979) because it assumes that overt behavior *corresponds* to an internal feature of the actor. It has come to be known, however, as the *fundamental attribution error* (FAE; Ross, 1977). This unflattering term is warranted because research has shown that people routinely underestimate the influence of external factors when explaining other people's behavior. Even when situational forces are made blatantly obvious, people persist in making internal rather than external attributions for an actor's behavior (e.g., Jones & Harris, 1967; Lord, Scott, Pugh, & Desforges, 1997; Ross et al., 1977). As Fritz Heider (1958) said decades ago in his depiction of social judgment, "behavior engulfs the field."

In a sense, the fundamental attribution error is a manifestation of the automatic tendency to make rapid inferences about people when observing them, a point that was discussed earlier. If inferences are made spontaneously on the basis of photographs (Willis & Todorov, 2006), it is hardly a stretch to assume that inferences are made on the basis of overt behavior. Angry behavior is attributed to a low threshold for anger, for example, while nervous behavior is attributed to the person's chronic anxiety, and cheerfulness is attributed to the person's agreeableness or sunny disposition.

This does not mean that people are oblivious to the context surrounding a person's behavior or ignore it when making an attribution for his or her behavior. But to override the FAE, a person must go beyond simply *observing* someone's behavior; he or she must *think* about the behavior (Gilbert, 1993). Such thinking does not come easy when one's executive resources are depleted (Baumeister et al., 1998), or when one is using these limited resources for some other purpose. This suggests that when people are tired, distracted with another activity or topic to think about, or simply unmotivated to think a little more deeply, they are especially inclined to commit the FAE.

Research by Daniel Gilbert and his colleagues demonstrate the automatic nature of dispositional inferences and the deliberative processing required to make allowances for situational factors. In this line of research, participants observe a person behaving in a certain manner (e.g., friendly, hostile, nervous) and are asked to judge the extent to which the person has the corresponding personality trait (friendliness, hostility, anxiety). To test whether executive resources are relevant to these judgments, the researchers introduce a manipulation designed to undermine the resources that participants can devote to the judgment task. Participants experiencing this *cognitive busyness* manipulation are expected to make dispositional inferences for the observed behavior, whereas participants whose executive resources are not undermined are expected to take situational information into account and adjust their inferences accordingly.

In an early test of this idea, participants viewed a videotape (without sound) of a young woman being interviewed (Gilbert et al., 1988). The woman appeared nervous throughout the tape, biting her nails, twirling her hair, tapping her fingers, and shifting in her chair from "cheek to cheek." Half the participants were told that she was responding to a series of anxiety-inducing questions (e.g., about her sexual fantasies and personal failings). The other participants were told instead that she was responding to rather innocuous questions (e.g., great books, world travel). Half the participants in each of these conditions simply watched the videotape without any distraction, but the other half were asked to memorize a list of words while viewing the woman twirling her hair and the like.

Gilbert predicted that participants with this extra demand on their resources (cognitively busy) would not take into account the type of questions responded to by the woman and so would not make the appropriate adjustment to their judgment of her as an anxious person. So even when the woman was asked personally embarrassing questions, she was assumed to be an anxious person by the cognitively busy participants. The results, presented in Figure 7.2, confirmed this prediction and support the idea that the FAE is likely to go uncorrected when people's mental resources are drained or diverted to another task.

This reasoning provides insight into why seemingly minor issues can sometimes lead to major altercations. Consider barroom brawls. It is no accident that fights are more likely to break out when people (usually men) interact in an establishment devoted to alcohol consumption than in establishments devoted to caffeine consumption. One of the first features of mind to go when a person is intoxicated is his or her capacity for higher-level mental processes—the ones necessary to override automatic processes and take context into account. So when a person who has had a few drinks is bumped by someone, he (or maybe she) is unlikely to consider all the factors in the situation that might have prompted the bump (e.g., the crowded and dark conditions). Instead, the bumpee may automatically assume that the bump reflects something personal about the bumper—his (or her) rudeness, desire to show dominance, or lousy personality. Fortunately, motor skills also take a hit when one is intoxicated, so the bumpee's intended retaliation against the bumper may not be executed well enough to do much damage.

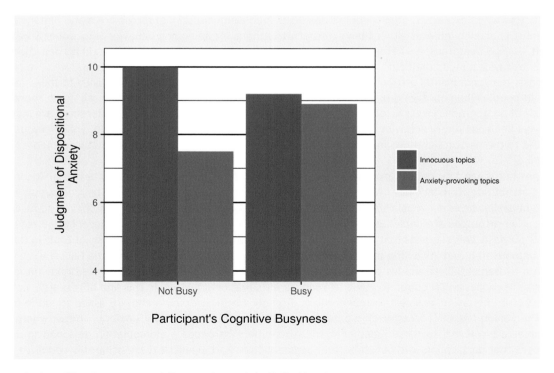

FIGURE 7.2 Cognitive Busyness and the Fundamental Attribution Error
Source: Adapted from Gilbert et al. (1988)

Actor-Observer Differences

To this point, the concern has been with how people attribute responsibility for the behavior of someone else. But people also assign responsibility for their own behavior. Maybe your car, not another person's, careens off the road into a ditch. Maybe you get nervous during an interview. Maybe you ace an exam—or for that matter, score near the bottom. If you attribute responsibility for your own behavior (as the *actor*) in the same way you attribute responsibility for others' behavior (as an *observer*), you would blame yourself for the car in the ditch, you would view yourself as a nervous person, and you would consider yourself a strong or weak student, depending on whether you aced or failed the exam.

As you may have guessed from these examples, you do not follow the same rules as an actor as you do as an observer when attributing responsibility for behavior. And you're right (which means people would consider you an insightful person!). Theory and research have identified two *actor-observer differences* in attribution.

First, you are less prone to the fundamental attribution error (Jones & Nisbett, 1971; Nisbett, Caputo, Legant, & Maracek, 1973; Robins, Spranca, & Mendelson, 1996; Taylor & Fiske, 1975; Watson, 1982). Whereas your judgment about another person's behavior is biased toward internal attributions—his or her traits and motives—you are more inclined toward external attributions for your own behavior. Unless you are doing something in isolation from everything else (e.g., singing in the shower, doing homework by yourself, reading a book), your actions are connected to features of the situation that require attention and thus involve controlled rather than automatic processing. So although you can ignore the context surrounding other people's actions, your actions are in response to forces in the situation (expectations, social norms, incentives, pressures, the behavior of others) and cannot be ignored. When asked why you were anxious during an interview, for example, you could point to features of the situation—the hard questions being asked, the importance of doing well in the interview, the unfriendly person asking the questions, and so forth—as reasonable causes of your discomfort. And if you get angry when someone questions your intellect or moral compass, you probably feel your behavior is an appropriate response to an insult rather than a reflection of your anger management issues.

The second actor-observer difference is a bit less flattering about the way you explain your own actions. Most people want to feel good about themselves and they can usually find a way to do so—even if that involves distorting reality a bit. This can color the way people assign responsibility for their behavior. When considerations of praise (for good actions) and blame (for bad actions) are at issue, people tend to display a *self-serving bias* (Baumeister, Stillwell, & Wotman, 1990; Greenberg, Pyszczynski, & Solomon, 1982; McAllister, 1996; Mezulis, Abramson, Hyde, & Hankin, 2004; Miller & Ross, 1975; Pronin, Lin, & Ross, 2002; Riess, Rosenfeld, Melburg, & Tedeschi, 1981; Sicoly & Ross, 1979; Zuckerman, 1979). If the behavior is clearly wonderful, or if it signifies personal success, people mysteriously lose sight of the situational foundations of what they have done. A victory in a sporting event or an A on an exam, for example, are attributed to one's personal skill or effort. But when the behavior is not so great or results in failure, people tend to be highly attentive to all the pressures, distractions, and sources of unfairness responsible for the bad or undesirable action.

The self-serving bias may not apply to everyone. Some people have a negative view of themselves and tend show a *reversal* of the self-serving bias because positive actions are inconsistent with their negative self-view (Swann, 1990). They are thus inclined to accept greater personal responsibility for failure than for success. So, for example, if a low self-esteem person does well on an exam or manages to impress a new acquaintance, he or she is likely to attribute the success to the relative ease of the task ("the exam was a no-brainer," "that person probably likes everyone") or simply to luck or chance ("that will never happen again").

Social Judgment in Context

What Factors Affect People's Judgments of One Another?

Social judgment is not a detached enterprise. When we form impressions, make evaluations, and assess responsibility, we usually do so in real-world settings stacked with personal concerns, social norms, incentives, and distractions. To understand the process of social judgment, it is important that these factors are given the attention they deserve. Fortunately, social psychologists have been pretty good about doing this. The factors that have been identified can be grouped into three basic categories: *mental effort*, *accessibility and priming*, and *culture*.

Mental Effort

Thinking can be hard work. As discussed in Chapters 3 and 6, the use of higher-level "executive" resources requires mental energy. The task of thinking becomes especially strenuous when one is confronted with other demands on one's limited mental resources, as demonstrated in the research on *cognitive busyness* described earlier. The amount of mental effort devoted to social judgment is not simply a matter of competing demands on limited resources. All the resources in the world would not matter if people were not motivated to understand someone. By the same token, even if mental resources were devoted to parallel tasks, motivation to think deeply about a person might override the tendency to make simplistic judgments. The motivated nature of social judgment has been investigated in several ways.

Mood

As discussed in Chapter 4, positive and negative moods have different functions. A positive mood signals that things are basically fine, so that there is no need to change course or be particularly vigilant regarding threats or dangers. So when a person is happy or content, he or she is especially likely to employ cognitive shortcuts, such as the heuristics discussed earlier, in thinking about people and events (Park & Banaji, 2000; Ruder & Bless, 2003). In fact, a positive mood can promote stereotypical thinking about people, with little consideration to the things that make each person unique (Bodenhausen et al., 1994).

A negative mood has a very different function. It signals that things are not basically fine, and thus promotes a mindset attuned to vigilance and problem solving (Frijda, 1988). When a person is sad, for example, he or she is sensitive to his or her losses and setbacks, and to how things might get worse. So rather than relying on cognitive shortcuts, the person in a negative mood is likely to think more thoroughly, noticing things that might be lost on a person in a positive mood (Forgas, 1995; Schwarz, 1990). People who are mildly depressed, for example, think more thoroughly about social events (Gannon, Skowronski, & Betz, 1994) and are more accurate in judging the links between actions and outcomes (Alloy & Abramson, 1979). A negative mood thus tends to focus a person's attention on specific characteristics and actions, resulting in a judgment that is differentiated rather than global and simplistic.

Mood can also impact social judgment because of its effect on the *breadth of attention*. Whereas negative mood narrows the breadth of attention, positive mood tends to broaden a person's attentional scope (Frederickson & Branigan, 2005; Rowe, Hirsh, & Anderson, 2007). This effect has implications for how we perceive and evaluate other people (Avaramova, Stapel, & Lerouge, 2010). People in a negative mood tend to focus squarely on a target person, noticing his or her specific actions and characteristics, with relatively little attention to the larger context. People in a positive mood are attentive to both the target person and his or her situation. So although a positive mood can promote a less nuanced view of the person's characteristics, it heightens sensitivity to situational factors that impact the person's behavior.

Cognitive Needs

Because mental effort is required to override the automatic nature of social judgment (e.g., cognitive heuristics, snap judgments based on appearance), one might expect people to differ in their willingness to put forth such effort. Research supports this idea. Some people opt for quick and easy judgments, which they are unwilling to question once they are generated. Other people, however, are willing to expend mental effort when trying to figure out what someone is really like. This difference among people has been investigated in various ways.

Need for cognition (Cacioppo, Petty, Feinstein, & Jarvis, 1996) represents the degree to which people enjoy thinking. People with high need for cognition enjoy solving puzzles—from riddles and crossword puzzles to societal problems—and thrive on learning new ideas and challenging existing ones. They also seek accurate rather than convenient understanding. So rather than relying on snap judgments and cognitive heuristics when thinking about others, people with a high need for cognition are motivated to expend the extra effort needed to make accurate inferences about others' personality and to assess whether their own behavior reflects personal dispositions or external circumstances. People with low need for cognition, in contrast, take the low-effort route to understanding. They rely on heuristics and have no problem with making snap judgments and not looking back.

This difference is demonstrated in a study by D'Agostino and Fincher-Kiefer (1992) concerning the correspondence bias. Participants read a speech that either favored or opposed legalized abortion. They were told that the speechwriter was assigned to one position or the other and thus had no choice in which point of view to express. Participants were asked to indicate whether the speechwriter actually believed the position he or she advocated (an internal attribution). Participants low in need for cognition did not take the lack of choice into account, but instead assumed that the speechwriter was committed to the position he or she advocated. Those high in need for cognition, however, were far less certain that the speechwriter truly believed what he or she wrote. Rather than showing the correspondence bias, they took into account the external factor (assignment to particular point of view) and resisted the temptation to make an internal attribution for the speech.

Need for closure (Kruglanski & Webster, 1996) gets at essentially the same idea as need for cognition. Everyone wants to gain clarity and reach firm conclusions when considering an event or a person, but some people are especially motivated to achieve "closure" in their judgments (Webster & Kruglanski, 1994). Someone with a high need for closure tends to "seize" a conclusion (e.g., a trait inference, a good versus bad evaluation, an assessment of responsibility) without considering all the relevant information. And once they do, they "freeze" on the judgment and display strong resistance to contrary judgments or to information that contradicts their judgment. In contrast, a person with a low need for closure is open to information and different conclusions, and is willing to reconsider his or her judgment when presented with contradictory information or alternative conclusions.

Need for closure shapes the way people make judgments about others. Compared to people with low need for closure, those with high need tend to rely more on stereotypes when forming impressions of someone who is identified as a member of a particular category and they pay less attention to information specific to the person (Kruglanski & Freund, 1983). People with high need for closure, moreover, tend to recall less behavioral information after forming an impression, a tendency which is consistent with their "freezing" tendencies.

Dijksterhuis, Knippenberg, Kruglanski, and Schaper (1996) demonstrated these differences in a study involving impressions of soccer hooligans—a category for which there is a negative stereotype. Participants read a series of behavioral descriptions about each member of a group of soccer hooligans and were asked to form an impression of this group. For example, one of the descriptions read, "Hank sometimes starts a fight in a bar." After reading the descriptions, participants judged the group on four personality trait dimensions, two of which were consistent with the hooligan stereotype (intolerant and selfish) and two of which were inconsistent (intelligent and industrious). Participants with high need for closure rated each member more strongly on the hooligan-stereotype traits than did those with relatively low need for closure. The closure-prone participants also indicated that there was less variability among the hooligans than did those less motivated by closure concerns. Most interesting of all, participants with low need for closure were especially attentive to the *inconsistent* information, whereas those with high need for closure recalled more information that was *consistent* with the hooligan stereotype. Having judged each member in terms of the group stereotype, the high-closure participants demonstrated "freezing" by ignoring behavior that contradicted the stereotype (see Figure 7.3).

Social Interdependence

Whether people make good use of their executive resources or instead make snap judgments or rely on cognitive heuristics depends in part on the degree to which there is *social interdependence* (Kelley & Thibaut, 1978) with the target of judgment. *Low interdependence* means that the actions of two (or more) people have little or no impact on one another. Your connection to strangers and entertainers qualifies as low interdependence. Under these conditions, people have little hesitation in generating judgments based on minimal information and even less mental energy. *High interdependence* means that each person's actions have important implications for one another. Your connection to close friends, family members, teammates, and co-workers qualify as high interdependence. In such relationships, people resist the allure of simplistic snap judgments (Brewer, 1988; Fiske & Neuberg, 1990). They invest mental energy in learning about and judging each other, whether in forming an impression, making a global evaluation, or assessing responsibility for an event.

Research by Neuberg and Fiske (1987) demonstrates how social interdependence affects impression formation. College students participated in a program they thought was designed to help long-term hospital patients of the same age become adjusted to everyday life. To get acquainted with the patients (who were actually accomplices of the researchers), the students were told that they and a former patient (whose name was Frank) would work together to create interesting games for which they could receive cash prizes. Some students were told that the prizes would be awarded on the basis of individual effort (*low interdependence* with the former patients), but others were told that their joint efforts with Frank would determine whether they received a prize (*high interdependence*).

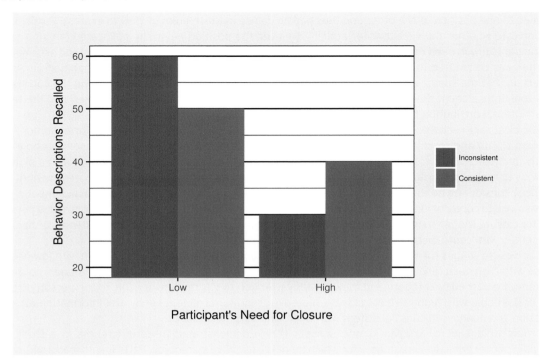

FIGURE 7.3 The Recall of Behavioral Descriptions that Were Consistent versus Inconsistent with the Soccer
Hooligan Stereotype
Source: Adapted from Dijksterhuis et al. (1996)

All students were told that Frank had been hospitalized for schizophrenia, a very serious psychological disorder. They then read a personal statement that ostensibly had been written by Frank, after which they were asked to indicate their impressions of him. Students who had a low interdependent relationship with Frank tended to provide impressions of Frank that amounted to a stereotypical description of a schizophrenic (e.g., emotionally unstable, mentally confused), regardless of the rather sensible statement that Frank had written. But students who were interdependent with Frank tended to provide impressions that were less stereotypical and more in touch with the details that Frank had provided in his statement.

Social Status

People's social and economic standing in a society can shape the way they view themselves, other people, and events (Kraus, Piff, & Keltner, 2009). People with lower socioeconomic status have a relatively weak sense of personal control and thus tend to explain their experiences—whether personal, political, or economic—in terms of their opportunity structures, life circumstances, and social forces. Their bias, then, is to make external attributions for their behavior and for the behavior of people generally. People with higher socioeconomic status see the world and their role in it far differently. They have a stronger sense of personal control and they project this internal causation to others as well (Kluegel & Smith, 1986; Kraus et al., 2011). For them, accomplishments reflect personal attributes rather than life circumstances, social forces, and the like. They are thus inclined to make internal attributions for their own behavior as well as other people's behavior.

Social status affects social judgment in another, perhaps more surprising way. Who do you think would be accurate in judging people's emotional expressions—low-status or high-status members of society? Research by Kraus, Côté, & Keltner (2010) suggests that the edge goes to those with lower social and economic status. Presumably, their accuracy in judging nonverbal displays of emotions is due to their greater sensitivity to the social context and their awareness of their interdependence with others. In effect, they are good at reading how other people feel because it is to their advantage to do so.

One could argue that people who differ in their socioeconomic status simply differ in their ability to perceive emotions, regardless of any difference in their respective interdependence. To rule out this possibility, Kraus et al. (2010) manipulated social-class status in a subsequent study, with participants randomly assigned to relatively low- versus relatively high-social status. This was accomplished in a very clever way. Participants were presented with an image of a ladder with 10 rungs and told to think of the ladder "as representing where people stand in the United States." They were then randomly assigned to experience either low or high social class by asking them to compare themselves to either someone near the bottom of the ladder (low status) or near the top of the ladder (high status). This manipulation (which sounds a bit like empathy) worked: when participants were asked where they would place themselves on the ladder, those who thought about a lower-rung person placed themselves closer to the bottom of the ladder than did those who thought about a higher-rung person.

They then viewed 36 pictures, each portraying the expression of different emotions (e.g., nervous, playful, hostile) through muscle configurations around the eyes. For each picture, they chose from four options the emotion word that best described the picture. Participants who temporarily experienced a low-status state proved to be more accurate at identifying the emotions conveyed in the pictures. Simply imagining that one has low social status makes one sensitive to the external social context and thus more attuned to the emotions of other people.

Accessibility and Priming

Life is filled with events and situations that are open to interpretation. The same comment (e.g., "You are totally wrong in your belief about the economy") could be perceived by as hostile by one observer, for example, but as direct and constructive by another observer. What determines how people reduce the inherent ambiguity of social life? The general answer is that we interpret people's actions through the lens of the schemas, traits, or concepts that are in our mind at the time. The more specific answer is that people's impressions are influenced by *accessibility*— the extent to which particular schemas, traits, and concepts are at the forefront of a person's mind and thus likely to color his or her judgments about what he or she perceives (e.g., Ford & Thompson, 2000; Higgins, 1996; Todorov & Bargh, 2002).

There are two ways by which concepts become accessible and function in this manner. First, some concepts are *chronically accessible* because of past experience (e.g., Dijksterhuis & van Knippenberg, 1996; Higgins & Brendl, 1995; Rudman & Borgida, 1995). Because they are always lurking beneath conscious attention, they are always on call to interpret ambiguous actions and situations. If you have experienced or witnessed a great deal of violence in the past, for example, you might be inclined to view confrontational behavior in a social situation as aggressive or hostile. However, if you have more often experienced or witnessed straightforward and constructive interactions in the past, the same confrontational behavior might be viewed as an honest attempt to clear the air between the people involved.

Second, a concept can become accessible because of a recent experience that has little to do with the general pattern of one's past experiences (Bargh, 1996; Higgins & Bargh, 1987; Stapel & Koomen, 2000). The process by which recent experiences increase the accessibility of a schema, trait, or concept is known as *priming*. Research by Higgins, Rholes, and Jones (1977) demonstrates the role of priming in making sense of behavior that could be judged in very different ways. Participants were asked to engage in what they thought were two unrelated tasks. In the first, which was described as a study of perception, they were asked to identify different colors while memorizing a list of words at the same time. In the second task, which was said to involve reading comprehension, they were asked to read a paragraph about someone named Donald and then indicate their impressions of him. This is the description they read:

> Donald spent a great deal of time in his search of what he liked to call excitement. He had already climbed Mt. McKinley, shot the Colorado rapids in a kayak, driven in a demolition derby, and piloted a jet-powered boat—without knowing very much about boats. He had risked injury, and even death, a number of times. Now he was in search of new excitement. He was thinking, perhaps, he would do some skydiving or maybe cross the Atlantic in a sailboat. By the way he acted, one could readily guess that Donald was well aware of his

ability to do many things well. Other than business engagements, Donald's contacts with people were rather limited. He felt he didn't really need to rely on anyone. Once Donald made up his mind to do something, it was as good as done, no matter how long it might take or how difficult the going might be. Only rarely did he change his mind, even when it might well have been better if he did.

The description was designed to paint an ambiguous portrait of Donald's actions, which could be seen as positive and admirable or as negative and reckless. Attempting to sail across the Atlantic, for example, could be seen as adventurous and indicative of self-confidence or as irresponsible and indicative of recklessness.

So how did the participants in this study perceive Donald and his actions? As illustrated in Figure 7.4, it depended on the words they were asked to memorize in the first study. The participants who had memorized *adventurous, self-confident, independent*, and *persistent* tended to form positive impressions of Donald. Most of them (70%) saw him as a likable man who enjoyed new challenges. But participants who had memorized *reckless, conceited, aloof*, and *stubborn* tended to form negative impressions of Donald. The majority of these participants (90%) considered him to be a stuck-up person who needlessly took dangerous chances. Not all positive and negative words were influential in shaping impressions of Donald. If participants memorized positive words like *neat* or negative words like *disrespectful*, they did not show a clear bias in their impressions of Donald. The memorized words had to prime concepts that were relevant for reducing the ambiguity of Donald's actions. *Adventurous* and *reckless* make sense of Donald's actions, but *neat* and *disrespectful* do not.

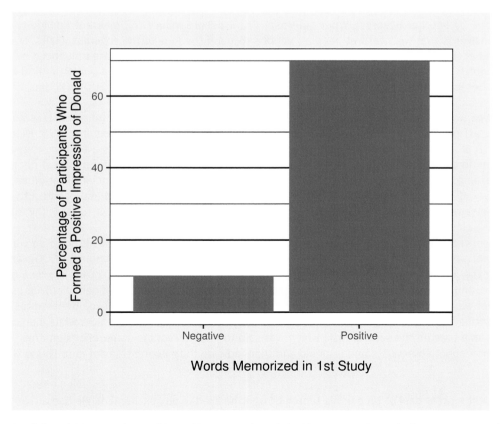

FIGURE 7.4 Participants' Impressions of Donald Were "Primed" by the Types of Words they Had Memorized in an Earlier "Unrelated" Study

Source: Adapted from Higgins et al. (1977)

When judging others, people typically are not aware that they are applying concepts or schemas they had been thinking about earlier. The unconscious and automatic nature of priming is demonstrated in research in which words are flashed on a computer screen too rapidly for people to recognize them. John Bargh and Paula Pietromonaco (1982), for example, flashed words related to hostility (e.g., *hostile, unkind*) or neutral words (e.g., *water, between*) on a computer screen so quickly that participants could not consciously perceive them, seeing only a flash of light. Participants then read a paragraph that described a person who behaved in a way that could be interpreted as hostile or as benign (e.g., "A salesman knocked on the door, but Donald refused to let him enter"). Participants who had been primed by the hostile words judged Donald to be more hostile than did people who had been primed by the neutral words.

Culture

People everywhere make inferences about personality, evaluate one another, and assess responsibility. But different aspects of these processes are on greater display in some cultures than in others. Every culture is unique, but as noted at various points in earlier chapters, one can distinguish between cultures that emphasize *individualism and independence* and those that emphasize *collectivism and interdependence* (Markus & Kitayama, 1991; Nisbett, 2003; Triandis, 1995). This distinction is relevant to basic processes of social judgment.

The Correspondence Bias

The correspondence bias is a basic principle of social thinking, but individualistic and collectivistic cultures differ in the strength of this tendency (e.g., Choi, Nisbett, & Norenzayan, 1999). Individualistic cultures (e.g., the United States, most European countries) place emphasis on individual freedom and autonomy, whereas collectivistic cultures (many Asian, African, and Latin American countries) place greater emphasis on group membership, interdependence, and conformity to group norms. People in collectivistic cultures show greater awareness of how situational factors can affect behavior and take these into account to correct for the correspondence bias (Choi, Dalal, Kim-Prieto, & Park, 2003; Choi & Nisbett, 1998; Choi et al., 1999; Krull et al., 1999; Miyamoto & Kitayama, 2002). The tendency in collectivistic cultures to override the correspondence bias is especially likely when the situational information is highlighted (Choi et al., 2003; Lieberman, Jarcho, & Obayashi, 2005; Trope & Gaunt, 2000).

This difference in cultural emphasis is reflected in the tendency to make internal versus external attributions. In an early demonstration of this difference, Joan Miller (1984) asked Hindus living in India (a collectivistic culture) and Americans living in the United States (an individualistic culture) to provide examples of behavior by their friends and then to explain why they behaved in that fashion. The American participants tended to provide dispositional explanations (internal attributions) for their friends' behaviors, whereas the Hindu participants were more likely to provide situational explanations (external attributions) for their friends' behavior. At this point, you might think, "well, maybe the Americans and Hindus simply generated different behaviors, with the former providing unique actions reflecting individual differences and the latter providing common actions that most anyone would perform." Even if you did not come up with this clever interpretation, Miller did. To rule it out, she asked the American participants to explain some of the behaviors generated by the Hindus. The Americans still tended to make dispositional inferences to explain Hindus' behavior.

Cultural differences in the correspondence bias can even be observed in newspaper articles. Morris and Peng (1994) looked at reports of two mass murders, one committed by a Chinese graduate student in Iowa, the other committed by a Caucasian postal worker in Michigan. They looked at how these murders were reported in the *New York Times* and in the *World Journal*, a Chinese-language US newspaper. Compared to journalists writing for the *World Journal*, those writing for the *New York Times* tended to describe both murders in dispositional terms. In the *Times* articles, for example, one of the murderers was described as having a "sinister edge to his personality." In the *World Journal* article, the same murderer was characterized as "not getting along with his adviser" and as experiencing "isolation from the Chinese community."

The Self-Serving Bias

One might expect to observe a stronger self-serving bias in individualistic cultures than in collectivistic cultures. There is greater emphasis on individual identity and goals in individualistic cultures, which enhances the tendency to boost and protect self-esteem. People in such cultures are thus motivated to stand out from the group and highlight their individual talents and accomplishments. This makes them inclined to attribute their successes to internal qualities and to find external reasons for their shortcomings and failures. People in collectivistic cultures, in contrast, are more concerned with how they fit in a group as opposed to how they stand out in a group. They certainly wish to pursue personal goals and develop their unique abilities, but these desires are tempered by deference to the groups with which they identify. So whereas an American might take personal credit for his or successes, a person from a more interdependent society might downplay his or her personal role in a successful venture (Al-Zahrini & Kaplowitz, 1993; Hooghiemstra, 2008; Schuster, Forsterlung, & Weiner, 1989).

When Chinese students perform well, for example, they no doubt feel good but they attribute the success to their teachers or parents, or to the high quality of their school (Anderson, 1999; Bond, 1996). It is not that Chinese students cannot grasp the feeling of internal causation. To the contrary, they readily make internal attributions—but more so when they have failed rather than succeeded! (Anderson, 1999; Fry & Ghosh, 1980; Lee & Seligman, 1997; Oishi, Wyer, & Colcombe, 2000). The contrast between cultures is not limited to China and the United States. When over 200 studies from around the world were reviewed, the strongest self-serving bias was found in the United States, Canada, Australia, and New Zealand (Mezulis et al., 2004)—countries that top the charts with respect to individualism. People everywhere can resonate with self-serving attributions, but this tendency, like the actor-observer difference, can be overridden by cultural values stressing one's interdependence with others.

Stability Versus Change in Social Judgment

What Determines Whether People Resist Change in Their Judgments?

There are advantages to maintaining a judgment in the face of new information and other challenges to the accuracy of the judgment. The impressions we form of other people provide a platform for our interactions with them, reducing uncertainty about how we should act. If we felt compelled to rethink our assessments every time they were challenged, we would be perpetually "buried in thought" (Tolman, 1932) and unable to act in a decisive manner from one situation to the next. But there are disadvantages to holding onto a judgment as well, particularly when these judgments have important consequences and rest on questionable evidence. To maintain contact with reality means remaining open to new information that might call into question our conclusions about other people's characteristics and overall goodness or badness. Social judgment thus is a balancing act. There are mental and behavioral processes that promote stability in our conclusions, but there also processes that unlock our assessments and make us willing and able to change the way we think about someone.

Biases in Thinking

The mind is designed to make sense of one's experiences, not necessarily to forge an accurate view of reality. Accuracy is a laudable goal, of course, but the more fundamental goal is achieving a coherent and stable view of one's social world. Once a coherent judgment is forged, the mind is designed to protect the judgment from facts and events that threaten its validity. To fulfill this function, the mind has a broad range of tools at its disposal. These cognitive tools are of two basic types—one shaping what events we notice and how we interpret them, the other shaping how we test our hypotheses and beliefs about issues and other people.

Selective Attention

We cannot attend to everything. Attention is necessarily selective, which means that much of what happens goes unnoticed. Even when observing a trivial event that takes place in a short period of time, there is simply too much information available for it all to be noticed, let alone remembered. Imagine watching a crowd of people crossing a downtown street in the middle of the day. Did you notice the guy with dark slacks or the reflection of people in the store window? If you did, that means many other features of the event went unnoticed.

The focus of attention is partly driven by its salience. An action that is unexpected or unusual, for example, can capture our attention, as can an action with positive or negative consequences. But the focus of attention is also influenced by our biases and preconceptions. If you consider someone dishonest, for example, you are likely to be especially attentive to any action on his or her part that looks deceptive or to any statement that looks to be untrue.

But someone else may consider the same person to be honest and be especially attentive to instances of sincerity and candor in his or her actions and statements.

In the battle for attention, bad things tend to win against the good things. We are more sensitive to threats than to rewards, for example, and to the negative attributes of a person than to his or her positive attributes—especially if the person is a stranger who is in a position to affect our experiences (e.g., Kanouse & Hanson, 1971). In impression formation, for example, this *negativity effect* means that people give greater weight to negative actions and characteristics than to positive actions and characteristics. The negative qualities of a person, moreover, can cancel his or her positive qualities, but the reverse is far less likely—positive qualities do not cancel negative qualities. Someone may be smart, open to new ideas, and friendly, for example, but learning that he or she is insincere can quickly burst the bubble and promote a decidedly negative judgment. However, learning that a thoroughly dishonest person is highly intelligent and has great social skills is unlikely to change the impression from negative to positive.

There are two explanations for the negativity effect. The *figure-ground* perspective centers on people's expectations for behavior. In a typical day, most of our social interactions are pleasant—maybe not warm and intimate, but certainly cordial and lacking in threat and antagonism. Negative events are infrequent in part because they violate informal social norms about appropriate interpersonal conduct (Jones & Davis, 1965). A negative event is therefore likely to stand out as the "figure" and be readily noticed against the "background" of pleasant occurrences. Friendly behavior by a new acquaintance, for example, may not be seen as particularly revealing about his or her personality; instead, it is likely to be chalked up to situational factors that call for such behavior. Unfriendly behavior, in contrast, is infrequent and thus is given a great deal of weight in forming an impression of the person.

The second explanation—*vigilance*—trades on the idea that "bad is stronger than good" (Baumeister et al., 2001). The first order of business for any species is to avoid injury and death, a concern that promotes heightened sensitivity to negative events and vigilance regarding those who represent danger. Pleasant events are "frosting on the cake"—we cannot focus on them until we feel comfortable that potential dangers are not on the horizon. Sensitivity to "bad" is a reasonable way to engage the world. It is more important to know whether someone will hurt us than to know whether he or she will be pleasant to us.

Although most everyday events are good, or at least neutral, *extreme* negative events are probably more common than extreme positive events. In any given day, the likelihood of a severe accident while driving a car is far greater than winning a million-dollar lottery. Life is filled with a succession of minor pleasant events, punctuated on infrequent occasions with very unpleasant events (e.g., a serious illness, a natural catastrophe, a national emergency, the death of a loved one). Bad events may be infrequent, but when "stuff" happens, we pay attention.

Behavior Interpretation

Life would be far simpler, and erroneous judgments of one another would be far less frequent, if our behavior had an obvious meaning that was shared by everyone. Some actions are pretty clear and are seen in the same way by most people. But these are usually extreme events like murder (unambiguously bad) and heroism (unambiguously good). In daily life, things are not so obvious. An act that seems positive—complimenting someone, for example—could be viewed in unflattering terms—as manipulation or phoniness. Likewise, an act that seems negative—a harsh criticism of someone, for example—could be interpreted in positive terms—as a constructive assessment or a demonstration of honesty in communication.

It may seem ironic, but actions that are more "objective"—identified in terms of basic movements, gestures, and the like—are more open to interpretation than are actions that are identified in more global terms that reflect intentions, motives, and values. If a man puts his hand in his pocket, for example, we could make any number of interpretations of this behavior. Perhaps he is reaching for his keys, or maybe he is reaching for a weapon. When people focus on the basic features and details of an action, their mental machinery is called upon to infer a higher-level meaning of the action (Vallacher & Wegner, 1987).

Because of the "interpretative elasticity" of lower-level actions, two people viewing the same behavior can come away with very different views of what was done and what the actor is like (e.g., Duncan, 1976). This is likely when different observers have different judgments of the actor to begin with. An observer who may have a positive view of the actor is likely to see a smile as an expression of warmth and a moment of silence as a sign of introspection. For an observer with a negative view of the actor, the smile might be seen as insincere or perhaps as a manipulation attempt, and the silence might be viewed as awkwardness or disinterest.

Confirmation Bias

It is hard to imagine an idea or a belief about which there is not both supportive and contrary evidence. Think of any hotly contested issue of the day–the death penalty, legalization of marijuana, gun control, climate change, the effect of tax policy on the economy, and so on. One would think that people–the brainiest species on earth–would evaluate the evidence on both sides of these issues before coming down on one side or the other. Especially in the age of easy access to information (e.g., internet search engines), people can reasonably be expected to check the sources and critically evaluate both sides of an argument.

As reasonable as this sounds, it couldn't be further from the truth (although we recommend you consider evidence to the contrary!). After all, people disagree intensely about each of the above issues and feel as though the evidence points only in their direction. This issue has not gone unnoticed in social psychology, and the preponderance of evidence points unequivocally to a very different model of how people consider whether ideas or beliefs are valid. Even if people are not strongly invested in the idea or belief, but are simply interested in whether it might be true, they tend to display a *confirmation bias* (e.g., Klayman & Ha, 1987; Shermer, 2011; Skov & Sherman, 1986). People tend to test a proposition by searching for evidence that would support it and ignoring evidence that does not support it.

Let's say you are curious whether washing your car makes it likely that it will rain the next day–a fairly popular superstition, actually. This is a rather silly idea and you wouldn't want to bet money on it. Still, in thinking about the matter, you probably think primarily about the number of times car washing was followed by rain. What you don't consider–but should, of course–are the three other combinations and their relative occurrence: the times you didn't wash the car and it rained anyway, the times you didn't wash the car and it didn't rain, and the times you washed the car and it didn't rain. Even if all four combinations occurred with equal frequency–let's say 10–you would count as evidence the 10 times your suspicion was confirmed, giving little credence to the other 30 cases that don't confirm it.

The confirmation bias is particularly strong when people are committed to an idea or belief (Dawson, Gilovich, & Regan, 2002; Ditto & Lopez, 1992; Gilovich, 1983; Kruglanski & Webster, 1996; Kunda, 1990). Consider, for example, how information about the effectiveness of the death penalty is processed by people who support the death penalty and by those who don't. Lord, Ross, and Lepper (1979) asked people on both sides of this controversial issue to read two different (bogus) state-by-state comparisons. In one, the comparisons showed that crime rates are not any lower in states with the death penalty, but that the crime rate went down in a few states as soon as the death penalty was put in place. In the other, the evidence was the opposite: crime rates were lower in states with the death penalty, but the crime rate when up in a few states as soon as they implemented the death penalty. The question was how participants on either side of the death penalty debate would make use of this information.

In line with the confirmation bias, both proponents and opponents of the death penalty came away more convinced than ever of their belief (see Figure 7.5). They did this by emphasizing the data that supported their position and dismissed as irrelevant or flawed the contradictory data. When exposed to state-by-state comparisons showing that crime rates were not lower in death penalty states but that the crime rate dropped in a few states when the death penalty was adopted, the anti-death penalty participants focused on the first point but pro-death penalty participants focused on the second point. However, when exposed to contradictory comparisons–showing that crime rates were lower in death penalty states but that crime rate increased in a few states after the death penalty was adopted–the anti-death penalty participants focused on the second point, whereas the pro-death penalty participants focused on the first point.

The confirmation bias is not limited to big issues, but plays a prominent role in everyday life, shaping how people think about one another. Think of a good friend whom you consider to be friendly and sensitive to other people's feelings. The confirmation bias suggests that when asked for evidence in support of this judgment, you would recall the many instances in which the person acted in a friendly manner. There may be evidence to the contrary–occasions in which the person was critical or downright nasty–but this evidence is not given equal air time when discussing the person. By the same token, if you know someone else that you consider critical and insensitive, your natural tendency would be to consider only evidence that supports this conclusion, even if the person gets along just fine with most people much of the time.

Illusory Correlation

Sometimes people are not looking to confirm an existing impression, or even to test whether a person has a particular trait. To the contrary, they may want to understand what someone is like, without having preconceptions. Even here,

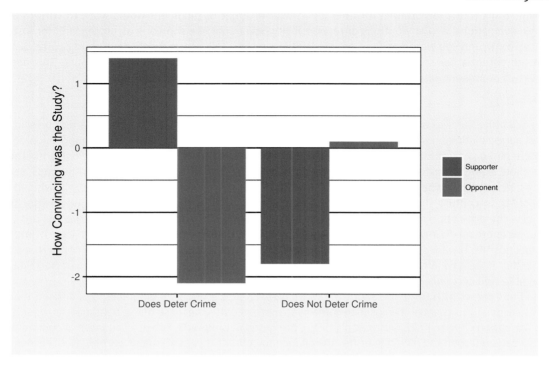

FIGURE 7.5 Confirmation Bias by People Holding Opposing Opinions on the Death Penalty. Positive Numbers Indicate Agreement.
Source: Adapted from Lord et al. (1979)

however, they may still come away with an inaccurate judgment. In fact, people often see things as related when they are not. This tendency is known as the *illusory correlation* (Chapman & Chapman, 1969; Eder, Fiedler, & Hamm-Eder, 2011; Hamilton & Gifford, 1976; Murphy et al., 2011; Ratliff & Nosek, 2010).

The most common form of illusory correlation is the tendency to see a connection between two infrequent or distinctive events. Imagine that you happen to think about someone you haven't seen in years and then later that day the person sends you an e-mail message. You might find it difficult not to see a connection between these—you might even entertain the idea that thinking about things can make them happen! From a statistical point of view, this is silly. Consider how many people you think of each day and how many daily e-mail messages you receive. In the vast majority of cases, there is no connection whatsoever—you think about one person but get a message from someone else. But the one-time pairing of these two unusual events carries more weight than does a statistical analysis. The mind's tendency to see patterns (Shermer, 2011) is operative even when an apparent pattern does not hold up to careful analysis.

Biases in Action

Sometimes you observe others at a distance and have little or no expectation that you will encounter them, let alone develop some sort of relationship. Politicians, movie stars, sports figures, and high-profile criminals provide examples of this type of social judgment. More commonly, your judgments of others take place in an interpersonal context, or at least in a context where interaction with the target of judgment is possible. Acquaintances, fellow students, coworkers, neighbors, and store clerks provide familiar examples of this type of judgment. Your degree of interdependence with such targets may be quite low, but the mere possibility of social interaction can nonetheless influence the social judgment process.

You might think that the potential for interaction with a target of judgment would work to correct erroneous impressions, evaluations, and attributions of responsibility. You might see someone as unpleasant, for instance, but then realize how wrong you were once you get to know him or her. This can certainly happen, of course. But it is also likely that the potential for social interaction only serves to strengthen an erroneous judgment. This possibility is reflected in two prominent action biases: *autistic hostility* and the *self-fulfilling prophecy*.

Autistic Hostility

All serious scientific theories are put to the test—that's what makes them serious. The same cannot be said for some of the most serious judgments that people develop about each other. A person may form an impression of someone else, evaluate him or her on some basis, or allocate responsibility for an action to him or her, but bring the process to a halt without going the extra step to see whether the impression, evaluation, or causal attribution is warranted.

This is especially likely when the judgment in question is negative. Theodore Newcombe (1947) coined the term *autistic hostility* to capture this asymmetry in testing the validity of positive and negative judgments. The asymmetry reflects the distinction between approach and avoid that was discussed in Chapter 4. If we feel positive about something, we approach it; if we feel negative toward something, we avoid it. This is clearly the case in interpersonal life. If we feel positive toward someone, we are motivated to seek out him or her for interaction or perhaps to build a relationship. But if we have a negative assessment of someone, we keep our distance from him or her, avoid contact if at all possible, and certainly do not cultivate a relationship.

If we do not interact with someone about whom we have formed a negative judgment, it is difficult if not impossible for the judgment to change—except to become even more negative because of the potential for thought-induced attitude polarization (Tesser, 1976; Wilson et al., 1995), discussed in Chapter 3. The unwillingness to communicate with a negatively valued target and give him or her the chance to counter this assessment perpetuates feelings that may be totally unwarranted. This is troubling enough in interpersonal encounters. It is especially troubling when the target of a negative judgment is an entire group of people (e.g., a racial or ethnic group, a religion, a foreign country).

Self-Fulfilling Prophecy

Sometimes our hypotheses are tested—and the results only seem to confirm our assessments. What we don't recognize, however, is our role in producing biased results. Even if the judgment is totally unwarranted, acting on the basis of the judgment can set in motion a chain of events that produces a new reality. This chain of events is commonly referred to as the *self-fulfilling prophecy* (Darley & Fazio, 1980; Jussim, 1986; Smith, Jussim, & Eccles, 1999).

Rosenthal and Jacobson (1968) provided a dramatic demonstration of the self-fulfilling prophecy in an unexpected setting: a grade school classroom. Children in an elementary school in San Francisco took an intelligence test. Beyond providing a measure of each child's IQ at the time, the test was said to predict whether the child would "bloom" and show significant gains in IQ over time. The teachers were actually the unwitting participants in this study. They were told that some of the children (about 20% in each classroom) had scored quite high on the "blooming" portion of the test and thus were likely to show impressive gains in intellectual development over the next several months. This information was false—the children identified as "bloomers" were chosen completely at random. And of course, the children knew nothing about their test scores. So the issue was whether teachers' expectations—which were not grounded in reality—would have any effect on the children's performance.

To test this possibility, the children were administered the same IQ test at the end of the school year. The results were dramatic—and sobering (see Figure 7.6). The children who were labeled—randomly—as "bloomers" did in fact show larger gains in IQ than did their "non-bloomer" classmates. The halo effect for "bloomers" extended to a host of personality qualities as well—compared to "non-bloomers," the "bloomers" were seen as better adjusted, more appealing, more affectionate, and less needy for social approval from others. Some of the children in the "non-bloomer" group also demonstrated gains in IQ. But rather than perceiving these children in the same positive terms as the "bloomers," the teachers tended to react negatively to their unexpected improvement. In fact, the more a "non-bloomer" student's IQ increased, the more that he or she was viewed as poorly adjusted, uninteresting, and unaffectionate! Apparently, behavior that contradicts one's negative expectations can be a source of irritation rather than admiration.

The self-fulfilling prophecy is not limited to special contexts such as the classroom, but is a fairly common feature of everyday social situations (Darley & Fazio, 1980). Imagine talking to someone whom you have been led to believe

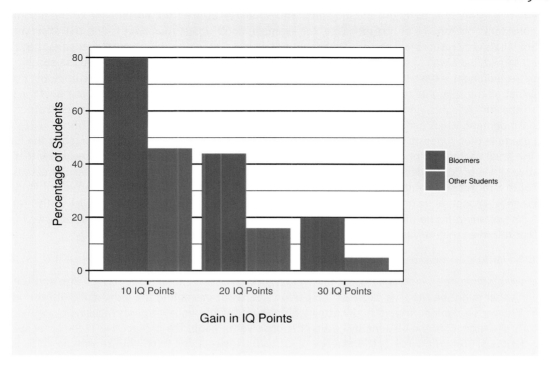

FIGURE 7.6 The Self-Fulfilling Prophecy in the Classroom
Source: Adapted from Rosenthal & Jacobson (1968)

(falsely) is feeling stressed and is a little sensitive and edgy. Just expecting the person to act in this manner can promote actions on your part that cause the expectation to be fulfilled—even if that's the last thing you want to happen. For example, you might stand a little further apart than you normally would, you might smile a bit too much and come off as insincere, and you might steer the conversation to the most benign and least upsetting topics imaginable ("what a nice day today—and so many birds!"). Now consider the effect of your well-intended behavior strategy on the other person. He or she might feel patronized by your tone of voice, body language, and choice of things to talk about. Or the person might note your discomfort and become self-conscious about his or her behavior. The person might not be stressed at the outset, but as the awkward conversation continues to degenerate into pointless utterances, he or she might very well show signs of discomfort and stress. Just the sort of behavior you would expect from an edgy, stressed-out person!

Change in Social Judgment

The biases in thinking and action create the impression that once a judgment is formed, nothing can be done to change it. People can change, of course, or else there would never be growth in people's thinking, nor would a meeting of minds be possible between people with different points of view. But what does it take for a firmly held judgment—a trait inference, an evaluation, or an attribution—to lose its grip and give way to another way of thinking?

Disassembly and Reconfiguration

You might think that if someone has an erroneous judgment about a target person, the best strategy for correcting the judgment is to point out the errors in the person's assessment. This strategy is actually doomed to failure—if anything, it runs the risk of making the person double down on his or her assessment. People react defensively when their beliefs and attitudes are challenged. Sometimes, in fact, challenges are taken as an insult and can promote a hostile or even an aggressive response (e.g., Baumeister et al., 1996).

An alternative strategy is to ignore the judgment altogether—or at least the bottom line of the judgment. If an observer considers someone to be irresponsible, for example, don't waste your time telling the observer that the person is actually a very responsible person. That could end up in a "is too!" versus "is not!" battle that goes nowhere. Instead, you should find a way to *disassemble* or *deconstruct* the judgment, calling attention to the specific thoughts upon which the judgment is based. Remember, the primary motive in social judgment is not accuracy, but *coherence*—the feeling that all the thoughts relevant to a judgment are mutually consistent and support one another. By calling attention to specific thoughts, and isolating these thoughts so they are not considered together with other thoughts or the global judgment, you are in a position to introduce incoherence into the person's judgment.

A vivid example that suggests a different way of thinking about the actor, for example, can start the ball rolling. From this low-level vantage point, you are in a position to rebuild the person's judgment in a new way that provides an alternative sense of coherence for the specific thoughts. Simply asking a person to consider the details of his or her behavior in a recent social encounter, for example, can make him or her vulnerable to subsequent feedback suggesting that he is a cooperative or a competitive person (Wegner et al., 1986). Davis and Knowles (1999) refer to this process as *disrupt and reframe*—first *disrupt* the coherence of a person's way of thinking or acting, then introduce a new idea that *reframes* the relevant information in a way that reestablishes coherence.

Perspective Taking

Inferences about someone's personality occur fairly automatically and commonly fail to take into account features of the context that might be the true cause of the person's behavior prompting the judgment. With this in mind, to change an observer's judgment—that is, to undermine his or her trait inference—requires focusing his or her attention on the actor's situation. This can be done by getting the observer to adopt the perspective of the actor and imagine how he or she feels. This, of course, is the essence of *empathy*. Instructions to empathize with an actor essentially turn observers into actors. This approach thus redirects the observer's attention from the actor to the actor's situation (e.g., Regan & Totten, 1975).

So while an uninstructed observer is inclined to explain an actor's nervousness by inferring corresponding personality traits (e.g., insecurity, anxiety), the empathic observer is more inclined to identify causes for nervousness in the actor's situation—perhaps the person with whom he or she is interacting, for example, or the stressful nature of the interaction setting. In the absence of taking the actor's perspective, "behavior engulfs the field" (Heider, 1958), so that the forces in the situation are not considered. If the observer can be induced to take the actor's perspective, however, he or she sees things differently—the field in a sense engulfs the behavior.

SUMMING UP AND LOOKING AHEAD

- **People spend a substantial portion of time thinking about and judging one another, a tendency that has proven highly adaptive in evolutionary history and continues to be adaptive in contemporary life. Three types of judgment are especially useful in social life: identifying the important characteristics of individuals (personality inference), distinguishing between good and bad people (evaluation), and assessing responsibility for behavior (causal attribution).**
- **People make inferences about one another's personality rapidly and on the basis of minimal information. Cognitive heuristics are used to infer qualities about a target even when direct evidence is lacking. In addition to inferring the target's behavioral dispositions (traits), people attribute mental states to the target, a process that is biased by their evaluation of him or her.**
- **Specific characteristics of someone tend to be integrated to promote a global evaluation of the person. People employ two basic dimensions of evaluation—warmth and competence—with other people seen as having personalities that reflect various combinations of these dimensions.**
- **In assessing responsibility for behavior, people distinguish between causes that are internal to the actor and those that reside in the situation in which the action occurred. The default tendency is to see the actor as primarily responsible for his or her behavior by making inferences about his or her personality that correspond to the behavior. When making attributions for their own behavior, however, people are sensitive to the forces and expectations in the action context. People also demonstrate a self-serving bias in explaining what they have done, attributing good behavior to their personal qualities and bad behavior to the action context.**

Rarely
Sometimes
Often
- How often do you feel starved for company?
Never
Rarely
Sometimes
Often
- How often do you feel shut out and excluded by others?
Never
Rarely
Sometimes
Often

Source: Russell (1996)

Loneliness may be subjective and differ widely across individuals, but it is not unpredictable. For one thing, loneliness is about 50% heritable—some people are predisposed from birth to be especially sensitive to the pain of feeling socially isolated (Boomsma et al., 2005). Loneliness also displays predictable patterns across the life span. Adolescents, for example, are more likely than adults to equate being alone with feeling lonely (Larsen, Csikszentmihalyi, & Graef, 1982). As one gets beyond the tumultuous teen years, one can function comfortably without the presence of others. Loneliness picks up again among senior citizens, however, as they lose important social connections and are at risk for becoming socially isolated (Cacioppo & Hawkley, 2013). Contemporary society attends to the financial and medical conditions of older adults, but gives very little attention to their social needs. They are on their own if they have few people whom they trust or with whom they can interact, yet this is the predicament in which older people find themselves in today's world. A survey conducted in 2010 revealed a 50% increase since 2001 in loneliness among people 45 years of age and older in the United States (Edmondson, 2010).

Both sexes experience loneliness, but they tend to do so under somewhat different circumstances. Males feel lonely when they are isolated from group interactions, whereas females feel lonely when they lack close one-on-one relationships (Berg & McQuinn, 1986; Stokes & Levin, 1986). This difference plays to sex-role stereotypes, with males valuing teamwork (e.g., sports, coordinated activities) and females placing greater value on face-to-face interaction (e.g., sharing feelings and personal information). But the difference is a matter of degree and there are certainly important exceptions. Anyone, whether hyper-masculine or hyper-feminine, can experience loneliness if deprived of meaningful social connections (e.g., Stroebe, Stroebe, Abakoumkin, & Schut, 1996).

Loneliness is more than an unpleasant feeling. It can have enormous consequences for one's health—physical as well as psychological—and it can interfere with many areas of life, including those that have little to do with being around other people (Allen, Uchino, & Hafen, 2015; Cacioppo & Hawkley, 2009). Loneliness is associated with social anxiety, depression, and suicidal ideation and behavior. It is also a serious risk factor for alcoholism, obesity, and cardiovascular disease (Holt-Lunstad, Smith, & Layton, 2010). In response to stressful events (e.g., preparing to give a speech or taking a challenging test), lonely people experience greater inflammation—an immune mechanism with links to a host of physical maladies—than do people who are not lonely (Jaremka et al., 2013). And because loneliness is associated with stress and vigilance to social threats, it can function as a *cognitive load* that diminishes executive resources (Cacioppo & Hawkley, 2009). As noted in Chapter 6 ("Personal Control"), when executive resources are depleted (e.g., by stress, alcohol, or excessive self-regulation), people have a difficult time controlling their impulses and resisting temptations of various kinds—from eating candy bars to reacting angrily to an annoying person.

Loneliness can be looked upon as a signal that prompts people to renew social connections by changing their behavior (Cacioppo & Hawkley, 2013). In that sense, it is like any other aversive state (e.g., hunger, thirst, physical pain) that motivates people to take corrective action. At the same time, though, loneliness promotes suspicion and negativity in judging others' actions, which can work at cross-purposes with restoring social connections. In effect, when people feel lonely, they experience an *approach-avoid conflict* in their social relations—they want to affiliate with others but they have low expectations that their overtures will be accepted or reciprocated. As noted in Chapter 7 ("Social Judgment"), negative expectations can bias the way another person's behavior is interpreted and can even promote the very behavior one fears. Loneliness, in other words, can become a self-fulfilling prophecy.

You might think that loneliness is a thing of the past because of social media and electronic communication. Even if a person feels as though he or she could enter a room filled with peers and yet go unnoticed, he or she has plenty of other options in today's world for connecting with others. With a simple mouse click, anyone can create, or at least tap into, social networks that are often buzzing with online interaction. And the number and variety of people with whom a person can connect far exceed the number and variety that even the most popular person could encounter through old-fashioned face-to-face interaction. Arguably the biggest advance in this new form of social interaction is the smartphone, which burst upon the scene in 2007 with the introduction of Apple's iPhone. These devices are small enough to be carried in one's pocket, making them a potential source of constant communication with others, whether by voice or text message. Not surprisingly, they have become an ubiquitous feature of social life, enabling a person to be in contact with others as often as he or she desires. And people, especially young people, have acted upon this potential—by 2017, 75% of American teens owned an iPhone.

Has this new means of social interaction gratification brought an end to loneliness? The short answer is "no"—far from it. In fact, as documented by Jean Twenge in *iGen* (2017), a book that documents the habits, lifestyles, and emotional lives of Americans born since 1995, loneliness has shown a dramatic *increase* since the introduction of the iPhone (see Figure 8.1). For this generation, the sudden potential for electronic communication without the need for face-to-face interaction coincided with the emerging preoccupation with social relations and fitting in that character-izes the adolescent years. Unlike all previous generations of teens, iGen teens could attempt to forge and maintain social relations without the benefit (or embarrassment) of eye contact, facial expressions, and gestures that define

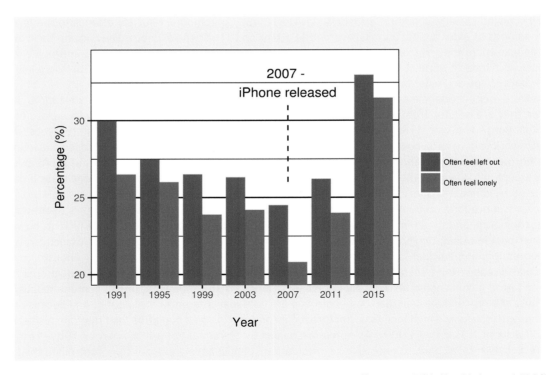

FIGURE 8.1 Percentage of 8th, 10th, and 12th Graders Who Agree or Mostly Agree With the Statement "I Often Feel Left Out of Things" or "A Lot of Times I Feel Lonely"
Source: Adapted from Twenge (2017)

face-to-face interaction. As we shall see in a later section, these features of *nonverbal communication* typically carry greater weight in conveying people's thoughts and feelings toward one another than do the words they exchange. The bonding that occurs in social relations, moreover, is created through the reciprocity and synchronization of eye gaze, hand gestures, and bodily posture (e.g., Chartrand & Bargh, 1999). Twenge (2017) points to many reasons why the heavy reliance on smartphones (and other means of electronic communication) is associated with increased loneliness (and the stress and depression promoted by loneliness), but the absence of nonverbal signals in smartphone communication is no doubt an important factor.

Social Rejection

It is bad enough to feel lonely, with one's need for social contact going unfulfilled. It is all the more devastating when one has established a connection with someone, only to experience *social rejection* by the person (Baumeister & Tice, 1990; Williams, 2001). Rejection by a close friend or a romantic partner is particularly painful, of course, but even feeling excluded by total strangers in a setting devoid of intimacy can be unpleasant. The pain associated with such exclusion has been demonstrated by Kip Williams and his colleagues in the "ball toss" paradigm (Williams, Cheung, & Choi, 2000). In this procedure, three people simply toss a ball back and forth. Only one of them, however, is a naïve participant. The other two are accomplices of the experimenter and follow a pre-arranged script. In a common variation, the participant is excluded from the activity after a few tosses and never gets the ball again. This may seem fairly trivial in comparison to romantic rejection, but it is sufficient to make the excluded participant feel quite bad—not simply angry or frustrated, but anxious and despondent as well.

Social exclusion in this paradigm can induce negative emotions even if one is excluded by members of a disliked group such as the Ku Klux Klan (Williams, 2001). Exclusion hurts even when one is playing with strangers over a computer hook-up. *Cyberball* is a virtual "ball toss" game in which the participant is led to believe he or she is playing with two other participants sitting at computers elsewhere who can toss the ball to either player. The participant is included for the first few minutes, but then excluded by the other players for the remaining 3 minutes. This short time period of ostracism produces significant increases in self-reported levels of anger and sadness. People feel rejected even if they know they are only playing against the computer! (Zadro, Williams, & Richardson, 2004). The aversive nature of being excluded is experienced even when exclusion is associated with a financial reward and inclusion entails a financial loss. Money, it seems, cannot make up for feeling rejected.

The pain associated with rejection is not all in one's head. It can be felt physically as well. Everyone knows what it is like to get an "icy stare," a "cold shoulder," or a "chilly reception" as opposed to getting a "warm reception" or feeling a "warm glow." You might think that cold and warm are simply metaphors. When people reject someone, after all, their eyes and shoulders don't show a sudden drop in temperature, nor do their faces literally become warmer when they meet someone they like. True enough, but recent research suggests that these metaphors for social experience are reflected in people's experience of and preference for actual temperatures.

Zhong and Leonardelli (2008) asked participants to recall occasions in which they were either socially included or excluded and then to estimate the temperature of the lab room. Those who recalled an exclusion episode felt that the room was cooler than did those who recalled an inclusion episode. In a follow-up study, participants had an online virtual interaction during which they were either excluded or included by the other (bogus) individuals. Afterward, they were asked to express their preference for a warm food (soup), a warm drink (coffee), or a cold drink (Coke). Compared to participants who experienced the "warmth" of inclusion, those who experienced exclusion reported greater preference for warm food and drinks—presumably to make up for the "coldness" of their social experience (see Figure 8.2).

The effects of rejection go beyond feeling bad. In fact, rejection can motivate a variety of behaviors. Some behaviors are benign or even positive. When rejected, a person might try extra hard to reestablish the social connection or perhaps establish new connections to make up for what he or she has lost. But other behavioral responses to rejection can be dysfunctional or destructive. People chosen at random to receive messages of social exclusion become more aggressive, more willing to cheat, less willing to help others, and more likely to pursue short-term over long-term goals (Twenge, Catanese, & Baumeister, 2002).

Not everyone has the same reaction to rejection. People who have low self-esteem or are high in social anxiety are especially vulnerable to rejection (Zadro et al., 2004). There are also gender differences in response to social rejection. Women tend to show greater nonverbal engagement by initiating eye contact and leaning toward the person who seems to be rejecting them. Men tend to disengage when rejected and display face-saving techniques, such as

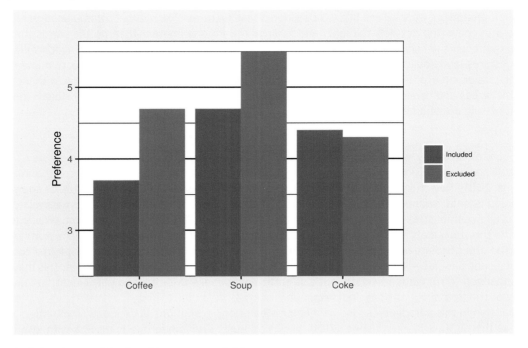

FIGURE 8.2 Ostracism and Feeling Warm versus Cold
Source: Adapted from Zhong & Leonardelli (2008)

pretending to be unaffected and uninterested. This suggests that women are motivated to regain a sense of social belonging, whereas men are more interested in regaining the self-esteem they lost because of the rejection. It is noteworthy that virtually all of the school shootings reported over the past several years have involved male students (Leary, Kowalski, & Smith, 2003). When female students are rejected, they might try to regain social connections or become despondent. Male students might have these reactions as well, but they are also inclined to seek vengeance on those who have rejected them because of the toll that rejection takes on their self-esteem.

Ostracism clearly hurts the person who is excluded, but it can also hurt the person responsible for the exclusion. Legate, DeHean, Weinstein, and Ryan (2013) demonstrated the double-edged nature of ostracism using *Cyberball*, the "ball toss" paradigm described earlier. Participants thought they were playing a computerized game with two people, but the moves of these individuals were actually controlled by a computer. In an *ostracized* condition, the participant was excluded by the two other players; in an *ostracizer* condition, however, the participant was instructed to exclude one player from the game. After the game, all participants were asked how they felt about their experience in the game.

Not surprisingly, the ostracized participants felt bad, but so did those who did the ostracizing. They were included in the game, but this did not make up for the bad feeling they experienced in making another person feel excluded. Although unpleasant, this feeling is adaptive because it inhibits us when we feel the temptation to exclude certain people from certain activities or our social network. Think how hard it is, for example, to reject a friend request on Facebook from a casual acquaintance, even if you aren't particularly interested in his or her vacation plans or feelings about the final episode of *Game of Thrones*.

Box 8.2   Can Social Rejection Make You Obese and Sick?

Social stress is not only bad for one's mental health, but it can also wreak havoc on one's physical health. Being excluded or ostracized from a group is especially damaging, but even low or uncertain status is a group can promote stress reactions that affect the body in unwanted ways. These sources of social discomfort can cause the body to deposit fat in the abdomen, which increases the risk of heart disease (Shively, Register, & Clarkson, 2009). Excess fat of any kind is bad, of course, but "belly fat" behaves differently than fat in other locations (buttocks, legs, etc.) and tends to have more serious health consequences.

To see how social status affects the development of heart disease, female monkeys were fed a Western-style diet that contained fat and cholesterol. The monkeys were housed in groups, enabling them to establish a pecking order from dominant to subordinate. The subordinate monkeys were frequently excluded from group grooming sessions (which often takes the form of checking for fleas, ticks, and other bugs in one another's body hair). They were also often the target of aggression by the other monkeys. The researchers found that this treatment had a physical toll: the subordinate monkeys developed more fat in the abdominal cavity than did the other monkeys. Social subordination causes the release of stress hormones that promote fat accumulation in the abdomen. This fat, in turn, promotes the build-up of plaque in blood vessels that leads to heart disease—the leading cause of death worldwide.

The results of this research suggest that the obesity epidemic in the United States and other developed countries is not a straightforward consequence of the availability of junk food. Sure, double-cheese bacon burgers are not a particularly wise culinary choice, but their effect is amplified by uncertain status in a social group—which may be just as prevalent today as the opportunities to purchase cheap junk food.

The Goals of Social Interaction

OK, people clearly need and value social connections. But we typically have some choice regarding the people we interact with. After all, we do not start talking to everyone we run into on the street. Why do we choose to interact with some people but not with others? And once a social contact is made, we have considerable latitude in how we interact with the person. What do we expect or want to get out of our face-to-face interactions? Of course, social interaction can satisfy a number of specific motives. When people talk to one another, they may seek answers to specific questions, exchange gossip, or simply pass time while waiting for the bus. But behind the surface motives of social interaction, what psychological concerns are activated?

Research suggests that people approach social interaction with a small number of basic agendas in mind. These motives may not be expressed explicitly (e.g., "I want you to like me!") but they nonetheless influence people's choice of an interaction partner and the way in which they interact with the chosen person.

Acceptance, Liking, and Respect

In light of the basic human need for social connectedness, it is not surprising that people's primary concern in social interaction is *acceptance*. When we seek out people, after all, we aren't looking to be rejected or ignored. But our motives for social interaction do not stop there. It is nice to belong, but it is also nice to be *liked* or even *respected*. But what if these concerns—acceptance, liking, and respect—cannot all be satisfied in our interactions with a particular person? To make it more interesting, imagine you are asked to choose between two people for a social interaction—*Person A*, who would like to strike up a relationship with you but isn't likely to shower you with liking and respect, and *Person B*, who is likely to express liking for you but isn't particularly interested in starting a new relationship. Whom would you choose—the accepting person or the admiring person?

In considering this choice, remember that the first order of business in social life is feeling connected to others—even if that connection is not necessarily based on a great deal of love and respect. Apart from the benefits that social connections provide (mutual activities, a shared reality, etc.), social connections are critical to the formation of a clear and positive self-concept. As noted above in the discussion of loneliness, a person who does not feel connected in some way to others is likely to feel insecure and have an unflattering self-image. This suggests that people's level of self-esteem can be looked upon as a measure of their social connectedness—people with high self-esteem feel more connected to others than do people with low self-esteem. Only after people feel connected and have a secure feeling about themselves can they raise their sights and concentrate on gaining the liking and respect of others.

This is the essence of the *sociometer hypothesis* (Leary et al., 1995), discussed in Chapter 5 ("Self-Concept"). Lower levels of self-esteem signify a relatively weak sense of social connectedness and thus a correspondingly strong desire to be accepted–even if the acceptance does not guarantee being respected or admired. In contrast, high levels of self-esteem signify satisfaction of belongingness needs. Secure in having social connections, high self-esteem people turn their attention to how positively they are viewed by their interaction partners. With this in mind, return to the choice posed above: interacting with someone who is accepting but does not feel particularly positive about you versus interacting with someone who has little interest in forming a relationship but nonetheless has a very high opinion of you.

Rudich and Vallacher (1999) presented this choice dilemma to college students who had low, moderate, or high self-esteem, based on tests completed at an initial session. The experimenter explained that two students (whose gender was the same as participants) had independently read their test responses and had written a brief summary of the impression they had formed based on these responses. Participants read both summaries, after which they were asked to decide which student they wanted to meet in a get-acquainted session. These summaries varied in two ways: (1) their evaluation of the participant (positive vs. negative), and (2) their interest in forming a friendship with the participant (acceptance vs. rejection).

This is how the *positive evaluation* was worded:

> Based on this person's responses, I believe that this person is socially self-confident. He (she) seems at ease with people he (she) does not know very well. He (she) seems to have little doubt about his (her) social competence and seems to be highly confident. I am highly certain of my evaluation.

This is how the *negative evaluation* was worded:

> From looking at this person's answers, he (she) appears to be ill at ease in social situations. There are probably times when he (she) is around other people and just doesn't know quite what to say. There are times when this person likes being around people, but in some social situations he (she) is uncomfortable and anxious. I am pretty certain that this accurately describes him (her).

This is how the *accepting evaluation* was worded:

> I am looking forward to meeting this person and we would probably make good friends.

This is how the *rejecting evaluation* was worded:

> I don't believe we would get along very well and we would not be likely to form a friendship.

Unbeknownst to the participants, the two potential interaction partners did not exist and their purported summaries were actually prepared by the experimenters. The interest was which student participants would choose to interact with, based on the combinations of evaluation and acceptance versus rejection conveyed in the two summaries. Of special interest was participants' choice when one student's summary expressed positive evaluation but no interest in friendship (*positive/rejecting*) and the other student's summary expressed negative evaluation but high interest in friendship (*negative/accepting*). Would participants base their choice on being accepted (even if that meant they were evaluated somewhat negatively) or on being evaluated positively (even if that meant they were likely to be rejected)?

The results, presented in Figure 8.3, are in line with the sociometer hypothesis. Participants with relatively low self-esteem displayed an overwhelming preference for the negative/accepting student (88% to 12%), as did those with moderate self-esteem (77% to 23%). Apparently, the prospect of being accepted in the subsequent get-acquainted session was more important to these participants than was being viewed favorably. Participants with high self-esteem, on the other hand, tend to choose the positive/rejecting student over the negative/accepting student (62% to 38%). Because high self-esteem signifies security with respect to belongingness, these participants were primarily concerned with being viewed in positive terms, even if the student who felt this way had little desire to form a friendship with them.

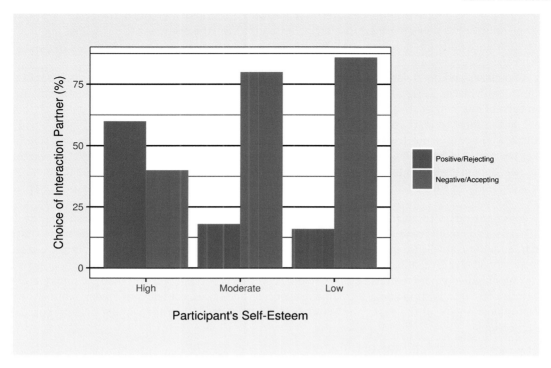

FIGURE 8.3 Self-Esteem and Choice of Interaction Partners
Source: Adapted from Rudich & Vallacher (1999)

Cognitive Clarity

When reality is ambiguous, people turn to one another to clarify matters. This is true for mundane events—the unexpected sound or the out-of-the-blue compliment—but it can also scale up to the level of ideology and values. Many public policy issues (e.g., healthcare, taxation) are complex and can be viewed as warranted or unjustified, depending on one's viewpoint. How other people make sense of such issues can play a larger role in achieving "understanding" than can independently checking the relevant facts. And if a collection of people has yet to form relationships with one another, the rapid convergence on social consensus in response to an ambiguous event can be the trigger that makes it happen. In the absence of the event, they might not have noticed one another, let alone taken the time to forge relationships.

Uncertainty is one thing; an uncertain danger is quite another. The anxiety and stress associated with adverse consequences that are not well-defined increase the importance of other people in clarifying reality (Schachter, 1959; Kirkpatrick & Shaver, 1988). This can be seen in people's response to national crises (e.g., the aftermath of the 9/11 terrorist attacks), social changes that upset traditional norms and values (e.g., gay rights, religious diversity), and proposed courses of action with unknown consequences (e.g., preparation for warfare). In such instances, there is an uptick in people searching out others—usually those in the same boat and with the same set of values and life experiences—to clarify what has happened and what should be done in response. The interaction may turn out to be fun, but that is frosting on the cake—the real motivation is achieving *cognitive clarity* and thereby reducing the uncertainty of an event.

The desire to seek out social interaction when faced with stressful circumstances is demonstrated in a study by Stanley Schachter (1959). College students were individually informed that they would receive an injection as part of the experiment concerning the effects of a new drug on color vision, but they were not told whether or not the shot would be painful. They were given the option of waiting by themselves or with other students anticipating the same event. As Schachter predicted, students by a wide margin chose to wait with the other students. A concern with cognitive clarity can promote social interaction, even with total strangers.

Sometimes the stress people experience dates to unpleasant or traumatic events in their past. In such instances, people may be reluctant to seek out others, preferring instead to keep the event and their feelings about it private. Is this advisable? When a person experiences something horrible and traumatic, is it better to bury it as deep as possible or to open up and discuss the event and the feelings it produces with other people?

James Pennebaker and his colleagues have investigated this issue in a series of experiments (Pennebaker, 1997; Niederhoffer & Pennebaker, 2002). Pennebaker and Beale (1986), for example, asked college students to spend 15 minutes on each of four consecutive nights writing about either a traumatic event (e.g., rape, death of a sibling) or a trivial event. In the short term, those who wrote about traumatic events felt worse (and had higher blood pressure) than did those who wrote about trivial events. But the long-term benefits favored those who described traumatic events. Over the next 6 months, they reported having fewer illnesses and were less likely to visit the health center. In a more dramatic demonstration of the power of "opening up," Holocaust survivors who disclosed the most about their World War II experiences showed improvement in their health over several months (Pennebaker, Barger, & Tiebout, 1989).

So why does opening up about traumatic events lead to better health? The reason appears to be the coherence that is achieved by communicating with someone about these events. People who improve the most are those who begin with fragmentary and disorganized descriptions of their problem, but end with coherent, organized stories that explain the event and give it meaning (Pennebaker, 1997). Once an event is given meaning, it not only loses its potential for inducing negative emotion, it also stops being a source of preoccupation and thought suppression (Wegner, Quillian, & Houston, 1996). Writing about a traumatic event—or better yet, confiding in others about it—helps people gain a better understanding of the event and allows them to move on in their life without being preoccupied by an unresolved problem.

Social Networks

Social interaction plays a role in social life that goes beyond people's immediate concerns and desires. Through contact and affiliation, people create *social networks* that can expand to include large numbers of people. This is the insight of *balance theory*, a classic perspective on social relations developed by Fritz Heider (1958). Balance theory starts with the basic assumption that people try to maintain consistency—or "balance"—among their beliefs, cognitions, and feelings. Heider suggested that the fundamental process can be seen in a 3-person set or *triad*. Picture yourself (A) as one of the three people, with two acquaintances (B and C) filling the remaining slots. Let's say you like both of them and that they like each other as well. This is a *balanced configuration*, with positive feelings defining each of the dyadic (2-person) relations—A and B, A and C, and B and C.

But now imagine that B and C can't stand one another, even though you have positive relations with both of them. This is an *imbalanced configuration*. Imagine what it would be like if the three of you had to spend an hour together with no possibility of escape. The interaction would be awkward, if not downright tense, with little likelihood of finding common ground as the interaction proceeds. You could try to agree with B and C, but since they are likely to disagree with each other, you would find it difficult to find something to say that doesn't offend one of them. In such situations, people expend psychological energy to restore balance. Your first choice might be to get B and C to like each other—this would produce a nice set of positive relations all the way around. Failing that, you might choose sides, continuing to like one (say, B) but developing a dislike for the other (C). Now you have created balance of a different kind: friendship in which two people (you and B) have a common enemy (C).

Heider examined triadic relations in terms of all possible combinations of positive (+) and negative (−) feelings. He then proposed a simple algebraic rule for determining whether each combination is balanced or imbalanced. Here's the rule: *things are balanced if the product of the three sentiments is positive*. Try a couple of examples. If your friend (+) is liked by another person (+), you can achieve balance (and avoid imbalance) by liking that person (+), since (+) *times* (+) *times* (+) = +. You may recognize this process at work in advertising, where the goal is to get people to like an unfamiliar product. An admired movie star or athlete (+), for example, expresses his or her liking (+) for a particular brand of shoes (or a political candidate), and you are expected to adopt the same feeling (+) toward the product (person), perhaps even purchasing it (or voting for it) without looking deeper into its (or his or her) quality (qualifications). As another example, imagine you have an enemy (−) who is disliked by another person (−). In this case, you can achieve balance by liking that person (+), since (−) times (−) times (+) = +. In effect, "the enemy of your enemy is your friend" (Aronson & Cope, 1968).

Research testing balance theory predictions employ one of two approaches. In one, two relationships are established in a triad and the focus is how participants feel about the remaining relationship. This approach characterizes the examples presented above: A knows how he or she feels about B and how B feels about C, and uses this information to form feelings toward C that create balance. In the other approach, participants are presented with triads in which all the relationships are specified, with the triads being either balanced or imbalanced. The focus in this approach is how participants feel about balanced versus imbalanced relationships and how well each type is remembered. The results show that people feel better about balanced relationships and tend to have an easier time remembering them as well (Gawronski, Walther, & Blank, 2005; Hummert, Crockett, & Kemper, 1990; Nowak, Vallacher, & Burnstein, 1998).

A concern with achieving and maintaining balance is a basic mechanism of mind and social relations. One does need a great deal of information in order to decide whether an unfamiliar object or idea is good or bad—one need only look to see how the object or idea is viewed by friends and enemies. And in deciding whether someone is a potential friend or enemy, one need only consider how this person relates to your current friends and enemies. In this way, expanding networks of social relations can be created without individuals having to form personal relations through one-on-one social interactions.

Box 8.3   Does the Size of Your Brain Predict the Size of Your Social Networks?

The size of your *amygdala*—a subcortical structure of the brain associated with basic emotions—might indicate how large and complex your social network is. Nonhuman primate species that live in larger social groups tend to have larger amygdalas. Bickart et al. (2011) wondered whether this connection holds for human as well, such that people with extensive social networks have amygdalas with greater volume. To find out, they measured two features of social networks in a large sample of adults. The first factor was *network size*—simply the total number of people with whom each participant has regular contact. The second factor was *network complexity*—the number of different groups that a participant's contacts can be divided into. These variables were then correlated with the size of participants' amygdala. They also looked at the correlations between the network variables and the size of participants' *hippocampus*—a different subcortical structure that regulates biological motives (e.g., hunger) and thus was not expected to vary in size based on participants' social network size or complexity.

Results revealed that the size of participants' amygdala was indeed correlated with both the size and complexity of their social networks. The correlation did not hold for other social factors, such as life satisfaction or perceived social support. Nor were network size and complexity correlated with the size of participants' hypothalamus, although three other regions in the cerebral cortex (the caudal inferior temporal sulcus, caudal superior frontal gyrus, and subgenual anterior cingulate cortex) were somewhat correlated with the network factors. These regions may have evolved along with the amygdala over millennia to deal with the complexities associated with growing human circles.

Keep in mind, though, the adage that "correlation is not causation." It may be that social network size and complexity promote growth in the amygdala, so that the amygdala increases in volume as people gain more friends and acquaintances. But the opposite causal direction is also plausible. Perhaps some people are born with larger amygdala and this enables (or motivates) them to create larger social networks. To settle the matter, scientists may have to start with babies and follow them through adulthood, measuring their brains and friends at various points along the way.

The Self in Social Interaction

How and Why Do People Try to Control How They Are Seen by Others?

When you interact with someone, you are actually focusing on two people—the other person, of course, but also yourself. Even in a simple conversation, you might be as concerned with how you are perceived by the other person as you are with how you perceive him or her. This dual focus is inevitable because of the human capacity for self-awareness, as discussed in Chapter 5. A person develops a self-concept in part by taking the perspective of others on him or herself, but long after a fairly stable self-view has been established, the person remains sensitive to the perspectives of others with whom he or she interacts (e.g., Carver & Scheier, 1998; Mead, 1934). The person's motivation changes, however, from a concern with forming a self-concept to a desire to project an image of what he or she is like. This simple motive is manifest in different ways, each of which has been thoroughly investigated.

Self-Verification

Sometimes the image that one attempts to create in the mind of an interaction partner matches the self-concept that one has formed over the years. If a person views him or herself as bright, eccentric, and not particularly athletic, for example, he or she wants others to share this view, and will attempt to correct those who don't. This is the essence of *self-verification theory* (Swann, 1990), introduced in Chapter 5. Self-verification is motivated by a desire to maintain and protect a coherent perspective on one's qualities, even those that are not particularly admirable. If a person with a negative view of his or her social skills elicits admiration and warmth in a conversation, for example, he or she might begin acting in a way that turns off the conversation partner's enthusiasm. Faced with being seen in an *accurate but negative* light versus being seen in a *positive but inaccurate* light, people in a self-verification mode opt for the former.

Apart from maintaining coherence in one's self-concept, self-verification facilitates social interaction (Swann, Stein-Seroussi, & Giesler, 1992). If both people in an interaction agree on what one another is like, the interaction is likely to proceed more smoothly. Imagine thinking of yourself as shy and reserved but interacting with someone who expects you to break into snappy patter and witty one-liners at any moment. That mismatch in perceptions of your behavioral tendencies could lead to awkward exchanges ("that's all you've got?"), if not frustration experienced by both of you ("this is not what I had in mind"). But if the other person behaves toward you in a way that matches your self-view, the conversation is far less likely to hit such road bumps and to proceed in accordance with mutual expectations for how to behave.

Beyond its immediate implications for social interaction, self-verification can preserve a social relationship over the long haul. You might be able to interact on a given occasion with someone who sees you differently than you see yourself, but over time the person may become disenchanted as he or she realizes the mistake. Or at least, you might worry that the person will eventually discover the truth about who you are and change his or her feelings about you accordingly. This concern could motivate you to get things straight at the outset of the relationship. So if you feel shy and reserved, you may want to emphasize these qualities in interacting with someone, even though these qualities may not be particularly exciting or match what the person is looking for. Better for the person to know what he or she is getting into than for him or her to become disappointed down the road.

Self-Presentation

The desire to be viewed by other people in a way that matches one's personal self-view can be overridden under some circumstances. Sure, it's nice to have one's self-perceived qualities recognized by others, but it may not always be advantageous. You might think of yourself as friendly and agreeable, for instance, but this is hardly the best quality to project when negotiating for a new car or standing up to someone who intends you harm. To optimize one's outcomes in various social contexts, one may try to create an impression of oneself in the eyes of others—even if the impression is not one that captures one's private self-concept. This feature of social interaction is sometimes referred to as *impression management* but more commonly as *self-presentation* (Goffman, 1959; Leary, 1995; Schlenker, 1980).

Modes of Self-Presentation

Some scholars have argued that social life is like a stage performance (Goffman, 1959). When we interact with other people, what we are really doing is putting on a show designed to elicit reactions in others, who effectively constitute an audience. This is a little strong—spontaneity and honesty in our social relations is common and highly valued, particularly in our relations with those who are close to us. But the attempt to present ourselves in a certain way is nonetheless a basic fixture of social life (Baumeister, 1982; Mead, 1934; Schlenker, 1980; Shrauger & Shoeneman, 1979). Think about occasions in your recent past where you were not only conscious of how you were viewed but also invested in trying to manage that view. What specific view of yourself were you trying to create? And what was your purpose in doing so? Chances are, your self-presentation corresponded to one of five basic modes identified by Edward Jones and Thane Pittman (1982).

These modes and their associated goals are presented in Table 8.1, along with the tactics and risks associated with each. The most frequent—and most thoroughly documented—mode is *ingratiation* (Jones, 1964). The goal is to be seen as a likable person. Besides being inherently rewarding, being liked is instrumental in achieving a variety of other goals, from securing a date to nailing a job interview. There are a variety of tactics at your disposal to get someone to like you. You can agree with everything the person says, compliment the person, offer to do favors for the person, or simply smile and hang on every word the person says.

There are risks to ingratiation, however. After all, the other person is aware of this self-presentation mode and thus is vigilant regarding your sincerity and the possibility of being manipulated. This risk—referred to as the *ingratiator's dilemma*—is especially high in situations where the person knows that it is to your advantage to be liked. In a job interview, for example, the interviewer is aware of your desire to be hired over plenty of other job candidates and so may not trust your expressions of agreement with everything he or she says, and may wonder just how sincere all your smiling really is (e.g., Jones, Davis, & Gergen, 1961).

Being liked is almost always advantageous, but sometimes it is more important to be seen as competent. This is the goal of the *self-promotion* mode. Everyone wants to be considered smart, strong, athletic, or talented in some way, and bragging about one's accomplishments and skills is a shortcut to achieving this view. There are risks in doing so, however. For one, it can run counter to the goal of being liked. After all, no one likes a person who comes across as overly boastful, conceited, and generally full of himself or herself. Beyond that, self-promotion runs the risk of being perceived as phony or even as covering up one's insecurity regarding competence. When a person brags about him or herself incessantly, others might begin to think he or she actually feels inadequate in some way.

When someone is truly competent and others are aware of this, he or she may *downplay* his or her accomplishments, creating an impression of *modesty* in the eyes of others. After a successful action, for example, a person can describe what he or she did in relatively low-level mechanistic terms instead of emphasizing its significance (Vallacher, Wegner, & Frederick, 1987). So rather than saying "I hit a homerun that won the game," a baseball player might say, "aw shucks, I just swung my bat and hit the ball." This combination—established competence but a self-presentation of modesty—can generate liking as well as respect.

Being liked is possible when one is a self-promotion mode, but all pretense of establishing warm relations is lost when one is in an *intimidation* mode. The goal is to be seen as powerful, willing and able to dominate others. This goal makes sense in a confrontation with enemies in everyday life or in a professional setting such as politics or

Table 8.1 Strategies for Managing People's Impressions of Themselves

	Ingratiation
Impression Goal	"I am likable"
Tactics	Give compliments, favors; smile and act attentive
Risks	Being perceived as phony, a sycophant
	Self-Promotion
Impression Goal	"I am competent"
Tactics	Make positive claims about one's self or performance
Risks	Being perceived as conceited or boastful
	Intimidation
Impression Goal	"I am powerful"
Tactics	Make threats, displays of dominance and aggression
Risks	Being perceived as a bully
	Exemplification
Impression Goal	"I am worthy"
Tactics	Make claims of moral superiority, self-denial, suffering
Risks	Being perceived as self-righteous
	Supplication
Impression Goal	"I am weak"
Tactics	Offer submission, plead, self-deprecate
Risks	Being perceived as overly needy

Source: Jones & Pittman (1982)

business where there is intense competition (Carnevale, Pruitt, & Britton, 1979). To create this image, the person might make overt threats or engage in displays of dominance, with icy stares and rigid postures replacing warm looks and smiles. This mode is hardly likely to generate liking. And if pushed too far, it can result in one being seen as a bully who deserves reprimand of some kind.

Competence and intimidation can generate respect and admiration, but so can *exemplification*—the presentation of oneself as morally worthy. Rather than bragging about one's accomplishments or engaging in dominance displays, the person trying to create an image of moral worthiness may make a point of his or her self-denial and suffering in service of some larger good. At a societal level, people who have forgone pleasures and economic security or risked imprisonment in order to further a social cause are admired as heroes and martyrs. Mahatma Gandhi, Martin Luther King Jr., and Mother Teresa are examples of people who made enormous personal sacrifices to improve conditions in their respective societies.

Exemplification is less common in everyday life, but you may know someone who goes out of his or her way to show his or her moral superiority in some way. This person presents him or herself as highly moralistic and makes it known how he or she has done the right thing while avoiding the temptations that mere mortals cannot resist. This self-presentation mode may have the additional effect of making others feel a bit small and guilty when in the person's presence (Gilbert & Jones, 1986). But the person also runs the risk of being perceived as self-righteous and attempting to look better than others—hardly a winning strategy in social relations.

The self-presentation modes to this point all have as their goal a desire to create a positive impression of oneself— as likable, competent, powerful, or moral. Sometimes, though, it is to a person's advantage to be seen as weak, needy, or even helpless. This mode of self-presentation, referred to as *supplication*, can occur when one is truly in need. Following a natural disaster, for example, a person might make it known how helpless he or she is to regain physical or economic security. But supplication can occur as well in everyday social relations. Perhaps you have known someone who looks for sympathy rather than respect, hoping to be taken care of and protected. Appearing weak and submissive can work, generating sympathy and nurturance in others (e.g., Weary & Williams, 1990). But it is a risky strategy because it opens the person up to exploitation, or even abuse. Short of producing these consequences, supplication can produce an image of oneself as overly needy, someone who should be avoided rather than embraced.

Cultural Differences in Self-Presentation

Recall the distinction between independent and interdependent cultures, introduced in Chapter 1 and noted in several contexts since then. You might expect that self-presentation, with its emphasis on self-enhancement, would be more prominent in independent cultures than in the interdependent cultures that characterize much of Asian, Latin American, and African societies. This expectation has been confirmed: whereas people in independent cultures wish to be seen in a positive light by others, people in interdependent cultures are more inclined to criticize themselves in social situations (e.g., Heine et al., 1999). College students in Canada (an independent culture) and Japan (an interdependent culture), for example, responded very differently when told they had done poorly on a test assessing creativity (Heine, Kitayama, & Lehman, 2001; Heine & Renshaw, 2002). The Canadian students tended to dismiss the negative feedback, wanting to maintain and project a positive image of themselves, whereas the Japanese students accepted the criticism and saw it as an opportunity for self-improvement.

But such differences may not reflect the presence versus absence of self-presentation concerns in different cultures. Perhaps independent and interdependent cultures simply differ in their emphasis on different modes of self-presentation. To be viewed positively in cultures like the United States, people emphasize the ways that distinguish them within a group. Wanting to be recognized for their unique talents and contributions, they are inclined to present themselves in ways that look self-enhancing. In cultures that value interdependence, on the other hand, people want to be recognized for fitting in with the group and emphasizing the group's accomplishments. To be seen in these terms, people in these cultures downplay their uniqueness, project an image of modesty, and advertise their willingness to support the group's interests over their own (Sedikides, Gaertner, & Yoshiyasu, 2003). Conceivably, this is a self-presentation strategy designed to achieve the same sorts of goals (e.g., liking, acceptance, respect) that motivate a very different self-presentation strategy in independent cultures.

Self-Monitoring

So there are two conflicting motives regarding the self in social interaction. People want to be seen as they see themselves (*self-verification*), but they also want to be seen in ways that are advantageous in their interactions, even if this means acting in ways that do not reflect their "true" self (*self-presentation*). Which motive predominates depends in part on the reason for interacting in the first place. If social interaction is in service of forming a relationship based on mutual affect and understanding, people want to be seen for who they really are (e.g., Jourard, 1964; Swann et al., 1992)—although there is usually a certain amount of self-presentation that goes in the initial stages of a relationship, when the goal is to impress one another. But if people engage in social interaction for explicitly strategic reasons— negotiating a purchase, getting hired by an employer, impressing others at a social gathering, gaining sympathy when in need, looking tough to an antagonist, and so on—they may put their true self on hold and attempt instead to create the desired image of themselves in the eyes of others.

Sometimes it is hard to predict whether people will project their personal self or instead project a self that is suited to the specific interaction or context in question. In an informal social setting, you may want to develop a warm relationship with someone but you might also want to act in a way that will be seen as admirable, or simply as appropriate, even if that behavior does not reflect your true attitudes or values. It turns out that people differ reliably from one another in how they navigate such situations. Some people are inclined to act in accordance with their self-perceived attitudes, values, and behavioral dispositions, regardless of what particular mode of self-presentation would be advantageous. Other people lean the other way: they monitor their behavior to ensure that it is appropriate to the current situation, even if this behavior has little correspondence with their private attitudes, values, and dispositions.

Mark Snyder (1974), a leading researcher in this area, developed an instrument—the *Self-Monitoring Scale*— that distinguishes among people on this basis. People who score as *high self-monitors* continually monitor their behavior and note how people react to it, making adjustments if necessary in order to gain the desired effect. People who score as low self-monitors are less likely to monitor and adjust their behavior to ensure that it is seen as appropriate in a given context or conform to the behavior of others. Instead, low self-monitors express their personal attitudes, values, and dispositions in a fairly consistent manner across different contexts. If you're curious about where you fall on the self-monitoring dimension, you can take the test (Box 8.4). But keep in mind that knowing what the test measures can influence how you will respond to the various items—especially if you're a high self-monitor!

Box 8.4   The Self-Monitoring Scale (Selected Items)

Read each statement and decide whether it is true or false as it pertains to you.

1. I find it hard to imitate the behavior of other people.
2. My behavior is usually an expression of my true inner feelings, attitudes, and beliefs.
3. At parties and other social gatherings, I do not attempt to do or say things that others will like.
4. I can only argue for ideas which I already believe.
5. I can make impromptu speeches, even on topics about which I have almost no information.*
6   I guess I put on a show to impress or entertain people.*
7. When I am uncertain how to act in a social situation, I look to the behavior of others for cues.*
8. I sometimes appear to others to be experiencing deeper emotions than I actually am.*
9. I laugh more when I watch a comedy with others than when I am alone.*
10. In different situations and with different people, I often act like very different persons.*
11. I am not always the person I appear to be.*
12. I would not change my opinions (or the way I do things) in order to please someone else or win their favor.
13. In order to get along and be liked, I tend to be what people expect me to be rather than anything else.*
14. I have never been good at games like charades or improvisational acting.
15. I have trouble changing my behavior to suit different people and different situations.
16. I may deceive people by being friendly when I really dislike them.*

Items marked with an asterisk (*) indicate high self-monitoring.

Source: Snyder (1974)

Individual differences in self-monitoring are manifest in many ways (Gangestad & Snyder, 2000). High self-monitors show greater variability in their behavior across situations—acting sober in one context but carefree in another—than do low self-monitors. High self-monitors also conform to the opinions and desires of other people, whereas low self-monitors express their personal feelings even if they run counter to the feelings of others. High and low self-monitors also differ in their social networks: the former compartmentalize, interacting with different people in different contexts, depending on who can provide the most rewarding experience. A high self-monitor is likely to choose one person to play racquetball with (someone with comparable experience and skills), for example, but choose someone else to go to a movie with (someone with similar movie interests). A low self-monitor, however, is likely to ask the same person (e.g., a close friend) for both activities, regardless of the person's skills and interests. In a related vein, high self-monitors tend to have a wider circle of acquaintances (including more sex partners) than do low self-monitors, who place greater value on stable relationships.

The Dynamics of Social Interaction

How Do People Interact With One Another?

In principle, there is no limit to the things that people can say and do when interacting with one another. Two individuals could greet each other by bobbing their heads and doing "jazz hands," for example, and then proceed to interact by walking in tight circles around each other while saying whatever pops into their respective minds. All this is rather unlikely, however. There seem to be some ground rules for how people engage one another, with social interactions of all kinds and in very different contexts conforming to a handful of common features.

Nonverbal Communication

When you think about the way people interact, you probably focus on the things they say to each other. In describing an encounter with someone at a party, you might note the topics that were discussed, the jokes and witty remarks each of you made, the gossip you exchanged about mutual acquaintances, or the personal information the two of you disclosed. Verbal communication is certainly a defining feature of social interaction, but it may not be the most important feature when in capturing the essence of interaction.

The Function of Nonverbal Behavior

The words exchanged do not count as much as the *nonverbal behavior* in an interaction (Ambady & Rosenthal, 1992, 1993; De Paulo & Friedman, 1998; Gifford, 1994). How close two people stand, how much eye contact they make, their facial expressions and posture—these features of social interaction convey the nature of the interaction, the degree to which the individuals agree with one another, and how they feel about one another (Henley, 1977; Knapp & Hall, 2006). Even speaking has important nonverbal components—the rate at which words are uttered, the intonation in a person's voice, the volume of vocalizations—that convey important information about the speakers and the nature of the relationship between them.

Charles Darwin is best known for his theory of evolution through natural selection, but he also provided what many consider to be the first scientific study of nonverbal communication (Darwin, 1872/1998). He documented the ways in which members of various species communicate their friendly versus hostile intent and their relative power when they come across one another. That animals communicate nonverbally is hardly surprising. They do not have much choice—dogs, monkeys, and antelopes can vocalize, but these sounds do not qualify as words or sentences. But Darwin noted that humans, despite being unique in having verbal skills, nonetheless communicate their thoughts and feelings in ways that are eerily reminiscent of the nonverbal displays of lesser species. Like chimps, for example, people communicate anger by puffing themselves up to full size, stiffening their backs, tightening their eyebrows, thrusting their chins forward, and leaning toward one another (Olson, Hafer & Taylor, 2001).

Verbal and nonverbal communication tend to serve different purposes (Argyle, 1988). The content of spoken language is used to communicate information about events external to the speakers, whereas nonverbal channels are used to establish and maintain the nature of the relationship between individuals. A person can gush, "I think you're wonderful," of course, but this sentiment is more tactfully (and perhaps more convincingly) communicated without being quite so explicit—perhaps by smiling and standing especially close to the person. In fact, the content of speech provides less than 10% of the affective meaning, with nonverbal channels signaling the bulk of each person's feelings about one another (Mehrabian & Ferris, 1967). Beyond conveying one's feelings about the other person, nonverbal behavior is a primary vehicle for managing self-presentation. Body posture, for example, conveys superior versus inferior status in an interaction in a manner that far outweighs what the respective individuals are saying.

Sometimes nonverbal behavior can contradict the content of a verbal message. When this occurs, the nonverbal signal usually carries the day (Mehrabian & Wiener, 1967). Someone who claims to be a superior being and points out that you are lucky to talk with him or her, for example, will not be taken seriously if he or she says this while hunched over and shaking in a near-fetal position. Although people attempt to avoid such contradictions, they can be employed for a desired effect. Consider sarcasm, for example. When a person responds to an insight on your part by saying, "Wow, that was brilliant!" while at the same time rolling his or her eyes, he or she is not exactly handing down a compliment.

Facial Communication

Nonverbal communication occurs through many channels (e.g., body posture, hand gestures, shoulder shrugs, stance), but the most important and diverse channels involve the face. There are numerous muscles that precisely control the mouth, lips, eyes, nose, forehead, and jaw. The combinations of these muscular contractions allow the face to display more than 10,000 different expressions—and people are able to recognize each of them (Birdwhistell, 1970; Ekman, 2003). These expressions convey a wide variety of emotions, including sadness, happiness, fear, anger, disgust, surprise, anguish, shame, and sexual interest. They occur spontaneously and are universally recognized, suggesting that they are rooted in biology, as Darwin suggested.

To a large extent, emotional displays are either negative or positive. Negative displays typically involve increased tension in various muscle groups—tightening of jaw muscles, furrowing of the forehead, squinting of the eyes, and lip occlusion (in which the lips seem to disappear). Positive emotions are displayed through relaxation of the muscles controlling the mouth, loosening of the furrowed lines on the forehead, and widening of the area around the eyes. When people feel especially relaxed, they may tip their head to one side and expose their neck—a very vulnerable area that animals protect when engaged in a hostile confrontation.

Of all the facial displays, the most important is *eye contact*. Looking directly into someone's eyes is the primary means by which people communicate their attention to and interest in the person. The duration of eye contact is especially important: the longer the mutual eye contact between people, the greater the liking and potential for feelings of intimacy (Ekman, Friesen, & Ancoli, 1980). Pupil dilation during eye contact is also a giveaway that individuals are attracted to one another. Disinterest, meanwhile, is signaled when people engage in little eye contact. The person who says, "I think you're wonderful," undercuts the credibility of this claim if his or her eyes are darting around the room or staring at a nearby exit.

Proxemics

The physical distance that people maintain in interaction can also convey critical information. The study of how people use and perceive the physical space around them is known as *proxemics* (Hall, 1966). Distance is a reliable indicator of the relationship between two people. Strangers stand further apart than do acquaintances, acquaintances stand further apart than friends, and friends stand further apart than romantic partners.

Sometimes, of course, these rules are violated. Recall the last time you rode 20 stories in an elevator packed with total strangers. The sardine-like experience no doubt made the situation a bit uncomfortable. With your physical space violated, you may have tried to create "psychological" space by avoiding eye contact, focusing instead on the elevator buttons (Argyle & Dean, 1965). By reducing closeness in one nonverbal channel (eye contact), one can compensate for unwanted closeness in another channel (proximity). Similarly, if you are talking with someone who is seated several feet away at a large table, you are likely to maintain constant eye contact—something you might feel uncomfortable doing if you were standing next to each other. People, in short, have a knack for adjusting their nonverbal communication to establish and maintain a comfortable psychological distance in their interactions with one another.

Nonverbal communication is a universal language for social interaction, but there are some notable differences among cultures in how people express their intentions and feelings in this language (Ekman, 1972; Hess, Beaupré, & Cheung, 2002). Physical distance, for example, signals relationship status everywhere, but the specific distances vary across cultures (Hall, 1966). People from the Middle East and Latin America, for instance, stand closer to one another when engaged in a conversation than do people from North America and Western Europe.

Cultural differences in proxemics can make for awkward interactions when people from different societies come into close contact with one another. If you get the chance sometime, watch a video of someone from Saudi Arabia interacting with someone from Germany—then speed up the video. It will look somewhat like a dance, with the Saudi leading the German around the room as the latter continually backs up to maintain what he or she feels is the appropriate distance for this level of acquaintanceship. The German could, of course, perceive the close proximity as a sign of the Saudi's desire to establish a closer relationship—in which case the dance might take on a far different meaning.

Behavioral Mimicry

Social interaction is not simply the simultaneous verbal and nonverbal displays of feelings and intentions of two or more people. The displays must be coordinated in time, with each person adjusting his or her utterances, gestures, facial expressions, and so forth, to take into account the other person's verbal and nonverbal behavior. To a surprising extent, these adjustments involve people imitating the nonverbal behavior of one another. When one person in an interaction smiles or folds his or her arms, the other person is likely to make similar facial and bodily adjustments. And just as nonverbal behavior occurs spontaneously, without a great deal of conscious awareness or control, so too do the adjustments made in response to these behaviors. As a highly social species, we are preprogrammed biologically to imitate one another (e.g., Dijksterhuis, 2005). So even if a person has a clear intention or feeling that he or she wishes to communicate in social interaction, much of his or her nonverbal behavior will amount to *behavioral mimicry* of the person with whom he or she is communicating.

The Chameleon Effect

Behavioral mimicry is sometimes referred to as the *chameleon effect* (Chartrand & Bargh, 1999). In case you need reminding, a chameleon is a lizard that changes its color to match its surroundings. Being a lizard, a chameleon does this without conscious deliberation—the chameleon doesn't think, "I'm near some leaves, so time to turn green!" Humans are not lizards, of course, and are not confined to reptilian autopilot operation in our actions. So it is all the more surprising to discover that people routinely mimic one another spontaneously and with little or no conscious awareness of doing so. Unconscious mimicry, in fact, occurs in 30% or more of an ordinary social interaction (Chartrand & Bargh, 1999; Lakin & Chartrand, 2003).

People's unconscious tendency to mimic the facial expressions, mannerisms, physical gestures, and even posture of others around them is well documented. In an early demonstration (Chartrand & Bargh, 1999), students were asked to describe a series of photographs from various magazines in two 10-minute sessions. In each session, participants were paired with another person, who was actually an accomplice of the experimenter. The accomplice in one session frequently rubbed his or her face, while the accomplice in the other session continuously shook his or her foot. In both sessions, the participant was secretly videotaped as he or she and the accomplice described the photographs. From the videotapes, it could be determined how much time participants spent rubbing their face or shaking their foot in each session.

In support of the chameleon effect, participants tended to mimic the nonverbal behavior of the accomplice in each session (see Figure 8.4). When paired with the face-rubbing accomplice, participants engaged in a great deal of their own face-rubbing. When paired with the foot-shaking accomplice, however, they followed suit and shook their own foot a great deal. This tendency to mimic an accomplice is particularly pronounced among people who have a high need to affiliate with others and among those who have a strong empathic orientation. Lakin and Chartrand (2003), for example, found that participants unconsciously primed with the concept of affiliation were more likely to mimic the behavior of a person seen on a videotape than were participants who were not primed to think about affiliation.

The Functions of Mimicry

Considerable research in recent years has shown that mimicry—even something so trivial as two people rubbing their respective faces—serves as "social glue" that binds people together (Dijksterhuis, 2005; Lakin, Jefferis, Cheng, & Chartrand, 2003). Mimicry within dyads fosters understanding and empathy, and enhances their perceived similarity with one another (Bernieri & Rosenthal, 1991; Chartrand & Bargh, 1999; LaFrance, 1979; Lakin et al., 2003; Stel, Van Baaren, & Vonk, 2008). When counselors mimic the arm and leg positions of a client, for example, the client perceives the counselor as having greater empathy for him or her (Maurer & Tindall, 1983). In classroom settings,

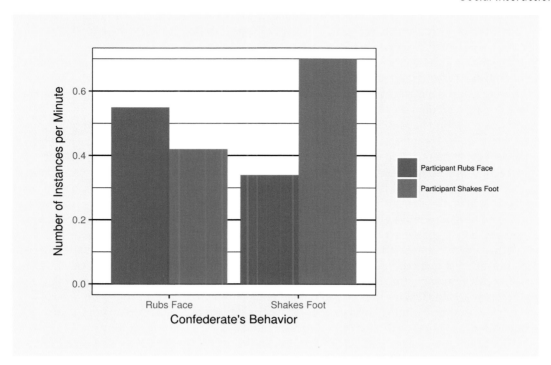

FIGURE 8.4 Unconscious Mimicry
Source: Adapted from Chartrand & Bargh (1999)

a teacher can establish rapport with students by coordinating his or her movements with those of the students (Bernieri, 1988).

Mimicry can also create mutual liking between the mimicker and the mimickee. Several studies have demonstrated that the person being mimicked (the mimickee) develops positive feelings toward the person doing the mimicry (the mimicker). Chartrand and Bargh (1999, study 2), for example, recruited participants to work on a task with a confederate who either mimicked their mannerisms or exhibited neutral, nondescript mannerisms. Those who were mimicked reported greater liking for the confederate and described their interaction with him or her as smoother and more harmonious. In a study of speed dating, male participants evaluated female confederates who mimicked them more positively than equally attractive female confederates who were just as friendly but did not mimic them (Gueguen, 2004). Mimicry also creates liking for the mimickee on the part of the mimicker (e.g., Stel & Vonk, 2010). When people observe another person, their liking for the person is greater when they mimic the person's gestures and facial expressions than when they inhibit such mimicry.

Beyond its effects on dyadic relationships, being mimicked makes people feel closer to other people in general and can promote prosocial behavior (Ashton-James et al., 2007; Lakin & Chartrand, 2003; Maddux, Mullen, & Galinsky, 2008). For example, people tend to leave more generous tips in a restaurant if the server has mimicked their facial expressions or gestures (Van Baaren, Holland, Steenaert, & Van Knippenberg. 2003). And an experimenter who mimics the posture of participants is likely to receive greater help from them if he or she "accidentally" drops pens on the floor (Van Baaren, Holland, Kawakami, & Van Knippenberg, 2004).

This does not mean that the more mimicry, the better. Quite the contrary, in fact—too much mimicry in some contexts can have negative effects. There are implicit standards for how much mimicry should occur in a given social interaction (Cheng & Chartrand, 2003; Dalton, Chartrand, & Finkel, 2010; Finkel et al., 2006), and violation of these implicit standards can promote feelings of disliking or even threat (Liu, Vohs, & Smeesters, 2011; Stel et al., 2010). This was demonstrated in a study by Leander, Chartrand, and Bargh (2012). A female experimenter interacted with male and female participants in either an informal manner signaling affiliation (e.g., saying "awesome" instead of "good") or a formal manner signaling a business-like interaction (e.g., talking only about the participants' task). The experimental task consisted of describing photographs. The experimenter handed the participant 10 photographs, one at a time, and asked him or her to describe each one verbally. Throughout this procedure, the experimenter either mimicked the participant's posture, gesture, and nonverbal mannerisms, or she did not mimic the participant at all. Following the photograph descriptions, participants completed a questionnaire that assessed how well a series of adjectives described how they felt at the moment. One of the adjectives was *physically cold*. The question is whether a sense of physical coldness can be brought on by inappropriate mimicry—either too much or too little.

The results, presented in Figure 8.5, revealed that participants experienced "the chills" in two conditions: when they were *not mimicked* by the informal (affiliation-oriented) experimenter and when they *were mimicked* by the formal (task-oriented) experimenter. Behavioral mimicry, it appears, is fine as long as it is appropriate and expected—as it is when interacting with someone who approaches the interaction in an informal manner. But mimicry can literally give people "the chills" when it is inappropriate and unexpected—as it is when interacting with someone who approaches the interaction in a business-like manner.

Mimicry can also have a negative effect when people attempt to control this unconscious tendency. In light of the benefits of mimicry, you might expect that people would take control of this process and engage in conscious imitation of one another's facial expressions, posture, movements, and the like (e.g., Swaab, Maddux, & Sinaceur, 2011). Of course, people can attempt to do so. You see someone smile and you make a point of smiling back. But conscious mimicry is not as effective as mimicry that occurs spontaneously and without awareness (e.g., Finkel et al., 2006). Mimicry simply is too complex and too fast for the conscious mind to monitor and control. People spontaneously synchronize their movements, for example, within 21 milliseconds—that's one-fiftieth of a second! (Condon & Ogston, 1967).

Beyond that, when mimicry is controlled rather than spontaneous, it can be recognized as insincere, even manipulative, and disrupt rather than facilitate social bonding. Getting liked by someone is a strategy used by people to gain influence (e.g., Cialdini, 2000), whether in formal settings like a job interview or the most informal settings like a first

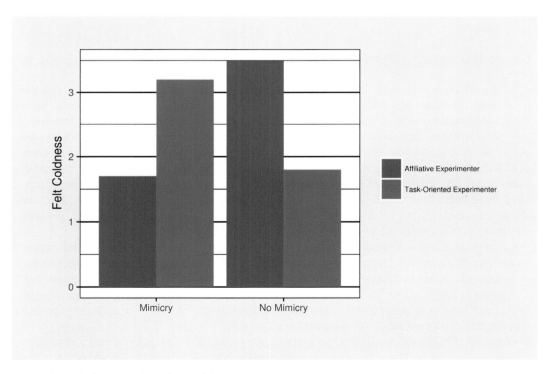

FIGURE 8.5 Being Mimicked and Feeling Cold
Source: Adapted from Leander et al. (2012)

date. As noted in the discussion of self-presentation, when people are aware of this influence strategy—often referred to as *ingratiation* (Jones, 1964)—they can be turned off rather than turned on when they see it coming. A job interviewer, for example, may become suspicious when his or her every change in body position is matched by the person being interviewed.

Mimicry is universal, but there are cultural differences in the how much mimicry is typically displayed (or expected) in social interactions. People tend to be more attuned to the emotions and behaviors of one another in collectivist cultures, and this sensitivity promotes sympathetic mirroring of one another's nonverbal behaviors (Sanchez-Burks, Bartel, & Bount, 2009). People in collectivist cultures expect mimicry and experience tension when this expectation is not fulfilled. People in individualist cultures expect mimicry as well, but this expectation is not as strong, at least in a formal situation like a job interview (e.g., Leander et al., 2012).

Emotional Synchrony

Everyone is familiar with the concept of *empathy*. When we see someone registering an emotion, whether unpleasant or pleasant, we may feel the same emotion to some degree. If we see a person cry because of sadness, for example, we may experience sadness as well. Empathy can be looked upon as *emotional synchrony*, the affective counterpart to behavioral mimicry. In fact, the potential for emotional synchrony is amplified by behavioral mimicry. If our facial muscles and posture mirror the facial muscles and posture of another person, we tend to experience the same emotion as the person as well.

Bases of Synchrony

This basis for emotional synchrony follows from the research on the *facial feedback hypothesis*, described in Chapter 4 ("Emotion"). Feedback from facial configurations (e.g., corresponding to a smile or a frown) promotes the associated subjective feeling (e.g., happiness or sadness). Feedback from voice, posture, and movement can also promote corresponding subjective experiences (e.g., Ekman, Levenson, & Friesen, 1983; Laird & Bresler, 1992; Scherer, 1982). So when people mimic one another, they tend to adopt at least a twinge of the emotional state conveyed in one another's facial expression, vocal quality, posture, or movement pattern. Emotional synchrony, however, can be achieved without behavioral mimicry. Neuroscience research has revealed that humans—as well as our fellow primates—have a special type of brain cell referred to as a *mirror neuron* (Gallese, Fadiga, Fogassi, & Rizzolatti, 1996; Rizzolatti, & Craighero, 2004; Rameson, Morelli, & Lieberman, 2011). These cells acquired this name because they respond the same way when we perform an action and when we observe someone else perform the same action. When you see someone laugh or yawn, for example, the mirror neurons for these acts in your own brain fire automatically and involuntarily—as if you were laughing or yawning yourself. So although empathy is considered a special feature of human nature that separates us from lower forms of life, it is nonetheless rooted in basic biology.

Empathy is a common occurrence in everyday interactions between individuals. In less frequent circumstances, emotional synchrony is experienced as *emotional contagion* (Hatfield, Cacioppo, & Rapson, 1993). This refers to the convergence on the same emotional state when people automatically mimic and synchronize expressions, postures, and movements of other people, whether or not social interaction is involved. Contagion is different from empathy. In a crowd, for example, people are not particularly empathic, looking at how others feel and then developing a similar internal state. Instead, people seem to "catch" the same feeling and might assume that everyone is responding to some external event rather than to each other (e.g., Neumann & Strack, 2000). Emotional contagion is especially likely in stressful circumstances that that make people feel threatened and uncertain (Gump & Kulik, 1997).

Anticipating Social Interaction

Simply anticipating interaction with someone, even a complete stranger, can motivate people to get in sync with the person once they meet, with a readiness to like him or her (Darley & Berscheid, 1967; Knight & Vallacher, 1981). Even if they are in a good mood, they may dampen down their feelings so that they are in a neutral mood, from which they can adjust as necessary to synchronize with the other person (Wegner, Erber, & Zanakos, 1993). They may even dampen their spirits a bit if they believe the other person is not feeling all that well.

Interpersonal Expectations

The tendency to coordinate actions and internal states suggests that people in social interaction can converge on a pattern of behavior, thought, and feeling that may be distinct from how either partner normally behaves (Nowak et al., 2005). Two people who are only moderately extraverted, for example, might become highly animated and downright giddy when they get together. But it is conceivable that one person adapts his or her behavior more than the other person does. This seems especially likely if one of them has clear expectations for how the other person is likely to behave. This possibility becomes all the more interesting when the person's expectations for the other person's behavior are wildly inaccurate. Do people in social interaction really conform to inaccurate expectations for their behavior? If so, is this tendency inevitable, or is it observed only under certain conditions?

Behavior Confirmation

Recall the discussion of *self-fulfilling prophecy* in Chapter 7. When people have a preconceived notion of what someone is like, they unwittingly engage in behavior that brings about the expected behavior in the person (Jussim, 1986; Snyder & Swann, 1978). If the person is expected to be competitive, for example, he or she is likely to be treated in a manner that brings out competition. But if the same person is expected to be cooperative, he or she is likely to be treated in a friendly and trusting manner that brings out his or her cooperative tendencies.

But let's say you are not entirely certain what someone is like and you want to find out prior to meeting him or her. Imagine, for example, that you want to find out whether another person is an extravert—someone who enjoys mingling with people, talking a lot, going to parties, and so forth. And let's say you can choose from a long list of questions those that you would ask the person in order to settle the issue. Some of the questions probe for extraversion (e.g., "What would you do to liven things up at a party?") and some probe for introversion, the opposite of extraversion (e.g., "In what situations do you wish you could be more outgoing?"). Which questions would you choose to ask?

This is the situation that Mark Snyder and William Swann (1978) presented to participants. Logically, participants should have chosen both kinds of questions—those probing for extraversion and those probing for introversion. A search for confirmatory information, however, trumped logic. In trying to determine whether the target was an extravert, participants chose almost exclusively from the list of extravert-relevant questions, skipping the questions that gave examples of introverted behavior an equal chance. Imagine the dilemma faced by a true introvert when asked these questions. If asked what he or should do to liven things up at a party, the introvert could challenge the premise of the question, but they rarely did this. Instead, they came up with reasonable answers (e.g., "I would suggest what songs to play or hang around people who are talking a lot"). (Of course, a clever introvert might answer the "liven up a party" question by saying, "I'd leave!"). The opposite bias was displayed by participants who were assigned the task of finding out whether the target person was an introvert. They chose almost exclusively from the list of questions probing for introversion (e.g., "In what situations do you wish you could be more outgoing?"). And again, the target complied by answering these questions as if they were reasonable (e.g., "I guess I could speak up more in my classes").

Snyder and Swann tape-recorded the interview sessions and played them to another group of participants who knew nothing about the purpose of the interview study. The questions were edited out, so that the observers heard only the target's responses. The observers were then asked to rate the degree to which the target was an extravert or an introvert. The results were straightforward. If they heard the target's responses to extravert-probing questions, they rated the target as an extravert—regardless of what the target was really like. But if they heard the target answering introvert-probing questions, they rated the target as an introvert—again, regardless of whether he or she was introverted.

Overcoming Behavior Confirmation

Does this mean that you are doomed to act in ways that confirm the preconceptions—even the inaccurate ones—that people have about you? Not necessarily. Self-fulfilling prophecies tend to occur under fairly specific conditions that characterize some social contexts but not all of them (Darley & Fazio, 1980; Jussim & Harber, 2005; Olson, Roese, & Zanna, 1996).

The likelihood that the target of an erroneous expectation will confirm the expectation is greatest when the person holding the expectation controls the social encounter and the target defers to this control (Smith, Neuberg, Judice, &

Biesanz, 1997; Snyder & Haugen, 1994). This power differential helps explain why students tend to confirm teachers' expectations (Rosenthal & Jacobson, 1968). Especially students with low power in the educational system—those who have low socioeconomic status, are minority group members, or are female—tend to be susceptible to erroneous (and often quite low) expectations (Jussim, Eccles, & Madon, 1996). The potential for behavior confirmation is inherent in other relationships with a power differential, such as interviewer and job applicant, employer and employee, and therapist and patient (Copeland, 1994). The likelihood of behavior confirmation is minimized, meanwhile, if the target of an erroneous expectation has a clear and stable sense of what he or she is really like. The expectation may prevail initially, but over time the person's true self may be revealed and correct the erroneous expectations held by his or her interaction partner (Swann & Ely, 1984).

The likelihood of self-fulfilling prophecies has also been shown to differ for men and women (Christensen & Rosenthal, 1982; Nelson & Klutas, 2000). Men are more likely to *create* self-fulfilling prophecies, whereas women are more likely to be *victims* of them, living up to erroneous (e.g., sexist) expectations. This may reflect the power differential noted above, if one assumes that men are socialized to take control of their social encounters, while women are socialized to be more deferential and accommodating in social encounters.

SUMMING UP AND LOOKING AHEAD

- **Humans have higher-order motives such as self-esteem and self-actualization, but these do not become pressing concerns until a person has achieved a sense of belongingness with others. The experience of loneliness is associated with dysfunctional psychological states and can lower the threshold for certain physical illnesses. Social rejection, even by strangers, has serious consequences for psychological and physical well-being and can promote antisocial behavior.**
- **People's level of self-esteem reflects the degree to which they feel they are connected to others. Because low self-esteem people are primarily concerned with gaining social acceptance, they prefer to interact with someone who expresses interest in forming a relationship, even if that person does not indicate a great deal of liking or respect for them.**
- **People seek out one another for social interaction when events or circumstances have ambiguous meaning, especially if they are consequential or stressful. Stressful events in the past can haunt people in the present, particularly if they have not come to grips with their causes and larger meanings. By focusing on such events in the context of social interaction, people can achieve cognitive clarity and closure, and experience psychological and physical health benefits.**
- **People attempt to achieve balance in their social networks, with a common feeling toward everyone in the network. This can bias people to feel positive toward "a friend of a friend" or "an enemy of an enemy." By the same logic, people are biased to feel negative toward "an enemy of a friend" or "a friend of an enemy," without considering the person's qualities.**
- **People attempt to manage their impressions in social interaction. They often want to be viewed in the same way they view themselves. If an interaction partner seems to hold an inconsistent view, people will attempt to "correct" the partner's impression—even if the impression is highly flattering. Sometimes people will forgo a concern with self-verification, attempting instead to create an impression of themselves that has strategic value in social interaction. People differ from one another in the extent to which they are concerned with self-verification versus strategic self-presentation. Low self-monitors attempt to display their "true self" regardless of the social context, while high self-monitors adjust their self-presentation in different contexts to maximize their personal gain.**
- **People's feelings about one another in social interaction are conveyed more by their nonverbal behavior than by their verbal behavior. People tend to mimic one another's nonverbal behaviors, and do so automatically and usually without awareness. Behavioral mimicry promotes positive affect in social interaction, although it can promote awkwardness rather than comfort and liking in some contexts.**
- **People also tend to synchronize their emotional states in social interaction. This basis for empathy can result from facial mimicry, with feedback from muscle configurations promoting emotions that correspond to the mimicked facial display. Emotional synchrony and empathy can also occur in the absence of mimicry because of mirror neurons that respond the same way to observing an action as performing the action.**

Synchronization of internal states also develops in groups by means of emotional contagion. Although emotional synchronization is an automatic process, it can be brought under conscious control. In preparing for social interaction, people often adjust their emotional state to match what they imagine is the emotional state of the interaction partner—even if that means dampening a positive mood to feel emotionally neutral.

- People often engage in social interaction with expectations about the characteristics of their interaction partner. These interpersonal expectations may be misguided or totally off-base, but they can bias how people behave, bringing about the behavior they expect—even if such behavior is at odds with the person's "true self."

When a close relationship develops between two individuals, they continue to mimic one another, present themselves in certain ways, and satisfy personal goals such as acceptance, liking, respect, and cognitive clarity. But they also conform to a set of principles that make these relationships unique. An overview of these principles provides the focus of the next chapter.

Key Terms

Need for social connections	Balance theory	The chameleon effect
Hierarchy of human needs	Self-verification	Facial feedback
Self-actualization	Self-presentation	Mirror neurons
Loneliness	Impression management	Empathy
Social rejection	Ingratiator's dilemma	Emotional synchrony
Acceptance, liking, respect	Self-monitoring	Emotional contagion
Sociometer hypothesis	Nonverbal communication	Self-fulfilling prophecy
Cognitive clarity	Proxemics	Behavior confirmation
Social networks	Behavioral mimicry	

9 Close Relationships

What could be better than being in love? If the sheer number of poems, novels, movies, and songs devoted to this topic is any indication, love is the holy grail of human relations, maybe of life itself. As far back as written records of human history go, love has been a preoccupation in our species. Love brings joy and meaning into our lives, and it creates the context in which people keep the human story alive, creating families and ensuring the continuation of our species for succeeding generations.

But love can be as much a curse as it is a blessing. The most devastating emotions we can experience are associated with love that is unrequited—or worse, love that was once reciprocated but now lost. In what has to count as one of humanity's cruelest ironies, people kill those with whom they have had an intimate relationship at a far higher rate than they kill people in any other kind of relationship—even bitter rivals with whom no love is lost. And short of these emotional and behavioral downsides, love by its very nature entails very notable trade-offs in satisfying personal needs. In forming a special relationship, people must relinquish a fair degree of autonomy and freedom in exchange for the companionship of someone else with his or her own autonomy and freedom concerns.

Love is clearly a double-edged sword. We elevate it to the highest levels of human desire, yet this heralded state can carry us to the deepest levels of unpleasant emotions and mental states. What makes this feature of interpersonal experience so special? Do people know what they are getting into when they fall in love, or do "fools rush in where wise men fear to tread"? For most of human history, these sorts of questions were left to poets, philosophers, novelists, and musicians. But in recent decades, social psychologists have entered the fray, investigating the nature of love from a detached and objective scientific perspective. Poets and philosophers still have the upper hand in capturing the essence of love, but psychologists have had their fair share of success in describing many aspects of this universal human proclivity. This chapter provides an overview of this accumulated wisdom. Much of what you will learn will come as little surprise, but you will almost certainly be enlightened, if not taken aback, by many of the insights that have been generated in research—sometimes in the sterile and non-romantic lab rooms in which psychologists conduct their research.

CHAPTER OVERVIEW

What Are You Going to Learn?

- **Why do people become attracted to one another?** We come into contact with dozens of people every day and many of them—perhaps the majority—are quite pleasant and have some degree of interest value. Yet, we are not drawn to all of them—certainly not a majority. How important is physical attractiveness in promoting liking? Are the bases for interpersonal attraction common to everyone, or do people differ in whom they find likable and attractive? Do people become attracted to others who are similar or to those who are opposite in certain ways?
- **Why do people fall in love?** Liking someone is one thing; loving that person is quite another. What distinguishes attraction from intimacy? Is love a biological phenomenon that reflects hormones and brain centers? How is love shaped by cultural values and traditions? What emotions are unique to love? How do people in love satisfy each other's needs while yet satisfying their own? Do males and females have similar agendas for romantic relations?
- **Why do people fall out of love?** Falling in love can seem effortless, but keeping the relationship alive can prove anything but. What are the common hazards that arise in close relationships? Do males and females differ in their experience of jealousy? In their potential for infidelity? Can the likelihood of disruption to a relationship be predicted from the partners' communication patterns?

Attraction

Who Likes Whom, and Why?

In principle, you could like everyone you meet. Of course, you could conceivably dislike everyone you come into contact with. In reality, of the total number of people you have met, the proportion you like is somewhere between 100% (everyone) and 0% (no one). Feeling drawn to some people but not to others is central to social experience, with important consequences for every other aspect of your life. You form friendships, choose roommates, join clubs, take trips, adopt music preferences and clothing fashions, and establish professional relationships in large part based on whether you like the people involved. And of course, there is the special form of attraction that can morph into an intimate relationship, thereby creating the potential for passing on one's genes and perhaps setting the genetic course for many generations to come.

Because liking plays such a prominent role in social life, it is one of the most investigated topics in social psychology. Thousands of experiments and correlational studies have been conducted to isolate the basic principles that determine "who likes whom, and why." It turns out that the answer to this simple question is quite complex. The multi-determined nature of interpersonal attraction may pose a challenge for developing a unified theory, but it does allow for people of all kinds to become the focus of liking and adoration in someone's eyes.

Physical Attraction

"Beauty is only skin deep" is a popular expression that captures our concern with focusing on a person's inner qualities—his or her character, values, and humanity—rather than on his or her outward appearance. This is a noble idea, but one that says more about human conceit than about human reality. To be sure, a person with a rotten disposition is unlikely to win many popularity contests, no matter how good-looking he or she is. But all other things being equal, people are

son might forge a bond, and a person with poor self-control might be drawn to someone with high self-control (Shea, Davisson, & Fitzsimons, 2013). Attraction might also develop between people with different talents and expertise (Wegner, Erber, & Raymond, 1991). A mathematician might hit it off with a musician, with both providing and gaining new insights and skills. Complementarity, however, does not bode well in the long run. There is a risk that divergent perspectives and personalities will degenerate into friction after the initial glow of novelty and discovery wears thin.

Actually, recent research has found evidence for a particular form of complementarity that does bode well for relationships—although this is not the kind of "opposites attract" with which you are likely to be familiar. In fact, even if you know what it is, you will not be conscious of it when it occurs in your own life, because it is rooted in the non-conscious mandates of evolutionary biology. The survival of any species—whether potatoes or humans—depends on diversity among its members in their immune responses to pathogens and infectious agents such as viruses, bacteria, and fungi. If everyone in a population had identical immune systems, they all would be at risk of dying if a certain pathogen infected the population. Such a fate, in fact, almost occurred during a 3-year period (1348-1350) in Europe, when the bubonic plague (the "Black Death") swept through much of the continent, killing between 75 and 200 million people. Those who survived apparently had an immune system that was distinct from the immune system of those who perished, and this difference enabled them to defend against the otherwise deadly pathogen (a bacterium).

Because diversity in immune response is so important to long-term survival, people have evolved preferences for mating with partners whose immune system can provide protection that complements that provided by their own immune system. Such complementarity has been identified with respect to the *major histocompatibility complex* (MHC), a protein complex that plays a role in a person's immunities. The more diverse a person's MHC, the better equipped he or she is to fend off pathogens and infectious diseases. From an evolutionary perspective, females should be attracted to a male with an MHC that is both diverse and different from their own, so that their offspring will acquire a diverse—and thus strong—immune system (Molinero et al., 2002). But how can a woman possibly know the status of a man's MHC? She can't. But she can smell, and the odors she detects signal a man's MHC and its similarity versus difference from her own MHC. The woman does not know anything about immune response, pathogens, and the like. All she knows is that the odor smells good or bad.

This remarkable effect has been demonstrated in yet another T-shirt study (Wedekind, Seebeck, Bettens, & Paepke, 1995). Males wore a T-shirt to bed for two consecutive nights without using any artificial scents (cologne, deodorant). Females then sniffed the T-shirts and classified the odor as attractive or unattractive. Females not using contraceptives (and thus potentially fertile) were more attracted to the scent of males with dissimilar MHCs, whereas females on contraceptives (and thus non-fertile) preferred the scent of men with MHCs similar to her own. Why did women on birth control show a similarity effect rather than a complementarity effect? The researchers speculated that birth control pills fool the body into "thinking" it is pregnant, so the woman's non-conscious strategy switches from genetic diversity to signals of similarity that are associated with bonding and protection.

Males, too, are sensitive to a woman's MHC. In their own T-shirt study, Randy Thornhill and his colleagues (2003) found that males were more attracted to the scent of females with dissimilar MHC than to the scent of females with similar MHC. Like the females in the Wedekind et al. (1995) study, the males were clueless as to the significance of their preferences. Evolution takes care of the heavy lifting in these matters; people can simply follow their noses.

The idea that people are not attracted to others who are too similar to them biologically finds expression in the *incest taboo*—a prohibition against sexual relations between closely related individuals, especially between parents and offspring and between siblings. With very few exceptions, cultures worldwide throughout history abide by the incest taboo (Bittles & Neel, 1994; Lieberman, Tooby, & Cosmides, 2003). Every culture has developed its own rationale for this prohibition, but the real reason has more to do with biology than with values and norms. Sex between closely related individuals increases the chance that their offspring will acquire the same recessive genes, which can prove harmful. And as noted above, related individuals are likely to have similar immune systems and thus possess a relatively narrow range of defenses against infectious diseases. To prevent these problems, humans (and other mammals) have evolved an aversion to sex with close relatives. This aversion is unconscious; people do not have to be told not to have sex with their parents or siblings, and unless they have received education concerning genetics, they cannot explain why they are turned off by the very idea.

Propinquity

When students head off to college, they no doubt imagine all the interesting and attractive people they are going to meet. They may look upon the college campus as an enormous social supermarket, with fellow students from all the aisles providing a wide range of choices for friendship and romance. This sounds great, but the reality is a bit different. Students, like people in virtually every other context, tend to like others based on their physical proximity or *propinquity*. Students are far more likely to make friends with fellow students who live in the same dorm or apartment building than with students who live in the neighboring housing complex (Festinger, Schachter, & Back, 1950; Segal, 1974). And *within* a dorm or apartment building, the likelihood of students becoming friends is related to how close their respective rooms are. A student is more likely to become friends with someone next door than with the students at the other end of the hall.

Propinquity increases the likelihood of chance encounters and the opportunity for people to get to know one another. The issue, then, is not really physical distance per se, but rather *functional distance*—features of the setting that encourage contact between certain people and discourage contact between others. In a two-story housing complex, for example, a person on the first floor is physically closer to the people in the room over his or head on the second floor than to the people two doors away on the same floor. In terms of functional distance, however, the people on the same floor are considerably closer, and thus more likely to become friends, because they are more likely to encounter one another on a chance basis. The most enduring and intense relationships develop between people whose paths cross frequently.

Emotion

One cannot say anything sensible about romantic attraction without giving a prominent role to emotion. We don't think we are in love—we *feel* in love. But as we saw in Chapters 3 ("Beliefs, Attitudes, and Values") and 4 ("Emotion"), emotions can be tricky and their relation to other mental processes can be even more so. Love may be special, but several points discussed in those chapters are relevant to the emotional processes associated with romantic attraction.

Affect and Preference

If we like someone, we usually have a reason for doing so. You might note that a new acquaintance is attractive or bright, and then develop a preference for being around him or her. This suggests that thinking precedes affect, with our highly evolved mental capacities shaping our feelings toward other people. Of course, non-conscious processes like the "smell of symmetry" can promote attraction to someone without a role played by consideration of the person's characteristics. But when these biological markers of attractiveness are not relevant, surely we rely on our mental faculties to decide how we feel about someone.

Well, not necessarily. In fact, our liking for someone can develop without even thinking about the person or forming impressions of his or her personality. Our *preferences* for a person, in other words, do not always depend on our *inferences* about him or her. Sometimes we come to like someone *merely because we are repeatedly exposed to him or her*. To test this *mere exposure effect*, Robert Zajonc (1968) created a set of Turkish words (e.g., *kadirga, afworbu, lokanta*) that were unfamiliar to participants in his study (and to most everyone else outside of Turkey). He then showed different words from this set to the participants 0, 1, 2, 5, 10, or 25 times. The participants were then asked to indicate the extent to which they felt each word referred to something good or bad. In line with the mere exposure effect, the more frequently participants saw a particular Turkish word, the more they assumed it referred to something good. If they were exposed to *kadirga* 10 times and to *lokanta* 2 times, for example, they had a more positive feeling about the former than about the latter. Zajonc observed the same effect when Chinese pictographs (symbols used in Chinese writing) were substituted for the Turkish words. The effect was observed again for college yearbook photos: participants expressed greater liking for the individuals whose photos they saw most often.

But why does repeated mere exposure to a person (or any stimulus) create positive feelings about him or her? The favored explanation involves *perceptual fluency*, a phenomenon introduced in Chapter 4. The idea is that people like stimuli—whether images, sounds, objects, or ideas—that are easy to process and do not tax mental resources (Reber, Winkielman, & Schwarz, 1998; Winkielman & Cacioppo, 2001). People prefer a high-resolution photo and a rhythmic sound over a faded photo and a dissonant sound, for example, because the former are easier to process. Familiarity promotes perceptual fluency: the more frequently we are exposed to something, the easier it is to recognize and process the features of the stimulus.

Repeated exposure to a person works the same way. The more frequently we encounter someone, the easier it is to process the person's appearance and behavior. Because perceptual fluency is pleasurable, we are inclined to feel positively toward the frequently encountered person. Exposure, of course, is no guarantee that we will like someone. An annoying person whom we encounter on a frequent basis may be disliked more than an annoying person we manage to avoid (Ebbesen, Kjos, & Koneci, 1976). The mere exposure effect simply increases the likelihood that we will come to like someone when other important factors (e.g., attractiveness, similarity) are not particularly relevant in shaping our desires.

Misattribution of Arousal

OK, so emotions can develop and be experienced without the aid of higher order mental processes (e.g., reasoning, evaluation). But when thoughts do enter the mix, emotional processes can become tricky and the resultant emotion can be a bit illusory. As explained in Chapter 4, when people have a stirred up physiological state (e.g., a fast heart rate), their thought processes are engaged to make sense of this arousal. Under certain conditions, the thoughts that arise can point to causes for the arousal that may be way off the mark. Arousal produced by a drug, for example, can be mistaken as feelings of euphoria or anger, depending on how the person processes relevant information in the surrounding situation (Schachter & Singer, 1962).

Even the special feelings of romantic attraction—especially passion—can also be subject to the *misattribution of arousal*. You might be mildly attracted to someone, for instance, but this emotion can be amplified to passionate feelings if your body is in an agitated state due to a cause that has nothing to do with the person. Maybe you are still experiencing the effect of three cups of morning coffee and don't make the connection to your agitated state (Zillman, 1978).

This perspective on romantic attraction was put to the test in a well-known field experiment (Dutton & Aron, 1974). The laboratory was a popular tourist site in North Vancouver, British Columbia, with two bridges. One, the Capilano Canyon Suspension bridge, is 5 feet wide, 450 feet long, constructed of wooden boards attached to wire cables, and spans a turbulent portion of the Capilano River, which is 230 feet below (see the photo below). This bridge is clearly not for the faint of heart—it wobbles when people walk on it, and it sways in the wind. Let's call it the "wobbly" bridge (although "scary" seems appropriate as well). The other bridge, a bit downstream, is built out of heavy wood and is only 10 feet above the river, which is quite peaceful at this point. Let's call this the "solid" bridge.

To test the misattribution of arousal hypothesis, Dutton and Aron arranged for a male or female research assistant to intercept an unaccompanied (and unsuspecting) male who was crossing one of the bridges. The assistant told the man that he or she was completing a psychology experiment and asked whether he would serve as a participant by writing an imaginative story in response to an ambiguous picture—and to do so right there, standing on the bridge.

The "wobbly" (scary) Capilano bridge in British Columbia

The man was informed that if he wanted to receive information about the results of the study, he could call the assistant later (with the phone number provided by the assistant).

Dutton and Aron were interested in whether the stories generated by the men were loaded with sexual imagery, and whether the men tried to contact the research assistant (ostensibly to learn about the study's results). Both measures produced results that were consistent with the misattribution model. Men contacted by the female research assistant on the wobbly bridge generated the highest degree of sexual imagery. And as is apparent in Figure 9.3, the men on the wobbly bridge were also the most likely to call the female assistant. Presumably, they experienced heightened arousal (e.g., elevated heart rate) because they were on a swaying bridge hundreds of feet in the air, but attributed their arousal to the female who intercepted them.

This conclusion is hardly ironclad. The participants were not randomly assigned to the two bridges, so the response of the men contacted on the wobbly bridge by the female assistant may say more about their personalities than about the bridge and female combination. Perhaps the men who chose to walk across the wobbly bridge were especially adventurous, both physically and sexually, than were the man who chose the solid bridge. To rule out this interpretation, Dutton and Aron repeated this experiment using only the wobbly bridge. On a random basis, half the men were contacted while on the bridge (as in the first study), and half were contacted after crossing the bridge and having had a chance to calm down. In line with misattribution model, the men contacted on the bridge by the female generated stories with the highest sexual imagery and were the most likely to attempt subsequent contact with her.

This study suggests that arousal can be interpreted as romantic attraction if the person would be still be viewed in mildly positive terms under neutral conditions. But what happens when one encounters someone who is viewed in mildly *negative* terms? Would the misattribution of physiological arousal (e.g., due to a wobbly bridge or a mega dose of caffeine) still promote heightened attraction to the person? Or would misattribution operate in the opposite direction—producing a strong *aversive* reaction to the person? Keep in mind that misattribution is ultimately in service of trying to make sense of one's arousal. If one encounters a person who is somewhat unappealing or unpleasant, it makes more sense to assume that one's arousal reflects aversion or repulsion rather than attraction. A mildly positive person may generate very warm feelings, but a mildly negative person is more likely to generate very cold feelings.

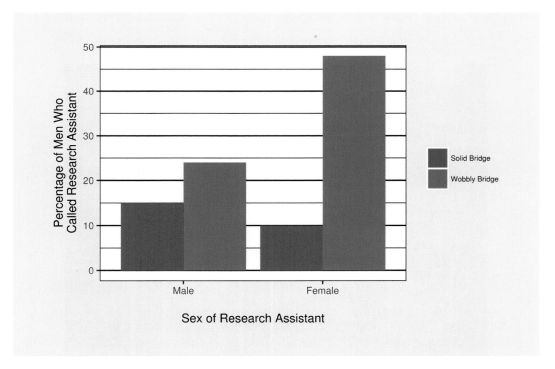

FIGURE 9.3 Attraction for the Male versus Female Research Assistant on the Solid Versus Wobbly Bridge
Source: Adapted from Dutton & Aron (1974)

This *polarization of affect* was demonstrated in a study by White, Fishbein, and Rutstein (1981). Male participants ran in place for two minutes (*high arousal*) or 15 seconds (*low arousal*). They then viewed a 5-minute videotape of a female whom they expected to meet for a get-acquainted date. The female (an experimental accomplice) was made up to look either *attractive* (e.g., she had nice hair and makeup, wore form-fitting attractive clothes, and talked energetically) or *unattractive* (e.g., she had unattractive makeup, wore loose-fitting, unattractive clothes, talked in a boring fashion, and had the sniffles). In both cases, she followed the same script in talking about her hobbies, career interests, and favorite dating activities. After viewing the tape, participants were asked how much they would like to date her, how much they would like to kiss her, and how attractive they considered her. The items were highly correlated and combined to create a measure of *romantic attraction*.

As revealed in Figure 9.4, the male participants in a state of low arousal felt more "romantic" toward the attractive female than toward the unattractive female, but not by very much. But look at how the male participants in a state of heightened arousal felt. Those who viewed the attractive female saw her in highly romantic terms (and were eager to meet her for the date), but those who viewed the unattractive female had virtually no romantic feelings toward her—if anything, they were somewhat repulsed by her. Generalizing from these results, one might expect people to fall in love with an attractive person if they encounter this person after a workout or an exciting movie. But by the same token, the workout or movie could generate intense dislike for someone who might otherwise be seen as not particularly desirable.

Social Exchange

It is nice to think of attraction as driven by desire and admiration, even if these feelings reflect biological processes that are often non-conscious (e.g., the smell of symmetry, MHC compatibility). But attraction has some practical constraints that are similar to the factors that influence our consumer behavior. We may want to purchase a Rolex or a Ferrari, but if these products are beyond our reach, we make do with a Timex or a Ford. In analogous manner, people adjust their criteria for social relations in accordance with their sense of what they can hope to achieve. This is the essence of *social exchange theory* (e.g., Thibaut & Kelley, 1959).

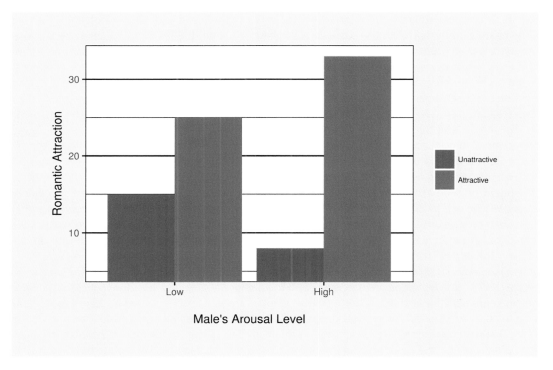

FIGURE 9.4 Arousal-Induced Polarization of Feelings toward an Attractive and an Unattractive Woman
Source: Adapted from White et al. (1981)

Comparison Levels

Theories that emphasize social exchange view interpersonal relations as analogous to a marketplace, with consumers negotiating for the best deal they can get in a friend, a teammate, or even a romantic partner. With enough marketplace experience, consumers develop a notion of what they can reasonably expect to obtain at a price they can afford. This expectation, referred to as a *comparison level* (*CL*), functions as the neutral point on a *goodness-of-outcome scale*. People with different *CL*s are likely to feel differently about the same product or experience. Think about this in monetary terms. A $50,000 income might be viewed as wonderful for someone whose comparison level is near the poverty level but as unbearable for someone whose comparison level is near the top 1% income level. People adapt to their experiences and develop expectations that determine the subjective value of subsequent experiences.

In social relations, a person's *CL* determines how attracted he or she is to people with a certain marketplace value (Thibaut & Kelley, 1959). If a person has a history of low-quality social relations, his or her *CL* will be correspondingly low, so that he or she may be attracted to others who are not particularly good looking or who have relatively bland personalities. But if the person's history consists of high-quality social relations, he or she has a higher *CL* and will only be attracted good looking people with an interesting personality.

Social exchange theory suggests that people with similar marketplace value are likely to match up. In a social situation (e.g., a party or a club), everyone may seek someone with maximum social desirability, but ultimately each person will narrow his or her focus to those who are close to his or her *CL*, since people who exceed this value are unlikely to reciprocate the person's interest. This makes it likely that people who have similar *CL*s will be mutually attracted. This does not necessarily mean that people with a low *CL* "settle" for undesirable people. Because the *CL* establishes the subjective value of potential partners, people who meet a person's *CL* may not be viewed as a compromise—just as earning a middle-class income is not seen by most people as "settling," despite the fact that some people are millionaires or billionaires. In becoming attracted to someone who meets one's *CL*, one is likely to appreciate the unique qualities of this person and can be truly attracted to him or her.

The social marketplace involves more than attraction. People may establish a connection with someone who falls short of their *CL* if there are no alternatives available. This feature of social exchange reflects a different reference point, known as the *comparison level for alternatives* (*CL alt*), that defines the quality of outcomes that is perceived to exist in the next best alternative to the current relationship (Rusbult, 1983; Thibaut & Kelley, 1959). A person with a low *CL alt* perceives (perhaps accurately, perhaps not) that there are few or no alternatives that are more desirable than his or her current relationship. A person with a high *CL alt*, meanwhile, feels that there are more desirable alternatives to his or her current relationship. So whereas a person's *CL* functions as a standard for determining his or her *attraction* to others, a person's *CL alt* functions as a standard for determining his or her *dependency* on others.

These two standards are often related. If we are attracted to someone, we may both "want" the person and "need" the person. But the *CL* and the *CL alt* are independent in principle—and sometimes in practice. A first-year college student, for example, may discover many people who are more interesting and more attractive than the students he or she knew in high school. Assume the person strikes up a relationship with one of his or her new acquaintances. He or she will be attracted to the new relationship partner (the relationship exceeds the person's *CL*) but he or she may not feel dependent on the partner (the relationship is below the person's *CL alt* because there are plenty of other attractive people who are available). The other conflict between one's *CL* and *CL alt* can occur as well. A student who gets stranded on a desert island with one other person, for example, may not be attracted to this person but in the absence of any alternative relationships, the student is dependent on the relationship with this person. In social exchange terms, the desert island partner is below the student's *CL* but above his *CL alt*.

A mismatch in partners' respective *CL alt* has implications for the *balance of power* in the relationship (Blau, 1964; Thibaut & Kelley, 1959). The less dependent person—with the higher *CL alt*—is in a position to dictate the terms of their relationship. In some traditional cultures, for example, women are highly constrained in their social behavior, while men are free to cultivate relations with other people. With virtually no possibility of forming an alternative relationship, the women in such cultures have a *CL alt* that is effectively zero. Because the men do have alternatives and thus a far higher *CL alt*, they have a monopoly on the power in the relationship and can dictate how the women behave. They may not exploit this basis for power, but the potential is inherent in the relationship.

Reciprocity of Liking

The most basic form of social exchange is *reciprocity* (Gouldner, 1960). When people give us gifts, help us out of a jam, or offer us advice, we feel obligated to return the favor in some fashion. Reciprocity prevails as well in social life. If someone pays us a compliment, we feel obliged to say something nice in return. And if someone appears to like us, we are inclined to reciprocate this positive feedback by expressing liking for him or her. Because we tend to assume that others will act positively toward us when we first meet them, the mere expectation of an interaction with someone tends to generate positive feelings toward him or her (Darley & Berscheid, 1967; Knight & Vallacher, 1981).

The reciprocity-of-liking effect comes with two notable caveats. For one thing, feedback on one's personality does not take place all at once, but rather unfolds over time. Imagine, for example, that you are at a party and during the course of the evening you overhear another person describing his or her feelings about you. Let's say you hear one of four temporal patterns in the person's assessment: (1) the person starts out judging you harshly and doesn't change his or her tune on the subsequent occasions; (2) the person starts out gushing over your qualities and keeps this up on all the subsequent occasions; (3) the person starts out positive but becomes increasingly negative over time; or (4) the person starts out with a harsh assessment but becomes increasingly positive, with the final assessment being highly flattering. Which temporal pattern would make you like versus dislike the person the most?

You might think that you would *dislike* the person most if he or she displayed pattern (1), saying consistently negative things about you; and *like* the person most if he or she displayed pattern (2), saying consistently positive things about you. In both cases, there are more indications of disliking and liking, respectively, to reciprocate. According to *gain-loss theory* (Aronson & Linder, 1965), however, you would have the strongest reactions to the person if he or she changed his or her tune over time. If the person's feedback changed from positive to negative—so that you effectively *lost* his or her liking—you would dislike the person most intensely. But if the feedback changed from negative to positive—so that you effectively *gained* his or her liking—you would have the most favorable feelings about the person.

The gain-loss perspective has implications for the fate of close relationships. In getting to know someone, there is a certain thrill in seeing admiration or respect develop for you in the other person, especially if the initial encounters were a bit rocky in this regard. This is a theme, for example, in romantic comedies. The two people start out wary of one another, perhaps even expressing some degree of contempt, but by the end of the movie they have discovered one another and fallen madly in love, perhaps flying off in a hot-air balloon together. But close relationships can turn cold and even hostile under the other scenario. To have someone's love and respect, only to lose the person's positive regard over time, can be painful and promote harsh feelings. Love lost is felt more strongly than not having been loved in the first place.

The second caveat to the reciprocity of liking effect represents a dilemma for people with low self-esteem. Recall from Chapter 5 ("Self-Concept") that people do not necessarily crave positive feedback, but rather feedback that is consistent with the way they see themselves (Swann, 1990). Because most people hold themselves in high regard, the consistency effect boils down to a positive feedback effect. So when a high self-esteem person receives compliments from others, he or she is quite comfortable in reciprocating the positive regard because it verifies his or her own self-assessment. But for people who have a low opinion of their desirability, positive feedback is a source of inconsistency. Such feedback is initially savored, but over time the person disavows the compliments and affection as lacking in credibility. This wreaks havoc on the reciprocity of liking effect, and it hardly bodes well for smooth social encounters or a conflict-free romantic relationship.

Romantic Relationships

How and Why Do People Form Intimate Relationships?

We can feel attracted to many different people, and this interest may be reciprocated by a fair portion of them. But we don't form close relationships with all of them. Clearly, there is more to love than physical attraction, similarity, polarized arousal, and marketplace considerations. What are the missing factors that translate liking into loving? Are these factors universal or do they vary across different cultures? Do males and females approach romantic entanglement in the same way?

The Meaning of Love

When we love someone, we feel little need to explain it, let alone come up with a theory for it. But when philosophers, poets, songwriters, and novelists take on the task of explaining what love is, they inevitably come to appreciate the nuance and complexity of this fixture of human relations. Far from being a simple experience, love involves a mix of emotions, a trade-off among basic needs, and the interplay of fantasy and reality considerations.

Box 9.1   The Language of Flirtation

It can be risky to come right out and tell someone that you are attracted to him or her. Apart from the possibility that you might be rejected—and a bit embarrassed as a result—this straightforward approach might make the other person feel uncomfortable and it may convey an asymmetric power relationship with the person ("you may be more important to me than I am to you"). Beyond that, it can make for some awkward moments if the person doesn't know quite what to say—and you are at a loss for a follow-up comment. An alternative to blurting out your attraction to someone is to convey your interest through nonverbal channels—in other words, to flirt with the person.

Flirtation is a common occurrence and seems to occur effortlessly without a great deal of conscious control. Check out a nightclub sometime where singles (or those posing as singles) mingle and attempt to form a short-term relationship, perhaps with the hope that it evolves into a longer-term one. If you have better things to do, that's fine—researchers have taken up the challenge and spent hundreds of hours documenting the nature of flirtation that occurs in singles bars (e.g., Givens, 1983; Perper, 1985). This line of scientific inquiry has identified four phases of the flirtation scenario.

In the initial *getting attention phase*, men engage in exaggerated behaviors to advertise their resources or their potential for acquiring resources. They may roll their shoulders or stretch their arms to show off their muscles, or order an expensive drink in a loud voice and make sure that their expensive watches are visible as they hand their gold credit card across the bar to the bartender. For their part, women smile coyly, flick their hair, and walk in a way that captures attention and conveys sensuality (e.g., swaying their hips and arching their back).

In the *recognition phase*, the flirtatious individuals express their interest by raising their eyebrows, locking their gaze upon one another, talking in a sing-song voice, and laughing at even the most inane comments by one another. Assuming this phase goes well, the individuals progress to the *touching phase*. This can be tricky, so the individuals first move a bit closer to one another, creating the opportunities to touch one another with pats on the shoulder, "accidental" bumps against one another, and provocative brushes on one another's arms.

All this culminates in the *keeping-time phase*, which involves fairly precise coordination of body language. The individuals—who are well on the way to becoming romantic partners—line up their actions to express their own interest and assess one another's interest. They mirror one another's glances and laughter, all the while keeping their shoulders and faces aligned. At this point, their faces and hair touch as they continue to synchronize their various nonverbal channels of communication. They are saying things too, of course, but the verbal comments are secondary to what is being conveyed by their faces and bodies.

In view of the importance of nonverbal behavior in this dance of mutual seduction, it's interesting to consider the fate of matches that are initiated over dating services on the internet that are restricted to words and posed images. What may seem like a perfect match on Match.com or Tinder may fizzle when the individuals get together and the nonverbal flirtation ritual fails to seal the deal.

Universals of Love

Love may be complex and hard to describe, but it has features that are universal. Robert Sternberg (1986) has proposed and validated an especially intriguing model that identifies three independent factors that interact in various ways to generate the complexity and nuance of love relationships. The key components, depicted in Figure 9.5, are *passion*, *intimacy*, and *commitment*. Because these factors are distinct from one another and can coexist in different blends, Sternberg's model defines different types of love.

Passion is often, but not always, the lead player in romantic attraction. For many years, in fact, psychologists interested in close relationships focused on this component under the rubric of interpersonal attraction. Passion may be critical for love to blossom, but it does not hold up well over time. To be sure, couples can be together for decades and still stir each other in very basic ways. But for this to happen, the experience of love must take on one or both of the remaining components. Intimacy is critical because it means forming an emotional rather than merely a physical connection with one's partner. Long after the fires of a passionate relationship have begun to simmer, people can feel warm and connected with their partner because of the intimate connection they have. The converse is also true: deepening intimacy can fuel passion (Baumeister & Bratslavsky, 1999) and keep a relationship fresh and exciting.

In an emotionally intimate relationship, people let down their guards, dispense with the self-presentation strategies on display in interactions with other people (Chapter 8), and disclose secret thoughts, hopes, and fears, while listening to those of their partner. Such *self-disclosure* (Jourard, 1964) has a positive feedback loop with relationship satisfaction: the greater the self-disclosure, the greater the satisfaction, and the greater the satisfaction, the more self-disclosing the partners become (Collins & Miller, 1994; Neff & Karney, 2005; Sanderson & Cantor, 2001).

Self-disclosure in a relationship tends to be reciprocated but this *disclosure reciprocity* effect (Miller, 1990) is not always immediate. In fact, if one person reveals too much about him or herself too soon, it can put the brakes on a budding relationship. Some people tend to be especially skilled at getting others to open up, even those who normally are reluctant to do so (Miller, Berg, & Archer, 1983; Pegalis, Shaffer, Bazzini, & Greenier, 1994). Women tend to have the edge here, and they are also more willing than men to disclose their fears and weaknesses (Cunningham, 1981). With increasingly egalitarian gender-role attitudes in society, however, this difference is becoming less pronounced, with men today being more willing to reveal intimate feelings and experience mutual trust in self-disclosure.

The third component—commitment—is clearly critical to the long-term success of a romantic relationship. It is also the trickiest component. Passion and intimacy can create a desire for commitment, but other factors can prevent people from acting on this desire. People have basic tendencies that sound diametrically opposed to commit-

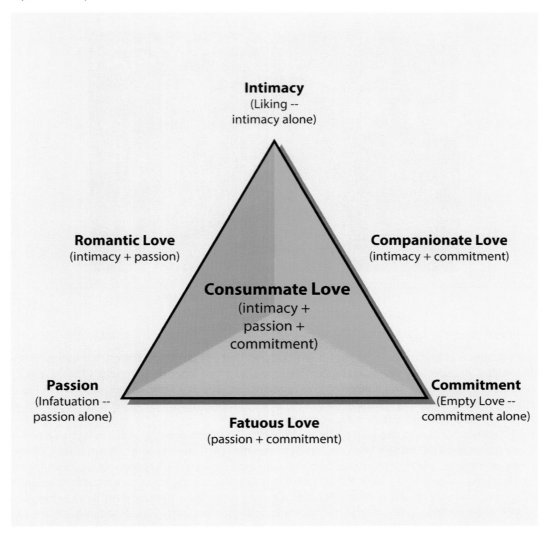

FIGURE 9.5 The Triangulation of Love
Source: Adapted from Sternberg (1986)

ment—impulse, personal autonomy, egoistic goals, self-determination, reactance, and personal freedom. Add to these features of individual psychology the relationship opportunities available in today's world. Unlike our ancestors, we can travel anywhere in the world, advertise ourselves online, and go to clubs and parties where there are likely to be potential mates. Why form a commitment with one person when there is a boundless supply of other possible partners waiting to be discovered?

Yet we do form commitments and achieve the third ingredient of love. Commitment obviously involves more than a rational assessment of one's likelihood of optimizing relationship opportunities. The forces in our ancestral environment that shaped our preferences for the right waist-hip ratios and symmetrical features also shaped a desire to become connected over time with one person. Without such desires, the pair-bonding essential for successful child-rearing would have not been possible—and we would not be here right now to discuss the matter.

Before people can become committed, they must feel both *satisfied with* and *dependent on* the relationship. Recall that a person's satisfaction is relative to his or her *CL* (how the rewards and costs compare to the person's expectations or past relationships), while his or her dependency is relative to his or her *CL alt* (how the rewards and costs compare with the rewards and costs in alternative relationships). To these considerations, Carol Rusbult (1983) added the person's *level of investment* in the relationship. If the person has devoted considerable time, energy, and finances to the relationship, he or she is likely to feel heavily invested in the relationship and reluctant to leave it. Taken together, then, satisfaction, dependency, and level of investment shape one's commitment to relationship. If the relationship is better than the person's past relationships, better than alternative relationships, and constitutes a substantial investment of time, energy, and resources, it stands a good chance of persisting over time.

Box 9.2   Which Relationships Have the Most Mental Staying Power?

Not all relationships work out. Some fizzle early, some run their course and gradually lose steam, and some last beyond expectation before taking a turn for the worse. But just because relationships fade or flame out doesn't mean they are forgotten. Some relationships are especially likely to pop into one's mind long after their demise, sometimes without warning or for any good reason. But which relationships have this staying power, even if one or both partners have moved on and would just as soon never think about one another again? We suspect you would make one of two predictions: the relationships that are the most intense or the ones that lasted the longest.

There is some wisdom to this prediction, but according to research reported by Wegner, Lane, and Dimitri (1994), there is another type of relationship that trumps both passion and commitment—relationships that were kept secret while they were ongoing. Office romances, for example, or affairs with the partner of one's best friend, are relationships that we try to keep quiet and out of the rumor mills. This may seem surprising, but it actually makes sense in light of what you learned about the ironic nature of thought suppression in Chapter 3. Attempts to suppress a thought (even a trivial thought about white bears) have the ironic effect of keeping the thought in mind—so that we can check whether the suppression has worked (Wegner, 1994). Suppression can prove successful if one devotes executive resources to the task. But this means that the suppressed thought is tied up with a lot of mental effort and time. And when the mental effort is withdrawn and devoted to other matters, the suppressed thought can burst back into consciousness. That office romance or secret liaison may have been brief and not all that intense, but it is not forgotten.

Chemistry of Love

We have all heard of "sexual chemistry," but most of us understand this popular cliché as a metaphor and do not take it literally. Perhaps we should. Earlier, we saw how the smells of symmetry, female fertility, and immune diversity can promote attraction between people. There is also evidence that a variety of neurotransmitters and hormones play a big part in cementing a romantic relationship (e.g., Acevedo, Aron, Fisher, & Brown, 2012).

Perhaps the most important chemical basis of romantic love is the hormone *oxytocin* (Carter, 1998; Taylor, 2006). This hormone is produced in the hypothalamus—a brain structure implicated in motivation and emotion—and there are receptors for it in many areas of the brain, including the brainstem, regions of the spinal cord that regulate the autonomic nervous system, and the olfactory system. Oxytocin increases pair-bonding and nurturing behavior in nonhuman species (Taylor, 2006). Two closely related rodent species, the prairie vole and the montane vole, differ in the location of oxytocin receptors in their respective brains (Carter, 1998), and this difference is associated with quite different mating patterns: the prairie vole mates with one partner for life, whereas the montane vole is highly promiscuous, showing little commitment to its many partners. When oxytocin is injected into a montane mole's brain, it drops its promiscuous habits and adopts the prairie vole's commitment to a life-long partner (Williams, Insel, Harbaugh, & Carter, 1994).

It is a stretch to say that oxytocin promotes romantic love in prairie voles. But remember that commitment is a major component of love in humans (Sternberg, 1986). And oxytocin affects humans in much the same way that it affects our rodent brethren. Oxytocin is released during female lactation and thus may play an important role in mothers' bonding with their offspring, and it is also released during the uterine contractions associated with female orgasm (Carter, 1998). Presumably, this release intensifies the feeling of bonding that accompanies sexual inter-course, and it promotes the "cuddling" that takes place upon orgasm. Research confirms that oxytocin is associated with love rather than sexual desire. When women were asked to recall an experience of warmth toward another person, for example, there was a greater release of oxytocin into their bloodstreams if they expressed displays of love than if they expressed displays of sexual desire (Gonzaga et al., 2006). Oxytocin, then, may be the "love molecule" that keeps commitment relevant in an age where it is all too easy to forge relationships solely on passion and to relinquish such relationships with the expectation that another one is just around the corner. Passion may set the stage for love, but the commitment fostered by oxytocin may seal the deal.

Cultural Differences

Romantic love exists everywhere, and it always has. The foundations and expression of this universal tendency, however, vary a great deal across cultures and have undergone many transformations throughout recorded history (Jankowiak, 1995; Murstein, 1974). Among the ancient Greeks, for example, romantic love was experienced primarily *outside* of marriage and was usually homosexual rather than heterosexual in nature. During the Roman era, homosexual love gave way to heterosexual love, but it was still considered something that occurred outside of marriage. When Christianity became firmly established in Roman society, the passionate component of love—sex—was devalued, with religious leaders arguing that sex was morally corruptive and tolerated only in marriage because it could not be avoided if people wanted to bear offspring. Romantic love made a comeback during the Middle Ages (AD 1000–1300), at least among European aristocrats who practiced "courtly love." This form of romance emphasized the majestic and spiritual nature of love, while downplaying the physical component. Courtly love, in fact, was never consummated—at least in theory, if not in practice.

Throughout these periods, marriage had little to do with passion and intimacy, but a lot to do with economics and politics. Marriages were arranged by the parents, with the partners themselves having little to say in the matter. To form an alliance or settle a conflict with a neighboring group, for example, a marriage between a man and a woman from the two groups would be arranged. Romantic love as a basis for marriage really did not occur until the 17th and 18th centuries, as the traditional considerations became less important (Stone, 1977). The link between romance and marriage appeared first in England, but became more pronounced in the "New World" when the English and other Europeans settled in America. Social class distinctions were less strongly enforced in America, and people felt free to choose their own partners (Rosenblatt & Cozby, 1972).

Our contemporary notion of romantic love—in Western society at least—is bit of a hybrid representing aspects of earlier traditions. Love leads to marriage, but it would be naïve to suggest that economics has nothing to do with partners' decision to make this commitment. Sex occurs outside of marriage, but voices are raised about the morality and appropriateness of this practice, with a small minority of young people today pledging chastity until they form a marital bond. Marriage has traditionally been heterosexual in nature, but there is an emerging acceptance of marriage between homosexual individuals of both genders.

Cultural differences are disappearing as the world gets increasingly interconnected, and this trend is almost certain to continue in the years to come. Perhaps this is a good thing, assuming that the coming homogeneity represents personal choice and discretion in forming a long-term commitment. It is hard for someone in the Western world to reconcile arranged marriages and inequality between men and women with fundamental human needs, dignity, and inalienable rights. But the loss of cultural diversity in close relationships may be a mixed blessing. Culture-specific values and norms may promote the long-term commitment that is threatened in societies where personal freedom and self-enhancement are the pillars of social relations.

Interdependence

Even a highly independent person in an individualistic society relies on other people for information, entertainment, and verification of his or her beliefs. This is true in casual relationships, although it is possible to interact with such people with limited goals in mind, and to look elsewhere when these goals are not met. Close relationships, however, have interdependence at their very core. People in a committed relationship depend on one another for everything from meal preparation, weekend planning, and the latest gossip to career guidance, validation of their personal worth, and emotional support during stressful times. The interdependence characterizing a close relationship not only covers a broader range, it also takes on qualitatively different forms than those observed in everyday social interaction.

Exchange and Communal Orientations

In interacting with a business partner or a college roommate, people are sensitive to the "deal" they are getting. Social exchange considerations are important in the early stages of a close relationship as well, but once the relationship is established, the tit-for-tat concerns are often relaxed. The relationship can be said to evolve from an *exchange orientation* to a *communal orientation* (Clark & Mills, 1993). Rather than focusing on one another's reliability in returning favors and doing his or her "fair share," people in a love relationship focus on one another's needs. If one of them falls on hard times, develops an illness, or has an emotionally upsetting experience, the other person will take over some of the responsibilities in the relationship. In doing so, the person does not look for a payback or convey the feeling that "you owe me!" In fact, if it appears that the relationship is defined in terms of reciprocity and exchange factors, it can promote awkwardness and even dissatisfaction. Events that would destabilize an exchange-based relationship can strengthen a communal relationship. If a person makes sacrifices that benefit his or her partner, he or she experiences positive emotions and expresses satisfaction rather than resentment (Kogan et al., 2010).

Attachment

Humans are born with virtually no survival skills and are totally dependent on their caretakers for well over a decade. They cannot flee predators, locate shelter, find food, feed themselves, or treat themselves when they become sick. No other mammal is as sorely equipped during youth for survival on its own as are humans. In order to survive and reach adulthood, human infants are programmed by evolution to form intense close relationships with parents (or parental figures). And this desire to form a close bond with someone does not end with childhood, but continues throughout humans' life span. Forming a close relationship is a prerequisite for mating and raising offspring—the ultimate evolutionary mandate.

John Bowlby (1969) recognized the evolutionary bases for bonding in human relationships and advanced *attachment theory* to explain how these bonds are established, and to predict the consequences for close relationships in adulthood that result from children's experience with caretaker bonding during childhood. Psychologists have expanded on Bowlby's theory and tested hypotheses about the influence of childhood experiences with their parents on adulthood experiences in close relationships (Hazan & Shaver, 1987; Simpson et al., 1996).

The central idea of attachment theory is straightforward. In forming attachments to their parents, children develop a *working model of relationships* (Baldwin et al., 1996). The specific model they develop reflects their experiences with how available their parents are and the extent to which their parents provide a sense of security. The most noteworthy attempt to identify attachment patterns, developed by Mary Ainsworth (1993), is based on the way children respond to separations and reunions with their caregivers. In the *strange situation* procedure, an infant and his or her caregiver enter an unfamiliar room containing interesting toys. As the infant explores the room and begins to play with the toys, a stranger walks in and the caregiver quietly leaves. After three minutes, the caregiver returns and greets the infant, comforting him or her if necessary. Not surprisingly, all infants experience some degree of distress when the caregiver leaves the room. The issue is how the caregiver and infant behave when the caregiver returns.

Three basic patterns of caregiver and infant behavior are commonly observed. In the *secure attachment* pattern, the caregiver responds quickly and reliably to the infant's distress cries. These infants are comfortable in moving away from the caregiver to explore the environment, although they glance at the caregiver once in a while to make sure things are OK. The infants apparently feel safe in a novel environment even if they are not in direct contact with their caregivers. In the *anxious attachment* pattern, caregivers are not reliable in their behavior toward the child. Sometimes they intrude on the infant's activities, but at other times they show little interest and seemingly reject the infant. These infants tend to cry or show anger when put in a novel environment and are not easily comforted by the caregiver when he or she attempts to provide it. In the *avoidant attachment* pattern, the caregiver is more reliable, showing disinterest and seeming rejection of the infant in the novel situation. The children of these parents often do not seek out the caregiver in the novel situation, and they may even reject attention when the caretaker offers it.

Table 9.1 Attachment Styles in Romantic Relationships

The proportion of participants who endorsed statements that best described their romantic relationships

Secure style   **56%**

"I find it relatively easy to get close to others and am comfortable depending on them and having them depend on me. I don't often worry about being abandoned or about someone getting too close."

Avoidant style   **25%**

"I am somewhat uncomfortable being close to others; I find it difficult to trust them completely, difficult to allow myself to depend on them. I am nervous when anyone gets close, and often love partners want me to be more intimate than I feel comfortable being."

Anxious style   **19%**

"I find that others are reluctant to get as close as I would like. I often worry that my partner doesn't really love me or won't stay with me. I want to merge completely with another person, and this desire sometimes scares people away."

Source: Hazan & Shaver (1987)

Knowing a child's attachment style may tell us a lot about the child, but is this knowledge relevant to how the child behaves many years later as an adult? There are many experiences on the path from childhood to adulthood, after all, so perhaps an infant's relationship with his or her parents fades in significance over time. That does not seem to be the case. To the contrary, evidence supports the contention that a person's attachment style as an infant shapes how he or she relates to other people—his or her friends, children, romantic partners—well into adulthood (Fraley & Spieker, 2003). Of course, attachment style is manifest differently by adults than it is by infants. Grown men and women do not cry and throw tantrums when their relationship partner leaves the room. So researchers have developed various self-report measures to assess adults' attachment style (Brennan, Clark, & Shaver, 1998).

In one popular approach, participants read three brief paragraphs and are asked to select the one that best describes the way they relate to other people (Hazen & Shaver, 1987). The paragraphs are presented in Table 9.1, along with the attachment style each paragraph represents and the proportion of participants who chose each paragraph to describe their romantic relationships.

People's self-reports on such measures predict how they actually approach intimate relationships (Collins & Feeney, 2000; Rholes, Simpson, & Orina, 1999; Simpson et al., 1996). Those with a secure attachment style are comfortable with intimacy and want to be close to others when dealing with threat or uncertainty. Individuals with an avoidant attachment style tend to distance themselves from others, becoming especially detached when they feel threatened or uncertain. And individuals with an anxious attachment style compulsively cling to others, especially when threatened or uncertain, and they obsessively worry about their relationships.

Not surprisingly, attachment style is related to relationship satisfaction (e.g., Cooper, Shaver, & Collins, 1998; Shaver & Brennan, 1992), with a clear advantage associated with secure attachment. In a 4-year longitudinal study (Kirkpatrick & Hazan, 1994), for example, far fewer secure individuals experienced a romantic breakup (25.6%) than did avoidant individuals (52.2%) or anxious individuals (43.6%). Not to be outdone, Klohen and Bera (1998) analyzed data from a longitudinal study of females that spanned 30 years. They found that secure women were more likely to be married in their fifties (82%) than were avoidant women (50%), and that the former reported significantly fewer marital tensions.

Male and Female Agendas

When issues of dating and mating are discussed, the question of differences between men and women is almost certain to become front and center. Both genders experience attraction and fall in love, of course, but laypeople and scientists alike wonder whether men and women have the same motives and agendas (some hidden) about forging the relationship. Do they want or expect the same benefits as a resulting of becoming partners? Do they differ in how willing they are to become intimate with potential partners? How important are social exchange or "marketplace" considerations in shaping how men and women relate to one another?

Currency of Social Exchange

As noted earlier, attraction and relationship formation reflects marketplace economics, with each person attempting to secure the best deal possible. This does not mean that men and women play with the same bargaining chips or want the same benefits. In blunt and overly simplistic terms, sex is a resource that women have and men want. In exchange for this resource, men have to provide resources that women want (Baumeister & Vohs, 2004; Buss & Schmitt, 1993; Symons, 1979), including respect, attention, and commitment. Men also offer security and protection in exchange for sex. In our ancestral environment, these resources took the form of status and dominance in relation to other males, characteristics that often boiled down to strength, energy, and health. In today's world, security and protection are also associated with money; this resource is a bigger bargaining chip than are V-shaped torsos and strong jawlines.

Why is sex such a lopsided resource favoring women? In evolutionary terms, a man's reproductive strategy is best served by having sex with many women in order to maximize his genetic contribution to succeeding generations (Buss & Schmitt, 1993; Symons, 1979). The sex act is a relatively low-cost investment for men, so there is little to inhibit them from seeking out multiple mates. To be sure, men do not seek out women for sex to fulfill a conscious desire to impregnate them. But evolved sexual desires have little to do with conscious considerations; evolution has selected for a variety of behavioral tendencies, from overeating to risk-taking, that proved adaptive in our ancestral environment.

Women, in contrast, are predisposed to bypass opportunities for casual sex and to be selective in their choice of sex partners. Sex is associated with possible pregnancy (with pain and the risk of death during childbirth). A woman must carry a baby for 9 months, then care for the offspring for close to two decades, all the while sacrificing other activities that might be rewarding in other ways. Contraception can certainly reduce some of this concern, of course, but keep in mind that our evolved mental mechanisms regarding sex have been in place for thousands of years, with birth control arriving on the scene only in the last few decades. So even if sex is pleasurable for a woman, it is considered in relation to its extensive potential costs. Women therefore tend to hold back on offering this resource, and men must offer compensatory benefits to make this exchange acceptable to the woman.

But is it really the case that men desire sex more than do women? There is an extensive literature on this issue, and a review of this evidence reveals that on virtually every measure, men display greater sexual motivation than do women (Baumeister et al., 2001). To be more specific, compared to women, men:

- Think about sex more often
- Have more frequent fantasies
- Are more frequently aroused
- Desire sex more often (both early and late in relationships and outside of relationships)
- Desire a higher number of sex partners
- Masturbate more frequently
- Are less willing to forgo sex and are less successful at celibacy (even when celibacy is supported by personal religious commitments)
- Enjoy a greater variety of sexual practices
- Take more risks and expend more resources to obtain sex
- Initiate more goal directed behavior to get sex
- Refuse sex less often
- Commence sexual activity sooner after puberty
- Have more permissive and positive attitudes toward most sexual behaviors
- Are less prone to report a lack of sexual desire
- Rate their sex drives as stronger than women's.

Men also expect (or hope) to have greater sexual variety. Buss and Schmitt (1993) surveyed male and female students about the number of sex partners they desired over different time periods, from one month to their entire lifetime. The results, presented in Figure 9.6, reveal big differences between the genders, even during the shorter time periods. For example, women expressed an interest in having two sex partners after 3 years, whereas males reached this number in less than six months—by 3 years, they expected (or hoped) to have 10 sex partners. Over the course of

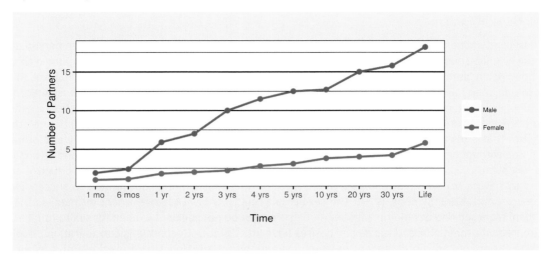

FIGURE 9.6 Number of Sex Partners Desired by Men and Women
Source: Adapted from Buss & Schmitt (1993)

their lifetimes, females indicated desire for six or fewer partners, whereas males on average indicated a desire to have sexual relations with close to 20 women.

Buss and Schmitt (1993) also found that men were more eager than women to bring sex into a relationship. When women were asked how long they would have to know a man before it was likely they would consider having sex with him, women indicated 3 months. When asked the same question about a woman, men indicated 1 day! But if men and women differ in their readiness to have sex, which gender tends to prevail? This issue was addressed by Cohen and Shotland (1996), who asked couples when they wanted to bring sex into the relationship and when they actually did. There was *zero correlation* between what the men in these couples wanted and what happened, but there was a very *strong correlation* between what the female partners wanted and the couple's activities. Men may want sex as soon as possible, but women are the ones who decide when it will happen.

Men may be more eager for sex, but this does not mean they are only interested in women for sexual reasons. In fact, men are more affected by love relationships in certain respects than are women. Men fall in love faster than women, and women fall out of love faster than men (Hill, Rubin, & Peplau, 1976; Kanin, Davidson, & Scheck, 1970). Men more often experience loving someone who doesn't reciprocate the feeling, whereas women more often receive love but do not reciprocate it (Baumeister, Wotman, & Stillwell, 1993). And when a love relationship breaks up, men suffer more intense emotional distress than do women (Hill et al., 1976).

Box 9.3   What Do Men and Women Regret About Their Sex Lives?

It is hard to imagine going through life without some regrets regarding one's behavior in sexual situations (Morrison & Roese, 2011). But do men and women regret the same things? Apparently not, according to research by Galperin and colleagues (2013). The authors reasoned that if women have a weaker sex drive, they can bypass opportunities for casual sex without feeling regretful. However, they might be inclined to regret sexual action on their part—particularly sexual liaisons involving casual sex with a man they hardly knew. Men, on the other hand, are motivated to seek out frequent sex, even with women they hardly know, because of their stronger sex drive. Because of their more pressing and persistent quest for sexual relations, they are likely to regret *inaction* on their part—missed opportunities or occasions where they did not manage to consummate a liaison with a woman.

To test this hypothesis, the researchers presented a checklist of regrets to male and female college students and asked them to indicate which regrets they had experienced. Some regrets referred to engaging in casual sexual encounters (*sexual action*), whereas others referred to *not* pursuing or engaging in casual sex (*sexual inaction*). The results provided support for the predicted gender difference. Below are five of the regrets experienced more often by women than by men—note that all refer to sexual *actions* rather than inactions.

- Lost virginity to "wrong" partner (24% of women, 10% of men)
- Relationship progressed "too fast" sexually (20% of women, 10% of men)
- Sex with a stranger (20% of women, 6% of men)
- Sex with someone who faked commitment (17% of women, 3% of men)
- One-night stand (12% of women, 4% of men).

Now, compare these regrets with five of the regrets experienced more often by men than by women—note that all refer to sexual *inactions* rather than actions.

- Too shy to indicate sexual attraction to someone (27% of men, 10% of women)
- Was not more sexually adventurous when young (23% of men, 7% of women)
- Was not more sexually adventurous when single (19% of men, 8% of women)
- Did not experiment enough sexually (18% of men, 8% of women)
- Did not lose virginity early enough (10% of men, 4% of women).

It is important to put the social exchange view in perspective. Men and women trade from different resource classes, but this does not mean that romantic relationships are simply a disguised version of prostitution. The bases for attraction and commitment go far beyond the cold, calculating marketplace economics at work when people shop for groceries or a new car. Keep in mind all the factors that promote passion, intimacy, and commitment that have been discussed in earlier sections. People are drawn to each other and fall in love because they share important attitudes and values, satisfy one another's needs, feel excited in one another's presence, want to open up to one another, desire to share experiences as a team, and enjoy the feeling of attachment. The point at which exchange of resources becomes important is not yet well understood. For some people, an exchange of sex and resources may function as an initial screen, narrowing the potential partners for consideration on other criteria (similarity, need fulfillment, etc.). But for others, the other considerations may arise first, with the currency of social exchange entering the picture when deciding whether to close the deal.

Sex Ratio and Social Exchange

On average, the number of men and women available for romance in a society is equal—for every man there is a woman and vice versa. But for a variety of reasons, the ratio of men to women—referred to as the *sex ratio*—can become a bit lopsided, with either "too many men" (a ratio greater than 1.0) or "too many women" (a ratio less than 1.0). Immigration to a new land, for example, can flood the new region with too many men, leaving too many women behind in the old region. Men seeking fortune in the "Wild West" of the United States in the 19th century or in frontier Alaska in the mid-20th century are examples of this scenario.

Restrictive family planning policies can also upset a society's sex ratio. In the late 20th century, for example, the Chinese government sought to curb population growth by restricting families to a single child. A sobering (and presumably unintended) consequence of this policy was infanticide of newborn females. In traditional parts of China (and in traditional cultures elsewhere), there is a premium placed on males because they carry on the family name and because they are expected to become working members of the society and perhaps leaders. So if a couple gave birth to a girl, this meant that the desire to have a boy could not be fulfilled. But if they killed the girl at birth and kept this a secret, they could try again, hoping for a boy. Now fast-forward a couple of decades, and the result is a society with an unbalanced sex ratio, with too many men competing for too few women.

Marcia Guttentag and Paul Secord (1983) investigated the implications of high versus low sex ratios for male-female relations, with social exchange dynamics in mind. Assuming men desire sex with women, their willingness to provide resources to women to satisfy this desire should reflect the availability of potential partners. If there are too many men (i.e., a shortage of women), women can dictate the terms of romance and make the price of sex very high. They can demand greater respect or material resources, for example, and withhold sex until the desired bargain is struck. For their part, men in a high sex-ratio environment attempt to impose prudish sex practices and place a high value on monogamy and fidelity in order to enhance their likelihood of finding a woman, to ensure that she does not stray with another man, and to discourage other men from attempting to steal her away. Females in these high sex-ratio societies are thus well respected and taken care of, but they are expected to be sexually modest and are not free to follow their sexual impulses.

A very different pattern of male-female relations is associated with a low sex ratio (too many women). In this marketplace, women cannot demand much in exchange for sex because men can find other women who are willing to provide this resource. In social exchange terms, men have a relatively high *CL alt* when there is an excess of available women, so they feel less need to provide resources to women in exchange for sex, and they are less concerned with protecting women's virtue or their accessibility to other men. So although women lose bargaining power, they are relatively free to follow their sexual impulses without incurring the reputational damage (or retaliation) they would incur under high sex-ratio conditions.

Guttentag and Secord (1983) observed these patterns in their analysis of unbalanced sex ratios in several cultures throughout history. Other researchers have provided evidence that a society's sex ratio influences the sexual market-place. In studying women's clothing fashions from 1885 to 1976, for example, Barber (1999) found that skirt length correlated with the sex ratio, with women wearing shorter skirts when there were too few men. If one looks upon wearing shorter skirts as advertising one's sexuality, this correlation is consistent with the weaker bargaining position of women when their numbers exceed those of men.

The sex-ratio thesis assumes that males have institutional power, so that females' only recourse is to negotiate interpersonal power. This is a reasonable assumption for much of human history and for many societies in the modern era. If women do not have opportunities to become leaders in government, business, and science, they must exercise their power by using resources they do control. However, societies worldwide have experienced substantial changes over the past few decades, with women now represented in politics, law, medicine, science, and business. It remains to be seen whether this leveling of the institutional playing field changes the way in which unbalanced sex ratios affect the currency of social exchange in male-female relations.

Homosexuality

The theories and research discussed so far seem to imply that close relationships develop only between individuals of the opposite sex. This clearly does not capture reality. Homosexuality is a fixture of human relations that can be found in every society throughout recorded history. And in important respects, same-sex relationships are not that different from opposite-sex romance and love. The desire for sexual variety, for example, is stronger among gay men than among lesbian women (Bell & Weinberg, 1978).

Homosexuality is hard to square with theories emphasizing the role of culture in shaping values and desires. Most cultures throughout history have condemned homosexual relations as sinful, with some cultures even treating this orientation as illegal and deserving of severe punishment. Of course, same-sex relations have gained acceptance in recent decades, especially in western societies (e.g., the United States, European countries), and even social conservatives are increasingly tolerant of gay marriage. But against the backdrop of human history, the contemporary acceptance of same-sex unions is analogous to the last minute or two on a 24-hour clock. For that matter, the frequency of homosexuality does not seem to be increasing despite the recent upsurge in tolerance—although reliable data concerning this possibility are lacking.

The universality of homosexuality despite cultural values that discourage such behavior suggests that this orientation has a biological basis. In fact, twin studies suggest that there are genes that predispose men toward a same-sex orientation (Bailey & Pillard, 1991). But same-sex sexual relations do not result in pregnancy, so why haven't "gay genes" disappeared from the population? Some have argued that gay genes are linked with other genes that have adaptive value, and that these adaptive genes are expressed in heterosexuals as well as homosexuals (Zietsch et al., 2008). In this view, the gay genes are carried by, but not expressed in, individuals who have genes for certain qualities (e.g., altruism, creativity). When such individuals mate, they pass on these genes—as well the genes for same-sex orientation—to their offspring.

The foundations for same-sex orientation may be somewhat different for men and women. There is evidence that women have greater *erotic plasticity*—the degree to which the sex drive is shaped or altered by cultural or situational factors (Baumeister, 2000). The sex lives of men are not affected by their level of education or their religiosity, for example, but these cultural forces can have a substantial effect on the sex lives of women. A man's sexual orientation at age 20 is likely to be the same when he reaches middle or old age, but a woman's orientation may switch back and forth between heterosexual and homosexual orientations during this time (Adams & Turner, 1985; Savin-Williams, 1990; Whisman, 1996). Women's greater elasticity may also reflect their somewhat weaker sex drive (Baumeister et al., 2001). Because women view close relationships in emotional rather than purely sexual terms, they are open to experiencing intimacy with other women.

Whatever the bases for homosexuality turn out to be, the desire for same-sex relations cannot be dismissed as an anomaly or as an abnormality in human functioning. It is expressed universally and it conforms to the same principles that characterize heterosexual relationships.

Dissolution of Relationships

Why Do Close Relationships Fail?

Marriage is defined in terms of commitment, often expressed in a public setting with religious overtone and dozens of witnesses, so one would expect the union to endure for a long time, maybe even until "death do you part." This is not the case, however: 50% of first-time marriages end in divorce (Myers, 2000). And for every marriage, there are dozens more romances, infatuations, and affairs. If half of marriages fail, one can only imagine the failure rate of these forms of intimacy. Particularly when a close relationship is formed on the basis of passion rather than commitment, it is primed for dissolution once passion begins to subside. Yet breaking up is hard to do. Beyond the emotional upheaval experienced during a break-up, there are often material costs (e.g., lawyer fees) incurred by both partners. Divorces have become easier to obtain, but they are not free and they can drag on for far too long. The assets that were acquired together—the music collection, DVDs, books, photo albums, mementos, and so forth—pose another problem in ending a relationship with some history.

So, what determines whether partners remain committed or decide to end the relationship? Three sources of trouble are especially noteworthy. First, the *social exchange dynamics* in the relationship may change, undermining the way the partners interact with one another. Second, beyond the gradual destabilization that can occur as a relationship evolves, catastrophic events can occur that threaten the foundation of the relationship. Foremost among these events are those associated with *cheating* (whether real or suspected). And third, several *signals of impending doom* have been identified that predict whether a couple can weather the ups and downs inherent in a relationship, long before these problems are experienced.

Social Exchange Dynamics

For a close relationship to succeed, the partners must feel they are getting a fair deal. True, the concern with social exchange gives way over time to a concern with mutual need satisfaction, but the sensitivity to exchange dynamics is never completely suppressed. What looks like a lopsided exchange, with one partner providing benefits without getting much in return, may really be social exchange on a longer timescale. Rather than expecting immediate reciprocity, as in business transactions, or on a daily or weekly basis, as in friendships, romantic partners may remain committed to a one-sided exchange for months, even years, because they assume that the other person will someday return the favor or at least provide evidence that he or she intends to do so. Even over shorter time spans, partners can question whether the relationship is such a good deal after all. Two factors in particular can undermine one's evaluation of a relationship: a *change in one's comparison levels* and the *perception of inequity* in the relationship.

Change in Comparison Levels

The concept of comparison level (*CL*) is simple enough: someone who is more attractive, intelligent, or interesting than others we have encountered is considered a great deal and we are motivated to become involved with him or her. That sounds like a recipe for a very nice long-term relationship, filled with rewarding interactions that keep us happy, appreciative, and fully engaged. But keep in mind that over time, our CL is updated to take into account the experiences in the current relationship, so that even experiences that were initially beyond our expectations become the norm rather than the exception and hence effectively neutral.

This suggests that over time, close relationships become increasingly based on mutual dependency rather than mutual attraction. This creates the potential for boredom and may motivate sampling again in the social marketplace (Aronson & Linder, 1965). This does not necessarily break up the relationship but it might promote "roving eyes" and flirtatious behavior when in the company of other potential partners. As long as one's partner is above one's comparison level for alternatives (*CL alt*), the relationship is likely to remain intact. But with the renewed interest in alternatives, there is the risk that one will encounter someone new who provides the spark that has diminished in one's current relationship (Lawson, 1988).

The perception that one has alternatives to the present relationship is a primary factor in break-ups (Rusbult, 1983). As illustrated in Figure 9.7, when people become committed to a relationship, the importance of their *CL alt* pales in comparison to their satisfaction with the relationship (their *CL*) and their level of investment in the relationship. But people's *CL alt* emerges as the dominant factor when people decide to break up with their relationship partner. In essence, people fall in love because of attraction (dictated by their *CL*) but fall out of love because perceived changes in their dependency (dictated by their *CL alt*).

The reassuring news is that a *CL alt* is not subject to updating in the same way that a *CL* is. A person might become accustomed to an exciting relationship partner, but his or her value in the social marketplace is less likely to change. There are circumstances, however, that can dramatically increase a person's *CL alt* and undermine his or her dependency on a relationship. Sudden fame or wealth, for example, can make a person desirable to others who previously would not have given him or her a second look. Of course, the person may wish to enjoy the change in status with his or her current partner, but there is always the risk that the person will be sensitive to the upward revision in his or her *CL alt*.

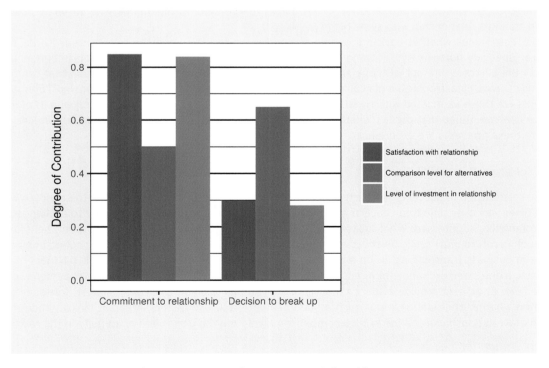

FIGURE 9.7 Issues in the Formation and Breakup of Long-Term Relationships
Source: Adapted from Rusbult (1983)

Fairness and Equity

Social life is regulated by norms of fairness as well as by the marketplace considerations associated with comparison levels. Whether in business or in close relationships, the parties to a relationship expect that the benefits each party receives should be proportional to their respective contributions to the relationship. This notion of fairness is referred to as the *norm of equity* (Adams, 1965; Deutsch, 1975). Equity is fairly straightforward in business and work relationships. The hardest working or best performing member of a work team, for example, is entitled to bigger compensation for his or her efforts than are the other team members.

Equity is not nearly as straightforward in close relationships (Walster, Berscheid, & Walster, 1973). One partner might have a higher income but the other partner plays a greater role in household management and childcare. Are their respective contributions equivalent, or is one more important than the other? And even if this issue can be resolved, how does one decide the benefits each person should receive? Romantic partners do not pay each other money. Perhaps the partner who contributes the most should be entitled to the most free time with his or her friends, to decide what the couple does on weekends or where to go on vacations, or to take control of the remote control when channel surfing on the TV.

The subjectivity in calculating equity in close relationships can pose serious problems (Walster et al., 1978). Partners commonly disagree on their respective contributions, usually by over-estimating their own contributions relative to the other person's (Sicoly & Ross, 1979). When marriage partners are each asked to estimate their own contribution to household maintenance, for example, the total contribution commonly exceeds 100%! Both of them, in other words, feel they are doing more than half the work in keeping the household running.

In a close relationship, the time frame for equity may be months, even years. In a marriage, for example, one partner may sacrifice his or her career ambitions to help the other partner get through graduate school or launch a business venture. In like manner, a marriage partner is likely to pick up the lion's share of household and financial responsibilities when his or her partner falls ill or suffers a serious accident. In such cases, the expectation is that the other person would do the same and that eventually equity will be restored to the relationship. When doubt creeps into these implicit calculations, however, the seemingly communal orientation is perceived as evidence of inequity. The sacrifices made by the under-benefited partner may begin to morph from "providing support" to "being exploited."

"Cheating"

People forming a close relationship expect commitment and exclusivity. Marriage is the ultimate expression of this expectation. In front of family members, friends, and religious leaders, the two individuals vow to be faithful to one another, resisting any and all temptations that may arise over the years and decades to come. Yet, despite all the personal promises and public vows, people often find that maintaining an exclusive relationship with one person can prove challenging and become tempted to form an *extradyadic relationship*—a passionate or emotional connection with someone else. Infidelity, whether actual or suspected, can prove highly disruptive to a relationship and is a primary cause of divorce among married couples (Wiederman, 1997). Even if a person has not acted on the temptation to get involved with someone else, his or her partner may nonetheless be concerned about this possibility, and this jealousy can undermine the warmth and trust that cemented the relationship in the first place.

Jealousy

Jealousy is sometimes rooted in suspicion rather than in reality. Some people are especially prone to paranoid jealousy, incorrectly thinking that their partner is interested in someone else and may act (or may have already acted) on this desire. These suspicions can promote *mate guarding*—actions designed to decrease the opportunity for the partner to become involved in an extradyadic relationship (Buss, 1988; Buss & Shackelford, 1997; Krems et al., 2016). The jealous partner might constantly check up on the other person, for example, or attempt to prevent him or her from meeting other people. This can prove self-fulfilling, with the suspected partner feeling the lack of trust and losing the sense of intimacy that is essential to maintaining commitment to a relationship. This feedback loop between unfounded suspicion and partner disengagement can spiral to the point that the suspicious partner goes into jealous rages and becomes physically violent toward the partner (Gondoff, 1985).

Both males and females experience jealousy, but they differ in the triggers that promote this feeling. According to evolutionary psychology, these triggers reflect differences between the reproductive systems of men and women. For women, there is little mystery concerning their genetic contribution to their offspring—when they give birth, they can be 100% certain that they are the baby's mother. Things are quite different for a man. Because his genetic contribution to the offspring—fertilization of the woman's egg—occurs 9 months before the baby's arrival, and because he certainly doesn't give birth, he cannot be absolutely certain that the baby is really his. There is a chance that the woman had sex with another man around the same time, and that this man's sperm, rather than his own, fertilized the woman's egg. Faced with *paternity uncertainty*, men are highly vigilant regarding the woman's involvement with other men. They guard their mates against the advances of other men and experience intense anger if they learn (or simply suspect) that she has had sex with another man. Indeed, suspected infidelity is a leading cause of abuse and even homicide of women by men (Wilson & Daly, 1996).

So what triggers jealousy in women? They are not concerned about their genetic contribution to the baby, but they are deeply concerned about caring for the baby once it is born and about their own protection during pregnancy and for years afterward while rearing the child. Strictly speaking, men's work is done at the moment of conception, but for women the work is just beginning. In the modern world, it is possible for pregnant women and mothers to fend for themselves—although they are certainly in need of assistance and support. But in our ancestral environment when humans' evolutionary mandates were established, women who were pregnant or caring for a baby were at a clear disadvantage in tending to their own needs. It was essential for them to gain and maintain the commitment of the child's father during this critical time. Because emotional intimacy sets the stage for commitment to a relationship, women are sensitive to their male partner's level of emotional involvement with them and are vigilant regarding his emotional involvement with other women. So although women have little need to be jealous of their male partner's sexual involvement with another woman, it is in their interest to be jealous of his potential emotional involvement with another woman.

The idea that men experience *sexual jealousy* but that women experience *emotional jealousy* was tested by Buss, Larsen, Westen, and Semmelroth (1992). They asked US college students to imagine two hypothetical incidents involving a close relationship partner: (1) their partner having a one-time sexual encounter with someone of their sex; (2) their partner having an emotionally intimate encounter with someone of their sex that did not include sexual intercourse. The students were asked which incident they would find more distressing. None of them, male or female. were thrilled with either incident. But when forced to choose which one was worse, the students' responses were consistent with the evolutionary rationale. As Figure 9.8 illustrates, the majority of men were more distressed by the sexual infidelity, whereas the majority of women were more distressed by the emotional infidelity.

This research inspired considerable controversy. Some critics suggested that this was a cultural phenomenon that said little about universal evolutionary adaptations. But the finding that males and females are differentially sensitive to emotional versus sexual infidelity has been replicated in many cultures (e.g., Buunk, Angleitner, Oubaid, & Buss, 1996). Other critics have offered a "double shot" interpretation (DeSteno, Bartlett, Braverman, & Salovey, 1996), such that sexual infidelity implies emotional infidelity and vice versa. So if men suspect that their female partner has had sex with another man, they assume that she has also experienced emotional intimacy with him. By the same token, women are likely to assume that if their male partner has had an emotional connection with another woman, he is eager to have sex with her as well. Presumably, both men and women have a difficult time separating sexual from emotional intimacy, so that priming them to think about one brings to mind the other.

With this possibility in mind, subsequent research has decoupled sexual and emotional intimacy in the narratives that are provided (Murphy et al., 2006). In the purely sexual narrative, it is made explicit that the partner had no emotional connection with the person with whom he or she had sex. In the purely emotional narrative, it is made clear that the partner did not have sex with the person with whom he or she had the emotionally intimate encounter. Rather than supporting the double-shot interpretation, the results reveal a *greater* disparity between men and women in what triggers the greatest jealousy. In other words, when men are asked to imagine their female partner having sex with a man but not having any emotional connection to him, they become especially jealous. From an evolutionary perspective, when a woman is seen as having emotionally detached sex with other men, it sensitizes a man

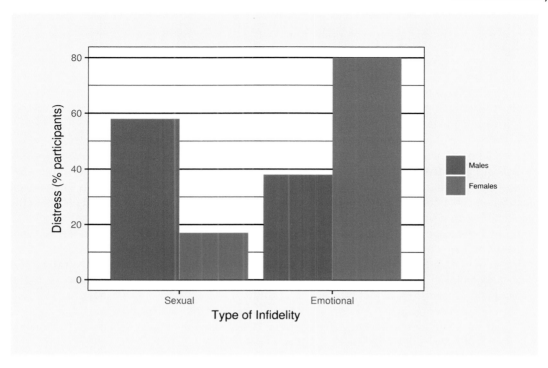

FIGURE 9.8 Sexual vs. Emotional Jealousy in Males and Females
Source: Adapted from Buss et al. (1992)

to a heightened risk that she could be impregnated by one of them, thereby increasing the likelihood that he would be investing resources in an offspring that is not his.

Nonetheless, there are individual differences in the experience of jealousy for both males and females. Levy and Kelly (2010) assessed the attachment style of college students and asked them whether they would be more distressed by their partner's emotional or sexual infidelity. They focused on two types of attachment—dismissive/avoidant and secure. A dismissive person sees little value in close relationships, placing primary value on his or her independence, whereas a secure person values relationships and is comfortable with intimacy. The securely attached students were more distressed by their partner's emotional infidelity, but those with a dismissive attachment style were more distressed by their partner's sexual infidelity. You might wonder why dismissive individuals were bothered by the thought of sexual infidelity. Levy and Kelly suggested that although dismissive individuals avoid intimacy, they still have a human need to feel some sort of connection to others—and sexual contact is a basic expression of that need.

Infidelity

A sure way to undermine, if not destroy, a romantic relationship is for one (or both) of the partners to have sex with another person—especially if that piece of information is brought to light. Particularly in marriage, the tolerance for infidelity is quite low. The vast majority of both men and women (over 90%) say that extramarital sex is "always wrong" or "almost always wrong," with a mere 1% saying it is "not wrong at all" (Laumann, Gagnon, Michael, & Michaels, 1994). Not surprisingly, then, people who remain faithful are more likely to stay together than are people who have sex with other partners (Laumann et al., 1994). Strictly speaking, this does not necessarily mean that infidelity causes break-ups. Some people may be deeply unhappy with their relationship and feel ready to move on prior to cheating, with their infidelity representing a *result* rather than a *cause* of a failing love connection.

Infidelity is not something that people advertise or admit to, so its frequency is hard to know for certain. The promise of anonymity in surveys helps, but there is no way of knowing whether the responses provided are honest. The most reliable data, however, suggest that cheating is not nearly as pervasive as one might infer from steamy novels, movies, and TV shows. The National Health and Social Life Survey (NHSLS), for example, found that more than 90% of wives and 75% of husbands claim to have been completely faithful throughout their marriage.

Cheating may be relatively rare, but inhibition of the desire to have sex outside of a relationship may be harder for men than for women. Males are commonly regarded as the more opportunistic of the two sexes when it comes to roving eyes and "openness to experience." As discussed earlier, males fantasize about sex more frequently and they are aroused by idea of sex with women with whom they have no desire to form a long-term relationship. In fact, when it comes to short-term relationships—a one-night stand, for example—males dispense with many of the criteria that would predict a meaningful long-term relationship.

This is illustrated in a study by Kenrick, Groth, Trost, and Sadalla (1993). Male and female students stated the minimum percentile of intelligence they would accept in considering someone for different levels of involvement: a *date*, a *one-night stand*, a *steady dating partner*, and a *marriage partner*. The results, presented in Figure 9.9, indicate that for high levels of commitment, both genders desire a partner of relatively high intelligence. Females keep the bar relatively high when contemplating a date or even a one-night stand. But males are willing to entertain the thought of a one-night stand with a woman with relatively low intelligence—someone they wouldn't want to have as a steady dating partner, let alone a spouse. This suggests that males may be easily tempted to stray, taking the opportunity to have sex with a woman who may not be desirable in other, more meaningful ways.

Of course, male-female differences in sexual desire could say more about males' fantasies than about their willingness to act on such fantasies. To see whether men really "walk the talk" in these matters, Clark and Hatfield (1989) conducted a very unorthodox study at Florida State University in the late 1980s. They arranged for an attractive male and an attractive female to approach students of the opposite sex and strike up a brief conversation. These conversations ended with the accomplice making one of three offers: "Would you like to go out sometime?" "Would you like to come to my apartment now?" or "Would you like to go to bed with me?"

The results, presented in Figure 9.10, revealed a striking difference between the men and women who were approached with these offers. When asked simply whether they would like to "go out," a sizable and fairly equal proportion of the men and women said yes. The research accomplice was attractive, after all, and the participants may have been interested in seeing him or her again. But when asked if they wanted to go to the accomplice's apartment, the men and women parted ways in their responses. A tiny percentage of women agreed to the offer, but the percentage of

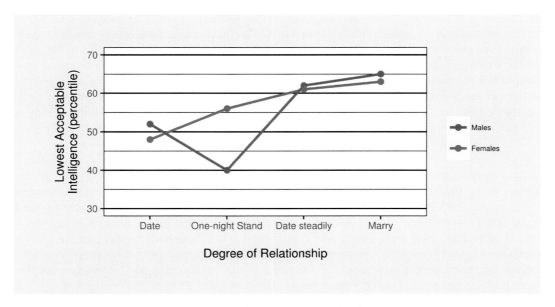

FIGURE 9.9 Where Men and Women "Set the Bar" for Different Levels of Involvement
Source: Adapted from Kenrick et al. (1993)

men who agreed was larger than the percentage that agreed simply to "go out." And when the offer was to "go to bed," none of the women said yes, while the majority of men did. These results are consistent with the suggestion that men tend toward opportunism in their sexual relations, and that women tend to put the brakes on fulfilling this tendency.

But females do not come off all that saintly either. As noted earlier, women have two agendas that are sometimes mutually incompatible. On the one hand, they want a male who is committed to the relationship and willing to invest in the care of their offspring. A sensitive and caring male fits the bill nicely. On the other hand, women want to mate with a man who has genes associated with desirable characteristics that will show up in their offspring. Strength, dominance, and independence are highly valued in men because it promotes alpha male status—or at least it did in humans' ancestral environment prior to the development of bank accounts and post-graduate degrees. Unfortunately, these characteristics are not always conducive to warmth and sensitivity. The males who are "players" in the dating scene may be a good bet for high rank in a dominance hierarchy, but they may not be such a good bet for commitment and fidelity.

How women handle these conflicting mate selection criteria depends on where they are in their menstrual cycle. As noted earlier, during their ovulatory phase—the time during which they can get pregnant through intercourse—women prefer men with masculine faces (e.g., Penton-Voak et al., 1999), presumably because such men are seen as stronger and more dominant and thus likely to be good breeding material. More to the point, fertile women express greater interest in having a "fling" with a man who has a lower, more masculine voice (Puts, 2005). If women acted on this hormone-inspired desire, one would expect a large number of children who are not biologically related to the man they believe is their father. DNA testing has in fact confirmed that out-of-wedlock pregnancies occur at a surprisingly high rate—between 5% and 15% of all pregnancies. Presumably, some of these are the result of "flings" with men who signal dominance and good breeding material.

It's interesting to consider gender differences in infidelity in terms of *power*. Power is great in many ways—it is synonymous with social influence and it is a sign of confidence, competence, and social skill. But there are downsides

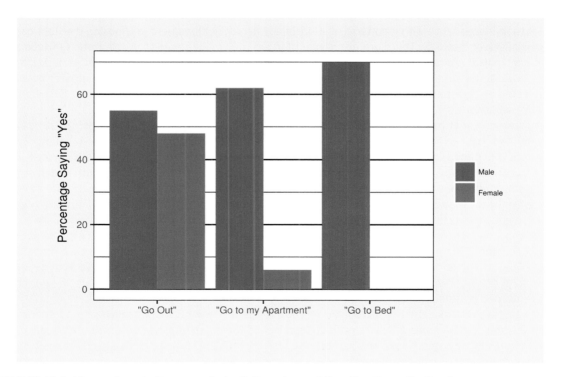

FIGURE 9.10 Male Versus Female Response to Invitations by an Attractive Opposite-Sex Person
Source: Adapted from Clark & Hatfield (1989)

to having power when it comes to being faithful. A survey of 1,275 professionals by Lammers et al. (2011) found that people who perceived themselves as very powerful had more intentions to commit infidelity and were more likely to cheat on their spouses than did those who perceived themselves as less powerful. This effect was just as true for women as it was for men. This calls into question the evolutionary rationale that men are more prone to engage in extramarital sex because this mating strategy increases the likelihood of passing on their genes (Buss & Schmitt, 1993). Throughout history, men have enjoyed greater power (politically, economically, interpersonally) than women—an asymmetry that still exists in most parts of the world. Perhaps men cheat more than women because of their power advantage. If so, we should expect the difference between men and women in their likelihood of straying from their wedded vows to dissipate as the gender gap in power diminishes in the modern world. Whether this should be looked upon as a positive consequence of gender equality is a different matter.

Nonetheless, modern humans are a monogamous species, with both males and females for the most part controlling their desires and resisting the temptations they experience. Males do not attempt to build harems, no matter what goes on in their fantasy life (Labuda, Lefebvre, Nadeau, & Roy-Gagnon, 2010). We may not be as faithful as the prairie vole and many bird species that mate for life, but we are far better at maintaining commitment to one partner than are a host of other species—gorillas, elk, and sea elephants, to name a few—that live in harems in which one male has reproductive access to many (up to a dozen in some cases) females.

Signals of Impending Doom

People do not form close relationships, let alone get married, with the expectation that they will break up some day. Yet most close relationships do come to an end; even 50% of first marriages, which are *defined* in terms of long-term commitment, end in divorce. Can we tell by looking at a marriage whether it will persist through children, lifestyle changes, misfortunes, and career transitions, or whether it is doomed to fail? The answer is yes. Some predictors are straightforward; others are subtle and often go unnoticed.

Consider first the straightforward column. Individuals with lower SES status (e.g., low education, low income, low occupational prestige) tend to have rockier marriages that end in divorce (Williams & Collins, 1995), presumably because of the stress these circumstances create. Individuals who marry at a young age tend to divorce, which probably reflects their inexperience with long-term relationships, their lack of judgment in choosing the right partner, and of course their lack of maturity. There are also straightforward personality predictors. Neurotic (anxious and emotionally volatile) individuals tend to have unhappy relationships and are primed for divorce (Karney & Bradbury, 1997; Kurdek, 1993). And, not surprisingly, individuals who are sensitive to rejection respond with greater hostility when they feel rejected by their partners (Ayduk et al., 1999; Murray, Holmes, MacDonald, & Ellsworth, 1998)—hardly a firm foundation for an enduring marriage.

Now let's take a look at the less obvious factors. John Gottman and Robert Levenson (1992, 2000) developed a laboratory method that can predict whether or not a couple (heterosexual, gay, or lesbian) will stay together or break up. Couples are videotaped while engaging in a 15-minute conversation concerning an issue both partners recognize as a source of conflict (e.g., finances, intimacy, parenting). These interactions are coded for both negative behaviors (anger, criticism, defensiveness, stonewalling, contempt, fear, sadness) and positive behaviors (e.g., affection, interest, humor). The frequency of negative behaviors during this brief interaction can predict with remarkable accuracy (up to 93%) which couples will break up over the next several years. Particularly toxic for a relationship are expressions of *contempt*, with one partner looking down on the other. Predictive power is also provided by the *ratio of positive to negative behaviors*. Partners in a close relationship can say negative, even nasty, things to each other, as long as these expressions are offset by an abundance of positive comments. In fact, the ratio of positive to negative must be at least 5 to 1. Anything short of that (e.g., 4 to 1) can spell doom for the couple within a few years. In relationships, as elsewhere in life, *bad is stronger than good*.

Another easy-to-overlook signal of a troubled relationship is the way partners explain one another's behavior. Recall from Chapter 7 that people attribute positive behavior to their own qualities but attribute negative behavior to external factors. In happy marriages, this self-serving bias is expanded to include one's partner: positive behavior is attributed to the partner's wonderful qualities but negative behavior is dismissed as a response to circumstances, stress, and so forth. In unhappy marriages, the self-serving bias does not include one's partner (Fincham et al., 1997; Karney & Bradbury, 2000; Miller & Rempel, 2004). The partner's positive behavior is attributed externally ("she's just trying to look good in front of others"), while his or her negative behavior is attributed to his or her traits or motives ("he's insensitive and uncaring").

SUMMING UP AND LOOKING AHEAD

* There are universal aspects of attractiveness that people everywhere recognize. Symmetry in physical features, which signals good health and high levels of sex hormones, heightens the attractiveness of both sexes. Faces that represent the average facial features in a culture are viewed as attractive by people in that culture.

* Men are attracted to females with a waist-to-hip ratio of 0.7 and who have high cheekbones and full lips. Men can detect when women are in the fertile phase of their menstrual cycle by odor cues and this non-conscious awareness produces a spike in their testosterone and lowers their threshold for sexual thoughts and risky decisions. Women's criteria for male attractiveness vary across their menstrual cycle. During ovulation, they are attracted to men who have masculine features associated with high levels of testosterone. During non-fertile phases, women are attracted to men with feminized features associated with sensitivity and commitment. In countries characterized by poor health and income inequality, women display heightened preference for men with masculine features.

* People are attracted to others who have similar attitudes, values, and personality characteristics. They are also attracted to others with whom they have frequent contact. People are not attracted to others with a complementary personality, but they are attracted to those whose immune system is different from their own because it enhances the resistance to pathogens in offspring resulting from sexual intercourse.

* People can become attracted to someone without first thinking about the person's characteristics if the person is encountered frequently. The mind plays a role, however, in assigning meaning to bodily states of arousal, and this attribution-of-arousal process can result in very different feelings about a person from the same set of physiological states. When highly aroused, these feelings—whether liking or disliking—become more polarized.

* Liking is based in part on marketplace considerations. Whether someone is liked depends on the market value of that person compared to one's past experiences and on the market value of the next best alternative to this person. When people feel that someone likes them, they reciprocate those feelings. The reciprocity effect is enhanced if the person's liking appears to increase over time. People with low self-esteem tend to discredit expressions of liking by someone because it is at odds with their self-concept.

* Love may start out as physical attraction, but for a relationship to become truly "close," the partners must become connected emotionally as well as behaviorally. The script for a close relationship is essentially a three-act play: Act 1 is *attraction* and a sense of passion; Act 2 is *intimacy* and a sense of mutual understanding; Act 3 is *commitment* and a desire to maintain the relationship even when the embers of passion fade a bit and rough patches are experienced.

* The initial stages of a close relationship reflect social exchange concerns, but over time the relationship becomes defined in terms of a communal orientation with the partners focusing on each other's needs. The degree to which a person can form close communal relationships in adulthood is constrained by the person's attachment to caretakers as an infant.

* Males and females differ in the resources they bring to the table when negotiating the terms of the relationship. Men have a stronger sex drive and this difference has implications for the exchange of benefits between the partners. These implications are enhanced or diminished depending on a society's sex ratio.

* Close relationships can be derailed when the social exchange established at the outset undergoes noticeable change. Relationships over time are driven by a communal orientation, and this can blunt the update in the exchange dynamics, although what appears to be a communal orientation can reflect an exchange orientation operating on a longer time scale. Inequity in a relationship can be tolerated for a long time, but eventually one or both partners may feel dissatisfied and lose their sense of commitment.

* Both men and women experience jealousy, but for different reasons. Men can never be certain of their paternity when children are born, so they are attentive to, and distressed by, signs of sexual infidelity in

their mate. **Women are concerned about maintaining the intimacy and commitment of their mate because of the demands and perils of pregnancy and carrying for the offspring for close to two decades.**

- **Males have a lower threshold for sexual temptation and desire greater sexual variety. Women are less open to extradyadic sexual relations, but their threshold for temptation is lower when they are in the fertile phase of their menstrual cycle. Compared to other species, humans are largely monogamous and are capable of maintaining long-term commitment to a relationship.**

- **A relationship headed for break-up can be detected years in advance by noting partners' communication when discussing stressful topics. When the ratio of positive to negative comments dips below 5 to 1, the relationship is in trouble. Relationship health is also revealed in partners' explanation for one another's behavior. In a healthy relationship, the partners credit the other person's qualities for desirable actions but blame circumstances or external factors for the other person's undesirable behavior. This pattern is reversed in unhealthy relationships.**

Social relations involve more than perceptions, judgments, and feelings about one another. In daily life, people attempt to influence one another to think a certain way or to engage in a particular course of action. In a close relationship, the partners are open to influence because of their shared reality and desire to please one another. But love and commitment do not characterize the majority of people's relationships, so effective social influence requires the use of other means, some of which are decidedly manipulative rather than transparent. Documenting the various forms of social influence provides the focus of the next chapter.

Key Terms

Facial symmetry	Equity	Attachment style
Smell of symmetry	Reciprocity of liking	Resource exchange
Incest avoidance	Gain-loss theory	Sex ratio
Waist-to-hip ratio	Flirtation	Male and female homosexuality
Fertility status and attraction	Triangulation of love	Extradyadic relationship
Similarity and attraction	Self-disclosure	Paternity uncertainty
Complementarity and attraction	Oxytocin	Mate guarding
MHC compatibility	Pair bonding	Erotic plasticity
Propinquity	Cultural differences in love	Sexual versus emotional jealousy
Functional distance	Misattribution of arousal	Infidelity
Mere exposure	Polarization of affect	Positive to negative ratio in communication
Perceptual fluency	Interdependence	
Misattribution of arousal	Exchange versus communal orientation	Biased attribution for positive and negative behavior
Comparison level	Mutual need satisfaction	
Comparison level for alternatives	Emotional coordination	
"Matching hypothesis"		

10 Social Influence

Social influence goes to the heart of social psychology. It pervades every aspect of social life, from everyday requests ("pass the cookies, please") to commercial advertising ("get a new Toyota for no money down!") to political propaganda ("vote for Senator Blowhard and your taxes will be cut!"). Even in simple conversations, people try to influence each other in various ways. In passing on gossip, you are trying to get someone to form an opinion about someone else; in telling a joke, you are hoping to make the other person break into laughter and perhaps stick around awhile. Some psychologists have argued that social psychology is essentially the study of social influence. In the 1954 *Handbook of Social Psychology*, for example, Gordon Allport defined social psychology as "an attempt to understand . . . how the thought, feeling, and behavior of the individual are influenced by the actual, imagined, or implied presence of others" (Allport, 1954a).

Influence may be central to social experience, but much of the time the point is not to change the way someone thinks or feels from then on. In asking someone for the time of day, you are influencing the person's behavior but you are not attempting to make the person feel differently about punctuality, nor to turn him or her into a compulsive observer of clocks. The research on social influence is more restricted, limited to those occasions in which the point *is* to change the way a person acts or the way he or she thinks or feels about something. That still leaves a lot to talk about. To make social influence a manageable topic, I distinguish three general means by which people attempt to alter someone's thought, feeling, or behavior. These forms differ in the degree to which they are direct and overt versus indirect and subtle.

The most direct form of social influence is *behavior control*. Reward and punishment are employed to achieve this end, but control can also come in the form of authority figures who simply tell people what to do. A less direct form of influence is *persuasion*, in which people attempt to convince others to think about issues and topics in a new way. The least direct form of influence is *manipulation*. The goal is to get a person committed to a way of thinking or acting with techniques that do not look like influence at all. This chapter provides an overview of each form of influence. Perhaps you'll behave differently from now on as a result of reading the following pages. And maybe you won't realize that you have changed.

CHAPTER OVERVIEW

What Are You Going to Learn?

- **What techniques do people use to control each other?** A person who has the power to provide rewards or threaten punishment can use this power to dictate how someone else should act. Even in the absence of such power, the person may control people's behavior if her or she has legitimate authority to exert such control. Will people do things that they find personally objectionable if they are told to do so by an authority figure? When do obvious attempts at behavior control backfire and produce behavior opposite to what the influence agent wants?
- **How and why does persuasion work?** People try to change the way other people think about issues and events. What personal characteristics enable someone to overcome people's resistance to persuasion and change their attitudes and beliefs? How should a persuasive message be presented in order to have the desired impact? How does the way people process information affect their openness to persuasion? What determines whether persuasion is short-lived or instead persists and grows stronger over time?
- **How do people manipulate other people's thoughts and feelings about engaging in behavior?** People can be induced to like doing things they would not otherwise consider. What strategies overcome people's reluctance to engage in a costly or effortful behavior? What psychological processes are engaged in people that enable these strategies to work?

Behavior Control

How Do People Exert Direct Control Over Others?

The most direct way of getting someone to do something is to apply the same principles that people use to control the behavior of pets and circus animals. You can talk until you are blue in the face trying to make your puppy understand why he should consider rolling over or walking on his hind legs, but such appeals are destined to fall on uncomprehending ears. JoJo can be induced to do these doggy tricks in short order, however, if you associate such behavior with bones and chew toys. And to stop JoJo from doing unwanted things (barking, making a mess on the carpet), you can associate such behavior with unpleasant consequences (a rolled-up newspaper, time-out in his crate). Pets and other animals also recognize power differences and readily submit to other animals (the Great Dane next door) and people (their owner) who have high ranking in their perceived power structure. If influence based on rewards, punishment, and authority is so effective with other species, perhaps it is effective in influencing people as well.

Reward and Punishment

Long before there was a science of social psychology, people recognized the power of reward and punishment in getting their fellow humans to do things. Even in the early decades of scientific psychology, the *behaviorist perspective* provided the authoritative word on influence. It was assumed that people, like rats and pigeons, were motivated by the prospect of receiving positive (pleasurable) outcomes or avoiding negative (aversive) outcomes. Psychological science has come a long way since then, but no one can deny that people are influenced in their actions by the outcomes associated with these actions.

Reward power is the ability to motivate people to do something in exchange for outcomes they desire. The rewards may be material (e.g., money, a nice gift), but in everyday social life they are tend to be non-material (e.g., approval, affection, compliments). People are more responsive to a request or an order if the influence agent provides social rewards (e.g., appreciation, a warm smile) when the request is made or the order is given. If responding to the request or order requires time and effort, the person making the request may need to increase the amount of social rewards. A nice smile might be all that is needed to induce someone to hold the door when exiting a room, for example, but a heartfelt "thank you, thank you!" may be necessary to induce the person to help drag a piece of furniture through the door.

Coercive power is the ability to provide aversive or unpleasant outcomes to someone if the person does *not* comply with a request or an order. Like reward power, coercive power can involve concrete outcomes, such as the use or threat of physical force, or it can involve outcomes that are considerably less concrete. The parent concerned with a child's messy bedroom, for example, might express strong disapproval for the child's failure to put away his or her toys.

Sometimes there is no alternative to coercive power. A thief who demands someone's smart phone is not likely to get very far by accompanying this demand with a warm smile, while neglecting to display a weapon. Even in everyday social encounters, people sometimes feel it is necessary to threaten one another with unpleasant consequences (e.g., "see if I ever do you a favor!") if their requests are not met. But coercion hardly forges a warm bond between people. People resent being threatened with punishment, even if they would otherwise enjoy the action that is demanded. Authoritarian parents who rely on threats to promote desired behavior tend to create rebellious children who lack intrinsic motivation for their actions (Baumrind, 1971).

Legitimate Authority

Every society has *social norms*—laws, regulations, customs, and expectations—that regulate personal and interpersonal behavior. Societies also entitle individuals in certain social roles to enforce these norms. The flight attendant who instructs 300 passengers to put their seats and tables in a full upright position does not have much reward or coercive power, yet this person is obeyed because of his or her *legitimate authority*. Legitimate power is critical for societal coordination. Imagine what traffic at a four-way intersection would be like if the signal lights failed and the police on the scene had to rely on gifts or their personal charm to gain the cooperation of each driver. But blind obedience to legitimate authority can also bring out the worst in people, sometimes to the detriment of themselves or others. Social psychologists have investigated legitimate power with special emphasis on these worrisome consequences of *obedience to authority*.

Obedience to Authority

Insight into the power of legitimate authority to promote obedience was provided by what is probably the most famous (or infamous) line of research in social psychology. Like many others, Stanley Milgram (1965) was disturbed, yet fascinated by key events during World War II. Under the Nazi regime in Germany, millions of innocent people, a majority of them Jewish, were singled out as less than human, put in concentration camps, and often herded into gas chambers. Genocide is a fixture in human history, but the scale of the Nazi campaign intensified the drive to understand how the few can influence the many in the name of legitimate authority.

Milgram obviously could not replicate the conditions that led to the Holocaust, but he did want to capture the psychological processes that were at work during that period. His specific aim was to investigate whether ordinary people will take orders from a legitimate authority figure when compliance with the order causes another person to suffer. He hoped to replicate in a benign setting the dynamics at work during wartime, when soldiers are given orders to kill enemy soldiers and citizens. In his experiments, which were ostensibly concerned with the psychology of learning, a participant "teacher" was asked to deliver electric shocks to a "learner" (a middle-aged man who was actually an accomplice of Milgram) every time the learner produced an incorrect response in a simple learning task. The naïve participant and the accomplice each drew a card to see who would be the teacher and who would be the learner, but the procedure was rigged so that the naïve participant always drew the "teacher" card.

With the teacher watching, the learner was strapped into a chair with his hand tethered to plate that was connected to the shock delivery apparatus (see photo below). The learner pointed out that he had a heart condition and expressed concern that the shocks would be dangerous for him. The experimenter dismissed this concern, telling the learner, "although the shocks may be painful, they are not dangerous." The teacher's role was to read a series of word pairs (e.g., blue/girl, glove/book, anvil/pope) to the learner over an intercom, then to read the first word of each pair (e.g., blue) and give the learner a few seconds to respond with the paired word (e.g., girl) by pressing a response key with his free hand. The learner's responses were highlighted on a panel in front of the teacher. If the response was wrong (e.g., "book" in response to "blue"), or if the learned failed to respond, the teacher's job was to punish him by holding down a toggle switch on a shock generator that presumably delivered a shock to the learner. No shocks were actually delivered to the learner, although he responded according to a standardized script to create the impression that he was experiencing the shocks.

The learner being strapped to the shock apparatus in Milgram's research
From the film *Obedience* ©1965 by Stanley Milgram. © Renewed 1993 by Alexandra Milgram. Distributed by Alexander Street Press.

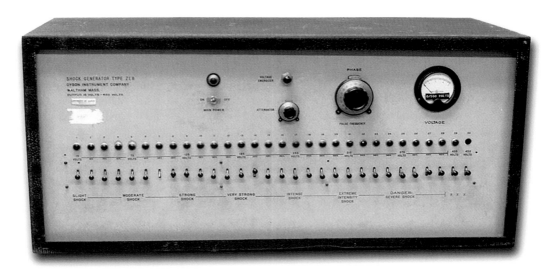

The shock generator used in Milgram's research
From the film *Obedience* ©1965 by Stanley Milgram. © Renewed 1993 by Alexandra Milgram. Distributed by Alexander Street Press.

The shock generator, pictured above, delivered shocks that ranged from 15 volts to 450 volts. Before the learning task began, the teacher received a 45-volt shock (the third toggle from the left) so he would realize the shocks he would be delivering to the teacher were in fact real—and painful. The teacher delivered 15 volts after the learner's first mistake and then increased the shock intensity in 15-volt increments after each subsequent mistake. Each level of shock intensity was associated with a description, ranging from *"slight"* (15 volts) to *"danger, extreme shock"* (360 volts). Beyond 360 volts, the remaining increments were labeled *"xxx,"* conveying the clear impression that words failed to describe the shock intensity. The learner's responses were actually pre-recorded, although teachers thought they were genuine. The sequence of responses was such that if Milgram's instructions were followed, the teachers would eventually deliver the maximum shock intensity. The question was how far teachers would go on this scale to punish the learner's incorrect responses before refusing to continue.

In one experiment, Milgram varied the proximity between the teacher and the learner. In the *remote-feedback* condition, the learner was in an adjoining room and could not be seen or heard by the teacher, except for one time when the learner pounded vigorously on the wall separating them. In the *voice-feedback* condition, the learner was again in the adjoining room and so could not be seen, but he could be heard. What teachers heard were vigorous protests about being shocked and experiencing pain as a result. This is the setup that is most often described in textbooks (and in movies and YouTube videos depicting the Milgram experiment). Listed below are the learner's responses to the increases in shock intensity in this condition.

Shock intensity	Learner's reaction
75 volts	Ugh!
90 volts	Ugh!
105 volts	Ugh! (louder)
120 volts	Ugh! Hey, this really hurts!
135 volts	Ugh!!!
150 volts	Ugh!! That's all! Get me out of here! I told you I had heart trouble! My heart is starting to bother me now! Get me out of here, please! My heart's starting to bother me! I refuse to go on. Let me out!
165 volts	Ugh!! Let me out! (shouting)
180 volts	Ugh!! I can't stand the pain! Let me out of here! (shouting)
195 volts	Ugh!! Let me out of here! Let me out of here! My heart's bothering me! Let me out of here! You have no right to keep me here! Let me out! Let me out of here! Let me out! Let me out of here! My heart's bothering me! Let me out! Let me out!
210 volts	Experimenter! Get me out of here! I've had enough! I won't be in the experiment anymore!
225 volts	Ugh!!
240 volts	Ugh!!
255 volts	Ugh!! Get me out here!
270 volts	Ugh!! (Agonized scream). Let me out of here! Let me out of here! Let me out of here! Do you hear? Let me out!
285 volts	Ugh!! (Agonized scream)
300 volts	Ugh!! (Agonized scream). I absolutely refuse to answer any more! Get me out of here! You can't hold me here! Get me out! Get me out of here!
315 volts	Ugh!! (Intensely agonized scream). I told you I refuse to answer! I'm no longer part of this experiment!
330 volts	Ugh!! (Intense and prolonged agonized scream). Let me out of here! Let me out of here! My heart's bothering me! Let me out, I tell you! (Hysterically). Let me out of here! Let me out of here! You have no right to hold me here! Let me out! Let me out of here! Let me out!
345–450 volts	(Silence—no response or verbalization from the learner)

In the *proximity* condition, the teacher and the learner were in the same room, 1.5 feet from each other. In the *touch-proximity* condition, the teacher was instructed to force the learner's hand onto the shock plate, using a sheet of insulation so that the teacher would not be shocked as well. The learner in these conditions followed the same script as did learners in the voice feedback condition (including the protests and agonizing screams). In all four conditions, the learner stopped responding to the word pair challenges after receiving 330 volts.

So how did the participant "teachers" react in these different conditions? Did anyone really go all the way to 450 volts (*xxx*) to punish a middle-aged man with a heart condition for making incorrect responses and who stopped

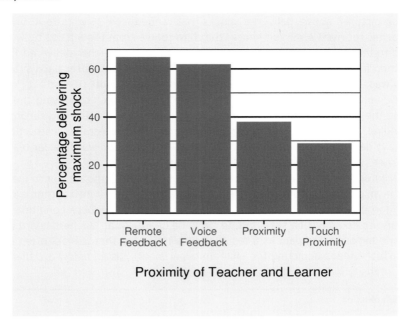

FIGURE 10.1 The Percentage of Teachers Who Delivered 450 Volts of Electricity to the Learner Under Different Conditions of Proximity
Source: Adapted from Milgram (1965)

responding altogether after experiencing a far less intense shock? The results, presented in Figure 10.1, are quite chilling (OK, shocking). In the *remote-feedback* condition, 65% of the teachers followed the experimenter's instructions and went all the way to the end, delivering 450 volts to the learner. This effect is startling, but perhaps somewhat understandable because there was no feedback from the learner that he was in pain. Without feedback from the learner, the only influence on the teacher came from the experimenter, who never wavered in his instructions to continue with the experiment.

But now look at the results for the *voice-feedback* condition—in which the learner made it very clear that he was in intense pain (beginning at 120 volts), wanted to end the experiment (150 volts), ultimately refused to go on (300 volts), and then fell silent (at 345 volts, far short of the maximum 450 volts). Despite the vigorous protests from the learner—not to mention the possibility that his silence signaled unconsciousness or even death—the degree of obedience was essentially the same (62.5%) as that observed in the *remote-feedback* condition. The direct and unequivocal feedback from the learner clearly did not deter most of the teachers from continuing to shock him when they were told to do so by the experimenter.

Figure 10.1 shows that the percentage of teachers who followed orders to the end dropped off quite a bit when they were in the same room as the learner. But even when teachers had to forcibly hold the learner's hand on the shock plate, about 25% of them continued to 450 volts. Seeing the victim of one's behavior and being physically engaged with him or her undermines the tendency to follow orders, but not entirely.

The results presented in Figure 10.1 were observed when the experimenter was in the same room, standing next to the teacher, creating visual and verbal proximity. In another set of studies, the experimenter left the room after giving the instructions and gave his orders by telephone. In the *voice-feedback* condition, the absence of the experimenter reduced the percentage of teachers administering the maximum shock to about 20%—less than one-third the percentage observed when the experimenter remained in the room. This suggests that people find it far easier to disobey an authority figure when that person is not in close physical contact.

So why were Milgram's participants so obedient? Why did they follow orders that caused discomfort and pain to another person who was merely there to take part in a psychology experiment? The first point is that participants did not mindlessly follow orders without pushing back against the experimenter. They experienced serious concern about what they were doing and became agitated as they delivered increasing levels of shock intensity. But their agitation was not sufficiently strong to get them to disobey the experimenter. So the question remains: why did so many participants obey the experimenter's orders?

The key factor was participants' feeling of *responsibility* for what they were doing. Strictly speaking, the teacher was responsible for shocking the learner—after all, he was the one pushing the keys on the shock generator. But recall from Chapter 6 ("Personal Control") that an action can be identified in many ways, from *low-level act identities* involving physical movements to *high-level act identities* that emphasize the consequences and reasons for the action (Vallacher & Wegner, 1987). So although the teacher was responsible for the low-level act identity of pushing keys, he or she may have felt little responsibility for the higher-level identities of the act—causing pain, ignoring the learner's pleas to stop, and so forth. Once the experimenter made clear that he, not the teacher, was responsible for these consequences, the teacher could continue with his or her end of the bargain—pushing keys and following orders.

This is what typically happened. At some point after the learner began to express his distress and demanded to be released, teachers invariably asked the experimenter, "who's going to take responsibility for the man's condition?" The experimenter responded by saying, "I am responsible . . . Now please continue with the procedure." With the responsibility for the action's possible consequences now residing with the experimenter, the teacher could continue with his lower-level act of pushing the keys and following orders.

Obedience to Authority in Perspective

Milgram's findings were unsettling to scholars and to the lay public at the time, and still have considerable shock value today. In the early 1960s, the horrors of World War II were still fresh in people's memories. People liked to think that those horrific events were exceptional, reflecting unique circumstances and twisted personalities. But Milgram's research suggested that Hitler's Final Solution revealed a feature of human nature that anyone could display under the right circumstances. Subsequent research employing Milgram's paradigm demonstrated comparable levels of obedience in other countries, including Australia, Spain, Germany, and Jordan (Kilham & Mann, 1974; Meeus & Raaijmakers, 1986). The tendency to defer to the demands of legitimate authority, even when these demands run counter to one's personal values and inhibitions, appears to be very strong.

Legitimate authority does not always need to be all that legitimate. Someone who lacks credible claim as an authority figure can still exercise power if he or she has symbols of authority, such as clothing or an impressive title. A man dressed as a security guard, for example, can get people to pick up litter even if the request occurs in a context where an actual security guard would not have such authority (Bickman, 1974). Sometimes even fictional authority figures are accorded legitimate power. This tendency is exploited a great deal in advertising. When an actor states at the outset of a commercial pitch for cough medicine that "I am not a doctor, but I play one on TV," a significant portion of the viewing audience will follow his recommendations if he is dressed in a white lab coat and brandishes a stethoscope.

Legitimate authority is not simply a necessary evil in human affairs. To the contrary, it serves important social functions. Perceived legitimacy is necessary for elected representatives, police officers, and school crossing guards to secure compliance as they carry out their duties. And although teachers want to be liked and valued as experts by their students, their power in the classroom is due in large part to students perceiving them as legitimate authority figures. Even parents, who have many other bases of power (reward, coercion, expertise) over their children, must from time to time remind Jason and Heather who is in charge in order to maintain control over their behavior. Like other aspects of feature of social life, whether legitimate authority promotes good or evil behavior depends on the restraint and judgment of those who exercise it.

Limitations to Behavior Control

The use of direct influence—rewards, punishment, legitimate authority—to control people's behavior may control behavior in the short-run but is likely to fail in the long run—sometimes producing a desire to behave in precisely the opposite manner. *Reactance theory* (Brehm & Brehm, 1981) is based on the assumption that people like to feel free to do what they want. So when personal freedoms are threatened, people act to reassert their autonomy and control. Commanding a 2-year-old child or a teenager not to do something runs the risk of eliciting an "I won't!" rebuttal, for example, or reluctant compliance that disappears as soon as the parent leaves the premises or simply looks away. All the bases of behavior control at the parent's disposal–reward, coercion, authority–pale in comparison to the child's distaste for having his or her tacit agreement removed from the parent-child exchange.

This effect has been cleverly demonstrated in the *forbidden toys paradigm* (Aronson & Carlsmith, 1963). The experimenter showed nursery school children five toys and asked them to say how much they liked each one. The experimenter then told the children that he had to leave the room for a while. Each child was told that he or she was free to play with the toys–except for his or her second favorite. This restriction was expressed in one of two ways. In the *mild threat* condition, the experimenter said he would "be annoyed" if the child played with the forbidden toy. In the *severe threat* condition, the experimenter said he "would be very angry" and "would have to take all of my toys and go home and never come back again." The experimenter then left the room, leaving the child alone with the toys.

While the experimenter was gone, each child was covertly observed with hidden cameras. None of them played with the forbidden toy, so both mild and severe threats were effective in getting children to follow orders. But this masked how the children felt about the forbidden toy. When the experimenter returned, they were asked to reevaluate all five toys. The results, displayed in Figure 10.2, revealed that the children who received the mild threat tended to like the forbidden toy about the same as before or liked it even less. But in the severe threat condition, the majority of children expressed *greater* liking for the forbidden toy–and none of them liked it less. Warning the children in harsh terms not to play with the toy worked at the behavioral level, but had a boomerang effect at the attitude level. The lesson here is simple: harsh warnings to a child to avoid doing something may work in the short run, but such warnings run the risk of intensifying the motivation to engage in the forbidden activity later on.

Reactance theory calls into question the basis for various public policy initiatives. In a study comparing ways to reduce alcohol consumption, for example, participants who received a strongly worded anti-drinking message subsequently drank more than did those who received a moderately worded message (Bensley & Wu, 1991). Participants apparently viewed the strongly worded message as a threat to their personal freedom, prompting them to react by

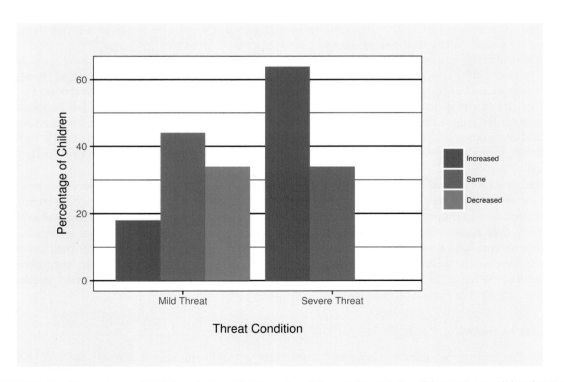

FIGURE 10.2 The Percentage of Children in the Mild Threat and Severe Threat Conditions Whose Liking for the Forbidden Toy Increased, Stayed the Same, or Decreased
Source: Adapted from Aronson & Carlsmith (1963)

drinking more rather than less in an effort to assert their sense of control. Such findings question the wisdom of the "Just Say No" mantra of drug education programs aimed at young people. Because it short-circuits personal decision-making, the slogan has in fact backfired in some instances, promoting increased rather than decreased consumption of illegal substances—although it's not entirely clear that this is due solely to reactance (Donaldson, Graham, Piccinin, & Hansen, 1995).

Heavy-handed forms of influence are especially vulnerable to reactance effects, not only because they are a restriction of freedom for targets, but also because they are transparent to targets. Letting someone know that you're trying to influence him or her is a decidedly poor strategy—unless, of course, your real goal is to get him or her to do the opposite.

Box 10.1   Does Torture Work?

Most people are uncomfortable with the idea of torture—inflicting serious physical or psychological pain on another person. Even a person convicted of mass murder is expected to receive humane treatment during his or her period of punishment—unless, of course, the punishment includes execution. In the aftermath of the September 11, 2001, terrorist attacks in the United States, however, the use of torture has become a contentious issue, with many politicians and laypeople putting aside their moral qualms in favor of pragmatic concerns that they feel warrant "enhanced interrogation techniques"—the euphemism for torture. The claim is that extreme measures are necessary to elicit information that a suspect might not give up by any other means.

As we have seen, however, overt and intense forms of influence can backfire because it does not address the internal motivation of the recipient, and in fact can induce motivation to act in opposition to such influence attempts. So a terror suspect is likely to become all the more antagonistic to his or her captors, and to their country, if he or she is subjected to water boarding, extreme sleep deprivation, and the like. But the hardening of a suspect's attitudes and motives can be overlooked as worth it if he or she provides useful information that leads to the capture of a high-profile enemy or that prevents an attack that could destroy property and kill innocent citizens. From this perspective, the question is whether torture works. Does it produce valuable information that could not be obtained through means that do not entail the trade-off with morality and civilized rules of conduct?

Some politicians and commentators feel the use of torture can be effective, as do many laypeople (Janoff-Bulman, 2007). When Osama bin Laden was killed on May 1, 2011, for example, some suggested that the water-boarding of detainees at Guantanamo Prison in Cuba several years earlier had elicited information that proved instrumental in learning Bin Laden's location. Others argued, however, that any relevant information obtained through these techniques was not decisive, but rather offered a relatively insignificant component of the vast array of information constituting a pattern that pinpointed Bin Laden's whereabouts. It was the intelligence gathering and interpretation that proved decisive, not any one piece of information.

The effectiveness of torture in Bin Laden's case is a matter of controversy, but the effectiveness of torture in general is not. There is consensus among professional interrogators that not only does torture not work, but that it can produce information that is useless, or worse, misleading and designed to direct attention away from a suspect or an impending "ticking time bomb" (Bennett, 2007; Arrigo & Wagner, 2007). Beyond that, the use of torture can have ripple effects that undermine a country's sense of morality and damage its reputation in the international community (Vallacher, 2007). Remember the lesson of cognitive dissonance theory: when people engage in an activity they find unappealing, they tend to change their attitude toward the activity so that it now seems like a perfectly justifiable way of behaving. This is particularly true if the behavior is hard to justify in terms of rewarding outcomes.

Torture fits this bill nicely. Most people find it unappealing but once it becomes part of a country's interrogation program, they may reconsider its worth and downplay its negative moral overtones. The irony here is that this collective rationalization is especially likely if torture proves to be ineffective and does not result in saved lives and cities. The lack of rewarding outcomes, in other words, may motivate people to rationalize torture as inherently appropriate—perhaps as a legitimate means of dealing with terrorists and other bad people.

Persuasion

How Do People Change Other People's Opinions, Beliefs, and Values?

You can order a person to do something but you cannot tell a person what attitudes and beliefs to have. Yet sometimes we want to change how people think. The strategy for doing so seems simple enough: we should present a sound argument why the new way of thinking is correct or desirable. However, persuasion often has little to do with logic or factual support. What does matter are *the characteristics of the communicator, how the communicator presents the message*, and *how the audience processes the message* (Hovland, Janis, & Kelley, 1953).

Characteristics of the Communicator

Someone can make all the compelling arguments in the world in favor of a point of view but the message will fall flat, while another person can elicit agreement and vigorous head nods with a far less compelling rationale. Such differences can spell victory versus defeat in a political campaign, and you may have observed wide variation in persuasion effectiveness in your own social network. Two personal characteristics are especially important in persuasion: *credibility* and *likability* (Hovland et al., 1953).

Credibility

A communicator is seen as credible if (a) he or she knows what he or she is talking about, and (b) he or she is communicating this knowledge honestly. The first component refers to the person's *expertise*. The role of expertise in shaping attitudes was demonstrated in a classic study by Hovland and Weiss (1951). Participants read a speech advocating the development of atomic submarines, a controversial issue at the time. Half were told that the speech was given by a well-known physicist (Robert J. Oppenheimer), whereas the other half were told that it was given by a writer for the Communist Party newspaper, *Pravda*. In matters of atomic power, it's safe to say that a physicist has the edge in expertise over a political writer. When participants were asked for their opinions after reading the speeches, they were more favorable toward developing atomic submarines if the speech was attributed to the credible source (Oppenheimer).

Expertise promotes persuasion even if it has nothing to do with the topic. Someone who is seen as intelligent and successful is commonly assumed to have expertise and thus can change opinions on topics for which he or she has no credentials (Eagly & Chaiken, 1998). Who knows, perhaps Oppenheimer could have persuaded people to buy a new Ford or take a trip to Colorado, even though his expert credentials were in physics, not automobiles or vacation planning.

The second feature of credibility is the communicator's *trustworthiness*. An expert's communication is likely to fall on deaf ears if the audience has reason to question whether he or she can be trusted to tell the truth. In part, this reflects judgments about the communicator's personality—whether he or she is basically an honest person. But this judgment is hard to come by for people in certain occupations, regardless of their personality or moral compass. Which occupations come up short in the trustworthiness category? According to a 1997 Gallup poll, the general public considers advertisers, insurance salespeople, lawyers, and car salespeople as the least trustworthy people. The people considered most trustworthy? Topping the poll were pharmacists, clergy, physicians, and professors (really, trust me on this one).

Box 10.2   Can We Tell When Influence Agents Lie to Us?

People are always trying to influence one another. Knowing this, you might think that everyone would be wary of attempts to change the way he or she thinks or acts. Particularly when the consequences of change are important or costly, people should be sensitive to deception and outright lies in persuasion attempts. And indeed, people are on guard when subjected to influence attempts and they often resist adopting the communicator's point of view or recommendation for how they should act. But such suspicion is largely based on the communicator's personal qualities (e.g., attractiveness, credibility) and the degree to which he or she has vested interests in persuasion (Lehman & Crano, 2002). As we saw in Chapter 7 ("Social Judgment"), people are also adept at reading one another's minds, so you might think that they would be able to detect insincerity when exposed to an influence agent's attempts at persuasion—regardless of how attractive, knowledgeable, or trustworthy he or she is.

In fact, there are certain clues that can indicate whether a communicator is honest or is simply trying to change your opinions and actions. When people are telling a lie, they tend to have more speech hesitations, touch their face more often, jiggle their legs, show sudden rises in the pitch of their voice, increase their eye contact, and display subtle signs of negative emotion (DePaulo, Lanier, & Davis, 1983; Mehrabian & Williams, 1969). Despite these well-documented and fairly easy-to-read clues, however, people are not particularly adept at noticing them (Ekman & O'Sullivan, 1991). In the research on this issue, participants watch videotapes of someone who is either lying or telling the truth, and then indicate whether the communicator is being honest or not. On average, participants are correct in making this distinction about 57% of the time—slightly better than chance (50%).

OK, but perhaps some people are better than others at picking up on cues to honesty versus dishonesty. Some occupations, for example, rely on the ability to judge human character. Shouldn't clinical psychologists, prosecutors, and judges excel at reading a person's nonverbal behaviors and arrive at informed decisions regarding his or her honesty? Actually, these professionals are no more accurate than the average person in reading cues to lying and deception. There is one group, however, that has better-than-average ability in catching liars: secret service agents. These professionals, whose job it is to protect public figures, are trained in the social psychology of lying and therefore highly sensitized to the cues noted above. Of course, with the benefit of learning about these cues, you too may become a master of lie detection from now on.

The low trust in people in certain occupations reflects in part their *vested interests* (Lehman & Crano, 2002) in getting people to believe them. If they have something to sell (e.g., cars, insurance policies), their motivation is somewhat suspect. Suspicion about vested interests can undermine a communicator's trustworthiness, even if he or she has expertise. A physician may know a lot about pharmaceuticals, but his or her claims about the effectiveness of a particular drug may be viewed with skepticism is he or she works for the company that produces the drug. But someone who makes an argument that goes *against* his or her self-interest can be especially persuasive. Imagine listening to a speech that criticizes a company for polluting a river. Now imagine that the speech was delivered either by a political candidate with a business background or by an environmentalist. Because the former is arguing against business interests, he or she is likely to be more persuasive, even though the environmentalist probably knows more about the causes and consequences of river pollution (Eagly, Wood, & Chaiken, 1978).

Likability

Likability is influenced by many factors, but two stand out in the context of persuasion: *similarity* and *physical attractiveness*. People who are similar to us are influential because they provide a common frame of reference for evaluating ideas and events. The bases of such *reference power* can be deep, representing similarity in personality traits, values, and worldviews. But similarity can also prove effective if it is based on relatively superficial qualities, such as clothing, residency, and sports preferences. Imagine, for example, that you are asked to read a speech advocating the use of SAT scores in college admissions. Now imagine that the person who wrote the speech is a fellow student at your university or a student at another university in a different part of the country. The two speechwriters may be equally credible and trustworthy, but they differ in their similarity to you on an important dimension—where they go to college. Because of his or her greater reference power, you are likely to find your fellow student to be more persuasive (Mackie, Worth, & Asuncion, 1990).

Similarity can be trumped by how physically attractive a communicator is (Chaiken, 1979; Dion & Stein, 1978). Attractive political candidates, for example, are more successful in persuading people to vote for them than are their less attractive opponents (Budesheim & DePaola, 1994; Eagly & Chaiken, 1975)—even though voters deny they are swayed in this fashion. In part, the impact of attractive communicators reflects the *beautiful is good stereotype* discussed with respect to close relations (Chapter 9). We assume that attractive people possess many desirable qualities, including intelligence and emotional stability.

But attractive people are also persuasive simply because they provoke a positive reaction in us, and we are interested in what they think and do. Think about the commercials you see on TV. Do they typically provide an abundance of information relevant to the wisdom of purchasing the product in question? Or do they instead simply associate an attractive person with the product? Even if the product is costly, the likelihood of people making a purchase reflects the physical appeal of the person associated with the product. To get people to buy an expensive Lincoln SUV, advertisers don't busy the TV audience with a barrage of relevant information (e.g., gas mileage, turning radius, back seat leg room, resale value). Instead, they simply show actor Matthew McConaughey looking introspective and talking about his liking for Lincolns while driving one on a darkened road. And this works. In the case of Lincoln, for example, sales shot up by 25% when the McConaughey commercial was aired.

Characteristics of the Message

The same idea can be communicated in very different ways, and these differences can make or break the persuasion attempt. An idea that is logical and makes a great deal of sense might fall on skeptical ears, and one that is senseless or even illogical can elicit agreement if it is presented in the right way. And there are several "right" ways.

Self-Confidence

A message delivered with self-confidence and passion tends to be influential, even if the speaker is not considered an expert and little is known about his or her trustworthiness (e.g., Erickson, Lind, Johnson, & O'Barr, 1978; Newcombe & Arnkoff, 1979). Self-confidence plays a big role in eyewitness testimony in criminal justice proceedings (Kassin, Ellsworth, & Smith, 1989; Smith, Kassin, & Ellsworth, 1989). A jury is inclined to believe an eyewitness if he or she expresses no doubt in identifying a defendant as the perpetrator. This sounds reasonable, but there is actually a very weak correlation between confidence and accuracy of eyewitness testimony (Wells, Olson, & Charman, 2002): an accurate eyewitness account may be presented with hesitation, and a totally inaccurate account can be presented without the slightest hesitation.

Speech Rate

Have you ever noticed (and wondered why) commercials are spoken at a rate that sounds like the speaker has had far too many drinks of Red Bull that day? The answer is simple: rapid speech works. Although annoying, a speech or sales pitch delivered at a rapid rate tends to be more persuasive to listeners than the same message expressed more slowly (Miller, Maruyama, Baeber, & Valone, 1976; Smith & Shaffer, 1995). In part, this is because speech rate is sometimes used to infer the intelligence and competence of the speaker (Brown, 1980). Rapid speech also cuts short any unfavorable thoughts that might otherwise occur to the audience as it listens to the message (Smith & Shaffer, 1995). Of course, if a speaker talks so rapidly that the audience cannot absorb the message, his or her effectiveness is undermined rather than enhanced (Petty & Wegener, 1998; Street, Brady, & Putnam, 1983).

One-Sided Versus Two-Sided Messages

Imagine you're a politician trying to convince voters of the benefits of a change in tax policy or the need for military intervention. Should you emphasize only the points in favor of your point of view? This would constitute a *one-sided message*. Or should you also acknowledge the opposing arguments and then shoot them down? This would be a *two-sided message*. Let's consider both sides of this issue.

One-sided messages are fine if the audience already agrees with you. "Preaching to the choir" tends to characterize political rallies that are attended primarily by a candidate's fervent supporters. In today's world, it is possible for people to avoid both sides of an argument because of the splintered and internally homogeneous forums for learning how to think about various social, economic, and political issues. Just look at certain cable TV channels (e.g., Fox, MSNBC), internet sites, or blogs that fervently emphasize a particular point of view as if there was no other way to think about the political and economic issues of the day. So although we no longer live in small villages that emphasize single points of view, we have found our own virtual villages in cyberspace that serve the same function.

Two-sided messages run the risk of undermining the intended message, but they are necessary if the audience is well informed and likely to seek out or simply encounter different perspectives (Hovland, Lumsdaine, & Sheffield, 1949). If nothing else, a two-sided message can inoculate the audience against the other way of thinking. Of course, for this approach to be effective, the communicator must refute the arguments on the other side (Allen, 1991; Crowley & Hoyer, 1994; Lumsdaine & Janis, 1953). Two-sided messages are also more effective if the audience is comprised of people who are on the fence regarding the message—and this strategy is essential if the audience initially disagrees with the message (see Figure 10.3).

Communicating First Versus Last

Is it better to get your point of view out front first, or is it better to "have the last word"? If the speeches are given back to back and there will be no delay before people make up their minds, it is best to go first. This represents a *primacy effect*. But if there is a delay between the speeches and the audience members have a chance to make up their mind right after hearing the second one, it is best to go last. This *recency effect* occurs because people remember the second speech better than the first one (Haugtvedt & Wegener, 1994; Miller & Campbell, 1959).

Emphasis on Gains Versus Losses

Persuasive messages are more effective when they are custom-tailored to reflect the interests and concerns of the intended audience (Hirsh, Kang, & Bodenhausen, 2012; Lee & Aaker, 2004). The advertising industry is sensitive to the importance of resonating with the needs of its target audience. By activating people's desires, those with a product to sell can arouse interest in something that would otherwise be viewed with far less enthusiasm. Of course, not everyone has the same desires, so an attempt to prime a particular desire may be effective for some members of a target audience but fall flat for others. The variation among people in their specific interests and concerns is

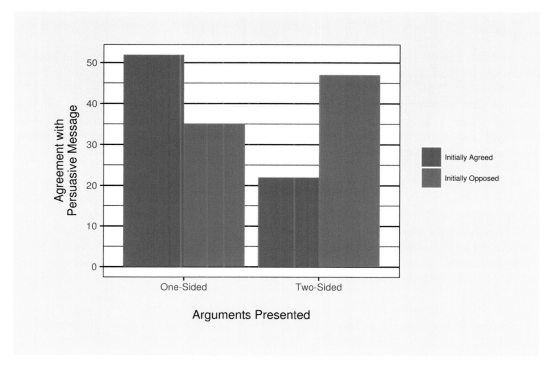

FIGURE 10.3 Persuasion by One-Sided versus Two-Sided Arguments for People Who Initially Opposed Versus Initially Agreed With the Message
Source: Adapted from Hovland et al. (1949)

enormous, making it impractical for a message to be modified to reflect every conceivable point of view. Fortunately (for advertisers, at least), psychologists are quite adept at grouping specific concerns, interests, and desires into basic categories, and doing so makes the framing of messages considerably more doable.

A popular categorization is people's relative concern with *gain* versus *loss*. According to *regulatory focus theory* (Higgins, 2000), for example, people differ in the extent to which they focus on achievement and positive outcomes (*promotion-focus*) versus obligations and avoidance of negative outcomes (*prevention-focus*). Influence is more successful when there is a "fit" between the framing of the influence attempt and the person's focus: promotion-focused people are more seduced by a message emphasizing the attainment of positive outcomes, whereas prevention-focused people respond more favorably to a message emphasizing the alleviation or prevention of unwanted effects (Cesario, Grant, & Higgins, 2004).

Consider, for example, how an advertiser might frame an ad to boost sales of a particular brand of grape juice (Lee & Aaker, 2004). The ad might emphasize the positive benefits of drinking the grape juice by stating that "preliminary research suggests that drinking purple grape juice may contribute to the creation of greater energy." Or the ad could tap into people's concern with prevention by stating that "preliminary research suggests that drinking purple grape juice may . . . reduce the risk of some cancers and heart disease." People who are promotion-focused should respond more favorably to the former ad, whereas those with a stronger prevention focus are more likely to be swayed by the latter ad. Research like this has shown that the success of an ad campaign is greater when there is a "fit" between the promotion versus prevention emphasis in the ad and the promotion- versus prevention-focus of the target audience (Brendl, Higgins, & Lemm, 1995; Lee & Aaker, 2004).

There are cultural differences in the relative persuasive appeal of promotion- and prevention-focus ads. Aaker and Lee (2001) found that people in individualistic societies (such as the United States) respond more favorably to ads that emphasize the positive benefits of a product (e.g., a health drink that promises greater energy), whereas people who have an interdependent orientation—more common in collectivist societies such as those in parts of Asia and Africa—are more influenced by ads that emphasize how the product prevents or alleviate negative experiences (e.g., the health drink reduces fatigue).

Appeals to Fear

Is making people fearful an effective way to influence their attitudes and behavior? Using a fear-arousing communication certainly makes intuitive sense. If you want people to stop smoking, for example, you might be tempted to point out the long-term health consequences of smoking, which include just about every life-threatening disease there is—not to mention facial wrinkles, yellow teeth, gum disease, and bad breath. Public service ads commonly rely on fear as well. Practice safe sex or you will get AIDS; wear seat belts or you will die in a head-on collision; avoid drugs or your brain will turn on you. And fear appeals are often employed in political campaigns, usually by pointing the dire consequences for the country (e.g., terrorist attacks, moral decay, loss of privacy, end of free-market economy) if you vote for the opponent.

But is fear really effective? It can be, but only if done in the right way. First of all, communications that arouse a *moderate level of fear* are more effective than those that arouse intense fear. If people become terrified by a communication, they are likely to become defensive, which may be manifest as denying the importance of the threat and an inability to think rationally about the issue (Janis & Feshbach, 1953; Liberman & Chaiken, 1992). Telling a smoker that he or she will die a painful death due to lung cancer if he or she doesn't kick the habit is likely to promote vigorous counter defense, usually along the lines of pointing to a grandmother who smoked three packs a day and lived to be 95. The response may not be rational but it defends against the intense anxiety that the person might otherwise experience.

Even inducing a moderate level of fear can fail to change people's behavior unless the message includes clear suggestions how to avoid the dire consequences (Hoog, Stroebe, & de Wit, 2005; Janis & Feshbach, 1953; Ruiter, Abraham, & Kok, 2001). If people believe that attending to a message's recommendations will eliminate the threat, they are motivated to analyze the message carefully and experience a shift in their thinking (Rogers, 1983). To reduce smoking, for example, a health expert might present a film depicting the likely health consequences of smoking, then provide the audience with a pamphlet describing concrete steps on how to stop smoking (Leventhal, Watts, & Pagano, 1967). The scary film alone won't do the trick. Scaring people, then leaving them hanging without a clear course of action, only intensifies the anxiety and can leave them looking for rationalizations and effective denials.

The Message and the Medium

Are communicators more effective if they present their message complete with the complexity that typically surrounds important issues? Or are they better off with simple messages that get right to the point without spending time on the rationale or relevant facts? In making a case for military intervention in another country, for example, one could present a message loaded with details about the historical context, the number of troops required, and the project costs of the intervention. Alternatively, one could present the case in very simple terms as the need to stop an enemy in its tracks before it threatens the homeland. Which message is most likely to convince the audience that intervention is the appropriate course of action?

The answer itself is somewhat complex, not simply a case of one approach or the other being the winner. One of the key factors is the medium in which the message is presented. Messages presented in written form (e.g., newspapers, magazines, and books) are more persuasive when they are complex. Having the time to go over the text enables careful consideration. If, however, the message is presented in a video format (e.g., a video presentation), the persuasive advantage goes to simple messages. Visual information is processed in a more superficial fashion, with the audience's attention engulfed by vivid perceptual cues such as the appearance of the communicator or the vocal quality of his or her voice. In a sense, "a picture can be worth a thousand words."

The advantage of simplicity over complexity in visual media is on full display in political campaigns. Have you ever wondered where all the money (millions of dollars) goes in presidential campaigns? A large proportion of it goes to 30-second spots on TV, each of which can cost half a million dollars. These spots are hardly a source of detailed information that stimulates deeper reflection. Instead, they convey a simple positive message about the preferred candidate (e.g., that he or she is a patriot or a dutiful spouse and parent) or an equally simple but negative message about the candidate's opponent (e.g., he once visited a strip club, he or she takes money from corporate lobbyists). Even when political communication is extended in time, as during a 90-minute televised debate between the candidates, people remember the clever one-liners (e.g., "There you go again!" "You're no Jack Kennedy!") and nonverbal behaviors (e.g., maintaining rigid rather relaxed posture), not the substance of what either candidate said.

This can be looked upon as a cause for concern. In recent years, the visual media—television, movies, internet videos—have become a more common way of conveying information than print media, such as magazines, newspapers, and yes, even books. Yet, the issues that confront us in contemporary life are becoming increasingly complex, with events often open to more than one simple interpretation. This is a dangerous mix. With increasing complexity, people are attending to media that are best suited for simple messages. One can wonder what this means for the future of decision-making regarding political and economic issues, as well as lifestyle and personal conduct. Will society consist of an increasingly simple-minded public, unable to grasp or control the complexity of world events or make informed choices in their own life? Maybe a nice video on the topic would clarify things. Or maybe not.

Mode of Processing

The discussion so far may give the impression that persuasion has little to do with logic or solid evidence in favor of a position. This is not always the case. Sometimes people can overlook the communicator's appearance, speech rate, and the like, focusing instead on the quality of his or her arguments. The question is, when are people influenced by the intrinsic features of an argument, and when are they instead influenced by other factors?

Central Versus Peripheral Processing

Two influential theories of persuasive communication—the *heuristic-systematic model* of persuasion (Chaiken, Wood, & Eagly, 1996) and the *elaboration-likelihood model* (Petty & Cacioppo, 1986) offer similar answers to this question. Both models acknowledge that people are sometimes motivated to pay attention to the facts presented in a communication and more persuaded when these facts are compelling and logically consistent. Carefully thinking about the content of a communication and elaborating on it represents the *central route to persuasion* (Petty & Cacioppo, 1986) in the elaboration-likelihood model and the *systematic route to persuasion* in the heuristic-systematic model (Chaiken et al., 1996). Persuasion occurs in this manner when people are motivated to attend to the facts and have the ability to do so. A message that has relevance for one's life, for example, is likely to be attended to carefully.

When people lack such motivation, however, they pay less attention to what is said and focus instead on surface or peripheral features of the message—the length of the message, for example, or whether the communicator is attractive or has solid credentials on the topic. This is referred to as the *peripheral route to persuasion* in the elaboration-likelihood model (Petty & Cacioppo, 1986) and as the *heuristic route to persuasion* in the heuristic-systematic model (Chaiken et al., 1996). Figure 10.4 depicts the two different routes to persuasion.

A study by Petty, Cacioppo, and Goldman (1981) illustrates the distinction between these two routes. College students listened to a speech arguing that all students should be required to pass a comprehensive exam in their major in order to graduate. Half the students were told that their university was considering whether to adopt the exam right away, and half were told that the university might adopt the exam but that it would be implemented 10 years later (long after they had graduated). Two other variables were employed that could impact whether students agreed with the speech. The first represented a *central cue*. Half the students heard arguments that were strong and relevant (e.g., "the quality of undergraduate teaching has improved at schools with the exams"), and half heard arguments that were weak and pointless (e.g., "the risk of failing the exam is a challenge most students would welcome"). The second variable represented a *peripheral cue*. Half the students were told that the speaker was an eminent professor at Princeton University, and half were told that the speaker was a high school student.

The question was which set of cues would prove most effective in getting students to agree with the recommendation to adopt comprehensive exams. In line with the elaboration-likelihood model (and the heuristic-systematic model), the answer depended on the personal relevance of the exam issue to students. Look first at the left panel in Figure 10.5, which displays the agreement with the message by students who felt they might have to take the

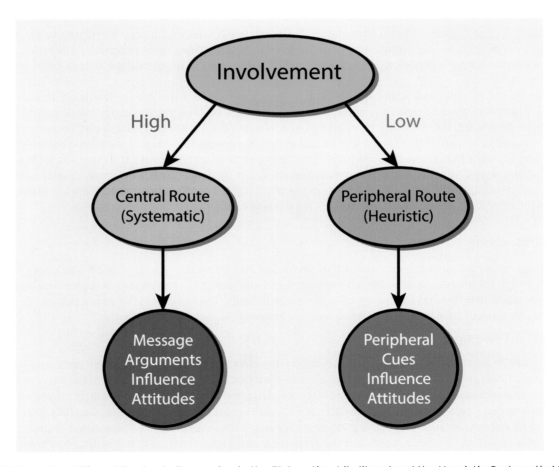

FIGURE 10.4 Two Different Routes to Persuasion in the Elaboration-Likelihood and the Heuristic-Systematic Models

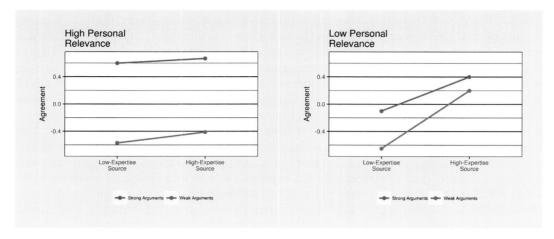

FIGURE 10.5 Personal Relevance and Persuasion
Source: Adapted from Petty et al. (1981)

comprehensive exam. Because the issue had *high personal relevance*, these students were influenced far more by the strong arguments than by the weak arguments (central cue), and largely ignored the prestige of the speaker (peripheral cue). Even a lowly high school student proved persuasive if he or she made a solid case for the comprehensive exams.

Now look at the right panel in Figure 10.5, which displays agreement with the message by students who would not be affected by the implementation of comprehensive exams. Because the issue had *low personal relevance*, these students were more influenced by the prestige of the speaker (peripheral cue) than by the strength of his or her arguments (central cue).

Personal relevance captures the *motivation* to process persuasive messages via the central versus peripheral routes. But which persuasion route is employed also depends on people's *ability* to process messages with respect to the central route. To some extent, this ability varies across people. For example, people who routinely engage in effortful cognitive activities—a tendency referred to as high *need for cognition* (Cacioppo et al., 1996)—form their attitudes by paying close attention to strong and relevant arguments (i.e., via the central route). People with low need for cognition, in contrast, can be persuaded by weak arguments if the communicator is attractive or has high prestige (i.e., via the peripheral route).

The ability to process information via the central route, however, can be diminished for even intellectually curious people under certain circumstances. Sometimes there are distractions (e.g., noises, distracting images, other people) that make it difficult to concentrate on the quality of the argument presented. When unable to pay attention to the argument's quality, people tend to be persuaded by peripheral cues (Petty, Wells, & Brock, 1976).

The central route is also trumped by the peripheral route if the topic is complex or difficult to understand (Chaiken et al., 1996). Climate change, proposed changes in tax policy, and military intervention in another country are highly important and personally relevant issues, but they involve complex and sometimes contradictory information, making it difficult for a person to attend to the facts that are presented. When exposed to strong arguments on both sides of such issues, people tend to switch from the central to the peripheral route in deciding how they feel about the issue. The most charismatic, likable, or prestigious communicator, for example, might win the debate. Such a person can rely on anecdotes and clever one-liners and still prevail over a less desirable opponent who makes his or her case with facts and logic.

In light of the media effects described earlier, the likelihood of people following the peripheral (heuristic) route is enhanced with visual media (e.g., TV). By the same token, someone who is inclined to think about the issue in terms of peripheral (heuristic) cues—because he or she is uninvolved with the issue, perhaps, or because the issue is complex— is likely to turn on the TV rather than go to the trouble of reading up on the issue.

Disassembly and Emergence

Another persuasion strategy plays on people's need to have a coherent and meaningful interpretation of an issue or a recommended course of action. It works by temporarily preventing people from thinking about the issue or recommendation in a unified manner. This is done by inducing people to think about the details of the issue or the specific features of the recommendation. Because people desire to have a meaningful "high-level" understanding of the issue or recommendation, those whose thoughts have been disassembled into "lower-level" pieces in this manner are vulnerable to influence agents who can put the pieces back together for them (Vallacher & Wegner, 1987).

This scenario underlies the *disrupt-then-reframe technique* of persuasion (Davis & Knowles, 1999). The influence agent overcomes a target's resistance to persuasion by disrupting the target's own high-level view of an issue, and then quickly reframes the issue in a way that is likely to be acceptable to the target. To demonstrate this technique, researchers posed as door-to-door salespeople (Davis & Knowles, 1999). When a person answered the door, he or she was offered a pack of eight high-quality greeting cards for $3.00. When the salesperson simply stated this price, the majority of people (65%) resisted the offer. Even when the salesperson pointed out that $3.00 was "a bargain," 65% of the people said "no thanks." For some of the people, however, the salesperson disrupted their negative attitude by saying "these cards sell for 300 pennies ... that's $3; it's a bargain." This detailed presentation of the offer reduced people's resistance dramatically—only 35% resisted the pitch, with the remaining 65% agreeing to pay $3.00 for the cards. Calling their attention to a large number of pennies disrupted their ready-made attitude about what constituted a bargain price for the greeting cards.

Temporal Effects

Psychological processes rarely occur all at once, but rather unfold over time (Vallacher et al., 2015). An initial reaction to an event or new information can generate a response that gets stronger over time, or conversely, a response that diminishes or even reverses over time. Theory and research on persuasion have focused on two such effects—one showing an increase in persuasion over time, the other showing a decrease.

The Sleeper Effect

Persuasion may not be obvious at first. An audience may listen to a speaker and appear to disregard what he or she has to say. Over time, however, the message may begin to sink in and generate a change in attitude in line with the speaker's message. This delayed reaction to persuasion, illustrated in Figure 10.6, is known as the *sleeper effect* (Kumkale & Albarracín, 2004; Pratkanis et al., 1988; Weiss, 1953). Imagine hearing a compelling argument about the need to rebuild the infrastructure (roads, bridges, etc.) of the United States, but that the argument is presented by a politician representing a political party you dislike. Because of your dislike for the messenger, you might ignore the message or downplay its significance. Over time, however, the points he or she raised (e.g., the US infrastructure is not only outdated but also represents a danger for travel) begin to resonate with your concerns. When asked how you feel about the need to improve the US infrastructure, you might now show agreement with the position you initially rejected.

In part, the sleeper effect occurs because persuasion induced by facts and logic (the central route) tends to be more enduring than persuasion induced by peripheral features such as a communicator's appearance (the peripheral route). People who form an attitude based on a careful analysis of the arguments are more likely to maintain this attitude over long periods of time, are more likely to behave consistently with this attitude, and show greater resistance to counter-persuasion than are people who form their attitude based on cues related to the speaker's characteristics and style of communication (Chaiken, 1980; Mackie, 1987; Petty & Wegener, 1998). So although the peripheral cues may promote a negative response initially—the communicator was decidedly non-charismatic, for example—these tend to lose their effect over time, allowing the facts and logic of the communicator's message to become prominent in your consideration of the issue. This assumes, of course, that the issue had some personal relevance in the first place, so that at least some degree of central processing had taken place.

Emotional Appeals

The opposite temporal effect is also plausible under some circumstances. As we learned in Chapter 4 ("Emotion"), affective states tend to decay fairly rapidly—certainly more rapidly that we expect them to. This suggests that a

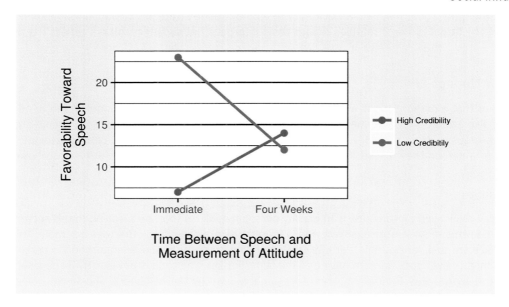

FIGURE 10.6 The Sleeper Effect

persuasive appeal based primarily on emotion might be highly effective in the short term, but lose its power over time as the emotional state begins to dissipate. A message emphasizing fear, for example, might change people's attitudes in the intended direction—provided the fear arousal is moderate and the message provides recommendations about what to do. But fear, like other emotions, decays fairly rapidly. If the target of the message has not acted on his or her initial fears, the impact of the message may become increasingly negligible.

By the same reasoning, a message may be enthusiastically embraced if it generates positive feelings in the target audience. Humor, for example, is a reliable means of getting people to embrace a communicator's message—whether in a political debate, an advertising campaign, or a university classroom—because it makes the source likable (Gruner, 1985) and because it gets people to pay attention to the message (Duncan & Nelson, 1985). But as the pleasant feeling begins to dissipate, the impact of the message may dissipate as well.

Although emotional appeals seem to produce temporal effects opposite to those of the sleeper effect, they can be understood as representing the same psychological process. In both cases, the initial reaction is governed by peripheral cues—the characteristics of the messenger in the case of the sleeper effect, the feelings generated in the case of emotional appeals. So, just as an audience might initially be persuaded by the characteristics of the influence agent—as in the sleeper effect—an audience might also be whipped into a frenzy by a strong emotional appeal. Over time, however, the peripheral cues lose their impact, and the quality of the message itself becomes the deciding factor whether the audience is persuaded. The difference between the sleeper effect and emotional appeals lies in the audience's initial reaction. The sleeper effect is observed when the message is *disregarded* because the messenger is not seen as credible or likable. In the case of emotional appeals, the message is initially *embraced*, not rejected, because of the fleeting feelings that are aroused.

Manipulation

How Do People Manipulate Others' Preferences, Decisions, and Actions?

Behavior control can be effective in promoting change in people's overt actions, but when the force is relaxed, they are likely to revert to their previous ways of acting—perhaps more strongly than ever. To bring about a lasting change that is internalized by the person, it is necessary to change the person's preferences while preserving his or her sense of freedom and control. If the influence agent has an agenda that doesn't coincide with the target's initial preferences and concerns, then, the agent may find it necessary to employ subtle strategies designed to manipulate the desires and choices of the target. Some strategies reflect basic interpersonal dynamics; others reflect the power of basic social norms.

Manipulation Through Liking

We noted earlier that a person who is well liked can play on this sentiment to persuade people to adopt ideas and beliefs. Liking also proves effective when trying to get people to adopt a course of action. People are more willing to comply with requests from someone they like than from someone they couldn't care less about—and certainly more than from a person they dislike. There are many bases for liking, and each is put to good use in service of manipulation.

Personal Qualities

One surefire way to be liked by someone is to display personal qualities that are pleasing to the person. It can prove difficult to turn down a request from a person who is friendly, nice, pleasant, or otherwise desirable. Think about how Girl Scout cookies are sold, for example. Parents send their daughter around the neighborhood to peddle cookies that the neighbors might never consider purchasing at the supermarket. The child is not exactly a seasoned salesperson, but she is a representative of the parent, who is presumably liked by the neighbors. The same principle is used by door-to-door salespeople who ask customers for names of their friends whom they might call. When subsequently contacted, these friends find it hard to reject the salesperson's pitch, since they would be in effect rejecting the referring person.

Similarity

People like those who are similar to them, so it is not surprising that similarity is often incorporated into the repertoire of sales people. A car dealer may claim to come from a customer's home state ("Nebraska? Me too!"), and a salesperson at the mall may tell an undecided customer trying on a dress that she purchased the very same outfit yesterday. The power of similarity to promote compliance has been observed even when the similarity is decidedly superficial. During elections, for example, voters tend to vote for candidates with familiar sounding names (Grush, 1980). Sometimes similarity in clothing is all that is necessary. Emswiller, Deaux, and Willits (1971), for example, had accomplices dress as either "straight" or "hippie" and ask fellow college students for money to make a phone call. Compliance was observed less than half the time when the confederate-target pair differed in clothing type, but over two-thirds of the time when the accomplice and target subject were similar in their attire.

Flattery

Perhaps even more basic than our readiness to do things for those we like is our need to be liked by those we know. Because flattery is hard to resist, it has a long history as an effective compliance technique, both inside and outside the laboratory (Carnegie, 1936/1981; Dractman, deCarfuel, & Insko, 1978). People offering praise are liked even if the compliments are recognized as inaccurate by the target. So influence agents need not bother gathering facts to support their compliments; simply expressing positive comments may be sufficient to woo the target and gain his or her compliance. But flattery can backfire if the target is aware, or simply suspicious, that the flattery is being strategically employed for manipulative purposes. This stumbling block to successful manipulation is known as the *ingratiator's dilemma* (Jones, 1964), discussed in Chapter 8 ("Social Interaction"). For that matter, the influence agent can simply overdo the flattery and come across as disingenuous and obsequious.

Manipulation Through Scarcity

People desire what they don't have—from toys in childhood to fancy cars, whiter teeth, or greener grass in adulthood. This tendency can be exploited by making a product scarce and hard to obtain. The lure of the unattainable, for example, can spark competition and fuel sales in commercial settings (Cialdini, 2007). Cries of "today and today only" and "in limited quantities" drive shoppers like lemmings toward the red tag special, and convenient Christmastime shortages of Tickle Me Elmos or Furbys stoke the fires of demand for these things.

With this in mind, consider the tendency for censorship efforts to backfire, creating a stronger demand than ever for the forbidden fruit. The prohibition of alcohol in the 1920s, for example, only whetted people's appetite for liquor and spawned the rise of secret establishments (the "speakeasy") that provided access to the scarce commodity. Anti-pornography crusades have the same effect, increasing interest in the banned books and magazines, even among people who might not otherwise consider this particular genre. Telling people they cannot read or see something can increase—or even create—a desire to take a peek at the hard-to-find commodity. Once the censorship or prohibition is lifted, interest in the object in question tends to wane.

There are several plausible reasons why there is enhanced desire for scarce items. The first centers on reactance: people don't like having their freedom threatened and making an item difficult to obtain or forbidding an activity clearly restricts people's options with respect to the item and the activity. The second reason centers on simple supply-and-demand economics: the lower the supply-and-demand ratio with respect to an item, the more those who control the resource can jack up the price and still count on willing customers. The third reason follows from evolutionary considerations: the conditions under which we evolved were harsh and uncertain, and there may have been selection pressures favoring our hominid ancestors who were successful at securing and hording valuable but limited food supplies and other resources.

The fourth plausible reason centers on people's simultaneous desires to belong and to individuate themselves from the groups to which they belong (Brewer, 1991). Scarcity has a way of focusing collective attention on a particular object, and there may be a sense of social connectedness in sharing the fascination with others. Waiting in line with throngs of shoppers hoping to secure one of the limited copies of the latest *Harry Potter* volume, for example, is arguably an annoying and irrational experience, but it does make the person feel as though he or she is on the same wavelength as people who would otherwise be considered total strangers. At the same time, if the person is one of the "lucky few" who manages to secure a copy before the shelves are cleared, he or she has individuated him or herself from the masses. Scarcity may be effective because it provides a way for people to belong to, and yet stand out from, the crowd, in a world where he or she may routinely feel both alienated and homogenized.

Manipulation Through Norms

Compliance is driven to a large extent by standards of behavior that are internalized by group members. These norms provide a moral compass for deciding how to behave in situations that might offer different action alternatives. The norm of social responsibility (Berkowitz & Daniels, 1964), for example, compels us to help those less fortunate than ourselves, while the norm of equity prevents us from claiming excessive compensation for minimal contribution to a group task (Walster, Berscheid, & Walster, 1973). By tapping into norms, social influence agents can extract costly commitments to behavior from targets without having to flatter them.

The Norm of Reciprocity

All human societies adhere to the *norm of reciprocity* (Gouldner, 1960). Because reciprocity creates a sense of future obligation, it promotes and maintains both personal and formal relationships, lending predictability, trust, and stability to the larger social system (Eisenberger, Cotterell, & Marvel, 1987). Transactions involving material goods are regulated by reciprocity, but so are favors and invitations. Christmas cards are sent to those who send them, and compliments are rarely accepted without finding something nice to say in return (Cialdini, 2007). Even when gifts and favors are unsolicited (or unwanted), the recipient feels compelled to provide something in return. The ability of uninvited gifts to produce feelings of obligation in the recipient is successfully exploited by many organizations, both charitable and commercial. People may not need personalized address labels or hackneyed Christmas cards, but once they are received, it is difficult not to respond to the organization's request for a "modest contribution" (Berry & Kanouse, 1987).

Reciprocity can increase the recipient's liking for the gift- or favor-giver, but the norm can be exploited successfully without liking playing a role (Regan, 1971). Affect does enter the picture, however, when people *fail* to uphold the norm. Non-reciprocation runs the risk of damaging an exchange relationship (Cotterell, Eisenberger, & Speicher, 1992) and may promote reputational damage for the offender (e.g., "moocher," "ingrate") that can haunt him or her in future transactions. Negative feelings can also be created when the reciprocity norm is violated in the reverse direction. You might think that someone who provides a gift but doesn't allow the recipient to repay would be viewed as generous, unselfish, or altruistic. But such a person may be disliked for violating exchange etiquette (Gergen, Ellsworth, Maslach, & Seipel, 1975). This tendency is universal, having been demonstrated in US, Swedish, and Japanese samples.

Cooperation is a form of reciprocity. Just as giving a gift prompts repayment, cooperative behavior elicits cooperation in return (Braver, 1975) and can promote compliance with subsequent requests (Bettencourt, Brewer, Croak, & Miller, 1992). This is not lost on the car salesperson who declares that he or she and the customer are on "the same side" during price negotiations, and takes up the customer's fight against the sales manager. Even if their alliance comes up short and the sales manager purportedly holds fast on the car's price, the customer may feel sufficiently obligated to repay the salesperson's cooperative overture with a purchase.

"Door in the Face"

A related form of reciprocity is the tactical use of concessions to extract compliance from those who might otherwise be resistant to influence (Cialdini & Trost, 1998). The strategy is to make a request that is certain to meet with a resounding "no," if not a rhetorical "are you kidding?" The request might call for a large investment of time and energy, or perhaps for a substantial amount of money. After this request is turned down, the influence agent follows up with a more reasonable request. In effect, the influence agent is making a concession and, in line with the reciprocity norm, the target now feels obligated to make a concession of his or her own.

A study by Cialdini et al. (1975) illustrates the effectiveness of what has come to be known as the *Door-in-the-Face* technique. Posing as representatives of a youth counseling program, the researchers approached college students to see if they would agree to chaperon a group of juvenile delinquents for several hours at the local zoo. Not surprisingly, most of them (83%) refused. The results were quite different, though, if they had first asked the students to do something even more unreasonable—spending two hours per week as counselors to juvenile delinquents for a minimum of 2 years. After students refused this request (all of them did), the smaller zoo-trip request was agreed to by 50% of the students—a tripling of the compliance rate.

"That's Not All!"

The power of reciprocal concessions is also apparent in the *That's Not All!* technique, which is a familiar trick of the trade among salespeople (Cialdini, 2007). The tactic involves making an offer or providing a come-on to a customer, then following up with an even better offer before the target has had time to respond to the initial offer. This technique is used to push big-ticket commercial items. A salesperson, for example, quotes a price for a large-screen TV, and while the interested but skeptical couple is thinking it over, he or she adds, "but that's not all—if you buy today, I'm authorized to throw in a free Blu-ray player." This strategy is effective because of the contrast between the initial and follow-up concession and because it creates a felt need in the target to reciprocate the agent's apparent concession (Burger, 1986).

Knowing that people tend to reciprocate concessions provides a cornerstone of negotiation and dispute resolution. The bargaining necessary to reach a compromise solution in such instances invariably hinges on one party making a concession with the assumption that the other party will follow suit with a concession of his or her own. This phenomenon can be seen at work in a wide variety of contexts, including business, politics, international diplomacy, and marriage.

Manipulation Through Commitment

Although it is not a social norm, *commitment* can influence behavior as much as reciprocity, equity, responsibility, and other basic social rules and expectations (Kiesler, 1971). Once people have committed themselves to an opinion or course of action, it is difficult for them to change their minds or otherwise fail to stay the course. A commitment that is expressed publicly, whether in front of a crowd or to a single individual, is especially effective in locking in a person's opinion or promise, even if there are good reasons for reconsidering the commitment.

"Foot in the Door"

Perhaps the best-known tactic is referred to as the *Foot-in-the-Door*, which is essentially the mirror image of the "door-in-the-face" tactic. Rather than starting out with a large request and then appearing to make a concession by making a smaller request, the foot-in-the-door specialist begins with a minor request that is unlikely to meet with resistance. After securing commitment with this request, the influence agent ups the ante by making a far more costly request that is consistent with the initial request. Because of commitment concerns, it can be very difficult at this point for the target to refuse.

A series of clever field experiments (Freedman & Fraser, 1966) provide compelling evidence for the effectiveness of this tactic. In one study, suburban housewives were contacted and asked to do something which most of them (78%) refused to do: allow a team of six men from a consumer group to come into their homes for two hours to "enumerate and classify all the household products you have." Another group of housewives was contacted and presented with a much less inconvenience-producing request—simply answering a few questions about their house-hold soaps (e.g., "What brand of soap do you use in your kitchen sink?"). Nearly everyone complied with this minor request. These women were contacted again 3 days later, but this time with the larger home-visit request. Over half the women (52%) complied with the request and allowed the men to rummage through their closets and cupboards for 2 hours.

The commitment process underlying this tactic goes beyond the target's concern with maintaining consistency with the action per se. It also engages the target's self-concept with respect to the values made salient by the action. The women who complied with the initial request in the Freedman and Fraser (1966) studies were presumably sen-sitized to their self-image as helpful, public-spirited individuals. To maintain consistency with this suddenly salient (and perhaps newly embraced) self-image, they felt compelled to comply with the later, more invasive request. The foot-in-the-door tactic thus holds potential for influencing people's thought and behavior long after the tactic has run its course.

Freedman and Fraser (1966) noted a parallel between their approach and the approach employed by the Chinese military on US prisoners of war captured during the Korean War in the early 1950s. A prisoner might be asked to indi-cate his agreement with mild statements like "the United States is not perfect." Once the prisoner agreed with such minor anti-American statements, he might be asked by the interrogator to elaborate a little on why the United States is not perfect. This, in turn, might be followed by a "request" to make a list of the "problems with America" he had identified, which he was expected to sign. The Chinese might then incorporate the prisoner's statement in an anti-American broadcast. As a consequence of this ratcheting up of an initially mild anti-American statement, a number of prisoners came to label themselves as "collaborators" and to act in ways that were consistent with this self-image (Schein, 1956).

"Throwing a Low-Ball"

Commitment underlies a related tactic known as *Throwing a Low-Ball*, which is routinely employed by salespeople to gain the upper hand over customers in price negotiations (Cialdini, 2007). Automobile salespeople, for example, will seduce customers into deciding on a particular car by offering it at a very attractive price. To enhance the cus-tomer's commitment to the car, the salesperson might allow the customer to arrange for bank financing or even take the car home overnight. But just before the final papers are signed, something happens that requires changing the price or other terms of the deal. Perhaps the finance department has caught a calculation error or the sales manager has disallowed the deal because the company would lose money at that price. At this point, one might think that the customer would back out of the deal—after all, he or she has made a commitment to a particular exchange, not simply to a car. But many customers accept the new terms and proceed with the purchase. In making the initial commitment, the customer takes "mental possession" of the object and is reluctant to let it go (Burger & Petty, 1981; Cioffi & Garner, 1996).

Changing the terms of the deal without undermining the target's commitment is not limited to shady business practices. Cialdini, Cacioppo, Bassett, and Miller (1978), for example, contacted students in Introductory Psychology to see if they would agree to participate in a study on "thinking processes" that began at 7:00 a.m. As this would entail waking up before the crack of dawn, few students (24%) expressed willingness to participate in the study. For another group of students, however, the investigators threw a low-ball by not mentioning the 7:00 a.m. element until after the students had indicated their willingness to take part in the study. A majority of the students (56%) did in fact agree to participate, and *none* of them backed out of this commitment when informed of the starting time. Once committed to a course of action, new details associated with the action—even aversive details that entail unanticipated sacrifice—can be added without undermining the psychological foundations of the commitment.

"Bait and Switch"

Like the low-ball tactic, the *Bait and Switch* tactic works by first seducing people with an attractive offer. But whereas the low-ball approach changes the rules by which the exchange can be completed, the bait and switch tactic nixes the exchange altogether, with the expectation that the target will accept an alternative that is more advantageous to the influence agent. Car salespeople once again unwittingly have furthered the cause of psychological science by their shrewd application of this technique (Cialdini, 2007). They get the customer to the showroom by advertising a car at a special low price. Taking the time to visit the showroom constitutes a tentative commitment to purchase a car. Upon arrival, the customer learns that the advertised special is sold, or that because of its low price, the car doesn't come with all the features the customer wants. Because of his or her commitment to purchase a car, however, the customer typically expresses willingness to examine and purchase a more expensive model—even though he or she wouldn't have made the trip to look at these models in the first place.

Manipulation Through Mood

Suppose you receive a phone call from a charitable organization asking you to volunteer time to help with its cause in some fashion—calling potential contributors, perhaps, or going door-to-door asking for contributions. This is a tough sell; simply pointing out the worthwhile nature of the cause may fail to get you involved. But what if the caller manages to manipulate your mood? He or she might try to make you feel good (happy or relaxed) or alternatively, the person might try to put you in a bad mood—sad, perhaps, or even guilty. Assuming your mood is successfully affected, would that make you more open to the request? If so, which mood is likely to the trick—a good mood or a bad mood?

Positive Mood

The answer to this question seems obvious: if you are in a good mood, you should be more likely to comply with the request. And in fact, there is considerable evidence that people are more responsive to requests when they are feeling happy, relaxed, and content (Cialdini, 2007; Isen, Clark, & Schwartz, 1976). Positive moods make people more compliant for two reasons. First, mood can color how events are interpreted. So people in a good mood see a request, even from strangers, in positive terms, overlooking its intrusive nature (Carlson, Charlin, & Miller, 1988; Forgas, 1998a). They take the request at face value and are unlikely to get paranoid about the possible deceptive nature of the request. If you're in a good mood, a fellow student who asks to see your class notes is seen as truly in need of such help rather than lazy and irresponsible.

The second reason is people's desire to keep a positive feeling going. This tendency, referred to as *mood maintenance*, promotes actions that sustain positive feelings (Wegener & Petty, 1994). There are many things that can do this, of course—watching a funny video or eating a nice cookie might do the trick, for example. But sometimes the opportunity that presents itself is doing something nice for another person (e.g., Dunn, Aknin, & Norton, 2008). Helping someone in need or responding to a request for assistance can make one feel good inside—certainly more so than hurting the person in need or turning down the request. This is a nice feature of human nature, of course, but you can see how it can be exploited by an influence agent to gain compliance with a request that does not directly benefit the influence target.

Negative Mood

If positive feelings promote compliance with requests, negative feelings would seem to make a person anything but agreeable. And this is certainly true of some unpleasant emotions. Making a person angry before asking him or her for a favor is not exactly a strategy destined for success. But some negative emotions can make a person vulnerable to influence. *Sadness*, for example, can motivate people to help someone in need or donate to a charitable cause. Looking at pictures of pitiful puppies in a dog pound waiting for a home (or for euthanasia), for example, can make even the most heartless person teary-eyed and responsive to requests from Sarah McLaughlin to donate "just 30 cents a day" to save them.

In part, sadness can amplify empathy for others (even puppies) and promote compliance with requests that might end their perceived suffering. When sad, it is easy to feel another's pain. But complying with requests when in a sad mood can also have the effect of making one feel better. People typically do not want to feel sad and will take advantage of opportunities to feel better. The idea that helping others is really a way of helping oneself is known as the *negative state relief hypothesis* (Cialdini, Darby, & Vincent, 1973).

Sadness can set people up for influence, but it doesn't come close to *guilt* in this respect. As discussed in Chapter 6 ("Personal Control"), guilt is a uniquely human emotion—and a uniquely powerful motive for doing whatever it takes to feel better. Sadness can be overcome in many ways (e.g., eating a nice meal or meditating) but feelings of guilt are not so easily eliminated. Guilt is an emotional response to inappropriate or harmful interpersonal behavior (Baumeister et al., 1994). To reduce guilty feelings thus requires making amends for such behavior. The upshot for influence is straightforward: make a person feel guilty and he or she is likely to be compliant with requests that might make up for his or her "bad" behavior.

This connection between guilt and vulnerability to influence has been demonstrated in many contexts. The recipe of such studies is simple. Naïve participants are led to feel guilty by arranging for them to cause inconvenience or problems for someone else (who is usually an accomplice of the experimenter). For example, they may inadvertently break a camera or screw up while helping with an important task. They are then asked if they are willing to help someone—not necessarily the one they inconvenienced—and their willingness to do so is assessed (Cialdini et al., 1973).

These studies show that participants who are duped into feeling guilty are highly responsive to subsequent requests, even if these requests have nothing to do with the problem they caused. Cialdini et al. (1973), for example, arranged for participants to cause carefully arranged computer cards (a means of storing data that was used last century) to fall into a disorganized heap on the floor. Participants were then asked if they would be willing to make phone calls to students as part of a large-scale survey. They were quite willing to do so—far more than were participants who hadn't made the computer card blunder. You might be wondering, by the way, if the experimenters felt a bit guilty as well. After all, they had faked the computer card incident and duped participants into actions that made them feel bad! Who knows, maybe the experimenters were especially compliant to requests from colleagues or spouses later that day.

Manipulation Through Priming

If influence is more effective when it is subtle rather than explicit, it should be especially effective if the target does not even know he or she has been influenced. This general tack is feasible in light of what psychologists have discovered about *unconscious processing* (Bargh & Chartrand, 1999; Bowers & Meichenbaum, 1984; Kihlstrom, 1987). It may seem strange, but a great deal of information is received and processed below the level of conscious awareness. This raises the possibility that messages can be delivered under people's mental radar and that these messages can impact their subsequent conscious thoughts and feelings.

This idea was seized upon in the 1950s by some in the advertising industry, most notably by those wishing to boost sales at the concession counter in movie theaters. While people were paying (conscious) attention to what was happening on the movie screen, a picture of popcorn or a soft drink would pop up, but only for a few frames so that viewers would not recognize that anything was amiss. But a few milliseconds were considered sufficient for the picture to be unconsciously processed, presumably activating thoughts about the popcorn or drink.

This attempt at *subliminal priming* is generally considered to have been a failure, but the rationale underlying this approach—the activation of mental content by stimuli that are presented out of conscious awareness—has since been thoroughly investigated in research (e.g., Bornstein, Leone, & Galley, 1987; Zajonc, 1968). As we saw in Chapter 7 ("Social Judgment"), people's evaluation of a stranger can be influenced by positive and negative words presented too quickly for them to be recognized (Bargh & Pietromonaco, 1982; Higgins et al, 1977).

The effect of priming has been demonstrated in behavioral contexts as well. Imagine someone trying to convince you that you should walk like a senior citizen—slowly and perhaps a little hunched over. That would probably be a hard sell—if anything, you might pick up your pace so as to reaffirm your youthful vitality. But what if you were primed with the "elderly" concept without being consciously aware of this attempted mental activation? This is the tack employed by Bargh, Chen, and Burrows (1996). Participants performed a sentence completion task in a study said to be concerned with "language proficiency." They were given 30 sets of 5 words each and were asked to form a grammatical sentence using 4 of the 5 words. For half the participants, many of the words were associated with stereotypes of the elderly—for example, "gray," "wrinkle," "bingo," and "Florida." These words were expected to prime the concept of elderly for these participants. Participants in the control condition were exposed to neutral words that are not associated with senior citizens, so the elderly concept was not activated for them. After completing the task, all participants were told the study was over and sent on their way.

Actually, the study was far from over. Unbeknownst to the participants, a second experimenter timed how long it took them to walk from the laboratory to the elevator down the hall. Because "slow" is a characteristic associated with the elderly, the investigators predicted that elderly-primed participants would take more time to reach the elevator than would participants for whom this concept was not activated. This prediction was confirmed: participants who used words associated with the elderly to perform the sentence completion task took 13% longer to reach the elevator. When subsequently asked about their walk to the elevator, none of the primed participants mentioned thinking about the elderly—or anything else about the task they had completed. The concept of elderly was primed but they did not realize it.

The power of priming without people's awareness has been demonstrated in a number of contexts. For example, activating "rudeness" makes people behave more assertively when they have been inconvenienced (Bargh et al., 1996) and activating achievement goals leads people to persevere longer at difficult tasks (Bargh et al., 2001). In a study with commercial applications, playing French music resulted in increased sales of French wine at the expense of German wine, but playing German music increased sales of German rather than French wine—in both cases, without customers realizing (consciously) what type of music they were exposed to (North, Hargeaves, & McKendrick, 1999).

Priming can prove more effective than overt attempts at manipulation that play on people's conscious processes. If people know they are being influenced, they can try to counteract the manipulation (Lepore & Brown, 2002; Lombardi, Higgins, & Bargh, 1987). Such resistance is taken off the table when the influence occurs through unconscious channels. To influence people, it helps if they don't realize they are being manipulated.

SUMMING UP AND LOOKING AHEAD

- **Laws, regulations, and orders by legitimate authority figures are often effective in getting people to do things they might not otherwise do—even acts they find personally objectionable. But this general strategy can backfire because it threatens people's sense of freedom and thus can create a desire to do precisely the opposite of what is demanded.**

- **A less heavy-handed and potentially more effective influence strategy is to change people's opinions, beliefs, and values with principles of persuasion. The effectiveness of this approach has little to do with the logic or evidence associated with a persuasive communication. What matters instead are characteristics of the communicator (e.g., his or her credibility, likability, trustworthiness, similarity to the audience, and physical appearance) and the manner in which the persuasive message is presented (e.g., how confidently it is presented, whether it presents both sides of the issue, its emphasis on gains versus losses, whether the advocated message is presented before or after an opposing argument, and whether the message arouses fear).**

- **The effectiveness of communicator and communication variables depends on characteristics of the target audience. A one-sided message is likely to be persuasive when addressing those who are inclined to believe the message, but a two-sided message is necessary to convince those who initially disagree with the message. A message that emphasizes the positive benefits of adopting a point of view is likely to be persuasive for people who focus on achieving rewarding outcomes, but a message that emphasizes the alleviation or prevention of negative events may be necessary to persuade a person who focuses on prevention rather than promotion in his or her orientation to life. Prevention-focused messages also tend to be more effective persuading people who have an interdependent (or collectivist) orientation rather than an independent (or individualistic) orientation.**

- **Communicator and communication variables also differ in their effectiveness depending on the medium in which the message is presented. Complex messages can be effective when presented in written form (e.g., books, newspapers, magazines) but simple messages are more effective when visual media (e.g., TV, video clips) are employed. Visual media also enhance the persuasive power of an attractive communicator.**

- **People process persuasive communication in either a controlled mode that utilizes higher-level mental processes or an automatic mode that encodes the peripheral features of the communication. The distinction between the central (systematic) and peripheral (heuristic) modes of processing has implications for the effectiveness of communicator and communication variables. Visual media tend to activate the peripheral** mode, although this tendency can give way to the central mode when the persuasive message has high personal relevance for the target audience or if the audience is predisposed to engage in effortful cognitive activities.

- To overcome resistance to influence, an influence agent can play on people's desire for coherent understanding by focusing on message details or otherwise undermining the target's understanding of the message. From this disrupted state, the influence agent can frame the message in a way that provides a new understanding of the message.

- The acceptance or rejection of a persuasive communication can change over time. An idea that is initially rejected because of undesirable communicator characteristics (e.g., low credibility) can show a sleeper effect, gaining acceptance over time as these characteristics lose their salience. Conversely, a message that initially wins adherents because of its emotional appeal may be rejected over time as the emotional impact weakens.

- Requests that might otherwise be refused can be accepted if the person making the request flatters the target, appears to like the target, or seems similar to the target in some way. A target audience can be induced to desire a product that it might not otherwise care about by creating the impression that the product is in scarce supply.

- People's willingness to engage in an effortful or unpleasant action can be manipulated by making them feel obligated to do so. Giving a trivial gift to a stranger can induce him or her to reciprocate the favor, even if this involves a costly action. An outrageous request that is turned down by the target ("door in the face") can make promote compliance with a more reasonable request in the spirit of compromise. The same tactic underlies the "that's not all!" technique, in which an unacceptable offer likely to be rejected is quickly followed by another offer that seems reasonable in comparison. The opposite ("foot in the door") tactic works as well—a trivial action request that is accepted commits the person to subsequent action requests that are far more costly. "Throwing a low-ball" also plays on commitment, as when a salesperson changes the terms of an offer after the customer has agreed to the initial terms. The "bait and switch" tactic goes one step further by scrapping the initial deal altogether and offering something else instead.

- People can be induced to comply with requests by manipulating their mood. Putting people in a positive mood makes them agreeable to requests they might otherwise turn down. But a person in a negative mood (e.g., sadness, guilt) can also be induced to comply with a request if the requested action is viewed by the person as a way to feel better.

- The lack of awareness associated with manipulation is maximized in techniques based on subliminal priming—the activation of mental content by stimuli that are unconsciously processed. Exposing a person to positive or negative words, for example, can shape the person's mental set for subsequent action in line with the valence of these words. If the target is aware of the intended connection between stimuli exposure and subsequent judgments, however, he or she is likely to resist the influence.

As noted at the outset, social influence is at the heart of all social relations. This chapter has emphasized subtle but effective means of changing a person's behavior by changing the way he or she thinks and feels. Sometimes, though, people are simply concerned with affecting one another's outcomes—for better or worse. This can take the form of behavior that harms another person or a group of people. Such behavior is frowned upon in most social contexts and thus can be looked upon as *antisocial behavior*. But having direct impact on the outcomes of others can also take the form of compassion, help, and altruism. This class of behavior is valued and admired in social systems and thus can be looked upon as *prosocial behavior*. The next chapter provides an overview of what science has learned about these expressions of social behavior that are embedded in a societal context. As such, it represents our initial foray into the nature of collective experience.

Key Terms

Reward power
Coercive power
Social norms
Legitimate power
Obedience to authority
Reactance theory
Communicator characteristics
Vested interests
One-sided versus two-sided
  messages
Primacy versus recency
Gain versus loss
Regulatory focus
Promotion focus
Prevention focus

Appeals to fear
Simple versus complex messages
Elaboration likelihood
Central versus peripheral
  processing
Systematic versus heuristic
  processing
Need for cognition
Disassembly and emergence
  scenario
Disrupt-then-reframe technique
Sleeper effect
Emotional appeals
Manipulation
Flattery

Ingratiator's dilemma
Norm of social responsibility
Norm of equity
Norm of reciprocity
Door-in-the-face
That's not all!
Commitment
Foot-in-the door
Throwing a low-ball
Bait and switch
Mood maintenance
Negative state relief
Unconscious processing
Subliminal priming

PART IV

COLLECTIVE EXPERIENCE

11 Antisocial and Prosocial Behavior

It is hard to believe that Adolf Hitler and Mahatma Gandhi are members of the same species. Hitler was a power-hungry demagogue bent on taking over the world and eliminating entire groups of people. He was the epitome of what we call *evil*. Gandhi was a humble man who was willing to experience deprivation and risk imprisonment in order to establish justice and freedom for the people of India. He was the epitome of *good*. The extremes of human nature captured in Hitler and Gandhi are not exceptions, but can be observed in everyday life. Just turn on the national news—or the local news, for that matter. It seems that for every story about an admirable person—a hero, a philanthropist, a Nobel Prize winner—there is a story about an equally despicable person—someone guilty of child abuse, corporate fraud, even murder.

When we hear about such people, or when we encounter nasty versus wonderful people in our daily lives, we are tempted to make broad brushstrokes about human nature. In experiencing a nasty person, we may wonder whether human nature is inherently selfish and if everyone is capable of such behavior, with good behavior possible only through learning self-restraint and embracing a higher morality. When exposed to a virtuous person—for example, a hero highlighted at the end of a nightly news program to counter the preceding 25 minutes of tragic events—we may feel that people are inherently good, rather than evil being at the core of human nature. Or we may conclude that good and evil represent fault lines that divide humanity into one category or the other: some people are bad and unworthy, others are good and admirable.

Contemplating the capacity for good and evil in human nature is a preoccupation of social psychologists as well. Social psychology blossomed as a discipline in the years following World War II in large part because of the horrendous behavior that occurred during the war—much of it inspired by Hitler. That interest in the dark side of human nature continues to this day. But there is also intense interest in the potential for admirable behavior—from simple acts of generosity to acts of altruism that benefit other people or mankind generally. This chapter gives you an overview of what the field has learned about both sides of human nature. But instead of framing the issue as good versus evil, psychologists speak of *antisocial and prosocial behavior*. Both categories of human behavior are latent in human nature, each ready to be triggered by a wide assortment of factors that are all around us in our daily lives.

CHAPTER OVERVIEW

What Are You Going to Learn?

- **Where do antisocial and prosocial behavior fit into human nature?** Does one orientation or the other best capture the true nature of being human, with the other representing an override to how people really operate, or do both orientations reside at our core? What benefits did these conflicting orientations provide to our ancestors in the course of evolution? What biological factors give rise to both extremes of human behavior?
- **What factors in social life have the potential to trigger antisocial behavior in people?** What social contexts and physical circumstances activate people's predisposition to act in a hostile manner toward others? How does a person's experience within a family or social environment lower his or her threshold for harming others? What societal conditions and cultural factors tip the scales in favor aggressive behavior? What personal factors make some people especially sensitive to the triggers of antisocial behavior?
- **What factors in social life motivate people to engage in prosocial behavior?** Very few people are natural heroes, but many of us—perhaps the majority of us—can rise to the occasion and engage in positive behavior toward one another, even if such behavior does little to further our self-interest. What social contexts enhance the likelihood of such behavior? What intrapersonal processes are at work when people behave in a prosocial manner? Acting in a selfless manner is a fragile tendency, easily derailed by factors that reactivate concerns with personal gain and safety. What are the factors in everyday life that have this potential to undermine people's desire and willingness to engage in helpful and altruistic action?

Good Versus Evil in Human Nature

Are People Basically Selfish and Hostile or Socially Concerned and Helpful?

This issue is central to social psychology and has been addressed in two related ways. One increasingly popular approach is to identify the evolutionary foundations of human behavior. If hostility or helpfulness reflects human nature, this tendency presumably was adaptive for solving persistent problems of survival faced by our ancestors millennia ago. The other approach—also gaining in popularity—is to explore the biological bases of behavior. If either antisocial or prosocial behavior represents a basic human tendency, it should have a genetic basis and its expression should be linked to hormones, activation in brain centers, and other biological factors.

Before considering these perspectives, it is important to clarify what exactly qualifies as "good" and "bad" social behavior. One person's noble deed, after all, might be blasted by someone else as insensitive or downright wicked. Throughout history, people have fought one another and nations have gone to war in the firm belief that they are on the side of goodness and that their antagonists are motivated by far less desirable impulses and goals.

Expressions of Good and Evil

Sometimes it is easy to declare an action to be good or evil. Going out of one's way to help someone in need would seem to represent the former; going out of one's way to harm someone would seem to represent the latter. But sometimes it is not so easy to make this distinction. Helping a mass murderer escape when he or she is surrounded by the police is great for him or her, but such an act hardly qualifies as good if it means the person can continue generating carnage. If anything, hurting such a person might quality as a good act, worthy of admiration by society. Aware of the problems that arise when focusing only on overt behavior, psychologists go a bit deeper to identify the internal states, motives, and perceived consequences associated with helpful and harmful behavior. This approach has resulted in some distinctions that have proven helpful in generating insight into the good and bad in human nature.

Types of Hurting

Two distinctions are commonly made when investigating *aggression*—behavior intended to hurt someone. The first is *direct versus indirect aggression* (Walker, Richardson, & Green, 2000). *Direct aggression* is behavior aimed at hurting someone in a face-to-face context. This can take a physical form, as when someone punches or shoots another person, but it can also be expressed verbally, as when the person threatens or insults someone. *Indirect aggression* is harmful behavior that occurs without face-to-face conflict. Spreading rumors or malicious gossip behind someone's back on social media captures this form of aggression.

The second distinction involves the mental state of the person. *Emotional aggression* is generated by angry feelings that find expression in harmful behavior. Punching someone during a heated argument is an aggressive act that springs directly from losing one's temper. This stands in contrast to *instrumental aggression*, harmful behavior that is service of some other goal (Berkowitz, 1993). In robbing a store, a person may feel little or no anger toward the store clerk but threaten or harm him or her anyway in order to carry out the robbery. Sometimes it is hard to determine the mental state associated with an aggressive act. Aggressive behavior in response to an insult, for example, could be motivated by anger or by a desire to maintain one's image in the eyes of bystanders. For that matter, both mental states could be at work when attempting to harm someone (Bushman & Anderson, 2001). Examples of the four types of aggression generated by these two distinctions are displayed in Table 11.1.

Types of Helping

Everyday life is filled with many examples of helpful acts, from holding open a classroom door for someone, to picking up books that a person has dropped, to giving up a seat on a crowded bus for a senior citizen. Helpfulness can also play out in extraordinary circumstances, as when people donate money to a charity or offer aid to victims of a natural disaster.

Some prosocial acts are truly selfless, in that the person does not benefit in any obvious way from behaving in this fashion. When the motivation is purely to offer help without expectation of any reward, psychologists speak of *altruism*. A donation to charity, for example, is motivated by a desire to help those in need. The same can be said for a simple act of courtesy, such as helping an elderly person cross a busy street, without expecting compensation or even admiration by bystanders. The altruistic nature of such acts is amplified when they are costly to the helper or incur risks to him or her. The donation to charity, for example, could deplete the person's savings account, and helping someone cross a busy street might run the risk of being hit by a car.

But prosocial acts are often far less selfless, reflecting instead an expectation of social or material rewards. A person who donates money to charity could be motivated by a tax break or by a desire to be seen as a noble person by friends and perhaps the mass media. The person who helps a senior citizen cross the street might do so because he or she wants to be recognized as a good person by friends and bystanders, or perhaps because he or she hopes the senior citizen will express his or her gratitude in a material manner. Sometimes it can be hard to tell whether a person's helpful behavior is truly altruistic or motivated by the expectation of some reward. For that matter, prosocial behavior can reflect both altruism and a desire to help oneself. A person might donate money to charity because he or she wants to relieve people's suffering and because he or she expects to receive a tax break for doing so.

Table 11.1 Examples of Different Types of Aggressive Behavior

	Direct	Indirect
Emotional	A man punches a peer who questions his manhood	A man pours a soft drink on an enemy's computer keyboard
Instrumental	A man shoots a clerk while committing a robbery	A man posts intimate photos of his ex-girlfriend on *Facebook* to impress his friends

Evolutionary Foundations

Perhaps people are basically selfish but learn to help others because it is in their long-term interest to do so. Or perhaps people's natural tendency is to help others, with harmful actions occurring in response to instigations that override our helpful nature. Or perhaps both helping and hurting are ingrained in human nature. To resolve this issue, we need to consider the extent to which helping and hurting have been selected for in the course of human evolution.

Aggression

Long before there were police, courts, and lawyers, people had to settle disputes in a considerably more basic manner. In competing over scarce resources or dealing with a threatening adversary, our ancestors had to stand their ground and take forceful action to prevail in the dispute. Those who were not willing to fight when challenged by others ("OK, you win") were unlikely to gain access to resources or avoid being defeated by an adversary, and thus were at a disadvantage in the struggle for survival. Natural selection favored individuals with a genetic predisposition to act in an aggressive manner under such circumstances (Buss & Duntley, 2006; Shackelford & Hansen, 2013).

The evolutionary basis of aggression is on display in forming intimate relationships—which may seem ironic, given the tenderness and affection we tend to associate with love. In many animal species, though, males must compete for mates, with competition expressed in aggressive encounters that can lead to death of the loser. Such aggression increases dramatically just before the mating season (Gould & Gould, 1989), with males butting heads or clawing at each other in their attempt to demonstrate their dominance and impress nearby females. Throughout human history, males have also aggressed against one another in competition for mates—and as in other species, such aggression can result in severe injury and even death (Daly & Wilson, 1994).

Bull elk lock horns and battle, sometimes for hours and sometimes with one of them dying, in competition for access to fertile and sexually receptive females. Such behavior has parallels in many other species—including humans.

Today, men can impress one another with their bank accounts, credentials, and other signs of their social rank. But before there were banks or advanced university degrees, males had to demonstrate their mate value in physical means. This evolved strategy is still at work in males when they reach puberty but have yet to acquire "civilized" means of demonstrating their rank in the social hierarchy (Weisfeld, 1994). With wealth and social status out of reach until adulthood, teenage males—like the males of other species—compete by attempting to dominate, or at least intimidate, one another, and this goal is often accomplished by violent encounters.

Prosocial Behavior

Prosocial behavior is found in all human societies, which suggests it has adaptive value, both for societies and for individuals who behave in this manner (M. Nowak, 2006). The need to put aside personal self-interest in order to help one another was present at the dawn of our species, when everyday survival depended on collective action. A selfish individual living in the harsh conditions of our ancestral environment would not have fared well in the face of predators, uncertain food supplies, and hostile neighbors. By forming groups and working together to defend against predators, hunt prey animals and grow crops, and stand together against antagonistic tribes, individual humans—which are arguably the weakest, pound for pound, of all mammals—not only survived but managed to build civilizations, develop science and technology, create art and music, and transform the earth in countless ways.

Prosocial behavior comes naturally to us in today's world. People hold doors for one another, offer assistance to those in need, donate money to charitable organizations, and even risk their lives to save the lives of others under certain circumstances (e.g., rescuing a child from a burning car, jumping into raging water to save someone from drowning). In the United States—perhaps the most individualistic society on the planet—70% of all households donate to charities, almost half (44%) of all adults volunteer in public service organizations, and millions of people donate their blood for those in need (Giving USA, 2003; Piliavin & Callero, 1991). Natural disasters such as hurricanes, earthquakes, and floods, routinely elicit an outpouring of help from people, even those living in distant lands.

This is all fine, but how can we account for altruistic acts that put one's life at risk from an evolutionary perspective? After all, the driving force in human (and animal) nature according to evolutionary theorists is the non-conscious desire to pass on one's genes to succeeding generations. To do so, people must ensure that they survive, at least long enough to mate and produce offspring. Shouldn't this mean that people only help one another if there is a direct personal benefit and they can avoid personal sacrifice—particularly sacrificing their own lives—altogether? Altruistic sacrifice may make sense in the long run, but in the short run such behavior flies in the face of "watching out for number one."

There are three answers to this apparent riddle. The easiest answer is that there is no riddle at all—people help one another, and even risk their lives to do so, to ensure their genetic survival. The key here is *genetic*, not personal survival. This idea is central to *inclusive fitness theory*, formulated originally by W.D. Hamilton (1964) and expanded upon and popularized by several others (e.g., Dawkins, 1976). Think about this in terms of simple mathematics. A person shares 50% of his or her genes with a sibling, 25% with a first cousin, 12.5 % with a second cousin, and so on. If our evolutionary mandate is ensuring the survival of our genes, personal survival is certainly important—but no more than the survival of two siblings (50% ÷ 2 = 100%) or four cousins (25% ÷ 4 = 100%). This implies that we help others to the extent that we share genes with them. By helping two or more siblings survive, our own genes survive and the evolutionary mandate is served, even if our help comes at the expense of our personal survival.

This seems strange. Human history predates scientific knowledge of genes by thousands of years, and even today most people have no insight into the mathematics of shared genes beyond that of their immediate family. But remember that evolution does not require insight into the distal causes of our behavior. People eat fatty and salty food because it tastes good, for example, without any understanding of the need of our ancestors to store food in fat cells to get them through periods of limited food availability or outright famine. In similar fashion, although we are motivated to help our kin because we like them or see them as familiar or similar to us, these desires and cues are just nature's way of ensuring that we protect our genetic lineage.

There is considerable evidence to support this idea. Many animal species feed, defend, and assist their closest relatives more than distant relatives, and will sacrifice themselves if need be. Humans are not different in this regard—we tend to help those who are genetically close relatives (Burnstein, Crandall, & Kitayama, 1994; Neyer & Lang, 2003). This helping takes many forms, from donating a kidney to save the life of a relative to depleting a bank account to help a relative down on his or her luck financially.

But people do not limit their helpfulness and altruism to relatives. People will help neighbors and friends in times of need, despite not sharing any genes with them. Robert Trivers (1971) addressed this issue by pointing out the basic tendency toward *reciprocity* in interpersonal relations. People feel obligated to repay the benefits and favors they receive from others. If someone loans you money, you pay it back; if someone pays you a compliment, you are likely to say something nice in return. The notion of *reciprocal altruism* extends this idea to helpful behavior, even actions that may be risky for the helper. In effect, people engage in prosocial behavior because it creates the likelihood that they will be helped some day when they need it. So what looks like pure altruism in the short run is really enlightened self-interest in the long run. Reciprocal altruism is reinforced by cultural traditions, although it appears in many other animal species (E. O. Wilson, 2012), suggesting that it has an evolutionary foundation.

But even reciprocity does not fully capture the extent to which people engage in prosocial behavior. As noted above, people donate money to charitable organizations, pitch in to help with relief efforts after a natural disaster, and join campaigns to raise awareness of societal problems (e.g., poverty, child abuse) and diseases (e.g., cancer, ALS). In such cases, there is no expectation that the help provided will be reciprocated by those who are helped. To provide an evolutionary account for prosocial behavior that goes beyond inclusive fitness and reciprocal altruism, several theorists have proposed that natural selection is *multi-level*, operating at the level of *the group* as well as at the level of *the individual* (Caporael, Dawes, Orbell, & van de Kragt, 1989; D. S. Wilson & E. O. Wilson, 2008). *Group selection* occurs when a social structure promotes the fitness of group members, thus favoring individuals who are predisposed to form and maintain that structure. Wolves associate in packs, for example, because that facilitates the capture of prey. Hence, wolves possessing genes that predispose them to form this social structure are favored by natural selection over those that do not possess these genes.

The notion of group selection is somewhat controversial (Dawkins, 1976; Pinker, 1997). Advocates note that the survival of a group would be impossible without mutual helping and altruism among all group members. If an individual acted only in line with his or her personal genetic interest, aiding genetic relatives or those who can repay the aid, the social system might not survive, in which case the individual's genes would not survive anyway. Altruism for the benefit of strangers may be risky for individuals, but it is less risky than selfishness. Critics argue that helping others regardless of personal benefit would not occur without reinforcement by society or religious traditions. However, experiments (Goodnight & Stevens, 1997; Wade, 1977) and computer simulations (e.g., M. Nowak & Highfield, 2011) have demonstrated the viability of group selection and shown how this tendency could have shaped the course of human evolution. Beyond that, the human capacity for *empathy*—which is a direct consequence of *theory of mind* (Premack & Woodruff, 1978)—places this form of altruism well within the boundaries of human nature. Because we have the mental capacity to imagine how others think and feel, we are motivated to alleviate their suffering and aid them when they need help.

Biological Bases

Evolutionary pressures represent the distal causes of aggression and prosocial behavior, but they ultimately are expressed through biological processes. Research has identified two ways in which basic biology underlies both expressions of human nature: *genetics* and *gender*.

Genetic Variation

Selective breeding research has shown that aggression is inheritable in mice (and several other species) (Nelson, 2006). Researchers identify mice that differ in their aggressive tendencies, and ensure that the mice with similar tendencies mate with one another. This procedure is then followed for the offspring of these two groups—the most aggressive offspring mate with other aggressive offspring and the least aggressive offspring mate with other unaggressive offspring. When this procedure is repeated for several generations, the offspring become increasingly aggressive versus increasingly nonaggressive.

For obvious practical and ethical reasons, scientists cannot use selective breeding to determine whether human aggression has a similar genetic component. People live too long to wait several generations to get the answer, and it is clearly ethically wrong to dictate with whom people can mate. An alternative strategy is to compare the aggressive tendencies of *monozygotic* (identical) twins, who share all of their genes, and *dizygotic* (fraternal) twins, who share on average half of their genes. This research strategy has shown that identical twins are more similar in their aggressive tendencies (as well as many other traits) than are fraternal twins (Bock & Goode, 1996). Everyone is capable of acting aggressively, but people are primed by their genes to differ from one another in their threshold for such behavior.

Like aggression, prosocial behavior shows individual variation, with some people more cooperative and altruistic than others. And as with aggression, individual differences in prosocial behavior are partly attributable to inheritance.

This has been established by comparing the similarity in helping tendencies of identical and fraternal twins. Among children as young as 14 months, as well as among adults, identical twins are more alike in their helpfulness toward others than are fraternal twins (Rushton et al., 1986). All people are inclined to help, but some enter the world especially inclined to do so.

Gender

In the discussion of the evolutionary bases for aggression, you may have noticed that the factors apply primarily to men rather than women. *Males* fight for dominance, *males* defend territory, and *males* battle one another for mating opportunities (Daly & Wilson, 1994). The statistics confirm the greater readiness for violence on the part of males. In the United States, the probability of a male committing a violent crime is almost nine times greater than the comparable probability for a female. A male is eight times more likely to commit aggravated assault, 10 times more likely to commit murder, 13 times more likely to commit armed robbery, and 44 times more likely to commit sexual assault. Most prisoners are male, and 98.4% of those on death row are male. Worldwide, men commit about 90% of assaults and virtually all rapes (Graham & Wells, 2001). This gender difference begins early in development. Among children, boys show higher rates of physical aggression than do girls, and infant boys display more anger and poorer emotional regulation than do infant girls (Loeber & Hay, 1997).

This does not mean that females are devoid of aggressive tendencies. Women are just as prone to anger as are men, and like men they are inclined to act on these feelings (Bettencourt & Miller, 1996). They just go about this differently. Males opt for physical, often violent aggressive behavior—hitting, pushing, kicking, and the like. Females opt for less physical forms of aggression, such as shouting, insulting, spreading rumors, and excluding others from activities (Archer & Coyne, 2005; Graham & Wells, 2001; Österman et al., 1998).

What is it about men that sets the bar so low for physical aggression, even in circumstances that seem devoid of evolutionary significance? Socialization by parents and societal norms play a role, but perhaps the most important factor is a particular hormone: *testosterone*. Women have some testosterone circulating in their bodies, but this amount pales in comparison to the level of testosterone in men's bodies. This hormone is essential for the secondary sex characteristics that men acquire at puberty (e.g., facial and body hair, upper body muscle mass, body size), and it creates the sex drive that is necessary for mating. But higher levels of testosterone are also associated with aggressive behavior in males (Archer, 2006b; Dabbs & Morris, 1990; Ellis, 1986). Because aggression, particularly when it is manifest as assault or murder, is frowned upon by society, men with high levels of testosterone are prone to antisocial behavior and thus are over-represented in the criminal justice system.

The link between testosterone and aggression is a bit misleading. What testosterone *really* does is promote attempts at seeking and maintaining social dominance (Mazur & Booth, 1998). Of course, aggression is an obvious way to accomplish these goals. In infrahuman animals, it is typically the *only* way to establish dominance hierarchies. The alpha male, loaded with testosterone, spends much of his time engaging in threat displays, sexual mounting, and violent behavior intended to intimidate a rival. Aggression has also provided a means by which humans seek dominance for much of our history. Individuals dominate one another by fighting, while groups assert dominance by attacking one another with military forces.

Among humans in the modern era, there are alternative means of establishing and maintaining dominance. Males—and females, for that matter—can acquire and display resources and symbols of power and can rise to leadership positions in industry, science, and politics. Presumably, a person who has the opportunity to command respect in a government or a large corporation—or in sports or entertainment—can satisfy the testosterone-based need for dominance without physical confrontations and aggression. Nations, too, can achieve dominance through economic success, scientific and technological advances, and leadership in international relations, without resorting to military intervention.

Research relevant to this point has shown that the relationship between testosterone and aggression exists for men in lower socioeconomic classes whose opportunities for achieving dominance by other means is limited (Dabbs & Morris, 1990). But as Figure 11.1 illustrates, among middle- and upper-middle-class men, the association between testosterone and aggression vanishes. Men with opportunities for dominance in business, government, politics, and science can bypass the need to assert their strength through physical aggression.

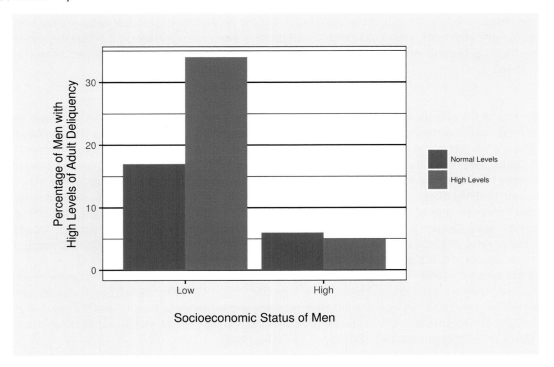

FIGURE 11.1 Risk of High Levels of Testosterone for Antisocial Behavior Among Men with Low versus High
Socioeconomic Status
Source: Adapted from Dabbs & Morris (1990)

Causes and Triggers of Aggression

What Promotes Antagonistic and Hostile Interpersonal Behavior?

To say that there are evolutionary and biological bases for aggression does not mean that people wander around ready to lash out at each other without warning and for no reason. Even the most aggressive person by virtue of genes and hormones spends the majority of his or her time acting in a nonaggressive fashion. The study of aggression has given a great deal of attention to the factors and conditions of social life that act as triggers for aggressive behavior.

Social Learning

Aggression is a special class of behavior, but according to *social learning theory* (e.g., Bandura, Ross, & Ross, 1961; Mischel, 1973), it is acquired in much the same way that more mundane types of behavior are. Like *behaviorism* (Pavlov, 1927; Skinner, 1938), social learning theory assumes that people acquire a new behavior if it is associated with rewards of some kind (e.g., food, money, admiration). But social learning goes beyond this basic idea by describing how people acquire new forms of behaviors without having to actually perform them. Instead, people (like other intelligent mammals) learn through observation. If they observe someone perform an action that results in receiving a reward, they will enact this behavior under similar circumstances and perhaps incorporate it into their own behavioral repertoires.

Parents and Peers

The role of *modeling* in the development of aggressive tendencies is especially pronounced during childhood, when children are learning behaviors of every kind. Young children are dependent on their parents and look to them for guidance in how to do just about everything, from getting dressed to interacting with people. They note how their parents behave and use this behavior as a model for how they can and should behave when left to their own devices. Note that this route to acquiring aggressive behavior has little to do with anger or other emotions, and thus is more in line with instrumental aggression. Kids learn through observation that aggression can be an effective means for achieving goals.

As children grow older, they increasingly model the behavior of those with whom they play or desire to have as friends (Harris, 1995; Scarr, 1992). By the time children are in their late teens, their behavior patterns better reflect the lessons they have learned from peers than all the early lessons modeled by their parents. So even if Mom and Dad model patience and helpful behavior, their kids are at risk for antisocial behavior of various kinds (e.g., aggression, intolerance) if their peers provide models for this approach to social relations.

Media Violence

For most of human history—remember, we've been around in our present form for over 150,000 years—the range of role models was quite limited. People came into contact with, and observed the actions of, others with whom they shared the same geographical space. Even with the development of cities, the number of people who could have significant impact on a child's social orientation was relatively small. People learned how to handle conflicts and challenges by observing teachers, religious figures, community leaders, and especially their peers.

These role models still affect what children learn, but their function has been usurped to some extent by a new source of social learning: the mass media. This form of influence expanded rapidly with the advent of movies in the early 20th century, television in the middle 20th century, and video games and the internet in the late 20th century. Children today can observe the actions of hundreds of people with whom they will never have contact, and thus can learn many different ways of handling situations involving potential conflict. Do these opportunities for social learning produce patterns of behavior that conflict with, or take precedence over, social learning in the home and neighborhood? Do children learn how to behave by watching what perfect strangers do on movie screens and on their TVs and computers?

Here are a few chilling statistics. The average child in the United States spends 40 hours per week consuming mass media (Rideout, Foehr, & Roberts, 2010). This is equivalent to holding down a full-time job. There are more television sets in the United States than there are toilets. This might not be a cause for concern if televised content centered on science, adventure, and goofball humor. But that is clearly not the case. The lion's share of TV content—about 60%—involves violence and other forms of antisocial behavior. By the time an average American child has finished the primary grades, he or she will have witnessed about 100,000 violent acts—including about 8,000 murders (Huston et al., 1992). This violence, moreover, is often presented in a way that makes it appear trivial—or worse, as glamorous (Bushman & Phillips, 2001).

The massive degree of exposure to violence on TV has prompted concern that children today are learning that aggression is a common and acceptable form of behavior. Particularly when the violence seems to solve a problem, children may learn that "might makes right," so that no matter what the relative merits of a dispute are, the side that is stronger, has more weapons, or displays better fighting skills is the winner. With this concern in mind, psychologists have conducted hundreds of studies since the 1960s on the impact of media violence on the attitudes and behaviors of children (Anderson et al., 2003). This work have been quite consistent in showing that indeed there is something to worry about. Children who watch TV shows that portray people attempting to hurt or kill one another tend to act aggressively toward their peers, particularly if their interaction with the peers involves frustration or conflict of some kind.

But does this mean that watching violent TV *causes* children to be aggressive? It is tempting to make that interpretation, but keep in mind that *correlation is not causation*. Sure, there is a link between exposure to TV violence and aggressive behavior by young viewers, but it could be that kids who are predisposed to violence seek out TV shows that feature violence. For that matter, perhaps some third factor—poverty, for example, or short-tempered parents—independently increases aggressive tendencies in children and creates a desire to see violence glamorized on TV. As many as 22 such "third factors" have been identified (Belson, 1978)—although the link between TV viewing and violent behavior remains when each of these causes is removed with statistical techniques (Anderson et al., 2017).

To show that exposure to TV violence causes viewers to be aggressive, it is useful to conduct an experiment. Since the 1960s, when TV violence was first recognized as a potential problem, hundreds of studies have been performed in which participants are randomly assigned to view varying degrees of violence on TV and then put in a situation that provides an opportunity or excuse for aggression toward someone else.

Zillman and Weaver (1999), for example, recruited college students to watch either violent or nonviolent films for four nights in a row. They then participated in what they thought was an unrelated study and were provided an opportunity to harm the experimental assistant who acted in a provocative manner toward some of them. The results were clear: the students fed a 4-day diet of violent programming were more aggressive toward the assistant, even if she did nothing to provoke them. The causal impact of violent media has been established in dozens of other experiments (e.g., Green, 1998; Leyens, Camino, Parke, & Berkowitz, 1975; Parke et al., 1977).

The causal impact of media violence, however, depends on other factors that amplify the power of social learning. People are more likely to be violent after viewing films in which the perpetrator is someone with whom they can identify—a "good guy" or someone of the same gender and background (e.g., Leyens & Pincus, 1973). The modeling effect of media violence is also magnified when the violence is justified, as when it is directed against "bad guys" (Berkowitz, 1965). And violence in the context of violent pornography in which women are dominated or humiliated tends to increase aggressive behavior by men toward women (Donnerstein, 1980; Donnerstein & Berkowitz, 1981).

Although the causal impact of violent media in these studies is well documented, the effect is not very strong (Wood, Wong, & Chachere, 1991). Sometimes fancy statistical analyses are required to show that media violence promotes aggressive behavior, and some studies have failed to demonstrate this effect at all (e.g., Freedman, 1984; Friedrich-Cofer & Huston, 1986; McGuire, 1986; Wiegman, Kuttschreuter, & Baarda, 1992). This might make you wonder if the impact is also temporary, with little to worry about how it influences children's behavior in the long run as they progress toward adulthood. The immediate impact of an aggressive TV show or movie could be short-lived, giving way to a person's typical way of thinking and acting acquired in interactions with his or her parents, siblings, and peers.

Of course, the opposite scenario can also be envisioned—the immediate impact of exposure to media violence might feed on itself, resulting in a long-term effect that is even stronger. Which long-term scenario best characterizes the impact of violence in mass media? Is it just a short-term effect that dissipates as soon as the child is distracted by something else? Or is it more like a time bomb, with effects that become increasingly manifest as the child grows older, presumably because the lessons learned have become internalized, creating the seeds for a pattern of behavior that is self-sustaining?

Leonard Eron, Rowell Huesmann, and their colleagues have tackled this question by using longitudinal research methods. Children who watch varying degrees of TV violence are followed for years, even decades, to determine the long-term impact (if any) of the earlier mass media exposure (e.g., Huesmann, Moise-Titus, Podolski, & Eron, 2003). This line of research has established that the amount of TV violence watched by 8-year-old boys predicts not only their aggressiveness in adulthood, but even their likelihood of criminal activity by the time they reach 30 years of age! (See Figure 11.2). You might argue that aggressive boys watch more violent TV, so that their criminal behavior in adulthood is simply an extrapolation of their youthful tendencies. The researchers were sensitive to this possibility and obtained a pure measure of the link between childhood TV viewing and adult crime by employing statistics that controlled for the boys' aggressive tendencies. This pure measure revealed that exposure to heavy doses of TV violence in childhood did in fact "cause" criminal behavior in adulthood.

Females are less influenced by the violence depicted in mass media (Bartholow & Anderson, 2002; Eagly & Steffen, 1986). This gender difference is interesting in light of evidence that the modeling effect of TV violence may be partly responsible for spousal abuse. Huesmann et al. (2003) found that a heavy dose of TV violence during children's formative years was associated with spousal aggression when these kids got married. This effect, however, was considerably stronger for men (husbands) than it was for women (wives). This may reflect the disproportionate amount of violence on TV committed by men than by women. If so, as women become more aggressive in TV and movies, we may see equality in spousal aggression in the years to come. Whether this represents the sort of equality we want is another question.

Beyond its modeling effect, exposure to violence can promote aggressive behavior if it leads children to believe that such action is commonplace in social life. In a study by Orue et al. (2011), several hundred children between 8 and 12 years old completed questionnaires twice, 6 months apart, concerning their exposure to violence, their own aggressive behavior, the aggressive behavior of peers, and their normative beliefs about aggression. Witnessing violence predicted increases in children's aggression 6 months later, and that this effect was due to changes in their normative

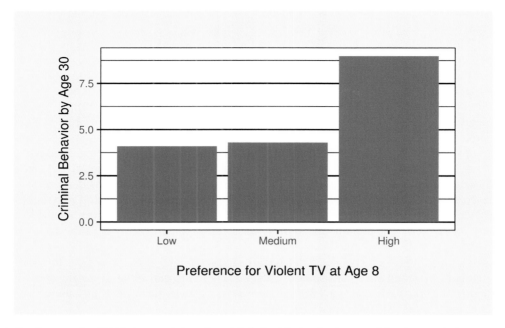

FIGURE 11.2 Preference for TV Violence at Age 8 and Criminal Behavior by Age 30. The *Y*-axis is Based on Two
Measures: The Number of Criminal Convictions and the Seriousness of Each Crime.
Source: Adapted from Huesmann (1986)

beliefs. When children think that violence is common in many contexts, they are more likely to incorporate aggressive behavior into their own lives.

If the effects of TV are due to social learning, then should not desirable effects result from TV shows with positive social messages? Mass media that portray friendliness, cooperation, and helpfulness do increase prosocial behavior in children, while reducing aggressive behavior (Greitemeyer, 2011). But keep in mind that the most vivid and attention-getting TV shows and movies are loaded with violent imagery, revenge, and outright aggression. So the prosocial effect of nonviolent mass media is destined to pale in comparison to the effect of violent mass media—at least until the proportion of violent to prosocial media somehow begins to reverse.

Violent Video Games

Everyone watches TV, but for today's youth, this pastime is giving way to playing video games as the default activity when not attending classes, interacting with peers, or taking care of business. Toward the end of the 20th century, when video games were still relatively novel, 85% of American teens engaged in this activity on a regular basis (Anderson & Bushman, 2001). Preteen boys (8 to 13 years old) are also quite taken with video games, playing them more than 7.5 hours per week on average (Rideout et al., 2010). Like TV programs, video games are often loaded with violent content. Individuals battle each other and competing nations fight to the death, often with a "good versus evil" theme that justifies the violence. Perhaps playing video games has a greater impact on aggressive tendencies than does watching a violent TV show or movie (Anderson & Bushman, 2001). The person controlling a person or an army battalion in a video game is not simply a spectator, passively noting what is happening, but rather is an active participant in the carnage. It is noteworthy that playing violent video games activates the same brain regions as does real-life aggression (Weber, Ritterfeld, & Mathiak, 2006)

To test whether video games promote aggression, researchers randomly assign participants (usually college students, sometimes teenagers) to one of two video games, one defined in terms of violent conflict between individuals or groups and one involving physical activity but without violence (e.g., Anderson & Dill, 2000). The violent game might be *Mortal Kombat*, in which the player's goal is to kill six other characters, and to do so as violently as possible.

The nonviolent game might be *PGA Tournament Golf*, in which the player chooses the appropriate clubs and attempts shots that are best suited to wind conditions, trees, and sand traps.

After playing one of these games, all participants play a competitive game with someone they think is another naïve participant, but who is actually an experimental accomplice (or a computer program). The winner of this game gets to "punish" the loser by delivering a blast of aversive white noise to him or her. The game is rigged, so that sometimes the true participant wins and sometimes the accomplice (or program) wins. The dependent measure is the intensity and duration of the white noise used by the participant when he or she is the winner. The results are clear: participants who play the violent game (e.g., *Mortal Kombat*) give longer and more intense blasts of aversive noise to the loser than do those who played the nonviolent game.

In reviewing the results of many studies of this kind, Anderson and Bushman (2001) concluded that playing violent video games not only increased aggressive behavior (e.g., delivering intense blasts of noise), but had other worrying effects as well. Participants assigned to play violent video games experience an increase in aggressive thoughts and emotions, and increased blood pressure and heart rate—physiological responses associated with fighting (and fleeing, for that matter). Violent video games also decrease the likelihood of prosocial acts such as helping, cooperation, and altruism. And it's not just men who are affected in these ways. Adult women display the same tendencies, and so do children.

The aggression-promoting effect of violent video games can persist long after the game is finished. Bushman and Gibson (2011) randomly assigned male participants (college students) to play either a violent or a nonviolent video game for 20 minutes. Half the participants in each condition were asked to think about the game and its meaning; the others were not asked to engage in this rumination. The next day, all participants competed with another male (actually a computer program). If they won, they could punish the loser with painful noise blasts through his headphones. Those participants who had played the violent video game made greater use of this punishment than did those who had played the nonviolent game—but only if they had spent time ruminating about their gaming experience. Playing a violent video game is one thing, but ruminating about the experience keeps aggressive thoughts, feelings, and behaviors fresh in the player's mind. By the same reasoning, if something prevents a person from reflecting on his or her experience dispatching enemies, he or she may be less likely to act aggressively later on.

The player's active involvement in video games can also promote *dehumanization*—perceiving enemies (and out-group members generally) to lack higher-order mental processes and emotions and thus to be less than fully human (Bandura, 2002; Haslam, 2006; Haslam, Loughnan, Reynolds, & Wilson, 2007). The enemies in video games, in fact, are typically presented as less than human (Hartmann & Vorderer, 2010). This is worrisome since dehumanization is a predictor of interpersonal aggression (Haslam et al., 2005) and intergroup aggression (Struch & Schwartz, 1989). Carried to the extreme, dehumanization can provide justification for sanctioned mass violence, including massacres and genocide (Kelman, 1973). Video games are a recent invention, so it remains to be seen whether they increase the risk for aggression against members of an out-group. But the evidence to date is cause for concern.

Society and Culture

Apart from the personal experiences that shape each person's pattern of thought and behavior, there are forces in society that affect everyone to some degree. Some of these factors pervade social life, but others are more prominent in certain cultural contexts than in others.

Income Inequality

Income inequality has received attention in recent years, as many countries have seen tremendous gains in wealth for a small percentage of their population. This has prompted concern that the increasing gap between the very rich and everyone else may have implications for societal well-being. Wilkinson and Pickett (2009) tackled this issue by investigating the relationship between income inequality and several measures, including a society's murder rate. Their measure of inequality was the difference in the percentage of wealth owned by the richest members of society (the top 20%) and the poorest members (the bottom 20%). They then compared this measure with the society's homicide rate (the number of homicides per million).

Figure 11.3 shows the relationship for industrialized countries, primarily those in North America, Europe, and East Asia. In those countries with higher income inequality, there is a correspondingly high homicide rate. Note that the

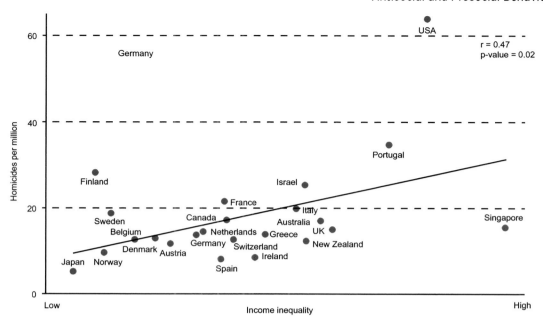

FIGURE 11.3 The Relationship Between Income Inequality and Murder in Industrialized Societies
Source: Wilkinson, R., & Pickett, K. (2009). *The spirit level: Why more equal societies almost always do better.* New York: Bloomsbury Press; reprinted from https://www.equalitytrust.org.uk/violence.

United States, for example, has a high degree of income inequality and by far the highest homicide rate of these countries. Wilkinson and Pickett offer several plausible reasons for this relationship. People at the bottom of the income ladder might feel powerful feelings of social rejection and resentment, for example, which can trigger violence. Inequality also has the potential to undermine the cohesiveness and sense of shared fate in a society. In effect, individuals in a highly unequal society may lack a feeling of good will and have little trust toward one another. Inequality also creates competition among males for economic resources and access to females. These two sources of conflict that can motivate criminal behavior, including murder (Daly, Wilson, & Vasdev, 2001).

Cultural Differences

Not all societies are equally violent. The United States has a high homicide rate compared to industrialized countries—largely those in Europe and parts of Asia—but this rate (about 10 per 100,000 people) is far lower than in other countries, particularly those in South America and certain areas of Africa. The lower murder rates in developed countries points to the importance of stable democratic institutions and a relatively high standard of living (e.g., Archer, 2006a).

Cultures also differ in their respective rates of rape, a particularly disturbing form of violent antisocial behavior. The coercive forcing of sex upon another person (typically male on female) can have very negative and long-lasting consequences for the victim, including generalized anxiety, distrust toward men, and problems in romantic relationships. To address what makes some cultures more rape-prone than others, Peggy Reeves Sanday (1997) looked at archival records from 156 cultures dating back to 1750 BC and continuing to the 1960s. Of course, the statistics on rape are open to serious reservations. Most troublesome is that rapes often go unreported—either because the victim is ashamed or fears repercussions, or because others do not wish to acknowledge the event for various reasons (e.g., social taboos, suspicions about the victim's "true" role in the rape). This reticence on the part of both the victim and the larger society may be more pronounced in those societies in which rape is more common.

Nonetheless, Sanday (1997) was able to formulate a few generalizations based on her archival analyses. *Rape-prone cultures* tend to have high levels of violence, a history of frequent warfare, and an emphasis on male toughness and machismo. Rape also tends to be most prevalent in cultures in which women have lower status than men. In many such cultures, women are denied access to education and political participation. Women in cultures relatively free of rape, in contrast, tend to have equal status with men. Knowing that these features characterize rape-prone cultures can actually be seen as good news. Despite some notable exceptions, the countries of the world are becoming increasingly democratic and in touch with equal rights for women (Pinker, 2011). Assuming this is a reliable trend, perhaps we can look forward to a world in which the incidence of rape is dramatically reduced.

Culture of Honor

The differences between cultures in murder rates and other indices of antisocial behavior do not tell the full story. Any culture is complex, comprising distinct and sometimes contradictory traditions that are associated with different regions (urban vs. rural, northern vs. southern) and demographics (education, income, population density, religiosity, etc.). This is certainly true of the United States. Richard Nisbett and Dov Cohen have documented that states in the South are more prone to violence than are Northern states (Cohen & Nisbett, 1997; Nisbett, 1993; Nisbett & Cohen, 1996). They suggest that the South is characterized by a *culture of honor*, which essentially means that people are concerned with their reputation for toughness, machismo, and willingness and ability to avenge a wrong or an insult.

To some extent, every culture shares these concerns, but two factors heighten them. First, Nisbett and Cohen (1996) note that people from Southern states historically were more likely to raise livestock, whereas people in Northern states tended instead to be farmers. Unlike the crops grown by the Northerners, the herds in the South were mobile and vulnerable to theft, making it difficult for law enforcement officials to protect them. This vulnerability gave rise to firm rules of politeness and other means by which people explicitly recognize the honor of others. But these rules constitute a double-edged sword: they lend stability to social relations and reduce the risk of violence, but they make people highly sensitive to slights and insults, which obligates them to respond with violence in order to protect or reestablish their honor. To succeed in an environment where theft was always a temptation, a man had to build a reputation for strength, toughness, and willingness to use swift, and sometimes violent, punishment against thieves.

The second factor concerns the reliability of institutions and the effectiveness of authorities (Nowak et al., 2016). Particularly in environments that are vulnerable to theft and exploitation, such as those noted by Nisbett and Cohen, honor cultures emerge if institutions and authorities cannot be counted on to protect people and property. In effect, people must fend for themselves, which makes them sensitive to signs of disrespect.

Data reported by Nisbett (1993) showed that people raised in the South are more likely than those raised in the North to respond with aggression when their honor is slighted. This is apparent in homicide rates. Southern and Northern states do not differ from one another in the rate of murders committed in the context of a felony (e.g., burglary). But murders that occur in the context of arguments and personal disputes are noticeably higher in the South and Southwest, especially in small towns (see Figure 11.4). Presumably, disputes can escalate to murder because inhabitants in these regions have greater reason to be concerned with their reputations being known throughout their communities.

But what happens when the person leaves the South and heads north? If a cultural norm has been internalized, the person should maintain a low threshold for respect-based aggression. But social psychology likes to emphasize the "power of the situation." If people respond to expectations in the immediate context, the aggressive tendencies of Southern men should be tempered when they accommodate to the local norms in a non-Southern part of the country.

These alternative predictions were put to the test at University of Michigan, which is located in a northern region of the United States (Cohen, Nisbett, Bowdle, & Schwarz, 1996). They arranged for each male participant and a male research assistant to walk down a narrow hallway from opposite directions. The assistant, an accomplice of the researchers, did not give way to the participant but rather bumped into him and then insulted him. Compared with Northerners, southern students exhibited greater physiological signs of being upset, had higher testosterone levels, engaged in more dominant behavior (by later giving firmer handshakes), and were less willing to yield to a subsequent "research assistant" in the hallway (see Figure 11.5). It appears you can take the boy out the country, but not the country out of the boy.

Triggers of Aggression

A wide range of situations encountered in daily life hold potential for triggering aggressive actions, and these can overcome the cultural norms, societal expectations, and personal values that normally prevent such outbursts.

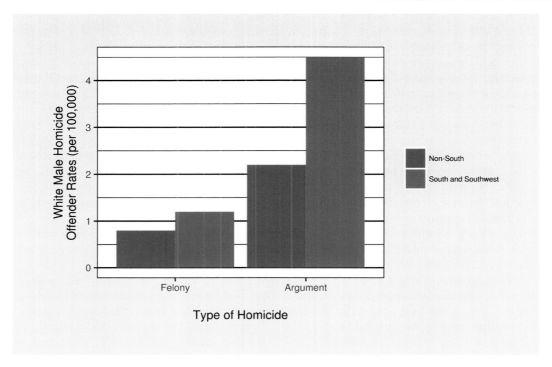

FIGURE 11.4 Homicide Rates for Argument-Related and Felony-Related Murders
Source: Adapted from Nisbett (1993)

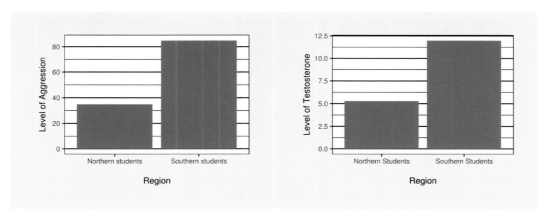

FIGURE 11.5 Aggressive Behavior and Testosterone Levels of Northern versus Southern Students After Being Insulted
Source: Adapted from Cohen et al. (1996)

Frustration and Discomfort

Feelings of discontent and negativity can lower the threshold for such action. Unpleasant emotions come from many sources, but certain sources are especially likely to trigger aggression. Early research put special emphasis on one emotional trigger in particular: *frustration*. For several decades, in fact, the *frustration-aggression hypothesis* (Dollard et al., 1939) was the leading contender in theoretical accounts of aggressive behavior. Frustration is experienced when a person's (or an animal's) attempt to achieve a goal is thwarted. This covers a lot of territory—from fairly trivial events such as not being able to open a window on a balmy day to more consequential events such as missing an important appointment because of an hour-long traffic jam or being blocked for promotion in one's occupation.

Frustration is a fairly common experience but aggression is not. The likelihood of aggression increases in proportion to four factors: (1) the amount of satisfaction the person anticipates before the goal is blocked; (2) the more completely the person is prevented from achieving the goal; (3) the more frequently the person is blocked from achieving the goal; and (4) the closer the person is to achieving the goal (Miller, 1941). Imagine, for example, that you are waiting in a long line to purchase lunch at the college cafeteria when a stranger cuts in line. Whether you are mildly irritated or provoked to the point of hostile behavior toward the line-cutter will depend on (1) how hungry you are, (2) how clear it is that you will not get to the front of the line in time to get lunch, (3) how often you have experienced line-cutting in the past, and (4) how close you were to the front of the line. So if you are especially hungry, if the food is gone before you get a chance to order, if you have had a similar experience several times during the semester, and if the person cuts in just before you reach the front of the line, you may lash out at him or her—verbally if not physically—in a particularly intense fashion.

Beyond resonating with intuition, the frustration-aggression hypothesis has some noteworthy implications. Perhaps the most unsettling manifestation is that the *target* of frustration-induced aggression does not have to be the *source* of the frustration. When laboratory rats are shocked, for example, they don't tackle the shock apparatus or the experimenter; instead they attack other rats that happen to be in the vicinity (Berkowitz, 1993). In much the same way, people may display *displaced aggression* by attacking innocent people who are convenient targets. The person who is frustrated by his or her boss at work, for example, may come home and lash out at his or her family members.

All this is true, but the singular importance of frustration was overstated by theorists. For one thing, frustration—even when it meets the four standards noted above—does not always produce aggressive impulses. Under some conditions, in fact, extreme and prolonged frustration can produce *learned helplessness* (Seligman, 1975)—complete passivity rather than a readiness to fight and remedy the situation. As discussed in Chapter 6 ("Personal Control"), this state is experienced when a person's goals are blocked and he or she feels no control over the matter. Beyond that, aggression is not always motivated by strong emotion, but sometimes serves an instrumental function. The burglar who threatens or harms witnesses to his or her crime may have little or no personal antipathy toward the victims—he or she simply wants to ensure that the witnesses don't become the state's evidence.

The contemporary view is that if frustration promotes aggression, it is because frustration makes people angry, irritated, or uncomfortable (Berkowitz, 1989). By this reasoning, anything that produces discomfort and unpleasant feelings can set the stage for aggressive action. Hot weather can be unpleasant, for example, particularly when experienced in the middle of a city rather than at the beach, and it has been shown to have the potential to amplify interpersonal tensions into violent confrontations. With this in mind, Craig Anderson (1987, 1989) assessed the number of days in which the temperature was greater than 90° F in 260 United States cities. He found that this measure predicted increases in the rates of violent crimes, but not nonviolent crime rates—cities with more days above 90° had the higher rates of assaults, murder, and rape. Anderson was careful to rule out other possible causes, including the city's level of unemployment, per capita income, and average age of residents.

Violence short of crime also shows a spike on hot days. In Major League Baseball, for example, pitchers throw more "bean balls"—pitches that hit the batter—on hot days (Reifman, Larrick, & Fein, 1991). This is not because the pitchers are less competent or more fatigued on these days, because they do not throw more wild pitches or walk more batters. They simply throw the ball at the batter more often, presumably because the heat induces unpleasant feelings of anger, which they take out on their opponent—the batter.

Revenge

Aggression, ironically enough, is often undertaken in the name of justice. Justice comes in many forms, but perhaps the most basic form is *revenge*. Revenge is the flipside of reciprocity. By much the same reasoning that people repay favors and exchange gifts and compliments of comparable value, they are motivated to extract "an eye for an eye, a tooth for a tooth" when they have been harmed, inconvenienced, insulted, or otherwise treated unfairly. The role of revenge in antisocial behavior cannot be overstated. One of every five homicides in the United States is attributable to revenge, often in response to an insult or some other sign of disrespect (McCullough, 2008). Young males are especially likely to seek revenge through violent action against those who are judged to have "done them wrong."

People assume that taking revenge will make them feel good and that not taking revenge will simply make bad feelings simmer and amplify. Instead of quenching hostility, however, revenge can prolong the unpleasantness of the original offense, making the person feel worse rather than better (Carlsmith, Wilson, & Gilbert, 2008). And instead of delivering justice and settling the matter, revenge often creates a cycle of retaliation. After all, the person on the receiving end of vengeance may feel he or she has been unjustly treated and seek revenge on the person who acted vengefully in the first place. Conflicts of all kinds, whether between acquaintances, gangs, or nations, are often defined in terms of spiraling hostility as each party to the conflict acts to avenge the other party's behavior—which itself was motivated by revenge.

Loss of Self-Control

Many social factors and personal experiences can loosen the restraints on impulsive actions, including aggressive actions. But these factors can be overcome if an individual has the "willpower" to do so. In contemporary social psychology, willpower is conceptualized and investigated in terms of *self-regulation*, discussed in Chapter 6. Humans can reflect on their actions, and this capacity creates the potential for inhibiting behavior fueled by strong emotions such as lust and anger (Baumeister, Vohs, & Tice, 2007; Denson, DeWall, & Finkel, 2012).

Self-control is not easy. It is not an *automatic process*, but rather a *controlled process* that requires mental effort. Much like a muscle that gets fatigued from strenuous effort, a person's capacity for self-control can get exhausted from a sustained period of checking impulses, resisting temptations, delaying gratification, and making tough decisions (Baumeister et al., 2007). Such *ego depletion* can make a person vulnerable to outbursts that he or she might normally be able to contain. When frustrated, provoked, or simply uncomfortable, a person might give in to his or her impulses and act aggressively toward an antagonist, or toward others who happen to be the immediate vicinity (DeWall, Baumeister, Stillman, & Gailliot, 2007).

Ironically, the effects of ego depletion can be minimized by exercising self-control—the very thing that produces ego depletion in the first place! Think again about the analogy to muscles. Sure, after a workout a person's muscles are exhausted, making it difficult for him or her to continue exercising. But over time, the workouts strengthen a person's muscles, enabling him or her to lift heavier objects, run for longer periods of time, and hit balls harder. In like manner, sustained practice at self-control can enhance a person's capacity to resist impulses, including aggressive ones, and to act in accordance with social norms and personal values despite provocations, frustrations, and other triggers of antisocial action.

To test this means of building self-control, Denson et al. (2011) asked participants to use their non-dominant hand for everyday tasks (e.g., eating, brushing their teeth) for 2 weeks. Subsequently they were provoked by an accomplice posing as a naïve participant, and given an opportunity to retaliate against this person by administering aversive noise blasts. Participants who had practiced self-control by using their non-dominant hand administered less intense noise blasts than did the participants who had not practiced self-control. This effect was observed even among participants who scored high on a test assessing aggressive tendencies.

Threatened Egotism

The loss of self-control in aggressive behavior suggests that self-awareness should inhibit violent outbursts. This is true as long as the focus is on one's internalized standards of appropriate behavior (e.g., Diener, 1980). A focus on one's overall self-worth, however, can have precisely the opposite effect. No one likes to have his or her personal worth challenged, but some people are especially sensitive to insults and snarky comments, and experience intense anger in response. The potential for defensive and aggressive action by a person who has been criticized is investigated in terms of *threatened egotism* (Baumeister, Smart, & Boden, 1996), a concept introduced in Chapter 5 ("Self-Concept").

At the heart of threatened egotism is high self-esteem, a subjective state that is normally associated with personal and social adjustment. This is fine as long as a person's flattering self-regard is based on a clear and confident sense of his or her personal qualities and skills. In the absence of such clarity, high self-esteem is fragile and open to disconfirmation. An unflattering comment that might be dismissed by someone with a confident self-view could prove highly threatening to someone else with an inflated self-view with a shaky foundation. There are many ways to deal with threatening information. One could simply avoid contact with those who say things one does not want to hear, for example, or find others who can come to one's defense. But research suggests that threatened egotism often sets the stage for aggressive action toward those who question the person's inflated self-view (Baumeister et al., 1996;

Bushman & Baumeister, 1998). The classroom bully, for example, is typically a boy who has a very high opinion of himself and cannot take criticism (Salmivalli & Nieminen, 2002).

Social Isolation and Rejection

When rejected, a person might try to reestablish the social connection or perhaps establish new connections to make up for what he or she has lost. But other behavioral responses can be dysfunctional, self-defeating, or even antisocial. People chosen at random to receive messages of social exclusion, for example, become more willing to cheat, less willing to help others, and more likely to pursue short-term over long-term goals (Twenge, Catanese, & Baumeister, 2002). Rejection also lowers the threshold for aggressive behavior (Downey, Irwin, Ramsay, & Ayduk, 2004; Twenge, Baumeister, Tice, & Stucke, 2001)—in the extreme, even murder.

Weapons

The triggers noted so far—frustration, revenge, frustration, diminished self-control, threatened egotism, social isolation and rejection—by themselves may not be sufficient to overcome personal and social restraints against aggressive behavior. But if there are features in the social context associated with aggression, they may serve to "prime" aggressive behavior at the expense of other possible ways of behaving. Berkowitz and LePage (1967) provided an early demonstration of such priming. They arranged for a male participant and a male confederate to work on a series of problems in a laboratory situation. They took turns evaluating each other's performance by delivering electric shocks for performance that needed improvement. They could choose between 1 and 10 shocks to convey their evaluation, with 10 shocks indicating that the other person's performance was pretty bad and in need of considerable improvement.

The participants worked on the problems first. Half the participants were paired with a confederate who delivered only one shock, and half were paired with a confederate who delivered several shocks. The participants who received multiple shocks were presumably angrier as a result than were those who received the minimum number of shocks—hence, this was a *no anger versus anger* manipulation. But there was another manipulation in this study that was hypothesized to be critical in turning anger into aggression. In a *neutral object* condition, there was a badminton racket and a couple of shuttlecocks near the shock machine. In an *anger-relevant object* condition, a handgun and a shotgun were near the shock machine. And in a control *no object* condition, there was nothing near the shock machine.

After receiving the confederate's "evaluation" (one vs. multiple shocks), it was the participant's turn to evaluate the confederate's performance. Berkowitz and LePage predicted that anger alone would promote aggression toward the confederate—if nothing else, the participant would be "returning the favor" in line with reciprocity. But this effect was expected to be amplified when there were nearby objects associated with aggression. This prediction was confirmed: Participants who were angered by receiving multiple shocks from the confederate responded with more shocks of their own when there were violent weapons (guns) as opposed to harmless objects (badminton rackets) or no objects in the immediate vicinity (see Figure 11.6).

If the presence of a gun can prime aggressive responding in a simple laboratory study, one can wonder whether the presence (and ready availability) of guns in everyday life can prime aggression as opposed to other forms of dealing with frustration, annoyance, or social rejection. Statistics on gun availability and homicide rate support this connection. Gun ownership is especially high in the United States (88 guns per 100 people)—far higher than in any other high-income country. Figure 11.7, meanwhile, shows that the rate of firearm homicides (number of such homicides per 100 people) in these countries is by far the highest in the United States. Associations such as this do not prove causation, of course. Nonetheless, the link between availability of guns and their use to commit murder is something to think about.

What Triggers School Shootings?

In recent years, there have been highly publicized accounts of American students who have entered their schools and used guns to shoot their classmates and teachers. This is a disturbing trend that begs for explanation. In light of the causes and triggers of aggression discussed so far, there is no shortage of plausible explanations for this extreme form of antisocial behavior.

To begin with, those who commit school violence are invariably young males. This suggests that testosterone is a key factor. Keep in mind, though, that the connection between testosterone and violence is observed among those who feel that socially acceptable means of achieving dominance are blocked. By this reasoning, young males from

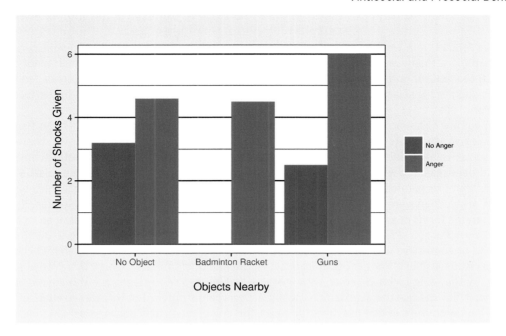

FIGURE 11.6 Number of Shocks Delivered to Partner When Participant is Angered or Not Angered and is Primed by the Presence of Guns
Source: Adapted from Berkowitz & LePage (1967)

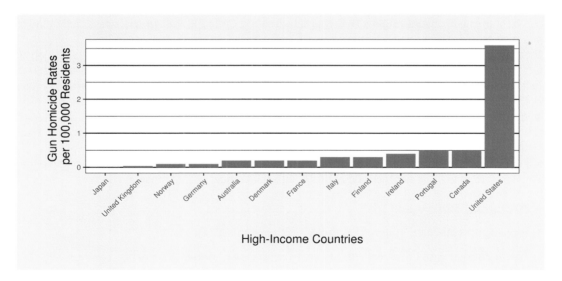

FIGURE 11.7 The Rate of Gun-Related Deaths in High-Income Countries
Source: Adapted from https://upload.wikimedia.org/wikipedia/common/2/2e/2010_homicide_suicide_rates_high-income_countries.png

minority groups should be the most likely candidates for resorting to violence against classmates and teachers. But the young males who go on murderous school rampages tend to be White and middle-class, thus not lacking the opportunities that are often denied nonwhite males living in poorer neighborhoods. Testosterone may be a necessary factor but other factors must be in play before this male hormone is expressed in this form of extreme antisocial behavior.

Another lead follows from what has been learned about the culture of honor. Over a 20-year period, culture-of-honor states had more than twice as many school shootings per capita as did non-culture-of-honor states (Brown, Osterman, & Barnes, 2009). And the students from these regions who lashed out in this manner tended to feel disrespected. This suggests that acts of school violence are attempts to defend one's honor in the face of perceived social humiliation.

But even in culture-of-honor regions, school violence is extremely rare. What is it about the handful of young males in these regions that puts them (and their classmates) at risk for murderous rampages? There is compelling evidence that social isolation and rejection are primary factors. An analysis of 15 school shootings between 1995 and 2001 found that peer rejection was present in 87% of the cases—all but 2 of the 15 (Leary, Kowalski, & Smith, 2003). The experiences that precipitated these mass shootings included chronic rejection, but also single episodes of rejection. The forms of rejection were varied, from simple avoidance to bullying, and romantic rejection. It is sadly ironic, but the most extreme forms of antisocial behavior are committed by those with the greatest need to establish social connections.

The likelihood of aggressive action is increased if social isolation is combined with threatened egotism. A lonely male who has a clear sense of his or her personal qualities can find other outlets for his frustration at lacking a viable social network. By the same token, a person with unstable and inflated self-esteem—the threatened egoist—who has social connections may not feel the need to take violent action against others. But threatened egotism and social isolation can be a dangerous mix. In rare but dramatic cases, this combination may push the person to harmful behavior toward others—in the extreme, even murder.

The final trigger is the availability of guns. There are more guns per capita in the United States than in any other country and it is easy for almost anyone, including young males, to get hold of them. More students from culture-of-honor regions bring a weapon to school than do students from non-culture-of-honor regions (Brown et al., 2009). The presence of guns amplifies the tendency for people to become aggressive when angered (Berkowitz & LePage, 1967). Young males in other countries are presumably just as prone to experience threatened egotism and feeling socially isolated, but without the exposure to guns that characterizes the United States, they are less likely to express their anger by shooting their teachers and classmates.

Taken together, these lines of research paint a picture of the person who is at greatest risk for shooting classmates and teachers. The person, first of all, is a young male from a culture-of-honor state who feels disrespected and thus primed to act violently. The risk is amplified if he has an inflated but shaky view of himself. And if he is socially isolated or rejected, the risk is all the greater. Finally, if he has easy access to guns, this can provide a means by which to act on his anger and frustration. Fortunately, it is rare for all these factors—young male, culture of honor, threatened egotism, social rejection, access to guns—to line up together, and even if they do, the likelihood of acting out in such extreme manner is still very low. Nonetheless, knowing the key dynamics at work in school shootings may prove useful in identifying those at risk and, more important, devising programs to minimize the unfortunate but inevitable tendency for school-age children to reject one another and activate antisocial tendencies of those at risk.

Bases of Prosocial Behavior

Why Do People Help One Another and Engage in Altruistic Behavior?

Prosocial behavior coexists with other features of human nature—self-interest, dominance, revenge, and so forth—that are at odds with cooperation and helping. Prosocial behavior is thus a fragile tendency that requires the support of cultural forces and the triggering of personal motives in order to be expressed.

Culture and Society

Some features of social life that promote prosocial behavior are universal, shaping how people everywhere respond to the needs of one another. Other social forces are more or less unique to different cultures or regions of a country. Yet others represent variability in the conditions experienced in a society or region.

Universal Norms

In any functioning social system, whether a family or a nation, there are *social norms* that dictate how we ought to behave. Some norms are specific. There was a time when men were expected to tip their hat when meeting a woman, for example. Hats are not worn much these days, and it would look strange indeed if a man at a dinner party who happened to be wearing one spent the evening tipping it upon encountering each woman he met. But some norms are quite general and seem to be universal in scope. Two in particular are worth noting.

Perhaps the best documented "ought" is the *norm of reciprocity* (Gouldner, 1960). This norm reflects the idea of reciprocal altruism (Trivers, 1971), discussed earlier. When we help others, we expect to be helped in return—if not immediately, then sometime in the future. By the same token, when others help us, we feel the obligation to return the favor in some fashion.

The reciprocity norm operates when people are in an exchange relationship with one other. But sometimes we encounter (or learn about) others whom we have not met or are even likely to meet. And sometimes such people would be unable to reciprocate even if we did encounter them. Yet we often help people anyway if they are in need of assistance. Such acts reflect the *norm of social responsibility*—the belief that people ought to help those who need help, without expectations of future reciprocity (Berkowitz, 1972; Schwartz, 1975). Socially responsible behavior is often motivated by *sympathy* (Rudolf, Roesch, Greitemeyer, & Weiner, 2004). We offer aid to those who are impoverished, attempt to remove the burdens of those who are disabled, and make donations to charitable foundations to help victims of natural disasters. But sometimes we act in a socially responsible manner because we feel it is the right thing to do. If a complete stranger asks for directions on a busy street, we stop for a moment to provide the needed information, without feeling all that sorry for him or her.

The likelihood of helping depends to a large degree on the attribution of responsibility for the needy person's dilemma. Victims of natural disasters are likely to have their needs addressed, but not if they are judged to have created their own misfortune—by lacking foresight, for example, or by being lazy or immoral (Weiner, 1980). And someone who collapses on a subway because he or she is drunk is less likely to be helped than is someone who collapses due to an apparent heart attack. Political conservatives are especially sensitive to a victims' personal responsibility in deciding whether to help them (Skitka & Tetlock, 1993).

There is a sexist element in the decision to help others in need. Women are more likely to receive help than are men, even if their circumstances are the same, presumably because women are perceived as less competent and more dependent (Eagly & Crowley, 1986). A woman standing next to a disabled car, for example, is likely to get more offers of help (especially from males) than is a man (Penner, Dertke, Achenbach, 1973; Pomazal & Clore, 1973; West, Whitney, & Schnedler, 1975). Female hitchhikers receive far more offers of a ride than do males or male-female couples (Pomazal & Clore, 1973; Snyder, Grether, & Keller, 1974). Of course, motives other than social responsibility cannot be ruled out in such cases. Men may be seen as posing a potential threat, for example, which could inhibit helping. And women may receive greater help by men because of men's romantic interest in women. In support of this latter effect, men are more likely to help attractive women than unattractive women (Mims, Hartnett, & Nay, 1975; Stroufe, Chaikin, Cook, & Freeman, 1977; West & Brown, 1975).

Cultural Differences

The social responsibility norm looms larger in collectivist cultures than in individualistic cultures (Baron & Miller, 2000). The greater sense of interdependence in collectivist nations—those in much of Asia, Africa, and Latin America—sensitizes people to one another's needs and motivates them to offer assistance when tough times or bad events are experienced. But even in the most individualistic societies, such as the United States and western European countries, help is commonly extended to those in need without any expectation of repayment. However, the attribution of personal responsibility plays a larger role in the decision to offer assistance in individualistic cultures. Someone who collapses on a subway due to heat exhaustion, for example, is likely to be helped in both cultures, but someone who collapses because he or she is drunk is more likely to elicit help in a collectivist culture.

Within any culture, there are regional differences that can affect the likelihood of helping someone in need. Regions differ in many respects, but perhaps the most important distinction is between *urban* and *rural* regions of a country. Imagine, for example, that while visiting someplace new, you get disoriented and cannot find your way around. Asking a stranger for help is a reasonable thing to do in this circumstance. But where would your request be more likely to receive a helpful response—in a large metropolitan area or in a small rural town?

Nancy Steblay (1987) answered this question by reviewing 35 studies that compared the helping rates in urban and rural environments. The forms of helping in these studies varied from granting simple requests ("can you tell me what time it is?") to helping people in need (e.g., an injured pedestrian) and intervening to stop a crime (e.g., an assault). For every form of helping, the results were clear: strangers are more likely to be helped in rural regions (see Figure 11.8). This effect boiled down to population size, with a decrease in helping as towns and cities increased in size from 1,000 to 50,000 citizens. So a town with 5,000 people is more helpful than is a town with 10,000 people, which in turn is more helpful than is a town with 20,000 people. Once a city hits 50,000, future increases in population size do not mean a decreased rate of helping. So if you expect to get lost on your next trip to Florida, try to do so in Pompano Beach rather than in Miami Beach. This tip, unfortunately, may not prove particularly helpful—getting lost in the former locale is far less likely than getting lost in the latter.

What is it about small towns that promotes greater helping? Three explanations have been offered by those who have investigated this issue. The focus of each is not so much why small towns are helpful, but why big ones are not. First, modern urban environments provide a great deal of stimulation, which can cause people to tune things out so as not to be overwhelmed. In this *stimulus overload* account (Milgram, 1970), people's normal tendency to notice and react to someone's troubles is inhibited in much the same way that many of the sights and sounds around them go largely unnoticed. Selective attention and concern are critical if one is trying to navigate a busy street filled with people, cars, honking horns, and construction barricades.

The second explanation is *diffusion of responsibility* (Darley & Latané, 1968). A person may feel that providing help is warranted but assume that someone else on the crowded avenue will step up and do the right thing. The third explanation centers on the greater *diversity* in large metropolitan areas. As discussed in Chapter 9 ("Close Relationships"), we like others who are similar to us. This bias extends to offering help: people are more likely to help others who are similar to themselves, including those who are similar in race and ethnicity (Dovidio & Gaertner, 1981; Latané &

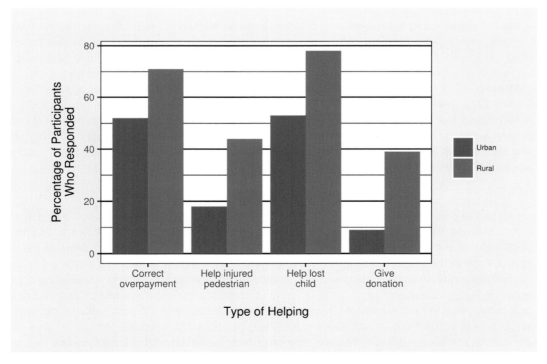

FIGURE 11.8 The Percentage of People Who Provide Help in Urban Versus Rural Environments
Source: Adapted from Steblay (1987)

Nida, 1981). Large urban areas have a greater range of people than do small towns, and this diversity is represented among those in need of assistance. An individual who needs help in a big city is likely to be dissimilar in various ways—including race or ethnicity—from potential helpers, and this can prevent the individual from receiving help, even on a boring street.

Variable Resources

You might assume that material well-being in a society or region would promote sharing and altruism ("giving back"). When personal security is assured, after all, people can afford to help others in need. Harsh or uncertain conditions, in contrast, should promote selfish concern ("looking out for number one") and undermine charitable and helpful behavior. It is certainly true that many wealthy people contribute a great deal to charities and causes that help the unfortunate. But this tendency is not always widespread in societies with economic security. Nor does economic insecurity in a culture undermine cooperation and assistance. In fact, when people are faced with the prospect or reality of scarce resources, they tend to display cooperative rather than competitive forms of interaction characterized by strong adherence to the norm of reciprocity (Andras, Lazarus, & Roberts, 2007; Smaldino, Schank, & McElreath, 2013).

Although somewhat counterintuitive, this feature of social experience is understandable. As long as social and economic conditions are stable, group members tend to see differences in income and resources as fair and appropriate. This takes the pressure off those who are on top from sharing with those who are at the bottom. But when resources become variable and unpredictable, with each year bringing the possibility of losing income and resources, the tendency to justify inequality is undermined. Those who are less well-off become dissatisfied with their relative lot in life, and those who are better off become more charitable.

Tough times do not always bring out the prosocial side of human nature. Resource uncertainty and scarcity can promote conflict between nations (Vallacher et al., 2010) and competition between groups and individuals within a nation (Hovland & Sears, 1940). For cooperation and reciprocity to characterize social life in a world of increasing demand (population growth) and diminishing supply (e.g., water, land), people must recognize their interdependence and shared fate (Sherif et al., 1961/1988).

Personal Motives

Against the backdrop of cultural factors that set the tone for prosocial behavior, there are personal considerations that can motivate people to engage in cooperative and altruistic actions. These personal motives are not unique to prosocial behavior, so it takes specific circumstances and social cues for them to be expressed in this manner.

Social Approval

Social approval can be a reward for doing things that one might not otherwise do. If that exchange calculation were the driving force in prosocial behavior, helping others would essentially take on the status as work, something that is done for extrinsic benefits rather than for intrinsic reasons. In fact, social approval can *dampen* a person's intrinsic desire to help a person in need (Warneken & Tomasello, 2008), in the same way that offering a prize to children for playing with a toy can undermine their enjoyment of the toy (Lepper, Greene, & Nisbett, 1973)—a point that was made in Chapter 6. But this raises a question: what are the intrinsic reasons for helping other people?

Emotion

Helping someone in need might simply feel good. If so, being in a positive mood should breed good will and a desire to help those in need. People want to keep their good mood going, and helping someone in need can provide this effect. There is evidence that positive feelings do increase the likelihood of helping. Almost any source of positive feelings can have this effect: sunny weather (Cunningham, 1979), imagining a Hawaiian vacation (Rosenhan, Salovey, & Hargis, 1981), and even eating a cookie (Isen & Levin, 1972).

But as you might expect from almost every topic we have discussed so far, things are not that simple. In fact, there is evidence that *bad feelings* can sometimes increase the likelihood of helping others. This connection is easy to understand when a person's bad feelings are in response to the plight of someone else. By helping a person in distress, the person can relieve his or her own distress. This idea is the premise of *negative state relief theory* (Cialdini, Darby, & Vincent, 1973). But the link between feeling bad and helping is not limited to the personal distress of seeing someone else in distress. The negative emotions could stem from something entirely different, such as guilt or shame, sadness, or hurt feelings. A person in a sad mood, for example, might take advantage of contributing to a worthy cause because such action can make the person feel good about him or herself and thus enhance his or her mood. Feeling bad about one's past actions can also promote prosocial action—such behavior not only makes one feel better, it also makes amends for one's misdeeds. So, prosocial behavior is likely when one feels guilty and wants to make up for his or her shortcomings—the greater the guilt, the more likely one is to take action to reduce the guilt (Carver & Scheier, 1999).

The relationship between guilty feelings and prosocial behavior has surprising consequences. Imagine, for example, that you have an opportunity to confess all your questionable actions over the past few weeks and get a clean bill of spiritual health from someone you trust and admire in such matters. Now imagine that an opportunity to engage in a noble action that reflects well on your morality opens up around this time as well. Finally—and here's the kicker—imagine that this opportunity occurs either immediately *prior* to the confession or immediately *after*. On which occasion would you be more likely to act in a way to act nobly—before confessing your sins or after doing so?

Your first response might be to answer this question with notions of personal consistency in mind. After you've confessed, you have a clean slate and you may want to keep it that way by doing things that reflect your moral self. The reduction of guilt rationale, however, suggests you would have stronger motivation to behave in a moral fashion *before* confessing than afterwards. Prior to confessing, the discrepancy between your internal standards and your conduct is at its maximum because you're reviewing all the questionable things you've done for the last several weeks. This discrepancy between reality and standards is felt as negative emotion, an unpleasant state that you wish to terminate. After confessing, it's a brand new world. You're clean, there's no negative emotion, and thus there's no need to do things to make yourself feel better.

This point was made in a study by Harris, Benson, and Hall (1975) in the context of Catholic confession, an important tradition in this religion. The participants were men and women attending Catholic services that included an opportunity for formal confession to a priest. A March of Dimes donation table was set up outside the church entrance, providing an opportunity to donate money to a noble cause. This opportunity was made available *prior* to churchgoers' entering the service (prior to their confessions) or *after* the services had ended as they exited the church (presumably after they had confessed their sins). By comparing when people were more generous, the investigators could discover whether the churchgoers were more inclined to act morally in order to reduce standard-behavior discrepancies (before confession) or to maintain a psychological state devoid of such discrepancies (after confession). The results were clear: a higher percentage of the male churchgoers made donations prior to confession than afterward (see Figure 11.9) and their donations were more generous as well. (Fewer females made donations and their behavior did not differ before vs. after the service.) Confession, it seems, may be good for the soul but it doesn't make one a saint, at least not right away.

Guilt and other negative emotions (e.g., sadness) tend to promote prosocial behavior only if the action is relatively easy to perform and the benefits to others are significant (Carlson & Miller, 1987; Weyant, 1978). This is clearly the case in the study just described—the churchgoers simply had to drop money in a pot and the money went to a noble cause. But when considerable effort is required to make a small difference, a person feeling blue is unlikely to act. Positive moods, in marked contrast, motivate people to help others regardless of the effort required and even if the benefits to others are minimal.

Empathy

Another intrinsic basis for helping is *empathy* (Krebs, 1970; Regan & Totten, 1975). In imagining one someone feels, we experience a twinge of that feeling ourselves. We are thus motivated to reduce someone's distress to feel better ourselves. Seeing anyone suffer, even a total stranger, can create discomfort and generate empathy for him or her. This idea is central to the *empathy-altruism hypothesis* (Batson et al., 1991). Keep in mind, though, that helping is not the only available means of dealing with the distress caused by seeing someone suffer. A far less costly way of eliminating one's distress is simply to look the other way or leave the situation altogether. Yet people don't always opt out in this way, but instead try to help others in need. What pushes people one way or the other?

Daniel Batson and his colleagues investigated whether empathy can override the temptation to leave the situation when witnessing someone suffer (Batson et al., 1981). The study was presented to participants as a test of the effects of stress on performance. Using a rigged coin toss, another participant (who was an accomplice of the experimenter) was assigned to perform 10 trials of a task and receive random electric shocks on each trial. The real participant

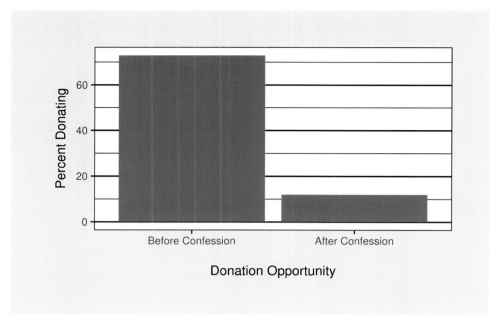

FIGURE 11.9 Donation to Charity Before versus after Confession
Source: Adapted from Harris et al. (1975)

watched all this over a video set-up. Before the trials began, the participant overheard a conversation between the experimenter and the other participant (Elaine). Elaine confided that she was once thrown off a horse and onto an electric fence, an experience that left her terrified of electricity. The experimenter understood how she felt, but pointed out that she would have to receive shocks anyway because she had lost the coin toss. Clearly, Elaine was set up to experience a great deal of distress, more than other people in this experiment were likely to feel.

To manipulate empathy (and the lack thereof), half the participants were told that Elaine had interests and values that were similar to their own (*high empathy*) and half were told that Elaine's interests and values were quite different from their own (*low empathy*). The experimenter also manipulated the ease with which participants could escape the situation, and presumably reduce their distress at Elaine's plight by moving onto something else. In the *easy-escape* condition, the experimenter informed participants that they could leave after watching Elaine receive shocks on the first 2 trials. In the *difficult-escape* condition, participants had to watch all 10 trials. After watching Elaine show considerable suffering on the first 2 trials, the experimenter asked participants in all the conditions if they would be willing to trade places with her for the remaining 8 trials so that she would not have to suffer any more.

The results illustrated the importance of empathy under these conditions. In the low-empathy condition, participants offered to switch positions with Elaine—but only if they could not leave after watching the first 2 trials. If they had the opportunity to escape, most of them did just that. Things were different in the high-empathy condition. Most of these participants (who felt similar to Elaine in interests and values) offered to switch positions, even if they could have left after witnessing the first 2 trials (see Figure 11.10). Apparently, high-empathy participants were more concerned with the victim's need than with their own personal distress.

Prosocial Behavior Derailed

Although people are intrinsically motivated to help one another, this tendency is always in danger of being overpowered by other forces and considerations. Several factors play important roles in stopping prosocial action before it has had a chance to play out. Among the most investigated are *pluralistic ignorance, diffusion of responsibility*, and *disbelief in free will*.

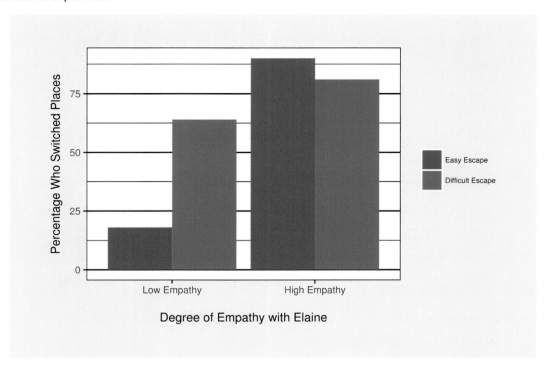

FIGURE 11.10 Altruistic Behavior under Low versus High Empathy When there is or is not a Chance to Escape the Situation
Source: Adapted from Batson et al. (1981)

Pluralistic Ignorance

Sometimes it is painfully obvious that a person needs help. When we see someone injured in a car accident or getting assaulted on a city street, there is little mystery that he or she would benefit if bystanders came to his or her aid. But events in everyday life are not always so clear. If we see a group of teenage boys pushing a couple of other boys, it is hard to know whether they are simply fooling around or engaging in bullying behavior. If we hear a woman shriek in an adjoining room, we could interpret this as a serious situation calling for intervention or as a startle response to something unexpected but non-threatening. Whether we offer help in such circumstances clearly depends on how we interpret what has happened. An event that warrants helping might generate little or no response if it is interpreted in benign terms.

As we saw in Chapter 10 ("Social Influence"), when observing an event that can be interpreted in different ways, people look to others to clarify what is really going on. This process can promote accurate and useful interpretations—but it can also lead us to conclusions that are off the mark and prevent action that is called for. Several classic experiments have demonstrated how people's reliance on social reality operates in the context of helping behavior.

In one such study, male undergraduates were asked to complete some questionnaires in one of three conditions (Darley & Latané, 1968). Some participants completed the questionnaires alone in a laboratory room. Others did so in the same room but with two other participants. Yet others did so in the presence of two accomplices posing as participants; their role was to remain unconcerned and passive, no matter what happened while completing the questionnaires. And what happened was quite interesting. While participants completed the questionnaires, smoke began to filter into the room underneath the door, gradually filling the room.

You might consider this event an obvious cause for concern and probably leave the room. In fact, this is what most participants did when they were alone. But the presence of other guys in the room changed things. Participants may have been concerned about the smoke but they were also concerned about overreacting in front of strangers. So before they expressed alarm, they checked the reaction of the two other men in the room. But this is what the other men were doing as well. You can picture this scene. Each person is holding his reaction in check, waiting to see the others' reaction. And what they see is no reaction! In effect, they promote an interpretation of the smoke that did not call for action. This phenomenon, in which people who are uncertain about the meaning of an event assume that nothing is wrong because other people are not expressing alarm, is referred to as *pluralistic ignorance*. As Figure 11.11 illustrates, the effect of pluralistic ignorance was especially pronounced when the two other men in the room were following a "no big deal" script. But even when the other men were true participants, the smoke was not interpreted as an emergency in the majority of cases (62%).

Diffusion of Responsibility

Emergency situations sometimes arise in public settings in full view of many people. Someone might be assaulted or experience a medical emergency, with this event noticed by everyone in the vicinity. You might assume that the presence of bystanders would guarantee that one of the bystanders—if not all of them—would intervene in such circumstances. Each individual feels the norm of responsibility, so the more people present, the more the feeling of responsibility adds up. The accumulation of responsibility with an increase in the number of potential helpers may make sense, but a highly publicized event in 1964 cast doubt on this idea. A young woman, Kitty Genovese, was murdered outside her apartment in full view of three dozen neighbors who heard the commotion and looked out their windows. The attack lasted over half an hour, yet none of the witnesses intervened to help—or even called the police! The fact that it took place in New York City provided an explanation for many social commentators. For them, this incident exemplified the desensitization and lack of concern for others that takes hold in large metropolitan areas, with New York epitomizing this new reality of human experience.

But a far less cynical explanation soon emerged. In their analysis of the *bystander effect*, John Darley and Bibb Latané (1968) suggested that rather than reflecting the *sum* of individuals' sense of responsibility, the likelihood of helping in an emergency reflects a *division* of responsibility across the potential helpers. The presence of two potential helpers doesn't double the likelihood of helping—it cuts it in half. And the presence of four potential helpers

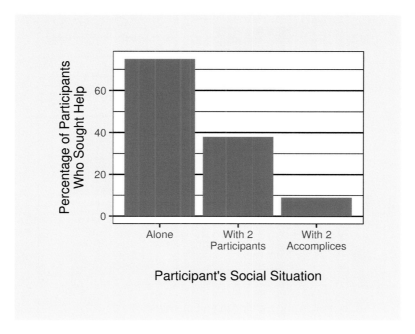

FIGURE 11.11 Response to an Emergency as a Function of Other People's Reaction
Source: Adapted from Latané & Darley (1968)

doesn't quadruple the liking of helping—it cuts it to 25%. Each person may feel strongly that help should be provided, but the *diffusion of responsibility* across potential helpers leads him or her to feel that someone else will intervene. Rather than being an issue of desensitization characterizing big cities, the bystander effect is a psychological process that in principle could occur on a farm if there were enough people present.

Darley and Latané launched a program of research to make the case. In their first study, they recruited New York City college students to take part in what they thought was a get-acquainted conversation. Over an intercom system, the students took turns expressing their thoughts and feelings about life as a new student or whatever else came to mind. What they did not know was that they were actually alone—the comments they heard over the intercom were recordings synchronized to seem like a conversation. After a few rounds of this faux conversation, one of the students seemed to experience an epileptic seizure and explicitly asked for help. The issue was whether participants' likelihood of helping, and their delay in doing so, would depend on the number of other people taking part in the conversation. Some participants thought it was a two-person conversation between them and the "victim." Others thought there was a third student, and thus another potential helper, in the conversation. Yet others thought they were talking with four other students, each of whom represented a potential helper.

The results were consistent with the diffusion or responsibility hypothesis (see Figure 11.12). Among participants who thought they were alone with the seizure victim, a majority (85%) left their cubicle to get help, and they did so almost immediately. The rate of helping dropped to 62% when participants thought there was one other potential helper, and to 31% when they thought four other students heard the cry for help. Participants were not unconcerned with the plight of the victim when other students were present; they simply did not feel the full weight of responsibility for taking action. This does not let city life completely off the hook, however. As noted in the earlier discussion of cultural differences, people in small towns and rural areas are more likely to help others than are people in large metropolitan areas. But the explanations for such differences do not invoke the cynical assumptions that were first expressed by the media and other talking heads in the aftermath of the Kitty Genovese incident.

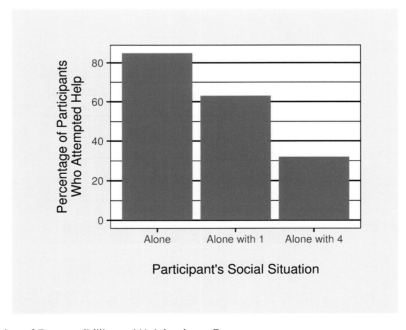

FIGURE 11.12 Diffusion of Responsibility and Helping in an Emergency
Source: Adapted from Darley & Latané (1968)

Box 11.1   What About Good Samaritans?

Everyone knows the biblical story of the Good Samaritan. The story is quite simple. Three different men walk by a man who has been beaten, stripped, and robbed. The first to walk by is a priest who is in a hurry to get somewhere. Although he is obviously a religious person and thus concerned with those in need, he does not take time out from his busy schedule to help the man. The second person is a Levite, who is also religious by training and presumably by disposition. Yet he too fails to stop and provide assistance to the man. The third person is a resident of Samaria, a group that follows quite different religious customs and is despised by the majority of people in this region. Upon seeing the half-dead man, the Samaritan stops to help him, even taking him to an inn and providing money for food and clothes. This help does the trick and restores the man's well-being.

Darley and Batson (1973) created a simulation of this story to reveal the conditions that can promote and undermine people's inclination to help those in need. Students at Princeton Theological Seminary were asked to give a talk to undergraduates elsewhere on campus. For some seminary students, the topic of the talk was the jobs that are available for seminary students after graduation. But for other students, the topic was—you guessed it—the story of the Good Samaritan. Students in a *no hurry condition* were told that they had plenty of time to get to the designated room across campus. Students in a *moderate hurry condition* were told that they would have to hustle a bit to get to the room on time. And those in a *high hurry condition* were told that they were already late for the talk and that the undergraduates were waiting to hear what they had to say. On the path across campus to the room, the students encountered—you guessed it—a man (an experimental accomplice) who was slumped over and groaning. The question here is obvious: did the seminary students act like the Good Samaritan by stopping to help the man?

You might think that students who were preparing to talk about the Good Samaritan story would act like the Good Samaritan. In fact, students primed in this manner were slightly more likely to help the slumped-over man than were those who were prepared to talk about jobs. But this effect paled in comparison to the effect of being in a hurry. The students who were in a hurry to give the talk were six times less likely to stop and attend to the man than were those who felt less hurried. In fact, only 10% of the students in the *high hurry* condition stopped to provide help.

This study illustrates just how fragile prosocial tendencies are. All the participants in this study were preparing for life in the ministry, and half of them were primed to think explicitly about the Good Samaritan parable—which is intended to serve as a reminder that we should not ignore those in need just because we are in a hurry. Yet when the seminary students were in a hurry, this is exactly what the majority of them did! Preaching about how one *should* act is apparently no guarantee that one will walk the talk. Perhaps the sermon should have been titled "Do as I say, not as I do."

Disbelief in Free Will

Most people assume they have free will and thus are responsible for their actions. However, anyone's belief in free will can be undermined, at least temporarily, by persuasive essays about the biological and social forces that shape and direct thought and behavior (Baumeister, 2008). Research has shown that the malleability of belief in free will has important consequences for personal conduct. When this belief in undermined, so that people feel their actions are the result of biological and social forces beyond their control, they lose the inhibition against cheating (Vohs & Schooler, 2008), they become less willing to help others (Baumeister, Masicampo, & Dewall, 2009), and they have a lower threshold for aggression when experiencing the various triggers discussed earlier (Baumeister, 2009).

So even if responsibility cannot be diffused to other people (e.g., when there are many bystanders), a person can evade responsibility for intervening to help others in need if he or she feels that factors beyond his or her control—whether brain mechanisms or social forces—are in charge of what he or she does.

SUMMING UP AND LOOKING AHEAD

- Human behavior is characterized by two opposing tendencies—antisocial behavior (e.g., aggression) and prosocial behavior (e.g., altruism)—each with evolutionary foundations that have proved adaptive over human history. There are also genetic and hormonal bases for antisocial and prosocial behavior that give rise to individual differences in both tendencies.

- Like other forms of behavior, aggression is learned and responsive to experiences in the family as well as in the larger social context. Modeling of aggression by parents and peers is influential for children, but media portrayals of violence and violent video games provide new avenues of social learning that increase the likelihood that aggressive tendencies will become internalized during childhood. Playing violent video games can also promote derogation of out-groups due to the dehumanizing portrayal of enemies in such games.

- Violence is lower in developed countries with stable democratic institutions and a high standard of living. However, developed countries with a large disparity between rich and poor have high violent crime rates. Some societies and regions are characterized by a culture of honor, such that the perception of disrespect (e.g., insults) can trigger aggressive action, including homicide. Honor-based aggression is especially likely in rural regions, particularly those in which the effectiveness of institutions and authorities is relatively weak.

- Frustration is a precondition for aggression—toward scapegoats as well as the source of the frustration—but research has shown that this effect is mediated by the aversive feelings and discomfort associated with frustration. Aggression can be triggered by revenge, which is the most basic form of justice and plays a significant role in the criminal justice system.

- People who have an inflated but fragile self-concept tend to experience threatened egotism, which lowers their tolerance for critical feedback regarding their personal qualities and can promote an aggressive response. Social isolation and rejection can trigger resentment and anger toward others and thus increase the likelihood of aggressive behavior, even toward strangers.

- The availability of weapons (e.g., handguns, semi-automatic rifles) can lower the threshold for aggression when personal factors (e.g., threatened egotism, social rejection) are experienced. This is consistent with statistics showing that countries with high rates of gun ownership (e.g., the United States) have higher rates of homicide—although the causal basis of this association is somewhat controversial.

- Prosocial behavior is promoted by social norms—most notably, reciprocity and social responsibility—that are universal but vary in their salience in different cultural contexts. Social responsibility is experienced more strongly in interdependent cultures than in cultures that place greater emphasis on individuality. Within societies, people in rural areas and small towns tend to be more helpful to those in need than are people in large urban areas characterized by population density and diversity. Societies with scarce resources often show greater reciprocity and cooperation, in recognition of their common fate and their concern with the reputational damage associated with selfishness in times of collective need.

- Personal concerns can motivate prosocial behavior beyond that prescribed by social norms. People sometimes help one another in order to gain social approval, but this runs the risk of undermining their intrinsic motivation to engage in such behavior. Positive emotions tend to bring out people's prosocial tendencies, but so can certain negative emotions such as guilt if such behavior can alleviate the aversive emotional state. Because the mechanism is the reduction of personal distress, however, prosocial action can be inhibited if other means of reducing distress are available. Empathy can motivate efforts to help others in need, even if other avenues of behavior that draw attention away from the suffering are available.

- Prosocial behavior is a fragile tendency. People may fail to offer help in ambiguous settings if everyone withholds his or her emotional responses, creating pluralistic ignorance regarding the need to take action. Even when the context is unambiguous and clearly calls for intervention, people may fail to offer assistance because their sense of responsibility is diffused across the potential helpers. Because prosocial behavior is motivated in part by a sense of personal responsibility, it can be undermined by the belief that human thought and action is determined by forces beyond personal control rather than a reflection of free will.

    The tendency to act in an antisocial or a prosocial manner is enhanced when the triggers for these actions are experienced in a group setting. Indeed, a great deal of individual psychology is amplified or otherwise transformed due to the various pressures people feel when in the context of interacting individuals. The ways in which groups modify the psychological principles characterizing individual thought and behavior provide the focus of the next chapter.

Key Terms

Direct versus indirect aggression	Social learning theory	Ego depletion
Emotional versus instrumental aggression	Modeling	Threatened egotism
	Media violence	School shootings
Altruism	Video games	Norm of reciprocity
Inclusive fitness theory	Dehumanization	Norm of social responsibility
Reciprocal altruism	Income inequality	Stimulus overload
Multi-level selection	Rape-prone cultures	Negative state relief theory
Group selection	Culture of honor	Empathy-altruism hypothesis
Theory of mind	Frustration-aggression hypothesis	Pluralistic ignorance
Selective breeding	Displaced aggression	Bystander effect
Monozygotic and dizygotic twins	Learned helplessness	Diffusion of responsibility
Testosterone	Revenge	Free will belief
Dominance hierarchy	Self-regulation	

12 Group Dynamics

Everyone recognizes that humans are a highly social species. We have an intense need to belong, we have fun together, we desire close relationships, we talk about (and evaluate) one another incessantly, and we worry about what others think of us. But to a large extent, these activities and motives do not require large numbers of other people. Feeling connected can be attained by having a few friends, a good time can be had with one person, a close relationship centers on one person (at a time), gossip can be whispered between two people, and obsessing over other people's evaluation of us can be done in private.

There is more to our social lives, however, than casual get-togethers with friends and intense get-togethers with someone special. We spend a fair amount of our time in groups—often very sizable groups. In this, we are not alone. Indeed, our affinity for groups is on par with that of many species. Chimpanzees, our closest relatives in the animal kingdom, spend most of their time in the presence of many other chimps. But behavior in the context of large groups also characterizes such distant species as buffalo, wolves, salmon, and butterflies.

Your affinity for groups is not exactly like that of buffalos, wolves, and salmon, of course. You don't travel in herds, packs, or schools—although first-year college students come eerily close—but you do move from one social setting to another throughout the day. In principle, you could attend a lecture by yourself, eat in an unoccupied part of the cafeteria, or watch a movie in an empty theater. And you may look upon these daily events as solo activities with respect to their purposes (learning, reducing hunger, getting entertained). But these activities would not be the same if there weren't other people doing the same thing at the same time and in the same place. Even if the other people are total strangers with whom you have no meaningful interaction, it's unlikely you would sit by yourself in a class, visit an empty cafeteria, or take a seat in an empty theater to watch your favorite movie. And when you are alone, much of the time you remain connected to others through the magic of technology. How long can you sit by yourself without checking e-mail, looking at Facebook or Twitter, or having vicarious social experiences by watching fellow humans interact on TV or the internet?

CHAPTER OVERVIEW

What Are You Going to Learn?

- **What exactly do we mean by a group?** What are the key factors that create a feeling that one is part of a group as opposed to a concentration of individuals who happen to be in the same place at the same time? Why are we drawn to groups in the first place?
- **How do groups change the way we think, feel, and make decisions?** Does our personal psychology give way to a "group mind?" Do groups make us more moral or more intelligent? Or do they have the opposite effects?
- **What do groups do and how do they do it?** What enables a collection of people to function as a meaningful and effective unit? How do people get their ideas across to other group members? How do group members coordinate their behavior to achieve a group goal? How do leaders facilitate group action? Do groups increase our motivation to do well, and does this motivation translate into better performance? Or would we better off doing things on our own? Are groups really worth the trouble?
- **Are social networks changing the nature of social relations?** Are social networks—which are freed from the constraints of physical proximity because of the internet and smartphones—displacing groups (which occupy a common location) as the basis for our identities, decisions, opinions, support, and action? If so, what are the implications for our species of this transition as we move forward in the 21st century?

Individuals and Groups

What Are Groups and Why Do People Form Them?

A group has little to do with the number of people assembled in one place. There may be several hundred people walking on a busy city street or waiting for the light to change at an intersection, but most of them are not thinking about their status as a member of a group. Even if everyone is shoulder to shoulder, with constant jostling for a place to stand or a path to travel, the ensemble of people is experienced as a crowd, but not as a group in the way that, say, a basketball team or a jury is. Under the right conditions, however, a gathering as small as three people might feel decidedly group-like—much more so than a gathering ten times that many.

If numbers alone do not define a group, what does? We address this issue by highlighting the factors that promote group formation, whether the group consists of 5 people or 5,000. We then consider why people are drawn to groups, even when this often means surrendering autonomy, relinquishing personal control, and suspending the pursuit of self-interest.

The Defining Features of Groups

Several dozen people standing at a bus stop may look like a group to an alien spacecraft looking down from several miles up. But it's unlikely that anyone at the bus stop would characterize the collection of humanity as a group. Now, if the alien makes its presence known, inadvertently turning off its invisibility cloak perhaps, the collection of individuals may transform immediately into what psychologists would call a group. There is no leader, no one knows anyone else, and they didn't plan to meet this morning. The sudden "groupness" derives from other factors: a *common focus of attention* ("what is that thing?!"), the potential for *mutual influence* ("what do you think—should we run?"), a readiness to embrace a *shared reality* ("it's an alien!"), and a *common course of action* ("run away!" "hold our ground!").

Common Focus

Groups come into their own when the members are all concerned about the same thing. This is clearly the case in task-oriented groups, factories, businesses, or corporations where there is a commonly recognized goal—solving a puzzle, making a car, selling paper, or marketing computers. Having a common focus is also central to informal groups that lack a concrete task. The people at a party are not there to build cars, but they do share a common concern with having fun, playing games, and impressing one another.

Even complete strangers can experience a taste of group feeling when there is a common focus. People meandering in a park or on a trendy downtown street, for example, hardly constitute a group but should they all witness an attention-grabbing event—a street performer, perhaps—the sense of being part of a group is enhanced a bit. If the event transpires for a while and has some uncertainty associated with it (e.g., will the street performer stumble?), the collection of people might develop a sense of having a shared experience and perhaps engage in conversations or listen in on other people's conversation.

If the only thing the collection of people have in common is observing a novel event, the group feeling is rather shallow and will dissipate as soon as they stop attending to the same thing. But it does create the potential for a more meaningful sense that one is part of a group. The potential stands a chance of becoming manifest if the following factors come into play.

Mutual Influence

People in groups acknowledge each other's existence, at the least, and typically interact with each other as well. Social interaction serves many functions (as we saw in Chapter 8), but none so central as social influence. In the absence of a group, influence is typically in service of each person's personal motives and concerns. But in a group context, people influence each other for shared reasons (e.g., Festinger, Schachter, & Back, 1950; Latané, 1981; Mac-Coun, 2012; Tanford & Penrod, 1984). They may convince one another to cooperate on a task, for example, or to share information. The goal of influence could be as simple as getting everyone to line up or take turns when talking, but still instill in each person a sense that he or she is part of a group.

Social influence can take many forms, from tactics that are overt and forceful (e.g., orders, threats, the promise of reward) to those that are so subtle that they are not even recognized as influence (e.g., expressions of liking). Sometimes just knowing what others think is enough to motivate a group member to adopt the same opinion or prefer the same course of action.

Shared Reality

One of the ironies of having an enormous brain is that we are easily confused by even a trivial event. An unexpected sound might signify nothing but "run away" to a dog, but cries out for an explanation when heard by a human. Receiving a compliment from a complete stranger can mean any number of things, from a superficial nicety to a tactic to soften us up for a manipulation attempt. Particularly in today's world with its nonstop flow of information and potential for sensory overload (Milgram, 1969), we need a means for deciding what events are important and how they should be interpreted. The problem is amplified when different sources of expertise offer conflicting interpretations. Try sometime to reconcile the opposing views of political reality provided by competing cable TV channels (e.g., Fox News, MSNBC).

Groups do not put up with ambiguity and conflicting interpretations for long. An unexpected event might promote temporary confusion but the group is likely to settle quickly on an interpretation that is embraced by all. This is true for mundane events—the unexpected sound or the out-of-the-blue compliment—but it is just as true for ideology, values, and notions of life and death. Many public policy issues (e.g., healthcare, going to war, taxation) are complex and can be viewed as legitimate and warranted or illegitimate or unjustified depending on one's viewpoint. How other people in one's group make sense of such issues can play a more significant role in achieving "understanding" than can independently checking the relevant facts. And if a collection of people has yet to form a group, the rapid convergence on social consensus in response to an ambiguous event can turn the gathering into a group. In the absence of the event, they might not have noticed one another, let alone taken the time to forge relationships.

Coordinated Action

As we saw in Chapter 8, people are predisposed to mimic one another's actions (Chartrand & Bargh, 1999). Two people in conversation will adopt similar postures and if they are sitting with their legs crossed, they will swing the crossed legs in unison. Such synchronization would seem impossible to achieve when there are many people involved. It turns out, though, that even large crowds of strangers can suddenly achieve synchronization and operate as if orchestrated by a conductor (Strogatz, 2003). Fans at a football game can readily form a "wave" that sweeps across a stadium, and revelers at a street party can spontaneously move back in forth in unison without stumbling over each other.

Coordination in a group may seem surprising in light of our concern with personal agency, discussed in Chapter 6. No one admits to following the crowd or being influenced by what those around one do. But some actions occur spontaneously without conscious knowledge, let alone conscious control (Chartrand & Bargh, 1999; Marsh, Johnston, Richardson, & Schmidt, 2009). The coordination that occurs in groups can promote behaviors that might not have occurred otherwise. Consider the contagious laughter that erupts in response to a joke that might elicit nothing more than a smile—or perhaps a grimace or an eye roll—when experienced in private.

The coordination that defines a group goes beyond the imitation of facial expressions, bodily movements, and other basic features of action. Sometimes, in fact, coordination means behaving *differently* from others in the group. Particularly when the task facing the group is complex and extended in time, successful execution of the action requires different people in the group to do different things at different times. In these instances, a *role structure* develops—or is sometimes imposed—to facilitate the group's larger goal.

The Attraction of Groups

Why bother to join a group? Unless one is the leader, being a group member often means relinquishing a sense of autonomy and freedom, suspending the luxury of doing whatever one pleases, waiting to do things, following rules, and worrying about what other people think. There are several reasons underlying people's natural inclination to form groups; some are pragmatic and under conscious control, others are less strategic and less open to introspection.

Evolutionary Foundations

Why would someone spend $50 to attend a rock concert that is jammed with other people, most of them complete strangers, when one could get a much better view of the onstage action on a widescreen TV at home, and do so for free? Despite the technology that enables us to experience events without social clutter, hassles, and considerable expenses, we forgo technology to attend football games, concerts, and public lectures, and to eat at restaurants in the most trafficked part of town. It's not about the game, the music, the lecture, or the food. It's about the presence of other people.

To understand why people are programmed to operate this way, it is useful to consider the evolutionary foundations of human psychology (Brewer & Caporael, 2006; Buss, 2015). Evolution is not concerned with maximizing an organism's enjoyment, but rather is concerned with survival and adaptation. Organisms develop cognitive and behavioral tendencies that increase the likelihood that they will live long enough to pass on their genes to their offspring. A tiger or a grizzly bear can spend the majority of its life without social contact—except, of course, when mating becomes an issue—and is likely to view another member of its species as a competitor rather than as a potential ally (or close friend). These solitary animals are quite adept at acquiring food on their own and they have little to fear from other predators.

Wild dogs and wolves, on the other hand, are considerably smaller and need the help of others to bring down their favorite prey, which are typically much bigger than they are (buffalo, elk, etc.). Individually, they are also more vulnerable to attack or stealing of their prey by other predators—including tigers and bears. So the pressures of survival and adaptation have selected for sociality in these animals. Those who didn't feel like being part of the group were hard pressed to live long enough to produce offspring.

Humans are more like wild dogs and wolves than tigers and grizzlies. Long before the invention of farming tools, hunting weapons, and defensive technologies (e.g., weapons, physical barriers) to protect them from predators, our ancestors adapted to the unforgiving nature of their environment by living in groups. Those who felt little use for such an arrangement probably did not last long, let alone experience success in finding mates and raising a family.

Humans, even athletes and bodybuilders, are pathetically weak in comparison to other primates (e.g., an adult male chimpanzee is seven times stronger than an adult human male of the same weight) and not well equipped to fend off predators on their own (nails instead of claws, barely noticeable canine teeth). Nor are we, in the absence of tools and weapons, able to secure a stable food source, whether agricultural or prey animal.

Of course, people aren't thinking about perpetuation of their genetic makeup or their survival when they participate in group activities. Evolution, however, doesn't demand much in the way of awareness. When people avoid mating with siblings, for example, it's not because they are concerned about the concentration of shared recessive genes that could lead to problems in their offspring. People don't have intimate relations with their siblings simply because they have no desire to do so. In like manner, people join groups for personal reasons that are rather distant from the evolutionary rationale that mandates such behavior. We are not dependent on groups today in the same way that our ancestors were thousands of years ago, but we still feel compelled fit in with various social groups and attend overpriced concerts.

When a person fails to gain acceptance in a group, there are psychological consequences. Loneliness is the most immediate effect. The brain activation of lonely people suggests that they are less rewarded by happy depictions but more attentive to depictions of social distress (Cacioppo et al., 2009). When loneliness becomes chronic, people are at risk for depression (Schultz & Moore, 1984) and eating disorders (Gilbert & DeBlassie, 1984). Even if all other essential needs are met—material success and accomplishments—the failure to achieve and maintain membership and status in a social group can undermine psychological well-being.

Individual Motivation

Evolutionary reasons aside, sometimes people are drawn to groups for purely selfish reasons of which they are quite aware. In principle, a student could prepare a term paper individually by checking out books from the library, looking up information on relevant (and trustworthy!) internet sites, thinking through all the ideas and points to be made, and editing the various drafts that are prepared. But a little help from one's friends (or classmates) wouldn't hurt and might save some time and energy. So the student might seek out classmates and arrange for a study or term paper group, in which the members trade reference material, exchange insights, and edit one another's work. The group in such instances is a means to a personal end. The student doesn't have a need to belong so much as a need to get a good grade.

Selfish interests may seem at odds with group cooperation, but the seeming contradiction is resolved from the perspective of *social exchange*. This concept, introduced in Chapter 8, is based on the assumption that groups (and social relations generally) operate according to an economic model in which people trade resources with each other, while trying to secure the best deal they can. The student attempting to complete his or her term paper seeks out others to obtain help with reference information, but in exchange he or she must offer something of value—an offer to edit someone's paper or perhaps a deep insight or two. Theories of social exchange have a long history in social psychology (e.g., Blau, 1964; Foa & Foa, 1975; Homans, 1961; Thibaut & Kelley, 1959) and are considered by many social scientists to provide the driving force in group dynamics (e.g., Axelrod, 1984; Messick & Liebrand, 1995).

Individuals are highly sensitive to how good a deal they have made. They evaluate the group experience according to whether the costs they incur (e.g., time and effort) are balanced by the positive outcomes they achieve (e.g., success, enjoyment, material rewards). The greater the perceived benefits relative to the perceived costs, the greater their satisfaction with group membership (Adams, 1965). People differ in what they consider to be the "break even" point in the benefits versus costs of group membership. Two people may experience the same benefits and costs, but whereas one person may consider this a great deal, the other person might feel he or she is getting a raw deal and decide to leave the group.

Social exchange in a group context entails commitment to norms of *reciprocity* and fair play. The student who offers his editorial help in exchange for reference information expects that the other person will hold up his or her end of the deal. When this expectation is violated—the other person accepts the student's help but gives nothing in return—the result is not simply dissatisfaction with the deal, but a sense of betrayal and injustice as well.

The importance of perceived justice in shaping people's feelings about social experience is demonstrated nicely in the *Ultimatum Game* (Gale, Binmore, & Samuelson, 1995; M. Nowak, Page, & Sigmund, 2000). The game is simple: one individual (A) is given an amount of money (e.g., $10) to divide between him- or herself and another individual (B). When A announces how the money is to be divided, B must decide whether to accept the offer. If B accepts the offer, that is how the money is divided. But if B refuses the offer, neither A nor B get any money. From a rational point of view, B should accept any portion of the total reward. Even $1 is better than nothing. But that is not how things typically work out. In fact, any offer less than 20% is typically rejected. Even if it is against their monetary self-interest, people will punish those who are seen as taking advantage of them. People may enter groups with a selfish agenda, but they quickly develop a notion of fair play in their exchanges with others, and this emergent motive can trump the motive that brought them there in the first place.

Group Functions

Some activities simply cannot be done by individuals acting alone. It takes the coordinated action of many people to move a boulder, play football, orchestrate a space mission, overhaul the health care system, or clean up the environment. These group activities are out of the reach of lone individuals. For that matter, some of these activities might not have occurred to individuals in the first place, were it not for the group.

The functions served by a group are not always task-oriented in nature. Some groups are predominantly social in their orientation. Families and social clubs, for example, spend most of their time doing things that are intended to be interesting and fun, not necessarily useful. And when students get together to study or prepare a term paper, it's hardly all work and no play.

Social Identity

Personal identity is clearly important, but people also adopt a shared identity with fellow members of groups. This *social identity* can transcend, or at least incorporate, people's idiosyncratic sense of who they are and what they are like (e.g., Smaldino, Pickett, Sherman, & Schank, 2012). As noted in Chapter 5, some cultures emphasize the role of the group in self-definition more so than do other cultures (Markus & Kitayama, 1991). But even in the most individualistic societies—the United States being an exemplar—people's identities go beyond their personal talents and attitudes to encompass their membership in groups of various kinds—family, ethnicity, career, lifestyle, sexual orientation, and religion serving as prime examples.

People take their social identities seriously, especially when there is competition with people holding different social identities. Willingness to go to war or engage in terrorism, for example, is hard to imagine without the driving force of social identity. A young person with decades of life ahead of him or her will risk it all for the sake of his or her national identity, even if this means doing things that are at odds with his or her personal identity and without an expectation of material rewards or even individual recognition. An unthinkable behavior from a personal identity perspective can become an unthinking response from a social identity perspective.

The Group Mind

How Do People Think in Groups?

People in groups tend to think alike. They may have different points of view when first getting together, but something happens that causes them to converge in fairly short order on a common idea, belief, or emotion. This tendency has been noted over the years by social commentators, psychologists, and laypeople—often in unflattering terms. Gustave Le Bon (1895), a French sociologist (and amateur physicist) in the late 19th century, was especially harsh in his assessment of people's thought processes in groups. He argued that people in groups lose their ability to think as reasonable human beings, functioning instead at a lower level, on par with that of animals. Most commentators haven't gone quite that far, but many suggest that congregations of people often inspire a *group mind* (McDougall, 1908) that synchronizes everyone's thinking and promotes a high degree of uniformity with little critical analysis.

The animal depiction is actually quite telling. Have you ever observed a school of fish make a sudden 90 degree turn to the left or right? It is as if the entire school, composed of perhaps dozens of fish, behaved as a single unit with a shared script for what to do at a precise moment. The thoughts and actions of people in groups sometimes resemble a school of fish. Consider the synchronization of mood and behavior in the throng of people on New Orleans' Bourbon Street during Mardi Gras, the synchronized hand-clapping of audience members at the finale of an exciting concert, the sudden eruption of yelling at a contentious town hall meeting, or the coordinated giggling among friends as they watch a comedy show on TV.

Uniformity in Groups

People are attuned to one another in group settings and readily develop a shared reality and common course of action. But how do they do this? Perhaps each person independently responds to an external event in the same way, so that uniformity is simply a coincidence. Or perhaps someone in the group functions as a leader who influences everyone to respond in the same way to event, regardless of how each would have responded individually. A third possibility is that people imitate the thoughts and actions of those who are nearby, with this local influence rippling through the group to produce a synchronized group-level response.

All three explanations have merit. People clearly respond to external stimuli, follow the lead of influential individuals, and influence each other to adopt a common way of thinking and acting. But the third model has the widest generality, promoting group-level uniformity when there might otherwise be idiosyncratic reactions to an event and when no one has emerged as a leader for the group. Once a group has achieved a common psychological state, moreover, anyone who expresses a contrary view is likely to experience enormous pressure to change. If the person doesn't cave in to such pressure, he or she is likely to be rejected from the group (Schachter, 1951), a fate that can be devastating for the person (Williams, 2007). This pervasive tendency for people to adopt and maintain the mental states of nearby group members is of keen interest to social psychologists. Three expressions of this tendency are particularly notable.

Conformity

Conformity is a "change in behavior or belief toward a group as a result of real or imagined group pressure" (Kiesler & Kiesler, 1976). Pressures toward uniformity invariably exist in groups and are brought to bear on the individual so that he or she will conform to the opinions and behavior patterns of the other group members (Festinger, 1950). If one of two diners at a table for two says that he or she finds the food distasteful and the other person expresses a more favorable opinion, the first person may not change his or her views to match those of his or her companion. However, the addition of several more dinner companions, each holding the contrary position, may well cause the person to rethink his or her position and establish common ground with the others. If he or she has yet to express an opinion, the likelihood of conforming to the others' opinions is all the greater.

To investigate the variables at work in this sort of context—group size, unanimity of group opinion, and the timing of the person's expressed judgment—Solomon Asch (1956) performed a series of experiments that are widely regarded as classics. Asch's original intention actually was to demonstrate that people do *not* conform slavishly and uncritically in a group setting. Asch put his hope for humanity to a test in a simple and elegant way. Participants thought they were in a study concerned with perception. They sat facing a pair of white cardboards on which vertical lines were drawn (see Figure 12.1). One card had a single line, which provided the standard for participants' perceptual judgments. The second card had three lines of varying length, one of which was clearly the same length as the standard. Participants were simply asked to indicate which of the three lines matched the standard. The correct answer was usually obvious, and in fact when tested individually, participants rarely made a mistake.

To give conformity a chance, Asch (1956) placed a naive participant in a group setting with six other people, who were actually experimental accomplices pretending to be naïve participants. By arrangement, the participant always made his judgment after hearing the others make their judgments. For the first two trials, the accomplices (and, of course, the participant) gave the obviously correct answers. After creating this group consensus, the accomplices gave a unanimous but incorrect answer on the third trial—and again on trials 4, 6, 7, 9, 10, and 12. To Asch's surprise, over 80% of participants conformed to the incorrect majority on at least one trial, and 7% conformed on all seven of the critical trials. Though not his intent, Asch had shown that even when there is a clear reality, people are still inclined to go along with the crowd.

Presumably, Asch's participants conformed because they wanted the other group members to like them or because they were fearful of ridicule if they failed to go along. During post-experimental interviews, participants typically mentioned these concerns as their motivation for concurring with obviously inaccurate judgments. And when Asch allowed participants to make their responses privately in writing as opposed to publicly by voice, the extent to which they conformed showed a marked decrease.

Social approval does not exhaust the possible motives for conformity, however. Several years prior to Asch's research, Muzafer Sherif (1936) had concocted an equally compelling experimental situation relevant to conformity, but one that played on the often ambiguous nature of physical reality rather than concerns with acceptance, rejection,

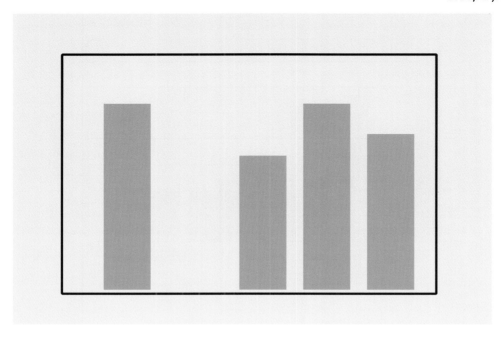

FIGURE 12.1   The Stimuli Used in the Asch Experiment—A Standard and Three Bars of Different Height, One of Which Matched the Standard

and the like. Sherif felt that groups provide important information for individuals and interpretative frameworks for making coherent judgments about information. People have a need for *cognitive clarity* (Schachter, 1959), but sometimes they lack an objective yardstick for determining the "true" nature of their experiences. In such instances, people turn to others, not to gain approval but rather to obtain social clues to reality. People are highly prone to rumors, for example, even from unreliable sources, when they hear about goings-on for which no official explanation has been provided. A sudden noise or a hard-to-read message can similarly make people prone to the assessments of others in an attempt to clarify what has happened.

To test this motivation for conformity, Sherif (1936) needed a situation in which the physical environment lacked ready-made yardsticks for understanding, so that the operation of social standards could be observed. His solution was to take advantage of the *autokinetic effect*—the apparent motion of a stationary spot of light in a dark room. The idea was to place a group of participants in this type of situation and ask them to make estimates of the light's movement. Participants, of course, were not informed that the light's movement was illusory. When tested individually, participants varied considerably in their estimates, from virtually no movement to more than 10 inches.

He then brought together three participants who had previously made estimates in private, and asked them to announce their individual judgments aloud and in succession. Despite their initial differences, participants converged fairly quickly (often within three trials) on a single estimate that functioned as a group standard for the light's movement (see Figure 12.2). Sherif went on to show that once a group defined reality for participants, they continued to adhere to the group judgment even after they left the group.

Normative and Informational Influence

Deutsch and Gerard (1955) recognized that people can conform for different reasons and formally distinguished between *normative influence*, which captures the essence of the Asch situation, and *informational influence*, which reflects subjects' motivation in the Sherif situation. Normative influence refers to conformity in an attempt to gain approval, whereas informational influence refers to conformity in an attempt to gain clear knowledge about reality.

Sometimes it is difficult to determine which basis of conformity is operative in a given situation. Imagine, for example, that you observe someone following the lead of others at a classical music concert. When they sit, he or

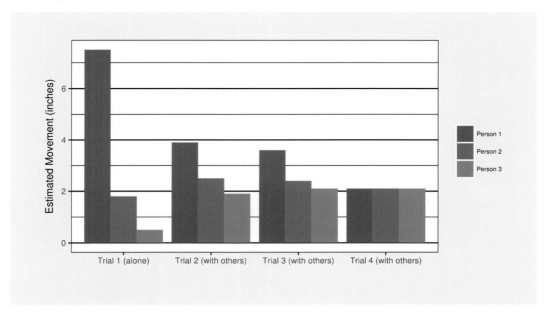

FIGURE 12.2 Convergence on a Group Norm in Perception of Physical Reality
Source: Adapted from Sherif (1936)

she sits. When they give a standing ovation, he or she follows suit. The group influence in this case could be normative, informational, or perhaps both, depending on the person's primary source of uncertainty. If unsure of his or her standing among the fellow concert-goers, the person's conformity could be driven by desire for approval or fear of ridicule. If unfamiliar with classical music, however, the behavior of others might provide all-important clues about the quality of the performance.

Normative influence is especially salient when the group controls important material or psychological rewards (e.g., Crutchfield, 1955), when the behavior is public rather than private (Insko et al., 1983), or when the person is eager for approval (Crowne & Marlowe, 1964). Someone attending the concert with prospective colleagues, for instance, may be especially inclined to match their behavior, particularly if he or she is uncertain about their interest in his or her job candidacy and the concert hall has good lighting. The salience of informational influence depends on the person's confidence in his or her own judgment and his or her judgment of how well-informed the group is (Cialdini, 2000; Deutsch & Gerard, 1955; MacNeil & Sherif, 1976). A classical music neophyte who sees tuxedo-clad audience members leap to their feet upon completion of "The Rach 3" is more likely to follow suit than if he or she sees the same behavior by schoolchildren. A graduate of Julliard is unlikely to mimic such behavior in either case.

Informational influence tends also to take precedence, not surprisingly, when the judgment task is particularly difficult or ambiguous (e.g., Coleman, Blake, & Mouton, 1958). Even in the Asch situation, conformity is increased when the lines are closer in length and thus harder to judge (Asch, 1956), and when judgments are made from memory rather than from direct perception of the lines (Deutsch & Gerard, 1955), presumably because our memories are considered more fallible than our immediate perceptions.

Uncertainty is one thing; an uncertain danger is quite another. The anxiety associated with uncertain but potentially adverse consequences increases the importance of informational influence (Kirkpatrick & Shaver, 1988; Schachter, 1959). This can be seen in people's response to national crises (e.g., the aftermath of the 9/11 terrorist attacks), social changes that upset traditional norms and values (e.g., gay rights, religious diversity), and proposed courses of action with unknown (and potentially bad) consequences (e.g., going to war). In such instances, there is an uptick in people searching out others—usually those in the same boat and with the same set of values and life experiences—to clarify what has happened and what should be done in response.

Groupthink

Conformity clearly serves important functions, but there are downsides as well. A particularly troublesome aspect is *groupthink* (Janis, 1982). Janis borrowed this term from George Orwell's *1984* to refer to a mode of thinking dominated by a concern for reaching and maintaining consensus, as opposed to making the best decision under the circumstances. Groupthink essentially entails "a deterioration of mental efficiency, reality testing, and moral judgment that results from group pressure" (Janis, 1982, p. 9). Rather than examining all possible courses of action, people in the grips of groupthink expend their mental energy on achieving and maintaining group solidarity and opinion unanimity. See Figure 12.3 for the sequence of stages involved in groupthink.

The potential for groupthink exists in any group context, but the most intriguing examples concern decisions with far-reaching consequences by people normally considered "the best and the brightest." Janis (1982) analyzed several such situations, including the Bay of Pigs invasion during the Kennedy administration, the bombing of Pearl Harbor that prompted US entry into World War II, and the Vietnam War. In each case, crucial decisions were made in small groups whose members had considerable mutual respect and liking. Positive regard is certainly preferable to disinterest or disrespect, but it can inhibit criticism and close examination of one another's suggestions. The group members also exhibited collective rationalization, discrediting or ignoring all information contrary to the prevailing group sentiment. They also tended to develop strong feelings that their mission (e.g., invading Cuba, implementing a massive troop buildup in South Vietnam) was moral and that the opposite side was not only immoral but also stupid. To further cocoon the group, self-appointed "mind-guards" precluded members from accessing information that was

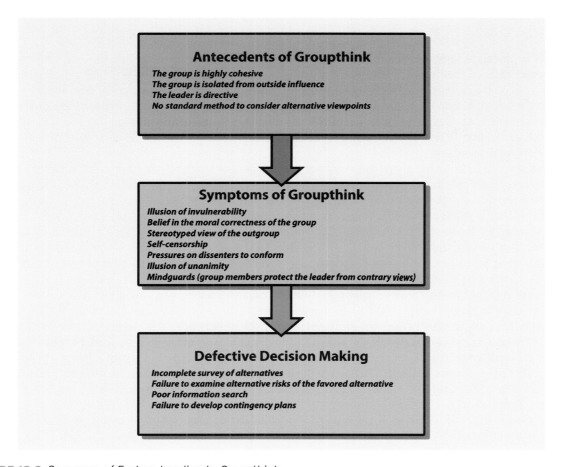

FIGURE 12.3 Sequence of Factors Leading to Groupthink

inconsistent with the party line. The upshot is something akin to tunnel vision, in which a single perspective is seen as the only viable perspective—not because of a rational assessment of the facts but because of the group's irrational *esprit de corps*.

Groupthink is not inevitable but it takes concerted efforts to prevent it from dominating the interpersonal dynamics in a group. A smart leader (e.g., someone one who has read what psychologists say about groupthink) can implement the following strategies to inoculate the group against this approach to decision-making (Flowers, 1977; McCauley, 1989).

- The leader can remain impartial, rather than taking a directive role in the process. Members can therefore express their opinions without fear of challenging the leader.
- The leader can invite opinions from people who are not members of the group. Because outsiders are less concerned with massaging the egos of group members and reinforcing their mutual love fest, they are better able to offer contrary points of view.
- The leader can assign one of the members the task of playing "the devil's advocate." This person's role is to adopt a position that challenges the emerging consensus in the group. This negative can stall the march toward coherence underlying groupthink.
- The leader can break the group into subgroups. Each subgroup is likely to develop somewhat different recommendations, so when they meet together in the larger group, they can evaluate the various recommendations and forge an enlightened policy.
- The leader can ask group members to express their opinions anonymously (e.g., in writing) or conduct a secret ballot to assess how each member thinks about the issue. This "frees" members to give their true opinions, without fearing group recrimination.

Group Polarization

Groupthink is related to another phenomenon—*group polarization*—that was considered surprising when first noted by researchers (Stoner, 1961; Wallach, Kogan, & Bem, 1962). The conventional wisdom was that individuals in groups avoid going out on the proverbial limb, generating popular opinions and "safe" recommendations (Allport, 1924). This implies that a group decision is usually more conservative than the average of group members' individual decisions. This view is reflected in critics' laments about the bland and timid recommendations by committees in bureaucracies. What the research began to reveal, however, was quite the opposite tendency—greater endorsement of risky decisions as a result of group discussion.

This so-called *risky shift* is not surprising in light of groupthink. The sense of superiority and certainty fostered by an emphasis on cohesiveness can be a breeding ground for bold decisions that go beyond what an individual alone would contemplate. The shift toward risky decisions, however, was observed in contexts that didn't involve the intellectual and emotional incest displayed by highly cohesive groups of self-important people. Even groups of strangers brought together for a one-shot encounter in a laboratory setting were found to advocate courses of action with less guarantee of success than the recommendations volunteered by the group members prior to their discussion. Because this observation flew in the face of conventional wisdom, it generated a tidal wave of research for the next decade.

This research demonstrated greater risk-taking in many areas, including bargaining and negotiations (Lamm & Sauer, 1974), gambling behavior (Blascovich, Ginsburg, & Howe, 1975; Lamm & Ochssmann, 1972), and jury decisions (Myers, 1982). The risky shift was observed, moreover, when the consequences of a group's decision involved real as well as hypothetical consequences (Wallach et al., 1962). The risky shift was not limited to recommendations regarding courses of action. Even among strangers, group discussion seemed to intensify all sorts of attitudes, beliefs, values, judgments, and perceptions (Myers, 1982). Such shifts were observed for both sexes, in different populations and cultures (e.g., the United States, Canada, England, France, Germany, New Zealand), and with many kinds of group participants (Pruitt, 1971).

During this same period, however, some research hinted at the opposite effect of group discussion—a *cautious shift*. To complicate matters even further, research began to find evidence of movement in *both* directions after a group discussion (Doise, 1969; Moscovici & Zavalloni, 1969), suggesting that both risky and cautious shifts were different manifestations of a more basic phenomenon. Based on a review of this research, Myers and Lamm (1976) identified what they felt was the underlying process. According to their *group-polarization hypothesis*, the "average postgroup response will be more extreme in the same direction as the average of the pregroup responses" (Myers & Lamm, 1976, p. 603). Imagine two groups, each consisting of four individuals whose opinions vary in their respective preferences for risk. The average choice of members is closer to the risky end of the caution-risk dimension in one group, but closer to the cautious end of this dimension in the other group. The group-polarization effect, illustrated in Figure 12.4, predicts that the first group should become riskier as a result of group discussion (a risky shift), but that the second group should become more cautious during its deliberations (a cautious shift). The evidence cited by Myers and Lamm (1976) is consistent with this prediction and is widely accepted today as a valid empirical generalization regarding group dynamics.

This straightforward generalization initially proved to be resistant to a simple explanation, and a number of theories were put forward. Of these, two have stood the test of time (thus far). *Social comparison theory* holds that people attempt to accomplish two goals during group discussion: evaluating the accuracy of their position by comparing it with the positions of other group members, and creating a favorable impression of themselves within the group. The confluence of these two motives results in a tendency to describe one's own position in somewhat more extreme terms (Goethals & Zanna, 1979; Myers & Lamm, 1976). *Persuasive-arguments theory*, on the other hand, stresses the importance of the information obtained during group discussion. Whether there is a shift toward risk or toward caution depends on the relative persuasiveness of the arguments favoring each position (Burnstein & Vinokur, 1977).

The distinction between these two accounts corresponds to the distinction between normative and informational influence. Social comparison theory, with its emphasis on self-presentation attempts to match the perceived group norm, reflects normative influence. The persuasive-arguments perspective, meanwhile, is practically synonymous with the rationale of informational influence. As noted earlier, these two forms of influence often co-occur, so social comparison and persuasive arguments often work together to promote polarization in groups.

Individuality in Groups

Imagine if conformity was the only dynamic at work in social groups. One can envision groupthink and group polarization carried to the extreme, with the complete suppression of dissent and a resultant interpersonal homogeneity. Fortunately, there is more to social life than accommodation by everyone to the majority viewpoint. The pressures for

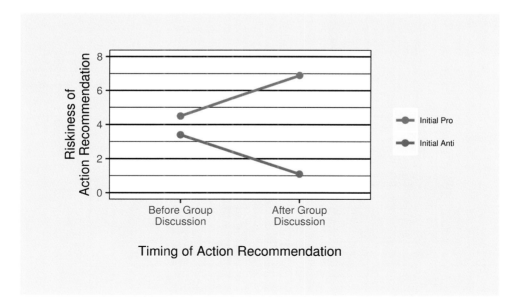

FIGURE 12.4 Polarization of Action Recommendations in Groups

uniformity can be strong, but under certain conditions people manage to hang onto their beliefs, values, and desires despite these pressures and with the possibility of being marginalized for doing so.

Experiments in the Asch tradition, for example, have found that both *group size* and *unanimity of the majority* have important effects on conformity. The relation between group size and conformity appears to be logarithmic: conformity increases with increasing group size up to a point, after which the addition of more group members has diminishing impact (Latané, 1981). In Asch's own research, even one dissenter among the confederates emboldened the naïve participant to resist group pressure and express his or her own judgment. This is true even if the dissenting confederate disagrees with the participant as well as the rest of the group (Allen & Levine, 1971). So the key factor is not agreement with the participant, but rather the recognition that nonconformity is possible and acceptable.

Research emphasizing the dynamics of group functioning has revealed an ironic twist: the survival of minority opinion is actually an inevitable consequence of group polarization. This is illustrated in a series of computer simulations of group dynamics performed by Andrzej Nowak, Bibb Latané, and their colleagues (Latané, Nowak, & Liu, 1994; Lewenstein, Nowak, & Latané, 1993; Nowak, Szamrej, & Latané, 1990). Figure 12.5 depicts how this process works.

Imagine a group of individuals—represented by the boxes in the figure—who get together to discuss whether a particular plan of action or a social policy is a good or bad idea. Assume, for example, they are discussing a controversial public option for healthcare in which the federal government would offer a medical care plan that would compete with private insurance companies. Let's say that prior to discussing this issue, 60% of the people are "pro" public option (the light colored boxes) and 40% are "anti" public option (the dark boxes), and that the "pro" and "anti" individuals are randomly distributed in space (e.g., in a large meeting room or an auditorium). Some individuals are more persuasive and more resistant to social influence than are others. The "strong" individuals may have greater expertise with respect to the topic, or they may possess personal attributes (e.g., intelligence, self-confidence, physical attractiveness) that make them persuasive in a variety of contexts. Strength is represented as the height of the boxes—the tall boxes are strong individuals, the short boxes are weak individuals.

What happens when everyone begins to discuss the issue? The model makes a small set of assumptions regarding this process, each of which is quite reasonable and consistent with empirical research on social interaction and influence (Latané, 1981).

- Each individual samples the degree of support for his or her position on the public option. Simply put, people want to know what other people in the group think.
- Each individual attaches greater weight (persuasive impact) to the opinions of others who are physically closest to him or her. In Figure 12.5a, each person (represented by a box) gives the most weight to the opinions of the

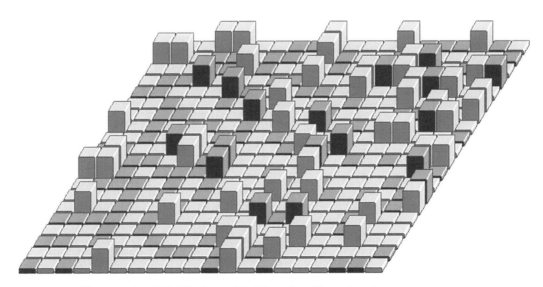

FIGURE 12.5a The Initial (Random) Distribution of Opinions in a Simulated Group

eight others who are immediately adjacent, and less weight to the opinions of others who are increasingly further away.
- The weight attached to a neighbor's opinion reflects the neighbor's relative strength. Two neighbors may both be immediately adjacent to the individual, but the stronger neighbor will have greater impact.
- Each individual's own opinion is given a great deal of weight by virtue of spatial immediacy (in a sense, there is zero distance between the individual and him or herself). But even here, the weight an individual attaches to his or her own opinion depends on his or her relative strength—a weak individual (short box) attaches less weight to his or her own opinion than does a strong individual (tall box).

After each discussion period, each individual compares the support for the "pro" and "anti" opinions and adopts the opinion with the strongest support. If an individual is "pro" public option and his or her immediate neighbors share this opinion, he or she will maintain the "pro" position. But if an individual is "pro" public option and five of the eight immediate neighbors are "anti" public option, he or she will change his or her opinion to match the local majority— unless he or she is strong and the neighbors are weak.

In the computer simulations, this procedure is repeated for each individual in the group, resulting in a new distribution of "pro" and "anti" positions. Then, the whole process is repeated—simulating further rounds of communication in the group—until the distribution of opinions stabilizes and shows no further changes. Sometimes the simulation process has to be repeated many times for this to happen—just as repeated rounds of group discussion are often necessary before everyone gets locked into a fixed position.

This simple process consistently reveals two basic phenomena, both of which are depicted in Figure 12.5b. First, the opinion that was slightly favored (60%) at the outset (Figure 12.5a)—in this case, the "pro" public option position— has increased substantially in favorability. Now an overwhelming majority of people in the group (90%) hold a "pro" public option opinion. This illustrates the tendency toward *polarization* (Moscovici & Zavalloni, 1969; Myers & Lamm, 1976) that has been emphasized so far. This is certainly a big change but not a total change. The minority position—the "anti" public option position—has managed to hang on. The way in which it manages to do so illustrates the second basic phenomenon—*clustering* of like-minded individuals within the larger group. The formation of clusters of "pro" and "anti" individuals is readily apparent in Figure 12.5b.

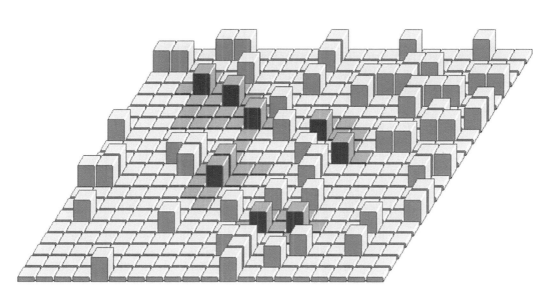

FIGURE 12.5b The Distribution of Opinions in the Simulated Group after Repeated Rounds of Discussion With Neighbors

Note that the minority clusters all contain strong individuals. As the majority opinion begins to polarize in a group, only the minority individuals who are strong (hard to convert) can maintain their stance. Clustering is critical to the preservation of minority opinions. By him or herself, a person holding a minority opinion is subject to the pressures of the majority and is always at risk of being converted. But within a cluster, the person's sampling of opinions yields a highly biased result: the opinions of like-minded neighbors create a local majority despite their minority status in the larger group. The cluster protects the minority opinion despite the pressure for uniformity that yields an entirely different result in the group as a whole.

Group Action

What Do Groups Do?

Groups come in many guises, from informal social gatherings to work groups charged with producing a product or deliberative bodies that forge social policies and enact legislation. Despite this diversity of group activity, there are some basic processes that underlie how groups get the job done. First and foremost, the members of the group must relinquish a bit of their autonomy and take their signals for what to do, and how to do it, from the group. But this general feature of group dynamics is manifest in different ways depending on the nature of the group and what it is trying to accomplish. Several factors are relevant here, including the emphasis on personal accountability, the development of social roles, and the style and function of leadership in the group. Let's discuss these factors in turn.

Deindividuation

There is always a loss in individuality and personal accountability in groups as people take their lead in deciding what to do from the group's composition and purpose. But under some conditions, this tendency can take rather extreme forms. Especially noteworthy is the phenomenon of *deindividuation*. Festinger, Pepitone, and Newcomb (1952) coined this term to describe a mental state defined by total submergence in a group. A deindividuated person feels he or she does not stand out as a unique individual, and this feeling leads to a reduction of inner restraints that can result in impulsive acts or other behaviors that might otherwise be inhibited. Although these behaviors may be benign or even desirable (e.g., spontaneous expression of feelings, laughing and dancing at a boisterous party), researchers have mainly focused on the potential for antisocial behavior associated with deindividuation (Diener, 1980; Zimbardo, 1970). Soccer hooligans committing random acts of violence, mobs rioting and looting stores, and gangs terrorizing their enemies are disturbing manifestations of this potential.

Several preconditions for deindividuation have been identified (Zimbardo, 1970). Being part of a large, unstructured group, for example, increases one's anonymity and thus can reduce feelings of personal responsibility for one's actions. The same can be said for clothing that conceals one's identity, the cover of darkness, sensory overload, the use of drugs or alcohol, and collective action of a simple, repetitive (or rhythmic) nature (e.g., marching, clapping, dancing).

The anonymity associated with deindividuating conditions decreases self-awareness (Duval & Wicklund, 1972) and thus undermines the salience of personal standards for acceptable conduct (Diener, 1980). Lacking the usual self-regulatory mechanisms for enacting and inhibiting behavior, the person is highly susceptible to influence from the group and the context in which the group is acting. The nature of this influence, however, does not map onto either normative or informational influence in a straightforward manner. Thus, the person is not consciously modifying his or her behavior to court approval from others, nor is he or she gaining a great deal of insight into physical reality from fellow group members.

One likely process is *behavioral contagion* (Le Bon, 1895), the rapid spread of behavior in a group context. Contagion occurs through simple imitation of others' behavior or the adoption of others' emotional state, and thus is not particularly taxing on people's mental processes. A related possibility concerns *emergent norms* (Turner & Killian, 1957), such that people in unstructured group settings without clear group goals are highly susceptible to cues to higher-order meaning and guides to action (norms) that develop (emerge) in the situation.

As a concrete example, imagine walking down New Orleans' Bourbon Street at 2 a.m. during Mardi Gras. This situation is ripe for deindividuation—maybe even prototypical. You are part of a large, unstructured group consisting of unfamiliar people, it's dark and no one is paying attention to you anyway, music is coming from all angles to overwhelm your powers of sensory integration, and there may have been a couple of "Hurricane Specials" consumed by this time. On top of that, there is no plan dictating your movements and shifts in attention. At this point, if others in the throng spontaneously broke into a rhythmic chant or began throwing plastic beads at a passing float, you might be tempted to follow suit. This collective action provides meaning for your experience and functions as an emergent norm. The norm doesn't imply acceptance or rejection by others—you could keep on walking and no one would care—but it does provide a guide that allows you to engage in concerted action rather than mere movement.

Viewed in this way, it is easy to appreciate how a state of deindividuation can promote widely divergent action trajectories—moral versus immoral, prosocial versus antisocial, effusive versus sullen, and so on. In effect, the deindividuated person is behaving in accordance with simple moment-to-moment action guides that are devoid of higher-level meaning. As we saw in the chapter on self-concept (Chapter 5) and again in the chapter on social influence (Chapter 10), this mental state is a precondition for emergent understanding (Vallacher & Wegner, 1987), making the person highly susceptible to whatever goals and plans become salient as the situation evolves. Should the situation resolve itself as an occasion for social camaraderie, the person might be inclined to laugh and dance with everyone he or she encounters. But should the opportunity for personal gain at the expense of others suddenly arise, the same person could just as easily behave in a decidedly unfriendly, even aggressive manner toward those who provide the opportunity. Social influence in this context provides personal, if somewhat fleeting, coherence and direction for individuals' otherwise disassembled and unregulated actions.

These pictures illustrate how deindividuation in an unstructured group can lead to mob violence (photo 1), joyous celebration (photo 2), or peaceful social protest (photo 3).

1. Mob scene with violence

2. Large crowd having fun (Mardi Gras, New Orleans)

3. Large crowd engaged in peaceful social protest

Social Roles

Fortunately, people in groups do more than simply suspend their personal identities and develop a mob-like agenda. The conditions required for deindividuation are rare, existing primarily in groups that have convened for social reasons rather than to perform a task or work toward a goal. The pressure for uniformity still exists in task-oriented groups but it is offset by the pressure to get things done effectively and efficiently. For this to happen, the members of the group sometimes must specialize, with different members performing different activities. The shared expectations about how particular people are supposed to behave constitute *social roles*. Some group tasks are simple and require the pooled efforts of everyone doing essentially the same thing. Pushing a car out of a ditch or generating solutions to a puzzle, for example, are tasks that do not require much specialization. But group tasks can be more complex, requiring individuals to fill distinct roles. Consider the roles necessary to assemble a car. Some workers specialize in installing the engine, others attach doors, yet others put on the wheels, and so forth. In formal groups, the various roles are specified in advance and procedures are employed to assign members to these roles. This is clearly the case in an organization, where people are recruited to fulfill certain roles—secretary, computer technician, salesperson, CEO, and so forth.

When there are clearly defined social roles, group members tend to feel satisfied and the group performs effectively (Bettencourt & Sheldon, 2001). These individual and group consequences are certainly desirable. But adherence to social roles can justify (or even legitimatize) behavior that may appear questionable to outsiders and create regrets on the part of the group members themselves when they look back on what they did. When roles are embedded in a hierarchical structure, for example, people may not feel personally responsible for actions that are expected and demanded by those in roles associated with leadership and decision-making. Recall the Milgram (1974) studies, discussed in Chapter 10, in which people who were assigned the role of "teacher" in a study they thought involved the psychology of learning followed orders from a "legitimate authority" to administer painful electric shocks to a someone assigned the role of "learner."

Box 12.1   "Brainstorming"

There are natural inhibitions that might stop a person in a large group from expressing an idea, volunteering information, or suggesting a solution, particularly if the idea is unusual or out-of-the-box. But perhaps there are ways around this, so that people feel comfortable in expressing themselves, even in a large group. This reasoning underlies *brainstorming.* In groups employing this strategy, everyone is encouraged to express whatever he or she is thinking, without concern for how it sounds or whether it will be greeted with cheers or an awkward silence. Surely, brainstorming would loosen up the group members and get new ideas on the table, some of which may prove valuable in solving the problem at hand. With more people tossing out ideas, the likely of a particularly creative and effective solution is increased.

This sounds good. Indeed, when people hear about brainstorming, they become convinced that they personally would do better in such a context than they would if they worked by themselves. Intuition notwithstanding, the research on brainstorming is not particularly supportive. There is no solid evidence that brainstorming produces great ideas, decisions, or courses of action (Mullen, Johnson, & Salas, 1991; Paulus, Dzindolet, Poletes, & Camacho, 1993; Stroebe, Diehl, & Abakoumkin, 1992). The interaction and exchange of ideas may feel good and promote an illusion of creativity, but all that thinking outside of the box may amount to very little outside of the group setting.

Leadership

The people comprising a group rarely have equal power or influence. Even in small and informal groups—friends who get together to watch football on Saturday or members of a neighborhood book club—one person is likely to take the lead in deciding what to do and when to do it. In large and formal groups, the asymmetry in power is more evident and is typically built into the structure of social roles, usually with one person occupying the role of leader. A leader is someone who makes decisions and coordinates the activities of group members. Leaders differ on at least two dimensions: the manner in which they exert influence (leadership style) and the concerns they focus on as leaders (leadership roles).

Leadership Style

Leaders differ in their tendency to be heavy-handed versus egalitarian and laid-back (Lewin, Lippit, & White, 1939). At one extreme is the *authoritarian* leader, a person who tells subordinates what to do and does not welcome questioning of his or her authority. At the other extreme is the *laissez-faire* leader, a person who essentially allows group members do what they like and provides only general guidelines for task-oriented behavior. Between these extremes is the *democratic* leader, a person who attempts to bring about the maximal involvement of group members in deciding what to do and how to do it. The democratic leader does not necessarily differ from the authoritarian leader in his or her power, but he or she differs a great deal in the way this power is exercised. This style of leadership involves spreading responsibility rather than concentrating it, so as to prevent the development of a hierarchical structure.

Research comparing these leadership styles has favored the democratic approach (Kelley & Thibaut, 1954). Laissez-faire leaders tend to fare the worst. Groups "led" in this fashion accomplish very little and have little enthusiasm for what they are doing. Authoritarian groups are more productive, but tend to be either more aggressive or more apathetic than democratic groups. Group members act submissively toward the leader but aggressively toward one another—sometimes treating each other as scapegoats for the anger they really feel toward the leader. And although the work in these groups can be constructive, this quality decreases when the leader is absent. Democratic groups, in contrast, maintain their level of constructive work in the leader's absence, and they tend to have a greater sense of unity than do authoritarian groups.

But there are caveats concerning the relative benefits of democratic and authoritarian leadership (e.g., Singer & Goldman, 1954). Democratic leadership is preferred in the long run, but group behavior under this arrangement requires some learning. People prefer authoritarian leadership when they are emotionally insecure or are in an ambiguous, stressful, or critical social situation. It is interesting in this regard that proportionally more German Protestants than German Catholics adopted the ideology of the Nazi party in World War II (Peak, 1945). In the unstable social order of Germany after World War I, the Catholics could meet their security needs by submitting to the authoritative leadership of the Catholic Church. The Protestants did not have such authoritative leadership, so they presumably found solace in submission to Adolf Hitler, who mapped a clear course of action and left little to individual choice.

Leadership Roles

Leaders also vary in the issues they focus on in groups and in their talent for dealing with these issues. In his *contingency theory of leadership*, Fiedler (1978) distinguished between two such issues: accomplishing the group's task and managing relations among group members. He argued that these functions required different skill sets and are often manifest in two kinds of leaders: the *task-oriented leader*, who is focused getting the job done; and the *relationship-oriented leader*, for whom members' feelings and relationships are the primary concern.

Neither type of leader is always more effective than the other. The critical factor deciding who will function better is the amount of control the leader has over the group. In *high-control work situations*, the leader has great relations with subordinates, his or her position in the group is viewed by everyone as powerful, and the work that needs to be done is well-defined. The opposite holds in *low-control work situations*: the leader has poor relationships with subordinates and the task facing the group is not well-defined.

Here is where the contingency enters the picture (see Figure 12.6). Task-oriented leaders are most effective in situations that are either *very high or very low in control*. When control is very high, group members are content, things are running smoothly, and there is no need to worry about members' feelings and relationships. This frees the task-oriented leader to focus his or her energies on getting the job done. When control is very low, the task-oriented leader excels at taking charge, imposing order on the ill-defined or confusing work environment. Leaders who are relationship-oriented shine in *moderate-control work situations*, where things are going fairly smoothly but some attention needs to be given to the feelings of group members and their relationships with one another. The leader who can address these issues is able to keep the group on track and getting the job done. Fiedler's theory has received considerable support for diverse leadership roles, including business managers, college administrators, military commanders, and postmasters (Peters, Hartke, & Pohlmann, 1985; Schriesheim, Tepper, & Tetrault, 1994).

Individual Versus Group Performance

Some activities and tasks require the joint action of many people. Factories, juries, footfall teams, corporations, and parties do not make any sense at the individual level. But some actions could be performed individually but nonetheless often take place in a group setting. Are there advantages to being with other people when trying to accomplish something? Are you better off studying for an exam in private, for example, or is there an added benefit (apart from

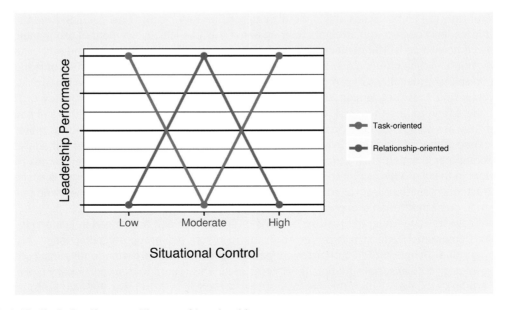

FIGURE 12.6 Fiedler's Contingency Theory of Leadership

fun and companionship) to studying in the company of fellow students? And when it comes to taking the exam, does it help or hurt to be surrounded by others enduring the same rite of passage? Do you do your best tennis (or chess, video gaming, running, aerobics, decision-making, etc.) when in the presence of others or in private? For that matter, does it make a difference whether you do something alone or in the context of other people?

There is support for all three answers—a group context can have no effect, an undermining effect, or a facilitating effect on an individual's performance. The factors associated with each effect are considered in turn below.

"Wisdom of Crowds"

A collection of individuals who gather for an event but have no other ties with one another would seem to be a recipe for pointless, if not foolhardy, behavior. Many scholars have lampooned the irrational responses of people making up spontaneous crowds. As noted earlier, such situations are a breeding ground for deindividuation and the impulsive behavior associated with this psychological state. A crowd can be exciting, even fun, but certainly not intelligent. Imagine the surprise of social scientists, then, when evidence began to surface that crowds are actually capable of highly intelligent action. More intelligent, in fact, than groups in which there is communication, information sharing, and influence among individuals. Indeed, disorganized crowds have even surpassed the intelligence of the very experts who derogated their abilities.

Consider the following scene. You are at a state fair and notice a contest to estimate the weight of a large steer (a castrated bull). A large crowd gathers to take part in the contest. Everyone can see the steer, but the contest is made more difficult by requiring people to estimate how much the animal would weigh after it is slaughtered and prepared for sale. People buy a ticket for a small price and write their estimates on the ticket. Some of the people who enter the contest are familiar with steers (e.g., butchers, cattle ranchers), but most know little about such matters and can only offer uninformed guesses. How accurate are these guesses likely to be?

Such an event was observed by Francis Galton, a 19th-century scientist whose ideas influenced psychology a great deal in succeeding decades. Galton did not have a particularly flattering opinion of people's intelligence and he felt that they became even dumber in groups. Expecting to find confirmation of his dour assessment of people and groups, he gathered the estimates the state fair crowd had made concerning the steer's weight. The correct answer was 1,198 pounds. To Galton's astonishment, the average of the 800 estimates was 1,197 pounds! (No one knows what Galton's own estimate was.) How could unintelligent, uninformed common folk operating in a herd generate such an accurate estimate?

In *The Wisdom of Crowds*, Surowiecki (2004) described the Galton experience and cataloged a variety of other instances in which the collective wisdom of large numbers of people exceeds that of experts. In predicting the outcome of a sporting event (e.g., the Super Bowl), for example, the final betting line—a direct reflection of the bets of many people—is consistently better than is the prediction made by a sport expert who is loaded with inside knowledge and relevant experience. The same pattern holds for anticipating what the stock market will do—expert stockbrokers cannot consistently pick winning stocks better than the market as a whole.

You may have witnessed this first-hand if you are one of the millions of people who watched the television show *Who Wants to Be a Millionaire?* The contestants on this game show could win large sums of money by giving correct answers to a series of multiple-choice questions on various topics (rarely social psychology, though—and never about the wisdom of crowds!). If the contestant was uncertain about the correct answer, he or she could call an expert—quite likely, his or her brightest or best informed friend or family member—or poll the audience for their response. When Surowiecki analyzed the success rate of these "lifelines," he found that experts provided the correct answer 65% of the time. This is quite good. But polling the studio audience—composed of people who aren't exactly hand-picked for their brains or knowledge—provided the correct answer a remarkable 91% of the time. So a crowd of ordinary people in a television studio show greater intelligence than do carefully chosen experts.

The "wisdom of crowds" phenomenon suggests that the larger the group, the more accurate the pooled response. But the crowds in this research hardly qualify as groups in a meaningful sense. True, they have a common focus of attention, but they lack the other defining features noted at the outset of this chapter: mutual influence, shared reality, and coordinated action. Essentially a crowd that behaves intelligently is a collection of people acting individually despite their spatial proximity. What happens when people influence each other, adopt a shared reality, and coordinate their ideas and actions? Are 10 heads still better than one?

Social Loafing

Sometimes the whole is less than the sum of its parts. This feature of group dynamics was first observed in an experimental setting by Max Ringelman in the 1920s. Using a gauge to measure effort exerted by tug-of-war participants, Ringelman found that the collective effort was always greater than that of any single participant, but less than the sum of all participants (Kravitz & Martin, 1986). If two people working alone could each pull 100 units, for example, their combined output was only 186—not the 200 one would expect if each pulled as hard as he or she could. Similarly, a three-person group did not produce 300 units, but only 255, and an eight-person group managed only 392 units—less than half the 800 possible.

Ringelman suggested that two mechanisms were responsible for this phenomenon. The first, *coordination loss*, reflects difficulties individuals have in combining their efforts. On a rope-pulling task, for example, people may not synchronize their respective pulls and pauses, and this can prevent each person from reaching his or her full potential. The second mechanism, referred to today as *social loafing* (Latané, 1981), refers to diminished effort by group members. People may simply not work as hard when they feel other people can pick up the load.

Latané, Williams, and Harkins (1979) attempted to replicate the Ringelman effect and to determine which of his proposed mechanisms accounted for it. In one study, participants were simply asked to shout or clap as loud or as hard as they could, while wearing blindfolds and headsets that played a stream of loud noise. When tested alone, subjects averaged a rousing 9.22 dynes/cm²—about as loud as a pneumatic drill or a teenager's stereo system. But in dyads, subjects performed at only 66% capacity, and in six-person groups, their performance dropped to 36% capacity. The results thus revealed an inverse relationship between the number of co-performers and the output each one generated.

To separate the impact of coordination loss and social loafing, Latané and his colleagues tested noise production in "pseudo-groups." Participants thought that either one other participant or five other participants were cheering with them, although they were actually cheering alone (the blindfolds and headsets came in handy here). Because there were no other group members, any drop in individual production could not be due to coordination loss, but instead would reflect social loafing. Results revealed that social loafing was indeed the operative mechanism. If participants thought they were cheering with one other person, they shouted at 82% of their capacity. Their productivity dropped to 74% if they thought five others were working with them.

The decrement in personal contribution with increasing group size has been documented on a variety of tasks, including maze performance, typing, swimming, vigilance exercises, creativity problems, job-selection decisions, and even brainstorming (Weldon & Mustari, 1988; Forsyth, 1990). Social loafing does not always occur, though. Group members loaf less when they are working on interesting or challenging tasks (Brickner, Harkins, & Ostrom, 1986). Loafing is also minimized when each member's contribution to a group project can be clearly identified, presumably because identification creates the potential for evaluation by other group members (Harkins & Jackson, 1985; Jackson & Latané, 1981; Williams, Harkins, & Latané, 1981).

Social loafing is also partly attributable to the diffusion of responsibility that takes place in groups and crowds. Bystanders to emergency situations feel less compelled to intervene if there are other potential helpers (Darley & Latané, 1968), for example, and restaurant patrons leave pitiful tips if there are many people in the dinner party (Latané & Darley, 1970). Beyond feeling that someone else will make up the difference, group members feel they can get away with not helping because the blame is shared by everyone in the group.

The tendency to loaf is greater among men than among women (Karau & Williams, 1993). Presumably, this is because women on average have greater *relational interdependence*, which is the tendency to focus on and care about interpersonal relationships, and this orientation inhibits the temptation to exploit others by letting them do the lion's share of the work (Eagly, 1987; Wood, 1987). People in Western cultures (e.g., the United States, western Europe) have a stronger tendency to loaf than do people in Asian cultures (Karau & Williams, 1993). This is consistent with the idea, described in Chapter 5 ("Self-Concept"), that Asians are more likely to have an *interdependent view of the self*. Defining oneself in terms of one's social relations reduces the temptation to sit back and let others do the heavy lifting.

The research on social loafing has largely examined groups that do not have a role structure in which people specialize on different parts of the task. Neither simultaneous shouting nor tug-of-war, after all, captures the essence of groups that build machines or solve human relations problems. Many group goals are defined in terms of distinct sub-acts that must be accomplished by different group members. For such activities, the quality of the group's performance depends on how well members' respective contributions are synchronized in time. Assembling a car on a production line requires such role differentiation, as does maintaining a household, moving heavy pieces of furniture, or implementing plans to manually recount votes in a close presidential election. Decrements of group performance in such instances may reflect coordination loss more than a decrease in the intensity of individual effort.

Social Facilitation

People's motivation in a group setting does not always center on how to get away with doing the least. Quite the contrary, people often enter social contexts with an intense desire to put forth the best effort they can, outperforming others and impressing observers in the process. When you take a midterm exam, you probably aren't thinking, "relax, someone else in the class will figure out the answers." Indeed, the motivation to perform well is probably enhanced by the prospect of competing with other people and being evaluated by those witnessing your performance. Does this enhanced motivation translate into better performance? Do you perform better on the midterm if you take it in a crowded classroom full of competitors (i.e., fellow classmates)? Is your learning curve on a new activity (e.g., tennis, chess) faster when other people are watching you step on the court or take a seat at the table?

The intuitive answer is yes, anything that enhances the motivation to do well will facilitate the quality of one's performance. Early research on this topic validated this intuition. As noted in Chapter 1, the first experiment in social psychology, conducted over a century ago, showed that a social context improves individual performance. In observing bicycle races, Triplett noted that cyclists who raced alone against the clock were usually slower than were those who raced against other cyclists. To test the generality of such *social facilitation*, Triplett (1898) asked research participants to wind fishing reels as fast as they could. Those who did this task alone were slower than those who did it when competing with someone else.

Subsequent research showed that competition was not the sole key to the social facilitation effect. Individuals seemed to perform better when other people were simply present, observing them performing the task (Cottrell, Wack, Sekerak, & Rittle, 1968; Seta & Seta, 1995). This was said to reflect *evaluation apprehension*: people increase their effort when others are present because they want the others to admire their performance and evaluate them positively. But things are not quite so simple and straightforward. In fact, social facilitation turns out to be a bit of a misnomer—sometimes the presence of others can *impair* performance. Even if one is competing against the other people and highly motivated to do well, the quality of performance can take a big hit under some conditions. So what are these conditions?

Insight into this issue was provided by Robert Zajonc (1965). He noted that the presence of other people tends to heighten an individual's physiological arousal. The effect may be subtle, but your heart beats a bit faster when in the company of other people, particularly if you are the center of attention or if the context is competitive in nature. Zajonc then pointed out that arousal does not simply provide an energy boost and enhance performance on any type of task. Rather, arousal promotes an organism's *dominant response tendencies*, while undermining response patterns that are less central or frequently enacted.

To get a feel for this idea, think about how your behavior differs when you are relaxed versus somewhat agitated or moderately excited. In the relaxed state, you can pick and choose how to act, perhaps even behaving in ways that are unusual for you. You may try out new ways of interacting with people ("maybe I'll try listening for a change") or vary the way you perform a physical act ("let's see if I can make a basket with my eyes closed"). Such flexibility is lost when you are tense or even aroused in a positive way. The heightened arousal gets in the way of deliberation, focusing one instead on habits and well-rehearsed ways of behaving that are enacted without considering less familiar actions. You may have recently been shown how to hit a tennis ball correctly, for example, but in the heat of a match when your adrenaline is peaking, you are likely to revert to your old way of stroking the ball despite its ineffectiveness.

The implications for the quality of task performance are straightforward (Cottrell, 1972; Zajonc, 1965). It is easy to think carefully and creatively when one is motivated but not supercharged. Arousal beyond a certain point can interfere with the efficiency of executive processes needed to choose among action alternatives. Now, if you are doing something that is familiar or personally easy (because you have mastered the action), the presence of others should facilitate your performance—the dominant response is likely to be the correct response. Deliberation of alternative courses of action is unlikely, but also unnecessary.

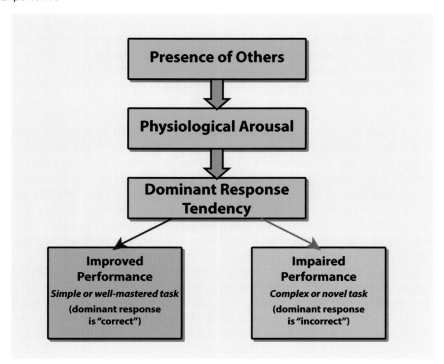

FIGURE 12.7 When Does the Presence of Other People Enhance or Impair Performance?

But what if the action is novel or not that well learned? In this case, the arousal brought about by other people should interfere with–not facilitate–your performance because your dominant response is likely to be incorrect or ineffective. Rather than trying out different alternative strategies, you are likely to persist in a rigid sequence of acts without switching gears, even if this behavior produces nothing but poor results. Attempting to solve a difficult seven-letter anagram or taking a standardized test requires deliberation and flexibility, but the required executive processes may be in short supply if you undertake these actions in a room full of other people, each trying to outperform one another and make a favorable impression on observers. Figure 12.7 depicts this connection between the presences of others and task performance.

The relationship between the presence of others and performance on difficult versus easy acts can also be understood in terms of the "optimality" hypothesis of action identification theory (Vallacher & Wegner, 1987), described in Chapter 6. The presence of other people, particularly if they are looking at and evaluating you, can magnify the high-level significance and implications of what you are doing. You are not simply performing an action, you are trying to impress the observers (or not embarrass yourself). If the action does not require attention to lower-level details–which is the case when an action is familiar or easy–a focus on the action's higher-level meanings can facilitate performance. But if the action is best enacted by focusing on its details–because the action is unfamiliar, complex, or novel–the focus on higher-level identities brought on by the presence of (or evaluation by) other people can prevent one from focusing your attention where you should–on the task's lower-level features.

Social Networks

How Are People in a Society Connected to Each Other?

When the group consists of two people–a dyad–the structure of communication is mind-numbingly simple and obvious. Even if one person does most of the talking, the structure of communication is complete and bidirectional, with both people sending messages back and forth. The situation is much the same in a three-person group or even in groups consisting of several people. Everyone talks to everyone else, although some people usually have a lot more to say than others. But as the size of the group increases, the communication structure becomes considerably less egalitarian. Think of your interactions at a large party, for example. Even if you spend several hours in a very social mode, it's unlikely you will have talked to everyone in attendance by the end of the evening. And you might note that one or two people seem to be the "social stars," commanding most of the attention.

Selective and unequal communication characterizes groups of all kinds. Ask any college professor who has taught a large enrollment course. Despite attempts on his or her part to facilitate class participation, the percentage of students asking questions or offering opinions decreases as the size of the class increases. In a seminar with half a dozen students, everyone talks; in a lecture hall filled with 300 students, less than 10% take part in class discussion.

What is astonishing about the structure of communication in groups is how universal the principles are. The connections among people in a classroom or at a party follow the same rules as do the connections that characterize an entire society! Because of this universality, many scientists have changed their focus from group dynamics to the dynamics of *social networks* (Barabasi, 2001; Christakis & Fowler, 2009; Westaby, Pfaff, & Redding, 2014). In this approach, communication among people who are near each other physically (as in a classroom or at a party) is really a special case of the flow of communication that characterizes people regardless of their physical proximity. Presumably, the structure of networks crosses the oceans and spans the globe. A social network, in this sense, is a group without physical boundaries.

Network Properties

To get a feel for social networks, try the following exercise. In the middle of a blank piece of paper, draw a small circle and place your initials in it. Now think about your friends and other people that you talk to most often. Draw a small circle for each of these people, with the circles arranged in a circular pattern around your circle. Position the circles so that people who know each other are close to each other. In each circle, write the initials of the person that the circle represents. Use a line to connect each circle to your circle. Finally, use lines to connect people (circles) who know each other.

The picture you have created represents your personal social network. It probably looks very similar to Figure 12.8. Each circle represents a *node* in the network and each line represents a *tie* or a *connection* between two nodes. In your picture, the nodes represent individuals and the ties represent friendship ties. But individuals can be linked in other ways, such as kinship, work relations, or frequency of contact. The nodes, too, can represent entities other than individuals. Depending on the context, the nodes might represent organizations, or even nations, with the ties representing financial connections, perhaps, or political alliances.

Different configurations in a social network convey distinct information about the relation between the nodes (see Figure 12.9). A *clique* is a subset of the network in which the individuals are connected with one another. It can be

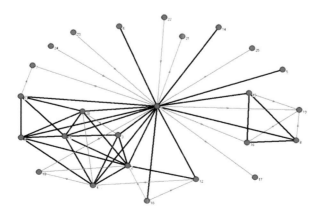

FIGURE 12.8 A Typical Personal Network (Friendship)

looked upon as a group within the larger network of relations. Because of frequent and mutual communication with a clique, the individuals often have the same information and adopt the same opinions. A *bridge* connects different parts of a network. An individual who occupies a bride position is critical to the maintenance of relations within a network. This person knows what the nodes on either side of the bridge knows, and can control what information is passed between the two sets of nodes. Look back to the personal network you created. Do some of your friends or acquaintance exist in cliques? Do others function as bridges between different cliques? What about you? Are you more like a member of a clique or do you function as a bridge in your social relations?

In most social situations, people are introduced to others by people they already know. Those people who already know the most individuals (i.e., those people representing a node with many connections) are introduced most often and so acquire new connections at the fastest rate. Indeed, their rate of meeting new people gets progressively faster in an accelerating fashion. In contrast, the number of new connections of those who have few connections grows very slowly, because only a small number of people can introduce them to others.

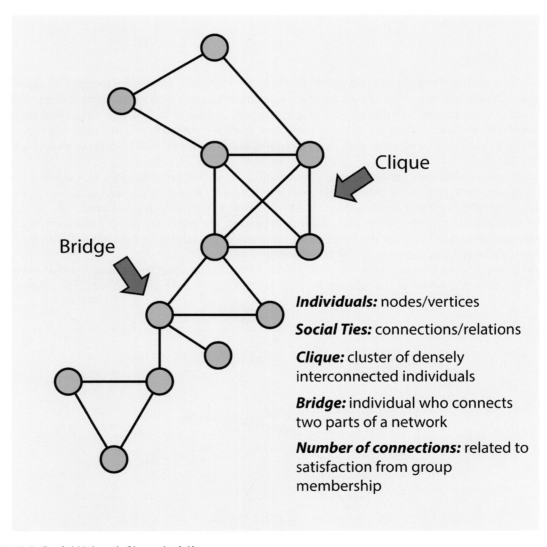

FIGURE 12.9 Social Network Characteristics

The differences between highly connected individuals and those with a small number of connections increases over time. This process results in many nodes with a relatively small number of connections and a few nodes with a very high number of connections. The highly connected nodes are referred to as *super-hubs*. This unequal distribution of connections is called *scale-free* because the distribution looks the same regardless of the size of the network (see Figure 12.10). Very small and very large networks have essentially the same distribution of super-hubs and nodes with relatively few connections. Scale-free networks characterize all types of social relations—from friendship ties to corporate alliances.

Small-World Phenomenon

The nature of social networks and their independence of group size have an intriguing and surprising implication concerning connections in the modern world. Conventional wisdom has it that each of us is cut off from other people, with little connection to people in our own neighborhood, let alone to people in other neighborhoods—or other countries. It turns out that quite the opposite is true in today's world. In fact, you are probably no more than five or six links away from someone in the farthest region of the world—a bus driver in Stockholm, a goat herder in Kenya, or a lumberjack in Manitoba. You may not know them, or ever come face to face with them, but you are linked to them nonetheless by virtue of network dynamics. The remarkable short chain of acquaintances required to connect anyone to anyone else in the world is referred to as the small world phenomenon.

The small world phenomenon was first demonstrated in 1967 by Stanley Milgram. In this novel experiment, people in Nebraska were individually asked to reach a target person in Boston by passing a message along a chain of acquaintances. The person has no clue who the target person is, but he or she might know someone in that area—New York City, perhaps. The New York contact, in turn, knows several people in Boston and passes the message onto one of them. This person then passes the message onto another link in the chain that is closer yet to the target person, and so on, until the target person is finally reached by an acquaintance. Milgram (1967) found that the average length of successful chains was about five intermediates—indicating six separation steps. Hence, the phrase "six degrees of separation" was born.

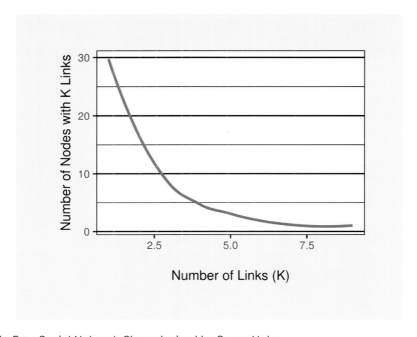

FIGURE 12.10 Scale-Free Social Network Characterized by Super Hubs

Research on the small world phenomenon has been updated to take into account internet-based communication technology, which has supplemented, or even supplanted, the telephone and postal systems available when Milgram ran his original study. Duncan Watts (2003), for example, has shown that between five and seven degrees of separation are sufficient for connecting any two people through e-mail.

Social Capital

A person's power in a group is often described in terms of personal characteristics, such as his or her intelligence, physical prowess, material resources, emotional stability, or charisma. These attributes are certainly important (Albright & Forziati, 1995; Chemers, Watson, & May, 2000; Hogan, Curphy, & Hogan, 1994; Judge, Bono, Ilies, & Gerhardt, 2002), but they do not mean a thing until they are translated into network dynamics. If a charismatic or wealthy person achieves social power and exercises influence over others, it is because these qualities have enabled him or her to occupy a special place in a network with useful social connections.

The value of network connections is easy to appreciate. Imagine two male college students—John and Peter—each of whom wants to buy a used car at an affordable price. John buys a 5-year-old Jeep advertised in the newspaper for $8,000. Peter, however, tells his friends that he is looking for a car. One of the friends has a friend who just bought a new car and is eager to get rid of his old car—a 5-year-old Jeep—and responds to the inquiry by asking $5,000. Both John and Peter acquire a car, but Peter saved $3,000 by using his social connections.

The potential value associated with social connections is referred to as social capital. Individuals who have high social capital are in a position to achieve many goals. They can better obtain needed information, they can reach out to and influence other people, and they can receive help and support from others. They also tend to be more satisfied with their life because their social needs are more fully satisfied. Of the various network properties, social capital is best reflected in the number of connections a person has. This factor can be approximated by noting how many telephone numbers or e-mail addresses a person has in his or her directories or contact lists. Not all connections carry the same weight in determining social capital, however. Connections to people in power—upward connections—increase social capital more than do connections to those low in power.

Social capital also depends on a person's position in a social network. People in a clique might seem to have power by virtue of being surrounded by like-minded others who can provide social support when their ideas and actions are challenged. But because of the closed nature of a clique, each member knows what the other members know, so the information is redundant and less likely to be updated than is information in interlinked parts of the network. A less obvious but more important position is the bridge. The person occupying a bridge position may not be the center of attention, but he or she has what Mark Granovetter (1973) calls the *strength of weak ties*. By serving as a link between different parts of a network, the bridge has access to different sources of information and can make this information available to the parts—including different cliques—that do not communicate directly and thus would not otherwise be privy to the information. The person who controls information in a social system is in a position to exercise significant influence over other people.

A group or network as a whole can have varying degrees of social capital. People in high capital networks have many acquaintances and friends, and these ties are associated with trust and cooperation. The social norms in such networks tend to be strong, moreover, ensuring that people will abide by rules of honesty, reciprocity, and fair play. In networks with low capital, people do not have many friends or acquaintances. As a result, they tend to be lonely and distrustful of others. Lacking social contacts and interpersonal trust, it is difficult for people in such networks to organize common projects and achieve shared goals.

Networks Versus Groups in Modern Society

In our ancestral environment—indeed, throughout history until a few decades ago—our primary social contacts lived right next to us, so there was no way of escaping the attitudes, beliefs, and lifestyles of those around us. We still have neighbors, but it is easy to maintain psychological distance from them and ignore or disregard what they think and believe. Does this mean that the principles of group dynamics are a relic of a bygone era? If we are inherently a pack animal, does the decreased salience of physical groups change our psychology in fundamental ways? Are people in modern society cut adrift from the pressures of conformity, free to follow their own agendas and develop their own attitudes and beliefs?

Well, not really. The vacuum left by the loss of physical groups has been filled by an increase in social net-works—links to others who may be in a different town or country but who nonetheless shape and constrain our thoughts and actions every bit as much as local groups did in the past. We may avoid our next-door neighbors but we are highly attentive to people we interact with by means of e-mail and networking sites such as Twitter, Facebook, and Instagram. The rise in social networking has consequences for social life that are not yet fully investigated, let alone understood. But we can sketch out some implications, some of which are manifest to some degree already.

Clustering and Polarization

We noted earlier that people in groups tend to develop similar thoughts and feelings, producing clusters of like-minded individuals. Something similar happens in a social network, even if people are physically distant from one another (Christakis & Fowler, 2009). Two people may live 20 feet apart in a small town or neighborhood, yet have entirely different social networks and thus very different beliefs and lifestyles. Both feel like their attitudes reflect local majorities, though, because they are in contact with dozens, maybe thousands, of others who share their views and provide support against challenges to the validity of their ideas.

Even happiness seems to cluster in social networks. Fowler and Christakis (2008) identified clusters of happy and unhappy people within the networks they examined, with a reach of three degrees of separation in these clusters. A person's happiness or unhappiness, in other words, was associated with the level of happiness of their friends' friends' friends. Similar clustering tendencies were also observed for obesity (Fowler & Christakis, 2007). The social support and behavioral contagion that produces like-minded people in groups and networks apparently produces like-bodied people as well.

If anything, the emergence of clusters may be enhanced in social networks. In a group, there is bound to be someone with a dissenting view, and this minority view can change the majority thinking. But in social networks, if we hear something we don't like, we can simply cut the tie. People, in other words, can self-select themselves into virtual communities of like-minded others, and this self-selection process can be continually updated to ensure survival of a point of view. Without exposure to opposing ideas, the clusters of like-minded people can drift further apart, undermining the center of gravity that operates in physical groups to maintain a shared reality (Vallacher, 2015). As a result, virtually any belief can take root in a society. Think of all the conspiracy theories that abound today. From the assassination of President John F. Kennedy to the birth status of President Barack Obama, one can find support for any idea that would not persist if information was exchanged between, not sim-ply within, clusters.

Social networks also amplify the tendency toward polarization. On the internet, some ideas or stories go "viral," sweeping across networks in an astonishingly quick and effective manner. It is one thing for panic to occur in a crowded theater, with dozens of people suddenly fearing a roof collapse or fire; it is quite another for a frightening but unsubstantiated rumor or a piece of malicious misinformation generated on Twitter to ripple through the entire society.

The Future of Social Relations

Life in the modern world is a bundle of contradictions. We are connected to everyone on the planet by about six links, yet we may not know who lives next door or down the block. We are aware of vastly different lifestyles and values, yet we are better able than ever to selectively attend only to viewpoints with which we already agree. We spend less time in physical groups than did our ancestors—or our parents, for that matter—yet our social needs seem to be sufficiently met to keep us happy for the most part.

There is no turning back the clock. We live in a world of networks and this fact of social life is changing the way in which we interact and undermining the importance of spatial proximity. But then again, maybe not—or at least, not entirely. Despite the availability of electronic communication that enables networks around the world to be established, it is unlikely that networks will ever defuse the desire, honed by thousands of years of evolution, to meet face-to-face and, and as a result, form deep alliances—and antagonisms. As a species, we are experiencing a very interesting set of selection pressures that may pose problems as we accelerate into new technological and social landscapes, each with its own promises and perils.

SUMMING UP AND LOOKING AHEAD

- **Assembling a large number of people is not sufficient to create a group. But providing a bunch of unacquainted individuals the slightest sense of shared reality or social identity can transform them into a viable group that can take precedence over the decision-making and choices of the individuals. People have powerful social needs rooted in our evolutionary background, and are primed to congregate with others, develop a common focus of attention, and coordinate their behavior to achieve goals that are sometimes at the expense of their individual goals and that maintain social order.**

- **Group formation builds on people's natural and largely unconscious tendency to mimic one another's mental states and behaviors in social interaction. The local bidirectional influences among people can ripple through the larger group, promoting the emergence of a "group mind."**

- **This process is enhanced by personal concerns about "fitting in" and being liked (normative influence) and achieving a coherent view of something that is otherwise ambiguous (informational influence). The result is often large-scale synchronization of perceptions, thoughts, interpretations, and action tendencies, even in groups consisting of total strangers. This is certainly preferable to large-scale conflict, with everyone fighting to make his or her particular point of view the dominant one. But the press for uniformity in groups can promote an inaccurate view of reality (conformity), bad decisions (groupthink), and judgments that are considerably more extreme than that of each individual in the group (polarization).**

- **For some activities—such as having fun, engaging in mob violence, or showing support for a cause—interpersonal synchronization can be effective. But for more complex tasks, simple uniformity in thought and behavior can get in the way of getting the job done. People in task-oriented groups develop a role structure that promotes specialization for different features of the task. Leadership is also critical, but this special role can be enacted in different ways (laissez-faire, authoritarian, democratic) and focus on different concerns (task vs. social relations). Democratic leaders are generally the most effective; whether a task or a social focus is most effective depends on the clarity of the task and the degree of harmony in the group.**

- **Whether the group facilitates or impairs individual performance depends on the structure of the task, the degree to which the person feels accountable for his or her efforts, and the personal difficulty of the task. Heightened motivation to do well translates into effective behavior, but only if the task is relatively easy. If it is personally difficult, heightened motivation can impair rather than facilitate performance in a social context, particularly if the person is concerned with how he or she is evaluated or how well he or she performs relative to others. Such concerns get in the way of the task from novel vantage points and they also keep the individual's attention focused on the outcomes of the task rather than on the details necessary to perform the task.**

- **Because of electronic communication (the internet, e-mail, networking sites, search engines), many of the functions of groups (information exchange, opinion formation, social bonding) are increasingly achieved through networks that can form ties across the ocean while leaving your next-door neighbor out of the loop. Networks can develop in many different realms (friendship, mutual interests, politics, business, etc.) and they can vary in size from a handful of people to a sizable portion of the planet. Yet, some basic properties are common to all these variations. The separation of opinions, interests, and lifestyles into distinct clusters that is central to group dynamics may be amplified by our increasing reliance on social networks.**

   The basic principles established in this chapter have important implications for other aspects of collective experience, including the stereotyping and discrimination that often characterizes relations between groups (Chapter 13) and the dilemmas of social life posed by the tension between the interests of the individual and the interests of the society in which he or she lives (Chapter 14). Having set the stage, we are now ready to examine each of these topics in some detail.

Key Terms

Social influence
Interdependence
Shared reality
Behavioral coordination
Role structure
Need to belong
Social exchange
Justice in groups
Ultimatum Game
Social identity
Ingroup favoritism
Minimal groups
Group mind
Coherence
Conformity
Autokinetic effect
Cognitive clarity
Normative influence
Rejection of deviates

Ostracism
Informational influence
Groupthink
Group polarization
Risky shift
Cautious shift
Social comparison theory
Persuasive arguments theory
Emergence
Clustering
Minority influence
Deindividuation
Behavioral contagion
Emergent norms
Social roles
Brainstorming
Authoritarian leadership
Democratic leadership
Laissez-faire leadership

Contingency theory of leadership
Task-oriented leader
Social-emotional leader
Wisdom of crowds
Social loafing
Coordination loss
Diffusion of responsibility
Social facilitation
Evaluation apprehension
Dominant response
Non-optimal level of thinking
Social networks
Scale-free network
Small world phenomenon
Six degrees of separation
Social capital
Networks versus groups

13 Prejudice, Stereotypes, and Discrimination

The world is full of nasty thoughts and horrendous deeds directed by people toward others who are different in some way. So much so, that it warrants special attention in a text like this. As noted in Chapter 1, the concern with antagonistic attitudes and relations between groups was a prime mover as social psychology emerged as a major concentration in the social sciences after World War II. But although demeaning thoughts and hostile actions stand apart from the thoughts and actions that most of us have on a daily basis, they are not an aberration of normal mental processes. The more psychologists learn about this dark side of mind and action, the more they recognize that it reflects principles underlying mundane processes. Thus, the points conveyed in earlier chapters provide the foundation for the troubling processes at work when people in one group derogate people in another group and treat them unfairly.

CHAPTER OVERVIEW

What Are You Going to Learn?

- **Why do groups so easily come to dislike each other?** People develop interpersonal preferences, valuing some individuals over others. These preferences have many sources, from physical appearance to similarity in worldviews. What additional factors shape how people in different groups think and feel about one another? What causes people to go beyond negative thoughts and feelings to treat members of different groups in a discriminatory fashion? When do such actions progress to the level of violence and denial of basic human rights?

- **How do groups maintain negative thoughts and feelings about each other?** Applying a blanket characterization and evaluation to everyone in a group makes little sense, particularly since people tend to actively avoid contact with the individuals in the targeted group. Yet even when there is evidence that contradicts a stereotype, people manage to hang on to their preconceived thoughts and feelings. What factors enable people to maintain views for which there is slim or contradictory evidence? Overt prejudice is not valued in contemporary society. Does this mean that stereotypes are becoming a thing of the past? Or has its expression simply become more subtle and covert? How can hidden stereotypes and prejudice be exposed?

- **How can prejudicial attitudes and antagonism be minimized or corrected?** The seeming inevitability of stereotypical thinking and prejudicial feelings paints a grim picture of humanity, particularly since we live in an increasingly interconnected world in which people from very different backgrounds are destined to come into contact. Does this mean we are helpless in overcoming the human tendency to view difference as deviance? What features of human psychology can be brought to bear to overcome broad generalizations, negative feelings, and discriminatory behavior in the relations between people from different groups?

In-Group and Out-Group Dynamics

How and Why Do People Judge Members of Other Groups Negatively?

It makes sense that people form impressions of the individuals they encounter, observe, or hear about. These impressions can be misguided, are biased in various ways and resistant to updating, and are almost always judgmental, as we saw in Chapter 7 ("Social Judgment"). But at least the thoughts and feelings we have about an individual are based on *something*—his or her physical appearance, actions, or reputation. One would think that people would be reluctant to form impressions of individuals about whom they have no information whatsoever—let alone, to make highly evaluative judgments of such individuals. But people do just that. They routinely attribute characteristics to, and develop firmly held judgments of individuals they have not met—and are unlikely to encounter—if these individuals fit into a familiar category of humanity.

The Interplay of Prejudice, Stereotyping, and Discrimination

As a first step in understanding this aspect of human experience, it is important to identify three ways in which it is manifest. *Prejudice* is a negative attitude or generalized negative feeling toward a distinguishable group of people and all the members of the group. A *stereotype* is a belief that the members of a group share certain physical, mental, and behavioral characteristics. *Discrimination* is unjustified negative or harmful behavior toward people based on their membership in a group. Taken together, these three concepts capture people's *emotions, thoughts*, and *actions* with respect to a group and its members.

Just as thoughts are more complex than feelings, a stereotype is more complex than prejudice—the former may consist of many distinct beliefs (e.g., regarding intelligence, moral character, appearance, physical abilities), whereas the latter is a global state characterized by negativity. Stereotypes, moreover, vary a great deal across different groups (e.g., African Americans, homosexuals, Muslims, CEOs, athletes), whereas prejudice represents much the same emotional response to different groups (e.g., African Americans and CEOs may both elicit negative feelings in some people). And just as thoughts and feelings are not always expressed in action—a point emphasized in Chapter 3 ("Beliefs, Attitudes, and Values")—stereotypes and prejudice do not invariably lead to discrimination.

In practice, though, it is hard to separate stereotypes, prejudice, and discrimination—just as it is difficult to understand thoughts, emotions, or actions without appreciating how they influence one another. Prejudice and stereotypes typically go hand in hand, with causality working in both directions. If a person has a negative affective response to a group (prejudice), he or she is likely to develop and maintain specific beliefs about the characteristics of members of that group (a stereotype). Conversely, the person may have beliefs about group members' characteristics (stereotype) and develop an emotional reaction (prejudice) that integrates these beliefs into a global assessment. Reciprocal influence also characterizes the relationship between stereotypes and prejudice on one hand and discrimination on the other. A person's derogatory beliefs and negative feelings can promote unfair behavior toward someone, but mean-spirited behavior could bolster, or even create, beliefs and feelings that justify the behavior. Figure 13.1 depicts the feedback among stereotypes, prejudice, and discrimination.

Social Identity

As we saw in Chapter 5 ("Self-Concept"), people are keenly sensitive to their individuality and identify themselves in terms of their personal traits, goals, values, social skills, and physical characteristics. But people are a highly social species with a strong tendency to coordinate their thoughts, feelings, and actions with those of others. In doing

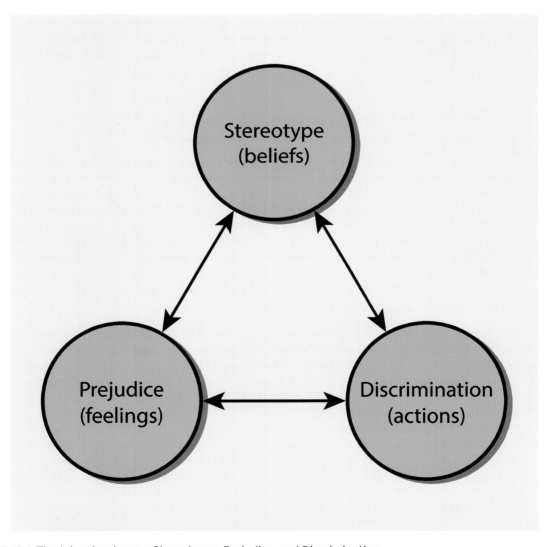

FIGURE 13.1 The Interplay Among Stereotypes, Prejudice, and Discrimination

so, they form a *social identity* that supplements—and constrains—their individual identity. This commitment is very strong—strong enough, in fact, that people will even sacrifice their lives to defend their group and the social identity it represents.

People rarely, if ever, have a single social identity (Brewer & Gardner, 1996; Roccas & Brewer, 2002). Think about yourself for a minute. You are a member of a family. You are a resident of a city and a citizen of a country. You are a member of an ethnic or a racial group. You are a college student, and within that category you probably have a major or at least a set of academic interests. You may be a member of a sports team, a fraternity or a sorority, or a friendship group that gets together for fun. For that matter, you are a member of one gender or the other, and think about yourself at least partly in terms of that basic category.

If people have multiple social identities, what determines which identity is likely to be most salient? Sometimes the answer is obvious. If you're having Thanksgiving dinner with your parents and siblings, you're probably thinking more about your identity as a family member than as a student (unless, of course, you've had your share of the proceedings and are fantasizing yourself back at school). But there is more to it than simply being around those who share the identity. Henry Tajfel (1982), a leading figure in theory and research regarding such matters, argued that people embrace those identities most strongly that enhance their self-esteem.

An interesting example of this is a phenomenon known as *basking in reflected glory* (BIRG). When the group with which you identify experiences a success, you get a self-esteem boost and identify more strongly than ever with the group—even if you had nothing whatever to do with the success. BIRG is on full display when your college's football or basketball team plays a rival team. Do you go to the stadium or arena simply hoping that the best team wins, or not caring who wins as long as the game is well played and exciting? That might be rational, but it certainly does not capture how games are normally seen. Assuming you identify with the team—they represent your college, after all—you hope they win and are willing to overlook or rationalize lucky breaks or bad calls that work in your team's favor.

Against this backdrop, the strength of your identification with the team—and your self-esteem—is affected by the game's outcome. If the team wins, you feel great and see yourself as one of them; if the team loses, your self-esteem takes a hit and you create some space between yourself and the team. Robert Cialdini and his colleagues (1976) provided interesting evidence of this at Arizona State University. After a football game, students were contacted by phone and asked about the game. If ASU won, the students typically said, *"we* won!" But if the team lost, the more common response was *"they* lost." Depending on the game's outcome, in other words, students' identification with the team was enhanced ("we") or diminished ("they"). Further evidence was provided by the way students dressed on the following Monday. If the team was victorious, students proudly displayed their ASU identification by wearing ASU T-shirts and sweatshirts; if the team lost, they looked elsewhere in their closets.

In-Group and Out-Group Evaluation

Identifying with a football team is harmless, even admirable in showing school spirit. But delighting in the victory of one's group over another group can have consequences that are not so harmless. It shapes how people perceive members of their own group and the members of the other group. And under some conditions, these views of the in-group and the out-group can find expression in behavior that does not exactly reflect the better angels of our nature.

In-Group Favoritism and Out-Group Derogation

Individuals in a group must get along and coordinate their actions to achieve common goals and avoid common threats, so having positive feelings toward members of an in-group is highly adaptive. In principle, this tendency might not have implications for feelings about members of groups with which one does not identify. One could imagine a world in which we loved everyone in our inner circle but felt warmly toward those who were not included. It doesn't seem to work that way. There is often a zero-sum relationship between in-group favoritism and out-group derogation: the more connected people feel with their in-group, the greater the antagonism they feel toward out-groups.

The readiness to distinguish between one's own group and other groups is quite remarkable. And the effects of making such distinctions on how people think and behave are far-reaching. Even if you are provided a fleeting and seemingly arbitrary identity, your thoughts and actions tend to fall in line, shaping the way you respond to events and other people. The ease with which people develop in-group versus out-group distinction has been demonstrated in the *minimal group paradigm*, developed by Henry Tajfel (Tajfel & Billig, 1974), in which groups of strangers are formed on stunningly arbitrary bases. Tajfel (1982), for example, asked college students to express their opinions about paintings by artists they probably knew nothing about—Klee and Kandinsky—and then assigned them to a group based on their on-the-spot preferences.

Once the students become members of either the Klee or Kandinsky group, they had no interaction with one another. Yet they were asked to indicate how much they liked the members of their group and the members of the other group. These are hardly informed judgments, yet the students indicated a great deal of liking for those in their own group, but not so much for those in the other group. They also indicated that members of their own group were likely to have pleasant personalities; again, not so much for members of the other group.

Even more stunning was how the students responded when they were asked to allocate money to members of their group and to those in the other group. They did more than simply give more money to their own group—they actually took a hit if that was necessary to make sure their group received a bigger share. For example, the participants were willing to give themselves only $2 if that meant giving those in the other group $1, but they were unwilling to give themselves $3 if that meant those in the other group would receive $4 (Brewer, 1979; Hogg & Abrams, 1988; Mullen, Brown, & Smith, 1992). Apparently maximizing their personal gain took a back seat to ensuring that their group did better than the other group.

Recall from Chapter 7 that there are two major dimensions of interpersonal evaluation: *warmth* and *competence*. Because they are separate dimensions, one can envision people who are good (or bad) on one dimension, but bad (or good) on the other dimension. In the context of in-group and out-group evaluation, however, these dimensions tend to lose their independence (Judd et al., 2005). In judging members of one's in-group, the dimensions are often positively correlated—a person who is judged as competent, for example, may be assumed to be warm as well. But in judging a member of an out-group, the dimensions sometimes are negatively correlated. This tendency is observed when the out-group person appears positive on one of the dimensions. To maintain their negative evaluation, people compensate the positive judgment by emphasizing the person's poor standing on the other dimension. So if he or she appears competent at some occupation or get noticed for a particular talent, people are inclined to maintain an overall negative evaluation by seeing him or her as especially cold, selfish, or immoral. By minimizing the out-group member's warmth, people can maintain their overall negative evaluation of the person.

Box 13.1   Do Hormones Bias People Toward Their In-Group and Against the Out-Group?

Conformity to the opinions of one's in-group is a basic feature of social life. The universality of this tendency suggests that it may have a biological basis. A likely candidate is the hormone *oxytocin*, which promotes social bonding in humans and other animals. But in light of the connection between in-group favoritism and out-group derogation, could this so-called love molecule have a dark side as well? Research by Stallen et al. (2012) suggests this may in fact be the case.

The researchers asked participants to rate the attractiveness of unfamiliar visual stimuli, after first administering either oxytocin or a placebo to the participants. While viewing each stimulus, participants were shown what they thought were ratings of the stimulus provided by members of their in-group and members of an out-group. For some trials, these ratings were different (e.g., positive by the in-group, negative by the out-group). The question was whether participants' ratings would be influenced by the ratings of in-group and out-group members. When administered a placebo, participants showed little bias—their ratings were not influenced by what they thought were the ratings of in-group and out-group members. But participants administered oxytocin showed a clear in-group/out-group bias: they conformed to the opinions of in-group members, and this tendency was more pronounced when these opinions conflicted with those of out-group members. The bonding effect associated with oxytocin apparently has a zero-sum quality. It may promote liking for fellow group members, but this favoritism is at the expense of positive feelings for those who are not part of the group.

Out-groups cannot get a break even when they do something positive. Recall the *self-serving bias* discussed in Chapter 7, in which people attribute their good behavior to their inner qualities but attribute bad behavior to external forces and circumstances. Essentially the same bias exists at the group level (Pettigrew, 1979; Schlenker & Miller, 1977). When one's own group acts in a noble or competent fashion, it is seen as an expression of the group's wonderful qualities. Less admirable behavior by one's group is attributed to external circumstances or random events. This bias is flipped when assessing responsibility for the actions of out-group members. If they do something wonderful, it is seen as a reaction to external circumstances, not as representative of their inner motives and traits. But their personal qualities are invoked as responsible when they act in an immoral or incompetent fashion.

This tendency to draw a line between one's group and other groups, and for positive and negative feelings to follow suit, is enhanced under conditions of threat. This is readily apparent at the societal level when one's country is threatened by outside forces associated with a different nation, ideology, or religion. After the terrorist attacks on the United States on September 11, 2001, for instance, there was a dramatic increase in anti-Muslim sentiment. Prior to that event, Muslims had largely lived peacefully alongside people of different faiths in the United States. There was some tension due to the fact that for the majority of US citizens, Islamic religion and cultural traditions marked Muslims as an out-group despite their common citizenship with other Americans. But this tension usually did not promote overt prejudice or hostility. In the aftermath of the 9/11 attacks, however, anti-Muslim sentiment became very intense in certain segments of the population. The vast majority of Muslims in the United States—and worldwide, for that matter—condemned the attacks, but this did not prevent the latent hostility inherent in in-group/out-group relations from becoming manifest.

The threat that can unleash in-group/out-group tensions need not be physical in nature. Hostility toward an out-group can become very intense when in-group members experience a threat to their self-worth. When a person's self-image is shaken by frustration and failure, for example, he or she is more likely to derogate members of stigmatized groups (Crocker, Thompson, McGraw, & Ingerman, 1987; Sinclair & Kunda, 2000; Spencer et al., 1998).

Fein and Spencer (2007) demonstrated this effect at the University of Michigan. Student participants took an intelligence test and were given bogus feedback that they had either performed quite well or quite poorly. They then participated in another study in which they evaluated a job candidate's personality and qualifications. Some of the students learned that the female job candidate was Jewish, which presumably activated the stereotype of "Jewish American Princess." Other students learned that the candidate was Italian, which presumably did not activate a negative stereotype for this population. Students who thought they had done well on the intelligence test evaluated both candidates in equally favorable terms. However, students who thought they had done poorly on the test evaluated the Jewish applicant much less favorably than the Italian candidate. Those who derogated the Jewish candidate subsequently showed increases in their self-esteem, suggesting that people can restore threatened self-esteem by derogating members of groups for which there are readily available negative stereotypes.

Stereotyping

In thinking about members of an out-group, people go beyond global evaluative judgments (prejudice) to shower them with a host of specific characteristics. *Stereotyping*—the tendency to attribute specific characteristics to others based solely on their group membership—occurs no matter how the human pie is sliced (Allport, 1954b; Devine, 1989; Fiske, 1998). Lest you consider yourself exempt from this tendency, think about the following individuals and note how little difficulty you have in applying traits to him or her.

- A high school cheerleader
- A used car salesman
- A fraternity guy
- A New Yorker
- A surfer dude
- An engineering student

Now, many of these people do you actually know? Why is it so easy—even natural—to assign traits to these individuals, sight unseen? Thinking in broad categorical terms about people does have the advantage of anticipating what a person from a category is like, and this can help decide whether to seek out the person and how to communicate with him or her when you do. Knowing the person is an engineering student, for example, you can be fairly sure that he or she is good at math. But stereotypes have two serious downsides that can undermine a fair assessment and perhaps cause you to avoid contact with someone you might really like.

First, stereotypes in a sense contain *too much* information about the people in different groups. It is fine to assume that an engineering student is good at math, but your assumptions probably do not stop there. You may assume that he or she—and most often, a "he" is assumed—is a bit nerdish, not particularly social, and unlikely to have strong interest in contemporary music, movies, and literature. And these assumptions might determine your interest, or lack thereof, in getting to know the person. If your assumptions are wrong, you are making an uninformed choice about getting to know the person.

Second, stereotypes gloss over individual differences. In thinking about the characteristics that seemingly apply to everyone in a group, you do not appreciate how each person in that group has a distinct set of talents, values, interests, and life experiences—characteristics you are sensitive to in your own circle of acquaintances and friends. The tendency to assume that "they're all alike" when thinking about members of different slices of humanity is known as the assumption of *out-group homogeneity* (Linville, Fischer, & Salovey, 1989; Ostrom & Sedikides, 1992; Park & Rothbart, 1982; Quattrone & Jones, 1980; Read & Urada, 2003).

Viewing the members of a group as if they were cut out of a common mold is a recipe for blanket discrimination. This may be adaptive in wartime when soldiers must fight and kill members of the opposing nation or group without worrying about their distinctive personalities. But this becomes a serious problem in everyday life. It's one thing to assume that engineering students are not party animals or that fraternity men are; it is quite another to assume that all African American men have criminal tendencies, that all Jews are clannish and stingy, and that all Muslims are intolerant of other religions and willing to attack those they consider heathens.

Inferring the Minds of Out-Group Members

As noted in earlier chapters, people are unique in their capacity for "theory of mind." When people observe someone, they infer what the person is thinking and use these inferences in forming judgments about him or her. This capacity is a prerequisite for empathy and thus can set the stage for altruistic action, as discussed in Chapter 11 ("Antisocial and Prosocial Behavior"). You might assume, therefore, that inferring the mental states of other people, rather than simply judging their overt behavior, would scale back the tendency to derogate members of an out-group. "Getting inside their heads," in other words, might prevent one from assuming the worst about people who don't happen to share one's group identity.

It doesn't work this way. In fact, the research on *mind perception* leads to a quite different conclusion. As pointed out in Chapter 7, we infer that the people we like have a greater capacity for abstract mental representations and acting in accordance with plans, goals, and long-term consequences than do people we dislike (Kozak, Marsh, & Wegner, 2006). Knowing nothing about a person other than that he or she is an out-group member—and therefore disliked—people are predisposed to assume that the person does not think deeply and engages in actions without a conscious concern for the action's consequences and implications.

It gets even worse when inferences about emotions enter the picture. As we learned in Chapter 5, humans differ from other animals in their ability to experience higher-level emotions such as guilt, shame, and pride. These complex emotions imply the existence of complex minds. So if out-group members are denied sophisticated mental states and abilities, they are also denied these higher-level "human" emotions. Research supports this connection. In-group members assume that out-group members have the same basic emotions—anger, fear, disgust, joy, and the like—as they do, but do not credit them with complex, sophisticated emotions such as pride or sympathy. The denial of complex emotions to out-group members elevates the feeling of moral superiority on the part of in-group members (Vaes et al., 2003), making it easier to engage in discriminatory and hostile action toward the out-group.

In effect, this process denies out-group members full membership in the human species, promoting a process known as *dehumanization* or *infrahumanization* (Cortes et al., 2005; Haslam, 2006)—the attribution of animal-like qualities to out-group members. The tendency to see out-group members as animals (Epley & Waytz, 2009), robots (Haslam, 2006), objects (Fredrickson & Roberts, 1997), or as otherwise less than fully human (Harris & Fiske, 2006) depends in part on our unique human ability to deconstruct their minds. In denying out-group members the advanced cognitive capacities we value in ourselves, we see them as less capable of acting on the basis of abstract concerns (Gray, Gray, & Wegner, 2007) or moral considerations (Gray & Wegner, 2009). The belief that out-group members' minds are not worth preserving is thus instrumental in leading people to treat each other as less than human.

Prejudice in Action

People with different social identities do not routinely act on the basis of their prejudicial feelings and stereotypes, but sometimes they do. And when they do, it can two basic forms: *discrimination* toward members of an out-group and *violent conflict* between members of different groups. The issue is *when* and *how* such translation of thought into action occurs.

Discrimination

People who differ in subjectively important ways can get along with one another most of the time. People in urban environments, for example, encounter members of different groups on a daily basis and rarely get embroiled in conflict. They may hold views of one another that are not particularly flattering, but they usually do not go out of their way to deny each other's freedom of action. The latent hostility in prejudice can become manifest, however, when members of a group feel threatened or frustrated due to events they experience collectively. Economic uncertainty during a recession, for example, can create feelings of competition over scarce resources (e.g., jobs, housing), and a threat to a group's status can promote hostility toward another group whose status is perceived to be increasing at their expense. Personal setbacks and frustrations can also intensify prejudicial feelings and create the potential for translating these feelings into direct action (e.g., hostile treatment of an out-group member) or support for policies that harm an out-group (e.g., denial of voting rights or educational opportunities).

These factors can be understood in term of the *frustration-aggression hypothesis* discussed in Chapter 11 ("Anti-social and Prosocial Behavior"). A person whose progress toward a goal is blocked experiences unpleasant arousal (e.g., anger) and this internal state can result in aggressive action toward the source of the frustration—or to anyone who is perceived to be associated, rightly or wrongly, with the frustration (Dollard et al., 1939). This can set the stage for hostility toward members of an out-group. If a person feels frustrated in his or her attempt to achieve personally significant goals—high social status, for example, or a job that pays a good salary—his or her negative feelings about members of an out-group may become intensified to the points of aggressive action. This *displaced aggression* occurs when the true source of a group's frustration is not a tangible, identifiable target, or if the source is powerful and likely to retaliate against the group (Marcus-Newhall, Pederson, Carlson, & Miller, 2000). Under these conditions, hostility is displaced onto identifiable, "convenient" targets who are unlikely to attack in return. In effect, the convenient target becomes a *scapegoat* for a group's troubles.

The treatment of Jews in Nazi Germany during World War II has been discussed in these terms. After World War I, the Germany economy was devastated and certain segments of the population—working class people, in particular—felt especially frustrated because they could not maintain the standard of living to which they had become accustomed and desired to maintain. Although the cause of their frustration was the war's aftermath and the collapse of the economy, these were hardly easy-to-identify targets and there was no obvious way to attack them. The Jews, however, were identifiable and were vulnerable to attack without fear of retaliation. Spurred on by the anti-Jewish propaganda espoused by Adolf Hitler and his fellow Nazis, the Jews became convenient scapegoats for the frustration experienced by many Germans.

This scenario played out as well in the southern United States in the decades following the Civil War as African Americans were freed from slavery and granted citizenship (though with vastly limited rights and opportunities). During Reconstruction, the economy of the South went through several periods of economic downturn, with farmers especially feeling frustrated by events over which they had no control. In what has to count as one of the most sobering manifestations of the frustration-aggression hypothesis, the number of lynchings of young African American males correlated over the years with the price of cotton—as the prices dropped, signifying an economic downturn, the number of lynchings increased (Hovland & Sears, 1940). Newly freed yet powerless, African Americans served as convenient scapegoats for the woes of working-class White Americans.

People can translate their prejudicial feelings and stereotypes into action without having experienced events that arouse negative emotions. Simply being prompted to think in a certain way, with these thoughts devoid of emotion, can promote discriminatory behavior. As discussed in previous chapters, people's thoughts can vary in their level of abstraction, from concrete details to broad generalizations (Trope & Lieberman, 2003; Vallacher & Wegner, 1987). There are important advantages to thinking about things in abstract, higher-level terms. Sticking to a plan of action and resisting distractions, for example, is easier when focusing on the goals (high-level act identities) of what one is doing rather than on the moment-to-moment details (low-level act identities) of the behavior (Fujita & Carnevale, 2012; Vallacher & Wegner, 1987).

But thinking in high-level terms has a serious downside when the object of one's thoughts is a member of an out-group. In focusing on the general properties of such a person—his or her group identity, race, gender, and so forth—less attention is paid to the person's unique characteristics. Rather than seeing José or Barbara as unique individuals, a person thinking in high-level terms is inclined to see them as a Mexican American and a female, respectively. Research has shown that abstract as opposed to concrete thoughts tend to increase decision makers' reliance on stereotypes (McCrea, Wieber, & Myers, 2012). When the person evaluates these people for a job, he or she may do so in based on his or her stereotype about Latinos and women, overlooking their unique qualifications for the job (e.g., Cuddy, Fiske, & Glick, 2007).

It is easy to maintain a high-level view of a person when an interaction with him or her is in the distant future. But when the interaction is imminent, one's attention begins to center on the person's unique characteristics rather than his or her presumed stereotypical qualities. Milkman, Akinola, and Chugh (2012) demonstrated this *temporal discrimination effect* in an academic setting. They arranged for a large sample of college professors (over 6,000) to receive e-mail messages from fictional prospective doctoral students who requested a meeting either the same day or in one week. The students' names suggested that each student was a male or female and one of five races: Caucasian (White), African American, Hispanic, Indian, or Chinese. The question was whether the professors would grant the meeting with the prospective student.

If the professors had negative feelings or thoughts about women or minority groups, they were more likely to grant the meeting request to Caucasian males than to the women and minorities—as long as the requested meeting was in one week. This discriminatory behavior, however, did not occur when the prospective students requested a meeting the same day. The immediacy of the interaction prompted the professors to think about the specific individuals making the request and to suspend their judgments about the groups to which they belonged.

The role of level of thinking in discrimination may explain why people can hold negative views of those who belong to out-groups, yet get along with such people on a daily basis. In the 1930s, for example, hotel owners did not discriminate against Chinese couples who requested a room in person, although a majority of them (91%) indicated that they would do so when contacted several weeks afterward as part of an alleged survey (LaPiere, 1934). With the event in the distant past, the owners were expressing their categorical level of thinking; when exposed to the couples in the present, the owners were expressing their immediate reactions, which reflected individuating features of the couples rather their identity-based stereotypes.

Intergroup Conflict and Violence

Discrimination is an asymmetric affair. One group, usually the one with greater power, treats members of the other group, typically the one with less power, in a prejudicial and unfair manner. But the tension inherent in in-group–out-group dynamics is sometimes manifest instead as conflict between the groups, with neither willing to accept a subordinate status. Human history, not to mention life in the modern world, is characterized by international warfare, revolutions, civil wars, genocide, and gang battles, with each group viewing one another in highly evaluative terms that minimize individual differences.

Conflict between competing parties is not invariably bad. It is central to political democracy and economic capitalism, not to mention team sports. It plays an important role in constructive social change, as people come into contact with others with different tools, lifestyles, food sources, fashions, belief systems, and scientific knowledge. Conflict can also be a source of creativity and innovation, as different groups reconcile differing points of view, lifestyles, and skill sets (Johnson, 2010). And even when conflict turns destructive, it is usually resolved in short order without lasting repercussions.

Nonetheless, a small percentage of intergroup conflicts—about 5%—become highly destructive and protracted over time, with resolution seemingly impossible (Coleman, 2011). These *intractable conflicts* can turn ugly and cause irreparable harm (Vallacher et al., 2010). They can take on a life of their own, showing strong resistance to intervention that, from a rational or even a selfish perspective, should defuse the source of tension and animosity. Even when the issues that launched such a conflict are resolved, the parties to the conflict may maintain hostile relations that can erupt into violence.

What determines whether in-group/out-group dynamics progress to conflict and violence? The specific causes are numerous and specific for different conflicts, but four factors apply to destructive conflicts of all kinds (Vallacher et al., 2013). Destructive conflicts are spawned, first of all, by *perceived incompatibility of interests* between the parties (Deutsch, 1973; Pruitt, Kim, & Rubin, 2004). When two groups vie for scarce resources (e.g., water, food supplies, land suitable for agriculture, for example, the zero-sum nature of this competition can result in overt hostility. By itself, this factor does not invariably produce violent conflict; although a precondition for discrimination, it usually does not generate overt conflict between groups.

Perceived incompatibility of interests can erupt into overt conflict when there is noteworthy *social change* (Vallacher et al., 2010). As long as conditions are fairly stable, groups—even those on the receiving end of discriminatory behavior—justify the status quo. People believe in a *just world* (Lerner, 1980)—not one in which everyone has equal resources and opportunities, but one in which everyone gets what he or she deserves and deserves what he or she gets. So a group that does not enjoy the same benefits and respect as other groups may nonetheless accommodate to its lot in life because of this *system justification* tendency (Jost, Banaji, & Nosek, 2004). But this belief can be called into question when a society experiences noteworthy changes in its societal norms and values (Nowak & Vallacher, 2019).

In today's world, such change is everywhere. There are dramatic political changes in many parts of the world. Many societies, and regions within societies, are experiencing urbanization that is eclipsing the traditions and lifestyles of agrarian life. The revolutionary changes in technology in recent decades have changed virtually every aspect of social life, from the way we communicate (e.g., social media, smart phones) to the way we shop (e.g., internet shopping, eBay). There has been a deterioration of trust in institutions of all kinds—Congress, the political process generally, Wall Street, organized religion, professional sports. Social norms have undergone dramatic change with regard to gay marriage, having children out of wedlock, and recreational drug use. And there have been shocks to the economic systems of many countries, which have resulted in economic recessions, stock market crashes, and increasing income inequality between the rich and everyone else. In the face of so many changes taking place simultaneously, people in groups that had previously justified the status quo begin to question the legitimacy of their position vis-à-vis other groups. Such questioning can breed discontent and frustration, which can highlight the incompatibilities of competing groups.

A third factor than can transform tense relations into open conflict is social identity based on a worldview or ideology that elevates one's own group while demeaning the value or humanity of other groups. A group or country with a fervently held political ideology can view groups or countries with different ideologies as a threat, or simply as a foe that needs to be converted—or eradicated. The Nazi and Communist ideologies of the 20th century are noteworthy examples.

The final factor promoting conflict is the *clustering of like-minded people* into homogenous groups that exist alongside other groups with whom they have little overt contact (Nowak & Vallacher, 2019). This may seem a bit ironic. After all, if people interact primarily with like-minded people, the likelihood of coming into contact with people from different groups is reduced accordingly. No contact, no conflict, right? But in forming clusters, people are not exposed to different points of view and instead receive constant reinforcement for their own ways of seeing the world. Such insulation can promote intolerance towards those with differing perspectives, so that when intergroup contact does occur, it is likely to be characterized by conflict rather than accommodation to a shared reality.

The clustering of like-minded people clearly occurs when religions, ideologies, and traditions are distributed in different nations. But clustering also occurs *within* nations, such that people with similar views and traditions are geographically segregated from people with dissimilar views. When such groups come into contact or feel they are in competition for jobs and other resources, their differences can translate into open conflict. In some European countries, for example, Muslims tend to cluster into homogeneous communities whose contact with people outside these communities is a potential source of conflict. And in the United States, there is geographical clustering of conservative and liberal attitudes, with cultural conservatives concentrated in rural areas, especially in the southern and western states, and cultural liberals prevalent in urban areas, especially on the east and west coasts.

In today's world, cluster formation is not restricted to geographical proximity. The internet and social media enable like-minded people in different regions of a country or in different parts of the world to communicate with one another and provide validation for their beliefs and lifestyles. A Muslim might live next door to a Christian or Jew, for example, but most of his or her contacts might be with other Muslims around the world. The virtual communities fostered by the rise of electronic communication has much to recommend it, but its role in creating self-contained echo chambers is worrisome because of the potential for intergroup conflict it creates.

Box 13.2   What About Religion?

Religion is a double-edged sword when it comes to destructive and protracted conflict between groups. On the one hand, religion clearly has value for humanity in promoting self-control and emphasizing standards of morality. But religious faith can also pose problems for intergroup harmony. Most religions divide mankind into good versus evil, saints versus sinners. The distinction between good and evil is often manifest as the distinction between those who share one's religious beliefs and those who don't. Thus, even if someone from a different faith behaves in a morally commendable fashion, he or she may be judged negatively (e.g., as an infidel) by virtue of worshipping a different god or embracing a different creation story.

When religious faiths fall along ethnic, regional, demographic, or national lines, religiosity tends to intensify the natural tendency to favor one's in-group (e.g., one's nation) over an out-group (e.g., another nation) (Dunkel & Dutton, 2016). If other conditions promote in-group versus out-group conflict (e.g., competition over land or resources), the polarization of in-group favoritism associated with religion can enhance rather than defuse the conflict. And by viewing out-group members as evil or damned, the constraints against aggression are weakened. Religion can thus promote behavior that contradicts the moral values it proclaims as sacred.

From this perspective, it is not surprising that many intense and prolonged conflicts today are associated with religious differences. Because the central controversies cannot be resolved conclusively (e.g., determining which god is the real one or which prophet is likely to be vindicated), religious-based conflicts are often protracted, with victory and defeat (or genocide, at the extreme) representing the only perceived means of terminating the conflict. This gloomy scenario is especially likely under conditions that reinforce a group's conviction that other groups must recognize the zero-sum nature of moral and cosmological truth.

Although religion has been associated with intergroup conflicts throughout human history, other factors often must be operative before religion can foster serious conflict and warfare. Religion is often used to justify aggression that is actually undertaken for very different reasons. And leaders sometimes exploit religious differences to engage citizens who would otherwise not be inclined to aggress against the out-group. It is also the case that most religions converge on moral codes that are beneficial for social relations. Efforts designed to emphasize these rules of interpersonal behavior can offset the intolerance associated with good versus evil categorization. There are numerous instances in history when calls to a higher morality have defused conflicts and brought about interpersonal and intergroup harmony.

Maintenance of Prejudice and Stereotypes

Why Are Broad Generalizations About Other People Resistant to Change?

The feedback between mind and action makes it difficult to change the way people relate to members of an out-group. If a stereotype existed in isolation from feelings and action, one could work on the stereotypical beliefs, showing them to be unwarranted and invalid. But disembodied stereotypes, cut off from feelings and behavior, are the exception rather than the rule. Instead, unflattering beliefs about a group are associated with negative feelings toward the group, and such beliefs and emotions are associated with the potential for discriminatory behavior.

The feedback among stereotyped beliefs and prejudicial feelings is particularly strong, in the same way that thoughts and emotions are strongly linked. This mutual support system makes each component highly resistant to change, even when people are confronted with facts and logical arguments to the contrary. Attack the stereotype with facts, and one's prejudicial feelings and emotions come to the rescue to twist, reinterpret, or deny the facts. Attack the prejudice, and one's beliefs come to the rescue, providing support for the emotional feelings (and justifying discriminatory behavior in the bargain). Beyond the mutual support system characterizing prejudice and stereotypes, several intrapersonal and interpersonal processes that perpetuate these mental states have been documented. Here are the primary ones.

Personality and Prejudice

Not everyone is equally prejudicial in his or her thoughts and feelings about out-group members. It is quite reasonable, then, to look for the causes of prejudicial thinking in peoples' personalities. This sensible idea provided the basis for much of the early theory and research on prejudice, and this tradition is alive and well today.

The Bigoted Personality

It is tempting to see prejudice as a sign of personality traits and motives that characterize some people, making them intolerant and prejudicial. That certainly makes the rest of us feel immune to prejudicial thinking, and therefore better than the bigots. And in fact, there is considerable evidence that prejudicial tendencies are far more pronounced in some people than in others. These tendencies, moreover, are not only expressed when thinking about some out-groups, but rather are apparent when prejudiced people think about *any* out-group. Participants who are prejudiced toward homosexuals, for example, also tend to be prejudiced toward women, immigrants, and persons with disabilities (Akrami, Ekehammar, & Bergh, 2010).

The assumption that prejudice is rooted in personality was widely held in the early days of social psychology on the heels of World War II. On the basis of extensive testing, psychologists identified a set of cognitive and emotional factors associated with prejudice and intolerance toward people who belong to different groups. In this view, bigots have an *authoritarian personality* (Adorno et al., 1950), characterized by deference to those in power and hostility to those lacking in power, unwillingness to introspect about one's feelings, the projection of one's hostile impulses onto others, conventional goals, intolerance of ambiguity, and disdain for modern art that plays with incongruities and asymmetries (e.g., Picasso paintings).

The tests employed to test authoritarianism also found that bigoted people tended to be politically conservative. To this day, those who are most prejudicial tend to score high on *right-wing authoritarianism* (Altemeyer, 1981) and related measures such as *social dominance orientation* (Sidanius & Pratto, 1999). Many felt this was an unfair indictment of politically conservative people and noted that some of the items used to assess authoritarianism were phrased to make conservative ideology seem prejudicial. In subsequent years, purer measures of the bigoted personality have been developed that give liberals an equal chance of revealing their prejudicial tendencies. The *Dogmatism* scale (Rokeach, 1960), for instance, captures the *closed-mindedness* associated with prejudice. Dogmatic (closed-minded) people are intolerant of ambiguity, are not sensitive to different perspectives, and resist change in their thinking once they have reached a conclusion. More recently, Arie Kruglanski and his colleagues have developed the *Need for Closure* scale (Kruglanski & Webster, 1996), which captures the need for people to reach quick conclusions and forgo further information processing. The tendency to "seize" and "freeze" on the part of those high in need for closure promotes and maintains stereotypical judgments about out-groups (Kruglanski & Freund, 1983).

There is also a relationship between prejudice and personality traits that are not defined in terms directly linked to prejudice. Of the *big five personality traits* (Costa & McCrea, 1995), for example, *agreeableness* and *openness to experience* stand out in this regard. People who score as disagreeable and not particularly open to experience or intellectually curious tend to hold prejudicial attitudes and express stereotypical judgments (Sibley & Duckitt, 2008).

Box 13.3   Is There a Genetic Basis for Prejudice?

The fact that prejudiced and non-prejudiced people differ in their personalities raises the possibility that some people are born with a predisposition toward prejudicial thinking. After all, personality is inherited to a notable extent, so perhaps the roots of prejudice can be traced to people's genetic makeup. In fact, there is evidence in support of this idea. Lewis and Bates (2010) compared the degree of in-group favoritism—which is often at the expense of out-group derogation–among two types of twins: *dizygotic* (who share about half of their genetic makeup) and *monozygotic* (who are genetically identical). Both types of twins share the same family environment, so if the monozygotic (MZ) twins are more similar in their degree of in-group favoritism than are the dizygotic (DZ) twins, this would suggest that the formers' shared genes play an important role in promoting their similarity.

The researchers looked at three expressions of in-group favoritism: *religious*, *ethnic*, and *racial*. In other words, to what degree did the participants hold more favorable attitudes toward those who belong to their religion, have the same ethnicity, or are members of the same racial group (e.g., "How much do you prefer to be with other people who are the same religion as you?"). For each type of in-group favoritism, they computed the correlation for the MZ and DZ twins. As Figure 13.2 shows, the MZ twins were considerably more similar for all three types. So if John has prejudicial views, his identical twin Josh is likely to have such feelings as well. Note, though, that the MZ correlations are far from perfect and that the DZ twins were also similar in their prejudicial tendencies. So although biology is important, it is not destiny. The environment in which children are raised is clearly important. This is fortunate and a potentially hopeful fact–it is far easier to change a person's environment than his or her genetic makeup.

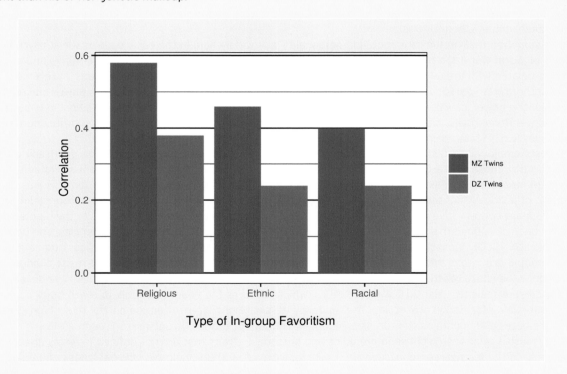

FIGURE 13.2 Similarity in Three Types of In-Group Gavoritism in MZ and DZ Twins
Source: Adapted from Lewis & Bates (2010)

Self-Esteem

As noted earlier, people emphasize their identification with a group to enhance their feelings about themselves (Tajfel, 1982). This suggests that people with relatively low self-esteem are more inclined to hold an especially positive view of the groups with which they identify (Crocker & Schwarz, 1985). Basking in the glory of one's in-group can help prop up a person's shaky self-image. People with poor self-regard also tend to derogate out-groups (Wills, 1981). In effect, they live in a world of perpetual threat, preparing to be outperformed by other people. So when exposed to out-group members who appear superior in some way (e.g., better performance, more friends, a stronger reputation), low self-esteem people double-down on their defensive reaction and blast the individuals and the out-group as a whole.

As reasonable as these conclusions are, they do not tell the full story. Research has shown that under some conditions, the relation between self-esteem and prejudice is flipped: people with *high* self-esteem tend to favor their own group more strongly and derogate out-groups more intensely (Aberson, Healy, & Romero, 2000; Guimond, Dif, & Aupy, 2002). This is especially likely to be the case when high self-esteem people are threatened by personal failure.

A study of sorority women at Northwestern University illustrates this idea (Crocker et al., 1987). Sororities (like male fraternities) are status-conscious and are recognized as falling into either the high status or low status camp by students. The researchers wondered how women with high versus low self-esteem would react if they wound up in a low-status versus a high-status sorority. Because low self-esteem people show in-group favoritism and out-group derogation regardless of their personal experience, the low-esteem women were expected to derogate the sorority to which they were not accepted—whether it was low-status or high-status. Because high self-esteem people only show out-group derogation when they are personally threatened, however, they were expected to blast the sorority to which they were not accepted only if it had higher status than the one that accepted them.

This is what happened (Figure 13.3). Low self-esteem women tended to derogate both low-status and high-status sororities to which they did not belong, but high self-esteem reserved their contempt for the high-status sororities. If they belonged to a high-status sorority, there was no need to blast the poor low-status sororities. But belonging to a low-status sorority threatened their positive self-view. To reduce this threat, they took the higher status sororities down a notch by derogating them and making their own sororities seem better by contrast.

Cognitive Biases

Identifying people who are inclined toward prejudicial thinking does not let the rest of us off the hook. Sure, some people have a lower threshold for such thinking than do others, but the processes involved in assessing one another,

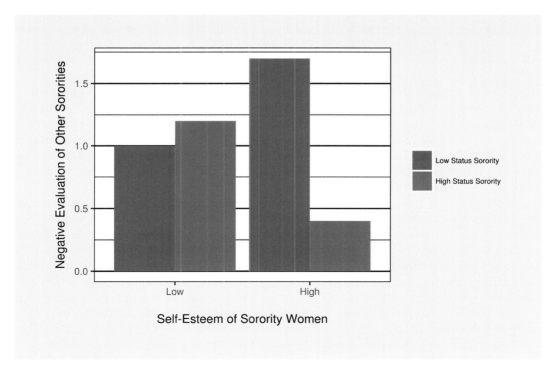

FIGURE 13.3 Self-Esteem, Threat, and Derogation of an Out-Group
Source: Adapted from Crocker et al. (1987)

described in Chapter 7, virtually guarantee that even the most socially sensitive person is predisposed to hang onto sweeping generalizations about the members of various groups. Prejudicial feelings and stereotypes concerning out-groups are not necessarily motivated by nasty motives, but rather reflect the same principles that enable us to form impressions of people at a party or in a classroom.

Confirmation Bias

Like social psychologists, laypeople attempt to understand and predict the actions of others (Nisbett & Ross, 1980; Wegner & Vallacher, 1977). But psychologists and laypeople test their ideas in very different ways. Whereas the scientist considers all relevant data and creates tests that could *falsify* his or her predictions, the layperson searches only for evidence that *supports* his or her beliefs, ignoring evidence that could falsify them. If a person has a negative view of an acquaintance or a public figure, for instance, he or she is highly sensitive to the target's shortcomings and overlooks evidence of the target's virtues. This asymmetry in assessing one's beliefs, discussed in Chapter 7, is known as the *confirmation bias* (Gilovich, 1991; Klayman & Ha, 1987; Skov & Sherman, 1986; Shermer, 1997). This bias is especially strong for firmly held beliefs (Dawson, Gilovich, & Regan, 2002; Ditto & Lopez, 1992; Kruglanski & Webster, 1996; Kunda, 1990; Lord, Ross, & Lepper, 1979). Because a stereotype is a firmly held belief, it can promote a tendency to consider only the information that fits the stereotype.

The confirmation bias comes in handy for prejudiced people in today's world. With the decline of many formal policies and cultural traditions that historically prevented African Americans from achieving success in different realms, for example, a racist is confronted with evidence of success that should give him or her pause about his or her attitudes. But not all evidence is created equal when one has a firm stereotype guiding one's observations and assessment of facts. A racist can overlook the accomplishments of African Americans, focusing his or her attention instead on those instances in which they come up short. When observing an interview, for example, a racist might ignore all the sensible things an African American says but take a single poorly expressed statement as proof of his or her intellectual inferiority.

The same bias is apparent when a sexist "tests" his or her hypotheses about women. In a work setting, for example, a woman may display impressive calm under stressful circumstances, but should she express irritation or frustration on a few occasions, that would provide evidence that women are not cut out for high-pressure occupations. The same pattern of behavior on the part of men would provide support for the sexist's view of men as well-suited to handle pressure.

Behavior Interpretation

Human action is often ambiguous and open to alternative interpretations. Does a loud noise coming from another room suggest an emergency situation or a clumsy act? When a male pushes another male, is he being playful or aggressive? When a stranger on a street late at night reaches into a bag, is he reaching for a sandwich—or a gun? The ambiguity of action usually does not pose a problem in everyday life, as people can easily generate higher-level meanings for the sights, sounds, and movements they witness (Vallacher & Wegner, 1987). But the ease with which people impose meaning on ambiguity can have the effect of reinforcing stereotypes about out-groups and promoting discriminatory behavior toward members of such groups.

To illustrate this idea, think about high-profile events in the recent past that have involved conflict between White and African American males. In 2012, an unarmed African American teenager, Trayvon Martin, was shot and killed by George Zimmerman, a self-appointed neighborhood watchman in a small Florida town. From Zimmerman's perspective—which was sufficiently persuasive to generate a *not guilty* verdict when he was tried for homicide—the fact that Martin was walking through the neighborhood late at night and wearing a hoodie was probable cause that he was "up to no good." Would Zimmerman have thought this if Martin had been a White teenager? We cannot know for sure, of course, but we do know that many people—Blacks as well as Whites—have a stereotype of young Black males as dangerous, potentially violent, and inclined to criminal behavior. So even though Martin was simply returning to a relative's home from a convenience store with a bag of Skittles, this behavior was sufficiently ambiguous that it could be interpreted in terms of the dangerous-Black-male stereotype and thus "justified" Zimmerman's stalking of Martin.

Not long after the Zimmerman-Martin incident, several other widely publicized White-Black incidents occurred that revolve around the Black male stereotype. In Ferguson, Missouri, on August 9, 2014, a White police officer, Darren Wilson, shot and killed an unarmed Black teenager, Michael Brown, after a physical altercation that occurred when the officer confronted and attempted to question Brown. Wilson shot Brown nine times at distances ranging from point blank to 12 feet. Lacking a video recording of the event, the specific behaviors of both Wilson and Brown are unknown and open to interpretation. From the perspective of many Whites—and the members of a grand jury, which decided that no charges should be brought against Wilson—Brown likely attacked the officer and attempted to grab his gun. This fits the stereotype of the dangerous Black male. But from the perspective of many African Americans, Brown was stopped and harassed for no reason other than being a young Black male. This fits the stereotype of widespread racism in police departments that is held by many African Americans.

Several experiments have revealed the role of stereotypes in interpreting ambiguous behavior by members of minority groups (Dunning & Sherman, 1997; Eberhardt, Goff, Purdie, & Davies, 2004). A light push is not seen as aggressive when done by a White male, for example, but is viewed as a violent shove when done by a Black male (Duncan, 1976; Sagar & Schofield, 1980). If this bias occurs for relatively innocuous physical contact in an everyday setting, imagine how it is manifest when the behavior involves potentially lethal behavior in a dangerous setting. Police officers are often faced with this sort of situation as part of their job. To the extent that they are aware of the dangerous-Black-male stereotype, they may make a split-second decision to shoot a Black male who is doing something that could be considered threatening—like reaching for a gun—but which is actually innocent—like reaching for a wallet.

Various takes on this scenario have been investigated in recent years (Payne, 2006). Consider, for example, the rather troubling results of a study by Correll, Park, Judd, and Wittenbrink (2002). College students were recruited to see how they would respond to a situation that is commonly confronted by police offers. The situation was not real, of course, but rather used a video game format, which can simulate reality quite effectively. Images of a young adult male who was either armed (holding a gun) or unarmed (holding a gun-sized object such as a black cell phone or a silver camera) appeared unexpectedly in a variety of contexts (e.g., a train station terminal, a hotel entrance, a city sidewalk). The male was either a Black or a White. If the students "saw" a gun, they were to "shoot" the person as quickly as possible by pushing a *shoot* button; if they "saw" an object other than a gun (e.g., a cell phone), they were to push a *don't shoot* button as quickly as possible. The point was to determine when the students would make a correct decision—shooting the armed person and not shooting the unarmed person—or make an error—shooting the unarmed person and not shooting the armed person.

The results, displayed in Figure 13.4, showed how the dangerous-Black-male stereotype influences perception when a split-second decision must be made. The Black male was more likely to be incorrectly shot—that is, when he was holding a harmless object—than was the White male. Under time pressure, the students had a difficult time distinguishing between a gun and a harmless object, but they were ready to treat an object held by Black males as if it were a gun, and to act on this decision by shooting him. This tendency was observed even when participants were trying not to be influenced by race—a finding that has been confirmed in other studies of this kind as well (Greenwald, Oakes, & Hoffman, 2003; Payne, 2001; Payne, Shimizu, & Jacoby, 2005). Simply knowing the stereotype that Black men are dangerous is apparently sufficient to create this bias, which can have unfair—and sometimes deadly—consequences.

The maintenance of stereotypes through behavior interpretation can be seen as well in *sexism*—the tendency to view males and females as having different characteristics, with the advantage usually going to males. Perceiving and evaluating men and women by different standards has been pervasive throughout history and continues to be on display in contemporary society. Even when men and women engage in the same behavior and demonstrate the same degree of success, people tend to perceive the respective behavior by men and women differently. You may think that college students would be too enlightened to think this way. This is indeed an enlightened thought, but it may not be all that insightful. Consider, for example, a classic study by Deaux and Emswiller (1974), in which male and female undergraduates were asked to describe how a fellow student managed to succeed at a complex task. If the student was a male, both men and women attributed his achievement almost entirely to his ability. But if the student was a female, there was a tendency for everyone—women as well as men—to see her achievement as largely a matter of luck.

This gender bias is not limited to specific tasks, but can color judgments about achievement in a career as well. Feldman-Summers and Kiesler (1974), for example, found that when males learned about a successful female physician, they judged her to be less competent than a successful male physician. Females saw things a bit differently. They assumed that the male had an easier time of it. Both men and women attributed higher motivation to the female physician. Seeing a female as highly motivated is flattering, but it implies that she had less skill than the successful male—"she may not be all that talented, but she tried really hard to make it."

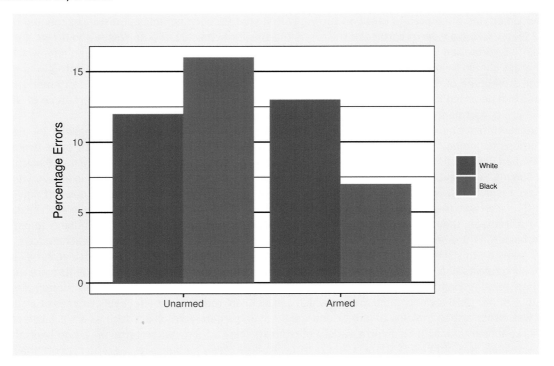

FIGURE 13.4 Percentage of Errors as a Function of Race of Target and Armed versus Unarmed. For Unarmed Targets, "Shooting" is an Error; for Armed Targets, "Not Shooting" is an Error
Source: Adapted from Correll et al. (2002)

Level of Action Description

Prejudice is reflected in the language used to describe actions by in-group versus out-group members (Maass, Ceccarelli, Rudin, 1996; Von Hippel, Sekaquaptewa, & Vargas, 1997). As noted earlier, any action can be described in varying degrees of abstraction, from very detailed and concrete ("he pushed a button") to very abstract ("he shocked another person"), with the more abstract (higher-level) descriptions saying more about the person performing the action (Vallacher & Wegner, 1987). The choice between lower-level (concrete) and higher-level (abstract) action descriptions is useful in maintaining an out-group stereotype in the face of contrary evidence. Whereas good behavior by an in-group member is described in higher-level terms, the same behavior by an out-group member is described in lower-level terms. So while an in-group member's action might be described as "demonstrating altruism," the same action by an out-group member might be dismissed as "putting money in a container."

The reverse bias occurs for a negative action—it is described in high-level terms if performed by an out-group member but in lower-level terms if performed by a member of one's in-group. While an in-group member might "drop a paper cup," the same act by an out-group member might be described as "showing disregard for the environment." In effect, out-group members are blamed for bad behavior but not given personal credit for good behavior.

Illusory Correlation

People can form hard-to-shake stereotypes without having any malice. To the contrary, they may attempt to understand what members of a group are like without an initial bias in mind. As noted in Chapter 7, this can happen because of the tendency for people to see *illusory correlations*—associations between events, characteristics, or categories that are not actually related (Chapman & Chapman, 1969; Fiedler, 2000; Klauer & Meiser, 2000; Hamilton & Gifford, 1976). These false but persuasive associations are based on the perceived connection between distinctive or infrequent events. Assume, for example, that you have witnessed very few car accidents and are not accustomed to seeing senior citizens on a daily basis. Now, if you were to witness a car accident involving a senior citizen, you might see a connection between the two and conclude that senior citizens are more likely than younger people to be unsafe drivers. This is actually an erroneous conclusion—young people, especially males, are over-represented in car accidents—but the distinctiveness of senior citizens and accidents makes their co-occurrence seem like a reasonable and generalizable connection.

The illusory correlation phenomenon has implications for prejudice regarding minority groups. By definition, members of a minority group are less frequent than are members of the majority group, and they tend to be distinctive as well because of differences in physical characteristics such as skin color. Criminal activity, too, is relatively infrequent and distinctive against the backdrop of everyday behavior. So when people hear of a crime—a robbery or an assault, for example—committed by a minority group member, they are primed to conclude that this category of humanity is predisposed to criminal behavior. The same behavior by someone in the majority group does not generate this conclusion because such a person is not distinctive. Even without an initial racial bias, then, many people associate criminal conduct (an infrequent behavior) with African Americans or Latinos (distinctive minority groups in the United States).

Subtyping

There is always a possibility that the biases discussed so far fail to defend one's stereotype of people in an out-group. In today's world especially, there is abundant evidence to contradict virtually every stereotype. African Americans, for example, are highly represented in all spheres of life, from arts and entertainment to science and government. Oprah Winfrey often tops the poll of "most admired person," Neil DeGrasse Tyson is perhaps the most visible scientist in the public eye, and Barack Obama was elected president of the United States—twice.

So what does a racist do when faced with such stereotype-shattering individuals? Ironically, he or she maintains the stereotype by looking upon these individuals as precisely that—as individuals rather than as exemplars of the group to which they belong. If there are enough individuals who do not fit the stereotype, the racist is likely to group them into a separate sub-category that represents an "exception to the rule." This means of maintaining a stereotype is called *subtyping* (Kunda & Oleson, 1995; Queller & Smith, 2002; Richards & Hewstone, 2001).

Subtyping essentially allows a prejudiced person to have it both ways. In thinking about a female scientist, for example, a sexist might subtype her as a non-traditional woman who probably is unattractive, unlikable, and more like a man than a woman in her personality. In one sense, the agility with which people can form subtypes is testament to their ability to see differences and create new categories. But in a more sobering sense, subtyping is a reminder of just how hard it is to open up a closed mind when it comes to issues of prejudice and tolerance.

Self-Fulfilling Prophecy

The various cognitive biases describe above assume that people have distorted perceptions or make systematic errors in drawing inferences about the behavior of out-group members. However, stereotypes can be maintained without calling into question people's perceptual or cognitive abilities. Instead of judging out-groups in an erroneous fashion, people can create a reality in which their judgments turn out to be accurate. The stereotypical judgment may not be fair but the target may unwittingly cooperate in providing evidence in support of it. Such *self-fulfilling prophecies* can manifest in two ways.

Behavioral Confirmation

In Chapter 7, you learned how people's expectancy regarding someone's behavior can influence that person to behave in a way that confirms the expectancy. If you expect a new acquaintance to be warm and friendly, you are likely to act in a warm and friendly fashion toward him or her, and he or she is likely to reciprocate this behavior—thereby providing *behavioral confirmation* for your expectancy (Darley & Fazio, 1980; Jussim, 1986).

Essentially the same thing can occur in an intergroup context, as first noted by the sociologist Robert Merton (1957). Even if a person is not prejudiced toward a particular group, he or she may approach members of that group with expectancies that are ingrained in the culture. In encountering an African American male on a dark street, for example, a White male or female might adopt a defensive posture, avoid eye contact, or even cross the street "just in case." If the African American male experiences this suspicious attitude on a regular basis, he may become a bit jaded about his experiences with Whites and not be particularly inclined to approach them with warmth. The White individuals, in turn, would see this behavior as evidence in support of his or her expectancy that African Americans are hostile toward Whites. This is hardly a great recipe for positive interracial relations. The same feedback loop can be at work with respect to criminal activity. If a member of a stereotyped minority group is expected to be dishonest and untrustworthy, he or she may come to see him or herself in these terms and perhaps establish a pattern of behavior that fulfills the low expectations of the majority group.

A similar feedback loop can occur when a sexist male interacts with a female. If he expects her to be uninterested in talking thoughtfully about serious matters such as politics or science, he is unlikely to bring up these topics, steering the conversation instead to what he considers to be topics of interest to females, such as celebrity gossip, fashion, or raising children. If the female responds to these overtures, she provides evidence for his assumptions. If she balks at these overtures and expresses resentment over his patronizing attitude, she may confirm another stereotype he may hold—that of a "bitch" who has a problem with men.

Behavioral confirmation of a stereotype is not inevitable. As pointed out in Chapter 7, it is most likely when there is a power differential between those holding the stereotype and the target of the stereotype. African Americans, for example, have less economic and political power than do White Americans. The civil rights and Black Power movements of the late 20th century redressed the power imbalance a great deal, and strides have been made toward greater equality since then. But in the early 21st century, there is still a disparity between African Americans and White Americans in educational opportunities, socio-economic status, and paths for upward mobility. The potential for behavioral confirmation by African Americans and other minority groups—and by women—remains strong.

Stereotype Threat

Something similar to self-fulfilling prophecy can exist with regard to one's own behavior. If a person is a member of a group for which there is a negative stereotype concerning performance in some domain (e.g., academics, athletics), the person's performance may confirm the stereotype. This self-fulfilling concern is referred to as *stereotype threat* (Steele, 1997). An African American or Latino student, for example, may fail to demonstrate his or her full academic aptitude on a standardized achievement test if he or she is mindful of the negative (and unfounded) stereotype that many people have about the intelligence of his or her racial group. But why should awareness of a negative stereotype about one's group undermine one's performance? The person may not believe the stereotype and he or she certainly does not want to confirm the negative perception of his or her group's ability. Should not the desire to disprove the stereotype motivate a person to be especially competent at the activity in question?

In a sense, the person can be *too* concerned about his or her performance. This heightened concern increases physiological arousal (Ben-Zeev, Fein, & Inzlicht, 2005; Murphy, Steele, & Gross, 2007) and reduces working memory capacity (Johns, Inzlicht, & Schmader, 2008; Schmader & Johns, 2003; Schmader, Johns, & Forbes, 2008). If a task is fairly easy or familiar, heightened arousal can energize one's performance and the reduced working memory capacity is not a problem because easy and familiar actions can unfold without a great deal of conscious attention (Rydell, Rydell, & Boucher, 2010). But on a difficult or familiar task, the heightened arousal and limited working memory associated with stereotype threat can prove deadly.

In an early test of stereotype threat, Claude Steele and Joshua Aronson (1995) administered difficult portions of the Graduate Record Exam (GRE), a test of aptitude and knowledge that is employed in the selection process for admission to post-graduate academic programs, to White and African American undergraduates. The test was identical for all students with one exception: half were told that the test was designed to measure their intellectual ability; the others were told that the test was just being developed and that their scores would mean nothing in terms of their actual ability. Steele and Aronson reasoned that the African American students led to believe that the test assessed intellectual ability would experience stereotype threat and underperform on the test relative to their SAT scores. But if their fears about racial differences on this test were minimized, the African American students should perform as well as their undergraduate SAT scores would predict. Because White students presumably do not experience stereotype threat on aptitude tests, their performance was not expected to be affected by which instructions they received—their scores should be consistent with their SAT scores in both cases. As Figure 13.5 shows, these predictions were confirmed by students' performance.

The performance impairment produced by stereotype threat seems to be a very general phenomenon. Consider, for example, the stereotype that women are not as good at math as are men. Spencer, Steele, and Quinn (1999) investigated whether women's performance on a test of mathematical ability might indeed be inferior to that of men—but only when women believe that the test is likely to show this gender gap. Men and women took the same test, but whereas half were told the test was designed to show gender differences in math abilities, the other half were told the test had nothing to do with gender differences. As Figure 13.6 shows, there was a pronounced difference between

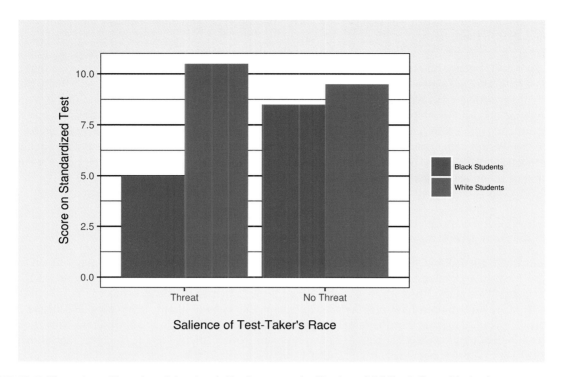

FIGURE 13.5 Stereotype Threat and Academic Performance by Black and White College Students
Source: Adapted from Steele & Aronson (1995)

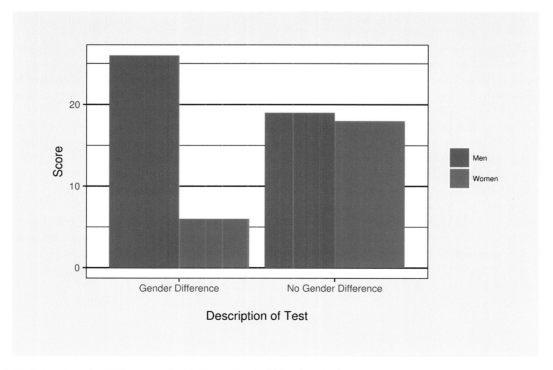

FIGURE 13.6 Are Gender Differences in Mathematical Ability Due to Stereotype Threat?
Source: Adapted from Spencer et al. (1999)

the men and women when the test was said to show such differences, but this difference was wiped out when the test was not described in these terms.

Researchers have shown the relevance of stereotype threat in yet other contexts. White males, for example, show relatively poor performance due to stereotype threat when their athletic performance is compared to that of African Americans (Stone, Lynch, Sjomeling, & Darley, 1999). Even if the activity is putting a golf ball—an activity that is associated with upper middle-class Whites—White males perform poorly if they are told the putting task is a measure of *athletic ability* as opposed to *athletic intelligence*. White males also show perform less well on a math exam when they think they are competing with Asian males—a group that is widely viewed as having superior math abilities. Elderly people, meanwhile, are commonly viewed as having poorer memory than younger people. And sure enough, elderly people do indeed show impaired performance on memory tasks—but only when they think their performance is compared to that of young adults (Mazerolle et al., 2012).

Box 13.4   Does Stereotype Threat Exist for Female Scientists?

In today's world, particularly in industrialized democracies such as the United States, the playing field for men and women has been leveled a great deal. Yet women today are greatly under-represented in almost all scientific disciplines. Why is this? And why are women more likely than men to abandon this career path if they do pursue it? Many explanations have been offered to explain this state of affairs. Some people—scholars as well as laypeople—have suggested that the female brain is different from the male brain, with the latter having the edge in mathematics and analytical skills (e.g., Baron-Cohen, 2003). Others point to the roles that women typically occupy (e.g., mother, homemaker) and suggest that these expectations and responsibilities are incompatible with the long hours and sacrifices required to become a scientist and develop a distinguished career.

The sexism identified by social psychologists offers another way to think about this issue. And so does stereotype threat on the part of women. Insight into how these two forces combine to undermine women's full engagement in a scientific career is revealed in how female scientist talk with their male and female colleagues. To provide unobtrusive samplings of such interactions, Holleran, Whitehead, Schmader, and Mehl (2011) asked male and female scientists at a research university to wear audio recorders as they went about their work. There was no difference in *how much* men and women had to say: both spoke about 17,000 words a day. But they differed in *what* they talked about, with this difference particularly notable when the topic was science. When male scientists talked to other male scientists about their research, they became energized and pursued this theme in their conversations. This effect was also observed when female scientists conversed with their female colleagues. But things were different when a female scientist talked with a male scientist. In discussing science (e.g., the latest research findings in their lab or in other labs), females tended to become increasingly disengaged, often expressing a lack of confidence in their own research. This loss of confidence and increased reticence was not observed, though, when the topic veered to topics other than science.

This pattern of interaction suggests that the female scientists experienced stereotype threat. Worrying that they would confirm the stereotype that females are not cut out for science, they did not focus on the substance of what they wanted to say, but rather on whether it reflected on their science acumen. And the more they worried about saying the wrong thing, the more they sounded insecure and incompetent. Their fear of confirming the stereotype, in other words, functioned as a self-fulfilling prophecy. This concern, moreover, motivated them to steer their awkward conversations with their male colleagues in a different direction. It is easy to appreciate how the disengagement from scientific topics when interacting with male colleagues, presumably motivated by stereotype threat, might lead women to disengage from their scientific careers.

Covert Prejudice

No one thinks he or she is a racist. People from all ethnic and racial groups are represented in high status occupations, and they are often viewed in wildly positive terms regardless of their group identity. Consider the widespread positive attitudes toward certain high-profile African Americans. Oprah Winfrey is arguably the most popular and influential woman in the United States. Michael Jordan and Muhammad Ali were considered the most recognizable people on the planet during their heyday and were widely regarded as charismatic and otherwise terrific. And then there's Barack Obama. He won the presidential election in 2008, and was reelected in 2012, and not just because of racial voting blocks. His first primary win, in spring of 2008, was in Iowa—hardly a bastion of minority groups. Does this mean that we now live in a post-racial era? Have we transcended the narrow-mindedness that once characterized the mainstream attitudes of White people toward people of color in the United States? It may be nice to think so, but there are reasons to hold off celebrating this apparent victory over prejudicial thinking.

Modern Racism

A case could be made that prejudice toward people in different groups has largely disappeared in the United States. But when one looks deeper, it appears that although overt racism has largely disappeared, it has been replaced by a more subtle counterpart (Kinder & Sears, 1981; McConahay, 1986; Pettigrew & Meertens, 1995; Sears & Henry, 2005). This *modern racism* rejects explicitly racist beliefs (e.g., that there are genetic differences between racial groups in their relative intelligence), but embraces suspicions that African Americans and other minority groups are undermining cherished beliefs of self-reliance, "family values," and fairness. In this perspective, for example, self-reliance is undermined by affirmative action policies, and family values are undermined by Black welfare recipients and unwed mothers.

Sam Gaertner and John Dovidio (1986; Dovidio & Gaertner, 2004) have offered a variation on this view. They suggest that many, if not most Americans hold egalitarian values and thus reject prejudice and discrimination, yet harbor unacknowledged negative feelings toward minority groups that reflect in-group favoritism and defense of the status quo (Sidanius & Pratto, 1999). These feelings may not lead to discriminatory behavior, particularly if the situation does not offer a convenient justification or "disguise" for such behavior. But if such excuses and disguises are available, the prejudice of the modern racist will be revealed.

Gaertner and Dovidio (1977) tested this idea by looking at the conditions that influence whether White individuals will offer aid to a White or Black person in need of medical assistance. If the participants believed that they were the only ones who could offer this assistance, they did so for the Black victim somewhat more often than they did for the White victim (94% vs. 81%). But if they thought there were other potential helpers, they could justify lack of aid to the Black victim in nonracial terms by thinking that someone else (perhaps with better expertise) would intervene. With this rationale in hand, they helped the Black victim substantially less than they did the White victim (38% vs. 75%). In effect, they could discriminate without appearing, or perhaps even feeling, prejudicial toward African Americans (Saucier, Miller, & Doucet, 2005).

This effect has been demonstrated in the context of evaluating applicants for college (Hodson, Dovidio, & Gaertner, 2002). The participants completed the *Attitudes Toward Blacks Scale*, which assesses subtle prejudice toward African Americans, then were asked later to rate White and Black applicants for college. When the applicants either excelled, or were below par on all relevant dimensions (e.g., GPA, SAT scores), the prejudiced and unprejudiced participants rated White and Black applicants the same way. But if the applicants excelled on some dimensions and were below average on others, the prejudiced participants rated the Black applicants less favorably than did the unprejudiced participants. Low ratings by the prejudiced participants could be disguised—defended as nonracial—by claiming that the dimensions on which the Black applicants fell short were more important than those on which they excelled.

Sexism—the view that women are inferior to men in important ways—and homophobia—the negative and hostile feelings toward homosexual men and women on the part of some heterosexuals—can be understood in similar terms (Haddock, Zanna, & Esses, 1993). A sexist might not derogate women explicitly, but endorse traditional gender roles, differential treatment of men and women, and stereotypes about lesser female competence (Swim, Aikin, Hall, & Hunter, 1995). For example, he or she might point to the breakdown in family life that he or she believes results when women take on careers. A homophobic person, meanwhile, might not derogate the sexual preferences of people directly, but rather point to what he or she feels are the unwanted consequences of homosexuals having contact with children or serving in the military.

Implicit Prejudice

No one likes to think he or she is bigoted. For some people, denying prejudice and stereotypical thinking is insincere. They really harbor negative thoughts about various groups but do not like to admit it. But for other people, the denial of prejudice may be genuine—at least at the conscious level. Yet they may harbor thoughts and feelings about various groups that rarely, if ever, reach consciousness. The possibility that people have attitudes of which they are consciously unaware sounds paradoxical. As discussed in Chapter 3, however, a great deal of thinking occurs without awareness (e.g., Dijksterhuis & Nordgren, 2006) and even the output of thought processes (attitudes and beliefs) may remain hidden from conscious awareness (Greenwald & Banaji, 1995). A person could be a racist or sexist and not even know it.

Several procedures have been developed to measure implicit prejudice (Wittenbrink & Schwarz, 2007). The most widely researched of these is the *Implicit Association Test* (IAT), developed by Greenwald, McGhee, and Schwartz (1998), described in Chapter 3. The IAT measures how quickly a person can associate different concepts. If two concepts are quickly associated, this presumably means that they have similar meaning for the person. If it takes more time to associate another pair of concepts, this suggests that they have different or perhaps conflicting meaning for the person. The extension to prejudice is straightforward. Consider racism, for example. If a person can quickly associate pictures of White faces with positive words, but takes longer to associate pictures of Black faces with positive words, the former association is presumably more "natural" or "spontaneous" than the latter and thus occurs automatically, without conscious awareness.

To assess implicit attitudes, a series of words or pictures is presented on the monitor and respondents are asked to sort them into one of two categories—usually "positive" and "negative"—as quickly as possible by pressing one of two keys. In tests of racism, the series might consist of pictures of White and Black faces and positive and negative words presented in random order. In the first part of the test, respondents press the "d" key when either a White face or a positive word (e.g., *pleasant, good*) pops up and press the "k" key when either a Black face or a negative word (e.g., *unpleasant, bad*) appears. In the second part of the test, the rule is switched: respondents press "d" when either a White face or a negative word appears and "k" when a Black face or a positive word appears. If it takes longer to press the correct key in the second part, this means that the association between Black faces and positive words is not spontaneous, but requires at least momentary deliberation. The greater the difference between response times on the first and second parts of the test, the greater the respondent's unconscious (implicit) racism.

Over a million people have taken the Web version of the IAT for a wide variety of topics (https://implicit.harvard. edu/ implicit/), including racism. About two-thirds of White respondents (and half of Black respondents) show some degree of prejudice in favor of Whites over Blacks (Nosek, Banaji, & Greenwald, 2002). But does how quickly a person presses computer keys really measure prejudice? Perhaps people respond more quickly on Black-negative trials than on Black-positive trials simply because they are aware of the negative Black stereotype but do not endorse it. Their responses, in other words, may say more about what they *know* about their culture than about how they *feel* about this knowledge.

The issue is not yet definitively decided, but there is evidence to support the validity of the IAT approach (e.g., Lane, Banaji, Nosek, & Greenwald, 2007; Rudman & Ashmore, 2007). McConnell and Leibold (2001), for example, had participants interact with a White experimenter, then take the IAT for racism, and then interact with a Black experimenter. Participants whose IAT scores suggested unconscious racism spoke less to the Black experimenter, and when they did speak to him, they had more speech errors. These differences were not observed for participants whose IAT scores did not suggest implicit racist attitudes.

The existence of implicit prejudice does not mean that people are at the mercy of their unconscious thoughts and are destined to act on them. As discussed in Chapter 6 ("Personal Control"), people can control how they act and what they say—and even what they think. But such *self-regulation* is a *controlled process* that requires executive resources (e.g., Wegner, 1994). And as noted in Chapter 6, controlled processes can give way to *automatic processes* under a variety of circumstances (e.g., Baumeister, Vohs, & Tice, 2007). When people are tired, experiencing stress, have consumed alcohol, or have simply depleted their mental resources by exercising too much self-control, they may give in to their impulses, emotions, and unconscious thoughts and desires. Automatic processes driven by unconscious thoughts can also override conscious control when people have to react quickly or make a split-second judgment. So although people can go about their daily lives acting on the basis of their values and notions of right and wrong, their behavior may reflect prejudicial biases when their ability to deliberate gives way to unconscious processes (Devine, 1989; Hugenberg & Bodenhausen, 2003, 2004).

Reducing Intergroup Conflict

How Can Stereotypes, Prejudice, and Intergroup Conflict Be Eliminated?

The picture painted so far sounds decidedly bleak. It is bad enough that people develop unfair thoughts and feelings about others with different social identities, and that they act on these stereotypical thoughts and prejudicial feelings under some circumstances. It is all the more disconcerting that the human mind often functions to defend stereotypes and prejudices against information that, rationally, should undermine them. The mind seems to make matters worse rather than better. But there are bases for optimism as well. Stereotypes and discriminatory action can give way to more benign, even positive orientations toward those we dislike.

Suppression of Prejudice

The most obvious way to reduce prejudicial thoughts is to exercise mental control. If you wish *not* to have a certain thought, simply make a point of not experiencing the thought. Things are not so easy, however. To suppress any thought, even one devoid of emotion, requires executive resources in service of controlled processing (Wegner, 1994). When such resources are stretched thin, as when one is engaged in a parallel task requiring conscious control, attempted thought suppression can backfire and ensure that the unwanted thought will capture one's attention. If thought suppression fails for innocuous topics (e.g., white bears), imagine how strongly it can backfire when the topic has significance and *should* be suppressed.

The ironic nature of thought suppression has implications for attempts to avoid thinking about members of a group in terms of the group's stereotype. A person may be able to do so when he or she has plenty of executive resources available, but his or her control over unwanted thoughts is likely to be ineffective if he or she is fatigued, stressed, or engaged in a parallel task that demands conscious attention. When people are instructed *not* to think about a stigmatized group (e.g., "skinheads") in stereotypical terms, for example, they may subsequently use such terms to describe the group with greater frequency than they would have in the absence of the suppression instructions (Gordijn et al., 2004). Ironically, the very attempt to transcend prejudicial thinking can ensure its survival.

More surprising and a bit frightening, suppression can promote prejudicial attitudes even if the person does not have them! Imagine, for example, that you are not at all a sexist but that you have been advised to *not* be a sexist. This challenge was put to college students by Wegner, Erber, and Bowman (1993, Exp. 2). They encouraged one group of participants to try not to be sexist as they completed a series of sentence stems. Some of the stems, derived from items on the *Attitudes Toward Women Scale* (ATW, Spence & Helmreich, 1972), prompted completions relevant to sexism. So, for instance, participants read "Women who go out with lots of men are…," and were asked to complete the sentence. An egalitarian completion might be something like "popular," whereas a sexist completion might be something like "cheap." For comparison, other participants were given no special instruction on how to respond. For some participants, cognitive load was imposed by asking for immediate responses; for others, cognitive load was reduced by allowing subjects up to 10 seconds to respond. The frequency of responses rated as sexist by coders was examined in each condition.

The rate of sexist sentence completions under low cognitive load was substantially reduced when participants were admonished not to be sexist. But under conditions of high cognitive load, the rate of sexist completions was significantly *increased* by the instruction not to be sexist (see Figure 13.7). This result was observed for both male and female respondents, and did not differ between participants who were high versus low in sexist attitudes as measured by the ATW. The ironic nature of thought suppression might be responsible for a fair proportion of the daily errors we least intend, from sexist remarks to *faux pas* of every kind.

Superordinate Goals

When kids get into a scuffle on the playground, teachers sometimes defuse the situation by getting the antagonists together in a different setting. The expectation (or hope) is that by interacting in a neutral setting, the kids will learn to respect each other, or perhaps learn to like one another. This certainly sounds reasonable. Getting antagonists to see

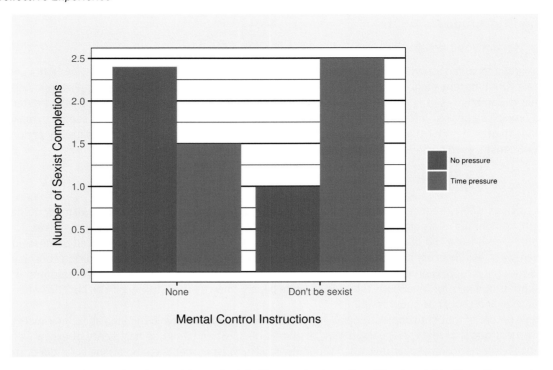

FIGURE 13.7 Ironic Effects of Trying Not to Be Sexist When under Low Cognitive Load (No Time Pressure) versus High Cognitive Load (Time Pressure)
Source: Adapted from Wegner et al. (1993); cited in Wegner (1994)

one another as individuals would seem to undermine the broad brushstroke thinking that characterizes stereotypes. However, research on the *intergroup contact hypothesis* (Pettigrew, 1997) has not been very encouraging (Pettigrew & Tropp, 2006). Putting individuals from antagonistic groups in contact does little to reduce their animosity and hostility (Bettencourt, Brewer, Croak, & Miller, 1992). Even supplementing contact with teaching individuals what members of the other group are like is not particularly effective (Bigler, 1999; Stephan, Renfro, & Stephan, 2004).

Contact can be effective, though, if individuals from different groups are presented with a task or challenge that can only be accomplished if everyone works together. When faced with a *superordinate goal*, the individuals must find a means of coordinating their behavior to achieve the goal. Their existing high-level judgment—a stereotype about the other group—gives way to an even higher-level concern—solving a common problem. Muzafer Sherif and his colleagues tested this insight in a context not unlike playground scuffles (Sherif et al., 1961). The participants were 22 fifth-grade boys who signed up for a 2.5-week summer camp at Robbers Cave Park in southeastern Oklahoma. The boys had all been screened to ensure that they were well adjusted (e.g., no school problems) and came from intact, middle-class families.

In the first phase of the study, the boys were divided into two groups and taken to separate areas of the park. Each group engaged in activities that fostered a sense of unity, such as preparing meals and pitching tents. For fun, they did typical summer camp activities—swimming and playing baseball during the day and putting on skits at night. Group cohesion developed fairly quickly and each group gave itself a name—the Rattlers and the Eagles.

Things changed dramatically in the second phase, when the groups were brought together for a tournament that lasted 5 days. The Rattlers and Eagles competed against each other in activities such as touch football, baseball, tug-of-war, and a treasure hunt. For each activity, the members of the winning team each received a medal and a pocket-knife, while the members of the losing team received nothing. It did not take long for things to go horribly wrong. From the beginning, the Rattlers and Eagles insulted each other with such colorful terms as "bums" and "stinkers." But the hostility went well beyond words. The Eagles stole and burned the Rattlers' flag, which naturally provoked a retaliatory capture of the Eagles' flag. The dining area became the site of food fights between the groups, raids on each other's cabins were undertaken, and challenges to engage in fights were issued. Keep in mind that the two groups did not differ in their appearance, background, social or economic status, and certainly not in their ideology (which was probably nonexistent—they were kids, after all). Merely identifying with a group and then engaging in competition with another group was sufficient to stoke intense conflict.

Fortunately, there was a third phase of the study, which was intended to see how (or whether!) the intergroup conflict could be resolved. Initially, the groups were simply brought together in non-competitive settings to see if their hostility would dissipate. It did not, even after seven such meetings. Then the investigators contrived several "crises" that could only be resolved if the two groups worked cooperatively. One crisis involved disruption of the water supply to the camp. To solve this crisis, the entire length of pipe from the reservoir to the campground had to be inspected, which was manageable only if all the boys inspected a certain length of the pipe. On another occasion, a truck carrying camp supplies broke down. As "luck" would have it, a large section of rope happened to be near the stalled truck. By using the rope to pull the truck, they managed to get it started—but this required that boys from the two groups worked as a team.

These superordinate goals had the intended effect. The name-calling and physical hostility quickly dropped off and friendships developed between Rattlers and Eagles. When the summer camp ended, the boys insisted that everyone return to Oklahoma City on the same bus rather than on the separate buses that had brought them to the camp. Figure 13.8 shows the percentage of nasty terms that were used by the boys to describe their own group versus the other group. The groups showed a clear in-group bias after the competition, but this prejudice (and its associated hostility) disappeared completely after the groups worked together to achieve shared goals.

In a sense, the superordinate goal approach amounts to scaling up the in-group versus out-group principle to a higher level: two groups that dislike one another become united into a larger group because of their dislike for a

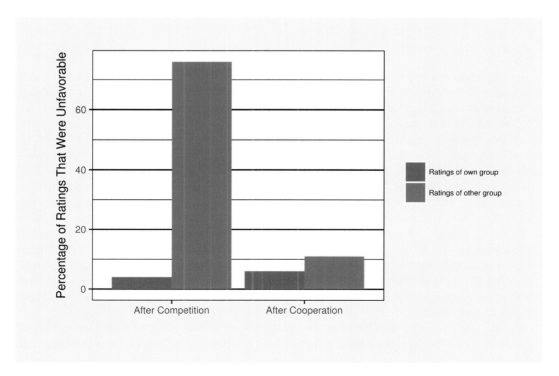

FIGURE 13.8 Unfavorable Feelings toward Members of One's Group Versus Members of the Other Group
Source: Adapted from Sherif et al. (1961)

common enemy. In the aftermath of the September 11, 2001, terrorist attacks in the United States, for example, there was a temporary suspension of animosity between different groups (e.g., Republicans and Democrats, urban and rural, Black and White) because of their common wrath toward Al Qaeda and other terrorist groups. In the Sherif et al. (1961) study, the common enemy was not another group, but the motivation for reducing animosity was essentially the same: forging solidarity in order to confront a common threat.

Cross-Cutting Social Identities

If people defined themselves in only one way, antagonism between groups would be difficult to overcome. Creating superordinate goals can work, but this approach plays on the tendency of people to protect their group against threats and thus is still rooted in hostility. But there is another way to view the problem of in-group/out-group antagonism. As noted in the discussion of social identity, people think of themselves in different ways, and these social identities tend to be *cross-cutting* (Brewer, 1991, 2000; Brewer & Pierce, 2005). Particularly in today's world, there is an enormous range of opportunities for self-expression, career choice, and other sources of identity creation. People may seek out others from different regions, or even from different countries, because of a common artistic preference, scientific interest, hobby, economic agenda, or simply because they want to interact in a video game.

These bases for social contact have the potential to override social identities rooted in tribalism and ethnicity. And because they are crosscutting, they can prevent polarization between groups from developing (Roccas & Brewer, 2002; Varshnay, 2002). The person in another country with whom one shares a hobby may have a different skin color, religion, or political persuasion. He or she may recognize these other bases of social identity, but minimize their importance because of the shared hobby. Cross-cutting identities, however, may be hard to maintain under stressful conditions. As discussed in Chapter 6, stress undermines complexity and nuance, promoting black-and-white thinking and a heightened need for closure (Kruglanski & Webster, 1996). This can cause people to retreat to a more basic social identity defined in terms of history, ethnicity, religion, demographics, or geographical region. So precisely when cross-cutting identities would be most useful—when stress aggravates tensions between groups—they are less likely to become the basis of personal identity.

Positive Mood

Positive moods are obviously more desirable than negative moods. They also may be more beneficial in preventing or reducing prejudicial thinking and discrimination. This is because positive moods tend to dissolve the mental boundaries between groups, a conclusion that follows from the work of Alice Isen (1987, 1993), described in Chapter 4 ("Emotion"). She showed that when people are induced to feel happy (e.g., by watching an amusing film clip), they tend to categorize objects in a more inclusive way. A happy person might consider a "cane" or a "purse" to be within the category of clothing, for example, while an unhappy person would define clothing in far narrower terms as things that are worn on one's body.

The flexibility associated with positive moods can prove important in situations of intergroup hostility, where it is important for each party to think "outside the box" by considering novel ideas and taking into account the positions and interests of the other party. Picking up on this idea, Barbara Fredrickson (2001) has proposed what she calls the *broaden-and-build hypothesis*, which holds that positive emotions broaden our thoughts and actions to help build emotional and intellectual resources. These resources, in turn, build our social resources—our friendships, collaborations, and social networks (Waugh & Fredrickson, 2006). For example, when people who are induced to feel a positive emotion, they tend to rate themselves as more similar to out-group members. This is consistent with the idea that positive moods promote broader categorization tendencies, so that people who might otherwise seem different are now seen as part of one's group.

There is a bit of irony associated with the effects of positive mood. Although it creates broader categories of inclusion, so that members of out-groups are embraced rather than rejected, it also promotes homogeneity in the perception of others. A person in a positive mood focuses more on the general qualities that people share rather than on the idiosyncrasies that distinguish them as individuals (Avaramova, Stapel, & Lerouge, 2010). This is an instance in which feeling that "they're all alike" is associated with liking rather than with prejudice.

SUMMING UP AND LOOKING AHEAD

- **Judging people on the basis of their group membership is hardly a testament to our humanity, and acting on the basis of such judgments is widely condemned as bigotry, intolerance, and ignorance. Yet the tendency to feel negatively toward out-group members, and to hold stereotypical views of them, is widespread in today's world, as it has been throughout human history. This is because prejudice, stereotyping, and discrimination are rooted in the human imperative to form a social identity distinguished from other social identities.**

- **Social identity is adaptive because it promotes trust and enables coordination with fellow group members. But in-group and out-group evaluation is often zero-sum, with the actions and perceived characteristics of out-group members considered less worthy and justifiable, representing a potential threat to the in-group. Out-group members are often seen as homogenous and interchangeable, lacking in fully human qualities, and devoid of higher-level thoughts and emotions, especially those involving issues of morality.**

- **The potential for out-group derogation and discrimination is likely when people feel threatened, either collectively or individually. If the source of threat cannot be identified or is immune to attack, people may displace their hostile feelings onto an out-group that is identifiable and less immune.**

- **Thinking in abstract as opposed to concrete terms has contradictory effects. Because higher-level thinking (e.g., focusing on values and standards) promotes self-regulation, it can inhibit aggressive and discriminatory behavior. But such thinking can reinforce broad categorical judgments, including stereotypes that overlook individual differences among out-group members. Thinking becomes more detail-focused when action is imminent, however, so people who endorse negative stereotypes in the abstract may be less inclined to act on such thoughts when confronted with an immediate situation and a particular out-group member.**

- **Conflict between groups is often adaptive, but a small proportion of intergroup conflicts become destructive and resistant to constructive resolution. This occurs when there is competition for scarce resources and rapid social change that upsets the balance of power between groups, particularly when the respective social identities of the warring groups reflect worldviews or ideologies that elevate the in-group and demean the value or humanity of the out-group. The ideological divide between groups is magnified by the tendency of like-minded people to seek out one another for validation and interpretation of ambiguous events and complex information. The ascendance of the internet and various social media in recent years promotes such clustering of opinions, and thus poses a challenge for maintaining tolerance and mutual respect among people with different beliefs and lifestyles.**

- **The potential for bigotry is greater for those with an authoritarian personality, those who are dogmatic in their views, those with a high need for closure, and those who are low in agreeableness and openness to experience. High self-esteem generally protects people against out-group antagonism, but it can enhance such feelings and behavior when a personal threat to self-esteem is experienced. There is also a genetic basis for individual variation in out-group antagonism.**

- **Several cognitive processes maintain stereotypes. People give greater weight to confirmatory than to disconfirmatory information, interpret ambiguous behavior in line with their preconceptions, and identify negative behavior by an out-group member as indicative of high-level intentions but identify positive behavior by this person in low-level terms devoid of significance. When an out-group member does something positive that cannot be denied, he or she may be seen as an exception that constitutes a subtype. Stereotypes can be formed and maintained without prejudice due to people's tendency to see associations between distinctive or infrequent events. Such illusory correlations are partly responsible for the belief that minority groups commit a disproportionate amount of antisocial (hence infrequent) behavior.**

- **Negative feelings and beliefs about out-group members can become self-fulfilling prophecies, with out-group members responding to in-group expectations in a way that verifies these expectations. A minority group member who is prejudged to be aggressive, for example, may respond with anger when treated as though he or she were aggressive. A related notion is stereotype threat, in which out-group members are concerned that their actions will confirm a stereotype. This concern can interfere with effective performance on actions that place demands on working memory. Stereotype threat helps explain why members** of minority groups and women often under-perform on tasks for which they are seen as having relatively low ability.

- Most people do not consciously harbor negative attitudes toward minorities and out-groups. Prejudice can still exist in covert form, disguised by values that paint out-groups in a negative light. An emphasis on traditional family values, for example, can provide justification for unfavorable evaluations of people (e.g., homosexuals, feminists) who are perceived as not abiding by these values. Prejudice and stereotypes can exist in the unconscious, but they can be revealed by the *Implicit Association Test*, which measures how quickly people can associate positive versus negative concepts or images with out-group members.
- The attempt to suppress prejudicial feelings and stereotypical thinking can backfire when mental resources are depleted (e.g., when one is under stress). Arranging contact between members of antagonistic groups is largely ineffective in reducing negative feelings, unless they are confronted with shared goals that require cooperation. Social identity may be at the root of in-group/out-group antagonism, but the multi-dimensional nature of social identity creates the possibility for people who differ in one way to share a common identity. Positive mood can reduce prejudice and stereotyping by creating a broader sense of identity that emphasizes similarities rather than differences among people.

The tendency to see the world in terms of in-groups and out-groups is problematic in an increasingly interconnected world in which resources must be shared and people from different backgrounds cannot be avoided. Such tension builds on the temptation to act in line with personal self-interest at the expense of other people's interests. Taken together, these human tendencies provide the breeding ground for social dilemmas that pit cooperation and trust against competition and exploitation. How these dilemmas of social life are manifest—and often resolved—is the focus of the next chapter.

Key Terms

Prejudice	Intractable conflict	Differentiation
Stereotype	Belief in a just world	Subtyping
Discrimination	System justification	Illusory correlation
Social identity	Authoritarianism	Modern racism
In-group favoritism	Dogmatism	Implicit prejudice
Minimal group paradigm	Need for closure	Thought suppression
Basking in reflected glory	Confirmation bias	Intergroup contact hypothesis
Out-group homogeneity	Behavior interpretation	Superordinate goals
Mind perception	Level of action description	Cross-cutting identities
Dehumanization	Subtyping	Broaden-and-build hypothesis
Frustration-aggression hypothesis	Self-fulfilling prophecy	
Displaced aggression	Stereotype threat	

14 Dilemmas of Social Life

You might think that life is a lot easier today than it was for our ancestors who did not have the benefits of modern science, technology, medicine, and government. But as daily life has become easier and safer in some ways, it has also become more complex and full of conditions that evolution did not prepare us for. We don't live in isolated villages and interact face-to-face with others who look like we do. And we don't have the luxury of talking exclusively with others who have the same background, speak the same language, and have the same values and worldviews. Particularly in light of the natural tendency to favor one's own group over other groups, the complexity and diversity of contact in today's world hold potential for fostering distrust, competition, conflict, and even overt hostility.

These changes in the patterns of social life pose three types of challenges as we proceed through the 21st century. First, our fate is increasingly linked to the actions and values of people who belong to different groups in our own society and different cultures around the world. This *social interdependence* with people near and far represents a dilemma in which our personal interests are often at odds with the interests of others. Second, as the social world becomes increasingly complex, diverse, and interdependent, how do we decide what constitutes a fair distribution of resources, the appropriate punishment for criminal behavior, and the degree to which we are socially responsible for the welfare and security of people in our own country and in distant lands? Inequalities and various forms of suffering abound; deciding whether these constitute injustice is not an easy matter, and deciding how to resolve them in a just manner is all the more difficult. These challenges represent *justice dilemmas*. Third, how do we judge whether a course of action is to be valued or condemned? People want to have true north on their moral compass, but this can prove difficult in a rapidly changing and diverse world. Because the standard answers to issues of right and wrong, good and bad, are often qualified or called into question, we are often confronted with *moral dilemmas* in our daily lives.

CHAPTER OVERVIEW

What Are You Going to Learn?

- **How do people navigate the conflict between their personal interests and the interests of other people?** Social life can be viewed as an ongoing conflict between desires to maximize one's personal gain and the need to temper these desires in order to get along with others. How is this basic dilemma of collective experience played out in different social contexts? What factors influence how social dilemmas are resolved?
- **How important is justice to social life?** How do people decide whether the outcomes experienced by different individual and groups are fair and deserved versus unfair and undeserved? Are there universal foundations for beliefs about social justice? How does the justice motive influence people's judgments about their own fate and that of others? Do different notions of justice underlie and give rise to different political ideologies?
- **What are the psychological foundations of morality?** Collective experience would not be possible without agreed-upon notions of right and wrong, good and bad behavior. Throughout history and in every society, people have developed codes of morally acceptable versus unacceptable behavior for judging one another. To what extent are moral judgments based on universal notions of right and wrong? Does morality reflect rational processes or does it based on intuition and emotion? What role does religion play in moral judgment and moral behavior?

Social Interdependence

How Do People Balance Self-interest and the Interests of Others?

Whether we like it or not, we are connected to everyone else on the planet. As we saw in Chapter 12 ("Group Dynamics"), a mere six degrees of separation exists between you and someone in Iceland or Angola. The connection goes far deeper than the number of links between people. People are mutually dependent on one another—the separate actions of two people, groups, or societies have consequences for both parties. An incident in one part of the world (e.g., a street demonstration in Egypt) can have dramatic effects on different continents (North America). This *social interdependence* will only increase as we progress through the 21st century, posing pressing challenges for individuals and societies that must be confronted.

Social Dilemmas

We may be connected to other people, but this does not mean that our respective interests coincide. There is often tension between our own self-interest and the interests of others. We take turns when exiting a room even if we are in a hurry, we wait patiently in line at check-out stands behind someone who can't find his or her debit card, we listen to others when we would rather do the talking, and we pay a proportion of our income as taxes to benefit others we will never meet. Self-interest is always present, even in the most intimate of relations. Couples experience mutually desirable actions, of course, but sometimes the partners' respective desires and goals are in conflict, so that one of them must forgo his or her personal self-interest to maintain harmony in the relationship.

Because self-interest is never off the table, the concern with others' welfare is a fragile tendency that is easily derailed. The tensions between immediate self-interest and the interests of others are investigated as *social dilemmas* (Dawes, 1980; Komorita & Parks, 1996; Van Lange, Joireman, Parks, & Van Dijk, 2013). A social dilemma is a situation in which a selfish course of action is tempting for each individual, but in which such an action would result in poor outcomes for everyone if everyone succumbed to this temptation. Social dilemmas are inherent in diverse contexts, from two-person interactions to the relationships among groups and entire societies.

The term *tragedy of the commons* was coined by ecologist Garrett Hardin (1968). The "commons" is a grassy pasture located in the center of old English towns. Hardin was concerned with the sharing of such pastures, but "commons" is used more broadly to describe any shared but limited resource, including air, water, energy sources, food supplies, and land for farming or hunting. The tragedy occurs when some individuals or groups consume more than their share, but the cost of their behavior is shared by everyone. When this happens, it can cause the collapse of the commons—hence, the tragedy of the commons.

Life in today's world is filled with situations reflecting this scenario. In drought-stricken areas, people are encouraged to cut back on watering their lawns, washing their cars, and even taking long showers. If everyone does so, the community has a better chance to survive the drought. But from an individual's perspective, the best outcome is for everyone else to cut back on water usage, while he or she keeps the grass green, the car looking spotless, and his or her hair clean and shiny. The problem is that everyone is thinking the same way—"if others hold back, I won't have to." Other contemporary issues that pit personal interest against collective interest include the overgrazing of common farm land (Hardin's concern), the overharvesting of fish, the recycling of plastics and paper products, the buildup of greenhouse gas in the atmosphere due to the reliance on fossil fuels, and the destruction of the Brazilian rainforest.

The commons dilemma clearly has been simulated in psychology lab experiments. Kevin Brechner (1977), for example, gave groups of three college students a chance to earn a semester's worth of experimental credit (about three hours of time outside of class) in a mere half an hour if they could manage to win 150 points in a game. To win points, they simply had to press a button that took a point from a common pool and placed it in their respective personal accounts. The common pool was visible to all students as a board with 24 lights, with each light representing a point. Whenever a student took a point, one of the lights went out—the more points taken, the more lights that went out. As long as the pool was nearly full (18 or more lights), it replenished rapidly (every 2 seconds). If the pool dropped to between 12 and 18 lights, it replenished more slowly (every 4 seconds). If the pool dropped to between 6 and 12 lights, it replenished even more slowly (every 6 seconds). And if it dropped to fewer than 6 lights (one-fourth its full size), the replenishment rate was very slow (every 8 seconds). Once the last point was taken, the pool stopped replenishing altogether and students could take no more points.

If everyone was greedy and grabbed all the points he or she could, no one would win—after all, there were only 24 points in the initial pool. So in order to succeed (i.e., take 150 points), the students had to cooperate to keep the pool replenished. The fewer the points they took each time, the faster the pool would replenish and enable all the students to achieve their goal. This seems simple enough, but just like the farmers in Hardin's tragedy of the commons, the students ran the pool dry (they "overgrazed") and earned only 14 points on average—far short of the 150 required to get the semester's worth of experimental credit. When the students could communicate with one another, they did somewhat better, earning 70 points on average—but still far short of their goal. So even in an easy-to-understand commons dilemma, people have a tough time maintaining the resources necessary for both personal and group survival. Although the group benefits when individual members restrain themselves from taking too much of a common resource too quickly, the temptation to act selfishly can prove too difficult to resist.

You might think that the only way to get people to suspend their immediate self-interest for the sake of collective interest is to play on other, more fragile, aspects of human nature, such as the capacity for guilt and shame (Chapter 6), the need to belong (Chapter 8), or empathic concern for the needs of others (Chapter 13). Though important, these tendencies are not necessary for people to solve many of the dilemmas they face. The logic of social life, shaped by our evolutionary past, is conducive to the emergence of cooperation under certain conditions.

This approach to social dilemmas is demonstrated in the *Prisoner's Dilemma* (Axelrod & Hamilton, 1981). The dilemma centers on two individuals who have been arrested on suspicion of having committed armed robbery. There is some evidence to support this charge (e.g., they are carrying concealed weapons and were arrested in the vicinity of one of the burglaries), but it is not solid enough to guarantee a conviction. So the police create a dilemma for the individuals that might cause one or both of them to confess to the crime. They do this by interviewing them separately, inviting each to confess to the crime and betray his partner. What happens to either person depends on how both of them react to this invitation. Assume that prior to their arrest, the two agreed to hold out and not confess if they happened to get apprehended.

Because each prisoner has two options—*confess* or *do not confess*—there are four possible combinations, each with a particular pattern of outcomes for the two of them (Figure 14.1). (1) *Mutual cooperation*. Neither prisoner confesses to the crime, so they can only be convicted of a relatively minor charge (carrying concealed weapons) and receive a light jail sentence (one year). (2) *Cooperation/betrayal*. Prisoner A does not confess but Prisoner B does. A assumes that B will stay mum, but B takes advantage of this trust and betrays A to get a better deal for himself. Specifically, B is free to go but A gets nailed for a 10-year sentence. (3) *Betrayal/cooperation*. This is the reverse of the prior combination: A confesses but B does not. Now A is free but B gets the 10-year sentence. (4) *Mutual betrayal*. Both A and B confess, thus betraying one another in the hope of going free. In this case, they both get a moderate jail sentence (5 years).

The dilemma for each prisoner is whether to confess and betray his partner, or to hold out and cooperate with the partner. Although confessing betrays the partner, it protects the prisoner in case the partner also seeks to betray. Refusing to confess (cooperating) is risky because although it could bring a good outcome for both prisoners, it leaves each prisoner vulnerable to the longest sentence if the other prisoner decides to confess. Note that the best outcome for each prisoner occurs if he betrays the other prisoner (by confessing) and the other prisoner cooperates (by not confessing). But the best outcome for both prisoners occurs if both refuse to confess. The prisoner's dilemma is a *non-zero-sum game*, in that both parties can achieve a reasonably satisfactory outcome. This is in contrast to a *zero-sum game*, in which one person's gains are another person's losses, so that the gains and losses add up to zero. Many situations have a zero-sum quality—sporting events have a winner and loser, for example, as do elections and horse races. For that matter, some interpersonal relationships—even some marriages—are zero-sum in that the parties vie for dominance and victory in their interactions. Achieving cooperation in zero-sum situations can thus be quite difficult. In non-zero-sum situations, however, a mutually beneficial outcome is possible if the parties choose to cooperate.

The scenario in the prisoner's dilemma has been employed to see whether people can cooperate when there is a conflict between self-interest and collective interest, and if they can, what behavioral strategies are most conducive to cooperation as opposed to defection. People are not arrested and treated as criminals in this research. But the same pattern of mixed-motives for two players can be generated by substituting rewards (e.g., money) for punishments (jail sentences). The players use the payoff matrix shown in Figure 14.2. On each round, the players simultaneously choose whether to cooperate or to defect, after which both see the outcomes of their choices. The players then make their choices on the next round and see the outcomes of these choices. This process is continued for many rounds—sometimes as many as 200.

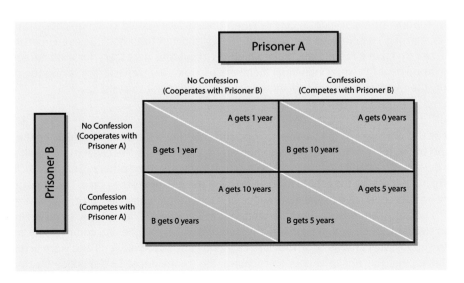

FIGURE 14.1 The Prisoner's Dilemma

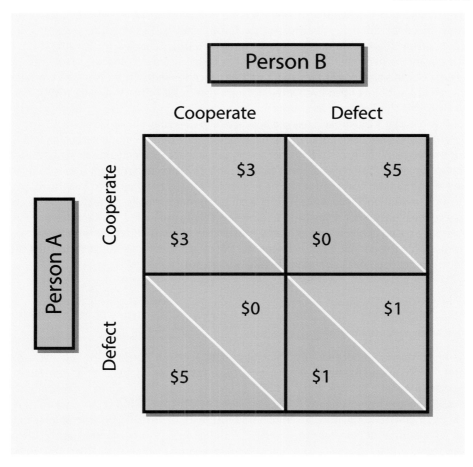

FIGURE 14.2 Mixed Motives in Prisoner's Dilemma Games

Many strategies are commonly employed in this game (Messick & Liebrand, 1995). A player might consistently cooperate or consistently defect, for example, or make a random choice on each round. Yet more complex strategies can be envisioned, such as a sequence of several cooperative choices followed by a switch to defection. Of all the strategies that have been tested, however, one has proven to be most effective at maximizing the gains of both players (Axelrod & Hamilton, 1981). That strategy—referred to as *tit-for-tat*—is based on the notion of reciprocity. On the first round, the player (A) cooperates. After that, he or she does what the other player (B) does. If B also cooperates, A and B continue cooperating and thereby maximize their collective outcomes. But if B defects on the first round, A reciprocates that behavior by defecting on the second round. If B continues to defect, A follows suit and defects as well. Mutual defection does neither player any good, so B is likely to switch to cooperation—which is then matched by A. Over time, then, both A and B see the benefit of cooperation and achieve better outcomes than the outcomes achieved by players employing different strategies.

Cooperation, though highly valued and encouraged in most societies, is a fragile tendency that is easily derailed. Still, it is part of human nature (M. Nowak, 2006; E. O. Wilson, 2012), and tends to emerge under certain conditions—including some surprising ones. What would you expect to happen, for example, when resources are scarce, so that there is not enough for everyone to feel personally satisfied? You might think that this would kill the willingness to cooperate, unleashing people's selfish desires to make sure they are not left out. Cooperation is great when there is enough to go around, but when things get tight, it's "every man for himself."

This sounds reasonable, but it is apparently not the case. Research with the Prisoner's Dilemma has shown that there is a tendency for cooperation to *increase*, not decrease, when environmental conditions are harsh or when resources are scarce rather than plentiful (Requejo & Camacho, 2011; Schank & McElreath, 2013). In the short run, defectors have the advantage because they can "sucker" the cooperators into sharing scarce resources and not giving anything in return. But this strategy is very short sighted. Once the defector's resources are exhausted, he or she cannot expect anyone to trust him or her. Even if the defector mends his or her ways and tries to cooperate with others, they are unlikely to see this behavior as sincere.

The essence of the Prisoner's Dilemma is easy to appreciate in everyday life with respect to a variety of resources, from food and water to class notes and parking spaces. Imagine, for example, students pulling into a parking lot with too few spaces for everyone. When two students get to the same space—the only one not taken—each has the choice of grabbing the space or letting the other student take it. Let's say that students are aware of this limited resource and have indicated ahead of time how they would deal with it. Perhaps they agree to take turns, so that each would voluntarily park in a distant lot once in a while. This is a situation that is ripe for defection. In the short run, the best strategy is to agree to the plan but not abide by it. So while everyone else makes the sacrifice once in a while, a defector grabs the desirable parking space when he or she is expected to head off to the remote lot. He or she wins—but only that day. The next time the parking issue is discussed, the other students are unlikely to trust the person and will exclude him or her from the cooperative strategy that is worked out.

Box 14.1   The Neurochemistry of Cooperation

Cooperation is understandable because it is vital to human survival. But in going against the grain of self-interest, it hardly seems a candidate for feeling good. The benefit of cooperation is the end result, not the intrinsic feeling. Or so we tend to think. It turns out that cooperation is often a pleasant experience at a biological level. James Rilling and his colleagues (2002) provided evidence that the brain is wired to make cooperation pleasing in the moment, not just in the anticipated future. In their study, 36 women played the Prisoner's Dilemma Game with another person over the internet, and their brains were scanned using fMRI technology as they did so. The results of the scans showed that when the women made cooperative choices (which they did frequently), reward-related regions of the brain (the nucleus accumbens, ventral caudate, and ventromedial/orbitofrontal cortex) lit up, indicating heightened neural activity. These regions of the brain are rich in dopamine receptors and are activated by a wide variety of rewards, from sweet tastes and smells to pictures of tropical vacations and pleasant skin sensations. Cooperation may represent enlightened self-interest, but it is apparently rewarding in a far more immediate sense as well.

Public Goods Game

The tendency for people to suspend their desire for immediate personal gain in order to reap long-term benefits has been revealed in the *Public Goods Game* (Gunnthorsdottir, Houser, & McCabe, 2007). A group of people sits around a table and each person is given a few dollars. They are told they can put as much money as they want in the community pot. The pot is doubled, and everyone then gets an equal portion back. Let's say there are 10 people, each of whom is given $2. If everyone puts in his or her money, there is $20 in the pot. This gets doubled to $40, so each person gets back $4. On each round, each person must decide how much money to contribute to the "public good." You might think that everyone would simply put in the maximum amount, so that everyone would double his or her money on every round.

But look at it another way. If everyone but you puts in $2 on the first round, the pot would be $18 and everyone—including you, who contributed nothing—would get back $3.60 ($18 doubled is $36, and $36 divided by 10 is $3.60). So you would now have $5.60—the original $2 plus the $3.60—instead of the $4 you would have had if you put in your $2. So, from a purely self-interested point of view, it makes more sense to withhold your money and benefit from the contributions of everyone else. But everyone else recognizes the personal benefit of selfishness too, and if everyone acts on this basis, the pot is empty and no one benefits.

So what do people typically do? Most people do not act selfishly at first. During the first round, most people contribute about half their tokens to the public pot. But as each round passes, and people see others free riding, the rate of contribution drops. By the last round, 70%-80% of the players are free riding, and the group as a whole is poorer than it would be otherwise. It only takes one cheater to make the economy sputter out. People would rather lose than help someone who is only taking and not giving. If the game is played so that everyone can see who puts in their fair share, the pot tends to grow for a while, but starts to shrink as people begin to test the water by withholding their money. The behavior spreads because no one wants to be a chump, and eventually the economy grinds to a halt.

Players fall into three general categories. Some are selfish and tend to free ride. Some are altruists, who contribute heavily to the public pot initially and continue to do so even as others ride free. But most players are "conditional consenters." They start out contributing some of their wealth, but watching others free ride makes them far less likely to keep putting money in it. By the last round, almost all the conditional consenters are no longer cooperating.

This game has implications for the temptation to cheat in paying taxes. From a public goods perspective, if everyone pays the taxes he or she owes, the pot—the money in the Treasury—grows and the government can pay its bills and provide services to the country's citizens. But from a selfish perspective, each person is tempted to payer fewer taxes than what he or she owes and free ride on the contributions of everyone else. But the results of the Public Goods Game suggest that when people sense that cheating is going on, they are inclined to follow suit, not wanting to be the chump in the system. The upshot is that many people, acting as "conditional consenters," find ways to avoid paying what they truly owe in taxes, a tendency that diminishes the revenue that could be used by the government for the public good.

Defection Versus Cooperation

Evolution has equipped us with enormous brainpower that enables us to cheat and enhance our own gain at the expense of others. But the same forces in our past equipped us with the ability to detect cheaters (Tooby & Cosmides, 1992). Essentially, then, there is a balance of forces in human nature—a natural inclination to deceive and cheat others, and built-in radar for detecting the expression of this inclination in others.

What factors dictate which side of the mixed-motive scenario people enact when they are in an interdependent relation with one another? You might expect that the answer boils down to personality. Some people are simply more selfish than others and thus more likely to defect when they think they can get away with it. And you would be right. There is indeed evidence to support the role of *individual differences* in the approach to social dilemmas. But regardless of personality, at least two other factors can influence how anyone is likely to behave in a social dilemma: people's *expectations and trust* concerning one another's behavior, and people's sensitivity to *personal standards* of appropriate behavior.

Individual Differences

Everyday observation suggests that people vary a great deal in their approach to social dilemmas (Griesinger & Livingston, 1973; Messick & McClintock, 1968). You may know some people who focus only on "what's in it for them" and attempt to enhance their own outcomes at the expense of other people's outcomes. But you probably know others who are genuinely concerned with how other people fare and cooperate rather than compete in social situations. For that matter, you might reflect on your own pattern of behavior and assign yourself to one orientation or another. How do these individual differences develop? What makes you such a sensitive soul and the guy down the street such a selfish jerk?

Paul Van Lange and his colleagues provide evidence that childhood experiences shape how people approach social dilemmas (Van Lange, Otten, DeBruin, & Joireman, 1997). In particular, they have documented a link between social orientation and *attachment style* (Bowlby, 1969; Hazen & Shaver, 1987), a basic pattern of social relations discussed in Chapter 9 ("Close Relationships"). People who are disposed toward cooperation are more likely to have a secure attachment in their romantic relationships—presumably modeled on the secure attachment they had with their parents—than are those with a more egoistic or competitive orientation. With less fear of abandonment, these individuals feel comfortable with others and are inclined to trust the people they encounter. This attitude primes them to approach social interactions, even those involving a potential conflict of interest, in a cooperative manner. In contrast, people who experienced insecure attachment in childhood are more likely to be wary of other people in adulthood and approach social relations with an egoistic or competitive orientation.

Individual differences in cooperative versus competitive orientations can also be acquired through interaction with siblings during childhood (Van Lange et al., 1997). Cooperative individuals tend to have more siblings than do egoists and these brothers and sisters tend to be older. In growing up in a home with several brothers and sisters, children learn that they cannot get by with selfishness, but rather must learn rules about sharing. Older siblings, too, are better at modeling these rules–and at enforcing them!

What happens when cooperators and competitors play social dilemma games? Cooperators see such games (and relevant situations in real life) as an issue of good versus bad behavior, with *cooperation as good*. Competitors see such games (and other interpersonal situations) as an issue of strong versus weak, with *cooperation as weak* (Liebrand, Wilke, & Wolters, 1986). When cooperators play other cooperators, the outcome is, not surprisingly, cooperation and the maximization of collective gains. When both players are disposed toward competition, the game quickly degenerates into mutual defection and both parties suffer. The interesting case is when a cooperator plays with a competitor. Unfortunately, the results confirm that "bad is stronger than good"–a point made in Chapter 7 ("Social Judgment"). Defection takes precedence over cooperation, and the game degenerates into a mutually antagonistic pattern, with both parties losing rather than winning (Kelley & Stahelski, 1970; Miller & Holmes, 1975).

Expectations and Trust

Regardless of their personal social orientations, people are likely to behave cooperatively if they believe that others will do so as well, and to behave competitively if this is what they expect from others. Such beliefs can operate as a *self-fulfilling prophecy*. As discussed in Chapter 8 ("Social Interaction"), if people expect someone to behave in a certain manner, they tend to elicit that behavior through their own actions (Darley & Fazio, 1980; Rosenthal & Jacobson, 1968; Snyder & Haugen, 1994). Such *behavioral confirmation* plays a role in determining whether people cooperate or defect in *mixed-motive games*.

The self-fulfilling nature of expectations is investigated by leading a person to think that his or her partner in a social dilemma game tends to be either cooperative or competitive (e.g., Snyder & Swann, 1978b). In fact, this information is misleading–the partner was chosen randomly from a pool of participants and so was not necessarily cooperative or competitive. But expectations can trump reality. If participants expect their partner to be cooperative, they approach the game in a cooperative manner and the partner responds in kind, so everyone comes out on top. If the participants expect their partner to be competitive, however, they "protect" themselves by behaving competitively–a strategy which promotes competition in the partner. The game results in poor outcomes for the participants and their partners.

Box 14.2   A Chemical Basis for Trust

Recall the discussion of *oxytocin*–the "love molecule"–in Chapter 9 ("Close Relationships"). The release of this peptide into the bloodstream turns promiscuous rodents into love-struck life partners, and it tends to promote feelings of love and commitment in humans as well. The significance of oxytocin may extend far beyond lovers, helping to cement social and economic transactions among total strangers. It does so by creating trust–an effect that has been demonstrated in the aptly named *Trust Game* (Kosfeld et al., 2005; Zak, 2005). This game is deceptively simple. Participants are given a certain amount of money (e.g., $10) and asked to give some of it, however much they want, to a stranger. The experimenter then triples the value of that gift, and the stranger gives some portion of the new amount back to the original participant.

Before the participant can feel comfortable giving away a sizable portion of his or her money, he or she clearly must trust that the stranger will return the favor by returning a sizable portion of the new (tripled) sum. Half the participants in the study inhaled oxytocin prior to playing the trust game, while the other half inhaled a saline solution. The differences between the two groups were striking: those who inhaled the oxytocin were more than twice as likely to give away the maximum amount of money.

If, as many economists argue, trust is the engine of cooperative relationships and the glue of healthy communities and nations, these findings have intriguing implications—and possible applications. Perhaps oxytocin should be dispensed during difficult negotiations between parties to a long-standing conflict. Or maybe oxytocin could be introduced in the context of marital therapy, economic transactions, and political campaigns. Of course, such intervention would have to be done in a subtle manner without the participants' awareness, to avoid their being on guard and reacting in the opposite manner. A bit of an irony here: the recipients of a manipulation designed to forge trust would have to be duped into this mental state without their consent.

Self-Regulation

People can think about what they do in many different ways (Vallacher & Wegner, 1987). These *act identities* range from those that are abstract and comprehensive (*high level*) to those that are concrete and specific (*low level*). This difference in how people think about their action has implications for how they view social dilemmas. For one thing, moral principles are more abstract than are specific behaviors (Carver & Scheier, 1999; Eyal, Liberman, & Trope, 2008; Vallacher & Wegner, 1987). So when thinking about behavior in higher-level terms, people should be sensitive to the collective good as opposed to their narrow self-interest. Beyond that, high-level act identities are associated with greater self-control and a focus on long-term as opposed to short-term consequences (Fujita, Trope, Liberman, & Levin-Sagi, 2006; Vallacher & Wegner, 1989). Perhaps inducing people to think in relatively high-level terms about their behavior could increase the likelihood of cooperation in social dilemmas.

OK, but how can people be induced to think about their behavior in relatively high- versus low-level terms? In everyday life, we are typically focused on the specific features of what we're doing, less so on the broader implications and meanings of the action. Recall from action identification theory, however, that we shift our attention to higher-level act identities when an action is familiar or relatively easy to perform (Vallacher & Wegner, 1987). Once we have become proficient at playing tennis or taking notes during a lecture, for example, we no longer focus on our hand movements or keystrokes, but focus instead on showing our skill or learning new course material. To the extent that people are familiar with contexts involving cooperation and competition, then, they might see the bigger picture in such contexts and control their behavior with long-term consequences rather than short-term gain in mind.

Even if people are unfamiliar with such contexts, they can be induced to think about them in higher-level terms. Asking people *how* they do something sensitizes them to the lower-level details of the action and thus takes their minds off the action's higher-level meaning. But asking people *why* they are doing something sensitizes them to the implications and consequences of their behavior (Freitas, Gollwitzer, & Trope, 2004; Wegner et al., 1984). Assuming this applies to how people think about their behavior in social dilemmas, it has implications for issues involving scarce resources. Whether the issue is energy conservation, water usage, or land management, individuals who are inspired (or induced) to think in abstract, comprehensive terms may be more inclined to act in accordance with the collective good than those who are inclined (or encouraged) to think about the means by which they perform their actions.

Social Justice

How Important Is Justice to Social Life?

The nature of social dilemmas implies that people are first and foremost concerned with maximizing their self-interest. If people suspend this concern in favor of collective interest, it is only because this generates a better personal outcome in the long run. There is another way, however, to think about people's willingness to set aside their personal self-interest and live with a state of affairs that may not be the most rewarding for them. This perspective on social life centers on the notion of *justice* (e.g., Deutsch, 1985; Homans, 1961; Lerner, 1980). The basic idea is that people are sometimes more concerned with members of group or society "getting what they deserve" than with getting the most for themselves. Thus, people are not only willing to accept less than maximal gains for themselves, they are *motivated* to accept less if doing so preserves their notion of what is fair and appropriate.

Justice is considered by social scientists of all stripes—political scientists, economists, anthropologists, and social psychologists—to be critical to social life. Inequality is a fact of life with respect to any outcome, whether wealth, status, popularity, health, or talent. To live with inequality without bitterness and competition, to achieve social harmony, and to coordinate efforts to achieve common goals, the members of a social system must agree on the terms of these inequalities. The failure to do so would promote continual conflict, with the group or society descending into chaos. But agreeing on what constitutes justice is hardly an easy matter. Wars are fought over competing notions of justice, and internal dissent in a society often has a perception of injustice as the primary cause.

Justice and Human Nature

You might think that justice is a feature of human behavior that falls on the nurture side of the *nature versus nurture debate*. Life is a struggle, and those without an innate tendency to "look out for number one" would seem to be at a disadvantage in this struggle. We have to overcome this natural tendency—with the help of childhood socialization, agreed-upon social norms, and experience in solving dilemmas of self- versus collective interest—to acquire a concern with justice in social relations. The games devoted to social dilemmas discussed to this point (e.g., the Prisoner's Dilemma) assume that people behave in a cooperative rather selfish fashion only because it is in their long-term self-interest to do so.

Learning, socialization, and long-term self-interest are clearly important, but research has highlighted the biological and evolutionary foundations of justice in human relations. Although sensitive to personal gain, people have an innate concern with fairness in their relations with one another. Justice, however, can mean different things and be manifest in various ways.

Revenge

Perhaps the most basic form of justice is *revenge*. When people feel they have been taken advantage of, cheated, or otherwise treated unfairly, they experience intense anger and a desire to seek vengeance and restitution for the injustice. The innate basis for this motive is evident in the social interactions of young children, who reserve their greatest anger for those who have treated them unfairly by taking a toy, telling a lie, or betraying a confidence. Striking evidence for the innate basis of justice comes from observations of other species (McCullough, 2008). Primates respond with anger and an eye toward revenge when a member of their group does something that upsets the order of the group or takes more than his or her fair share of resources. Even certain species of birds demonstrate what appears to be vengeful behavior.

The importance of revenge is apparent in the criminal justice system. Several reasons can be advanced for why someone who has been convicted of a serious crime should be incarcerated. These include *protection* (a person in prison cannot continue to commit crimes), *deterrence* (incarcerating a person sends a signal that deters others from acting in the same fashion), *rehabilitation* (prison time might motivate the person to mend his ways and resist behaving in a criminal fashion upon his or her release), and *revenge* (prison sentences are set in proportion to the crime's seriousness—with execution employed in a few countries to avenge the most heinous crimes). But when laypeople are probed for their beliefs about the rationale for incarceration, "just deserts"—essentially, revenge—tops the list (Carlsmith, Darley, & Robinson, 2002). This is especially true when they are asked to provide a rationale for the death penalty. We want the person who has committed a heinous crime to suffer for what he or she has done, even if a life sentence is thought to have as much deterrence power and even if the person could conceivably be rehabilitated—something that clearly is not accomplished by killing him or her.

Belief in a Just World

Justice is more than simply seeking vengeance for unfair treatment. Concerns with justice are salient in situations involving rewards and praise as well as punishment and condemnation. Justice broadly defined means that "people get what they deserve and deserve what they get" (Hafer & Bègue, 2005; Lerner, 1980). In a particularly influential theory, Melvin Lerner (1980) argued that people everywhere want to maintain a *belief in a just world*, and use this belief to allocate rewards and punishments to others and to judge the worthiness of others based on the rewards and punishments they receive. Thus, talented and hard-working people deserve to be compensated more than people with less talent or willingness to put forth effort. We lavish praise on people who contribute to science and the arts, talented athletes, and those who sacrifice for the well-being of others. By the same token, those who are lazy or untalented do not deserve to have the same positive outcomes as the rest of us, and we heap scorn on those who have behaved in an especially selfish or hurtful manner toward others.

Lerner argues that the belief in justice is more fundamental than a concern with self-interest. This is evident in research conducted in support of *equity theory* (Adams, 1965). If a person feels that his or her contributions to a group effort are not as good as the contributions of other group members, he or she is content with receiving correspondingly less compensation (e.g., Messé, 1971). Even when people are assured that no one will know that they have received more than they deserve, they nonetheless feel uncomfortable (e.g., guilty) with this distribution of rewards (Walster, Berscheid, & Walster, 1973). A concern with an equitable distribution of outcomes reduces antagonism and jealousy among people who differ in the quality of their experiences and it provides a common yardstick for determining how people should be compensated. This concern is more pronounced, though, in large-scale modern societies (e.g., the United States) than in smaller traditional societies where exchanges take place among individuals who are familiar with one another (Schafer, Haun, & Tomasello, 2015).

Box 14.3   Is Justice Uniquely Human?

A sense of fairness may not be a quality that only humans possess. Sarah Brosnan and Frans de Waal (2003) conducted an intriguing study featuring capuchin monkeys (see photo below). The monkeys (all female) were taught to trade pebbles in return for a slice of cucumber. Once they learned that pebbles equaled cucumber, the monkeys were paired together. At first, the trades were equitable, with both monkeys receiving cucumbers in exchange for pebbles. But as the research progressed, one monkey in each pair began receiving a grape—far more desirable than a cucumber to a monkey (and to most people, for that matter)—in return for pebbles. The other monkey, however, continued to get cucumbers. To make matters worse, some monkeys received grapes or cucumbers for doing nothing, while their partners still had to retrieve a pebble and bring it to the researcher.

As the inequitable trades continued, the shortchanged partners became noticeably upset. They did not want the cucumbers any more, and in some cases they threw the food out of their cage. The researchers also varied the amount of effort required to complete the exchange. When the monkeys had to expend more effort, they were especially sensitive to inequity and less likely to accept cucumber slices when their partners received grapes for equal or less work. For a monkey to refuse a perfectly fine food like a cucumber just because another monkey is getting something better is irrational from an economic perspective. Maximizing one's benefits requires that whenever one is given something, one should take it. So monkeys, like people, are sometimes more concerned with being treated fairly than with obtaining rewards. Justice, it seems, is a fundamental motive in social relations, at least among primates.

Source: Alamy.com

Ironic Justice

You might think that belief in a just world would motivate people to help those who suffer misfortune, or at least to promote sympathy for them. This is certainly true, but there are conditions that produce the *opposite* effect: the derogation of victims (Callan, Ellard, & Nicol, 2007; Lerner & Simmons, 1966). In fact, those with the strongest belief in a just world are sometimes the *most* likely to derogate victims (Rubin & Peplau, 1975). This seems strange, but it follows from the just world hypothesis. A belief in justice means not only that people should get what they deserve, but also that they *do* get what they deserve. Now, as long as a victim's plight is remedied, or stands a chance of being remedied, the belief in justice promotes sympathy and attempts to help the victim. But if the plight cannot be remedied, this raises the possibility that the world is not so just after all. To those who believe strongly in justice—which includes most everyone to some degree—this is an uncomfortable, if not downright threatening idea.

One way to make sense of misfortune that cannot be remedied is to see the misfortune as somehow deserved, which essentially means blaming victims for their plight (Kay, Jost, & Young, 2005; Lerner & Miller, 1978). For example, although most people feel compassion for female victims of rape, there is a tendency to blame the victim for what happened to her when the perpetrator of the rape is not apprehended (Jones & Aronson, 1973; Luginbuhl & Mullin, 1981). To maintain their belief in justice, observers tend to find fault with the personal character or the actions of the rape victim. Developmental psychologists have documented this mode of justice reasoning—which they refer to as *immanent justice*—in young children, but assumed that it gave way to more sophisticated reasoning by late childhood and adolescence (Piaget, 1932/1965). Apparently, people never fully outgrow this psychological tendency, even when serious issues of crime and punishment are at stake (Callan et al., 2007).

Victims can also be held responsible—getting what they deserve—if observers are sensitive to the role of choice in everyday life. A true victim, after all, does not choose to have things go wrong. It turns out that even thinking about the role of choice regarding mundane matters can undermine people's sympathy for the plight of someone who has experienced misfortune, even if observers know nothing about the choices the person actually made.

This point was made in a series of studies by Savani, Stephens, and Markus (2011). Participants in one study watched a 6-minute video of a male college student doing some very mundane activities in his apartment—opening mail, playing a CD, reading magazines, and eating chocolates. To activate the concept of choice, half the participants were instructed to press the spacebar whenever they saw the student make a choice. Participants in the control condition were instructed to press the spacebar whenever the student touched an object. Participants then read six vignettes that described people experiencing decidedly negative outcomes: having a heart attack, dropping out of high school, being physically abused, failing a high-school-diploma test, losing one's home because of a building collapse, and getting into a car accident. They were asked to rate the extent to which each victim was to blame for his or her outcome, and these ratings were averaged across the six vignettes.

The results were clear: participants who noted an actor making mundane choices tended to assign greater blame to victims for their misfortune than did participants who were not sensitized to choice. The effect of choice was especially strong for participants who described themselves as politically liberal as opposed to conservative (Figure 14.3). So although liberals are generally more sensitive than conservatives to the suffering of others (Graham et al., 2011), this difference is largely eliminated when liberals are induced to think about the role of choice in everyday life.

Choice had similar effects on participants' attitudes regarding social policies designed to remedy misfortunes. Compared to participants who noted whether the actor in the video touched objects, those who attended to his mundane choices indicated less support for affirmative action, banning violent video games, and reducing unhealthy foods in school lunches. When sensitized to choice, people feel that someone who suffers a misfortune is not truly a victim, but rather a causal agent who made choices that led to his or her unfortunate outcomes. Thinking about choice does not reduce people's support for any government policy, though. Savani et al. (2011) found that after focusing on choices, people were more supportive of policies like legalizing marijuana, which would reduce government's interference in people's lives.

The effect of choice on undermining sympathy for those who experience misfortune may be more pronounced in individualistic cultures, in which a high value is placed on personal responsibility. Savani et al. (2011) tested this idea by comparing the responses of American and Indian college students. Some participants were asked to make a series of rather mundane choices among various items, whereas others simply looked at the items without choosing among them. Afterward, participants read about a poor 7-year-old boy from the African country of Mali who was in danger

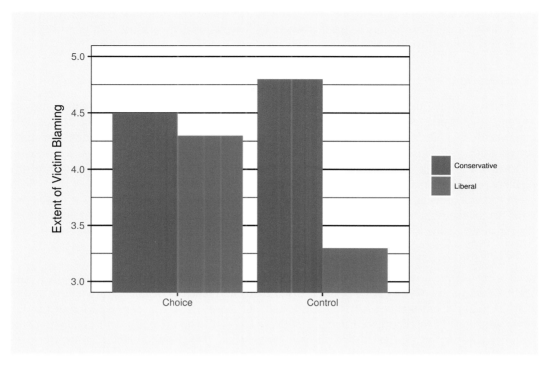

FIGURE 14.3 Sensitization to Choice and Blaming Others for their Bad Experiences
Source: Adapted from Savani et al. (2011)

of starvation. Americans who made choices were considerably less sympathetic and far less interested in helping the boy than those in the non-choice condition. The Indian students, in contrast, were not affected by the manipulation of choice. Presumably, people in India—and perhaps those in collectivist societies in general—view actions as part of a larger situational and cultural context rather than as matters of personal choice and responsibility.

The modern world provides an almost limitless array of choices that were not there for previous generations, creating the potential for greater personal control and intrinsic motivation. People can choose how to dress, what to eat, whom to marry, what occupation to pursue, what to eat, and what books to read. In light of the effect of choice on reactions to victims of misfortune, one can wonder whether the increased choice in our lives may impact the way we respond to people who suffer due to personal experiences or events beyond their control. Particularly with the ability of mass media to broadcast disasters wherever and whenever they occur, people may find it easier to dismiss the needs of victims, perhaps rationalizing their plight in various ways.

Ultimate Justice

Nonetheless, when faced with a clear injustice—as when a good person suffers or a bad person benefits—people may find it hard to restore justice by convincing themselves that the person deserved his or her fate. When a close friend suffers a tragic accident, for example, you are unlikely to start finding fault with his or her character or actions in his or her past. By the same token, when a despised person acquires a monetary fortune, you are unlikely to see him or her as a deserving person. In such instances, people engage in *ultimate justice* reasoning (Callan, Harvey, Dawtry, & Sutton, 2013; Hafer & Gosse, 2010). Essentially, this means that people imagine subsequent events that will restore the injustice: the good person who experiences a misfortune will later have fulfillment in his or her life, whereas the bad person who experiences fortune will encounter hardships or unpleasant outcomes in the future.

In a religious context, a concern with ultimate justice can reinforce people's notion of heaven and hell (Lerner, 1991). Particularly when the misfortune of a good person is long-term suffering or death, religious people comfort themselves and others by saying that the person has "gone to a better place," or is now in the company of God. When a bad person avoids punishment for his or her misdeeds, meanwhile, they invoke hell and eternal damnation as a means of restoring justice for what the person has done and for his or her wicked character.

System Justification

Equality has been the exception rather than the rule in societies throughout history. Even in nations built upon values emphasizing equal rights and laws designed to curb abuses of power, social and demographic groups differ in their social capital, wealth, and education, and these assets translate directly into differential influence in shaping public policy (Deutsch, 2006; Sidanius & Pratto, 1999). Yet, despite inequality in resources, income, and access to power, there is remarkably little conflict between the "haves" and "have-nots." To some extent, the lack of social unrest in the face of inequality reflects a realistic assessment by the disadvantaged of what would happen if they challenged the status quo. But the lack of social unrest goes beyond resignation on the part of groups with lower power. According to John Jost and his colleagues, there is a tendency for people to perceive inequality as legitimate and fair. How people come to this conclusion is the focus of *system justification theory* (Jost, Banaji, & Nosek, 2004).

Inequality and Fairness

The stability of a social system—whether a family, an organization, or a nation—can be maintained by force, coercion, and intimidation. But maintaining order by such means is costly and tends to be counterproductive in the long run. Those who are in power might feel fine with the status quo, but those who are on the receiving end of coercion are unhappy with their lot in life, feel oppressed, and are motivated to overthrow the oppressors (Sidanius & Pratto, 1999).

If authoritarian rule and intimidation do not maintain order in a system characterized by various forms of inequality, what does? The critical factor, according to system justification theory, is consensus among members of the system that the system is legitimate and that their experiences *vis-à-vis* one another are justified and appropriate. One might think that whether inequality is justified depends on which side of the inequality a person is on. It is hardly surprising that those who benefit from inequality tend to justify the status quo. But shouldn't those who are on the losing side of inequality—people from lower socio-economic classes, for example—resent people who are advantaged, question the nature of the system that promotes such inequality, and work to promote social change?

Such resentment does not seem to be case. Even if there is enormous income and social inequality, people on the losing end tend to feel that the distribution of money, power, and status is appropriate. There is evidence, in fact, that the members of low-status, disadvantaged, and marginalized groups are *more* likely than their high-status and advantaged counterparts to perceive the social system as legitimate and just (Jost, Pelham, Sheldon, & Sullivan, 2003). "Just world" beliefs (Lerner, 1980), moreover, are held with greater conviction in cultures with extremes of wealth and poverty than in cultures where wealth and status are more evenly distributed (Dalbert & Yamauchi, 1994; Furnham, 1993). India and South Africa both have extreme levels of income inequality, but people in these countries have a stronger belief in a just world than do people in the United States, Australia, Hong Kong, Great Britain, and Israel.

Even when disadvantaged people publicly express dissatisfaction with the status quo, assessment of their unconscious attitudes with the *Implicit Association Test* (Greenwald, McGhee, & Schwartz, 1998) often reveals a pattern of in-group and out-group evaluation that is consistent with the power asymmetry (Jost, Pelham, Brett, & Carvallo, 2002). In essence, there is implicit consensus among members of the society that the poor have less because they deserve less.

You might think that when attention is drawn to inequalities, people would be less inclined to justify this state of affairs. Actually, system justification actually *increases* in such instances. McCoy and Major (2003), for example, asked women to read about disadvantage suffered by women in general. If the women had previously been primed with system-justifying ideologies (e.g., meritocracy), they tended to blame themselves and women generally for the disadvantages, and to minimize the impact of discrimination. Even more surprising, these women also tended to endorse gender stereotypes and ascribe stereotypically feminine traits to themselves.

Psychological Compensation for Inequality

In justifying the status quo, people in the more powerful group do not simply assign bad traits to those with less power. To the contrary, people sometimes find a saving grace in the low power group's lot in life. It is easier to live with inequality if one feels that those on the losing end have experiences that make up for their poor economic or social status. Sure, they may be poor, but they are satisfied with life in their own way.

In support of this idea, Kay and Jost (2003) exposed participants to a rich person who was either happy or unhappy and to a poor person who was either happy or unhappy. After this exposure, participants completed a questionnaire that assessed their tendency to see the social and economic system as just. As Figure 14.4 illustrates, participants tended to demonstrate a high degree of system justification if they learned of a rich person who was unhappy or of a poor person who was happy. But their system justification tendency was weakened if the rich person was happy or the poor person was unhappy. Seeing someone as "poor but happy" seems to even the scales psychologically, enabling people to feel the system is basically just and appropriate.

Limits to System Justification

System justification is particularly likely under four conditions (Kay & Friesen, 2011). It is enhanced, first of all, when there is a perceived threat to the system. Especially when people from different countries challenge the legitimacy of the social system, people rally around the flag to deflect the challenge. Second, people are inclined to justify the status quo if they are dependent on the system, and would fare even worse if things were to change. Third, system justification is enhanced when there is no viable alternative to the status quo—in effect, when the system seems inescapable. Fourth, system justification tends to be greatest among those who have a weak sense of personal control. Feeling powerless to change things, such people are inclined to accept their fate and justify it as warranted and appropriate.

These conditions are often met in a stable social system in which issues of inequality are not called into question. But when circumstances upset the existing social order, assumptions concerning justice may be questioned and challenged. Individuals and segments of social system that have been on the losing end of inequality may gain a sense

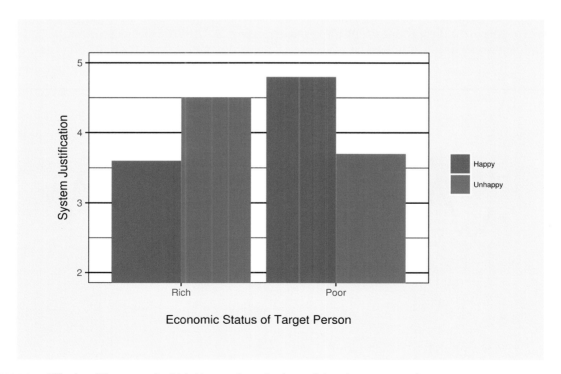

FIGURE 14.4 Effects of Exposure to Rich Versus Poor Protagonists Who Are Described as Happy Versus Unhappy on System Justification

Source: Adapted from Kay & Jost (2003)

of power and become motivated to challenge the status quo and essentially renegotiate what constitutes fairness and justice. Particularly if the current system is no longer seen as inescapable and an alternative system can be envisioned, inequalities that previously had passed for justice may be viewed as unacceptable. In effect, people stop justifying the system and begin working to bring about social change.

This scenario is epitomized by the civil rights movement that reached a peak in the United States in the 1960s. As barriers to education, housing, and employment were weakened through legislation, African Americans and other minority groups embraced the possibility of escaping poverty and discrimination. One might think that such progress would have been greeted with celebration and happiness by those whose parents and distant ancestors had lived with unequal treatment. But instead, these positive disruptions to the status quo undermined the system justification tendencies that had previously characterized the expectations of disenfranchised members of society. It's noteworthy that riots in the inner cities of Los Angeles, Detroit, and other metropolitan areas occurred with increasing frequency *after* civil rights legislation was passed by the federal government. In effect, the destabilization of system justification tendencies promoted a "revolution of rising expectations," with people's vision of a new social order outpacing the achievement of this state of affairs.

A similar scenario can be seen in other social movements, such as the push for women's rights and for marriage equality regardless of sexual orientation. The traditional division of roles between men and women were called into question as women entered the work force and achieved college education on par with men. And people with a homosexual orientation became increasingly dissatisfied with traditional views of what constitutes a "normal" relationship that precluded them from getting married and receiving the social and material benefits associated with that institution. With societal change, old assumptions gave way to new expectations, which often outstripped actual gains. The gap between expectation and reality continues to be experienced today as dissatisfaction and frustration in these and other segments of society.

The idea that noticeable changes in a system can undermine system justification tendencies is interesting to consider in light of the rather dramatic changes in income inequality that have occurred since the 1980s in the United States. People can live with inequality, but when the scale of inequality is magnified, their tendency to justify the system responsible for inequality is weakened, if not undermined entirely. Figure 14.5 shows the income share of the top 1% from 1913 to 2013 in the United States. Note the U-shaped pattern, with the high points occurring in 1928—just prior to the Great Depression—and in 2007—just before the Great Recession that began in 2008. After decades of stability

FIGURE 14.5 The Growth of Income Inequality in the United States
Source: https://inequality.org/facts/income-inequality/

following World War II, the share of national income experienced by the top 1% has increased dramatically and has regained its pre-war level. Dramatic changes such as this call into question the justifications for inequality.

Using General Social Survey data from 1972 to 2008, Oishi, Kesebir, and Diener (2011) found that Americans were on average happier in the years with less national income inequality. The relation between inequality and unhappiness was especially pronounced among lower- as opposed to higher-income respondents. This effect was not due to their lower household incomes, but rather reflected a lack of trust in others and a perceived lack of fairness. It is not inequality per se that promotes dissatisfaction, but rather the feeling that the system is unjust.

Rising inequality is associated with increasing political polarization in the US electorate, with Republicans and Democrats finding little common ground regarding economic, social, and international policies (Vallacher, 2015). This divide is illustrated in Figure 14.6, which presents the results of a Pew survey of liberal and conservative attitudes held by self-proclaimed Republicans and Democrats at three points in time–1994, 2004, and 2014. The lack of common ground during periods of increasing inequality may reflect a breakdown in trust. When people lose trust in one another, they stop justifying the system and retreat to their own ideological corners and have little use for compromise.

Political Orientation

World history has witnessed a wide variety of political orientations, each representing a set of assumptions and beliefs concerning the role of government in people's lives. Despite their unique features and specific policies expressed in different cultures, these various orientations reflect one of two general orientations. The *liberal* orientation emphasizes the importance of equality and related notions such as social justice, whereas the *conservative* orientation emphasizes the importance of freedom and personal responsibility (Rokeach, 1973). To ensure that people are treated fairly and not exploited by those with greater power and access to resources, liberals are willing to grant government

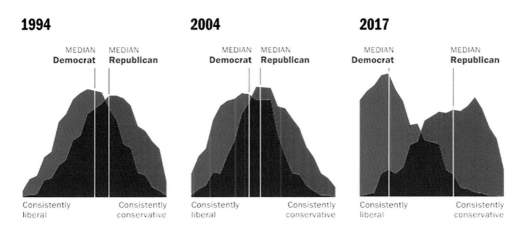

Democrats and Republicans more ideologically divided than in the past

Distribution of Democrats and Republicans on a 10-item scale of political values

Notes: Ideological consistency based on a scale of 10 political values questions (see methodology). The blue area in this chart represents the ideological distribution of Democrats and Democratic-leaning independents; the red area of Republicans and Republican-leaning independents. The overlap of these two distributions is shaded purple.
Source: Survey conducted June 8-18, 2017.

PEW RESEARCH CENTER

FIGURE 14.6 The Polarization of Republicans and Democrats in Liberal vs. Conservative Political, Economic, and Social Attitudes

Source: "Democrats and Republicans more ideologically divided than in the past." Pew Research Center, Washington, DC (October 4, 2017). http://www.people-press.org/2017/10/05/1-partisan-divides-over-political-values-widen/1_5-15/.

the right to control certain aspects of social life, such as economic transactions, educational opportunities, and health care. Conservatives, on the other hand, prefer to minimize the role of governmental control over people's lives, and are willing to risk inequality to preserve the autonomy and personal responsibility of individuals.

Is there a psychological foundation for these two orientations? Are liberals and conservatives fundamentally different in their emotional and mental makeup? Two lines of theory and research suggest an affirmative answer to this question, and thus provide insight into why a liberal and a conservative can be exposed to the same facts and events and arrive at diametrically opposed conclusions about what these facts and events mean and what should be done in response. The first theoretical perspective centers on the strength of fundamental values. The second centers on the strength of the ego-defensive function of attitudes.

The Values Perspective

The *values perspective* maintains that liberals and conservatives develop political attitudes that reflect their sensitivity to the five fundamental values identified by Haidt (2001), discussed in Chapter 3. Of these, *harm/care* and *fairness/reciprocity* come closest to tapping liberals' presumed concern with social justice and compassion, whereas the other values—*in-group/loyalty, authority/respect*, and *purity/sanctity*—reflect conservatives' concern with personal responsibility for appropriate conduct and their sensitivity to preserving the social order (Jost, Glaser, Sulloway, & Kruglanski, 2003). All these values sound laudable, so if you simply asked people if they endorsed each one, liberals and conservatives alike would say yes.

But what if you probed a bit deeper to see how strongly people felt about each value? One way to do this is to see how reluctant people are to engage in actions that *violate* each value. This is the approach taken by Jesse Graham, Jonathan Haidt, and Brian Nosek (2009). Participants, whose political orientation (from *very conservative* to *very liberal*) was assessed at a different session, were asked how much money it would take to engage in actions that reflect a violation of the five basic values identified by Haidt (2001). The monetary amounts ranged from zero ("I would do it for free") to a million dollars ("I would only do it if it made me rich"). In other words, participants were asked to "put your money where your values are." Below are examples of the specific acts participants were asked to consider with respect to each value.

Harm/care:

- Kick a dog in the head, hard.
- Stick a pin into the palm of a child you don't know.

Fairness/reciprocity:

- Steal from a poor person and use the money to buy a gift for a rich person.
- Say no to a friend's request to help him move into a new apartment, after he helped you move the month before.

In-group/loyalty:

- Burn your country's flag, in private (nobody else sees you).
- Publicly bet against your favorite sports team (so that lots of people know).

Authority/respect:

- Make a disrespectful hand gesture to your boss, teacher, or professor.
- Slap your father in the face (with his permission) as part of a comedy skit.

Purity/sanctity:

- Sign a piece of paper that says, "I hereby sell my soul, after my death, to whoever has this piece of paper."
- Get a blood transfusion of 1 pint of disease-free, compatible blood from a convicted child molester.

The results confirmed that liberals and conservatives differ in their sensitivity to basic values (see Figure 14.7). The politically liberal participants were willing to do things that violated in-group loyalty (e.g., betting against their favorite sports team), respect for authority (e.g., make a rude hand gesture to a boss), and purity (e.g., get a blood transfusion from a child molester) for less money than were their politically conservative participants. When it came to acting unfairly toward others, however, the liberal participants held out for as much money as did the conservative participants. And when the acts involving harming others, they held out for more money than did their conservative counterparts.

Sensitivity to the harm of people who fall on hard times may lead liberals to perceive injustice and direct their anger at the small percentage of people whose income and lot in life have dramatically improved. Conservatives, in contrast, are inclined to maintain belief in the fairness of the system because of their heightened sensitivity to freedom and respect for authority. Their belief in justice tends to take the form of blaming those who suffer rather than challenging the legitimacy of the system that has enabled rich and powerful people to become even richer and more powerful—particularly if it is not clear how the inequality could be easily reversed (Rubin & Peplau, 1975).

Conservatives are not totally insensitive to income inequality, but their concerns are motivated by different reasons than those that promote concerns among liberals (Chow & Galak, 2012). When income inequality is framed as the rich making more than the poor (as opposed to the poor making less than the rich), conservatives are more willing to support redistributive policies, in part because framing inequality in this way makes conservatives more likely to question whether the wealthy are responsible for their own success (Figure 14.8). For policymakers, these findings suggest one simple approach that can influence how individuals think about and respond to income inequality: change the language used to describe it.

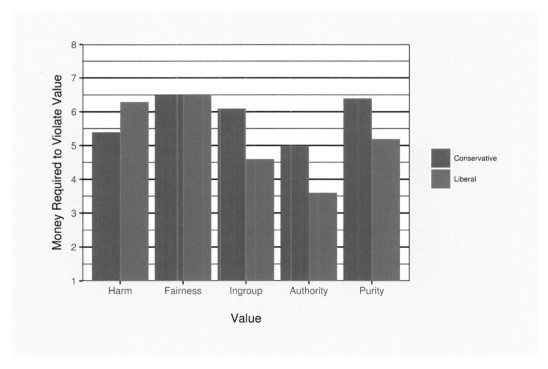

Figure 14.7 Amount of money required to violate value-related taboo for very liberal and very conservative participants. 1 = $0, 2 = $10, 3 = $100, 4 = $1,000, 5 = $10,000, 6 = $100,000, 7 = a million dollars, 8 = never for any amount of money.
Source: Adapted from Graham et al. (2009)

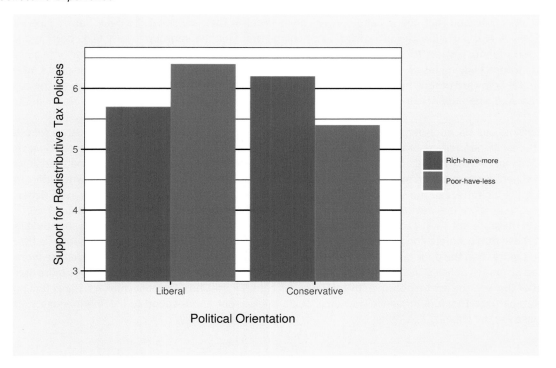

FIGURE 14.8 Support for Redistributive Tax Policies as a Function of Framing and Political Orientation. Scores on a Measure of Political Conservatism were used to Divide Participants into Conservative and Liberal Groups.
Source: Adapted from Chow & Galak (2012)

The Ego-Defensive Perspective

The *ego-defensive perspective* maintains that liberals and conservatives differ in their motivation to ward off certain anxieties. In a review of dozens of studies across several decades concerning different cultures, Jost et al. (2003) identified two core psychological components of political conservatism. The first is resistance to change. Conservatives are quicker to express reservations about change of almost any kind—whether it is a political revolution, a change in social conventions or sexual lifestyles, or a change in art and science. The second core component of conservatism is acceptance (or even endorsement) of social inequality. All societies have some degree of inequality in wealth, education, and access to resources. Conservatives are more willing than liberals to accept these inequalities as a fact of life.

What do these perspectives on change and inequality have to do with warding off ego-threatening anxieties? The research summarized by Jost et al. suggests that conservatives judge the world to be a more dangerous place, react more quickly to danger-related words, and even experience more nightmares (Fessler, Pisor, & Holbrook, 2017; Hibbing, Smith, & Alford, 2014). They also show less liking for unfamiliar music, show less interest in new technological innovations, and are less comfortable with changes in job requirements. To embrace each of these things requires some tolerance of uncertainty. To defend against fear and uncertainty, Jost et al. argue that conservatives gravitate toward beliefs that suggest the world that is orderly, structured, and predictable—even if that means living with long-standing inequalities.

If political conservatism is associated with sensitivity to threat and uncertainty, conditions that make everyone feel threatened or uncertain should tilt public opinion toward the conservative end of the spectrum. Particularly when the threat concerns the possibility of death, conservative candidates for public office should have the upper hand over their liberal opponents. A survey conducted during the 2004 US presidential election (Landau et al., 2004) supports this possibility. Respondents were asked their opinions about the Democratic challenger, John Kerry, or the

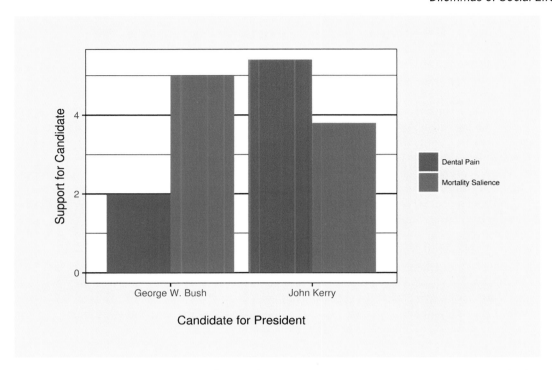

FIGURE 14.9 Mortality Salience and Support for President George W. Bush and Senator John Kerry During the 2004 US Presidential Election

Source: Adapted from Landau et al. (2004)

incumbent Republican president, George W. Bush. Some did so after being reminded of death and some did so after writing about a personal experience with dental pain. As the incumbent president, Bush was perceived by many as the leader of the fight against the Al Qaeda terrorist organization. Landau and his colleagues therefore predicted that the survey respondents would show a preference for Bush over Kerry after the mortality salience manipulation. This prediction was confirmed (see Figure 14.9).

Public opinion polls provided additional support for this idea. Support for Bush increased whenever the terrorist threat level announced by the Department of Homeland Security went up—presumably because these threat warnings made people aware of the possibility of death (Willer, 2004). Conservative candidates apparently have the upper hand when people are prompted with reminders of death, as long as they can convince voters that they are better equipped to handle the threats to their well-being.

Box 14.4   Startling Differences Between Liberals and Conservatives

The broad left (liberal) versus right (conservative) orientation is not unique to the United States or to the modern era, but rather pervades politics around the world and throughout history. The pervasiveness and persistence of this dimension suggests that it may have biological underpinnings. An intriguing study conducted by political scientists supports this contention (Oxley et al., 2008). White partisan Republicans and Democrats in Nebraska were quizzed on their views on a variety of topics, including the war in Iraq, same-sex marriage, pacifism, and the importance of school prayer. All the questions were designed to test how strongly people needed to guard against various internal and external threats.

Two months later, the researchers measured the volunteers' skin conductance, which is essentially moisture on the skin. Skin conductance is an index of threat response: when a person feels a threat, his or her skin releases more moisture. The release of moisture does not involve conscious thought, but rather is an automatic response of the sympathetic nervous system, which controls many of the body's "fight or flight" reactions. The researchers then showed the participants a number of disturbing images: a very large spider on the face of a terrified person, a person whose face had been bloodied, and an open wound filled with maggots. For comparison purposes, the participants also saw three decidedly non-disturbing images: a happy child, a bowl of fruit, and a bunny. The participants who held more conservative political attitudes had a stronger startle response to the disturbing images than did those with more liberal attitudes.

In a second experiment, the researchers startled the volunteers by playing a loud noise through headphones. This time, they measured how hard people blinked—blinking is an automatic reflex to startling sounds. The participants who held more conservative positions on political issues showed a stronger startle response than did their more liberal counterparts.

These results suggest an association between sensitivity to physical threats and sensitivity to threats affecting social groups and social order. People who are particularly sensitive to signals of visual or auditory threats also tend to adopt a more defensive stance on political issues, such as immigration, gun control, defense spending and patriotism. People who are less sensitive to potential threats, by contrast, are predisposed toward liberal positions on those issues. This difference does not mean that either liberals or conservatives are somehow abnormal for being more or less sensitive to threats. One could argue that it is bad to be jumpy, but one could just as reasonably argue that it is bad to be naïve about threats. From an evolutionary point of view, an organism needs to respond to a threat or it won't be around for very long. Thus, people who adopt political views you disagree with are not stupid or irrational. Rather, they may arrive at their positions in part because they are predisposed to be more or less worried about risk.

Morality

What Are the Psychological Foundations of Morality?

It's comforting to think that moral versus immoral behavior can be codified into a few simple rules. The problem is that any set of rules has caveats and exceptions. The Ten Commandments in the Old Testament of the Bible, for example, seem straightforward enough; abiding by them should make judgments of moral versus immoral behavior fairly simple. But consider the prohibition against killing. This sounds great, but what about capital punishment? War? Or self-defense? In each case, killing is not only permissible, it is considered by many people to be an appropriate and justifiable behavior. Or consider this horrible dilemma. A mother and her baby are hiding in a room with several other people, hoping to avoid detection by someone who wants to kill everyone in the group. But the baby begins to cry—a sound that would give away the hiding location. The only way to stop the baby from crying is to smother him or her. What is the right thing for the mother to do? Should she kill the baby in order to save everyone in the group? Or is killing a baby simply wrong, no matter what the consequences are?

The same complexity and nuance exists for other moral values. Lying is forbidden by the Ten Commandments, but what if one lies to a burglar about the location of a safe in one's house that holds one's valuables? Is lying in that context immoral? Respect and obedience to legitimate authority are important values, but as we saw in Chapter 10, such obedience can lead to horrendous behavior, as has been known to occur during war. Is it immoral to show disrespect for those with legitimate authority? Stealing is considered worthy of moral condemnation, but what about stealing to feed a starving child when no other options are available?

Rationality Versus Emotion

You get the picture. Rules about moral versus immoral behavior are easy to generate, but life is full of considerations that can override such rules without calling into question a person's morality. Deciding whether a particular action is the right thing to do can therefore present a *moral dilemma* for people in their daily lives. The question is how people resolve such dilemmas. One prominent point of view holds that people's higher-level thought processes are engaged when confronted with actions that could be considered either good or bad, right or wrong. But an alternative perspective maintains that people's moral judgments are influenced more by emotion than by reason. Let's see how you think and feel about each perspective.

Thinking and Moral Judgment

People have impressive minds and presumably put this brainpower to good use when deciding whether a particular course of action is moral and justifiable or immoral and unjustifiable. Lawrence Kohlberg (1969), a developmental psychologist, recognized this role of the mind and launched a program of research to identify how people reason about the appropriate course of action in situations involving moral dilemmas. Consider the following scenario:

> In Europe, a woman was near death from cancer. One drug might save her, a form of radium that a druggist in the same town had recently discovered. The druggist was charging $2,000—10 times what the drug cost him to make. The sick woman's husband, Heinz, went to everyone he knew to borrow money, but he could only get together about half of what it cost. He told the druggist that his wife was dying and asked him to sell it cheaper or let him pay later. But the druggist said, "No." The husband got desperate and broke into the man's store to steal the drug for his wife.
>
> (Kohlberg, 1969, p. 379)

Did Heinz act immorally? After all, he broke the law and committed a robbery. Or was his behavior justified? After all, his action was the only recourse left to him for saving his wife's life. For that matter, if Heinz had *not* stolen the drug, would that have been an immoral act? Letting someone die hardly seems a noble course of action. Kohlberg did not attempt to establish what defines moral versus immoral behavior—life is far too ambiguous for that. Rather, he focused on how people reason when confronted with actions that could be seen as either moral or immoral. How do people resolve the moral dilemmas they inevitably encounter in their lives?

Kohlberg theorized that people's reasoning about such dilemmas reflects one of three levels of moral thought. In the *preconventional level*, moral dilemmas are resolved in ways that satisfy self-serving motives. From this perspective, an act is moral if it enables the person to avoid punishment or obtain reward. In the *conventional level*—which represents how the majority of adults reason—moral dilemmas are resolved in a way that reflects societal laws and norms established by those in authority. An action is moral, in other words, if it maintains the social order or meets with social approval. In the *postconventional level*—attained by adults who have a relatively high degree of mental sophistication—moral thought is based on abstract principles such as equality, justice, and the value of life. In this approach, an act is moral if it affirms one's conscience, even if it violates the law and meets with little approval from others.

Keep in mind that the reasoning associated with each level could lead to diametrically opposed conclusions. Heinz's behavior, for instance, could be judged as moral or immoral regardless of one's level of moral reasoning. In Kohlberg's view, morality is not judged by an action's content but rather by the level of sophistication that leads to one conclusion or the other. In this view, a person's capacity for rendering moral judgments reflects his or her cognitive maturity and reasoning skills. Characterized to an extreme that is surely unacceptable to everyone, this perspective would suggest that very bright people can literally get away with murder, since they are very good at developing sophisticated rationales for their actions.

Emotion and Moral Judgment

To this point, you might have the impression that morality is relative rather than absolute, with the mind basically providing a tool that can lead to wildly different conclusions about good and bad, right and wrong. Stealing a drug can be seen as moral or immoral, for example. This perspective on moral judgment has been challenged in recent years by research emphasizing consensus among people when judging whether an action is moral or immoral. This does not mean that reasoning does not play a role, but rather that the reasoning process is influenced by emotions and unconscious motives that bias the way information is processed. Some behaviors are simply seen as immoral, others are seen as moral—and in both cases, little reasoning is involved in making the determinations.

To get a feel for this, consider the following (Haidt, 2001):

> Mark and Julie are brother and sister. They are traveling together in France on a summer vacation from college. One night they are staying alone in a cabin near the beach. They decide that it would be interesting and fun if they tried making love. At the very least it would be a new experience for each of them. Julie was already taking birth control pills, but Mark uses a condom, too, just to be safe. They both enjoy making love, but they decide not to do it again. They keep that night as a special secret, which makes them feel even closer to each other.

How would you judge what Mark and Julie did? Was it immoral? Your immediate reaction probably is something like, "Of course it is!" OK, but what makes it immoral? You might argue that it is dangerous to inbreed, which is what sex among siblings represents. But that is not an issue in this case, because Mark and Julie used birth control. Recognizing that argument to be irrelevant, you might argue instead that sex between siblings could hurt them emotionally. But the story makes clear that Mark and Julie felt closer as a result of their one-night adventure and have decided to remember it as something special.

If you have problems in explaining why Mark and Julie acted immorally, you are not alone. Nearly all college students who read this story not only view the incident as immoral, but also as disgusting (Haidt, 2001). When their logical reasons are refuted, students do not give in and reconsider the action's morality. Instead, they are likely to say, "OK, I can't explain why, but I just know it's wrong." It's not just students who react this way. Every culture in the world considers incest to be immoral (Brown, 1991). And it's not just incest that evokes these feeling-based moral judgments—judgments of virtue, character, and right versus wrong are often based on gut feelings (Batson, Engel, & Fridell, 1999a; Greene & Haidt, 2002; Greene et al., 2001).

Feeling-based judgments can be positive, as when we feel sympathy or compassion for others who suffer or are vulnerable (Batson & Shaw, 1991; Eisenberg et al., 1989). Even when we know a person has done something wrong, feelings of sympathy can soften our reaction to him or her. For example, knowing that a criminal defendant was raised in an impoverished environment or suffered abuse as a child can provoke sympathy in jurors, leading them to recommend less severe forms of punishment (Weiner, Graham, & Reyna, 1997).

However, research has more often focused on negative feeling-based judgments, such as anger and disgust, than on positive feeling-based judgments. Anger tends to be triggered when people's rights and freedoms have been violated—being denied fair access to an opportunity, for example (Rozin, Lowery, Imada, & Haidt, 1999). Disgust is triggered by the feeling that someone is impure in mind, body, or character (Haidt, Koller, & Dias, 1993; Wheatley & Haidt, 2005). A person who morally condemns cigarette smoking and meat consumption, for example, is likely to find these acts disgusting (Rozin & Singh, 1999). And people who condemn homosexuality as immoral are more prone to feel disgust than anger when judging this activity (Tapias et al., 2007; Van de Ven, Bornholt, & Bailey, 1996).

Sometimes these feelings are directed toward oneself. As discussed in Chapter 5 ("Self-Concept"), people experience *self-critical emotions*—embarrassment, guilt, and shame—when they feel they have violated social norms, moral codes, or ideas about character and virtue (Baumeister, Stillwell, & Heatherton, 1994; Higgins, 1987; Keltner & Anderson, 2000; Tangney, Miller, Flicker, & Barlow, 1996). People who experience these emotions less frequently or intensely are at greater risk for violent or criminal behavior (Beer et al., 2003; Keltner, Moffitt, & Stouthamer-Loeber, 1995). It is the bad feeling, not the recognition of bad conduct per se, that keeps people in line much of the time.

Does this mean that the mind is simply a tool for rationalizing one's automatic emotional reactions to events? Not necessarily. For one thing, sometimes events do not lend themselves to an automatic reaction based on our evolutionary history. Consider the dilemmas posed by Kohlberg (1969). Whether Heinz was justified or not for stealing the drug to save his wife is hard to judge based on purely emotional grounds. In such instances of moral ambiguity, the mind is called on to play a decisive role by considering the circumstances and the potential bases for making tough calls (e.g., respect for law or universal principles).

Higher-level mental processes can play a role even when a person has an automatic emotional reaction to a moral issue. Recall the distinction between *automatic* and *controlled processes*, first described in Chapter 3, and the factors that tip the balance in favor of one processing mode or the other. When people are distracted, stressed, or otherwise *cognitively busy* (Gilbert, Pelham, & Krull, 1988; Wegner, 1994), for example, they may find themselves unable to muster the executive resources necessary to overcome their automatic processes, including those based on emotional reactions. Automatic thought also dominates conscious deliberation when people's executive processes have been "depleted" by prior deliberation or self-control efforts (Baumeister, Bratslavsky, Muraven, & Tice, 1998).

The flipside is that when people are not depleted and are able to utilize their executive resources, they can override their immediate emotional reactions and make moral judgments in line with rational considerations. Simply priming people to think about issues in rational terms can enable them to take a fresh look at facts and circumstances that might otherwise provoke an automatic reaction reflecting emotional biases. The capacity for overriding emotional reactions is critical in the criminal justice system, where decisions about the fate of a defendant are too important to be based solely on feelings and gut reactions.

Religion

Religion is ubiquitous in human history. Every society has a creation story and a set of principles that dictate personal conduct and that constrain how people behave toward one another. Religion provides a foundation for moral behavior that enables people to determine right from wrong, good from bad, and to act in accordance with long-term purpose rather than immediate gratification. Religion tenets can override the power of everyday rewards and punishments in dictating what is important and meaningful—even worth dying for. These features of religiosity hold potential for fair and just behavior toward other people. Charities and good will are associated with religious institutions. People demonstrate genuine altruism when motivated by religious beliefs and are even willing to sacrifice their lives in the name of God.

Religion is commonly portrayed as a force that competes with biology and evolutionary imperatives. People pray to God in part to give them the strength to resist carnal desires, face tough challenges, forgive rather than seek revenge when treated poorly by others, and behave in a respectable rather than selfish fashion. But biology and religion may not actually be in conflict. In recent years, scholars have come to recognize that biology is not always biased in favor of self-interest, dominance, and competition, but rather can promote cooperative and altruistic actions that promote the needs of the collective as much as one's personal agenda. Humans are not alone in their ability and willingness to suspend their self-interest and attend to the needs of others. Franz de Waal (2007), a prominent primatologist, noted how chimpanzees—our closest relatives in the animal kingdom—nurture one another and engage in apparently altruistic actions. If a fellow chimp is injured, for example, one or more chimps will come to his or her aid. They also take care of one another's offspring, seek forgiveness for actions that cause harm, and even have a basic sense of justice when it comes to the allocation of food. This concern with what looks like morality is highly adaptive for a social species with a high degree of intelligence. By itself, high intelligence could be viewed as a powerful tool when competing with others, leading to deception and trickery. A moral sense constrains the use of this tool and allows groups to function with trust and harmony, and enables the coordination necessary to achieve common goals.

The biological basis for morality has gained traction in recent years to supplement the evolutionary perspective. As noted in Chapter 6 ("Personal Control"), self-control depends on executive processes in the brain. When the energy for this self-control is depleted—for example, by resisting the temptation to eat warm chocolate chip cookies—people become impulsive, more likely to cheat, and less willing to help others in need. When their executive resources are restored—after a rest, for example—people regain the ability to control their impulses, resist temptation, and otherwise act in a manner that is consistent with religious imperatives.

This does not mean that religion can be reduced to biological processes. Research suggests that religion can promote self-control beyond that provided by neural and physiological mechanisms. Rounding, Lee, Jacobson, and Ji (2012) proposed that religion emerged as a cultural adaptation necessary for self-control. In a series of experiments, they demonstrated that when religious themes were made salient in a subtle fashion, participants demonstrated greater self-control. This was observed even when participants' executive resources were depleted by having them engage in activities that required concentration and impulse control, making it difficult for them to exercise restraint on subsequent unrelated self-control tasks. The influence of religious primes, moreover, had a greater influence on self-control than did the priming of concepts related to morality per se or to death. Self-control may have a biological basis, but apparently there is a spiritual basis that can fill the void when biological fuel is depleted.

Moral Hypocrisy

There is clearly instrumental value in being viewed by others in ways that impress them. When interacting with certain people—a new acquaintance, for example, or a person who strikes you as desirable—you may be tempted to cultivate a highly positive image of your character and integrity ("I would never cheat on an exam"), even if this image does not reflect some of your actions particularly well. People who succumb to this temptation, but who are later discovered to have taken this self-presentation short cut, are at risk for being viewed as hypocrites.

Hypocrisy abounds in social life. People may profess a special trust with a friend but then later divulge the friend's secrets to other people. People commonly decry the portrayal of violence in the mass media but watch TV news coverage of murder. Catholic priests and other members of the clergy claim the moral high ground and condemn sexual predators, yet some of them engage in the sexual molestation of young children who are dependent on them. A politician campaigns for finance reform but routinely accepts expensive trips from lobbyists to famous golf courses overseas. Parents routinely admonish children for temper tantrums and aggression, but on occasion they may lose their temper and use physical force to punish them. And, believe it or not, some students present themselves as studious and honest but will cheat when they can get away with it.

No one likes a hypocrite. When a person is discovered to have violated the standards he or she espouses, the response is typically a loss of respect if not outright condemnation. Beyond these interpersonal deterrents, hypocrisy is a clear case of failing to act in a way that matches one's internal standards. As we saw in Chapter 6, discrepancy from standards produces self-critical emotions. What, then, motivates hypocrisy? Why do people do things that make them feel guilty or ashamed and that run the risk of eliciting anger and disgust from other people?

Hypocrisy has been investigated in two ways in recent years. Some psychologists have studied the discrepancy between what respondents think (or claim) is appropriate and how they actually behave (Batson et al., 1997; Batson et al., 1999b; Stone, Wiegand, Cooper, & Aronson, 1997). In effect, people sometimes preach one thing (striking a moral or self-righteous tone), but behave in another (considerably more self-serving) way. In another approach, psychologists emphasize the discrepancy between what respondents believe *other people* should do and what *they* actually would do in such a situation (Valdesolo & DeSteno, 2007, 2008).

Private Versus Public Action

People often give lip service to a social norm or universal value, but ignore these standards and behave in a self-serving manner when such behavior is likely to go undetected. This form of hypocrisy has been examined by Daniel Batson and his colleagues (1997, 1999b). Participants are presented with a clear conflict between choosing to benefit themselves or adhering to a more costly principle of fairness. The choice is between an appealing task that might earn them raffle tickets toward a $30 prize and a dull task that does not result in a prize. The participant has to assign him- or herself to one task and a second (non-existent) participant to the other. The experimenter emphasizes that the other participant will think the tasks were assigned by chance and assures the participant that the two of them will never meet.

Very few participants (5%) reported that assigning the positive task to themselves was the most moral thing to do. But did they act on this moral stance? In one experiment, the participants could assign the tasks by flipping a coin. Although this "fair" procedure should have resulted in about 50% of the participants assigning themselves to the positive task, 90% of them actually did so. OK, perhaps they decided what "heads" and "tails" meant after the coin toss, thus enabling them to rationalize the fairness of their decision. So in a subsequent experiment, each side of the coin had a sticker that specified what the coin flip would signify. Still, most participants (86%) who tossed the coin assigned the positive task to themselves.

This does not necessarily imply that people are inherently hypocritical or dishonest. Keep in mind people's remarkable capacity for interpretation, a tendency that all too easily can slip into rationalization of behavior that has personal benefit. In Batson's studies, people may have engaged in all sorts of justifications for their selfish behavior: "the experimenter said the choice was up to me—that means whatever I decide is OK," perhaps, or "if the tables were turned, the other person would take the fun task—why should I be a chump?" This was also a "winner takes all" situation, since one person would get the positive task and the other person would get nothing. It is hard to see how cutting oneself out entirely would be fair. So participants may have privately thought, "if we somehow could share the fun task, or even if I could be assured of getting *something* out of all this time here, I'd be happy to flip the coin and live with the outcome. But why should I take the chance of losing it all. How does a stupid coin flip justify the other person getting everything?!"

The upshot is that people can present themselves in a way that doesn't reflect how they are really inclined to behave, yet not feel terribly bad about such inconsistencies. The same mental powers that enable people to solve differential equations and interpret poetry also allow people to maintain a moral self-view while acting in ways that might not seem all that moral to others. Much of the time, hypocrisy is in the mind of the observer, not the mind of the actor.

Power and Double Standards

The other form of hypocrisy involves holding one standard of behavior for oneself and a different standard for everyone else. This *double standard* is especially prominent among people who enjoy high power or status (Kipnis, 1972). Adam Galinsky and his colleagues demonstrated this by inducing a sense of high versus low power in participants (Lammers, Stapel, & Galinsky, 2010). In one approach, participants were assigned to positions of high power (e.g., a prime minister) or low power (e.g., a civil servant) in a role-playing exercise. In another approach, they were simply asked to recall an experience of either high power or low power. The participants were then presented with moral dilemmas such as breaking traffic rules, cheating on taxes, and returning a stolen bike.

In the first experiment, for example, participants were told that they would be compensated with lottery tickets that could earn one of three fairly substantial monetary prize (approximately $35, $75, and $150). In a private cubicle, half the participants rolled two 10-sided dice (with the sides corresponding to zero through 9) to determine the number of lottery tickets they would receive—and hence, their likelihood of winning the lottery. Because the toss was done in private, participants were asked to report the total of the two dice. The possible values were between zero and 99, with an expected mean of 50. Cheating behavior would thus be indicated if participants reported a significantly higher amount than 50. The remaining participants did not roll dice and take part in the lottery. Instead, they were asked to indicate whether it is morally acceptable for people to overreport their traveling expenses.

Both high-power and low-power participants judged cheating (overreporting travel expenses) fairly harshly (close to *fully unacceptable*). But as illustrated in Figure 14.10, they parted ways when given an opportunity to cheat on the

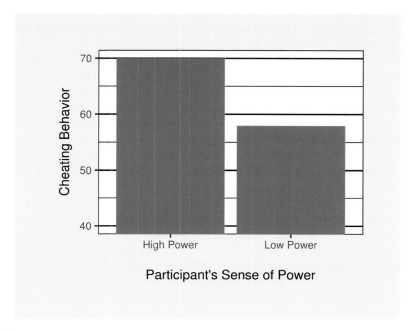

FIGURE 14.10 The Dice Toss Total Reported by High-Power and Low-Power Participants. Expressed Totals Greater than 50 Are Indicative of Overreporting and Hence Cheating.

Source: Adapted from Lammers et al. (2010, Experiment 1)

dice game. The high-power participants apparently had few qualms about cheating, claiming a higher total than would be expected by chance. They gave lip service to moral behavior but acted in a way that contradicted their expressed moral stance in order to optimize their chance of winning money. The low-power participants, however, acted in accordance with their moralistic stance by claiming a dice total that was close to what would be expected on a chance activity such as this. In other words, they "practiced what they preached."

A final experiment revealed that moral hypocrisy is most likely among people who are *legitimately powerful*. In fact, people who don't feel personally entitled to their power are actually *harder* on themselves than they are on others, a phenomenon the researchers dubbed *hypercrisy*. The combination of hypocrisy by the legitimately powerful and hypercrisy by the powerless may perpetuate social inequality. The powerful impose rules and restraints on others while disregarding these restraints on their own behavior, whereas the powerless do not feel the same entitlement and thus unwittingly collaborate in maintaining social inequality.

SUMMING UP AND LOOKING AHEAD

- **Social interdependence amplifies the natural tension between personal self-interest and the interests of others. This tension is manifest as two basic social dilemmas: deciding on and adhering to rules by which resources are shared (justice dilemmas) and agreeing on and conforming to standards of good versus bad behavior (moral dilemmas).**

- **Social dilemmas are simulated in mixed-motive games that present participants with a choice between an action that maximizes their immediate self-interest at the expense of others' interests and an action that reduces their immediate self-interest while maximizing the long-term mutual interest of themselves and others. The *Prisoner's Dilemma* and *Public Goods Game* are commonly used for this purpose.**

- **Several factors determine whether people cooperate or defect in mixed-motive situations. Personality plays a role, with some people inclined to cooperate or defect depending on their history of attachment and social learning during their formative years. If people expect defection, this acts as a self-fulfilling prophecy that ensures conflict and mutual exploitation. The likelihood of cooperation is enhanced by a self-regulation mindset centering on the higher-level meaning of action (consequences, implications).**

- **People believe in justice, but justice can be manifest in different ways. Revenge is the most basic form of justice and plays a prominent role in the criminal justice system. Equity, the allocation of outcomes in proportion to people's contributions, often overrides a concern with equality and can prevent people from exploiting others when given a chance to do so.**

- **The belief in a just world can perpetuate inequality and suffering because it provides a basis for inferring the actions and characteristics of people who differ in their material and social outcomes. The derogation of victims is heightened when people are primed to think about the role of choice in action. If injustice cannot be rationalized away, people may focus on ultimate justice (e.g., afterlife) that will eventually restore equity.**

- **The belief in justice is manifest at the societal level, with people on both sides of inequality feeling that the difference in outcomes experienced by different segments of society is legitimate. To compensate for such inequality, people ascribe intangible benefits (e.g., greater happiness) to those who experience lower tangible outcomes (e.g., money, status). System justification tendencies are undermined during rapid social change and when there are challenges to the status quo.**

- **Political liberals and conservatives have different views of justice that follow from their relative sensitivity to several universal values. Whereas liberals are primarily sensitive to the harm experienced by others, conservatives are more sensitive to in-group loyalty, respect for authority, and purity. Because of these differences, liberals are more inclined to favor redistribution policies to reduce inequality, whereas conservative are more inclined to demonstrate system justification and in-group favoritism.**

- **People everywhere are concerned with morality and judge themselves and others accordingly. Judgments of immoral versus moral behavior are heavily influenced by basic emotions (e.g., anger, disgust) and unconscious biases that can be traced to evolutionary adaptations (e.g., contamination, the incest taboo). The ascendance of emotion over reason is enhanced when people are distracted, depleted, or otherwise operating in line with automatic rather than controlled mental processes.**

- Religion can override selfish motives and sensitize people to social justice and standards of moral conduct. There may be biological bases for the self-regulatory nature of religion, but even when executive resources are depleted, people can act in accordance with religious principles if they are made mindful of these ideas.
- People sometimes demonstrate hypocrisy by judging others harshly for actions they justify in themselves. The likelihood of hypocrisy is enhanced when people have greater power (e.g., money, status) than others. Hypocrisy is less likely when the legitimacy of one's power is called into question.

This chapter has outlined the challenges and dilemmas of social life that each of us confronts, sometimes on a daily basis. That life in an interdependent world is rarely simple should come as no surprise in light of the various features of human experience we have explored in the previous chapters. Each of these topics—from the formation of personal attitudes and values to interactions with others from different walks of life—carries with it the potential for personal discomfort and interpersonal discord. But the human capacity for reflective thought, empathy, and personal control has also been front and center to this point. In principle, then, people are capable of navigating a path through life that satisfies their personal needs while taking into account the needs of others.

Making this potential manifest, however, is a different matter. How can the understanding of intrapersonal, interpersonal, and collective dynamics be put to use to maximize personal and social well-being in an increasingly diverse and complex world? How, in other words, can we move from theory to application? This issue is the focus of the concluding chapter, which shows how social psychology is relevant to the challenges of social life.

Key Terms

Social dilemma
Social interdependence
Mixed-motive game
Tragedy of the commons
Prisoner's Dilemma
Cooperation versus defection
Zero-sum versus non-zero-sum
Public Goods Game
Behavioral confirmation
Trust Game
Level of action identification
Belief in a just world

Equity theory
Ironic justice
Ultimate justice
System justification
Income inequality
Rising expectations
Liberal versus conservative
    political orientation
Freedom versus equality
Fundamental values and political
    orientation

Ego-defensive perspective on
    political orientation
Moral dilemma
Levels of moral reasoning
Emotion and moral judgment
Self-critical emotions
Religion and morality
Biological bases of morality
Moral hypocrisy
Private versus public action
Double standard
Moral hypercrisy

PART V

SOCIAL PSYCHOLOGY IN PERSPECTIVE

15 The Relevance of Social Psychology

The theories and ideas generated by social psychology are interesting, sometimes even counterintuitive, but if they are valid, they should also shed light on the difficulties people experience in today's world and prepare us for the challenges people will face in the years and decades to come. Does social psychology have practical utility for clarifying and resolving the problems faced by humanity in today's increasingly complex and interdependent world? Do the insights into the dynamics of human experience provided by social psychology allow prediction into what's in store as we proceed through the 21st century?

From Implications to Application

How Is Social Psychology Relevant to Issues in Contemporary Life?

Social psychology is rich in implications for the issues with which individuals and society as a whole must cope. These implications have been front and center in each chapter thus far. But the link between these implications and their applications in daily life—how a theory about *why* things happen can be translated into recommendations about *how* these things can be managed—is not always obvious. In this section, we consider how the lessons of social psychology can be applied to four features of contemporary life that could use a little help: *stress and modern life, happiness, law and criminal justice*, and *the environment*. Each topic warrants a chapter, if not an entire book, in its own right. The aim here is to outline the relevance of social psychology for each issue, suggesting how each can be approached in a more enlightened manner.

Stress and Modern Life

People today should be healthier than people at any time in history. Particularly in the developed and industrial societies of the modern world, people have ready access to resources, food, and healthcare, and they spend far less of their time attempting to maintain such access than did their ancestors of past eras. We have created elaborate infrastructures for transportation, sanitation, food distribution, and personal security, and most people have access to a social safety net for their senior years and times of hardship. Yet for all the benefits of modernity, people today are not as healthy as one would expect, and are prone to physical and mental issues that may represent an unwanted trade-off with the relative ease of life today. The rates of obesity, diabetes, and stress-related illnesses have increased dramatically over the past few decades in the western world, and this trend shows no signs of leveling off. What does social psychology have to say about these unintended consequences of today's lifestyle?

Modernity and Stress

Humans were not designed by natural selection to deal with the types of demands and challenges that we face today. We were remarkably successful in adapting to a threatening environment full of hostile neighboring tribes, we learned to consume fatty and sugary foods to get us through periods of shortage and famine, and we acquired a tendency to exploit and hoard resources. But in today's world, such adaptations often work against our personal health and collective well-being. In a diverse and interconnected world, defensive and antagonistic relations with out-groups (nations, ideologies, religions, races) create the potential for prejudice and sustained conflict. Fatty and sugary foods are no longer scarce, but rather are readily available and contribute to poor health (e.g., obesity, diabetes, heart disease). And our hoarding instinct promotes selfishness and gluttony while undermining the cooperation and willingness to sacrifice necessary to maintain social harmony. In short, the pull of human nature that served us so well in our ancestral environment is proving problematic in today's world.

Beyond being exposed to forces and opportunities in the modern world that promote unwise actions and decisions, we live in a far more complex and rapidly changing world than did our ancestors. Our sense of personal control has met its match in the multiple and sometimes conflicting demands of everyday life. On any given day, you are expected to be a conscientious student, a family member, and a member of an often volatile social network, while at the same time attending to tasks as diverse as navigating traffic, paying bills, pursuing hobbies, and keeping up with national and international news—which largely consist of events over which you have little or no control. Managing such complexity requires multi-tasking, with attention to many areas of life, each of which can drain our limited executive resources and undermine a sense of personal control. As discussed in Chapter 6 ("Personal Control"), the loss of personal control is at the core of psychological stress. Modernity may have substantial material benefits, but it also has psychological consequences that can offset these benefits. In a sense, stress is the price of choice and personal freedom associated with modernity (Baumeister, 1991).

Stress and Well-Being

Stress is not a simple cause-effect response to negative events. Imagine two people getting a traffic ticket. One of them may go to pieces over this, but the other person may take the event in stride, pay the fine, and move on to other matters. What distinguishes the two people is how they think about the unpleasant experience (Lazarus, 1966). The stressed-out person feels his or her life is out of control and worries excessively about future encounters with the criminal justice system. The move-on person is unlikely to feel happy about the ticket but feels he or she can avoid such events in the future by paying closer attention to traffic laws.

Beyond its cognitive and emotional consequences, stress can literally make people sick. More precisely, how people interpret and evaluate aversive events determines whether they are vulnerable to disease-causing factors. The common cold provides a good example. When people are exposed to a cold-causing virus, only between 20% and 60% of them actually get a cold. To find out who these people are, Cohen, Tyrrell, and Smith (1993) recruited people to spend a week at an English research institute. The stress of these participants was assessed by asking them to list recent events that had a negative impact on their lives. They were then given nasal drops that contained either the virus responsible for the common cold or saline (essentially salt water). Among those who reported the least amount of stress, 27% developed a cold within the next few days. The frequency of colds increased for people who reported more stress, reaching nearly 50% among those who experienced the most stress.

This mind-body connection may seem far-fetched or even a bit mystical. How can thoughts influence people's physical health? The connection actually is not all that mysterious. Stress, even when experienced over a short time period, can lead to a suppression of the immune system (Cacioppo, 1998). In laboratory settings, for example, students attempting to solve math problems continuously for six minutes show a suppressed immune response. The same effect can occur for people who are asked to deliver a speech to a critical audience on short notice.

Coping with Stress

The hassles and pressures of daily life are difficult to avoid—nor should you do so. Humans seek out challenges and are motivated to attain mastery. The trick is how to think about challenges, obstacles, and daily hassles in a way that does not provoke stress. This does not mean engaging in denial or repression. If confronted with term paper deadlines and a week of back-to-back final exams, you shouldn't shrug off these challenges as inconsequential and put them out of your mind. Instead, you should confront the challenges but put them into perspective and think about them in the "right way."

But what does it mean to think about challenges and hassles in a way that optimizes your behavior and does so without producing high levels of stress (and giving you a cold)? A concrete answer to this question comes from the contemporary concern with *mindfulness* (e.g., Brown & Ryan, 2003; Ekman, Davidson, Ricard, & Wallace, 2005). This concept has its origins in Buddhism but it has been reframed in recent years in terms that are familiar to students of psychology. In general terms, to be mindful is to adopt a non-judgmental awareness of one's current experience without becoming distracted by other thoughts. Meditation is commonly advocated as a means of achieving this mental state. Thus, sitting with one's eyes closed and focusing on one's breathing is said to produce a calm, present-focused state of mind.

Meditation is certainly helpful in reducing (or avoiding) stress, but people can't stop what they're doing every time a negative event is experienced, close their eyes, and concentrate on their breathing. A more general (and less eyebrow raising) way to think about one's experiences in a non-stressful manner follows from the notion of *optimal action identification* (Vallacher, Wegner, & Somoza, 1989), as discussed in Chapter 6. The key idea is that anything a person does can be understood at different levels of comprehensiveness or abstraction, from the action's mechanical details (*low-level act identities*) to its larger meaning, consequences, and self-evaluative implications (*high-level act identities*). The optimal level of identification depends on the action's personal difficulty or unfamiliarity. When attempting something difficult or challenging—or any action for the first time—effective performance requires attention to detail rather than a focus on the action's higher-level meaning. With less difficult or challenging actions, correspondingly less attention to the action's specific features is necessary; instead, the action can be effectively performed by focusing on the action's higher-level meaning.

Consider what it is like to give a speech to a large audience (Vallacher et al., 1989). For many people, this is a very stressful experience that produces tremendous anxiety and is performed in a halting, awkward manner. Others, however, experience little or no speech anxiety and they may even seek out opportunities to express themselves in front of a roomful of complete strangers. In both cases, speakers are sensitive to how they are evaluated and concerned with whether the audience will be entertained or persuaded. What determines whether this focus is stressful is the experience and skill that people have in giving a speech. Sensitivity to the speech's consequences and implications is *optimal* for the experienced speaker, who can deliver the speech without concentrating consciously on his or her voice, gestures, and the like. But the same focus is *non-optimal* for the novice speaker, who should be focusing on how to give the speech rather than on the consequences of the speech. The optimality perspective goes beyond this, however, to suggest that an experienced speaker is likely to experience self-consciousness and deliver a poor speech when he or she focuses on the lower-level features of speaking rather than what he or she is trying to accomplish. In effect, an experienced speaker who focuses on how to do what he or she does easily is "over-thinking" the action.

This simple idea may have wide generality. There is an optimal way to think about sport performance, taking an academic exam, maintaining a diet, and even having a conversation (Vallacher & Wegner, 2012). Each action can be enacted in a non-stressful fashion if it is enacted in line with a level of identification that matches your experience with, and mastery of the action. If a task is difficult or unfamiliar, you should deconstruct the action into manageable bites and tackle them rather than focusing on how your performance will reflect upon you. But if the task is familiar and you have a sense of mastery over it, focusing on the task's significance and implications is the appropriate way to approach it. Finding the optimal level of identification may not produce mindfulness in the Buddhist tradition—although it may help meditators maximize their experience (Parkin, Jarman, & Vallacher, 2015)—but it can go a long way in reducing the stress associated with the actions undertaken in everyday life.

Happiness

When people wonder about the meaning of life, to a large extent they are really wondering about what makes people happy. Happiness is the holy grail of psychological pursuit, the emotional state that everyone strives for. Indeed, the pursuit of happiness is considered a fundamental human right in the US Declaration of Independence, given equal billing with life and liberty. You might assume that positive emotions, including happiness, have a zero-sum relation with negative emotions—the greater one's positive emotional state, the less one's negative emotional state, and vice versa. But most researchers now agree that positive and negative affect are independent experiences, not opposite ends of a single dimension (Cacioppo & Gardner, 1999; Watson, Clark, & Tellegen, 1988). This means that happiness is not simply the opposite of sadness, but rather a unique state with its own set of sources and consequences. There is little mystery about what makes people unhappy—sad, anxious, angry, and so forth. But identifying the sources of happiness is a little more tricky.

Illusory Happiness

Despite its desirability, happiness is not that easily achieved. In part, this is because people do not understand the true sources of happiness, but rather attempt to become happy by focusing on the wrong things. Some things that people assume promote happiness do not have the expected effect, and some of the things that do promote happiness are not fully appreciated (Diener, Suh, Lucas, & Smith, 1999; Gilbert, 2006; Haidt, 2006).

The illusory nature of happiness is especially evident in the assumption that material well-being and comfort are a critical part of the equation (Myers & Diener, 1995). Who wouldn't be happy with winning a lottery or living in a part of the country with a nice climate? But chasing these things might take one down the wrong road (e.g., Diener, 2000; Myers & Diener, 1995). The relationship between material wealth and happiness has been investigated in two ways. Some studies have looked at the correlation *across* nations between each nation's wealth and the average happiness in each nation. In other words, are wealthy countries happy countries? Other studies have looked at the correlation *within* a nation between individual wealth and individual happiness. Are richer people in a nation happier than their less financially secure fellow citizens? In both cases, researchers employ brief questionnaires, most often the *Satisfaction with Life Scale* (Diener, Emmons, Larsen, & Griffin, 1985), that ask respondents how strongly they agree with straightforward statements, such as "If I could live my life over, I would change almost nothing" (strong agreement implies high subjective well-being).

Consider first the relationship between national wealth and national happiness. The evidence here is somewhat mixed (Diener et al., 1999). As Figure 15.1 illustrates, there is a tendency for wealthier countries to be happier places to live. The countries of northern Europe—Iceland, Denmark, Norway, Sweden, the Netherlands—have very high per capita gross national income (GNI) per person and also have the highest average scores on measures of subjective well-being. But there are two important caveats regarding this relationship.

First, the relationship is far from perfect. A closer look at Figure 15.1 reveals that beyond a relatively modest threshold of wealth—about $10,000 GNI per person—increased national wealth doesn't predict a nation's average level of happiness (Inglehart, 1990; Fischer & Boer, 2011). For example, happiness is about the same for the average person in Colombia and Sweden, even though the average Swede has more than twice the income.

The second caveat concerns the correlational nature of the data. When a correlation is observed between two variables, it may reflect the workings of other factors. This is the case for national wealth and subjective well-being. Wealthier countries tend to differ from poorer countries in several ways, including having a stable democracy, secure human rights, social equality, personal freedom, low income inequality, and a high level of average health. When these factors are statistically "removed" from the equation, the relationship between national wealth and happiness essentially disappears (Diener et al., 1999; Myers & Diener, 1995).

A similar pattern exists within nations. People with higher incomes are happier than those with lower incomes. The very poor tend to be unhappy, and increased wealth is associated with increased happiness—but only up to a point. There is a threshold for happiness that corresponds in the United States to a middle-class income. Beyond this threshold, people can feel fairly secure about their financial status and can turn their attention to other sources of personal fulfillment.

Money can actually have a *negative* impact on happiness, by undermining the pleasure of everyday experiences. Quoidbach, Dunn, Petrides, and Mikolajczak (2010) found that wealthy people report lower ability to savor positive experiences than do people with less money. Simply *thinking* about money can have this effect, even if one is not personally wealthy. When participants saw a picture of money, they ate chocolate faster and exhibited less enjoyment of it than did participants who viewed a neutral picture. So although money can provide access to many things, it may impede our ability to enjoy life's small pleasures. Because money provides an abundance of pleasurable experiences, it undermines the savoring of any one experience. Material outcomes—most notably, money—may have ironic implications

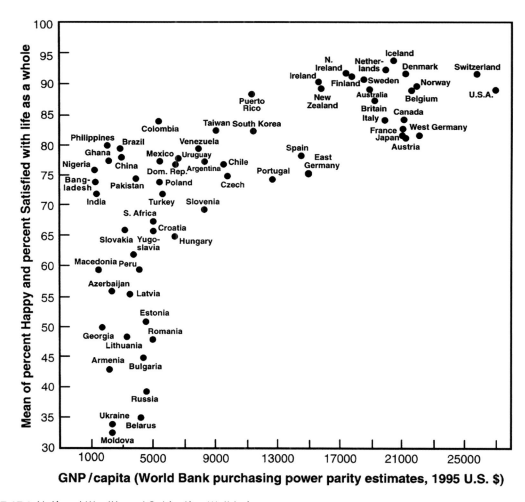

FIGURE 15.1 National Wealth and Subjective Well-being

for other psychological processes. As discussed in Chapter 6, the expectation of material rewards can undermine the motivation to engage in otherwise enjoyable activities. And as discussed in Chapter 10 ("Social Influence"), the promise of material rewards to influence people's behavior can backfire, undercutting their desire to do what is expected. Beyond that, simply being reminded of money can promote a self-sufficient orientation, so that people prefer to play alone, work alone, and even put greater physical distance between themselves and a new acquaintance (Vohs, Meade, & Goode, 2006). Money is certainly important for physical and material well-being, but it is by no means a guarantee of subjective well-being.

True Happiness

If money cannot buy happiness, what can? What are the factors that promote subjective well-being once a certain threshold of material well-being is met? Once again, this question can be addressed in two ways: what makes some nations happier than others, and what determines who is happy and who is not within a nation?

Consider first the relative happiness of nations. The best predictor of a nation's subjective well-being is the value placed on *individualism* (Fischer & Boer, 2011). Increasing wealth in a society may influence well-being, but it does so primarily by allowing citizens to experience greater autonomy and freedom in their daily life (Inglehart, Foa, Peterson, & Welzel, 2008).

But what about individual variation in happiness within a nation? Why are some people happier than their fellow citizens? As noted above, after a threshold of financial security is reached, increases in income do not lead to greater happiness. Nonetheless, money can promote happiness—provided it is used in the right way. Imagine you had $2,000 to spend. Would you buy the latest flat-screen 3D 4K 65-inch TV, or would you take a 2-week trip to a personally desirable location (another country, the Rocky Mountains, a white-sand beach in the Caribbean)?

This may seem like a tough question, but there is actually a clear answer: a memorable experience brings greater happiness than does acquiring a possession (Van Boven & Gilovich, 2003) and this happiness endures over a longer time. Possessions are important, even necessary, but their novelty wears off fairly quickly and they become absorbed into your everyday life. The TV might provide some initial joy, but it eventually becomes part of the furniture. An experience, in contrast, can be relived in one's memory and provide a topic of conversation in one's social relations. Photos and videos—that quaint outdoor café in Barcelona, the bear spotted running up the mountainside, the beautiful sunset on the beach—help to keep the experience fresh and exciting, bringing back (and embellishing) the feelings one had when the shots were taken. The vacation establishes memories that persist, or even get stronger and more pleasant over time (particularly when the fun parts are documented in photos and enhanced in story telling). Possessions do not have this power. One does not look at the TV day after day and become flooded with warm feelings, vivid memories of the sales transaction, and exciting fantasies about how your favorite show will look on a 65-inch screen.

Another factor influencing happiness is the tendency for people to compare themselves with others (Festinger, 1954; Parducci, 1995). Increasing one's income relative to that of others increases happiness, but increasing everyone's income (i.e., changes in a country's gross domestic product) does not affect happiness (Clark, Frijters, & Shields, 2008; Kassam, Morewedge, Gilbert, & Wilson, 2011). The wealthiest middle-class person in a small town or suburb, for example, is likely to have higher life satisfaction than is a millionaire in a posh community comprised of billionaires.

The type of social comparison also influences happiness. Engaging in *upward comparison* (comparing oneself to others who are better off financially) triggers negative feelings, while engaging in *downward comparison* (comparing oneself to others who are not doing as well) triggers positive feelings (Wheeler & Miyake, 1992). Not surprisingly, then, people who are happy are more likely to make downward comparisons than are their unhappy counterparts (Lyubomirsky & Ross, 1997).

Box 15.1 Tips on Savoring Positive Experiences

Having an experience can provide happiness. But to extract the full benefit of a positive experience, it must be *savored*. Savoring is a form of emotion regulation that people use to prolong and enhance positive experiences (e.g., Bryant, 1989, 2003; Kurtz, 2008). Four easy-to-implement strategies have been identified that can be employed alone or in combination to savor a positive event (Tugade & Fredrickson, 2007). Keep these in mind the next time something good happens to you.

- *Display your positive emotions nonverbally.* Rather than controlling your delight or enthusiasm, express your reaction with facial displays and gestures associated with positive feelings (e.g., open arms, hand-clapping). These displays should be natural, of course, and make sure you don't overdo it and ruin the event by eliciting stares and eye rolls from disapproving bystanders.
- *Stay focused in the moment.* Savoring a positive event is practically synonymous with attending to it and letting it sink in. People who linger on a positive experience tend to extract greater satisfaction from the experience than do those who quickly move on to another experience.
- *Think about the event before and after it is experienced.* Anticipation can enhance the pleasure of an event, as can reflecting on it after the fact. Don't let this get in the way of preparing for other experiences, of course, and don't dismiss the significance of less wonderful events that may also have value and are worth thinking about.
- *Tell others about the positive event.* A positive emotional response becomes even more positive when it is described to friends and acquaintances. Apart from enhancing the quality of the experience, sharing positive feelings with others can reinforce the closeness of your social relations. Be careful, of course, not to rub it in and make them envious—that could be an unpleasant event not worth savoring.

Financial security and social comparison aside, you might think that happiness is related to demographic factors such as age, sex, race, ethnic background, and educational level, or to personal factors such as IQ, athletic ability, or physical attractiveness. This is not the case, however (Diener et al., 1999). Contrary to intuition, received wisdom, and certain genre of literature, people are not less happy during middle age or in old age than they are during their young adult years. Men and women do not differ in their happiness, nor do White Americans and African Americans. College educated people are not happier than those without a college education, highly intelligent people are not happier than people with average intelligence, and beautiful women and handsome men are not any happier than their average-looking counterparts.

Happiness, however, does have some important sources. Social connections are especially important for personal well-being (e.g., Baumeister & Leary, 1995; Diener et al., 1999; Myers & Diener, 1995). This makes sense and confirms the centrality of belongingness needs in human psychology. We would never have made it out of the Pleistocene—the era during which modern humans evolved, about 150,000 years ago—if we didn't look to other people for support, comfort, and goal attainment. A happy society places value on individual freedom, but it is also one in which citizens trust one another and enjoy close social relationships (Oishi & Schimmack, 2010). And within a society, the happiest people are those who feel connected to others and have established close personal relationships (Myers & Diener, 1995).

A sense of personal meaning is also critical (Myers & Diener, 1995). People who believe that there is purpose in the universe and that there is something outside of themselves to believe in tend to be happier and more content than those who lack this worldview. They also tend to live longer than those who see less purpose in life (Hill & Turiano, 2014). Religion can satisfy this need and does so for many people. Purpose and meaning are not restricted to conventional religiosity, however. People may experience a profound connection with the forces at work in the universe—including those that are mysterious or unexplained—even if this connection does not correspond to a particular creation story or with belief in an afterlife. And although religiosity is associated with greater subjective well-being at the individual level (i.e., religious individuals in a nation tend to be happier than their non-religious counterparts), there is little association at the national level—nations with a high degree of conventional religiosity are not any happier than are nations in which conventional religions are less commonly practiced (e.g., those having low rates of church attendance).

Box 15.2   Why Is Holland, Michigan, a Happy Place to Live?

When one thinks of happy places to live, cities like Honolulu and Boulder, Colorado, might come to mind because of their wonderful climates, as might cities like New York, San Francisco, or Los Angeles, because of the abundance of cultural and lifestyle opportunities they provide. If pressed, people might dig a little deeper to find happy places, but it is unlikely anyone would guess Holland, Michigan—a city with a 17% unemployment rate, lousy weather, and virtually no attractions. Yet, Holland was the second happiest place in the United States in 2010 (Boulder was first, Honolulu was third). The rankings were based on more than 353,000 interviews with Americans who were asked questions about all aspects of their lives, including their physical and emotional well-being, healthy behaviors, work environment, and community.

So what is Holland's secret? It has lots of churches. Holland, in fact, is known as the "city of churches": there are 170 places of worship for its 35,000 residents—or about one church for every 200 people. Church attendance satisfies one of the true sources of happiness: finding purpose in life through religiosity. But the churches in Holland also satisfy another true source of happiness: strong and meaningful social connections. The churches form an informal network that promotes a strong community spirit, and this spirit is translated into a culture of sharing and giving. Indeed, despite its exceptionally high unemployment rate, Holland has over 100 volunteer-based service organizations fanned out through the city. The churches promote the informal social network necessary to help those in need. Holland's residents may not have a surplus of material well-being, but they more than make up for this deficit in their focus on the true sources of happiness.

Source: ABC News, February 17, 2010

Yet another source of happiness may strike you as strange, perhaps counterintuitive. As noted earlier, the enjoyment of everyday experiences may be undermined by financial wealth, because it promises an abundance of pleasurable experiences. By this reasoning, scarcity may *promote* happiness because it increases savoring of the scarce resource or event. For example, college seniors derive greater happiness from the final weeks of college when they realize that graduation is impending than when they think of graduation as being very far off (Kurtz, 2008).

Law and Criminal Justice

Criminal justice is at the intersection of several social psychological processes. Determining whether someone is guilty of a crime is not a simple matter of rational decision-making. Critical evidence can be lacking or inconsistent, and even when it is concrete and available, the jurors must process it to reach a conclusion. As we learned in Chapters 7 ("Social Judgment") and 13 ("Prejudice, Stereotypes, and Discrimination"), numerous factors bias the way people select and interpret information about other people. The verdict of guilt versus not-guilty often takes place in a jury context, moreover, so processes discussed in Chapters 10 ("Social Influence") and 12 ("Group Dynamics") are in play. And if a guilty verdict is reached, a judge or jury must decide how the defendant should be punished. Such decisions reflect people's sense of morality and justice, basic human concerns that were the focus of Chapter 14 ("Dilemmas of Social Life").

Evidence Credibility

Evidence relevant to a defendant's guilt or innocence can take many forms, but none prove more critical than eyewitness reports. Someone accused of robbing a store will find it tough proving his or her innocence if someone else observed the event and claims that the accused person was the culprit. *Eyewitness testimony* is often decisive in "solving" a crime, even if there is considerable evidence to the contrary. And the greater an eyewitness's confidence in what he or she claims to have seen, the more credible this evidence is considered to be.

However, research has established that the accuracy of eyewitness reports is often overestimated (Loftus, 1979; Lindsay, Wells, & Rumpel, 1981; Wells & Olson, 2003) and that a witness's confidence is only weakly correlated with his or her accuracy (Brewer & Weber, 2008; Lindsay, Read, & Sharma, 1998; Wells, Olson, & Charman, 2002; Wixted & Wells, 2017). Especially troubling is that people have been arrested and even wrongly convicted based on faulty eyewitness testimony (Brandon & Davies, 1973; Sporer, Koehnken, & Malpass, 1996; Wells, Wright, & Bradfield, 1999). Gary Wells and his colleagues (1998), for example, examined 40 cases in which DNA evidence, collected long after a jury trial, showed that a person convicted of a crime was actually innocent. In almost all these cases—36 of the 40—an eyewitness had "positively" identified the innocent person as the culprit in the crime.

A crime scene is far short of being optimal for making accurate observations and judgments. The person is a stranger and perhaps partially disguised; the action is unexpected, unfamiliar, and happens quickly; the context may be novel and the viewing conditions poor; and the situation is emotionally charged and stressful. Under these conditions, people's perceptions and judgments may say more about what they are feeling than about what they are seeing.

Even under optimal conditions—a familiar setting, adequate lighting, low stress—people can be wildly inaccurate in their eyewitness reports if the alleged perpetrator is a member of a different racial group. People are better at recognizing faces of the same race than of a different race because they are more familiar with the former. This *own-race bias* has been documented for various race combinations: Whites are better at recognizing white faces than black or Asian faces, Blacks are better at recognizing black faces than white faces, and Asians are better at recognizing Asian faces than white faces (Levin, 2000; Meissner & Brigham, 2001; Ng & Lindsay, 1994; Shapiro & Penrod, 1986).

This bias can also be understood in terms of *in-group variability versus out-group homogeneity*, as discussed in Chapter 13. People are sensitive to individual differences within their own group but tend to see members of other groups in terms of their common attributes. So when people examine same-race faces, they attend closely to features that distinguish that face from other faces (e.g., the height of the forehead). When examining a different-race face, however, they are more attentive to features that distinguish that face from their own race (Levin, 2000). This bias is not limited to racial in-groups and out-groups. College students, for example, can recognize faces of young people better than faces of middle-aged people, and middle-aged people are better at recognizing faces of people their own age than faces of college students (Wright & Stroud, 2002).

You might think that eyewitness problems might be minimized if eyewitnesses were asked to think carefully about what they saw, perhaps describing in words the face and other physical features of the person they saw committing the crime. Actually, that can make matters worse (Schooler, Fiore, & Brandimonte, 1997). Putting a face into words is not easy and attempting to do so can impair one's visual memory. An eyewitness might use *angry* to describe a robber's face, for example, but this label might focus the person's description on certain features (e.g., jaw tension, furrowed eyebrows) to the exclusion of other features that stood out at the time (e.g., hair color, nose shape). When later attempting to identify the culprit from a set of photos, the eyewitness might overlook features that were not verbalized, settling on photos that confirm his or her emphasis on angry features.

It is one thing to misperceive an event and its perpetrator—it's something else to say one has witnessed something that never happened at all. Yet this *false memory syndrome* is all too real (Kihlstrom, 1996). People can acquire vivid and detailed memories of events that they did not experience. This can be a tricky issue, especially when the event in question happened (or did not happen) during the person's childhood. Can a traumatic event such as sexual abuse be repressed for years, only to be recovered during adulthood? Such abuse certainly occurs and cries out for justice, but many researchers argue that the accuracy of *recovered memories* in adulthood cannot be accepted at face value (Loftus, 1993; Schooler, 1999; Schacter, 1996).

This does not mean that all recovered memories of traumatic childhood events are false (Bass & Davis, 1994; Schooler, 1999). However, the validity of repressed memories that suddenly resurface is questionable when another person—a psychotherapist, for example, or an attorney—suggests to the person that the event occurred (Johnson & Raye, 1981; Loftus, 1993). To avoid this problem, the person probing for the events should avoid leading questions that call for a confirmatory response (Hirt, McDonald, & Erickson, 1995; Loftus, 1979). Such questions can create false memories—which can lead to sending an innocent person to prison. Asking a possible victim *if* someone touched him or her in a sexual manner is less likely to produce a false memory than is asking the person *when and how* he or she was touched in a sexual manner.

Bias in Judging Guilt

Even with abundant evidence in hand, there is no guarantee that people will arrive at an objective and rational conclusion concerning a defendant's guilt versus innocence. Making such a determination is a special case of social judgment, a process that is open to well-documented biases and shortcomings, as discussed in Chapter 7 ("Social Judgment"). A juror might selectively attend to some information rather than to all the relevant facts, for example, or reinterpret the meaning of certain information to make it fit a prevailing interpretation. These features of human thought can shape the judgments regarding anyone, from a complete stranger to a loved one. They are likely to take on added importance in a criminal case if the defendant has characteristics that play into a juror's biases.

A defendant's physical attractiveness is one such characteristic. As noted in Chapter 7, people tend to see an attractive person in positive terms and interpret his or her behavior in a manner that maintains this positivity bias. That attractive people are judged more favorably in everyday life may seem unfair but it is not surprising. But this bias is at work in the criminal justice system as well. Better-looking defendants tend to receive more favorable treatment in the criminal justice system than do their average or unattractive counterparts (Castellow, Wuensch, & Moore, 1990; Zebrowitz & McDonald, 1991). Even when attractive defendants are found guilty of a crime, they often receive lighter sentences (Efran, 1974; Stewart, 1980).

Attractiveness can bias judgments in the criminal justice system, but this effect does not come close to the effect of a defendant's race on how justice is determined (Coker, 2003). The percentage of African Americans in prison or jail (close to 5,000 per 100,000) is almost 10 times higher than that of White males (about 500 per 100,000). And although African Americans constitute less than 13% of the US population, they make up 40% of the prison population (Lawrence, 2011). Of course, these statistics could simply mean that African Americans commit a disproportionate number of crimes. But a deeper look paints a more disturbing picture.

"Driving while Black," for example, refers to statistics showing that African Americans are four times more likely than Whites to be pulled over and have their cars searched. A study of the New Jersey turnpike found that although African Americans were 14% of the drivers and 15% of the speeders, they made up 35% of those pulled over and 70% of those arrested (Robinson, 2000). There is an especially marked racial disparity in the enforcement of drug laws. Although the rate of illicit drug use is similar for African Americans and Whites (10% vs. 8.7%), African Americans are arrested on drug charges at a far higher rate, are more likely to be convicted for the same drug crimes, and receive far stiffer sentences (i.e., greater prison time) for these crimes. African Americans tend to receive greater punishment than do Whites for most crimes. This is especially true for capital punishment. Blacks who killed Whites are sentenced to death 22 times more frequently than Blacks who killed Blacks and seven times more frequently than Whites who killed Blacks (Amnesty International, 2003, www.amnesty.org/en/library/info/AMR51/046; www.deathpenaltyinfo.org).

The issue of racial bias in the criminal justice system has been front and center in recent years, with several high profile cases that captured media and public attention. Several of these cases were discussed in detail in Chapter 13. What makes these cases so interesting (as well as tragic) is that one need not invoke explicit racism to explain the actions of the police officers involved. Police officers, and people generally, do not think of themselves as racially prejudiced and most of them probably are not—at least consciously. But as we saw in Chapter 13, people can harbor unconscious prejudicial attitudes that may bias their interpretations and overt behavior toward members of a minority group. Results obtained with the *Implicit Association Test* (IAT) suggest that many people hold unconscious assumptions about African Americans, particularly of young males, and that these biases can trigger reactions under stress and uncertainty that are less likely to be observed during an altercation with a White male.

Recall the studies documenting the potentially deadly effects of automatic stereotyping (e.g., Payne, 2001), discussed in Chapter 13. When a quick decision with life or death consequences is called for, people are more likely to identify a hidden object as a tool when a while male reaches for it, but as a gun when an African American male reaches for it. Stress functions as a *cognitive load* and can undermine the executive resources necessary to make a consciously reasoned decision. Lacking conscious mental control, people's behavior is at the mercy of unconscious attitudes that find expression in seemingly automatic fashion.

Action Identification in Judging Guilt

Even in the absence of bias (e.g., racism, sexism) or factors that undermine conscious control (e.g., stress, distraction), the determination of guilt versus innocence can be shaped by factors that can slant the judgment in very different directions. In fact, the very objectivity of information can engage judgment processes that seem anything but objective. To understand this apparent irony, recall the emergence scenario of *action identification theory* (Vallacher & Wegner, 1987), discussed in Chapters 5, 7, and 10. People's natural inclination is to understand an action in terms of its higher-level meanings and implications. So when they are induced to think about an action in lower-level terms (e.g., specific movements), they become eager to embrace higher-level identities of the action that are provided by others. The greater a person's absorption in the details of an action, the greater is his or her likelihood of showing emergent understanding of the action in line with the interpretations provided by the influence agent.

In the context of criminal justice, this means that when presented with detailed information concerning an alleged criminal act, a juror is vulnerable to the conclusions regarding guilt versus innocence he or she is offered (e.g., by police, prosecutors, defense attorneys, witnesses). From this perspective, an attorney can best shape jurors' verdict by getting them to focus on all the details of the events surrounding the alleged crime, and then offering an interpretation that provides an avenue of emergent understanding.

The "elasticity" of details and the potential for very different higher-level interpretations based on these details was demonstrated in a study involving an alleged rape incident (Vallacher & Selz, 1991). Male and female participants read a lengthy police interview (about 1,000 words) with either the alleged rapist (Larry) or the alleged victim (Jane), and then read a police summary concluding either that the perpetrator should be charged with rape or that there were insufficient grounds to press charges. The interviews contained the same details and sequence of events, but they differed with respect to implied intent, motivation, and responsibility. The sequence begins with a minor exchange in a college class (Larry borrowing a pencil from Jane) that is presented as innocent by Jane (complying with a request) but as seductive by Larry (compliance accompanied by a smile). The sequence continues with the buttons popping on Jane's skirt as she retrieves a dropped pen, Jane riding her bike home after class, Larry following Jane on his bike, Jane entering her apartment after briefly fumbling with her keys, Larry knocking on Jane's door, Jane allowing Larry to enter after he explains that he wants to return the pen, and culminates in Larry having forceful sex with Jane. Larry and Jane depict these events in manner that is consistent with their overall portrayal of what happened (i.e., seduction or rape).

In a *low-level action identification* condition, participants were told to pay close attention to the details of the events described in the interview. They were told to remember as many specific things as they could, including the particular words and actions of both Larry and Jane. In the *high-level action identification* condition, participants were told to pay attention to the meaning and implications of the events described in the interview. They were told to think about the motives and intentions behind the words and behaviors of Larry and Jane. After reading the interview under either the low-level or high-level perspective, participants read a "confidential summary report" prepared by the police officer who conducted the interview. For half the participants, the summary concluded that Larry had committed rape (*Larry to blame*); for the other half, the summary concluded that Larry had not committed rape but rather had responded to seductive behavior by Jane (*Jane to blame*).

Upon reading the police summary, participants were asked to judge Larry's responsibility for what happened (e.g., "Should Larry be held accountable?" "Did Larry do anything wrong?"), with higher numbers indicating greater responsibility. As Figure 15.2 illustrates, the police summary did not affect judgments of Larry's responsibility in the high-level identification condition—Larry and Jane were seen as equally responsible regardless of whom the report blamed. But the police summary influenced judgments in the low-level identification condition: they held Larry responsible if the police report concluded he was to blame but they were less likely to hold him responsible if the report concluded that Jane was to blame.

You might assume that to reach a fair judgment regarding a defendant in a criminal case, jurors should suspend their biases and "consider only the facts and nothing but the facts." The results of this study, however, call this assumption into question. To be sure, if jurors are encouraged to think about a defendant's behavior in high-level terms, they may interpret it in terms of unquestioned stereotypes, personal values, and other biases. But whereas a high-level perspective on behavior can bias how the facts in a case are interpreted, a low-level perspective can be problematic precisely because it is *not* biased. When jurors are instructed to focus on all the facts in a case, they can become vulnerable to whatever high-level interpretation is offered by those with official roles in the criminal justice system.

Even if jurors are not influenced by the presentation and interpretation of evidence in the courtroom, they become highly susceptible to influence in the jury room. As we saw in Chapters 10 and 12 ("Group Dynamics"), there is

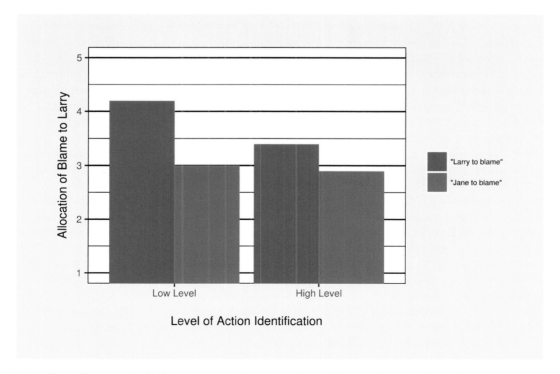

FIGURE 15.2 The Influence of a Police Summary ("Larry to Blame" Versus "Jane to Blame") on Judgments of Larry's Responsibility

Source: Adapted from Vallacher & Selz (1991)

pressure for consensus in group contexts, whether in an unstructured setting (e.g., *deindividuation*) or in a formal setting with a clear agenda (e.g., *groupthink*). The emergence of consensus occurs in juries as well (Myers, 1982). Indeed, the pressure to reach a group decision often plays a bigger role in reaching a verdict than does the independent consideration of the evidence by jurors, especially when the evidence is complex or ambiguous (e.g., Simon & Holyoak, 2002).

This does not mean that we should dispense with juries. But it does suggest that certain lessons of group dynamics could be introduced into the jury process. Particularly relevant are procedures that can weaken the tendency toward *groupthink*, as discussed in Chapter 12. The jury foreman (the person elected to lead the jury discussion), for example, can attempt to remain impartial rather than imposing his opinions on the other jurors, at least early in the jury's deliberations. He or she can also assign one of the jurors to play "devil's advocate" during the deliberations. In adopting a position that challenges the emerging consensus among jurors, this person could stall or perhaps reverse the pressure for consensus that underlies groupthink.

Another recommendation is to encourage individual judgment before group decision-making takes place. The jurors can be asked to express their opinions anonymously in writing, for example, or a secret ballot can be conducted to allow jurors the freedom to express their true opinions without worrying about recrimination from other jurors. These procedures are sometimes adopted by juries, but perhaps they could be made explicit in the instructions that are given to juries when they begin their deliberations.

Crime and Punishment

After a verdict is reached, it must be acted upon. Of course, a *not guilty* verdict means that the defendant is free to go on about his or her life. But if the verdict is *guilty*, the judge or jury must assign a punishment that is proportional to the crime: the more egregious the crime, the more consequential the punishment. Punishment in the criminal justice system typically takes the form of imprisonment. Incarceration may seem like the only reasonable way of punishing those who have run afoul of the law and pose a risk for engaging in such behavior again.

There are reasons, however, to be concerned about the effect of imprisonment on prisoners—and on those who guard them. Social psychology is known for controversial studies—the Milgram (1974) obedience to authority studies, for instance—but no study aroused greater controversy than the Stanford prison experiment (Haney, Banks, & Zimbardo, 1973). The plan was simple enough but the execution of the study quickly became very problematic. The researchers recruited undergraduates to play the role of guard or prisoner in a mock prison they built in the basement of the Psychology Department at Stanford University (see the photos below, taken from the experiment). The guards were dressed to look the part: they wore khaki shirts and pants, carried a whistle, and brandished a police nightstick. And they wore reflecting sunglasses. The prisoners' attire was considerably different and designed to signify their low-power status: a loose-fitting smock with an identification number stamped on it, a cap made from a nylon stocking, rubber sandals, and a locked chain attached to one ankle.

The students were randomly assigned to these roles, so any differences in their behavior during the course of the experiment did not reflect their personalities, but rather were in response to the role they were asked to play. And these roles made a big difference indeed. Within the first couple of days, the guards became aggressive and abusive, finding novel ways to harass and humiliate the prisoners, particularly if their orders were not followed without question. The prisoners, although defiant at first, became progressively passive, withdrawn, and helpless. The mock prison was scheduled to run for 2 weeks, but the situation rapidly deteriorated and had to be terminated after 6 days. Some prisoners became so depressed and anxious that they had to be released from the experiment earlier than that.

All the participants scored as perfectly normal on a battery of personality tests administered prior to the study. Their problematic behaviors therefore said little about them as individuals but spoke volumes about the nature of prison life. Incarceration certainly serves important functions, including protection of society and justice for bad behavior, and there may be no viable alternative to locking up people who have committed serious crimes. But in light of the roles that people so easily adopt in prison environments, there is little reason to expect prisoners to become rehabilitated during their sentence and to reenter society as better citizens.

What about the ultimate punishment—the death penalty? It certainly protects society from any possibility that the perpetrator will engage in the capital (or any) crime again. At the same time, though, it throws in the towel on rehabilitation. A person who is executed is hardly any better for the experience. Nonetheless, the majority of Americans in the early 21st century favor execution for certain capital offenses. Although the rationale for capital punishment is

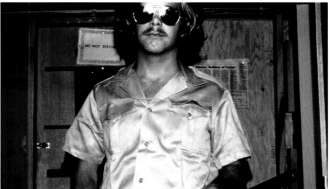

Photos from the Stanford prison experiment (© Stanford University)

often verbalized in terms of other motives—*deterrence* or *protection of society*—the evidence suggests that it really boils down to *revenge* (Carlsmith, Darley, & Robinson, 2002). People like to see the worst type of criminal punished by the legal system in the same way that they like to see a bully beaten up or an obnoxious person slip and fall flat on his or her face.

Of course, just because public support for capital punishment is motivated by revenge, this does not necessarily mean that executions do not have deterrence value. Perhaps knowing that the punishment for murder is getting killed by the government prevents people from acting on their murderous impulses. The deterrence value of capital punishment is a highly controversial issue. The overwhelming majority of America's leading criminologists, however, have concluded that capital punishment does not contribute to lower rates of homicide (e.g., Bedau, 1997; Radelet & Akers, 1996; Sorensen, Wrinkle, Brewer, & Marquart, 1999). In fact, there is evidence that executions are followed by an *increase* rather than a decrease in murders (Archer & Gartner, 1984; Bailey & Peterson, 1997). Perhaps society could be just as well-protected by locking up the offender for life or until he or she is too old to represent a threat to anyone.

The Environment

The earth has not grown in size since it was formed four and a half billion years ago. But the number of people populating the planet has grown from zero to almost seven billion. And most of that growth has occurred in the last 100 years—less than one-tenth of a second on a 24-hour clock representing the age of the earth. During that time, we have dramatically transformed the earth. Much of human-induced change is positive. We have built extensive infrastructures (sanitation, transportation, communication) that enable us to live in otherwise hostile environments (deserts, tropics, arctic tundra) and to do so with a population density that would have been impossible in ancient times. But we have also had an adverse effect on the environment. The overgrazing of land for agriculture, the slashing of tropical rainforests, the pollution of the atmosphere and the oceans, the depletion of natural resources—these consequences of modern life pose severe dilemmas today and will prove catastrophic in the future unless we find a way to deal with them. So what does social psychology have to offer in managing these human-created dilemmas?

Resolving Social Dilemmas

The research on social dilemmas, discussed in Chapter 14, has shown that selfishness may pay off in the short run, but cooperation tends to bring better payoffs to everyone in the long run. The question is how best to convince people to see modern social dilemmas—the sharing of scarce resources, cutting back on the use of fossil fuels, government policies that call for lifestyle changes—as beneficial in the long run when such changes might require personal sacrifices in their daily lives. What prevents people from defecting and letting others make the sacrifice?

You might think that people would inhibit the temptation to defect if they feared the consequences of acting in this manner. Laws, after all, keep people from running red lights, cheating on their taxes, and causing physical harm to others they do not like. However, the relationship between external constraints (e.g., the threat of sanctions or punishment) and cooperation versus defection is not that straightforward. Recall a key lesson from the discussions of *self-regulation* (Chapter 6) and *social influence* (Chapter 10). External forces can undermine a person's intrinsic reasons for doing something—in effect, the external forces replace an individual's personal desire to engage in an action.

This principle operates as well in social dilemmas. When there are opportunities for defection, it might seem natural to put in place means of monitoring to ensure that defection does not occur, and to punish people who defect. These measures can be quite effective while they are in place, but they can have the ironic effect or *increasing* the likelihood of defection once they are removed. If a person feels that the behavior of other people in a social dilemma is controlled by the threat of sanctions, he or she is likely to become wary of their behavior if sanctions are no longer employed.

Mulder, van Dijk, De Cremer, and Wilke (2006) tested this idea in a *Public Goods Game*. Participants learned that they were part of a four-person group, although they could not see or communicate directly with one another. They were presented two situations (A and B) in which they could earn money. In situation A, each participant was provided 100 chips worth about 10 cents each. Participants could give any number of these chips to the group (i.e., cooperate) or hold onto them (i.e., defect). The total number of chips given to the group would then be doubled and divided equally among the four participants. So it was better for all group members if individual members donated their respective chips. Each individual, however, profited more by hanging onto his or her chips if the other members donated theirs. In the *sanction condition*, participants were told that the two group members who donated the fewest chips would be fined about $7—a pretty strong incentive not to defect and take advantage of other group members. In the *no sanction condition*, there was no mention of punishing those who did not contribute to the pot. Participants were then asked how much they trusted the other group members and asked how many chips they decided to donate to the group.

Situation B was then presented. The procedure was identical to that employed in Situation A, except that participants in the *sanction condition* were told that the sanctioning system was no longer in place. Once again, nothing was said about sanctions in the *no sanction condition*. As in Situation A, participants were asked how much they trusted the other group members and how many chips they decided to donate to the group.

The results for both trust and number of chips donated supported the predicted undermining effect of sanctions. Figure 15.3 presents the results for chip donation. Participants who first played the game with sanctions in place (in Situation A) donated the largest number of chips. But their cooperative behavior dropped off in favor of defection when the sanctions were removed (Situation B). This switch from cooperation to defection was not observed when no sanctions were mentioned in Situation A. Parallel results were observed for trust: participants in the sanction

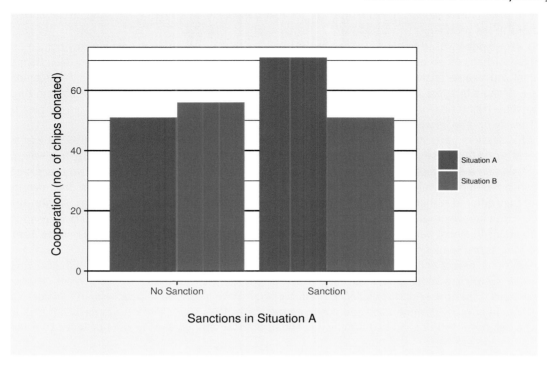

FIGURE 15.3 Cooperative Behavior in a Public Goods Game with and Without Sanctions for Selfish Behavior
Source: Adapted from Mulder et al. (2006)

condition tended to distrust the other group members when the sanctions were removed in Situation B, but a loss of trust did not occur for those in the no sanction condition.

The lesson here is simple. When there is a sanction on defection, people in social dilemmas doubt that cooperation by other people is internally motivated. So if the sanctions are lifted, people expect that others will revert to a competitive orientation and defect in order to maximize their outcomes. Expecting defection from one another, the players defect first in order to avoid being a chump. External sanctions may be necessary to prevent defection, particularly when there is a power differential (Kipnis, 1972) or if the parties do not anticipate repeated contact with one another (Axelrod, Riolo, & Cohen, 2002). But constraints, or at least their visibility, should be kept to a minimum, allowing cooperation to emerge from the coordination of self-interest among interdependent people.

Preserving the Environment

There are many assaults on the physical environment associated with an expanding global population, expectations of abundant food and energy, and the reliance on fossils fuels to maintain a modern lifestyle. Arguably, the biggest environmental problem of all is human-induced climate change. Overpopulation and increasingly scarce resources are certainly serious, but these problems tend to be geographically isolated, with some regions at greater risk than others, at least in the near future. But the increased concentration of carbon dioxide, methane, and other gases in the upper atmosphere has the potential to make life for humans unsustainable as the 21st century unfolds.

In view of the gravity of this worldwide problem, you might think that people everywhere would be eager to find a solution, even if that meant making some personal and societal sacrifices. Dire warnings by scientists regarding the danger of human-induced climate change have been voiced repeatedly, with the expectation that such warnings would convince people of the need for collective action. Yet nearly half the people in the United States are skeptical about human-induced climate change. This may seem surprising, but it actually follows from the research on *fear-based persuasion appeals*, discussed in Chapter 10. Such appeals tend to be ineffective, *especially* if they arouse high levels of fear (e.g., Janis & Feshbach, 1953). In order for fear appeals to be effective, they should be followed by possible solutions to the problem.

Can this knowledge be used to get people on board to deal with the impending doom posed by human-induced climate change? Perhaps so, according to a study by Feinberg and Willer (2011). They felt that scary depictions of climate change might provoke defensiveness in people, and that this reaction should be particularly intense among people who believe strongly in a *just world* (Lerner, 1980) because the dire consequences of climate change threaten this belief. However, a frightening depiction followed by possible solutions to the problem might soften people's defensiveness, particularly for people who feel that justice prevails in the long run.

In an initial session, participants completed a questionnaire (Dalbert, Montada, & Schmitt, 1987) assessing their belief in a just world (e.g., "I believe that people get what they deserve," "I am confident that justice always prevails"). At a second session a few weeks later, participants were randomly assigned to read one of two articles concerning climate change based on a United Nations report. Both articles provided the same information documenting climate change, but they differed in their final two paragraphs. The *dire-message* article detailed the devastation and possible apocalyptic consequences that could result from global warming. The *positive-message* article focused instead on potential solutions to global warming, emphasizing how technological ingenuity could possibly reverse its effects and find solutions to carbon emissions.

At both sessions—before and after reading the articles—all participants completed a survey that included two items assessing their skepticism about global warming: "How certain are you that global warming is actually occurring?" and "How likely is it that the scientific evidence used to demonstrate global warming is wrong?" Feinberg and Willer were interested in how the dire-message and positive-message articles changed participants' belief in global warming, and whether the effects of the two articles depended on how strongly participants believed that the world is basically just and orderly.

The results, illustrated in Figure 15.4, revealed that participants who believed strongly in a just world reacted very differently to the dire- and positive-message articles. Those who read the "doomsday" message became more skeptical

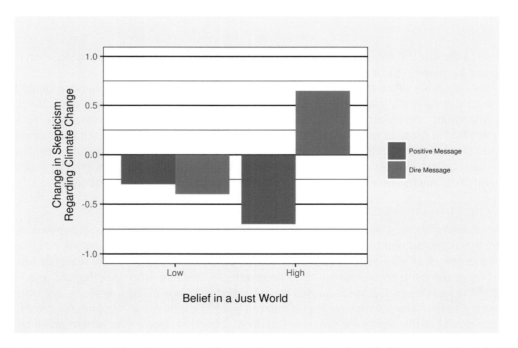

FIGURE 15.4 Change in Skepticism Regarding Climate Change for People with Strong vs. Weak Belief in a Just World. Positive Numbers Mean Increased Skepticism, Negative Numbers Mean Decreased Skepticism (Increased Acceptance).

Source: Adapted from Feinberg & Willer (2011)

of global warming, because it challenged their view that the world is generally a fair place. Defensiveness on their part overcame their consideration of the facts presented in the article. But if participants with a strong belief in a just world read an article that outlined solutions to climate change, their skepticism regarding global warming showed a significant *decrease* from their initial opinion. In other words, they trusted the science if the article aroused fears about the future but provided feasible ways of averting the crisis. Participants who believed less strongly in a just world were less affected by the articles. They became a bit less skeptical about climate change whether they read the dire-message or the positive-message version. Presumably, the dire consequences of climate change were less threatening to their idea of what the world is like.

Social Change

What Promotes Societal and Cultural Change?

The pace of change today is unprecedented in human history. This is great in many respects, particularly with regard to science, technology, and medicine. But the dynamics at work in contemporary life also pose dilemmas for people at the intrapersonal, interpersonal, and collective levels of experience. People's values can come under assault, traditional forms of social relationships may give way to new ways of relating to one another, and long-standing political and economic philosophies can be replaced by new ways of regulating how a society functions. To understand the consequences of social change, we must first understand the processes that promote such change. Are there common forces at work that drive change in different social systems? Are the resultant transitions in society incremental, with continuity over time in the scale of change, or are transitions sometimes sudden and dramatic, representing a wholesale change from the past? Will the processes of change promote disruptions to social order and stability in the years to come? Or will they pave the way to brighter and more peaceful future? What can we expect as the 21st century unfolds?

The Emergence of Norms and Values

Every society throughout history has developed beliefs, values, and rules of conduct that constrain the behavior of its citizens. Some broad norms and values—reciprocity, personal accountability, social responsibility—are basic to human nature and appear in every culture. But there is also considerable diversity among cultures in their practices and assumptions about social relations, morality, and justice. And although societies tend to maintain their respective norms and values despite changing circumstances and international relations, they can also evolve under some conditions—or even undergo catastrophic change. Can the principles introduced in this text explain these patterns of stability and change in social systems?

The Emergence of Social Structure

Social systems can undergo rapid and dramatic change in their form of government, economic institutions, and values regarding lifestyle. Insight into the nature of such change has been achieved by framing the underlying process in terms of principles that underlie transitions in complex systems studied in physics and chemistry (Nowak & Vallacher, 2019). The basic notion is that rapid changes in norms and values are remarkably similar to *phase transitions* in physical systems. Metaphorically, *islands of new* form in a *sea of old*, much like the formation of gas bubbles in a liquid as it nears the boiling point (e.g., Nowak, Szamrej, & Latané, 1990). As the transition proceeds, these islands—or *clusters*—grow, become connected, and encircle the remaining pockets of old. At some point, the new clusters represent the dominant perspective in the society, with the remaining clusters of *old* marginalized in the social system.

Such change was evident in the countries of Eastern Europe (e.g., Poland, Hungary) in the late 1980s with the collapse of Communism. These societies moved, seemingly overnight, from state-controlled to free-market economies, a major transition that ushered in a variety of significant political and social changes. Those who maintained their Communist sympathies survived in relatively small clusters of like-minded people and had little influence on government policy for several years.

This process of the *new* displacing the *old* is never complete, however, because the individuals who survive the pressure of the new tend to be strong and resistant to influence. And because they exist in clusters of like-minded people, they provide support for one another. This is an important but often overlooked feature of widespread and seemingly irreversible changes in society. If people become disillusioned with the *new*, for example, the *old* can mount a counterattack and restore their majority status. So what looks like a wholesale change in society can be just as easily be reversed when conditions change. This in fact happened in the eastern European case. Although the *old* (those with Communist leanings) were marginalized as the Communist empire imploded, they regained much of their influence in a few years because the political and economic reforms did not improve life in these countries as much as had been anticipated.

Computer simulations are useful for visualizing this scenario of dramatic social change. Take a look at Figure 15.5. Each cell in these grids represents an individual who holds one of two opinions (e.g., pro-communism vs. pro-democracy) represented by red and green. The height of each individual represents his or her strength, which can signify his or her persuasive power, resistance to persuasion by others, or expertise and knowledge. Each individual interacts with his or her neighbors and adopts the opinion that is most prevalent among his or her neighbors. If the individual is strong (i.e., a tall cell), he or she can maintain his or her opinion even if a slight majority of the neighbors hold a different opinion. This process of interacting with one's neighbors and maintaining or changing one's opinions as a result is repeated many times, with each time promoting an updating of the structure of opinions in the social system.

Figure 15.5 shows a typical course of change in opinions when a **bias** develops for the minority opinion (e.g., pro-democracy). In the starting configuration (*Panel A*), 10% of the population holds the minority opinion (green), with

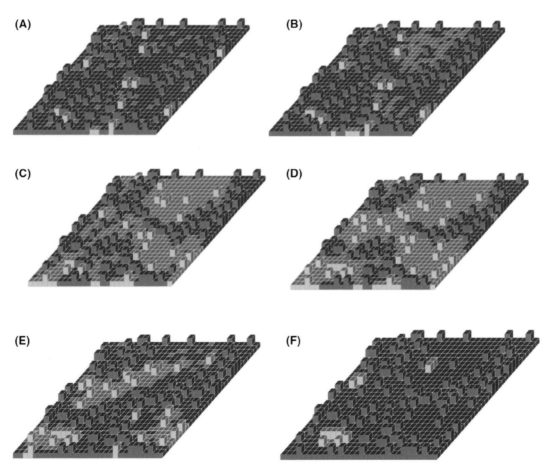

FIGURE 15.5 Computer Simulation of Social Change
Source: Nowak & Vallacher (2019)

these individuals randomly dispersed in the society. Because of the bias, the minority opinion begins to grow with the next round of social interaction (*Panel B*). The new opinion is beginning to form clusters around the original seeds of the new opinion. These clusters continue to grow in size and become connected (*Panel C*). In *Panel D*, the clusters of the new opinion—which initially was the minority point of view—are fully connected, and the initial majority is reduced to small, disconnected clusters.

The transition of an opinion from minority to majority status appears to be complete in *Panel D*, since the original majority opinion is now held by only 36% of the population. But note that these individuals, though small in number, tend to be stronger (i.e., taller cells) on average than the individuals holding the new majority opinion. This makes sense—they had to be strong in order to survive the bias sweeping through the social system. So when the bias weakens or is reversed (e.g., democratic reforms do not make life better), the old opinion, held by strong individuals, can show a rebound and reclaim its status as the majority opinion. In *Panel E*, the old opinion has grown to over 50%, and in *Panel F* it is once again the dominant opinion, held by 90% of the population. But this is still not the end of the story. If the societal bias in favor the new opinion (e.g., pro-democracy) returns, the new opinion will repeat its ascendance to majority status, relegating the old opinion to small clusters.

This scenario has noteworthy implications for social change. First, what looks like a fairly complete transformation of public opinion can be subject to dramatic reversal. This, in fact, is what happened in Eastern Europe. In the late 1980s and early 1990s, no Communist candidate was elected to Parliament. Those with Communist sentiment who managed to survive were strong, however, and they received support from like-minded individuals in coherent clusters. So when the bias in favor of free markets was reversed as people began to experience the costs of the transition to a free market economy, those with Communist sympathies could exert influence on their neighbors and regain a dominant role in society. More generally, this scenario predicts the emergence of well-defined strongholds for opposing norms and values, with the rest of the society switching between these perspectives, depending on the momentary bias favoring one over the other (Vallacher, 2015).

Consider this scenario in the light of the rapid and dramatic change in attitudes in the United States (and elsewhere) concerning gay marriage. Over just a few years, public opinion changed from a majority of the population opposing same-sex marriage to a majority that was supportive of these rights. But those individuals who have not changed are presumably very set in their opinions and exist in like-minded clusters that are defined either geographically or in terms of social networks that transcend geography. So although it appears that society has turned the corner on this (and many other) issues, there is a potential for a strong reversal in public opinion as those holding the marginalized point of view exert their influence and regain the majority.

In sum, norms and values in a society can appear stable, but they can show dramatic change in a short period of time. Such sudden reversals may become increasingly common as the world becomes increasingly interconnected. Because of the internet, social media, and smart phones, people are exposed to an enormous range of ideas and possibilities from around the world that can compete with the norms and values of their own society. These technologies allow thousands—if not millions—of people in different parts of the world to converge on a common narrative as if they were interacting face-to-face in a very big room. And in a sense, they are.

Minority Influence

It is one thing for a minority to survive despite being surrounded by a majority of group members (or citizens in a society) that considers their views deviant. It is quite another thing for the minority to challenge the majority viewpoint—and to prevail on occasion. Yet this happens. The power of a minority to change the views of the majority is vividly demonstrated in the film *12 Angry Men*. The central character (played by Henry Fonda) is Mr. Davis, a member of a jury deliberating the guilt versus innocence of a Spanish American man on trial for murdering his father—a crime that carried the death penalty in the case of a guilty verdict. The other members of the jury were convinced that the defendant was guilty and saw little need to discuss the matter at length in the jury room.

Mr. Davis was not so sure and was bothered by the haste with which the other jurors reached their conclusion. He insisted on deliberating the evidence and the merits of the prosecution and defense. This hardly endears him to the other jurors, who proceed to pressure him in much the same way that deviants have been shown to be pressured in the research on pressures for uniformity. But Mr. Davis sticks to his guns and holds out for deliberations. At the risk of spoiling the movie if you had planned on downloading it, Mr. Davis eventually prevails. Not only do the jurors deliberate the case, they become converted to Mr. Davis's point of view and vote unanimously to acquit the defendant—who, as I'm sure you have figured out, is innocent of the crime. The movie is interesting because it flies in the face of what we know about the power of the majority to win the day in a conflict with a minority opinion.

History abounds with examples of such *minority influence* (Crano, 2012; Moscovici, 1976). Facing the intense opposition of the Catholic Church, Galileo struggled for acceptance of his proof of the Copernican theory that the planets revolve around the sun. This acceptance did not come during his lifetime, but his influence lived on and eventually turned the intellectual tide for subsequent generations. Martin Luther King Jr. and Mahatma Gandhi both defied the prevailing norms of their respective cultures and brought about significant social and political change. Susan B. Anthony challenged people to confront the blatant but widely accepted sexist view—one that prevailed until well into the 20th century—that women did not warrant the right to vote. Scientific theory occasionally undergoes a "paradigm change" in response to a new idea that challenges conventional wisdom and is dismissed as nonsense by scientists working within the mainstream paradigm (Kuhn, 1970). New forms of entertainment are often marginalized when first introduced, only to become a fixture in pop culture over time.

Minority influence occurs in everyday life as well. People with opinions or lifestyles out of step with the majority often manage to preserve their personal perspective, sometimes even overcoming the majority's disapproval and winning acceptance. In recognition of these facts of social life, minority influence has emerged as an important topic in social psychology (Crano, 2012). Research on this topic has explored the conditions under which minority opinions not only survive, but also become influential to varying degrees in the group (e.g., Jarman et al., 2015). A primary conclusion is that minority members must marshal high-quality arguments and come across as credible. In other words, minorities must rely on *informational influence* to counter the *normative influence* associated with the majority position.

Photos: Individuals who epitomize minority influence

Galileo

DHXDXP (Galileo) Alamy stock photo

Mahatma Gandhi

FDGWYK (Gandhi) Alamy stock photo

Martin Luther King, Jr.

HPFB63 (MLK) Alamy stock photo

Susan B. Anthony

C13HR2 (Susan B Anthony) Alamy stock photo

Rosa Parks

C13HEW (Rosa Parks) Alamy stock photos

There are also specific factors that foster minority influence. Minorities are persuasive when they hold steadily to their views (Maass & Clark, 1984; Moscovici, Lage, & Naffrechoux, 1969), originally held the majority opinion (Clark, 1990; Levine & Ranelli, 1978), are willing to compromise a bit (Mugny, 1982), have at least some support from others (Asch, 1956; Tanford & Penrod, 1984; Wolf & Latané, 1985), appear to have little personal stake in the issue (Maass, Clark, & Haberkorn, 1982), and present their views as compatible with the majority but just a bit "ahead of the curve" (Kiesler & Pallak, 1975; Maass et al., 1982; Volpato, Maass, Mucchi-Faina, & Vitti, 1990). Minority influence also can prevail if the majority wants to make an accurate decision, since this gives the advantage to informational influence (Laughlin & Ellis, 1986).

The conditions associated with effective minority influence enable groups (and societies) to embrace new ideas, fashions, and action preferences. It is hard to imagine how societies and cultures—or social clubs and gangs, for that matter—could adopt new ways of thinking and acting without the potential for minority influence. Groups may be stacked in favor of pressures for uniformity, but they also operate in accordance with principles that enable the group to change course and embrace new perspectives. Under the right conditions, individuals or groups that are marginalized can promote significant changes in the larger social system.

What the Future Holds

To paraphrase Charles Dickens, "today is the best of times and the worst of times." Advances in science, technology, medicine—not to mention psychology!—provide a lifestyle and sense of security that would have been unimaginable to our grandparents, not to mention to their ancestors. Yet life today is constantly evolving, and these changes provide a breeding ground for personal adjustment issues, interpersonal discord, and collective antagonism. What does social psychology have to say about our accommodation to an increasingly "flat world" in which contact among cultures is increasing, with competition over scarce resources and clashes over ideology and customs? Is the future destined to be fraught with conflict between nation states and tension within them? Or will the future play out in ways that benefit humanity, with international and interpersonal harmony, as well as greater subjective well-being?

The Case for Pessimism

When one thinks of the many proximate causes for destructive relations between people, groups, and nations, a rather dreary scenario can be envisioned. The most pressing cause of intergroup conflict is competition over scarce resources. For the majority of human history, this basis for conflict occurred when two neighboring tribes or villages both laid claim to the same grazing territory, the same irrigable land for pastures, or access to the same source of water. In today's world, such disputes are not confined to local groups but play out in the context of intra-national and international relations.

The world's supply of fossil fuels, for example, could become depleted in coming decades, yet the demand for this resource is likely to increase dramatically in the years to come as countries that were primarily agrarian and rural in the 20th-century transition to industrial and urban economies. There are alternatives to oil and natural gas (e.g., solar, hydrothermal, wind, nuclear), but these have yet to become developed in an economically—and politically—feasible manner. For the foreseeable future, then, a decreasing supply of fossil fuels coupled with increasing demand is a recipe for conflict within countries and for warfare between nations.

Fuel is important and necessary in today's world, where machines rather than human labor are the driving force in production and consumption. But in principle, one can find and exploit alternatives to fossil fuels. Water is an entirely different matter. No matter how technologically savvy and innovative we become, there is no alternative to water for sustaining human life. We are totally dependent on water for drinking, sanitation, irrigation, fishing, transport on oceans, lakes, and rivers, and power generation. Water, like fossil fuel, is a limited resource and the demands for it, driven by population growth, rising standards of living, and climate change, are increasingly dramatically. Indeed, the water crisis may emerge in the 21st century as the primary basis for conflict over resources (Gleick, 1993).

Conflict is also fueled by the tendency to favor one's in-group over out-groups (Brewer, 1979; Tajfel, 1982), as discussed in Chapter 13. Especially when in-group/out-group relations center on ideology, norms, and customs, intergroup contact is a breeding group for stereotypes, negative feelings and attitudes, and violent confrontations. The world has always been diverse, with people in different regions showing marked differences on every conceivable dimension, from skin color and food preferences to economic systems and religion. Historically, however, physical distance and limited technology have prevented contact between people who differed on these dimensions and therefore did not unleash the potential for lethal intergroup contact.

The modern world has effectively erased the barriers between people in different parts of the world. One can reach virtually any spot on earth in less than a 15-hour plane ride, and people are increasingly taking advantage of this possibility. Even without traveling, people are exposed to people of different races, religions, and cultures on a daily basis because of mass media (movies, television), the internet, and social media. Because of the self-selection of people to mass media, internet sites, and social media, people are able to find and maintain social support for their views of out-groups—whether political, religious, or racial—and avoid exposure to information that might soften their views and promote tolerance (Christakis & Fowler, 2009). The "echo chamber" effect of selective communication, discussed in Chapter 12, has the potential to enflame the competition and animosity inherent in in-group/out-group relations.

And then there is the issue of immigration. People in increasing numbers are moving to other countries and bringing their national identities with them. Rather than assimilating to the new culture, as was common in earlier times, immigrants today are increasingly inclined to maintain their values, religious traditions, languages, and customs (Alba & Nee, 2005; Berry, 1997). Because immigrants and local residents live in a state of confined interdependence, the clash of cultures has the potential to tap the hostility latent in in-group/out-group relations.

Add to this mix the ongoing development of sophisticated weapons that can translate a simple conflict into an episode of destruction and death on an unimaginable scale. Fights between individuals and groups that were once fought with knives, clubs, spears, and swords are now fought with handguns and assault weapons. Interstate wars that were once engaged with troops and artillery are now fought with fighter planes, stealth bombers, ballistic missiles, and unmanned drones fired from a location thousands of miles away from the intended target. A battle that might produce a few thousand casualties can now decimate hundreds of thousands, if not millions of people. And the lack of face-to-face contact necessary to inflict harm on people reduces the constraints against the use of such means.

These factors are serious enough in isolation, but their combined impact can be all the more a cause for concern. The interdependence of different cultures amplifies competition over scarce resources, which in turn magnifies intergroup antagonism, which then reinforces the competitive approach to the resource dilemma. The availability of weapons of mass destruction in combination with their use at a safe distance increases the likelihood of destruction and death on scales unheard of in earlier times, which increases the desire of warring parties to stockpile and employ more deadly weapons. The increasing reliance on self-selected mass media and internet communication can reinforce out-group stereotypes, which can in turn reinforce avoidance of information and contact that might undermine such stereotypes. These feedback loops do not seem to bode well for the frequency and intensity of conflict in the years to come.

The Case for Optimism

This gloomy scenario is plausible, but there is another way to view the frequency and intensity of tension and conflict in the coming years and decades. Indeed, when hostility is viewed from a historical perspective, there is reason to be optimistic about the fate of interpersonal, intergroup, and international relations in the 21st century. Violence of all forms has shown a dramatic decline over the past few centuries (Pinker, 2011). Tribal warfare was nine times as deadly as war and genocide were in the 20th century. The homicide rate in medieval Europe was more than 30 times today's rate. Slavery, sadistic punishments, and executions were routine features of life for thousands of years, only to become targets for abolition in the last few centuries. Rape, battering, child abuse, animal cruelty, hate crimes, and deadly riots occur in today's world, but the frequency of each is dramatically lower today than in our past. The contemporary era, in fact, may be the least violent period in human history.

The decline in violence is attributable to a variety of factors that we can expect to become increasingly manifest as we move forward in the 21st century. In his analysis of the decline in interpersonal and intergroup violence, Steven Pinker (2011) points to the rise and spread of central governments, increased intranational and international trade, and the rise of urban centers and cosmopolitism. These factors have brought about self-control with respect to agreed-upon laws and norms, promoted bargaining and negotiation as a means of resolving disputes as alternatives to plundering and invasion, have debunked toxic ideologies and superstitions, and have encouraged the use of reason to reduce the temptations of violence and physical domination. The increased literacy occasioned by the rise of stable governments and enhanced standards of living has also contributed to the steady decline in violent confrontation because it has fostered empathy and perspective taking in social relations, and has familiarized people—at a safe distance—with the customs and traditions of different cultures.

The factors noted under the pessimistic scenario could actually work instead to make the world a *less* hostile and contentious place for interpersonal, intergroup, and international relations. The sharp increase in direct contact between people from different cultures in recent decades, for example, may inhibit rather than activate the conflict between groups. When people fly to distant parts of the world, they not only expect to observe different customs and norms, they are primed to appreciate these local features. Rather than competing with people in these cultures, visitors interact with them informally or through commercial transactions.

The portrayal of individuals representing different races, ethnicities, and religions in mass media and movies, meanwhile, can also soften the tension associated with intergroup conflict because this contact is devoid of the conditions such as resource competition and confined interdependence that bring out the worst in in-group/out-group relations. This assumes, of course, that the portrayal of diversity in entertainment and information media is largely positive and emphasizes variation rather than homogeneity within different groups—an assumption that seems to hold, at least in relatively affluent and democratic societies.

The likelihood of increasingly scarce resources—from fossil fuels and water to land for agriculture and population growth—would seem to increase competition and the potential for destructive conflict among groups and nations. But as noted in Chapter 11 ("Antisocial and Prosocial Behavior"), variable resources and harsh environmental conditions do not inevitably have this effect. When social systems are faced with the prospect or reality of scarce resources, they tend to display cooperative rather than competitive forms of interaction with strong adherence to the norm of reciprocity (Andras, Lazarus, & Roberts, 2007; Smaldino, 2013). For cooperation and reciprocity rather than competition and exploitation to characterize interpersonal and intergroup relations in a world of increasing demand (population growth) and limited supply (depletion of fuel, water, fish, and land suitable for agriculture), people must recognize their interdependency (e.g., Sherif et al., 1961/1988). It is difficult to ignore such interdependency in a world saturated with television, internet communication, large urban centers, and social media.

The contact between cultures may prove positive for yet other reasons. Recent decades have witnessed a sharp increase in emigration—movement from one country to settle in another country—and marriage between members of different ethnic groups and races. This has the effect of *increasing* the genetic and lifestyle variation within a culture and *reducing* these sources of variation between cultures. In the optimistic scenario, this blurring of group differences has the potential to reduce racism and ethnocentrism—which historically have been bases for intergroup prejudice and conflict.

The advances in technology witnessed in the past few years and decades may also contribute to an overall decline in hostile interpersonal and intergroup relations. Such technology, of course, has given us weapons that can transform a heated dispute into a homicide or shooting rampage, not to mention weapons of mass destruction that can decimate entire populations. But for every technological device conducive to harm, there are many more that are conducive to benign and positive social relations. Almost everyone in the modern world has a smart phone or access to the internet, web-based communication, and social media. These technologies enable people to form connections on a worldwide basis, and to do so with limited risk of becoming involved in zero-sum relations that produce winners and losers. In effect, people are poised to become world citizens rather than xenophobic and nationalistic members of a tribe or country.

As discussed in Chapter 12, people tend to self-select into virtual communities that echo their preconceived biases, beliefs, and concerns, and some bases for self-selection can serve to perpetuate stereotypes, misinformation, and intolerance. But people also use modern communication technology to build social networks that go well beyond the simple in-group/out-group dichotomies that dominated personal and social identity in the past. Today's world provides an enormous range of opportunities for self-expression, career choice, and other sources of identity creation. People may seek out others from different regions of the world because of a common hobby, artistic preference, economic agenda, or even because they wish to interact in a video game. These bases for social network formation not only displace shared identities rooted in tribalism and ethnicity, they also tend to be crosscutting in ways that prevent polarization between groups from developing (Brewer & Brown, 1998). The person in another country with whom one discusses entertainment preferences may well have different family customs, political persuasion, or skin color.

Historically, interpersonal aggression and intergroup violence have been launched and implemented largely by males (Daly & Wilson, 1988, 1994). This may reflect the fact that males historically have had a monopoly on institutional power, so that females have not been in a position to make decisions regarding warfare, nor to implement such decisions. But males may also be inclined toward aggression because of the male sex hormone, testosterone. Research across many mammalian species has documented a connection between levels of testosterone and aggressive behavior (Ellis, 1986; Monaghan & Glickman, 1992). Testosterone levels presumably have been stable across human history, so perhaps we are doomed to violent conflict no matter how much the factors cited above come to the fore in the modern era.

Even here, however, there is cause for optimism. As noted in Chapter 11, the immediate causal effect of testosterone is not aggression per se, but rather seeking and maintaining social dominance (Archer, 2006b; Mazur & Booth, 1998). Aggression, of course, is a basic means of establishing dominance hierarchies. And throughout much of human history, individuals dominated one another by fighting, while groups asserted dominance by attacking one another with military forces. Among humans in the modern era, however, there are alternative means of establishing and maintaining dominance. Males—and females, for that matter—can acquire and display resources and symbols of power. They can rise to leadership positions in industry, science, and politics. Presumably, a person who has the opportunity to command respect in a government or a large corporation—or in sports or entertainment—can satisfy the testosterone-based need for dominance without physical confrontations and aggression. Nations, too, can achieve dominance through economic success, scientific and technological advances, and leadership in international relations, without resorting to military intervention.

In the coming decades, then, one might expect a decrease in the expression of male-based aggression as opportunities for success and prominence become more widely available. Indeed, the same factor that historically has promoted horrific violence may be a driving factor in innovation and entrepreneurship as the new century unfolds. Of course, the expression of dominance could also take the form of totalitarian repression backed up by force. However, the forces noted earlier—democratic governments, cosmopolitism, literacy—are likely to provide a check on the rise of authoritarian regimes. The worldwide connectivity provided by smart phones, the internet, and social media also mitigate against this expression of dominance.

Which Scenario Will Prevail?

There is no guarantee that the trajectory of the last few hundred years, let alone the trajectory of recent decades, will continue in the same form in the coming years. In the study of *complex systems* (like a society), what looks like a consistent pattern or stable state on one time-scale can prove to be entirely different when viewed over a longer time span (Silver, 2012). So the decline in violence observed since the Middle Ages, and seen more dramatically with the advent of international trade, increasing standards of living, and a greater base-rate of literacy, may not forecast what is in store for the 21st century. Particularly in light of the accelerated rate of social and technological change in recent years, the decline in violence could show a dramatic reversal as the modern era continues to unfold. Even when conflict is not manifest with high frequency, it nonetheless exists as a latent pattern of behavior to which a social system can switch in response to various triggers. Conflict may be deeply ingrained into human nature as a result of natural selection (Wilson, 2012).

Which scenario will prevail? Are the factors that hold potential for enhancing the likelihood of conflict destined to embroil nations and identity-based groups into conflict? Or do the factors that have minimized conflict and violence in recent decades and centuries promise to make the world an increasingly peaceful place?

An understanding of how complex systems behave can offer some guidance—but no guarantee. Complex systems are governed by a press for progressive integration of system elements or parts into a higher-order state. Even in highly complex systems composed of many elements, there is a tendency for global states and patterns to emerge. The emergent state or pattern provides for coherence and stability in the system, while resisting the potentially destabilizing forces of new elements. In the context of social relations, this means that despite the vast amount of relevant information and the continuous flow of events, over time the respective parties—whether individuals, groups, or nation-states—will establish a stable way of perceiving and acting toward one another. The emergence of stable patterns that resist change is enhanced under conditions of heightened importance, urgency, and stress (Latané & Nowak, 1994; Vallacher et al., 2010). Because challenges and stresses are likely to characterize the 21st century, we can expect the formation of strong global patterns for social relations despite the enormous diversity of cultural, political, and economic agendas.

Another hallmark of complex systems is their potential for *bifurcation*—the same set of factors can result in the emergence of qualitatively different higher-order states (Kelso, 1995; Nowak & Vallacher, 1998; Ruelle, 1989). Thus, one can envision the emergence of positive social relations (in line with the optimistic scenario), but one can just as reasonably expect the emergence of malignant social relations (in line with the pessimistic scenario). For that matter, one can envision some pattern of temporal oscillation—periodic, quasi-periodic, or chaotic—between these very different scenarios as the 21st century unfolds.

Which scenario unfolds may not be entirely beyond prediction and control, however. To be sure, coherent higher-order states commonly emerge by means of self-organization, lending a noteworthy degree of unpredictability to the outcome. Lacking outside guidance, seemingly minor events can be determinative, shifting the balance in one direction or the other because of the amplifying effects of positive feedback. But emergence can also be guided by external forces and information—although only if these sources of influence are provided when the system is a state of disassembly (Vallacher & Wegner, 2012) and thus "ripe" for transformation (Coleman, 2000; Pruitt, 1997). The challenge for the 21st century is to provide the right cues for meaning at the right time. In the hands of malevolent forces that play to people's prejudices and fears, the future could re-launch patterns of entrenched conflict and destructive violence. But in the hands of others with the long-term benefits of all in mind, the optimistic scenario could play out. Now, perhaps more than ever, the fate of mankind is in our hands.

SUMMING UP AND LOOKING FORWARD

We assume you are completing this text knowing more about the nature of personal and social processes than you did before you opened the cover. But that raises another question about social experience that has not been discussed. Is it possible that knowing the reasons and mechanisms underlying what you and everyone else on the planet does is simply too much information? You have learned, for example, that falling in love is driven by a blend of marketplace considerations, hormones, and specialized "bonding" molecules that keep rodents together. Does knowing this take the romance and poetry out of forming a special attachment to someone? You have learned that conflict reflects primitive evolutionary mechanisms, emotionally biased judgments, and relativistic values. So what is the point of fighting for a cause or even getting agitated over differences in lifestyle and opinions? And consider free will. If it is an illusion, can you feel comfortable taking pride for doing good things or resisting bad things? Why feel bad about watching out for yourself and ignoring the plight of others—or even hurting them?

Shouldn't we feel silly about everything? If everything we do is constrained by biological, evolutionary, social, and cultural forces, aren't we just doing a walk-through in a script over which we have no role in editing, let alone writing?

There are three ways of dealing with the potential danger of "too much information." First, it may not matter how much we know. Doctors know how the body works, but this doesn't prevent them from getting headaches or growing older. Knowing the factors that make you fall in love does not prevent you from developing those special feelings for someone. You will still experience anger on occasion, no matter how much you know about our primate ancestry, brain structures, or hormones. And realizing that there are many causes, most of them invisible, of how you think and act won't stop you from feeling like you are a free agent, capable of making your own decisions and pursuing your own goals.

Second, understanding our own dynamics can be enlightening in a way that more than compensates for any existential concerns. With the knowledge of social psychology in hand, we can understand one another without passing judgment, we can avoid the traps set by our own biases, and we can recognize the benefits in the long run of resisting temptation in the short run.

Third, life is full of surprises, twists and turns. Just because your choices and actions are determined doesn't mean they can be predicted—by you or by anyone else. The science of complexity has taught us that even in a physical system, determinism does not guarantee prediction (Gleick, 1987; Lorenz, 1963). The factors that influence your thoughts, feelings, and actions are numerous, ranging from your genes and neurons to your family history and cultural background. These factors, moreover, interact with each other in an untold number of ways—the same genetic makeup, for example, can express itself in different patterns of thought and behavior depending on one's economic status or the beliefs and values in one's society.

Because these factors are interdependent, a slight change in one of them can, over time, lead to very different choices and life trajectories. So although psychology can identify specific factors that determine your internal processes and overt behavior, the interaction among these factors makes precise prediction of your destiny impossible. In this sense, the fact that so many things contribute to your psychological makeup grants you a sense of freedom.

There is a final point to consider. In the last analysis, self-knowledge is itself another psychological process. We can't help but reflect on our operating rules. And in that, we are unique in the animal kingdom. Now that's something to feel good about.

A Concluding Comment: Your Personal Conduct?

What you have learned in this text has no doubt affected the way you think about yourself, your relations with others, maybe even your role as a member of society. You may have learned the importance of self-control and also the factors that can undermine it. You may now recognize more clearly than before what shapes your judgments of other people, making you perhaps a bit more tolerant of behavior that you used to condemn strongly along with a harsh assessment of the person him or herself. You recognize how people can be manipulated into doing things that they otherwise would not consider—and how a person can maintain a way of thinking and acting despite enormous pressures to think and do the opposite. You may have a better sense of why commercials are effective, how political debates are won and lost, and why some people are more effective than others in getting their point of view accepted. You may understand why people hurt one another, why groups become locked into violent and protracted conflicts, why people judge one another on the basis of superficial features. And you may have learned what is required to get individuals and groups to suspend their egoistic agendas to cooperate and engage in mutually beneficial actions.

The question is whether all this knowledge will affect your conduct as you move on to other topics and to other spheres of life. You have the freedom to do so. But the lessons learned in this text will change your personal conduct only if these lessons have congealed into coherent ways of thought and behavior. Within the constraints provided by these new mental structures, you can freely choose to behave in ways that reflect what you have learned. Let's see what happens.

REFERENCES

Aaker, J. L., & Lee, A. Y. (2001). I seek pleasures and we avoid pains: The role of self-regulatory goals in information processing and persuasion. *Journal of Consumer Research, 28*, 33-49.

Abelson, R. P., Aronson, E., McGuire, W. J., Newcomb, T. M., Rosenberg, M. J., & Tannenbaum, P. H. (Eds.). (1968). *Theories of cognitive consistency: A sourcebook*. Chicago: Rand McNally.

Aberson, C. L., Healy, M., & Romero, V. (2000). In-group bias and self-esteem: A meta-analysis. *Personality and Social Psychology Review, 4*, 157-173.

Abramson, L. Y., Seligman, M. E. P., & Teasdale, J. D. (1978). Learned helplessness in humans: Critique and reformulation. *Journal of Abnormal Psychology, 87*, 49-74.

Acevedo, B. P., Aron, A., Fisher, H. E., & Brown, L. L. (2012). Neural correlates of marital satisfaction and well-being: Reward, empathy, and affect. *Clinical Neuropsychiatry, 9*, 20-31.

Adams, C. G., & Turner, B. (1985). Reported change in sexuality from young adulthood to old age. *Journal of Sex Research, 21*, 126-141.

Adams, H. E., Wright, L. W., & Lohr, B. A. (1996). Is homophobia associated with homosexual arousal? *Journal of Abnormal Psychology, 105*(3), 440-445.

Adams, J. S. (1965). Inequity in social exchange. In L. Berkowitz (Ed.), *Advances in experimental social psychology* (Vol. 2, pp. 267-299). New York: Academic Press.

Adorno, T. W., Frenkel-Brunswick, E., Levinson, D. J., & Sanford, R. N. (1950). *The authoritarian personality*. New York: Harper & Row.

Ainsworth, M. D. S. (1979). Infant-mother attachment. *American Psychologist, 34*, 932-937.

Ainsworth, M. D. S. (1993). Attachment as related to mother-infant interaction. *Advances in Infancy Research, 8*, 1-50.

Ajzen, I. (1985). From intentions to actions: A theory of planned behavior. In J. Kuhl & J. Beckman (Eds.), *Action-control: From cognition to behavior* (pp. 11-39). Heidelberg, Germany: Springer.

Ajzen, I., & Fishbein, M. (2005). The influence of attitudes on behavior. In D. Albarracín, B. T. Johnson, & M. P. Zanna (Eds.), *The handbook of attitudes* (pp. 173-221). Mahwah, NJ: Erlbaum.

Akrami, N., Ekehammar, B., & Bergh, R. (2010). Generalized prejudice: Common and specific components. *Psychological Science, 22*, 57-59.

Alba, R. D., & Nee, V. (2005). *Remaking the American mainstream: Assimilation and contemporary immigration*. Cambridge, MA: Harvard University Press.

Albarracín, D., & Wyer, R. S., Jr. (2000). The cognitive impact of past behavior: Influences on beliefs, attitudes, and future behavioral decisions. *Journal of Personality and Social Psychology, 79*, 5-22.

Albright, L., & Forziati, C. (1995). Cross-situational consistency and perceptual accuracy in leadership. *Personality and Social Psychology Bulletin, 21*, 1269-1276.

Allen, J. P., Uchino, B. N., & Hafen, C. (2015). Running with the pack: Teen peer-relationship qualities as predictors of adult physical health. *Psychological Science, 26*, 1574-1583.

Allen, M. (1991). Meta-analysis comparing the persuasiveness of one-sided and two-sided messages. *Western Journal of Speech Communication, 55*, 490-404.

Allen, V. L., & Levine, J. M. (1971). Social support and conformity: The role of independent assessment of reality. *Journal of Experimental Social Psychology, 4*, 48-58.

Allison, S. T., Messick, D. M., & Goethals, G. R. (1989). On being better but not smarter than others: The Muhammed Ali effect. *Social Cognition, 7*, 275-295.

Alloy, L., & Abramson, L. (1979). Judgment of contingency in depressed and nondepressed students: Sadder but wiser? *Journal of Experimental Psychology: General, 108*, 441-485.

Allport, F. H. (1924). *Social psychology*. Boston, MA: Riverside Editions, Houghton Mifflin.

Allport, G. W. (1954a). The historical background of modern social psychology. In G. A. Lindzey (Ed.), *The handbook of social psychology* (Vol. 1, pp. 1-46). Cambridge, MA: Addison-Wesley.

Allport, G. W. (1954b). *The nature of prejudice*. Reading, MA: Addison-Wesley.

Altemeyer, B. (1981). *Right-wing authoritarianism*. Winnipeg: University of Manitoba Press.

Alter, A. L., & Forgas, J. P. (2007). On being happy but fearing failure: The effects of mood on self-handicapping strategies. *Journal of Experimental Social Psychology, 43*, 947-954.

Al-Zahrini, S., & Kaplowitz, S. (1993). Attributional biases in individualistic and collectivistic cultures: A comparison of Americans with Saudis. *Social Psychology Quarterly, 56*, 223-233.

Amabile, T. M. (1996). *Creativity in context*. Boulder, CO: West View Press.

Ambady, N., & Rosenthal, R. (1992). Thin slices of expressive behavior as predictors of interpersonal consequences: A meta-analysis. *Psychological Bulletin, 111*, 256-274.

Ambady, N., & Rosenthal, R. (1993). Half a minute: Predicting teacher evaluations form thin slices of nonverbal behavior and physical attractiveness. *Journal of Personality and Social Psychology, 64*, 431-441.

Amnesty International. (2003). United States of America: Death by discrimination: The continuing role of race in capital cases. http://www.amnesty.org/en/library/info/AMR51/046.

Andersen, S. M. (1984). Self-knowledge and social inference: II. The diagnosticity of cognitive/affective and behavioral data. *Journal of Personality and Social Psychology, 46*, 294-307.

Anderson, C. A. (1987). Temperature and aggression: Effects on quarterly, yearly, and city rates of violent and nonviolent crime. *Journal of Personality and Social Psychology, 52*, 1161-1173.

Anderson, C. A. (1989). Temperature and aggression: Ubiquitous effects of heat on occurrences of human violence. *Psychological Bulletin, 106*, 75-96.

Anderson, C. A. (1999). Attribution style, depression, and loneliness: A cross-cultural comparison of American and Chinese students. *Personality and Social Psychology Bulletin, 25*, 482-499.

Anderson, C. A., Berkowitz, L., Donnerstein, E., Huesmann, L. R., Johnson, J., Linz, D., . . . Wartella, E. (2003). The influence of media violence on youth. *Psychological Science in the Public Interest, 4*, 81-110.

Anderson, C. A., & Bushman, B. J. (2001). Effects of violent video games on aggressive behavior, aggressive cognition, aggressive affect, physiological arousal, and prosocial behavior: A meta-analytic review of the scientific literature. *Psychological Science, 12*, 353-359.

Anderson, C. A., & Dill, K. E. (2000). Video games and aggressive thoughts, feelings, and behaviors in the laboratory and in life. *Journal of Personality and Social Psychology, 78*, 772-790.

Anderson, C. A., Lepper, M. R, & Ross, L. (1980). The perseverance of social theories: The role of explanation in the persistence of discredited information. *Journal of Personality and Social Psychology, 39*, 1037-1049.

Anderson, C. A., Suzuki, K., Swing, E. L., ... Petrescu, P. (2017). Media violence and other aggression risk factors in seven nations. *Personality and Social Psychology Bulletin, 43*, 986-998.

Anderson, N. H. (1968). Likeableness ratings of 555 personality-trait words. *Journal of Personality and Social Psychology, 9*, 272-279.

Anderson, N. H. (1974). Cognitive algebra applied to social attribution. In L. Berkowitz (Ed.), *Advances in experimental social psychology* (Vol. 7, pp. 1-101). New York: Academic Press.

Andras, P., Lazarus, J., & Roberts, G. (2007). Environmental adversity and uncertainty favour cooperation. *BMC Evolutionary Biology, 7*, 240.

Archer, D., & Akert, R. M. (1977). Words and everything else: Verbal and nonverbal cues in social interaction. *Journal of Personality and Social Psychology, 35*, 443-449.

Archer, D., & Gartner, R. (1984). *Violence and crime in cross-national perspective*. New Haven, CT: Yale University Press.

Archer, J. (2006a). Cross-cultural differences in physical aggression between partners: A social-role analysis. *Personality and Social Psychology Review, 10*, 133-153.

Archer, J. (2006b). Testosterone and human aggression: An evaluation of the challenge hypothesis. *Neuroscience and Biobehavioral Reviews, 30*, 319-345.

Archer, J., & Coyne, S. M. (2005). An integrated review of indirect, relational, and social aggression. *Personality and Social Psychology Review, 9*, 212-230.

Argyle, M. (1975). *Bodily communication*. New York: International Universities Press.

Argyle, M. (1988). *Bodily communication* (2nd ed.). Madison, WI: International Universities Press.

Argyle, M., & Dean, J. (1965). Eye-contact, distance, and affiliation. *Sociometry, 28*, 289-304.

Ariely, D., & Norton, M. I. (2007). Psychology and experimental economics: A gap in abstraction. *Current Directions in Psychological Science, 16*, 336-339.

Arkin, R. M., Cooper, H., & Kolditz, T. (1980). A statistical review of the literature concerning the self-serving attribution bias interpersonal influence situations. *Journal of Personality, 48*, 435-448.

Arkin, R. M., Lake, E. A., & Baumgardner, A. H. (1986). Shyness and self-presentation. In W. H. Jones, J. M. Cheek, & S. R. Briggs (Eds.), *Shyness: Perspectives on research and treatment*. New York: Plenum.

Arkin, R. M., & Maruyama, G. M. (1979). Attribution, affect, and college exam performance. *Journal of Educational Psychology, 71,* 85–93.

Armitage, C. J., & Conner, M. (2001). Social cognitive determinants of blood donation. *Journal of Applied Social Psychology, 31,* 1431–1457.

Aronson, E. (1992). The return of the oppressed: Dissonance theory makes a comeback. *Psychological Inquiry, 3,* 303–311.

Aronson, E., & Carlsmith, J. M. (1963). Effect of the severity of threat on the devaluation of forbidden behavior. *Journal of Abnormal and Social Psychology, 66,* 583–588.

Aronson, E., & Cope, V. (1968). My enemy's enemy is my friend. *Journal of Personality and Social Psychology, 8,* 8–12.

Aronson, E., & Linder, D. (1965). Gain and loss of esteem as determinants of interpersonal attractiveness. *Journal of Experimental Social Psychology, 1,* 156–171.

Aronson, E., Wilson, T. D., & Brewer, M. (1998). Experimentation in social psychological research. In G. Lindzey & E. Aronson (Eds.), *Handbook of social psychology* (4th ed., pp. 99–142). New York: McGraw-Hill.

Arrigo, J. M., & Wagner, R. V. (2007). Psychologists and military interrogators rethink the psychology of torture. *Peace and Conflict: Journal of Peace Psychology, 34,* 393–398.

Asch, S. E. (1946). Forming impressions of personality. *The Journal of Abnormal and Social Psychology, 41,* 258–290.

Asch, S. E. (1956). Studies of independence and conformity: I. A minority of one against a unanimous majority. *Psychological Monographs: General and Applied, 70,* 1–70.

Ashton-James, C., Van Baaren, R. B., Chartrand, T. L., Decety, J., & Karremans, J. C. (2007). Mimicry and me: The impact of mimicry on self-construal. *Social Cognition, 25,* 518–535.

Aspinwall, L. W., & Taylor, S. E. (1993). Effects of social comparison direction, threat, and self-esteem on affect, evaluation, and expected success. *Journal of Personality and Social Psychology, 64,* 708–722.

Atkinson, J. W. (1964). *An introduction to motivation*. New York: Van Nostrand.

Avaramova, Y. R., Stapel, D. A., & Lerouge, D. (2010). Mood and context-dependence: Positive mood increases and negative mood decreases the effects of context on perception. *Journal of Personality and Social Psychology, 99,* 203–214.

Averill, J. R. (1980). A constructivist view of emotion. In R. Plutchik & H. Kellerman (Eds.), *Emotion: Theory, research, and experience* (pp. 205–339). New York: Academic Press.

Axelrod, R. (1984). *The evolution of cooperation*. New York: Basic Books.

Axelrod, R., & Hamilton, W. D. (1981). The evolution of cooperation. *Science, 211,* 1390–1396.

Axelrod, R., Riolo, R. L., & Cohen, M. D. (2002). Beyond geography: Cooperation with persistent links in the absence of clustered neighborhoods. *Personality and Social Psychology Review, 6,* 341–346.

Ayduk, O., Downey, G., Testa, A., Yen, Y., & Shoda, Y. (1999). Does rejection elicit hostility in rejection sensitive women? *Social Cognition, 17,* 245–271.

Baars, B. J. (2005). Global workspace theory of consciousness: Toward a cognitive neuroscience of human experience. *Progress in Brain Research, 150,* 45–53.

Babad, E. (1999). Preferential treatment in television interviewing: Evidence from nonverbal behavior. *Political Communication, 16,* 337–358.

Babad, E. (2005). The psychological price of media bias. *Journal of Experimental Psychology: Applied, 11,* 245–255.

Bailey, J. M., & Pillard, R. C. (1991). A genetic study of male sexual orientation. *Archives of General Psychiatry, 48,* 1089–1096.

Bailey, J. M., Pillard, R. C., Neale, M. C., & Agyei, Y. (1993). Heritable factors influence sexual orientation in women. *Archives of General Psychiatry, 50,* 217–223.

Bailey, W. C., & Peterson, R. D. (1997). Murder, capital punishment, and deterrence: A review of the literature. In H. A. Bedau (Ed.), *The death penalty in America: Current controversies* (pp. 135–161). New York: Oxford University Press.

Baldwin, M. W., Keelan, J. P. R., Fehr, B., Enns, V., & Koh-Rangarajoo, E. (1996). Social-cognitive conceptualizations of attachment working models: Availability and accessibility effects. *Journal of Personality and Social Psychology, 71,* 94–109.

Bandura, A. (1971). *Social learning theory*. New York: General Learning Press.

Bandura, A. (1986). *Social foundations of thought and action: A social cognitive theory*. Englewood Cliffs, NJ: Prentice-Hall.

Bandura, A. (2002). Selective moral disengagement in the exercise of moral agency. *Journal of Moral Education, 31,* 101–119.

Bandura, A., Ross, D., & Ross, S. A. (1961). Transmission of aggression through the imitation of aggressive models. *Journal of Abnormal and Social Psychology, 63,* 575–582.

Bandura, A., Ross, D., & Ross, S. A. (1963). Imitation of film-mediated aggressive models. *Journal of Abnormal and Social Psychology, 66,* 3–11.

Barabasi, A. (2001). *Linked: How everything is connected to everything else and what it means for business, science, and everyday life*. New York: Penguin.

Barber, N. (1999). Women's dress fashions as a function of reproductive strategy. *Sex Roles, 40,* 459–471.

Bard, P. (1934). Emotion 1. The neuro-humoral basis of emotional reactions. In C. Murchison (Ed.), *Handbook of general experimental psychology.* Worcester, MA: Clark University Press.

Bargh, J. A. (1994). The four horsemen of automaticity: Awareness, intention, efficiency, and control in social cognition. In R. S. Wyer Jr. & T. K. Srull (Eds.), *Handbook of social cognition* (Vol. 1, pp. 1–40). Hillsdale, NJ: Erlbaum.

Bargh, J. A. (1996). Automaticity in social psychology. In E. T. Higgins & A. W. Kruglanski (Eds.), *Social psychology: Handbook of basic principles* (pp. 169–183). New York: Guilford Press.

Bargh, J. A., & Chartrand, T. L. (1999). The unbearable automaticity of being. *American Psychologist, 54,* 462–479.

Bargh, J. A., Chen, M., & Burrows, L. (1996). Automaticity of social behavior: Direct effects of trait construct and stereotype activation on action. *Journal of Personality and Social Psychology, 71,* 230–244.

Bargh, J. A., Gollwitzer, P. M., Lee-Chai, A., Barndollar, K., & Trotschel, R. (2001). The automated will: Nonconscious activation and pursuit of behavioral goals. *Journal of Personality and Social Psychology, 81,* 1014–1027.

Bargh, J. A., & Pietromonaco, T. L. (1982). Automatic information processing and social perception: The influence of trait information presented outside of conscious awareness on impression formation. *Journal of Personality and Social Psychology, 43,* 437–449.

Baron, J., & Miller, J. G. (2000). Limiting the scope of moral obligations to help: A cross-cultural investigation. *Journal of Cross-Cultural Psychology, 31,* 703–725.

Baron-Cohen, S. (2003). *The essential difference: The truth about the male and female brain.* New York: Penguin/Basic Books.

Bartholow, B. D., & Anderson, C. A. (2002). Effects of violent video games on aggressive behavior: Potential sex differences. *Journal of Experimental Social Psychology, 38,* 283–290.

Bass, E., & Davis, I. (1994). *The courage to heal: A guide for women survivors of childhood sexual abuse* (3rd ed.). New York: Free Press.

Batson, C. D., Batson, J. G., Slingsby, J. K., Harrell, K. L., Peekna, H. M., & Todd, R. M. (1991). Empathic joy and the empathy-altruism hypothesis. *Journal of Personality and Social Psychology, 61,* 413–426.

Batson, C. D., Duncan, B. D., Ackerman, P., Buckley, T., & Birch, K. (1981). Is empathic emotion a source of altruistic motivation? *Journal of Personality and Social Psychology, 40,* 290–302.

Batson, C. D., Engel, C. L., & Fridell, S. R. (1999a). Value judgments: Testing the somatic-marker hypothesis using false physiological feedback. *Personality and Social Psychology Bulletin, 25,* 1021–1032.

Batson, C. D., Kobrynowicz, K., Dinnerstein, J. L., Kampf, H. C., & Wilson, A. D. (1997). In a very different voice: Unmasking moral hypocrisy. *Journal of Personality and Social Psychology, 72,* 1335–1348.

Batson, C. D., & Shaw, L. L. (1991). Evidence for altruism: Toward a pluralism of prosocial motives. *Psychological Inquiry, 2,* 107–122.

Batson, C. D., Thompson, E. R., Seuferling, G., Whitney, H., & Strongman, J. A. (1999b). Moral hypocrisy: Appearing moral to oneself without being so. *Journal of Personality and Social Psychology, 77,* 525–537.

Baumeister, R. F. (1982). A self-presentational view of social interaction. *Psychological Bulletin, 91,* 3–26.

Baumeister, R. F. (1984). Choking under pressure: Self-consciousness and the paradoxical effects of incentives on skilled performance. *Journal of Personality and Social Psychology, 46,* 610–620.

Baumeister, R. F. (1990). Suicide as escape from the self. *Psychological Review, 97,* 90–113.

Baumeister, R. F. (1991). *Escaping the self: Alcoholism, spirituality, masochism, and other flights from the burden of selfhood.* New York: Basic Books.

Baumeister, R. F. (1998). The self. In D. T. Gilbert, S. T. Fiske, & G. Lindzey (Eds.), *Handbook of social psychology* (4th ed., Vol. 1, pp. 680–740). New York: McGraw-Hill.

Baumeister, R. F. (2000). Gender differences in erotic plasticity: The female sex drive as socially flexible and responsive. *Psychological Bulletin, 126,* 347–374.

Baumeister, R. F. (2008). Free will in scientific psychology. *Perspectives on Psychological Science, 3,* 14–19.

Baumeister, R. F., & Bratslavsky, E. (1999). Passion, intimacy, and time: Passionate love as a function of change in intimacy. *Personality and Social Psychology Review, 3,* 49–67.

Baumeister, R. F., Bratslavsky, E., Finkenauer, C., & Vohs, K. D. (2001). Bad is stronger than good. *Review of General Psychology, 5,* 323–370.

Baumeister, R. F., Bratslavsky, E., Muraven, M., & Tice, D. M. (1998). Ego depletion: Is the active self a limited resource? *Journal of Personality and Social Psychology, 74,* 1252–1265.

Baumeister, R. F., Catanese, K. R., & Vohs, K. D. (2001). Is there a gender difference in strength of sex drive? Theoretical views, conceptual distinctions, and review of relevant evidence. *Personality and Social Psychology Review, 5,* 242–273.

Baumeister, R. F., Dale, K., & Sommer, K. L. (1998). Freudian defense mechanisms and empirical findings in modern social psychology: Reaction formation, projection, displacement, undoing, isolation, sublimation, and denial. *Journal of Personality, 66,* 1081–1124.

Baumeister, R. F., & Heatherton, T. F. (1996). Self-regulation failure: An overview. *Psychological Inquiry, 7,* 1–15.

Baumeister, R. F., Heatherton, T. F., & Tice, D. M. (1994). *Losing control: How and why people fail at self-regulation*. San Diego: Academic Press.

Baumeister, R. F., & Leary, M. R. (1995). The need to belong: Desire for interpersonal attachments as a fundamental human motivation. *Psychological Bulletin, 117*, 97–529.

Baumeister, R. F., Masicampo, E. J., & Dewall, C. N. (2009). Prosocial benefits of feeling free: Disbelief in free will increases aggression and reduces helpfulness. *Personality and Social Psychology Bulletin, 35*, 260–268.

Baumeister, R. F., Mele, A. R., & Vohs, K. D. (2010). *Free will and consciousness: How might they work?* New York: Oxford University Press.

Baumeister, R. F., Smart, L., & Boden, J. M. (1996). Relation of threatened egotism to violence and aggression: The dark side to high self-esteem. *Psychological Review, 103*, 5–33.

Baumeister, R. F., Stillwell, A. M., & Heatherton, T. F. (1994). Guilt: An interpersonal approach. *Psychological Bulletin, 115*, 243–267.

Baumeister, R. F., Stillwell, A., & Wotman, S. R. (1990). Victim and perpetrator accounts of interpersonal conflict: Autobiographical narratives about anger. *Journal of Personality and Social Psychology, 59*, 994–1005.

Baumeister, R. F., & Tice, D. M. (1990). Anxiety and social exclusion. *Journal of Social and Clinical Psychology, 9*, 165–195.

Baumeister, R. F., & Twenge, J. M. (2003). The social self. In I. Weiner (Series Ed.) & T. Millon & M. J. Lerner (Vol. Eds.), *Handbook of psychology: Vol. 5. Personality and social psychology* (pp. 327–352). New York: Wiley.

Baumeister, R. F., & Vohs, K. D. (2004). Sexual economics: Sex as female resource of social exchange in heterosexual interactions. *Personality and Social Psychology Review, 8*, 339–363.

Baumeister, R. F., Vohs, K. D., & Tice, D. M. (2007). The strength model of self-control. *Current Directions in Psychological Science, 16*, 351–355.

Baumeister, R. F., Wotman, S. R., & Stillwell, A. M. (1993). Unrequited love: On heartbreak, anger, guilt, scriptlessness, and humiliation. *Journal of Personality and Social Psychology, 64*, 377–394.

Baumgardner, A. H. (1990). To know oneself is to like oneself: Self-certainty and self-affect. *Journal of Personality and Social Psychology, 58*, 1062–1072.

Baumgardner, A. H., & Bownlee, E. A. (1987). Strategic failure in social interaction: Evidence for expectancy disconfirmation process. *Journal of Personality and Social Psychology, 52*, 525–535.

Baumrind, D. (1971). Current patterns of parental authority. *Developmental Psychology, 4*, 1–103.

Beaman, A. L., Klentz, B., Diener, E., & Svanum, S. (1979). Self-awareness and transgression in children: Two field studies. *Journal of Personality and Social Psychology, 37*, 1835–1846.

Becker, E. (1973). *The denial of death*. New York: Free Press.

Bedau, H. A. (Ed.). (1997). *The death penalty in America: Current controversies*. New York: Oxford University Press.

Beer, J., Heerey, E. A., Keltner, D., Scabini, D., & Knight, R. (2003). The regulatory function of self-conscious emotion: Insights from patients with orbitofrontal damage. *Journal of Personality and Social Psychology, 85*, 594–604.

Beilock, S. L. (2007). Understanding skilled performance: Memory, attention, and "choking under pressure." In T. Morris, P. Terry, & S. Gordon (Eds.), *Sport and exercise psychology: International perspectives* (pp. 153–166). Morgantown, WV: Fitness Information Technology.

Beilock, S. L., & Gonso, S. (2008). Putting in the mind vs. putting on the green: Expertise, performance time, and the linking of imagery and action. *The Quarterly Journal of Experimental Psychology: Human Experimental Psychology, 61*, 920–932.

Beilock, S. L., & Gray, R. (2007). Why do athletes "choke" under pressure? In G. Tenenbaum & R. C. Eklund (Eds.), *Handbook of sport psychology* (3rd ed., pp. 425–444). Hoboken, NJ: John Wiley & Sons.

Bell, A. P., & Weinberg, M. S. (1978). *Homosexualities: A study of diversity among men and women*. South Melbourne: The Macmillan Company of Australia.

Belson, W. A. (1978). *Television violence and the adolescent boy*. Westmead: Saxon House, Teakfield.

Bem, D. J. (1967). Self-perception: An alternative interpretation of cognitive dissonance phenomena. *Psychological Review, 74*, 183–200.

Bennett, R. (2007). Endorsement by the seminar military interrogators. *Peace and Conflict: Journal of Peace Psychology, 34*, 391–392.

Bensley, L. S., & Wu, R. (1991). The role of psychological reactance in drinking following alcohol prevention messages. *Journal of Applied Psychology, 21*, 1111–1124.

Ben-Zeev, T., Fein, S., & Inzlicht, M. (2005). Arousal and stereotype threat. *Journal of Experimental Social Psychology, 41*, 174–181. doi:10.1016/j.jesp.2003.11.007

Berg, J. H., & McQuinn, R. D. (1986). Attraction and exchange in continuing and noncontinuing dating relationships. *Journal of Personality and Social Psychology, 50*, 942–952.

Berglas, S. C., & Baumeister, R. F. (1993). *Your own worst enemy: Understanding the paradox of self-defeating behavior*. New York: Basic Books.

Berglas, S. C., & Jones, E. E. (1978). Drug choice as a self-handicapping strategy n response to non-contingent success. *Journal of Personality and Social Psychology, 36,* 405-417.

Berkowitz, L. (1965). Some aspects of observed aggression. *Journal of Personality and Social Psychology, 2,* 359-369.

Berkowitz, L. (1972). Social norms, feelings, and other factors affecting helping behavior and altruism. In L. Berkowitz (Ed.), *Advances in experimental social psychology* (Vol. 6, pp. 63-108). New York: Academic Press.

Berkowitz, L. (1989). The frustration-aggression hypothesis: An examination and reformulation. *Psychological Bulletin, 106,* 59-73.

Berkowitz, L. (1993). *Aggression.* New York: McGraw-Hill.

Berkowitz, L., & Daniels, L. R. (1964). Affecting the salience of the social responsibility norm: Effects of past help on the response to dependency relationships. *Journal of Abnormal and Social Psychology, 68,* 275-281.

Berkowitz, L., & LePage, A. (1967). Weapons as aggression-eliciting stimuli. *Journal of Personality and Social Psychology, 7,* 202-207.

Bernieri, F. J. (1988). Coordinated movement and rapport in teacher: Student interactions. *Journal of Nonverbal Behavior, 12,* 120-138.

Bernieri, F. J., & Rosenthal, R. (1991). Interpersonal coordination: Behavior matching and interactional synchrony. In B. Rime & R. S. Feldman (Eds.), *Fundamentals of nonverbal behavior: Studies in emotion and social interaction.* New York/Paris: Cambridge University Press.

Berry, J. S. (1997). Immigration, acculturation, and adaptation. *Applied Psychology, 46,* 5-34.

Berry, S. H., & Kanouse, D. E. (1987). Physician response to a mailed survey: An experiment in timing of payment. *Public Opinion Quarterly, 51,* 102-114.

Bettencourt, B. A., Brewer, M. B., Croak, M. R., & Miller, N. (1992). Cooperation and the reduction of intergroup bias: The role of reward structure and social orientation. *Journal of Experimental Social Psychology, 28,* 301-319.

Bettencourt, B. A., & Miller, N. (1996). Gender differences in aggression as a function of provocation: A meta-analysis. *Psychological Bulletin, 119,* 422-447.

Bettencourt, B. A., & Sheldon, K. (2001). Social roles as mechanism for psychological need satisfaction within social groups. *Journal of Personality and Social Psychology, 81,* 1131-1143.

Bickart, K. C., Wright, C. I., Dautoff, R. J., Dickerson, B. C., & Feldman-Barrett, L. (2011). Amygdala volume and social network size in humans. *Nature Neuroscience, 14,* 163-164.

Bickman, L. (1974). The power of a uniform. *Journal of Applied Social Psychology, 4,* 61-77.

Bigler, R. S. (1999). The use of multicultural curricula and materials to counter racism in children. *Journal of Social Issues, 55,* 697-705.

Birdwhistell, R. (1970). *Kinesics and context.* Philadelphia: University of Pennsylvania Press.

Bittles, A. H., & Neel, J. V. (1994). The costs of human inbreeding and their implications for variations at the DNA level. *Nature Genetics, 8,* 117-121.

Bjorklund, D. F. (2007). *Why youth is not wasted on the young: Immaturity in human development.* Oxford, UK: Blackwell.

Blaney, P. H. (1986). Affect and memory: A review. *Psychological Bulletin, 99,* 229-246.

Blanton, H., Buunk, B. P., Gibbons, F. X., & Kuyper, H. (1999). When better-than-others compare upward: Choice of comparison and comparative evaluation as independent predictors of academic performance. *Journal of Personality and Social Psychology, 76,* 420-430.

Blascovich, J., Ginsburg, G. P., & Howe, R. C. (1975). Blackjack and the risky shift, II: Monetary stakes. *Journal of Experimental Psychology, 11,* 224-232.

Blau, P. N. (1964). *Exchange and power in social life.* New York: Wiley.

Bless, H., Clore, G. L., Schwarz, N., Golisano, V., Rabe, C., & Wolk, M. (1996). Mood and the use of scripts: Does a happy mood really lead to mindlessness? *Journal of Personality and Social Psychology, 71,* 665-679.

Bless, H., Mackie, D. M., & Schwarz, N. (1992). Mood effects on attitude judgments: Independent effects of mood before and after message elaboration. *Journal of Personality and Social Psychology, 63,* 585-595.

Bock, G. R., & Goode, J. A. (Eds.). (1996). *Genetics of criminal and antisocial behavior.* Chichester: John Wiley & Sons.

Bodenhausen, G. V., Kramer, G. P., & Susser, K. (1994). Happiness and stereotypic thinking in social judgment. *Journal of Personality and Social Psychology, 66,* 621-632.

Bodenhausen, G., Sheppard, L., & Kramer, G. (1994). Negative affect and social judgment: The different impact of anger and sadness. *European Journal of Social Psychology, 24,* 45-62.

Bond, M. H. (1996). Chinese values. In M. H. Bond (Ed.), *The handbook of Chinese psychology* (pp. 208-226). Hong Kong: Oxford University Press.

Boomsma, D. I., Willemsen, G., Dolan, C. V., Hawkley, L. C., & Cacioppo, J. T. (2005). Genetic and environmental contributions to loneliness in adults: The Netherlands Twin Register Study. *Behavior Genetics, 35,* 745-752.

Bornstein, R. F., Leone, D. R., & Galley, D. J. (1987). The generalizability of subliminal mere exposure effects: Influence of stimuli perceived without awareness on social behavior. *Journal of Personality and Social Psychology, 53,* 1070-1079.

Bosson, J.K., Swann, W.B., & Pennebaker, J.W. (2000). Stalking the perfect measure of implicit self-esteem: The blind men and the elephant revisited? *Journal of Personality and Social Psychology, 79*, 631-643.

Bouchard, T.J., Lykken, D.T., McGue, M., Segal, N.L., & Tellegen, A. (1990). Sources of human psychological differences: The Minnesota study of twins reared apart. *Science, 250*, 223-228.

Bower, G.H. (1981). Mood and memory. *American Psychologist, 36*, 129-148.

Bowers, K.S., & Meichenbaum, D. (1984). *The unconscious reconsidered*. New York: Wiley-Interscience.

Bowlby, J. (1969). *Attachment and loss: Vol. 1: Attachment*. New York: Basic Books.

Bowlby, J. (1980). *Attachment and loss, Vol. 3: Loss: Sadness and depression*. New York: Basic Books.

Brackett, M.A., & Salovey, P. (2004). Measuring emotional intelligence with the Mayer-Salovey-Caruso emotional intelligence test (MSCEIT). In G. Geher (Ed.), *Measurement of emotional intelligence* (pp.181-196). Hauppauge, NY: Nova Science Publishers.

Brandon, R., & Davies, C. (1973). *Wrongful imprisonment: Mistaken convictions and their consequences*. London: Allen & Unwin.

Braun, M.F., & Bryan, A. (2006). Female waist-to-hip and male waist-to-shoulder ratios as determinants of romantic partner desirability. *Journal of Social and Personal Relationships, 23*, 805-819.

Braver, S.L. (1975). Reciprocity, cohesiveness, and cooperation in two-person games. *Psychological Reports, 36*, 371-378.

Brechner, K.C. (1977). An experimental analysis of social traps. *Journal of Experimental Social Psychology, 13*, 552-564.

Brehm, J.W. (1956). Postdecision changes in the desirability of alternatives. *Journal of Abnormal and Social Psychology, 52*, 384-389.

Brehm, S.S., & Brehm, J.W. (1981). *Psychological reactance: A theory of freedom and control*. New York: Academic Press.

Brendl, C.M., Higgins, E.T., & Lemm, K.M. (1995). Sensitivity to varying gains and losses: The role of self-discrepancies and event framing. *Journal of Personality and Social Psychology, 69*, 1028-1051.

Brennan, K.A., Clark, C.L., & Shaver, P.R. (1998). Self-report measurement of adult attachment: An integrative overview. In J.A. Simpson & W.S. Rholes (Eds.), *Attachment theory and close relationships* (pp.46-76). New York: Guilford Press.

Brewer, M.B. (1979). In-group bias in the minimal intergroup situation: A cognitive-motivational analysis. *Psychological Bulletin, 86*, 307-324.

Brewer, M.B. (1988). A dual process model of impression formation. In T.K. Srull & R.S. Wyer (Eds.), *Advances in social cognition*. Hillsdale, NJ: Lawrence Erlbaum Associates.

Brewer, M.B. (1991). The social self: On being the same and different at the same time. *Personality and Social Psychology Bulletin, 17*, 475-482.

Brewer, M.B. (2000). Reducing prejudice through cross-categorization: Effects of multiple social identities. In S. Oskamp (Ed.), *Claremont symposium on applied social psychology: Reducing prejudice and discrimination* (pp.165-183). Thousand Oaks, CA: Sage.

Brewer, M.B., & Brown, R.J. (1998). Intergroup relations. In D.T. Gilbert, S.T. Fiske, & G. Lindzey (Eds.), *The handbook of social psychology* (4th ed., Vol. 2, pp.554-594). New York: McGraw-Hill.

Brewer, M.B., & Caporael, L.R. (2006). An evolutionary perspective on social identity: Revisiting groups. In M. Schaller (Ed.), *Evolution and social psychology* (pp.143-161). Philadelphia: Psychology Press.

Brewer, M.B., & Gardner, W.L. (1996). Who is this "we"? Levels of collective identity and self-representations. *Journal of Personality and Social Psychology, 71*, 83-93.

Brewer, M.B., & Pierce, K.P. (2005). Social identity complexity and out-group tolerance. *Personality and Social Psychology Bulletin, 31*, 428-437.

Brewer, N., & Weber, N. (2008). Eyewitness confidence and latency: Indices of memory processes not just markers of accuracy. *Applied Cognitive Psychology, 22*, 827-840.

Brickman, P., & Campbell, D.T. (1971). Hedonic relativism and planning the good society. In M.H. Appley (Ed.), *Adaptation-level theory* (pp.287-302). New York: Academic Press.

Brickman, P., Coates, D., & Janoff-Bulman, R.J. (1978). Lottery winners and accident victims: Is happiness relative? *Journal of Personality and Social Psychology, 36*, 917-927.

Brickman, P., Ryan, K., & Wortman, C.B. (1975). Causal chains: Attribution of responsibility as a function of immediate and prior causes. *Journal of Personality and Social Psychology, 32*, 1060-1067.

Brickner, M., Harkins, S., & Ostrom, T. (1986). Personal involvement: Thought-provoking implications for social loafing. *Journal of Personality and Social Psychology, 51*, 763-760.

Brosnan, S.F., & de Waal, F.B.M. (2003). Monkeys reject unequal pay. *Nature, 425*, 297-299.

Brown, B.L. (1980). Effects of speech rate on personality attributions and competency ratings. In H. Giles, P.W. Robinson, & P.M. Smith (Eds.), *Language: Social psychological perspectives*. Oxford: Pergamon.

Brown, D.E. (1991). *Human universals*. New York: McGraw-Hill.

Brown, J.D. (1993). Self-esteem and self-evaluation: Feeling is believing. In J. Suls (Ed.), *The self in social perspectives* (pp.27-58). Hillsdale, NJ: Erlbaum.

Brown, J.S. (1948). Gradients of approach and avoidance responses and their relation to motivation. *Journal of Comparative and Physiological Psychology, 41*, 450-465.

Brown, K.W., & Ryan, R.M. (2003). The benefits of being present: Mindfulness and its role in psychological well-being. *Journal of Personality and Social Psychology, 84*, 822-848.

Brown, R.P., Osterman, L.L., & Barnes, C.D. (2009). School violence and the culture of honor. *Psychological Science, 20*, 1400-1405.

Brummelman, E., Thomaes, S., & Sedikides, C. (2016). Separating narcissism from self-esteem. *Current Directions in Psychological Science, 25*, 8-13.

Bruner, J., & Taguiri, R. (1954). Person perception. In G. Lindzey (Ed.), *Handbook of social psychology* (Vol. 2). Reading, MA: Addison Wesley.

Bryant, F.B. (1989). A four-factor model of perceived control: Avoiding, coping, obtaining, and savoring. *Journal of Personality, 57*, 773-797.

Bryant, F.B. (2003). Savoring Beliefs Inventory (SBI): A scale for measuring beliefs about savoring. *Journal of Mental Health, 12*, 175-196.

Buck, R.W., & Parke, R.D. (1972). Behavioral and physiological response to the presence of a friendly or neutral person in two types of stressful situations. *Journal of Personality and Social Psychology, 24*, 143-153.

Bucy, E.P. (2000). Emotional and evaluative consequences of inappropriate leader displays. *Communication Research, 27*, 194-226.

Bucy, E.P., & Grabe, M.E. (2007). Taking television seriously: A sound and image bite analysis of presidential campaign coverage, 1992-2004. *Journal of Communication, 57*, 652-675.

Budesheim, T.L., & DePaola, S.J. (1994). Beauty or the beast? The effects of appearance, personality, and issue formation on evaluations of political candidates. *Personality and Social Psychology Bulletin, 20*, 339-348.

Burger, J.M. (1986). Increasing compliance by improving the deal: The that's-not-all technique. *Journal of Personality and Social Psychology, 51*, 277-283.

Burger, J.M., & Petty, R.E. (1981). The low-ball compliance technique: Task or person commitment? *Journal of Personality and Social Psychology, 40*, 492-500.

Burnstein, E., Crandall, C., & Kitayama, S. (1994). Some neo-Darwinian decision rules for altruism: Weighing cues for inclusive fitness as a function of the biological importance of the decision. *Journal of Personality and Social Psychology, 67*, 773-789.

Burnstein, E., & Vinokur, A. (1977). Persuasive argumentation and social comparison as determinants of attitude polarization. *Journal of Experimental Social Psychology, 13*, 315-332.

Bushman, B.J., & Anderson, C.A. (2001). Is it time to pull the plug on hostile versus instrumental aggression dichotomy? *Psychological Review, 108*, 273-279.

Bushman, B.J., & Baumeister, R.F. (1998). Threatened egotism, narcissism, self-esteem, and direct and displaced aggression: Does self-love or self-hate lead to violence? *Journal of Personality and Social Psychology, 75*, 219-229.

Bushman, B.J., & Gibson, B. (2011). Violent video games cause an increase in aggression long after the game has been turned off. *Social Psychological and Personality Science, 2*, 29-32.

Bushman, B.J., & Phillips, C.M. (2001). If the television program bleeds, memory for the advertisement recedes. *Current Directions in Psychological Science, 10*, 43-47.

Buss, A.H. (1980). *Self-consciousness and social anxiety*. San Francisco, CA: W.H. Freeman.

Buss, D.M. (1988). From vigilance to violence: Tactics of mate retention in American undergraduates. *Ethology and Sociobiology, 9*, 291-317.

Buss, D.M. (2015). *Evolutionary psychology: The new science of the mind* (5th ed.). New York: Taylor & Francis.

Buss, D.M., & Duntley, J.D. (2006). The evolution of aggression. In M. Schaller, J.A. Simpson, & D.T. Kenrick (Eds.), *Evolution and social psychology* (pp. 263-286). New York: Psychology Press.

Buss, D.M., & Schmitt, D.P. (1993). Sexual strategies theory: An evolutionary perspective on human mating. *Psychological Review, 100*, 204-232.

Buss, D.M., & Shackelford, T.K. (1997). From vigilance to violence: Mate retention tactics in married couples. *Journal of Personality and Social Psychology, 72*, 346-361.

Buss, D.M., Larsen, R.J., Westen, D., & Semmelroth, J. (1992). Sex differences in jealousy: Evolution, physiology, and psychology. *Psychological Science, 3*(4), 251-255.

Buunk, B.P., Angleitner, A., Oubaid, V., & Buss, D.M. (1996). Sex differences in jealousy in evolutionary and cultural perspective: Tests from the Netherlands, Germany, and the United States. *Psychological Science, 7*, 359-363.

Buunk, B.P., Oldersma, F.L., & de Dreu, C.K.W. (2001). Enhancing satisfaction through downward comparison: The role of relational discontent and individual differences in social comparison orientation. *Journal of Experimental Social Psychology, 37*, 452-467.

Byrne, D., Clore, G.L., & Smeaton, G. (1986). The attraction hypothesis: Do similar attitudes predict anything? *Journal of Personality and Social Psychology, 51*, 1167-1170.

Byrne, D., Griffitt, W., & Stefaniak, D. (1967). Attraction and similarity of personality characteristics. *Journal of Personality and Social Psychology, 5*, 82-90.

Cacioppo, J. T. (1998). Somatic responses to psychological stress: The reactivity hypothesis. In M. Sabourin & F. Craik (Eds.), *Advances in psychological science: Biological and cognitive aspects* (Vol. 2, pp. 87-112). Hove: Psychology Press.

Cacioppo, J. T. (2007). Psychology is a hub science. *APS Observer, 20*, 1-3.

Cacioppo, J. T., Berntson, G. G., Sheridan, J. F., & McClintock, M. K. (2000). Multi-level integrative analyses of human behavior: Social neuroscience and the complementing nature of social and biological approaches. *Psychological Bulletin, 126*, 829-843.

Cacioppo, J. T., & Gardner, W. L. (1999). Emotion. *Annual Review of Psychology, 50*, 191-214.

Cacioppo, J. T., & Hawkley, L. C. (2009). Perceived social isolation and cognition. *Trends in Cognitive Science, 13*, 447-454.

Cacioppo, J. T., & Hawkley, L. C. (2013). Perceived isolation. In D. Cervone, M. Fajkowska, M. W. Eysenck, & T. Maruszewski (Eds.), *Personality dynamics: Meaning construction, the social world, and the embodied mind* (pp. 91-105). Clinton Corners, NY: Eliot Werner Publications, Inc.

Cacioppo, J. T., Norris, C. J., Decety, J., Monteleone, G., & Nusbaum, H. (2009). In the eye of the beholder: Individual differences in perceived social isolation predict regional brain activation to social stimuli. *Journal of Cognitive Neuroscience, 21*, 83-92.

Cacioppo, J. T., Petty, R. E., Feinstein, J. A., & Jarvis, W.B.G. (1996). Dispositional differences in cognitive motivation: The life and times of individuals varying in need for cognition. *Psychological Bulletin, 119*, 197-253.

Cacioppo, J. T., Priester, J. R., & Bernston, G. G. (1993). Rudimentary determinants of attitude. II. Arm flexion and extension have differential effects on attitudes. *Journal of Personality and Social Psychology, 65*, 5-17.

Calder, B. J., & Staw, B. M. (1975). Self-perception of intrinsic and extrinsic motivation. *Journal of Personality and Social Psychology, 31*, 599-605.

Callan, M. J., Ellard, J. H., & Nicol, J. E. (2007). The belief in a just world and immanent justice reasoning in adults. *Personality and Social Psychological Bulletin, 32*, 1-13.

Callan, M. J., Harvey, A. J., Dawtry, R. J., & Sutton, R. M. (2013). Through the looking glass: Long-term goal focus increases immanent justice reasoning. *British Journal of Social Psychology, 52*, 377-385.

Campbell, J. D., Trapnell, P. D., Heine, S. J., Katz, I. M., Lavallee, L. F., & Lehman, D. R. (1996). Self-concept clarity: Measurement, personality correlates, and cultural boundaries. *Journal of Personality and Social Psychology, 70*, 141-156.

Campbell, W. K., & Sedikides, C. (1999). Self-threat magnifies the self-serving bias: A meta-analytic integration. *Review of General Psychology, 3*, 23-43.

Cannon, W. B. (1927). The James-Lange theory of emotion: A critical examination and an alternative theory. *American Journal of Psychology, 39*, 10-124.

Caporael, L. R. (2005). Psychology and groups at the junction of genes and culture. *Behavioral and Brain Sciences, 28*, 819-821.

Caporael, L. R. (2007). Evolutionary theory for social and cultural psychology. In E. T. Higgins & A. W. Kruglanski (Eds.), *Social psychology: Handbook of basic principles* (pp. 3-18). New York: Guilford Press.

Caporael, L. R., Dawes, R. M., Orbell, J. M., & Van de Kragt, A.J.C. (1989). Selfishness examined: Cooperation in the absence of egoistic incentives. *Behavioral and Brain Sciences, 12*, 683-739.

Carlsmith, K. M., Darley, J. M., & Robinson, P. (2002). Why do we punish? Deterrence and just deserts as motives for punishment. *Journal of Personality and Social Psychology, 83*, 284-299.

Carlsmith, K. M., Wilson, T. D., & Gilbert, D. G. (2008). The paradoxical consequences of revenge. *Journal of Personality and Social Psychology, 95*, 1316-1324.

Carlson, M., Charlin, V., & Miller, N. (1988). Positive mood and helping behavior: A test of six hypotheses. *Journal of Personality and Social Psychology, 55*, 211-229.

Carlson, M., & Miller, N. (1987). Explanation of the relationship between negative mood and helping. *Psychological Bulletin, 102*, 91-108.

Carnegie, D. (1936/1981). *How to win friends and influence people*. New York: Pocket Books.

Carnevale, P.J.D., Pruitt, D. G., & Britton, S. D. (1979). Looking tough: The negotiator under constituent surveillance. *Personality and Social Psychology Bulletin, 5*, 118-121.

Carruthers, P., & Smith, P. K. (Eds.). (1996). *Theories of theories of mind*. Cambridge: Cambridge University Press.

Carver, C. S. (1975). Physical aggression as a function of objective self-awareness and attitudes toward punishment. *Journal of Experimental Social Psychology, 11*, 510-519.

Carter, C. S. (1998). Neuroendocrine perspectives on social attachment and love. *Psychoneuroendrocrinology, 23*, 779-818.

Carver, C. S. (2003). Self-awareness. In M. R. Leary & J. P. Tangney (Eds.), *Handbook of self and identity* (pp. 179-196). New York: Guilford Press.

Carver, C. S., & Scheier, M. F. (1998). *On the self-regulation of behavior*. New York: Cambridge University Press.

Carver, C. S., & Scheier, M. F. (1999). Themes and issues in the self-regulation of behavior. In R. S. Wyer, Jr. (Ed.), *Advances in social cognition* (Vol. 12, pp. 1-105). Mahwah, NJ: Lawrence Erlbaum Associates.

Carver, C.S., & Scheier, M.F. (2002). Control processes and self-organization as complementary principles underlying behavior. *Personality and Social Psychology Review, 6*, 304-315.

Caspi, A., & Herbener, E.S. (1990). Continuity and change: Assortative marriage and the consistency of personality in adulthood. *Journal of Personality and Social Psychology, 58*, 250-258.

Castellow, W.A., Wuensch, K.L., & Moore, C.H. (1990). Effects of physical attractiveness of the plaintiff and defendant in sexual harassment judgments. *Journal of Social Behavior and Personality, 5*, 547-562.

Cesario, J., Grant, H., & Higgins, E.T. (2004). Regulatory fit and persuasion: Transfer from "feeling right." *Journal of Personality and Social Psychology, 86*, 388-404.

Chaiken, S. (1979). Communicator physical attractiveness and persuasion. *Journal of Personality and Social Psychology, 37*, 1387-1397.

Chaiken, S. (1980). Heuristic versus systematic information processing in the use of source versus message cues in persuasion. *Journal of Personality and Social Psychology, 39*, 752-766.

Chaiken, S., Wood, W., & Eagly, A.H. (1996). Principles of persuasion. In E.T. Higgins & A.W. Kruglanski (Eds.), *Social psychology: Handbook of basic principles* (pp. 702-742). New York: Guilford Press.

Chapman, L.J., & Chapman, J.P. (1969). Illusory correlations as an obstacle to the use of valid psychodiagnostic signs. *Journal of Abnormal Psychology, 74*, 271-280.

Chartrand, T.L., & Bargh, J.A. (1999). The chameleon effect: The perception-behavior link and social interaction. *Journal of Personality and Social Psychology, 76*, 893-910.

Chemers, M.M., Watson, C.B., & May, S.T. (2000). Dispositional affect and leadership effectiveness: A comparison of self-esteem, optimism, and efficacy. *Personality and Social Psychology Bulletin, 26*, 267-277.

Chen, M., & Bargh, J.A. (1999). Consequences of automatic evaluation: Immediate behavioral dispositions to approach or avoid the stimulus. *Personality and Social Psychology Bulletin, 25*, 215-224.

Cheng, C.M., & Chartrand, T.L. (2003). Self-monitoring without awareness: Using mimicry as a nonconscious affiliation strategy. *Journal of Personality and Social Psychology, 85*, 1170-1179.

Cherulnik, P., Donley, K., Wiewel, T., & Miller, S. (2001). Charisma is contagious: The effect of leaders' charisma on observers' affect. *Journal of Applied Social Psychology, 31*, 2149-2159.

Chirumbolo, A., Livi, S., Mannetti, L., Pierro, A., Kruglanski, A.W. (2004). Effects of need for closure on creativity in small group interactions. *European Journal of Personality, 18*, 265-278.

Chistensen, I. (1988). Deception in psychological research: When is its use justified? *Personality and Social Psychological Bulletin, 14*, 664-675.

Chiu, C., Morris, M.W., Hong, Y., & Menon, T. (2000). Motivated cultural cognition: The impact of implicit cultural theories on dispositional attribution varies as a function of need for closure. *Journal of Personality and Social Psychology, 78*, 247-259.

Choi, I., Dalal, R., Kim-Prieto, C., & Park, H. (2003). Culture and judgement of causal relevance. *Journal of Personality and Social Psychology, 84*, 46-59.

Choi, I., & Nisbett, R.E. (1998). Situational salience and cultural differences in the correspondence bias and actor-observer bias. *Personality and Social Psychology Bulletin, 24*, 949-960.

Choi, I., Nisbett, R.E., & Norenzayan, A. (1999). Causal attribution across cultures: Variation and universality. *Psychological Bulletin, 125*, 47-63.

Chow, R.M., & Galak, J. (2012). The effect of inequality frames on support for redistributive tax policies. *Psychological Science, 23*(12), 1467-1469.

Chow, S.M., Ram, N., Boker, S.M., Fujita, F., & Clore, G. (2005). Emotion as a thermostat: Representing emotion regulation using a damped oscillator model. *Emotion, 5*, 208-225.

Christakis, N.A., & Fowler, J.H. (2009). *Connected: The surprising power of our social networks and how they shape our lives.* New York: Little, Brown and Company.

Christensen, D., & Rosenthal, R. (1982). Gender and nonverbal decoding skill as determinants of interpersonal expectancy effects. *Journal of Personality and Social Psychology, 42*, 75-87.

Cialdini, R.B. (2000). *Influence: Science and practice* (4th ed.). Boston, MA: Allyn & Bacon.

Cialdini, R.B. (2007). *Influence: The psychology of persuasion.* New York: Harper Collins.

Cialdini, R.B., Borden, R.J., Thorne, A., Walker, M.R., Freeman, S., & Sloan, L.R. (1976). Basking in reflected glory: Three (football) field studies. *Journal of Personality and Social Psychology, 34*, 366-375.

Cialdini, R.B., Cacioppo, J.T., Bassett, R., & Miller, J. (1978). Low-ball procedure for producing compliance: Commitment, then cost. *Journal of Personality and Social Psychology, 36*, 463-476.

Cialdini, R.B., Darby, B.L., & Vincent, J.E. (1973). Transgression and altruism: A case for hedonism. *Journal of Experimental Social Psychology, 9*, 502-516.

Cialdini, R. B., & Trost, M. R. (1998). Social influence: Social norms, conformity, and compliance. In D. T. Gilbert, S. T. Fiske, & G. Lindzey (Eds.), *The handbook of social psychology* (Vol. 2, pp. 151-192). New York: McGraw-Hill.

Cialdini, R. B., Vincent, J. E., Lewis, S. K., Catalan, J., Wheeler, D., & Darby, B. L. (1975). Reciprocal concessions procedure for inducing compliance: The door-in-the-face technique. *Journal of Personality and Social Psychology, 31,* 206-215.

Cioffi, D., & Garner, R. (1996). On doing the decision: The effects of active versus passive choice on commitment and self-perception. *Personality and Social Psychology Bulletin, 22,* 133-147.

Clark, A. E., Frijters, P., & Shields, M. A. (2008). Relative income, happiness, and utility: An explanation for the Easterlin Paradox and other puzzles. *Journal of Economic Literature, 46,* 95-144.

Clark, M. S., & Bennett, M. E. (1992). Research on relationships: Implications for mental health. In D. Ruble, & P. Costanzo (Eds.), *The social psychology of mental health*. New York: Guilford.

Clark, M. S., & Mills, J. (1993). The difference between communal and exchange relationships: What is and is not. *Personality and Social Psychology Bulletin, 19,* 684-691.

Clark, R. D. (1990). Minority influence: The role of argument refutation of the minority position and social support for the minority position. *European Journal of Social Psychology, 20,* 489-497.

Clark, R. D., & Hatfield, E. (1989). Gender differences in receptivity to sexual offers. *Journal of Psychology and Human Sexuality, 2*(1), 39-55.

Clore, G. L., Gasper, K., & Garvin, E. (2001). Affect as information. In J. P. Forgas (Ed.), *Handbook of affect and social cognition* (pp. 121-144). Mahwah, NJ: Erlbaum.

Cohen, D., & Nisbett, R. E. (1997). Field experiments examining the culture of honor: The role of institutions in perpetuating norms about violence. *Personality and Social Psychology Bulletin, 23,* 1188-1199.

Cohen, D., Nisbett, R. E., Bowdle, B., & Schwarz, N. (1996). Insult, aggression, and the southern culture of honor: An "experimental ethnography." *Journal of Personality and Social Psychology, 70*(5), 945-960.

Cohen, I. I., & Shotland, R. L. (1996). Timing of first intercourse in a relationship: Expectations, experiences, and perceptions of others. *Journal of Sex Research, 33,* 291-299.

Cohen, J., & Andrade, E. B. (2004). Affect, intuition, and task-contingent affect regulation. *Journal of Consumer Research, 31,* 358-367.

Cohen, S., Tyrrell, D. A. J., & Smith, A. P. (1993). Negative life events, perceived stress, negative affect, and susceptibility to the common cold. *Journal of Personality and Social Psychology, 64,* 131-140.

Coker, D. (2003). Addressing the real world of racial injustice in the criminal justice system. *The Journal of Criminal Law and Criminology, 93,* 827-880.

Coleman, J. F., Blake, R. R., & Mouton, J. S. (1958). Task difficulty and conformity pressures. *Journal of Abnormal Social Psychology, 57,* 120-122.

Coleman, P. T. (2000). Fostering ripeness in seemingly intractable conflict: An experimental study. *International Journal of Conflict Management, 11*(4), 300-317.

Coleman, P. T. (2011). *The 5%: Finding solutions to (seemingly) impossible conflicts*. New York: Perseus Books.

Collins, N. L., & Feeney, B. C. (2000). A safe haven: An attachment theory perspective on support seeking and caregiving in intimate relationships. *Journal of Personality and Social Psychology, 78,* 1053-1073.

Collins, N. L., & Miller, L. C. (1994). Self-disclosure and liking: A meta-analytic review. *Psychological Bulletin, 116,* 457-475.

Condon, W. S., & Ogston, W. D. (1967). A segmentation of behavior. *Journal of Psychiatric Research, 5,* 221-235.

Cook, T. D., & Campbell, D. T. (1979). *Quasi-experimentation*. Boston, MA: Houghton Mifflin.

Cooke, R., & Sheeran, P. (2004). Moderation of cognition-intention and cognition-behavior relations: A meta-analysis of properties of variables from the theory of planned behavior. *British Journal of Social Psychology, 43,* 159-186.

Cooley, C. H. (1902). *Human nature and the social order*. New York: Scribner.

Cooper, J., & Worchel, S. (1970). Role of undesired consequences in arousing cognitive dissonance. *Journal of Personality and Social Psychology, 16,* 199-213.

Cooper, M. L., Shaver, P., & Collins, N. L. (1998). Attachment styles, emotion regulation, and adjustment in adolescence. *Journal of Personality and Social Psychology, 74,* 1380-1397.

Coopersmith, S. (1967). *The antecedents of self-esteem*. San Francisco: Freeman.

Copeland, J. T. (1994). Prophecies of power: Motivational implications of social power for behavioral confirmation. *Journal of Personality and Social Psychology, 67,* 264-277.

Correll, J., Park, B., Judd, C. M., & Wittenbrink, B. (2002). The police officer's dilemma: Using ethnicity to disambiguate potentially threatening individuals. *Journal of Personality and Social Psychology, 83,* 1314-1329.

Cortes, B. P., Demoulin, S., Rodriguez, R. T., Rodriguez, A. P., & Leyens, J. Ph. (2005). Infra-humanization or familiarity? Attribution of uniquely human emotions to the self, the in-group, and the out-group. *Personality and Social Psychology Bulletin, 31,* 243-253.

Cosmides, L. (1989). The logic of social exchange: Has natural selection shaped how humans reason? Studies with the Wason selection task. *Cognition, 31,* 187-276.

Costa, P. T., & McCrae, R. R. (1980). Influence of extraversion and neuroticism on subjective well-being: Happy and unhappy people. *Journal of Personality and Social Psychology, 38,* 668-678.

Costa, P. T., & McCrea, R. R. (1995). Domains and facets: Hierarchical personality assessment using the Revised NEO personality inventory. *Journal of Personality Assessment, 64,* 21-50.

Cota, A. A., & Dion, K. L. (1986). Salience of gender and sex composition of ad hoc groups: An experimental test of the distinctiveness theory. *Journal of Personality and Social Psychology, 50,* 770-776.

Cotterell, N., Eisenberger, R., & Speicher, H. (1992). Inhibiting effects of reciprocation wariness on interpersonal relationships. *Journal of Personality and Social Psychology, 62,* 658-668.

Cotterell, N. B. (1972). Social facilitation. In C. G. McClintock (Ed.), *Experimental social psychology* (pp. 185-236). New York: Holt, Reinhart & Winston.

Cottrell, N. B., Wack, D. I., Sekerak, G. J., & Rittle, R. H. (1968). Social facilitation of dominant responses by the presence of an audience and the mere presence of others. *Journal of Personality and Social Psychology, 9,* 245-250.

Cousins, S. D. (1989). Culture and self-perception in Japan and the United States. *Journal of Personality and Social Psychology, 56,* 124-131.

Crano, W. (2012). *The rules of influence: Winning when you're in the minority.* New York: St. Martin's Press.

Crick, F., & Koch, C. (2003). A framework for consciousness. *Nature Neuroscience, 6,* 118-126.

Crocker, J., & Park, L. E. (2004). The costly pursuit of self-esteem. *Psychological Bulletin, 130,* 392-414.

Crocker, J., & Schwarz, I. (1985). Prejudice and in-group favoritism in a minimal intergroup situation: Effects of self-esteem. *Personality and Social Psychology Bulletin, 11,* 379-386.

Crocker, J., & Wolfe, C. T. (2001). Contingencies of self-worth. *Psychological Review, 108,* 593-623.

Crocker, J., Thompson, L. L., McGraw, K. M., & Ingerman, C. (1987). Downward comparison, prejudice, and evaluations of others: Effects of self-esteem and threat. *Journal of Personality and Social Psychology, 52,* 907-916.

Cross, S. E., & Gore, J. S. (2003). Cultural models of the self. In M. R. Leary & J. P. Tangney (Eds.), *Handbook of self and identity* (pp. 536-566). New York: Guilford Press.

Crowley, A. F., & Hoyer, W. D. (1994). An integrative framework for understanding two-sided persuasion. *Journal of Consumer Research, 20,* 561-574.

Crowne, D. P., & Marlowe, D. (1964). *The approval motive: Studies in evaluative dependence.* New York: Wiley.

Crutchfield, R. (1955). Conforming and character. *American Psychologist, 10,* 191-198.

Csikzentmihalyi, M. (1990). *Flow: The psychology of optimal experience.* New York: Harper & Row.

Csíkszentmihályi, M. (1996). *Finding flow: The psychology of engagement with everyday life.* New York: Basic Books.

Cuddy, A. J., Fiske, S. T., & Glick, P. (2007). The BIAS map: Behaviors from intergroup affect and stereotypes. *Journal of Personality and Social Psychology, 92,* 631-648.

Cunningham, J. D. (1981). Self-disclosure intimacy: Sex, sex-of-target, cross-national, and generational differences. *Personality and Social Psychology Bulletin, 7,* 314-319.

Cunningham, M. R. (1979). Mood and helping behavior: Quasi experiments with the Sunshine Samaritan. *Journal of Personality and Social Psychology, 37,* 1947-1956.

Cunningham, M. R. (1986). Measuring the physical in physical attractiveness: Quasi-experiments on the sociobiology of female facial beauty. *Journal of Personality and Social Psychology, 50,* 925-935.

Cunningham, M. R., Barbee, A. P., & Pike, C. L. (1990). What do women want? Facial metric assessment of multiple motives in the perception of male facial physical attractiveness. *Journal of Personality and Social Psychology, 59,* 61-72.

Cunningham, M. R., Roberts, A. R., Barbee, A. P., Druen, P. B., & Wu, C. H. (1995). Their ideas of beauty are, on the whole, the same as ours: Consistency and variability in the cross-cultural perception of female physical attractiveness. *Journal of Personality and Social Psychology, 68,* 261-279.

Dabbs, J. M., Jr. (2000). *Heroes, rogues, and lovers: Testosterone and behavior.* New York: McGraw-Hill.

Dabbs, J. M., Jr., & Morris, R. (1990). Testosterone, social class, and antisocial behavior in a sample of 4462 men. *Psychological Science, 1*(3), 209-211.

D'Agostino, P. R., & Fincher-Kiefer, R. (1992). Need for cognition and the correspondence bias. *Social Cognition, 10,* 151-163.

Dalbert, C., Montada, L., & Schmitt, M. (1987). Glaube an eine gerechte Welt als Motiv: Validierungskorrelate zweier Skalen [The belief in a just world as a motive: Validity correlates of two scales]. *Psychologische Beiträge, 29,* 596-615.

Dalbert, C., & Yamauchi, L. A. (1994). Belief in a just world and attitudes toward immigrants and foreign workers: A cultural comparison between Hawaii and Germany. *Journal of Applied Social Psychology, 24,* 1612-1626.

Dalton, A. N., Chartrand, T. L., & Finkel, E. J. (2010). The schema-driven chameleon: How mimicry affects executive and self-regulatory resources. *Journal of Personality and Social Psychology, 98,* 605-617.

Daly, M., & Wilson, M. (1988). *Homicide*. New York: Aldine de Gruyter.

Daly, M., & Wilson, M. (1994). Evolutionary psychology of male violence. In J. Archer (Ed.), *Male violence* (pp. 253-288). New York: Routledge.

Daly, M., Wilson, M., & Vasdev, S. (2001). Income inequality and homicide rates in Canada and the United States. *Canadian Journal of Criminology*, 219-236.

Damaissio, A. (2009). *The feeling of what happens: Body and emotion in the making of consciousness*. Fort Worth, TX: Harcourt College Publishers.

Darley, J. M., & Batson, C. D. (1973). From Jerusalem to Jericho: A study of situational and dispositional variables in helping behavior. *Journal of Personality and Social Psychology, 27*, 100-108.

Darley, J. M., & Berscheid, E. (1967). Increased liking as a result of the anticipation of personal contact. *Human Relations, 20*(1), 29-40.

Darley, J. M., & Fazio, R. H. (1980). Expectancy confirmation processes arising in the interaction sequence. *American Psychologist, 35*, 867-881.

Darley, J. M., & Latané, B. (1968). Bystander intervention in emergencies: Diffusion of responsibility. *Journal of Personality and Social Psychology, 8*, 377-383.

Darwin, C. R. (1872/1998). *The expression of emotions in man and animals* (3rd ed.). New York: Oxford University Press.

Darwin, C. R. (1859). *The origin of species*. London: Murray.

Davidson, A. R., & Jaccard, J. J. (1979). Variables that moderate the attitude-behavior relation: Results of a longitudinal survey. *Journal of Personality and Social Psychology, 37*, 1364-1376.

Davies, M. F. (1997). Belief persistence after evidential discrediting: The impact of generated versus provided explanations on the likelihood of discredited outcomes. *Journal of Experimental Social Psychology, 33*, 561-578.

Davis, B. P., & Knowles, E. S. (1999). A disrupt-then-reframe technique of social influence. *Journal of Personality and Social Psychology, 76*, 192-199.

Davis, M. H., & Stephan, W. G. (1980). Attributions for exam performance. *Journal of Applied Social Psychology, 10*, 235-248.

Dawes, R. M. (1980). Social dilemmas. *Annual Review of Psychology, 31*, 169-193.

Dawkins, R. (1976). *The selfish gene*. Oxford: Oxford University Press.

Dawson, E., Gilovich, T., & Regan, D. T. (2002). Motivated reasoning and performance on the Wason selection task. *Personality and Social Psychology Bulletin, 28*, 1379-1387.

Deaner, R. O., Van Schaik, C. P., & Johnson, V. (2006). Do some taxa have better domain-general cognition than others? A meta-analysis of nonhuman primate studies. *Evolutionary Psychology, 4*, 149-196.

Deaux, K., & Emswiller, T. (1974). Explanations of successful performance on sex-linked tasks: What is skill for the male is luck for the female. *Journal of Personality and Social Psychology, 29*, 80-85.

De Bono, K. G., & Snyder, M. (1995). Acting on one's attitudes: The role of a history in choosing situations. *Personality and Social Psychology Bulletin, 21*, 629-636.

DeBruine, L. M., Jones, B. C., Crawford, J. R., Welling, L. L. M., & Little, A. C. (2010). The health of a nation predicts their mate preferences: Cross-cultural variation in women's preferences for masculinized male faces. *Proceedings of the Royal Society: Biological Sciences, 277*, 2405-2410.

DeCaro, M. S., & Beilock, S. L. (2010). The benefits and perils of attentional control. In M. Csikszentmihalyi & B. Bruya (Eds.), *Effortless attention: A new perspective in the cognitive science of attention and action*. Cambridge, MA: MIT Press.

deCharms, R. (1968). *Personal causation: The internal affective determinants of behavior*. New York: Academic Press.

Dechesne, M., Greenberg, J., Arndt, J., & Schimel, J. (2000). Terror management and sports fan affiliation: The effects of mortality salience on fan identification and optimism. *European Journal of Social Psychology, 30*, 813-835.

Deci, E. L., Koestner, R., & Ryan, R. M. (1999). A meta-analytic review of experiments examining the effects of extrinsic rewards on intrinsic motivation. *Psychological Bulletin, 125*, 627-668.

Deci, E. L., & Ryan, R. M. (1995). Human autonomy: The basis for true self-esteem. In M. H. Kernis (Ed.), *Efficacy, agency, and self-esteem* (pp. 31-49). New York: Plenum Press.

Deci, E. L., & Ryan, R. M. (2000). The "what" and "why" of goal pursuits: Human needs and the self-determination of behavior. *Psychological Inquiry, 11*, 227-268.

Denson, T. F., Capper, M. M., Oaten, M., Friese, M., & Schofield, T. P. (2011). Self-control training decreases aggression in response to provocation in aggressive individuals. *Journal of Research in Personality, 42*, 252-256.

Denson, T. F., DeWall, C. D., & Finkel, E. J. (2012). Self-control and aggression. *Current Directions in Psychological Science, 21*, 20-25.

De Paulo, B. M., & Friedman, H. S. (1998). Nonverbal communication. In D. T. Gilbert, S. T. Fiske, & G. Lindzey (Eds.), *Handbook of social psychology* (4th ed., Vol. 2, pp. 3-40). New York: McGraw-Hill.

DePaulo, B. M., Lanier, K., & Davis, T. (1983). Detecting the deceit of the motivated liar. *Journal of Personality and Social Psychology, 43*, 1096-1103.

Forgas, J. P. (1998c). On feeling good and getting your way: Mood effects on negotiation strategies and outcomes. *Journal of Personality and Social Psychology, 74*, 565-574.

Forgas, J. P., Fiedler, K., & Crano, W. D. (Eds.). (2015). *Social psychology and politics: 17th Sydney symposium of social psychology.* New York: Cambridge University Press.

Forgas, J. P., & Moylan, S. (1987). After the movies: Transient mood and social judgments. *Personality and Social Psychology Bulletin, 13*, 467-477.

Forster, J. L., & Jeffery, R. W. (1986). Gender differences related to weight history, eating patterns, efficacy expectations, self-esteem, and weight loss among participants in a weight reduction program. *Addictive Behaviors, 11*, 141-147.

Forsyth, D. R. (1990). *Group dynamics* (2nd ed.). Pacific Grove, CA: Brooks/Cole.

Fowler, J. H., & Christakis, N. A. (2007). The spread of obesity in a large social network over 32 years. *New England Journal of Medicine, 357*, 370-379.

Fowler, J. H., & Christakis, N. A. (2008). Dynamic spread of happiness in a large social network: Longitudinal analysis over 20 years in the Framingham heart study. *British Medical Journal, 337*, 2338.

Fraley, R. C., & Spieker, S. J. (2003). Are infant attachment patterns continuously or categorically distributed? A taxometric analysis of strange situation behavior. *Developmental Psychology, 34*, 387-404.

Frederickson, B. L., & Branigan, C. (2005). Positive emotions broaden the scope of attention and thought-action repertoires. *Cognition and Emotion, 19*, 313-332.

Fredrickson, B. L. (2001). The role of positive emotions in positive psychology: The broaden-and-build theory of positive emotions. *American Psychologist, 56*, 218-226.

Fredrickson, B. L., & Losada, M. (2005). Positive affect and the complex dynamics of human flourishing. *American Psychologist, 60*, 678-686.

Fredrickson, B. L., & Roberts, T. A. (1997). Objectification theory. *Psychology of Women Quarterly, 21*, 173-206.

Freedman, J. L. (1984). Effects of television violence on aggressiveness. *Psychological Bulletin, 96*, 227-246.

Freedman, J. L., & Fraser, S. C. (1966). Compliance without pressure: The foot-in-the-door technique. *Journal of Personality and Social Psychology, 4*, 195-202.

Freitas, A. L., Gollwitzer, P. M., & Trope, Y. (2004). The influence of abstract and concrete mindsets on anticipating and guiding others' self-regulatory efforts. *Journal of Experimental Social Psychology, 40*, 739-752.

Freud, S. (1920/1964). *Beyond the pleasure principle* (J. Strachey, trans.). New York: Norton.

Freud, S. (1933). *New introductory lectures on psychoanalysis.* New York: Norton.

Freud, S. (1936). *The ego and the mechanisms of defense.* New York: Hogarth Press.

Friedman, H. S., Mertz, T. I., & DiMatteo, M. R. (1980). Perceived bias in the facial expressions of television news broadcasters. *Journal of Communication, 30*, 103-111.

Friedrich-Cofer, L., & Huston, A. (1986). Television violence and aggression: The debate continues. *Psychological Bulletin, 100*, 364-371.

Frijda, N. H. (1988). The laws of emotion. *American Psychologist, 43*, 349-358.

Fry, P. S., & Ghosh, R. (1980). Attributions of success and failure: Comparison of cultural differences between Asian and Caucasian children. *Journal of Cross-Cultural Psychology, 11*, 343-363.

Fujita, K., & Carnevale, J. L. (2012). Transcending temptation through abstraction: The role of construal level in self-control. *Current Directions in Psychological Science, 21*, 248-252.

Fujita, K., & Roberts, J. C. (2010). Promoting prospective self-control through abstraction. *Journal of Experimental Social Psychology, 49*, 1049-1052.

Fujita, K., Trope, Y., Liberman, N., & Levin-Sagi, M. (2006). Construal levels and self-control. *Journal of Personality and Social Psychology, 90*, 351-367.

Furnham, A. (1983). Social psychology as common sense. *Bulletin of the British Psychological Society, 36*, 105-109.

Furnham, A. (1993). Just world beliefs in twelve societies. *Journal of Social Psychology, 133*, 317-329.

Gable, S. L., & Haidt, J. (2005). What (and why) is positive psychology? *Review of General Psychology, 9*, 103-110.

Gaertner, S. L., & Dovidio, J. F. (1977). The subtlety of white racism, arousal, and helping behavior. *Journal of Personality and Social Psychology, 35*, 691-707.

Gaertner, S. L., & Dovidio, J. F. (1986). The aversive form of racism. In J. F. Dovidio & S. L. Gaertner (Eds.), *Prejudice, discrimination, and racism* (pp. 61-89). Orlando, FL: Academic Press.

Gailliot, M. T., Baumeister, R. F., DeWall, C. N., Maner, J. K., Plant, E. A., Tice, D. M., Brewer, L. E., & Schmeichel, B. J. (2007). Self-control relies on glucose as a limited energy source: Willpower is more than a metaphor. *Journal of Personality and Social Psychology, 92*, 325-336.

Gale, J., Binmore, K. G., & Samuelson, L. (1995). Learning to be imperfect: The Ultimatum Game. *Games and Economic Behavior, 8*, 56-90.

Gallese, V., Fadiga, I., Fogassi, I., & Rizzolatti, G. (1996). Action recognition in the premotor cortex. *Brain, 119*, 593–609.

Gallup, G. G. (1977). Self-recognition in primates: A comparative approach to the bidirectional properties of consciousness. *American Psychologist, 32*, 329–338.

Gallup, G. G., & Suarez, S. D. (1986). Self-awareness and the emergence of mind in humans and other primates. In J. Suls & A. G. Greenwald (Eds.), *Psychological perspectives on the self* (Vol. 3, pp. 3–26). Hillsdale, NJ: Erlbaum.

Galperin, A., Haselton, M. G., Frederick, D. A., Poore, J., von Hippel, W., Buss, D. M., & Gonzaga, G. C. (2013). Sexual regret: Evidence for evolved sex differences. *Archives of Sexual Behavior, 41*, 1–17. doi:10.1007/s10508-012-0019-3

Gangestad, S. W., Simpson, J., Cousins, A., Garver-Apgar, C., & Christensen, P. (2004). Women's preferences for male behavioral displays change across the menstrual cycle. *Psychological Science, 15*, 203–207.

Gangestad, S. W., & Snyder, M. (2000). Self-monitoring: Appraisal and reappraisal. *Psychological Bulletin, 126*, 530–555.

Gangestad, S. W., & Thornhill, R. (1998). Menstrual cycle variation in women's preference for the scent of symmetrical men. *Proceedings of the Royal Society B: Biological Sciences, 265*, 927–933.

Gangestad, S. W., Thornhill, R., & Yeo, R. A. (1994). Facial attractiveness, developmental stability, and fluctuating asymmetry. *Ethology and Sociobiology, 15*, 73–85.

Gannon, K. M., Skowronski, J. J., & Betz, A. L. (1994). Depressive diligence in social information processing: Implications for order effects in impressions and for social memory. *Social Cognition, 12*, 263–280.

Gardner, R. A., & Gardner, B. I. (1969). Teaching sign language to a chimpanzee. *Science, 165*, 664–672.

Gawronski, B., Walther, E., & Blank, H. (2005). Cognitive consistency and the formation of interpersonal attitudes: Cognitive balance affects the encoding of social information. *Journal of Experimental Social Psychology, 41*, 618–626.

Gazzaniga, M. S. (1992). *Nature's mind: The biological roots of thinking, emotions, sexuality, language, and intelligence.* New York: Basic Books.

Gerdes, E. P. (1979). College students' reactions to social psychological experiments involving deception. *Journal of Social Psychology, 107*, 99–110.

Gergen, K. J. (1971). *The concept of self.* New York: Holt.

Gergen, K. J., Ellsworth, P., Maslach, C., & Seipel, M. (1975). Obligation, donor resources, and reactions to aid in three cultures. *Journal of Personality and Social Psychology, 31*, 390–400.

Gibbons, F. X. (1978). Sexual standards and reactions to pornography: Enhancing behavioral consistency through self-focused attention. *Journal of Personality and Social Psychology, 36*, 976–987.

Gibbons, F. X., Lane, D. J., Gerrard, M., Reis-Bergan, M., Lautrup, C. L., Pexa, N. A., & Blanton, H. (2002). Comparison-level preferences after performance: Is downward comparison theory still useful? *Journal of Personality and Social Psychology, 83*, 865–880.

Gifford, R. (1991). Mapping nonverbal behavior on the interpersonal circle. *Journal of Personality and Social Psychology, 61*, 279–288.

Gifford, R. (1994). A lens-mapping framework for understanding the encoding and decoding of interpersonal dispositions in nonverbal behavior. *Journal of Personality and Social Psychology, 66*, 398–412.

Gigerenzer, G., & Hug, K. (1992). Domain-specific reasoning: Social contracts, cheating, and perspective change. *Cognition, 43*, 127–171.

Gilbert, D. T. (1993). The assent of man: Mental representation and the control of belief. In D. M. Wegner & J. W. Pennebaker (Eds.), *The handbook of mental control* (pp. 57–87). Englewood Cliffs, NJ: Prentice Hall.

Gilbert, D. T. (2006). *Stumbling on happiness.* New York: Knopf.

Gilbert, D. T., Giesler, R. B., & Morris, K. A. (1995). When comparisons arise. *Journal of Personality and Social Psychology, 69*, 227–236.

Gilbert, D. T., & Jones, E. E. (1986). Exemplification: The self-presentation of moral character. *Journal of Personality, 54*, 593–615.

Gilbert, D. T., Lieberman, M. D., Morewedge, C. K., & Wilson, T. D. (2004). The peculiar longevity of things not so bad. *Psychological Science, 15*, 14–19.

Gilbert, D. T., & Malone, P. S. (1995). The correspondence bias. *Psychological Bulletin, 117*, 21–38.

Gilbert, D. T., Pelham, B. W., & Krull, D. S. (1988). On cognitive busyness: When person perceivers meet persons perceived. *Journal of Personality and Social Psychology, 54*(5), 733–740.

Gilbert, D. T., & Wilson, T. D. (2007). Prospection: Experiencing the future. *Science, 317*, 1351–1354.

Gilbert, E. H., & DeBlassie, R. R. (1984). Anorexia nervosa: Adolescent starvation by choice. *Adolescence, 19*, 839–846.

Gilmour, T. M., & Reid, D. M. (1979). Locus of control and causal attribution for positive and negative outcomes on university examinations. *Journal of Research in Personality, 13*, 154–160.

Gilovich, T. (1983). Biased evaluation and persistence in gambling. *Journal of Personality and Social Psychology, 44*, 1110–1126.

Gilovich, T. (1991). *How we know what isn't so: The fallibility of human reason in everyday life.* New York: Free Press.

Givens, D. B. (1983). *Love signals: How to attract a mate.* New York: Crown.

Glass, D. C., & Singer, J. E. (1972). *Urban stress: Experiments on noise and social stressors.* New York: Academic Press.

Glass, D. C., Singer, J. E., & Friedman, I. N. (1969). Psychic costs of adaptation to an environmental stressor. *Journal of Personality and Social Psychology, 12*, 200–210.

Gleick, J. (1987). *Chaos: The making of a new science.* New York: Viking-Penguin.

Gleick, P.H. (1993). Water and conflict: Fresh water resources and international security. *International Security*, *18*(1), 79-112.

Glocker, M.L., Langleben, D., Ruparel, K., Loughead, J., Gur, R., & Sachser, N. (2009). Baby schema in infant faces induces cuteness perception and motivation for caretaking in adults. *Ethology*, *115*, 257-263.

Goethals, G.R., & Zanna, M.P. (1979). The role of social comparison in choice shifts. *Journal of Personality and Social Psychology*, *37*, 1469-1476.

Goffman, E. (1959). *The presentation of self in everyday life*. Garden City, NY: Doubleday.

Goleman, D. (1995). *Emotional intelligence*. New York: Bantam.

Gondoff, E.W. (1985). *Men who batter: An integrated approach for stopping wife abuse*. Holmes Beach, CA: Learning Publications.

Gonzaga, G.C., Turner, R.A., Keltner, K., Campos, B., & Altremus, M. (2006). Romantic love and sexual desire in close bonds. *Emotion*, *6*, 163-179.

Good, K., & Chanoff, D. (1991). *Into the heart*. New York: Simon & Schuster.

Goodall, J. (1986). *The chimpanzees of Gombe: Patterns of behavior*. Cambridge, MA: Harvard University Press.

Goodnight, C.J., & Stevens, L. (1997). Experimental studies of group selection: What do they tell us about group selection in nature? *American Naturalist*, *150*, 59-79.

Gordijn, E.H., Hindriks, I., Koomen, W., Dijksterhuis, A., & Van Knippenberg, A. (2004). Consequences of stereotype suppression and internal suppression motivation: A self-regulation approach. *Personality and Social Psychology Bulletin*, *30*, 221-224.

Gottman, J.M., & Levenson, R.W. (1992). Marital processes predictive of later dissolution: Behavior, physiology, and health. *Journal of Personality and Social Psychology*, *63*, 221-233.

Gottman, J.M., & Levenson, R.W. (2000). The timing of divorce: Predicting when a couple will divorce over a 14-year period. *Journal of Marriage and the Family*, *62*, 737-745.

Gottman, J.M., Murray, J.D., Swanson, C.C., Tyson, R., & Swanson, K.R. (2007). *The mathematics of marriage: Dynamic nonlinear models*. Cambridge, MA: MIT Press.

Gottman, J., Swanson, C., & Swanson, K. (2002). A general systems theory of marriage: Nonlinear difference equation modeling of marital interaction. *Personality and Social Psychology Review*, *6*(4), 326-340.

Gould, J.L., & Gould, C.L. (1989). *Sexual selection*. New York: Scientific American Library.

Gouldner, A.W. (1960). The norm of reciprocity: A preliminary statement. *American Sociological Review*, *25*, 161-178.

Graham, J., Haidt, J., & Nosek, B.A. (2009). Liberals and conservatives rely on different sets of moral foundations. *Journal of Personality and Social Psychology*, *96*, 1029-1046.

Graham, J., Nosek, B.A., Haidt, J., Iyer, R., Koleva, S., & Ditto, P.H. (2011). Mapping the moral domain. *Journal of Personality and Social Psychology*, *101*, 366-385.

Graham, K., & Wells, S. (2001). The two worlds of aggression for men and women. *Sex Roles*, *45*, 595-622.

Granovetter, M. (1973). The strength of weak ties. *American Journal of Sociology*, *78*, 1360-1380.

Gray, H.M., Gray, K., & Wegner, D.M. (2007). Dimensions of mind perception. *Science*, *315*, 619.

Gray, K., & Wegner, D.M. (2009). Moral typecasting: Divergent perceptions of moral agents and moral patients. *Journal of Personality and Social Psychology*, *96*, 505-520.

Green, B. (2004). *The fabric of the cosmos*. New York: Random House.

Green, R.G. (1998). Aggression and antisocial behavior. In D.T. Gilbert, S.T. Fiske, & G. Lindzey (Eds.), *The handbook of social psychology* (4th ed., Vol. 2, pp. 317-356). New York: McGraw-Hill.

Greenberg, J. (1985). Unattainable goal choice as a self-handicapping strategy. *Journal of Applied Social Psychology*, *15*, 140-152.

Greenberg, J., Pyszczynski, T., & Solomon, S. (1982). The self-serving attributional bias: Beyond self-presentation. *Journal of Experimental Social Psychology*, *18*, 56-67.

Greenberg, J., Pyszczynski, T., & Solomon, S. (1986). The causes and consequences of a need for self-esteem: A terror management theory. In R.F. Baumeister (Ed.), *Public and private self* (pp. 189-212). New York: Springer-Verlag.

Greenberg, J., Pyszczynski, T., Solomon, S., Rosenblatt, A., Veeder, M., Kirkland, S., & Lyon, D. (1990). Evidence for terror management theory II: The effects of mortality salience on reactions to those who threaten or bolster the cultural worldview. *Journal of Personality and Social Psychology*, *58*, 308-318.

Greenberg, J., Simon, L., Porteus, J., Pyszczynski, T., & Solomon, S. (1995). Evidence of a terror management function of cultural icons: The effects of mortality salience on the inappropriate use of cherished cultural symbols. *Journal and Social Psychology Bulletin*, *21*, 1221-1228.

Greene, J.D., & Haidt, J. (2002). How (and where) does moral judgment work? *Trends in Cognitive Sciences*, *6*, 517-523.

Greene, J.D., Sommerville, R.B., Nystrom, L.E., Darley, J.M., & Cohen, J.D. (2001). An fMRI investigation of emotional engagement in moral judgment. *Science*, *293*, 2105-2108.

Greenwald, A.G., & Banaji, M.R. (1995). Implicit social cognition: Attitudes, self-esteem, and stereotypes. *Psychological Review*, *102*, 4-27.

Greenwald, A.G., & Farnham, S. (2000). Using the implicit association test to measure self-esteem and self-concept. *Journal of Personality and Social Psychology*, *79*, 1022-1038.

Greenwald, A. G., McGhee, D. E., & Schwartz, J. L. K. (1998). Measuring individual differences in implicit cognition: The implicit association test. *Journal of Personality and Social Psychology, 74*(6), 1464-1480.

Greenwald, A. G., Nosek, B. A., & Banaji, M. R. (2003). Understanding and using the implicit association test: I. An improved scoring algorithm. *Journal of Personality and Social Psychology, 85,* 197-216.

Greenwald, A. G., Oakes, A. M., & Hoffman, H. G. (2003). Targets of discrimination: Effects of race on responses to weapon holders. *Journal of Experimental Social Psychology, 39,* 399-405.

Gregory, S. W., Jr., & Gallagher, T. J. (2002). Spectral analysis of candidates' nonverbal vocal communication: Predicting U.S. presidential election outcomes. *Social Psychology Quarterly, 65,* 298-308.

Greitemeyer, T. (2011). Effects of prosocial media on social behavior: When and why does media exposure affect helping and aggression? *Current Directions in Psychological Science, 20,* 251-255.

Gresham, L. G., & Shimp, T. A. (1985). Attitude toward advertisement and brand attitude: A classical conditioning perspective. *Journal of Advertising, 14,* 10-17.

Griesinger, D. W., & Livingston, J. W. (1973). Toward a model of interpersonal motivation in experimental games. *Behavioral Science, 18,* 173-188.

Griffin, A. M., & Langlois, J. H. (2006). Stereotype directionality and attractiveness stereotyping: Is beauty good or ugly bad? *Social Cognition, 24*(2), 187-206.

Griffin, B. Q., Combs, A. L., Land, M. L., & Combs, N. N. (1983). Attribution of success and failure in college performance. *Journal of Psychology, 114,* 259-266.

Gross, J. J., Fredrickson, B. L., & Levenson, R. W. (1994). The psychophysiology of crying. *Psychophysiology, 31,* 460-468.

Gruber, J., & Tamir, M. (2011). A dark side of happiness? How, when, and why happiness is not always good. *Perspectives on Psychological Science, 6,* 222-233.

Grunberg, N. E., & Straub, R. O. (1992). The role of gender and taste class in the effects of stress on eating. *Health Psychology, 11,* 97-100.

Gruner, C. R. (1985). Advice to the beginning speaker on using humor: What the research tells us. *Communication Education, 34,* 142-147.

Grush, J. E. (1980). Impact of candidate expenditures, regionality, and prior outcomes on the 1976 Democratic presidential primaries. *Journal of Personality and Social Psychology, 38,* 337-347.

Gueguen, N. (2004). Mimicry and seduction: An evaluation in a courtship context. *Social Influence, 4,* 249-255.

Guerin, B. (1994). What do people think about the risks of driving? Implications for traffic safety interventions. *Journal of Applied Social Psychology, 24*(11), 994-1021. https://doi.org/10.1111/j.1559-1816.1994.tb02370.x

Guimond, S., Dif, S., & Aupy, A. (2002). Social identity, relative group status and intergroup attitudes: When favourable outcomes change intergroup relations... for the worse. *European Journal of Social Psychology, 32,* 739-760.

Gump, B. B., & Kulik, J. A. (1997). Stress, affiliation and emotional contagion. *Journal of Personality and Social Psychology, 72,* 305-319.

Gunnthorsdottir, A., Houser, D., & McCabe, K. (2007). Disposition, history and contributions in public goods experiments. *Journal of Economic Behavior & Organization, 62*(2), 304-315.

Guttentag, M., & Secord, P. F. (1983). *Too many women? The sex ratio question.* Beverly Hills, CA: Sage.

Haddock, G., Zanna, M. P., & Esses, V. M. (1993). Assessing the structure of prejudicial attitudes: The case of attitudes toward homosexuals. *Journal of Personality and Social Psychology, 65,* 1105-1118.

Hafer, C. L., & Bègue, L. (2005). Experimental research on just-world theory: Problems, developments, and future challenges. *Psychological Bulletin, 131,* 128-167.

Hafer, C. L., & Gosse, L. (2010). Preserving the belief in a just world: When and for whom are different strategies preferred? In D. R. Bobocel, A. C. Kay, M. P. Zanna, & J. M. Olson (Eds.), *The psychology of justice and legitimacy: The Ontario symposium* (Vol. 11, pp. 79-102). New York: Psychology Press.

Haidt, J. (2001). The emotional dog and its rational tail: A social intuitionist approach to moral judgment. *Psychological Review, 108,* 814-834.

Haidt, J. (2006). *The happiness hypothesis: Finding modern truth in ancient wisdom.* New York: Basic Books.

Haidt, J., & Joseph, C. (2007). The moral mind: How 5 sets of innate moral intuitions guide the development of many culture-specific virtues, and perhaps even modules. In P. Carruthers, S. Laurence, & S. Stich (Eds.), *The innate mind* (Vol. 3, pp. 367-391). New York: Oxford University Press.

Haidt, J., & Keltner, D. (1999). Culture and emotion: Multiple methods find new faces and a gradient of recognition. *Cognition and Emotion, 13,* 225-266.

Haidt, J., Koller, S. H., & Dias, M. G. (1993). Affect, culture, and morality, or is it wrong to eat your dog? *Journal of Personality and Social Psychology, 65,* 613-628.

Haken, H. (1978). *Synergetics.* Berlin: Springer.

Hall, E. T. (1966). *The hidden dimension.* Garden City, NY: Doubleday Anchor.

Hamilton, D. L. (1970). The structure of personality judgments: Comments on Kuusinen's paper and further evidence. *Scandinavian Journal of Psychology, 11*, 261–265.

Hamilton, D. L., & Gifford, R. K. (1976). Illusory correlation in interpersonal perception: A cognitive basis of stereotypic judgments. *Journal of Experimental Social Psychology, 12*, 392–407.

Hamilton, W. D. (1964). The evolution of social behavior. *Journal of Theoretical Biology, 1*, 295–311.

Hamner, W. C., & Foster, L. W. (1975). Are intrinsic and extrinsic rewards additive: A test of Deci's cognitive evaluation theory of task motivation. *Organizational Behavior and Human Performance, 14*, 398–415.

Haney, C., Banks, C., & Zimbardo, P. (1973). Interpersonal dynamics in a simulated prison. *International Journal of Criminology and Penology, 1*, 69–97.

Harackiewicz, J. M. (1979). The effects of reward contingency and performance feedback on intrinsic motivation. *Journal of Personality and Social Psychology, 37*, 1352–1363.

Harackiewicz, J. M., Manderlink, G., & Sansone, C. (1984). Rewarding pinball wizardry: Effects of evaluation and cue value on intrinsic interest. *Journal of Personality and Social Psychology, 47*, 287–300.

Hardin, G. (1968). The tragedy of the commons. *Science, 162*, 1243–1248.

Harkins, S. G., & Jackson, J. M. (1985). The role of evaluation in eliminating social loafing. *Personality and Social Psychology Bulletin, 11*, 457–465.

Harmon-Jones, E., & Winkielman, P. (Eds.). (2007). *Social neuroscience*. New York: Guilford Press.

Harris, J. R. (1995). Where is the child's environment: A group socialization theory of development. *Psychological Review, 102*, 458–489.

Harris, J. R. (1998). *The nature assumption*. New York: Free Press.

Harris, L. T., & Fiske, L. T. (2006). Dehumanizing the lowest of the low: Neuroimaging responses to extreme out-groups. *Psychological Science, 17*, 847–853.

Harris, M. B., Benson, S. M., & Hall, C. L. (1975). The effects of confession on altruism. *Journal of Social Psychology, 96*, 187–192.

Harris, R. N., & Snyder, C. R. (1986). The role of uncertain self-esteem in self-handicapping. *Journal of Personality and Social Psychology, 51*, 451–458.

Harter, S. (1986). Processes underlying the construction, maintenance, and enhancement of the self-concept in the children. In J. Suls & A. G. Greenwald (Eds.), *Psychological perspectives on the self* (Vol. 3, pp. 137–181). Mahwah, NJ: Erlbaum.

Hartmann, T., & Vorderer, P. (2010). It's okay to shoot a character: Moral disengagement in violent video games. *Journal of Communication, 60*(1), 94–99.

Harvey, J. H. (1976). Attribution of freedom. In J. H. Harvey, W. J. Ickes, & R. F. Kidd (Eds.), *New directions in attribution research* (Vol. 1, pp. 73–96). Hillsdale, NJ: Lawrence Erlbaum.

Haslam, N. (2006). Dehumanization: An integrative review. *Personality and Social Psychology Review, 10*, 252–264.

Haslam, N., Bain, P., Douge, L., Lee, M., & Bastain, B. (2005). More human than you: Attributing humanness to self and others. *Journal of Personality and Social Psychology, 89*, 937–950.

Haslam, N., Loughnan, S., Reynolds, C., & Wilson, S. (2007). Dehumanization: A new perspective. *Social and Personality Psychology Compass, 1*, 409–422.

Hassin, R. R., Uleman, J. S., & Bargh, J. A. (Eds.). (2005). *The new unconscious*. New York: Oxford University Press.

Hatfield, E., Cacioppo, J. L., & Rapson, R. L. (1993). Emotional contagion. *Current Directions in Psychological Science, 2*, 96–99.

Haugtvedt, C. P., & Wegener, D. T. (1994). Message order effects in persuasion: An attitude strength perspective. *Journal of Consumer Research, 21*, 205–218.

Hauser, M. D. (1996). *The evolution of communication*. Cambridge, MA: MIT Press.

Hazan, C., & Shaver, P. (1987). Romantic love conceptualized as an attachment process. *Journal of Personality and Social Psychology, 52*, 511–524.

Hazan, C., & Shaver, P. (1994). Attachment as an organizational framework for research on close relationships. *Psychological Inquiry, 5*, 1–22.

Hazen, C., & Shaver, P. (1987). Romantic love conceptualized as an attachment process. *Journal of Personality and Social Psychology, 52*, 511–524.

Heatherton, T. F., & Vohs, K. D. (2000). Interpersonal evaluations following threats to self: Role of Self-esteem. *Journal of Personality and Social Psychology, 78*, 725–736.

Heider, F. (1958). *The psychology of interpersonal relations*. New York: Wiley.

Heine, S. J., & Renshaw, K. (2002). Interjudge agreement, self-enhancement, and liking: Cross-cultural divergences. *Personality and Social Psychology Bulletin, 28*, 578–587.

Heine, S. J., Kitayama, S., & Lehman, D. R. (2001). Cultural differences in self-evaluation: Japanese readily accept negative self-relevant information. *Journal of Cross-Cultural Psychology, 32*, 434–443.

Heine, S. J., Lehman, D., Markus, H., & Kitayama, S. (1999). Is there a universal need for positive self-regard? *Psychological Review, 106*, 766–794.

Helgeson, V. S., & Mickelson, K. D. (1995). Motives for social comparison. *Personality and social Psychology Bulletin, 21*, 1200-1209.

Henley, N. M. (1977). *Body politics: Power, sex, and nonverbal communication*. Englewood Cliffs, NJ: Prentice Hall.

Henreich, J., Heine, S. J., & Norenzayan, A. (2010). The weirdest people in the world? *Behavioral and Brain Sciences, 33*, 61-83.

Hess, U., Beaupré, M. G., & Cheung, N. (2002). Who to whom and why: Cultural differences and similarities in the function of smiles. In A. Millicent (Ed.), *The smile: Forms, functions, and consequences* (pp. 187-216). New York: The Edwin Mellen Press.

Hibbing, J. R., Smith, K. B., & Alford, J. R. (2014). Differences in negativity bias underlie variations in political ideology. *Behavioral and Brain Sciences, 37*, 297-307.

Higgins, E. T. (1987). Self discrepancy: A theory relating self and affect. *Psychological Review, 94*, 319-340.

Higgins, E. T. (1996). Knowledge activation: Accessibility, applicability, and salience. In E. T. Higgins & A. W. Kruglanski (Eds.), *Social psychology: Handbook of basic principles* (pp. 133-168). New York: Guilford Press.

Higgins, E. T. (1997). Beyond pleasure and pain. *American Psychologist, 52*, 1280-1300.

Higgins, E. T. (1998). Promotion and prevention: Regulatory focus as a motivational principle. In M. P. Zanna (Ed.), *Advances in experimental social psychology* (Vol. 30, pp. 1-46). San Diego, CA: Academic Press.

Higgins, E. T. (2000). Making a good decision: Value from fit. *American Psychologist, 55*, 1217-1230.

Higgins, E. T., & Bargh, J. A. (1987). Social cognition and social perception. *Annual Review of Psychology, 38*, 369-425.

Higgins, E. T., & Brendl, C. M. (1995). Accessibility and applicability: Some "activation rules" influencing judgment. *Journal of Experimental Social Psychology, 31*, 218-243.

Higgins, E. T., Rholes, W. S., & Jones, C. R. (1977). Category accessibility and impression formation. *Journal of Experimental Social Psychology, 13*, 141-154.

Higgins, R. L., & Harris, R. N. (1988). Strategic "alcohol" use: Drinking to self-handicap. *Journal of Social and Clinical Psychology, 6*(2), 191-202.

Higgins, R. L., Snyder, C. R., & Berglas, S. (Eds.). (1990). *Self-handicapping: The paradox that isn't*. New York: Guilford.

Hill, C. T., Rubin, Z., & Peplau, L. A. (1976). Breakups before marriage: The end of 103 affairs. *Journal of Social Issues, 32*, 147-168.

Hill, P. L., & Turiano, N. A. (2014). Purpose in life as a predictor of mortality across adulthood. *Psychological Science, 25*, 1482-1486.

Hinduja, S., & Patchin, J. W. (2009). *Bullying beyond the schoolyard: Preventing and responding to cyberbullying*. Thousand Oaks, CA: Sage Publications.

Hiroto, D. S. (1974). Locus of control and learned helplessness. *Journal of Experimental Psychology, 102*, 187-193.

Hirsh, J. B., Kang, S. K., & Bodenhausen, G. V. (2012). Personalized persuasion: Tailoring persuasive appeals to recipients' personality traits. *Psychological Science, 23*, 578-581.

Hirt, E. R., Deppe, R. K., & Gordon, L. J. (1991). Self-reported versus behavioral self-handicapping: Empirical evidence for a theoretical distinction. *Journal of Personality and Social Psychology, 61*, 981-991.

Hirt, E. R., McDonald, H. E., & Erickson, G. A. (1995). How do I remember thee? The role of encoding set and delay in reconstructive memory processes. *Journal of Experimental Social Psychology, 31*, 379-409.

Hodson, G., Dovidio, J. F., & Gaertner, S. L. (2002). Processes in racial discrimination: Differential weighting of conflicting information. *Personality and Social Psychology Bulletin, 28*, 460-471.

Hoffman, C., Lau, I., & Johnsons, D. R. (1986). The linguistic relativity of person cognition: An English-Chinese comparison. *Journal of Personality and Social Psychology, 51*, 1097-1105.

Hofstede, G. (2001). *Culture's consequences: Comparing values, behaviors, and organizations across nations* (2nd ed.). New York: Sage Publications.

Hogan, R., Curphy, G. J., & Hogan, J. (1994). What we know about leadership: Effectiveness and personality. *American Psychologist, 49*, 493-504.

Hogg, M. A., & Abrams, D. (1988). *Social identifications: A social psychology of intergroup relations and group processes*. London: Routledge.

Holland, J. H. (1995). Can there be a unified theory of complex adaptive systems? In H. J. Morowitz & J. L. Singer (Eds.), *The mind, the brain, and complex adaptive systems*. Boston: Addison-Wesley.

Holleran, S., Whitehead, J., Schmader, T., & Mehl, M. (2011). Talking shop and shooting the breeze: Predicting women's job disengagement from workplace conversations. *Social Psychological and Personality Science, 2*, 65-71.

Holmes, T. H., & Rahe, R. H. (1967). The social readjustment rating scale. *Journal of Psychosomatic Research, 11*, 213-218.

Holt-Lunstad, J., Smith, T. B., & Layton, J. B. (2010). Social relationships and mortality risk: A meta-analytic review. *PLoS Medicine, 7*(7), e1000316. Retrieved from http://www.plos-medicine.org/article/info%3Adoi%2F10.1371%2Fjournal.pmed.1000316.

Homans, G. C. (1961). *Social behavior: Its elementary forms*. New York: Harcourt, Brace & World.

Hoog, N., Stroebe, W., & de Wit, J. B. F. (2005). The impact of fear appeals on processing and acceptance of action recommendations. *Personality and Social Psychology Bulletin, 31*, 24-33.

Hooghiemstra, R. (2008). East-west differences in attributions for company performance: A content analysis of Japanese and U.S. corporate annual reports. *Journal of Cross-Cultural Psychology, 39*, 618-629.

Hormuth, S. E. (1986). Lack of effort as a result of self-focused attention: An attributional ambiguity analysis. *European Journal of Social Psychology, 16,* 181-192.

Hovland, C. I., Lumsdaine, A. A., & Sheffield, F. D. (1949). *Experiments on mass communication.* Princeton, NJ: Princeton University Press.

Hovland, C. J., & Sears, R. R. (1940). Minor studies in aggression: VI. Correlations of lynchings with economic indices. *Journal of Abnormal and Social Psychology, 9,* 301-310.

Hovland, C. L., Janis, I. I., & Kelley, H. H. (1953). *Communication and persuasion.* New Haven: Yale University Press.

Hovland, C. L., & Weiss, W. (1951). The influence of source credibility on communication effectiveness. *Public Opinion Quarterly, 15,* 635-650.

Huesmann, L. R. (1986). Psychological processes promoting the relations between exposure to media violence and aggressive behavior by the viewer. *Journal of Social Issues, 42*(3), 125-139.

Huesmann, L. R., Moise-Titus, J., Podolski, C. L., & Eron, L. D. (2003). Longitudinal relations between children's exposure to TV violence and their aggressive and violent behavior in young adulthood: 1977-1992. *Developmental Psychology, 39,* 201-221.

Hugenberg, K., & Bodenhausen, G. V. (2003). Facing prejudice: Implicit prejudice and the perception of fatal threat. *Psychological Science, 14,* 640-643.

Hugenberg, K., & Bodenhausen, G. V. (2004). Ambiguity in social categorization: The role of prejudice and facial affect in race categorization. *Psychological Science, 15,* 342-345.

Hull, J. G. (1981). A self-awareness model of the causes and effects of alcohol consumption. *Journal of Personality and Social Psychology, 90,* 586-600.

Hull, J. G., & Young, R. D. (1983). Self-consciousness, self-esteem, and success-failure as determinants of alcohol consumption in male social drinkers. *Journal of Personality and Social Psychology, 44,* 1097-1109.

Hull, J. G., Young, R. D., & Jouriles, E. (1986). Applications of the self-awareness model of alcohol consumption: Predicting patterns of use and abuse. *Journal of Personality and Social Psychology, 51,* 790-796.

Hummert, M. L., Crockett, W. H., & Kemper, S. (1990). Processing mechanisms underlying use of the balance schema. *Journal of Personality and Social Psychology, 58,* 5-21.

Huston, A. C., Donnerstein, E., Fairchild, H., Feshbach, N. D., Katz, P. A., & Murray, J. P. (1992). *Big world, small screen: The role of television in American society.* Lincoln: University of Nebraska Press.

Hyde, J. S. (2005). The gender similarities hypothesis. *American Psychologist, 60,* 581-592.

Idson, L. C., & Mischel, W. (2001). The personality of familiar and significant people: The lay perceiver as a social-cognitive theorist. *Journal of Personality and Social Psychology, 80,* 585-596.

Inglehart, R. F. (1990). *Culture shift in advanced industrial society.* Princeton, NJ: Princeton University Press.

Inglehart, R. F., Foa, R., Peterson, C., & Welzel, C. (2008). Development, freedom, and rising happiness: A global perspective (1981-2007). *Perspectives on Psychological Science, 3,* 264-285.

Insko, C. A., Drenan, S., Solomon, M. R., Smith, R., & Wade, T. J. (1983). Conformity as a function of the consistency of positive self-evaluation with being liked and being right. *Journal of Experimental Social Psychology, 19,* 341-358.

Isen, A. M. (1987). Positive affect, cognitive processes, and social behavior. In L. Berkowitz (Ed.), *Advances in experimental social psychology* (Vol. 20, pp. 203-253). New York: Academic Press.

Isen, A. M. (1993). Positive affect and decision making. In M. Lewis & J. M. Haviland-Jones (Eds.), *Handbook of emotions* (pp. 261-278). New York: Guilford Press.

Isen, A. M., Clark, M., & Schwartz, M. F. (1976). Duration of the effect of good mood on helping: Footprints on the sands of time. *Journal of Personality and Social Psychology, 34,* 385-393.

Isen, A. M., & Levin, P. F. (1972). Effect of feeling good on helping: Cookies and kindness. *Journal of Personality and Social Psychology, 21,* 384-388.

Izard, C. E. (1990). The substrates and functions of emotion feelings: William James and current emotion theory. *Personality and Social Psychology Bulletin, 16,* 626-635.

Izard, C. E. (1994). Innate and Universal facial expressions: Evidence from development and cross-cultural research. *Psychological Bulletin, 115,* 288-299.

Jackson, J. C., Rand, D., Lewis, K., Norton, M. I., & Gray, K. (2017). Agent-based modeling: A guide for social psychologists. *Social Psychological and Personality Science, 20,* 1-9.

Jackson, J. M., & Latané, B. (1981). All alone in front of all those people: Stage fright as a function of number and type of co-performers and audience. *Journal of Personality and Social Psychology, 40,* 73-85.

Jackson, L. A., Hunter, J. E., & Hodge, C. N. (1995). Physical attractiveness and intellectual competence: A meta-analytic review. *Social Psychology Quarterly, 58,* 108-122.

James, W. (1884). What is emotion? *Mind, 19,* 188-205.

James, W. (1890). *Principles of psychology.* New York: Holt.

Janis, I.I., & Feshbach, S. (1953). Effects of fear-arousing communications. *Journal of Abnormal and Social Psychology, 48*, 78–92.

Janis, I.I., Kaye, D., & Kirschner, P. (1965). Facilitating effects of "eating-while-reading" on responsiveness to persuasive communications. *Journal of Personality and Social Psychology, 1*, 181–186.

Janis, I.L. (1982). *Groupthink*. Boston: Houghton Mifflin.

Jankowiak, W.R. (Ed.). (1995). *Romantic passion: A universal experience?* New York: Columbia University Press.

Janoff-Bulman, R. (2007). Erroneous assumptions: Popular belief in the effectiveness of torture interrogation. *Peace and Conflict: Journal of Peace Psychology, 34*, 429–436.

Jaremka, L.M., Fagundes, C.P., Peng, J., Bennett, J.M., Glaser, R., Malarkey, W.B., & Kiecolt-Glaser, J.K. (2013). Loneliness promotes inflammation during acute stress. *Psychological Science, 24*, 1089–1097.

Jarman, M., Nowak, A., Borkowski, W., Serfass, D., Wong, A., & Vallacher, R.R. (2015). The critical few: Anticonformists at the crossroads of minority survival and collapse. *Journal of Artificial Societies and Social Simulation, 18*(1), 6. <http://jasss.soc.surrey.ac.uk/18/1/6.html>

Jasienska, G., Lipson, S.F., Ellison, P.T., Thune, I., & Ziomkiewicz, A. (2006). Symmetrical women have higher potential fertility. *Evolution and Human Behavior, 27*, 390–400.

Job, V., Dweck, C.S., & Walton, G.M. (2010). Ego depletion: Is it all in your head? Implicit theories about willpower affect self-regulation. *Psychological Science, 21*, 1686–1693.

Job, V., Walton, G.M., Bernecker, K., & Dweck, C.S. (2015). Implicit theories about willpower predict self-regulation and grades in everyday life. *Journal of Personality and Social Psychology, 108*, 637–647.

Johns, M., Inzlicht, M., & Schmader, T. (2008). Stereotype threat and executive resource depletion: Examining the influence of emotion regulation. *Journal of Experimental Psychology: General, 137*, 691–705. doi:10.1037/a0013834

Johnson, D.B. (1983). Self-recognition in infants. *Infant Behavior and Development, 6*, 211–222.

Johnson, J.T., Ogawa, K.H., Delforge, A., & Early, D. (1989). Causal primacy and comparative fault: The effect of position in a causal chain on judgments of legal responsibility. *Personality and Social Psychology Bulletin, 15*(2), 161–174.

Johnson, M.K., & Raye, C.I. (1981). Reality monitoring. *Psychological Review, 88*, 67–85.

Johnson, S. (2001). *Emergence: The connected lives of ants, brains, cities, and software*. New York: Scribner.

Johnson, S. (2010). *Where good ideas come from: The history of innovation*. New York: Penguin.

Johnson, W. (2007). Genetic and environmental influences on behavior: Capturing all the interplay. *Psychological Review, 114*, 424–440.

Jones, B.C., DeBruine, L.M., Perrett, D.I., Little, A.C., Feinberg, D.R., & Law Smith, M.J. (2008). Effects of menstrual cycle phase on face preferences. *Archives of Sexual Behavior, 37*, 78–84.

Jones, B.C., Little, A.C., Penton-Voak, I.S., Tiddeman, B.P., Burt, D.M., & Perrett, D.I. (2001). Facial symmetry and judgments of apparent health: Support for a "good genes" explanation of the attractiveness: Symmetry relationship. *Evolution and Human Behavior, 22*, 417–429.

Jones, C., & Aronson, E. (1973). Attribution of fault to a rape victim as a function of the respectability of the victim. *Journal of Personality and Social Psychology, 26*, 415–419.

Jones, E.E. (1964). *Ingratiation: A social psychological analysis*. New York: Appleton-Century-Crofts.

Jones, E.E. (1979). The rocky road from acts to dispositions. *American Psychologist, 34*, 107–117.

Jones, E.E., & Berglas, S. (1978). Control of attributions about the self through self-handicapping strategies: The appeal of alcohol and the role of underachievement. *Personality and Social Psychology Bulletin, 4*(2), 200–206.

Jones, E.E., & Davis, K.E. (1965). From acts to dispositions: The attribution process in person perception. In L. Berkowitz (Ed.), *Advances in experimental social psychology* (Vol. 2, pp. 219–266). New York: Academic Press.

Jones, E.E., Davis, K.E., & Gergen, K.J. (1961). Role playing variations and their informational value for person perception. *Journal of Abnormal and Social Psychology, 3*, 302–310.

Jones, E.E., & Harris, V.A. (1967). The attribution of attitudes. *Journal of Experimental Social Psychology, 3*, 1–24.

Jones, E.E., & Nisbett, R.E. (1971). The actor and the observer: Divergent perceptions of the causes of behavior. In E.E. Jones, D.E. Kanouse, H.H. Kelley, R.E. Nisbett, S. Valins, & B. Weiner (Eds.), *Attribution: Perceiving causes of behavior*. Morristown, NJ: General Learning Press.

Jones, E.E., & Pittman, T.S. (1982). Toward a general theory of strategic self-presentation. In J. Suls (Ed.), *Psychological perspectives on the self* (Vol. 1, pp. 231–262). Hillsdale, NJ: Erlbaum.

Jordan, C.H., Spencer, S.J., Zanna, M.P., Hoshino-Browne, E., & Correll, J. (2003). Secure and defensive high self-esteem. *Journal of Personality and Social Psychology, 85*, 969–978.

Jost, J.T., Banaji, M.R., & Nosek, B.A. (2004). A decade of system justification theory: Accumulated evidence of conscious and unconscious bolstering of the status quo. *Political Psychology, 25*, 881–919.

Jost, J.T., Glaser, J., Kruglanski, A.W., & Sulloway, F.J. (2003). Political conservatism as motivated social cognition. *Psychological Bulletin, 129*, 339–375.

Jost, J. T., Pelham, B. W., Brett, W., & Carvallo, M. R. (2002). Non-conscious forms of system justification: Implicit and behavioral preferences for higher status groups. *Journal of Experimental Social Psychology, 38*, 586-602.

Jost, J. T., Pelham, B. W., Sheldon, O., & Sullivan, B. N. (2003). Social inequality and the reduction of ideological dissonance on behalf of the system: Evidence of enhanced system justification among the disadvantaged. *European Journal of Social Psychology, 33*, 13-36.

Jourard, S. M. (1964). *The transparent self*. Princeton, NJ: Van Nostrand.

Judd, C. M., James-Hawkins, L., Yzerbyt, V., & Kashima, Y. (2005). Fundamental dimensions of social judgment: Understanding the relations between judgments of competence and warmth. *Journal of Personality and Social Psychology, 89*, 899-913.

Judge, T. A., Bono, J. E., Ilies, R., & Gerhardt, M. W. (2002). Personality and leadership: A qualitative and quantitative review. *Journal of Applied Psychology, 87*, 765-780.

Jussim, L. (1986). Self-fulfilling prophecies: A theoretical and integrative review. *Psychological Review, 93*, 429-445.

Jussim, L., Eccles, J., & Madon, S. J. (1996). Social perception, social stereotypes, and teacher expectations: Accuracy and the quest for the powerful self-fulfilling prophecy. *Advances in Experimental Social Psychology, 29*, 281-388.

Jussim, L., & Harber, K. D. (2005). Teacher expectations and self-fulfilling prophecies: Knowns and unknowns, resolved and unresolved controversies. *Personality and Social Psychology Review, 9*, 131-155.

Kahneman, D., Knetsch, J. L., & Thaler, R. (1986). Fairness and the assumptions of economics. *Journal of Business, 59*, S285-S300.

Kahneman, D., Knetsch, J. L., & Thaler, R. (1991). The endowment effect, loss aversion, and status quo bias. *Journal of Economic Perspectives, 5*, 193-206.

Kahneman, D., & Tversky, A. (1972). Subjective probability: A judgment of representativeness. *Cognitive Psychology, 3*, 207-232.

Kanagawa, C., Cross, S. E., & Markus, H. R. (2001). "Who am I?" The cultural psychology of the conceptual self. *Personality and Social Psychology Bulletin, 27*, 90-103.

Kanin, E. J., Davidson, K. D., & Scheck, S. R. (1970). A research note on male-female differentials in the experience of heterosexual love. *Journal of Sex Research, 6*, 64-72.

Kanouse, D. E., & Hanson, L. R. (1971). *Negativity in evaluations*. Morristown, NJ: General Learning Press.

Karau, S. J., & Williams, K. D. (1993). Social loafing: A meta-analytic review and theoretical integration. *Journal of Personality and Social Psychology, 65*, 681-706.

Karney, B. R., & Bradbury, T. N. (1997). Neuroticism, marital interaction, and the trajectory of marital satisfaction. *Journal of Personality and Social Psychology, 72*, 1074-1092.

Karney, B. R., & Bradbury, T. N. (2000). Attributions in marriage: State or trait? A growth curve analysis. *Journal of Personality and Social Psychology, 78*, 295-309.

Kashima, Y., & Kashima, E. S. (2003). Individualism, GNP, climate, and pronoun drop: Is individualism determined by affluence and climate, or does language use play a role? *Journal of CrossCultural Psychology, 34*, 125-134.

Kassam, K. S., Morewedge, C. K., Gilbert, D. T., & Wilson, T. D. (2011). Winners love winning and losers love money. *Psychological Science, 22*, 602-606.

Kassin, S. M., Ellsworth, P. C., & Smith, V. L. (1989). The "general acceptance" of psychological research on eyewitness testimony: A survey of the experts. *American Psychologist, 44*(8), 1089-1098.

Katz, D., McClintock, C., & Sarnoff, I. (1957). The measurement of ego defense as related to attitude change. *Journal of Personality, 25*, 465-474.

Katz, I., Glucksberg, S., & Krauss, R. (1960). Need satisfaction and Edwards PPS scores in married couples. *Journal of Consulting Psychology, 24*, 205-208.

Kay, A. C., & Friesen, J. (2011). On social stability and social change: Understanding when system justification does and does not occur. *Current Directions in Psychological Science, 20*, 360-364.

Kay, A. C., & Jost, J. T. (2003). Complementary justice: Effects of "poor but happy" and "poor but honest" stereotype exemplars on system justification and implicit activation of the justice motive. *Journal of Personality and Social Psychology, 85*(5), 823-837.

Kay, A. C., Jost, J. T., & Young, S. (2005). Victim derogation and victim enhancement as alternate routes to system justification. *Psychological Science, 16*, 240-246.

Kelley, H. H. (1950). The warm-cold variable in first impressions of persons. *Journal of Personality, 18*, 431-439.

Kelley, H. H. (1967). Attribution in social psychology. *Nebraska Symposium on Motivation, 15*, 192-238.

Kelley, H. H., & Stahelski, A. J. (1970). Social interaction basis of cooperators' and competitors' beliefs about others. *Journal of Personality and Social Psychology, 16*, 66-91.

Kelley, H. H., & Thibaut, J. W. (1954). Group problem solving. In G. Lindzey & E. Aronson (Eds.), *The handbook of social psychology* (2nd ed., pp. 1-101). Reading, MA: Addison-Wesley.

Kelley, H. H., & Thibaut, J. W. (1978). *Interpersonal relations: A theory of interdependence*. New York: Wiley.

Kelly, G. A. (1955). *The psychology of personal constructs*. New York: Norton.

Kelman, H. C. (1973). Violence without moral restraint: Reflections on the dehumanization of victims and victimizers. *Journal of Social Issues, 29*, 25-61.

Kelso, J.A.S. (1995). *Dynamic patterns: The self-organization of brain and behavior*. Cambridge, MA: MIT Press.

Keltner, D., & Anderson, C. (2000). Saving face for Darwin: Functions and uses of embarrassment. *Current Directions in Psychological Science, 9*, 187-191.

Keltner, D., & Haidt, J. (1999). Social functions of emotions at four levels of analysis. *Cognition and Emotion, 13*, 505-521.

Keltner, D., Ellsworth, P.C., & Edwards, K. (1993). Beyond simple pessimism: Effects of sadness and anger on social perception. *Journal of Personality and Social Psychology, 64*, 740-752.

Keltner, D., Moffitt, T., & Stouthamer-Loeber, M. (1995). Facial expressions of emotion and psychopathology in adolescent boys. *Journal of Abnormal Psychology, 104*, 644-652.

Kenrick, D.T. (2012). Evolutionary theory and human social behavior. In P.A.M. Van Lange, A.W. Kruglanski, & E.T. Higgins (Eds.), *Handbook of theories of social psychology* (pp. 11-31). Thousand Oaks, CA: Sage Publications.

Kenrick, D.T., Groth, G.R., Trost, M.R., & Sadalla, E.K. (1993). Integrating evolutionary and social exchange perspectives on relationships: Effects of gender, self-appraisal, and involvement level on mate selection criteria. *Journal of Personality and Social Psychology, 64*, 951-969.

Kernis, M.H. (2003). Toward a conceptualization of optimal self-esteem. *Psychological Inquiry, 14*, 1-26.

Kernis, M.H., & Waschull, S.B. (1995). The interactive roles of stability and level of self-esteem: Research and theory. In M.P. Zanna (Ed.), *Advances in experimental social psychology* (Vol. 27, pp. 93-141). San Diego: Academic Press.

Kiesler, C. A. (1971). *The psychology of commitment: Experiments linking behavior to belief*. New York: Academic Press.

Kiesler, C.A., & Kiesler, S.B. (1976). *Conformity* (2nd ed.). Reading, MA: Addison-Wesley.

Kiesler, C.A., & Pallak, M.S. (1975). Minority influence: The effect of majority reactionaries and defectors, and minority and majority compromisers, upon majority opinion and attraction. *European Journal of Social Psychology, 5*, 237-256.

Kihlstrom, J.F. (1987). The cognitive unconscious. *Science, 237*, 1445-1452.

Kihlstrom, J.F. (1996). The trauma-memory argument and recovered memory therapy. In K. Pezdek & W.P. Banks (Eds.), *The recovered memory/false memory debate* (pp. 297-311). San Diego, CA: Academic Press.

Kilham, W., & Mann, L. (1974). Level of destructive obedience as function of transmitter and executant roles in the Milgram obedience paradigm. *Journal of Personality and Social Psychology, 29*, 696-702.

Kim, K., & Markman, A.B. (2006). Differences in fear of isolation as an explanation of cultural differences: Evidence from memory and reasoning. *Journal of Experimental Social Psychology, 42*, 350-364.

Kim, M.P., & Rosenberg, S. (1980). Comparison of two structural models of implicit personality theory. *Journal of Personality and Social Psychology, 38*, 375-389.

Kinder, D.R., & Sears, D.O. (1981). Prejudice and politics: Symbolic racism versus racial threats to the good life. *Journal of Personality and Social Psychology, 40*, 414-431.

Kipnis, D. (1972). Does power corrupt? *Journal of Personality and Social Psychology, 24*, 33-41.

Kirkpatrick, L.A., & Hazan, C. (1994). Attachment styles and close relationships: A four-year prospective study. *Personal Relationships, 1*, 123-142.

Kirkpatrick, L. A., & Shaver, P. (1988). Fear and affiliation reconsidered from a stress and coping perspective: The importance of cognitive clarity. *Journal of Social and Clinical Psychology, 7*, 214-233.

Kitayama, S., Duffy, S., Kawamura, T., & Larsen, J.T. (2003). Perceiving an object and its context in different cultures: A cultural look at new look. *Psychological Science, 14*(3), 201-206.

Kitayama, S., & Masuda, T. (1997). The cultural mediation model of social inference: A cultural psychological analysis of correspondence bias. In K. Kashiwagi, S. Kitayama, & H. Azuma (Eds.), *Cultural psychology: Theory and empirical research* (pp. 109-127). Tokyo: Tokyo University Press.

Klauer, K.C., & Meiser, T. (2000). A source-monitoring analysis of illusory correlations. *Personality and Social Psychology Bulletin, 26*, 1074-1093.

Klayman, J., & Ha, Y. (1987). Confirmation, disconfirmation, and information in hypothesis testing. *Psychological Review, 94*, 211-228.

Klohen, E.C., & Bera, S.J. (1998). Behavioral and experiential patterns of avoidantly and securely attached women across adulthood: A 30-year longitudinal perspective. *Journal of Personality and Social Psychology, 74*, 211-223.

Kluegel, J.R., & Smith, E.R. (1986). *Beliefs about inequality: Americans' views of what is and what ought to be*. Hawthorne, NY: Aldine de Gruyter.

Knapp, M.L., & Hall, J.A. (1997). *Nonverbal communication in human interaction*. Orlando, FL: Harcourt Brace.

Knapp, M.L., & Hall, J.A. (2006). *Nonverbal communication in human interaction*. Belmont, CA: Thomson Wadsworth.

Knight, J.A., & Vallacher, R.R. (1981). Interpersonal engagement in social perception: The consequences of getting into the action. *Journal of Personality and Social Psychology, 40*, 990-999.

Kogan, A., Impett, E.A., Oveis, C., Hui, B., Gordon, A.M., & Keltner, D. (2010). When giving feels good: The intrinsic benefits of sacrifice in romantic relationships for the communally motivated. *Psychological Science, 21*, 1918-1924.

Kohlberg, L. (1969). Stage and sequence: The cognitive-developmental approach to socialization. In D. A. Goslin (Ed.), *Handbook of socialization theory and research* (pp. 347–480). Chicago: Rand McNally.

Kolditz, T. A., & Arkin, R. M. (1982). An impression management interpretation of the self-handicapping strategy. *Journal of Personality and Social Psychology, 43*, 364–373.

Komorita, S. S., & Parks, C. D. (1996). *Social dilemmas*. Boulder, CO: Westview Press.

Konrath, S., Bushman, B., & Campbell, W. K. (2006). Attenuating the link between threatened egotism and aggression. *Psychological Science, 17*, 995–1001.

Kosfeld, M., Heinrichs, M., Zak, P. J., Fishacher, U., & Fehr, E. (2005). Oxytocin increases trust in humans. *Nature, 435*, 673–676.

Kosinski, M., Matz, S. C., Gosling, S. D., Popov, V., & Stillwell, D. (2015). Facebook as a research tool for the social sciences: Opportunities, challenges, ethical considerations, and practical guidelines. *American Psychologist, 70*, 543–556.

Kosinski, M., Wang, Y., Lakkaraju, H., & Leskovec, J. (2016). Mining Big Data to extract patterns and predict real-life outcomes. *Psychological Methods, 21*(4), 493–506.

Kozak, M. N., Marsh, A. A., & Wegner, D. M. (2006). What do I think you're doing? Action identification and mind attribution. *Journal of Personality and Social Psychology, 90*, 543–555.

Kraus, M. W., Piff, P. K., & Keltner, D. (2009). Social class, the sense of control, and social explanation. *Journal of Personality and Social Psychology, 97*, 992–1004.

Kraus, M. W., Côté, S., & Keltner, D. (2010). Social class, contextualism, and empathic accuracy. *Psychological Science, 21*, 1716–1723.

Kravitz, D. A., & Martin, B. (1986). Ringelman rediscovered: The original article. *Journal of Personality and Social Psychology, 50*, 936–941.

Krebs, D. (1970). Altruism: An examination of the concept and review of the literature. *Psychological Bulletin, 73*, 258–302.

Krems, J. A., Neel, R., Neuberg, S. L., Puts, D. A., & Kenrick, D. T. (2016). Women selectively guard their (desirable) mates from ovulating women. *Journal of Personality and Social Psychology, 110*, 551–553.

Krueger, J., & Clement, R. W. (1997). Estimates of social consensus by majorities and minorities: The case for social projection. *Personality and Social Psychology Review, 1*, 299–313.

Kruglanski, A. W., & Freund, T. (1983). The freezing and unfreezing of lay inferences: Effects of impressional primacy, ethnic stereotyping and numerical anchoring. *Journal of Experimental Social Psychology, 19*, 448–468.

Kruglanski, A. W., Pierro, A., Mannetti, L., & De Grada, E. (2006). Groups as epistemic providers: Need for closure and the unfolding of group-centrism. *Psychological Review, 113*, 84–100.

Kruglanski, A. W., & Webster, D. M. (1991). Group members' reactions to opinion deviates and conformists at varying degrees of proximity to decision deadline and environmental noise. *Journal of Personality and Social Psychology, 61*, 212–225.

Kruglanski, A. W., & Webster, D. M. (1996). Motivated closing of the mind: "Seizing" and "Freezing." *Psychological Review, 103*, 263–283.

Krull, D. S., Loy, M. H. M., Lin, J., Wang, C. F., Chen, S., & Zhao, X. (1999). The fundamental fundamental attribution error: Correspondence bias in individualist and collectivist cultures. *Personality and Social Psychology Bulletin, 23*, 1208–1219.

Kuhn, T. S. (1970). *The structure of scientific revolutions* (2nd ed.). Chicago: University of Chicago Press.

Kumkale, G. T., & Albarracin, D. (2004). The sleeper effect in persuasion: A meta-analytic review. *Psychological Bulletin, 130*, 143–172.

Kunda, Z. (1990). The case for motivated reasoning. *Psychological Bulletin, 108*, 480–496.

Kunda, Z., & Oleson, K. C. (1995). Maintaining stereotypes in the face of disconfirmation: Constructing grounds for subtyping deviants. *Journal of Personality and Social Psychology, 68*, 565–579.

Kuppens, P., Oravecz, Z., & Tuerlinckz, F. (2010). Feelings change: Accounting for individual differences in the temporal dynamics of affect. *Journal of Personality and Social Psychology, 99*, 1042–1060.

Kuppens, P., Van Mechelen, I., Nezlek, J. B., Dossche, D., & Timmermans, T. (2007). Individual differences in core affect variability and their relationship to personality and adjustment. *Emotion, 7*, 262–274.

Kurdek, L. A. (1993). Predicting marital dissolution: A 5-year prospective longitudinal study of newlywed couples. *Journal of Personality and Social Psychology, 64*, 221–242.

Kurtz, J. (2008). Looking to the future to appreciate the present: The benefits of perceived temporal scarcity. *Psychological Science, 19*, 1238–1241.

Kuusinen, J. (1969). Factorial invariance of personality ratings. *Scandinavian Journal of Psychology, 10*, 33–44.

Labuda, D., Lefebvre, J. F., Nadeau, P., & Roy-Gagnon, M. H. (2010). Female-to-male breeding ratio in modern humans: An analysis based on historical recombinations. *The American Journal of Human Genetics, 86*, 353–363.

LaFrance, M. (1979). Nonverbal synchrony and rapport: Analysis by the cross-lag panel technique. *Social Psychology Quarterly, 42*, 66–70.

Laird, J. D., & Bresler, C. (1992). The process of emotional feeling: A self-perception theory. In M. Clark (Ed.), *Emotion: Review of Personality and Social Psychology, 13*, 213–234.

Lakin, J. L., & Chartrand, T. L. (2003). Using nonconscious behavioral mimicry to create affiliation and rapport. *Psychological Science, 14*, 334–339.

Lakin, J.L., Jefferis, V.E., Cheng, C.M., & Chartrand, T.L. (2003). The chameleon effect as social glue: Evidence for the evolutionary significance of nonconscious mimicry. *Journal of Nonverbal Behavior, 27*(3), 145-162.

Lambert, A.J., Khan, S.R., Lickel, B.A., & Fricke, K. (1997). Mood and the correction of positive versus negative stereotypes. *Journal of Personality and Social Psychology, 72*, 1002-1016.

Lamm, H., & Ochssmann, R. (1972). Factors limiting the generality of the risky-shift phenomenon. *European Journal of Social Psychology, 2*, 99-102.

Lamm, H., & Sauer, C. (1974). Discussion-induced shift towards higher demands in negotiation. *European Journal of Social Psychology, 4*, 85-88.

Lammers, J., Janka, I., Stoker, J.I., Jordan, J., Pollmann, M., & Stapel, D.A. (2011). Power increases infidelity among men and women. *Psychological Science, 22*, 1191-1197.

Lammers, J., Stapel, D.A., & Galinsky, A.D. (2010). Power increases hypocrisy: Moralizing in reasoning, immorality in Behavior. *Psychological Science, 21*(5), 737-744.

Landau, M.J., Solomon, S., Greenberg, J., Cohen, F., Pyszczynski, T., Arndt, J., Miller, C.H., Olgilvie, D.M., & Cook, A. (2004). Deliver us from evil: The effects of mortality salience and reminders of 9/11 on support for George W. Bush. *Personality and Social Psychology Bulletin, 30*(9), 1136-1150.

Lane, K.A., Banaji, M.R., Nosek, B.A., & Greenwald, A.G. (2007). Understanding and using the implicit association test: IV: Procedures and validity. In B. Wittenbrink & N. Schwarz (Eds.), *Implicit measures of attitudes: Procedures and controversies* (pp. 59-102). New York: Guilford Press.

Lange, C.G., & James, W. (1922). *The emotions.* Baltimore, MD: Williams and Wilkins.

Langer, E.J. (1975). The illusion of control. *Journal of Personality and Social Psychology, 32*, 311-328.

Langer, E.J., & Rodin, J. (1976). The effects of choice and enhanced personal responsibility for the aged: A field experiment in an institutional setting. *Journal of Personality and Social Psychology, 34*, 191-198.

Langlois, J.H., & Roggman, L.A. (1990). Attractive faces are only average. *Psychological Science, 1*(2), 115-121.

Langlois, J.H., Ritter, J.M., Roggman, L.A., & Vaughan, L.S. (1991). Facial diversity and infant preferences for attractive faces. *Developmental Psychology, 27*, 79-84.

LaPiere, R.T. (1934). Attitude and actions. *Social Forces, 13*, 230-237.

Larsen, R.J. (1987). The stability of mood variability: A spectral analytic approach to daily mood assessments. *Journal of Personality and Social Psychology, 52*, 1195-1204.

Larsen, R.J. (2000). Towards a science of mood regulation. *Psychological Inquiry, 11*, 129-141.

Larsen, R.J., Csikszentmihalyi, M., & Graef, R. (1982). Time alone in daily experience: Loneliness or renewal? In L.A. Peplau & D. Perlman (Eds.), *Loneliness: A sourcebook of current theory, research, and therapy.* New York: Wiley.

Larsen, R.J., & Diener, E. (1985). A multitrait-multimethod examination of affect structure: Hedonic level and emotional intensity. *Personality and Individual Differences, 6*, 631-636.

Larsen, R.J., & Diener, E. (1987). Affect intensity as an individual difference characteristic: A review. *Journal of Research in Personality, 21*, 1-39.

Larsen, R.J., Diener, E., & Emmons, R.A. (1986). Affect intensity and reactions to daily life events. *Journal of Personality and Social Psychology, 51*, 803-814.

Larwood, L. (1978). Swine flu: A field study of self-serving biases. *Journal of Applied Social Psychology, 18*, 283-289.

Latané, B. (1981). The psychology of social impact. *American Psychologist, 36*, 343-356.

Latané, B., & Darley, J.M. (1968). Group inhibition of bystander intervention in emergencies. *Journal of Personality and Social Psychology, 10*, 215-221.

Latané, B., & Darley, J.M. (1970). *The unresponsive bystander: Why doesn't he help?* New York: Appleton-Century-Crofts.

Latané, B., & Nida, S. (1981). Ten years of research on group size and helping. *Psychological Bulletin, 89*, 308-324.

Latané, B., & Nowak, A. (1994). Attitudes as catastrophes: From dimensions to categories with increasing involvement. In R.R. Vallacher & A. Nowak (Eds.), *Dynamical systems in social psychology* (pp. 219-249). San Diego: Academic Press.

Latané, B., Nowak, A., & Liu, J. (1994). Measuring emergent social phenomena: Dynamism, polarization and clustering as order parameters of social systems. *Behavioral Science, 39*, 1-24.

Latané, B., Williams, K., & Harkins, S. (1979). Many hands make light work: The causes and consequences of social loafing. *Journal of Personality and Social Psychology, 37*, 822-832.

Laughlin, P.R., & Ellis, A.L. (1986). Demonstrability and social combination processes on mathematical intellective tasks. *Journal of Experimental Social Psychology, 22*, 177-189.

Laumann, E.O., Gagnon, J.H., Michael, R.T., & Michaels, S. (1994). *The social organization of sexuality: Sexual practices in the United States.* Chicago: University of Chicago Press.

Lawrence, K.O. (Ed.). (2011). *Race, crime, and punishment: Breaking the connection in America.* http://www.aspeninstitute.org/publications/race-crime-punishment-breaking-connection-america.

Lawson, A. (1988). *Adultery: An analysis of love and betrayal.* New York: Basic Books.

Lazarus, R.S. (1966). *Psychological stress and the coping process.* New York: McGraw-Hill.

Leander, N.P., Chartrand, T.L., & Bargh, J.A. (2012). You give me the chills: Embodied reactions to inappropriate amounts of behavioral mimicry. *Psychological Science, 23*(7), 772-779.

Leary, M.R. (1995). *Self-presentation: Impression management and interpersonal behavior.* Dubuque, IA: Brown & Benchmark.

Leary, M.R., Britt, T.W., Cutlip, W.D.I., & Templeton, J.L. (1992). Social blushing. *Psychological Bulletin, 112,* 446-460.

Leary, M.R., Kowalski, R.M., & Smith, L. (2003). Teasing, rejection, and violence: Case studies of the school shootings. *Aggressive Behavior, 29,* 202-214.

Leary, M.R., Tambor, E.S., Terdal, S.K., & Downs, D.L. (1995). Self-esteem as an interpersonal monitor: The sociometer hypothesis. *Journal of Personality and Social Psychology, 68,* 518-530.

Le Bon, G. (1895). *The crowd.* London: Unwin.

LeDoux, J.E. (1996). *The emotional brain: The mysterious underpinnings of emotional life.* New York: Simon & Schuster.

Lee, A.Y., & Aaker, J.L. (2004). Bringing the frame into focus: The influence of regulatory fit on processing fluency and persuasion. *Journal of Personality and Social Psychology, 86,* 205-218.

Lee, Y., & Seligman, M.E.P. (1997). Are Americans more optimistic than the Chinese? *Personality and Social Psychology Bulletin, 23,* 32-40.

Lefcourt, H.M. (1976). *Locus of control: Current trends in theory and research.* Hillsdale, NJ: Erlbaum.

Legate, N., DeHean, C.R., Weinstein, N., & Ryan, R.M. (2013). Hurting you hurts me too: The psychological costs of complying with ostracism. *Psychological Science, 24,* 583-588.

Lehman, B., & Crano, W.D. (2002). The pervasive effects of vested interest on attitude-criterion consistency in political judgment. *Journal of Experimental Social Psychology, 38,* 101-112.

Leotti, L.A., & Delgado, M.R. (2011). The inherent reward of choice. *Psychological Science, 22,* 1310-1318.

Lepore, L., & Brown, R. (2002). The role of awareness: Divergent automatic stereotype activation and implicit judgment correction. *Social Cognition, 20,* 321-351.

Lepper, M.R., & Greene, D. (Eds.). (1978). *The hidden costs of reward.* Hillsdale, NJ: Erlbaum.

Lepper, M.R., Greene, D., & Nisbett, R.E. (1973). Undermining children's intrinsic interest with extrinsic rewards: A test of the "overjustification" hypothesis. *Journal of Personality and Social Psychology, 28,* 129-137.

Lepper, M.R., Ross, L., Vallone, R., & Keavney, M. (1981). Biased perceptions of victory and media hostility in network coverage of presidential debates. (Unpublished data cited in Vallone, R.E., Ross, L., & Lepper, M.R. (1985). The hostile media phenomenon: Biased perception and perceptions of media bias in coverage of the "Beirut Massacre." *Journal of Personality and Social Psychology, 49,* 577-585).

Lerner, J.S., & Gonzales, R.M. (2005). Forecasting one's future based on fleeting subjective experiences. *Personality and Social Psychology Bulletin, 31,* 454-466.

Lerner, J.S., Gonzales, R.M., Small, D.A., & Fischhoff, B. (2003). Effects of fear and anger on perceived risks of terrorism: A national field experiment. *Psychology Science, 14,* 144-150.

Lerner, J.S., & Keltner, D. (2001). Fear, anger, and risk. *Journal of Personality and Social Psychology, 81,* 146-159.

Lerner, M.J. (1980). *The belief in a just world: A fundamental delusion.* New York: Plenum Press.

Lerner, M.J. (1991). The belief in a just world and the "heroic motive." *International Journal for the Psychology of Religion, 1,* 27-32.

Lerner, M.J., & Miller, D.T. (1978). Just world research and the attribution process: Looking back and ahead. *Psychological Bulletin, 85,* 1030-1051.

Lerner, M.J., & Simmons, C.H. (1966). Observer's reaction to the "innocent victim": Compassion or rejection. *Journal of Personality and Social Psychology, 4,* 203-210.

Levenson, R.W. (2003). Autonomic specificity and emotion. In R.J. Davidson, K.R. Sherer, & H.H. Goldsmith (Eds.), *Handbook of affective sciences* (pp.212-224). New York: Oxford University Press.

Levenson, R.W., Carstensen, L.L., Friesen, W.V., & Ekman, P. (1991). Emotion, physiology, and expression in old age. *Psychology and Aging, 6,* 28-35.

Levenson, R.W., Ekman, P., & Friesen, W.V. (1990). Voluntary facial action generates emotion-specific autonomic nervous system activity. *Psychophysiology, 27,* 363-384.

Levenson, R.W., Ekman, P., Heider, K., & Friesen, W.V. (1992). Emotion and autonomic nervous system activity in the Minangkabau of West Sumatra. *Journal of Personality and Social Psychology, 62,* 972-988.

Leventhal, H., Watts, J.C., & Pagano, F. (1967). Effects of fear and instructions on how to cope with danger. *Journal of Personality and Social Psychology, 6,* 313-321.

Levin, D.T. (2000). Race as a visual feature: Using visual search perceptual discrimination tasks to understand face categories and the cross-race recognition deficit. *Journal of Experimental Psychology: General, 129,* 559-574.

Levine, J.M., & Ranelli, C.J. (1978). Majority reaction to shifting and stable attitudinal deviates. *European Journal of Social Psychology, 8*, 55–70.

Levine, R.V. (2003). *The power of persuasion: How we're bought and sold*. New York: John Wiley & Sons.

Levy, K.N., & Kelly, K.K. (2010). Sex differences in jealousy: A contribution from attachment theory. *Psychological Science, 21*, 168–173.

Lewenstein, M., Nowak, A., & Latané, B. (1993). Statistical mechanics of social impact. *Physics Review A, 45*, 703–716.

Lewin, K. (1935). *A dynamic theory of personality: Selected papers* (D.K. Adams & K.E. Zener, trans.). New York: McGraw-Hill.

Lewin, K. (1948). *Resolving social conflicts: Selected papers on group dynamics*. New York: Harper & Brothers.

Lewin, K., Lippit, R., & White, R.K. (1939). Patterns of aggressive behavior in experimentally created "social climates." *Journal of Social Psychology, 10*, 271–279.

Lewis, G.J., & Bates, T.C. (2010). Genetic evidence for multiple biological mechanisms underlying in-group favoritism. *Psychological Science, 21*, 1623–1628.

Lewis, M. (1986). Origins of self-knowledge and individual differences in early self-recognition. In A.G. Greenwald & J. Suls (Eds.), *Psychological perspectives on the self* (Vol. 3, pp. 55–78). Hillsdale, NJ: Erlbaum.

Lewis, M. (1990). Self-knowledge and social development in early life. In L.A. Pervin (Ed.), *Handbook of personality* (pp. 277–300). New York: Guilford Press.

Lewis, M. (1995). Embarrassment: The emotion of self-exposure and evaluation. In J. Tangney & K. Fischer (Eds.), *Self-conscious emotions: The psychology of shame, guilt, pride, and embarrassment* (pp. 198–252). New York: Guilford.

Leyens, J.P., Camino, L., Parke, R.D., & Berkowitz, L. (1975). Effects of movie violence on aggression in a field setting as a function of group dominance and cohesion. *Journal of Personality and Social Psychology, 32*, 346–360.

Leyens, J.P., & Pincus, S. (1973). Identification with the winner of a fight and name mediation: Their differential effects upon subsequent aggressive behavior. *British Journal of Social and Clinical Psychology, 12*, 374–377.

Liberman, A., & Chaiken, S. (1992). Defensive processing of personally relevant health messages. *Personality and Social Psychology Bulletin, 18*, 669–679.

Libet, B. (1985). Unconscious cerebral initiative and the role of conscious will in voluntary action. *Behavioral and Brain Sciences, 8*, 529–566.

Libet, B. (1999). Do we have free will? *Journal of Consciousness Studies, 6*, 47–57.

Lieberman, D., Tooby, J., & Cosmides, L. (2003). Does morality have a biological basis? An empirical test of the factors governing moral sentiments relating to incest. *Proceedings of the Royal Society B: Biological Sciences, 270*(1517), 819.

Lieberman, M.D. (2007). Social cognitive neuroscience: A review of core processes. *Annual Review of Psychology, 58*, 259–289.

Lieberman, M.D., Jarcho, J.M., & Obayashi, J. (2005). Attributional Inference across cultures: Similar automatic attributions and different controlled corrections. *Personality and Social Psychology Bulletin, 31*, 889–901.

Liebrand, W.B.G., Nowak, A., & Hegselman, R. (Eds.). (1998). *Computer modeling of social processes*. London: Sage.

Liebrand, W.B.G., Wilke, H.A.M., & Wolters, F.I.M. (1986). Value orientation and conformity: A study using three types of social dilemma games. *Journal of Conflict Resolution, 30*, 77–97.

Linder, D.E., Cooper, J., & Jones, E.E. (1967). Decision freedom as a determinant of the role of incentive magnitude in attitude change. *Journal of Personality and Social Psychology, 6*, 245–254.

Lindsay, D.S., Read, J.D., & Sharma, K. (1998). Accuracy and confidence in person identification: The relationship is strong when witnessing conditions vary widely. *Psychological Science, 9*, 215–218.

Lindsay, R.C.L., Wells, G.L., & Rumpel, C.M. (1981). Can people detect eyewitness-identification accuracy within and across situations? *Journal of Applied Psychology, 66*, 79–89.

Lindsay-Hartz, J. (1984). Contrasting experiences of shame and guilt. *American Behavioral Scientist, 27*, 689–704.

Linville, P.W. (1987). Self-complexity as a cognitive bugger against stress-related illness and depression. *Journal of Personality and Social Psychology, 52*, 663–676.

Linville, P.W., Fischer, G.W., & Salovey, P. (1989). Perceived distributions of the characteristics of in-group and out-group members: Empirical evidence and a computer simulation. *Journal of Personality and Social Psychology, 57*, 165–188.

Liu, J., Vohs, K.D., & Smeesters, D. (2011). Money and mimicry: When being mimicked makes people feel threatened. *Psychological Science, 22*, 1150–1151.

Lockwood, P. (2002). Could it happen to you? Predicting the impact of downward social comparisons on the self. *Journal of Personality and Social Psychology, 82*, 343–358.

Loeber, R., & Hay, D. (1997). Key issues in the development of aggression and violence from childhood to early adulthood. *Annual Review of Psychology*, 371–410.

Loewenstein, G., & Lerner, J.S. (2003). The role of affect in decision making. In R.J. Davidson, K.R. Scherer, & H.H. Goldsmith (Eds.), *Handbook of affective sciences* (pp. 619–642). New York: Oxford University Press.

Loftus, E.F. (1979). *Eyewitness testimony*. Cambridge, MA: Harvard University Press.

Loftus, E.R. (1993). The reality of repressed memories. *American Psychologist, 48*, 518–537.

Lombardi, W. J., Higgins, E. T., & Bargh, J. A. (1987). The role of consciousness in priming effects on categorization: Assimilation versus contrast as a function of awareness of the priming task. *Personality and Social Psychology Bulletin*, *13*, 411-429.

Lopes, P. N., Brackett, M. A., Nezlek, J. B., Schütz, A., Sellin, I., & Salovey, P. (2004). Emotional intelligence and social interaction. *Personality and Social Psychology Bulletin*, *30*, 1018-1034.

Lord, C. G., Ross, L., & Lepper, M. (1979). Biased assimilation and attitude polarization: The effects of prior theories on subsequently considered evidence. *Journal of Personality and Social Psychology*, *37*, 2098-2109.

Lord, C. G., Scott, K., Pugh, M. A., & Desforges, D. M. (1997). Leakage beliefs and the correspondence bias. *Personality and Social Psychology Bulletin*, *23*, 824-836.

Lorenz, E. (1963). Deterministic nonperiodic flow. *Journal of Atmospheric Science*, *20*, 282-293.

Lorenz, K. (1950/1971). *Studies in animal and human behavior*. Cambridge, MA: Harvard University Press.

Lorenzo, G. L., Biesanz, J. C., & Human, L. J. (2010). What is beautiful is good and more accurately understood: Physical attractiveness and accuracy in first impressions of personality. *Psychological Science*, *21*, 1777-1782.

Lucas, R. E., Clark, A. E., Georgellis, Y., & Diener, E. (2003). Reexamining adaptation and the set point model of happiness: Reactions to changes in marital status. *Journal of Personality and Social Psychology*, *84*, 527-539.

Luginbuhl, J., & Mullin, C. (1981). Rape and responsibility: How and how much is the victim blamed? *Sex Roles*, *7*, 547-559.

Lumsdaine, A. A., & Janis, I. L. (1953). Resistance to "counterpropaganda" produced by one-sided and two-sided "propaganda" presentations. *Public Opinion Quarterly*, *17*, 311-318.

Lykken, D. T. (1999). *Happiness: What studies on twins show us about nature, nurture, and the happiness set point*. New York: Golden Books.

Lyubomirsky, S., & Ross, L. (1997). Hedonic consequences of social comparison: A contrast theory of happy and unhappy people. *Journal of Personality and Social Psychology*, *73*, 1141-1157.

Lyubomirsky, S., Sheldon, K. M., & Schkade, D. (2005). Pursuing happiness: The architecture of sustainable change. *Review of General Psychology*, *9*, 11-131.

Lyubomirsky, S., & Tucker, K. (1998). Implications of individual differences in subjective happiness for perceiving, interpreting, and thinking about life events. *Motivation and Emotion*, *22*, 155-186.

Ma, V., & Schoeneman, T. J. (1997). Individualism versus collectivism: A comparison of Kenyan and American self-concepts. *Basic and Applied Social Psychology*, *19*, 261-273.

Maass, A., Ceccarelli, R., & Rudin, S. (1996). The linguistic intergroup bias: Evidence for in-group-protective motivation. *Journal of Personality and Social Psychology*, *71*, 512-526.

Maass, A., & Clark, R. D., III (1984). Hidden impact of minorities: Fifteen years of research. *Psychological Bulletin*, *95*, 428-450.

Maass, A., Clark, R. K., & Haberkorn, G. (1982). The effects of differential ascribed category membership and norms on minority influence. *European Journal of Social Psychology*, *12*, 89-104.

MacCoun, R. J. (2012). The burden of social proof: Shared thresholds and social influence. *Psychological Review*, *119*, 345-372.

Mackie, D. M. (1987). Systematic and nonsystematic processing of majority and minority persuasive communications. *Journal of Personality and Social Psychology*, *53*, 41-52.

Mackie, D. M., Worth, I. T., & Asuncion, A. G. (1990). Processing of persuasive in-group messages. *Journal of Personality and Social Psychology*, *58*, 812-822.

MacNeil, M. K., & Sherif, M. (1976). Norm change over subject generations as a function of arbitrariness of prescribes norms. *Journal of Personality and Social Psychology*, *34*, 762-773.

Maddux, W. W., Mullen, E., & Galinsky, A. D. (2008). Chameleons bake bigger pies and take bigger pieces: Strategic behavioral mimicry facilitates negotiation outcomes. *Journal of Experimental Social Psychology*, *44*(2), 461-468.

Maier, S. F., & Seligman, M. E. P. (1976). Learned helplessness: Theory and evidence. *Journal of Experimental Psychology: General*, *105*, 3-46.

Major, B., & Gramzow, R. H. (1999). Abortion as stigma: Cognitive and emotional implications of concealment. *Journal of Personality and Social Psychology*, *77*, 735-745.

Mandler, G. (1975). *Mind and emotion*. New York: Wiley.

Mandler, G. (2002). *Consciousness recovered: Psychological functions and origins of conscious thought*. Philadelphia, PA: John Benjamins.

Mange, J., Senemeaud, C., & Michinov, N. (2013). Jotting down notes or preparing for the future? Action identification and academic performance. *Social Psychology of Education*, *16*, 151-164.

Manning, J. T., Scutt, D., & Lewis-Jones, D. I. (1998). Developmental stability, ejaculate size, and sperm quality in men. *Evolution and Human Behavior*, *19*, 273-282.

Marcel, A. J. (1983). Conscious and unconscious perception: An approach to the relations between phenomenal experience and perceptual processes. *Cognitive Psychology*, *15*, 238-300.

Marcus-Newhall, A., Pederson, W. C., Carlson, M., & Miller, N. (2000). Displaced aggression in alive and well: A meta-analytic review. *Journal of Personality and Social Psychology*, *78*, 670-689.

Marks-Tarlow, T. (1999). The self as a dynamical system. *Nonlinear Dynamics, Psychology, and Life Sciences*, 3, 311-345.

Markus, H. (1977). Self-schemata and processing information about the self. *Journal of Personality and Social Psychology*, 35, 63-78.

Markus, H., & Kitayama, S. (1991). Culture and the self: Implications for cognition, emotion, and motivation. *Psychological Bulletin*, 98, 224-253.

Markus, H., & Nurius, P. (1986). Possible selves. *American Psychologist*, 41, 954-969.

Markus, H., & Wurf, E. (1987). The dynamic self-concept: A social-psychological perspective. *Annual Review of Psychology*, 38, 299-337.

Marsh, K. L., Johnston, L., Richardson, M. J., & Schmidt, R. C. (2009). Toward a radically embodied, embedded social psychology. *European Journal of Social Psychology*, 39, 1217-1225.

Marsh, K. L., Richardson, M. J., Baron, R. M., & Schmidt, R. C. (2006). Contrasting approaches to perceiving and acting with others. *Ecological Psychology*, 18, 1-37.

Maslow, A. H. (1954). *Motivation and personality*. New York: Harper & Row.

Mast, M. S., Gatica-Perez, D., Frauendorfer, D., Nguyen, L., & Choudhury, T. (2015). Social sensing for psychology: Automated interpersonal behavior assessment. *Current Directions in Psychological Science*, 24, 154-160.

Masuda, T., & Nisbett, R. E. (2001). Attending holistically versus analytically: Comparing the context sensitivity of Japanese and Americans. *Journal of Personality and Social Psychology*, 81, 922-934.

Matsumoto, D., & Ekman, P. (1989). Japanese-American cultural differences in intensity ratings of facial expressions of emotion. *Motivation and Emotion*, 13, 143-157.

Maurer, R. E., & Tindall, J. H. (1983). Effects of postural congruence on client's perception of counselor empathy. *Journal of Counseling Psychology*, 30, 158-163.

Mayer, J. D., Gaschke, Y. N., Braverman, D. L., & Evans, T. (1992). Mood-congruent judgment is a general effect. *Journal of Personality and Social Psychology*, 63, 119-132.

Mayer, J. D., McCormick, L. J., & Strong, S. E. (1995). Mood-congruent memory and natural mood: New evidence. *Personality and Social Psychology Bulletin*, 21, 736-746.

Mayer, J. D., & Salovey, P. (1997). What is emotional intelligence? In P. Salovey & D. Sluyter (Eds.), *Emotional development and emotional intelligence: Implications for educators* (pp. 3-31). New York: Basic Books.

Mayer, J. D., Salovey, P., & Caruso, D. (2002). *Mayer-Salovey-Caruso Emotional Intelligence Test (MSCEIT): User's manual*. Toronto: Multi-Health Systems, Inc.

Mazerolle, M., Regner, I., Morisset, P., Rigalleau, F., & Huguet, P. (2012). Stereotype threat strengthens automatic recall and undermines controlled processes in older adults. *Psychological Science*, 23, 723-727.

Mazur, A., & Booth, A. (1998). Testosterone and dominance in men [Target article and commentaries]. *Behavioral and Brain Sciences*, 21, 353-397.

McAllister, H. A. (1996). Self-serving bias in the classroom: Who shows it? Who knows it? *Journal of Educational Psychology*, 88, 123-131.

McCauley, C. (1989). The nature of social influence in groupthink: Compliance and internalization. *Journal of Personality and Social Psychology*, 57, 250-260.

McConahay, J. B. (1986). Modern racism, ambivalence, and the modern racism scale. In J. F. Dovidio & S. L. Gaertner (Eds.), *Prejudice, discrimination, and racism* (pp. 91-125). Orlando, FL: Academic Press.

McConnell, A. R., & Leibold, J. M. (2001). Relations among the implicit association test, discriminatory behavior, and explicit measures of racial attitudes. *Journal of Experimental Social Psychology*, 37, 435-442.

McCoy, S. K., & Major, B. (2003). Group identification moderates emotional responses to perceived prejudice. *Personality and Social Psychology Bulletin*, 29, 1005-1017.

McCrae, R. R., & John, O. P. (1992). An introduction to the five-factor model and its applications. *Journal of Personality*, 60, 175-216.

McCrea, S. M., Hirt, E. R., & Milner, B. (2008). She works hard for the money: Valuing effort underlies gender differences in behavioral self-handicapping. *Journal of Experimental Social Psychology*, 44, 292-311.

McCrea, S. M., Wieber, F., & Myers, A. L. (2012). Construal level mindsets moderate self and social categorization. *Journal of Personality and Social Psychology*, 102, 51-68.

McCullough, M. E. (2008). *Beyond revenge: The evolution of the forgiveness instinct*. San Francisco, CA: Jossey-Bass.

McDougall, W. (1908). *Introduction to social psychology*. London: Methuen.

McGraw, K. O. (1978). The detrimental effects of reward on performance: A literature review and a prediction model. In M. R. Lepper & D. Greene (Eds.), *The hidden costs of reward* (pp. 33-60). Hillsdale, NJ: Lawrence Erlbaum Associates.

McGuire, W. J. (1986). The myth of massive media impact: Savagings and salvagings. In G. Comstock (Ed.), *Public communication and behavior* (Vol. 1, pp. 173-257). Orlando, FL: Academic Press.

McGuire, W. J., & Padawer-Singer, A. (1978). Trait salience in the spontaneous self-concept. *Journal of Personality and Social Psychology*, 33, 743-754.

McKenna, F. P., & Myers, L. B. (1997). Illusory self-assessments: Can they be reduced? *British Journal of Social Psychology, 88*(1), 39–51. https://doi.org/10.1111/j.2044-8295.1997.tb02619.x

Mead, G. H. (1934). *Mind, self, and society*. Chicago: University of Chicago Press.

Meeus, W. H. J., & Raaijmakers, Q. A. W. (1986). Administrative obedience: Carrying out orders to use psychological-administrative violence. *European Journal of Social Psychology, 16*, 311–324.

Mehrabian, A., & Ferris, S. R. (1967). Inference of attitudes from non-verbal communication in two channels. *Journal of Consulting Psychology, 31*, 248–252.

Mehrabian, A., & Wiener, M. (1967). Decoding of inconsistent communication. *Journal of Personality and Social Psychology, 6*, 109–114.

Mehrabian, A., & Williams, M. (1969). Nonverbal concomitants of perceived and intended persuasiveness. *Journal of Personality and Social Psychology, 13*, 37–58.

Meissner, C. A., & Brigham, J. C. (2001). Thirty years of investigating the own-race bias in memory for faces: A meta-analytic review. *Psychology, Public Policy, and Law, 7*, 3–35.

Merton, R. K. (1957). *Social theory and social structure*. Glencoe, IL: Free Press.

Mesquita, B., & Frijda, N. H. (1992). Cultural variations in emotions: A review. *Psychological Bulletin, 112*, 179–204.

Mesquita, B., & Leu, J. (2007). The cultural psychology of emotion. In S. Kitayama & D. Cohen (Eds.), *The handbook of cultural psychology* (pp. 734–759). New York: Guilford Press.

Messé, L. A. (1971). Equity in bilateral bargaining. *Journal of Personality and Social Psychology, 17*, 287–291.

Messick, D. M., & Liebrand, V. B. G. (1995). Individual heuristics and the dynamics of cooperation in large groups. *Psychological Review, 102*, 131–145.

Messick, D. M., & McClintock, C. G. (1968). Motivational bases of choice in experimental games. *Journal of Experimental Social Psychology, 4*, 1–25.

Mezulis, A. H., Abramson, L. Y., Hyde, J. S., Hankin, B. L. (2004). Is there a universal positivity bias in attributions? A meta-analytic review of individual, developmental, and cultural differences in the self-serving attributional bias. *Psychological Bulletin, 130*, 711–747.

Milgram, S. (1965). Some conditions of obedience and disobedience to authority. *Human Relations, 18*, 57–75.

Milgram, S. (1967). The small world problem. *Psychology Today, 2*, 60–67.

Milgram, S. (1969). Experience in living in cities. *Science, 167*, 1461–1468.

Milgram, S. (1970). The experience of living in cities. *Science, 167*(3924), 1461–1468.

Milgram, S. (1974). *Obedience to authority: An experimental view*. New York: Harper & Row.

Milkman, K. L., Akinola, M., & Chugh, D. (2012). Temporal distance and discrimination: An audit study in academia. *Psychological Science, 23*, 710–717.

Miller, D. T., & Holmes, J. G. (1975). The role of situational restrictiveness on self-fulfilling prophecies: A theoretical and empirical extension of Kelley and Stahelski's triangle hypothesis. *Journal of Personality and Social Psychology, 31*, 661–673.

Miller, D. T., & Ross, M. (1975). Self-serving biases in the attribution of causality: Fact or fiction? *Psychological Bulletin, 82*, 213–225.

Miller, G. A. (1956). The magic number seven plus or minus two: Some limits on our capacity to process information. *Psychological Review, 63*, 81–97.

Miller, G. A., Galanter, E., & Pribram, K. H. (1960). *Plans and the structure of behavior*. New York: Holt.

Miller, J. G. (1984). Culture and the development of everyday social explanation. *Journal of Personality and Social Psychology, 46*, 961–978.

Miller, L. C. (1990). Intimacy and liking: Mutual influence and the role of unique relationships. *Journal of Personality and Social Psychology, 59*, 50–60.

Miller, L. C., Berg, J. H., & Archer, R. L. (1983). Openers: Individuals who elicit intimate self-disclosure. *Journal of Personality and Social Psychology, 44*, 1234–1244.

Miller, N. E. (1941). The frustration-aggression hypothesis. *Psychological Review, 48*(4), 337–342.

Miller, N., & Campbell, D. T. (1959). Recency and primacy in persuasion as a function of the timing of speeches and measurements. *Journal of Abnormal and Social Psychology, 59*, 1–9.

Miller, N., Maruyama, G., Baeber, R. J., & Valone, K. (1976). Speed of speech and persuasion. *Journal of Personality and Social Psychology, 34*, 615–624.

Miller, P. J. E., & Rempel, J. K. (2004). Trust and partner-enhancing attributions in close relationships. *Personality and Social Psychology Bulletin, 30*, 695–705.

Miller, S. L., & Maner, J. K. (2010). Scent of a woman: Men's testosterone responses to olfactory ovulation cues. *Psychological Science, 21*(2), 276–283.

Miller, S. L., & Maner, J. K. (2011). Ovulation as a male mating prime: Subtle signs of female fertility influence men's mating cognition and behavior. *Journal of Personality and Social Psychology, 100*, 295–308.

Millgram, Y., Joormann, J., Huppert, J.D., & Tamir, M. (2015). Sad as a matter of choice? Emotion-regulation goals in depression. *Psychological Science, 26*, 1216-1228.

Mims, P.R., Hartnett, J.J., & Nay, W.R. (1975). Interpersonal attraction and help volunteering as a function of physical attractiveness. *Journal of Psychology, 89*, 125-131.

Mischel, W. (1973). Toward a cognitive social learning reconceptualization of personality. *Psychological Review, 80*, 252-283.

Mischel, W., Shoda, Y., & Peake, P.K. (1988). The nature of adolescent competencies predicted by preschool delay of gratification. *Journal of Personality and Social Psychology, 54*, 687-696.

Mischel, W., Shoda, Y., & Rodriguez, M.L. (1989). Delay of gratification in children. *Science, 244*, 933-938.

Miyamoto, Y., & Kitayama, S. (2002). Cultural variation in correspondence bias: The critical role of attitude diagnosticity of socially constrained behavior. *Journal of Personality and Social Psychology, 83*, 1239-1248.

Miyamoto, Y., & Wilken, B. (2010). Culturally contingent situated cognition: Influencing other people fosters analytic perception in the United States but not in Canada. *Psychological Science, 21*, 1616-1622.

Molden, D.C., Hui, C.M., Noreen, E.E., Meier, B.P., Scholer, A.A., D'Agostino, P.R., & Martin, V. (2012). The motivational versus metabolic effects of carbohydrates on self-control. *Psychological Science, 23*, 1130-1137.

Molinero, L.L., Marcos, C.Y., Mirbaba, F., Fainboim, L., Stastny, P., & Zwirner, N.W. (2002). Codominant expression of the polymorphic MICA alloantigens encoded by genes in the HLA region. *European Journal of Immunogenetics, 29*, 314-319.

Monaghan, E., & Glickman, S. (1992). Hormones and aggressiveness behavior. In J. Becker, S. Breedlove, & D. Crews (Eds.), *Behavioral endocrinology* (pp. 261-285). Cambridge, MA: MIT Press.

Moore, D.J., & Homer, P. (2000). Dimensions of temperament: Affect intensity and consumer lifestyles. *Journal of Consumer Psychology, 9*, 231-242.

Morris, M.W., & Peng, K. (1994). Culture and cause: American and Chinese attributions for social and physical events. *Journal of Personality and Social Psychology, 67*, 949-971.

Morrison, M., & Roese, N.J. (2011). Regrets of the typical American: Findings from a nationally representative sample. *Social Psychological and Personality Science, 2*, 576-583.

Moscovici, S. (1976). *Social influence and social change.* London: Academic Press.

Moscovici, S., Lage, E., & Naffrechoux, M. (1969). Influence of a consistent minority on responses of a majority in a color perception task. *Sociometry, 32*, 365-379.

Moscovici, S., & Zavalloni, M. (1969). The group as a polarizer of attitudes. *Journal of Personality and Social Psychology, 12*, 124-135.

Moskalenko, S., & Heine, S.J. (2003). Watching your troubles away: Television viewing as a stimulus for subjective self-awareness. *Personality and Social Psychology Bulletin, 29*, 76-85.

Mudrik, L, Breska, A., Lamy, D., & Deouell, L.Y. (2011). Integration without awareness: Expanding the limits of unconscious processing. *Psychological Science, 22*, 764-770.

Mugny, G. (1982). *The power of minorities.* London: Academic Press.

Mulder, L.B., Van Dijk, E., De Cremer, D., & Wilke, H.A.M. (2006). Undermining trust and cooperation: The paradox of sanctioning systems in social dilemmas. *Journal of Experimental Social Psychology, 42*, 147-162.

Mullen, B., Brown, R., & Smith, C. (1992). In-group bias as a function of salience, relevance, and status: An integration. *European Journal of Social Psychology, 22*, 103-122.

Mullen, B., Futrell, D., Stairs, D., Tice, D.M., Baumeister, R.F., Dawson, K.E., Riordan, C.A., Radloff, C.E., Goethals, G.R., Kennedy, J.G., & Rosenfeld, P. (1986). Newscasters' facial expressions and voting behavior of viewers: Can a smile elect a president? *Journal of Personality and Social Psychology, 51*, 291-295.

Mullen, B., Johnson, C., & Salas, E. (1991). Productivity loss in brainstorming groups: A meta-analysis. *Basic and Applied Social Psychology, 12*, 3-23.

Mullen, B., & Riordan, C.A. (1988). Self-serving attributions for performance in naturalistic settings: A meta-analytic review. *Journal of Applied Social Psychology, 18*, 3-22.

Mullen, B., Rozell, D., & Johnson, C. (2001). Ethnophaulisms for ethnic immigrant groups: The contributions of group size and familiarity. *European Journal of Social Psychology, 31*, 231-246.

Munroe, S.M., & Reid, M.W. (2009). Life stress and depression. *Current Directions in Psychological Science, 18*, 68-71.

Muraven, M., & Baumeister, R.F. (2000). Self-regulation and depletion of limited resources: Does self-control resemble a muscle? *Psychological Bulletin, 126*, 247-259.

Murphy, R.A., Schmeer, S., Vallee-Tourangeau, F., Mondragon, E., & Hilton, D. (2011). Making the illusory correlation effect appear and then disappear: The effects of increased learning. *Quarterly Journal of Experimental Psychology, 64*, 24-40.

Murphy, M.C., Steele, C.M., & Gross, J.J. (2007). Signaling threat: How situational cues affect women in math, science, and engineering settings. *Psychological Science, 18*, 879-885.

Murphy, S.M., Vallacher, R.R., Shackelford, T.K., Bjorklund, D.F., & Yunger, J.L. (2006). Relationship experience as a predictor of romantic jealousy. *Personality and Individual Differences, 40*, 761-769.

Murray, S.L., Holmes, J.G., MacDonald, G., & Ellsworth, P.C. (1998). Through the looking glass darkly? When self-doubts turn into relationship insecurities. *Journal of Personality and Social Psychology, 75,* 1459-1480.

Murstein, B.I. (1974). *Love, sex, and marriage through the ages.* New York: Springer.

Myers, D.G. (1982). Polarizing effects of social interaction. In H. Brandstatter, J.H. Davis, & G. Stocker-Kreichgauer (Eds.), *Group decision making.* New York: Academic Press.

Myers, D.G. (2000). *The American paradox.* New Haven: Yale University Press.

Myers, D.G., & Diener, E. (1995). Who is happy? *Psychological Science, 6,* 10-19.

Myers, D.G., & Lamm, H. (1976). The group polarization phenomenon. *Psychological Bulletin, 83,* 602-627.

Naumann, L.P., Vazire, S., Rentfrow, P.J., & Gosling, S.D. (2009). Personality judgments based on physical appearance. *Personality and Social Psychology Bulletin, 35,* 1661-1671.

Neff, L.A., & Karney, B.R. (2005). To know you is to love you: The implications of global adoration and specific accuracy for marital relationships. *Journal of Personality and Social Psychology, 88,* 480-497.

Nel, E., Helmreich, R., & Aronson, E. (1969). Opinion change in the advocate as a function of the persuasibility of the audience: A clarification of the meaning of dissonance. *Journal of Personality and Social Psychology, 12,* 117-124.

Nelson, D.W., Klein, C.T.F., & Irvin, J.E. (2003). Motivational antecedents of empathy: Inhibiting effects of fatigue. *Basic and Applied Social Psychology, 25,* 37-50.

Nelson, L.J., & Klutas, K. (2000). The distinctiveness effect in social interaction: Creation of a self-fulfilling prophecy. *Personality and Social Psychology Bulletin, 26,* 126-135.

Nelson, R.J. (Ed.). (2006). *Biology of aggression.* Oxford: Oxford University Press.

Neuberg, S.L., & Fiske, S.T. (1987). Motivational influences on impression formation: Outcome dependence, accuracy-driven attention, and individuating processes. *Journal of Personality and Social Psychology, 53,* 433-444.

Neumann, R., & Strack, F. (2000). "Mood contagion": The automatic transfer of mood between persons. *Journal of Personality and Social Psychology, 79,* 211-223.

Newcomb, T.M. (1947). Autistic hostility and social reality. *Human Relations, 1,* 69-86.

Newcomb, T.M. (1952). Attitude development as a function of reference groups: The Bennington study. In G.E. Swanson, T.M. Newcomb, & E.L. Hartley (Eds.), *Readings in social psychology* (pp. 420-430). New York: Henry Holt.

Newcomb, T.M. (1961). *The acquaintance process.* New York: Holt, Rinehart, & Winston.

Newcombe, D., & Arnkoff, D.B. (1979). Effects of speech style and sex of speaker on person perception. *Journal of Personality and Social Psychology, 37,* 1293-1303.

Newcombe, T.M. (1947). Autistic hostility and social reality. *Human Relations, 1,* 69-86.

Newtson, D. (1994). The perception and coupling of behavior waves. In R.R. Vallacher & A. Nowak (Eds.), *Dynamical systems in social psychology* (pp. 139-167). San Diego: Academic Press.

Neyer, F.J., & Lang, F.R. (2003). Blood is thicker than water: Kinship orientation across adulthood. *Journal of Personality and Social Psychology, 84,* 310-321.

Ng, W., & Lindsay, R.C.I. (1994). Cross-racial facial recognition: Failure of the contact hypothesis. *Journal of Cross-Cultural Psychology, 25,* 217-232.

Niedenthal, P.M. (2007). Embodying emotion. *Science, 316,* 1002-1005.

Niederhoffer, K.G., & Pennebaker, J.W. (2002). Sharing one's story: On the benefits of writing or talking about emotional experience. In C.R. Snyder & S.J. Lopez (Eds.), *Handbook of positive psychology* (pp. 573-583). London: Oxford University Press.

Nieuwenhuys, A., & Oudejans, R.R.D. (2011). Training with anxiety: Short- and long-term effects on police officers' shooting behavior under pressure. *Cognitive Processing, 12,* 277-288.

Nisbett, R.E. (1993). Violence and U.S. regional crime. *American Psychologist, 48*(4), 441-449.

Nisbett, R.E. (2003). *The geography of thought: How Asians and Westerners think differently: And why.* New York: Free Press.

Nisbett, R.E., Caputo, C., Legant, P., & Maracek, J. (1973). Behavior as seen by the actor and by the observer. *Journal of Personality and Social Psychology, 27,* 154-165.

Nisbett, R.E., & Cohen, D. (1996). *Culture of honor: The psychology of violence in the South.* Boulder, CO: Westview Press.

Nisbett, R.E., & Miyamoto, Y. (2005). The influence of culture: Holistic versus analytic perception. *Trends in Cognitive Science, 9,* 467-473.

Nisbett, R.E., Peng, K., Choi, I., & Norenzayan, A. (2001). Culture and systems of thought: Holistic versus analytic cognition. *Psychological Review, 108,* 291-310.

Nisbett, R.E., & Ross, L. (1980). *Human inference: Strategies and shortcomings of social judgment.* Englewood Cliffs, NJ: Prentice-Hall.

Nisbett, R.E., & Schachter, S. (1966). Cognitive manipulation of pain. *Journal of Experimental Psychology, 2,* 227-236.

Nisbett, R.E., & Wilson, T.D. (1977). Telling more than we can know: Verbal reports on mental processes. *Psychological Review, 84,* 231-259.

Noah, T., Schul, Y., & Mayo, R. (2018). When both the original study and its failed replication are correct: Feeling observed eliminates the facial-feedback effect. *Journal of Personality and Social Psychology, 114*(5), 657–664.

Nolen-Hoeksema, S. (1991). Responses to depression and their effects on the duration of depressive episodes. *Journal of Abnormal Psychology, 100*, 569–582.

Noller, P., Gallois, C., Hayes, A., & Bohle, P. (1988). Impressions of politicians: The effect of situation and communication channel. *Australian Journal of Psychology, 40*, 267–280.

Noor, F., & Evans, D.C. (2003). The effect of facial symmetry on perceptions of personality and attractiveness. *Journal of Research in Personality, 37*(4), 339–347.

North, A.C., Hargeaves, D.J., & McKendrick, J. (1999). The influence of store music on wine selections. *Journal of Applied Psychology, 84*, 271–276.

Nosek, B.A., Banaji, M.R., & Greenwald, A.G. (2002). Harvesting implicit group attitudes and beliefs from demonstration web site. *Group Dynamics: Theory, Research, and Practice, 6*, 101–115.

Nowak, A. (2004). Dynamical minimalism: Why less is more in psychology. *Personality and Social Psychology Review, 8*, 183–192.

Nowak, A., Gelfand, M.J., Borkowski, W., Cohen, D., & Hernandez, I. (2016). The evolutionary basis of honor cultures. *Psychological Science, 27*, 12–24.

Nowak, A., Szamrej, J., & Latané, B. (1990). From private attitude to public opinion: A dynamic theory of social impact. *Psychological Review, 97*, 362–376.

Nowak, A., & Vallacher, R.R. (1998). *Dynamical social psychology*. New York: Guilford.

Nowak, A., & Vallacher, R.R. (2019). Nonlinear societal change: The perspective of dynamical systems. *British Journal of Social Psychology, 58*, 105–128.

Nowak, A., Vallacher, R.R., & Burnstein, E. (1998). Computational social psychology: A neural network approach to interpersonal dynamics. In W. Liebrand, A. Nowak, & R. Hegselman (Eds.), *Computer modeling and the study of dynamic social processes* (pp. 97–125). New York: Sage.

Nowak, A., Vallacher, R.R., Tesser, A., & Borkowski, W. (2000). Society of self: The emergence of collective properties in self-structure. *Psychological Review, 107*, 39–61.

Nowak, A., Vallacher, R.R., & Zochowski, M. (2005). The emergence of personality: Dynamic foundations of individual variation. *Developmental Review, 25*, 351–385.

Nowak, M.A. (2006). Five rules for the evolution of cooperation. *Science, 314*, 1560–1563.

Nowak, M.A., & Highfield, R. (2011). *SuperCooperators: Altruism, evolution, and why we need each other to succeed*. New York: Free Press.

Nowak, M.A., Page, K.M., & Sigmund, K. (2000). Fairness versus reason in the ultimatum game. *Science, 289*, 1773–1775.

Nowak, M.A., & Sigmund, K. (1998). Evolution of indirect reciprocity by image scoring. *Nature, 393*, 573–577.

Oatley, K. (2004). *Emotions: A brief history*. Malden, MA: Blackwell.

Oatley, K., & Jenkins, J.M. (1992). Human emotions: Function and dysfunction. *Annual Review of Psychology, 43*, 55–85.

Ochsner, K.N. (2007). Social cognitive neuroscience. In A.W. Kruglanski & E.T. Higgins (Eds.), *Social psychology: Handbook of basic principles* (pp. 39–66). New York: Guilford Press.

Oishi, S., Kesebir, S., & Diener, E. (2011). Income inequality and happiness. *Psychological Science, 22*, 1095–1100.

Oishi, S., & Schimmack, U. (2010). Culture and well-being: A new inquiry into the psychological wealth of nations. *Perspectives on Psychological Science, 5*, 463–471.

Oishi, S., Wyer, R.S., & Colcombe, S.J. (2000). Cultural variation in the use of current life satisfaction to predict the future. *Journal of Personality and Social Psychology, 78*, 434–445.

Olivola, C.Y., & Todorov, A. (2010). Elected in 100 milliseconds: Appearance-based trait inferences and voting. *Journal of Nonverbal Behavior, 34*, 83–110.

Olson, J.M., Hafer, C.L., & Taylor, L. (2001). I'm mad as hell, and I'm not going to take it anymore: Reports of negative emotions as a self-preservation tactic. *Journal of Applied Social Psychology, 31*, 981–999.

Olson, J.M., Roese, N.J., & Zanna, M.P. (1996). Expectancies. In E.T. Higgins & A.W. Kruglanski (Eds.), *Social psychology: Handbook of basic principles* (pp. 211–238). New York: Guilford Press.

Olson, J.M., Vernon, P.A., Harris, J.A., & Jang, K.L. (2001). The heritability of attitudes: A study of twins. *Journal of Personality and Social Psychology, 80*, 845–860.

Orians, G.H., & Heerwagen, J.H. (1992). Evolved responses to landscapes. In J.H. Barlow, L. Cosmides, & J. Tooby (Eds.), *The adapted mind* (pp. 555–580). New York: Oxford University Press.

Orth, U., & Robins, R.W. (2014). The development of self-esteem. *Current Directions in Psychological Science, 23*, 381–387.

Orue, I., Bushman, B.J., Calvete, E., Thomaes, S., Orobio de Castro, B., & Hutteman, R. (2011). Monkey see, monkey do, monkey hurt: Longitudinal effects of exposure to violence on children's aggressive behavior. *Social Psychological and Personality Science, 2*, 432–437.

Osgood, C.E., Suci, G.J., & Tannenbaum, P.H. (1957). *The measurement of meaning*. Urbana: University of Illinois Press.

Österman, K., Björkqvist, K., Lagerspetz, K.M.J., Kaukiainen, A., Landau, S.F., Fraczek, A., & Caprara, G.V. (1998). Cross-cultural evidence of female indirect aggression. *Aggressive Behavior, 24*, 1-8.

Ostrom, T.M., & Sedikides, C. (1992). Out-group homogeneity effects in natural and minimal groups. *Psychological Bulletin, 112*, 536-552.

Oudejans, R.R.D., & Pijpers, J.R. (2010). Training with mild anxiety may prevent choking under higher levels of anxiety. *Psychology of Sport Exercise, 11*, 44-50.

Oxley, D.R., Smith, K.B., Alford, J.R., Hibbing, M.V., Miller, J.L., Scalora, M., Hatemi, P.K., & Hibbing, J.R. (2008). Political attitudes vary with physiological traits. *Science, 321*, 1667-1670.

Papaleontiou-Louca, E. (2008). *Metacognition and theory of mind*. Newcastle: Cambridge Scholars Publishing.

Parducci, A. (1995). *Happiness, pleasure and judgment: The contextual theory and its applications*. Mahwah, NJ: Erlbaum.

Park, B., & Rothbart, M. (1982). Perception of out-group homogeneity and levels of social categorization: Memory for the subordinate attributes of in-group and out-group members. *Journal of Personality and Social Psychology, 42*, 1051-1068.

Park, J., & Banaji, M.R. (2000). Mood and heuristics: The influence of happy and sad states on sensitivity and bias in stereotyping. *Journal of Personality and Social Psychology, 78*, 1005-1023.

Parke, R.D., Berkowitz, L., Leyens, J.P., West, S.G., & Sebastian, J. (1977). Some effects of violent and nonviolent movies on the behavior of juvenile delinquents. In L. Berkowitz (Ed.), *Advances in experimental social psychology* (Vol. 10, pp. 135-172). New York: Academic Press.

Parkin, S.S., Jarman, M.S., & Vallacher, R.R. (2015). On being mindful: What do people think they're doing? *Social and Personality Psychology Compass, 10*, 31-44.

Parrott, W.G. (1993). Beyond hedonism: Motives for inhibiting good moods and for maintaining bad moods. In D.M. Wegner & J.W. Pennebaker (Eds.), *Handbook of mental control* (pp. 278-305). Englewood Cliffs, NJ: Prentice-Hall.

Parrott, W.G., Sabini, J., & Silver, M. (1988). The roles of self-esteem and social interaction in embarrassment. *Personality and Social Psychology Bulletin, 14*, 191-202.

Patterson, M.L., Churchill, M.E., Burger, G.K., & Powell, J.L. (1992). Verbal and nonverbal modality effects on impressions of political candidates: Analysis from the 1984 presidential debates. *Communication Monographs, 59*, 231-242.

Paulus, P.B., Dzindolet, M.T., Poletes, G., & Camacho, L.M. (1993). Perfection of performance in group brainstorming: The illusion of group productivity. *Personality and Social Psychology Bulletin, 19*, 78-89.

Pavlov, I.P. (1927/1960). *Conditional reflexes*. New York: Dover Publications.

Payne, B.K. (2001). Prejudice and perception: The role of automatic and controlled processes in misperceiving a weapon. *Journal of Personality Social Psychology, 81*, 181-192.

Payne, B.K. (2006). Weapon bias: Split-second decisions and unintended stereotyping. *Current Directions in Psychological Science, 15*, 287-291.

Payne, B.K., Shimizu, Y., & Jacoby, L.L. (2005). Mental control and visual illusions: Toward explaining race-biased weapon misidentifications. *Journal of Experimental Social Psychology, 41*, 36-47.

Peak, H. (1945). Observations on the characteristics and distribution of German Nazis. *Psychological Monographs, 49*(276).

Pegalis, L.J., Shaffer, D.R., Bazzini, D.G., & Greenier, K. (1994). On the ability to elicit self-disclosure: Are there gender-based and contextual limitations on the opener effect? *Personality and Social Psychology Bulletin, 20*, 412-420.

Pelham, B.W. (1991). On confidence and consequence: The certainty and importance of self-knowledge. *Journal of Personality and Social Psychology, 60*, 518-530.

Pennebaker, J.W. (1997). Writing about emotional experiences as a therapeutic process. *Psychological Science, 8*, 162-166.

Pennebaker, J.W., & Beale, S.K. (1986). Confronting a traumatic event: Toward an understanding of inhibition and disease. *Journal of Abnormal Psychology, 95*, 274-281.

Pennebaker, J.W., Barger, S.D., & Tiebout, J. (1989). Disclosure of traumas and health among Holocaust survivors. *Psychosomatic Medicine, 51*, 577-589.

Pennebaker, J.W., & Francis, M.E. (1996). Cognitive, emotional, and language processes in disclosure. *Cognition and Emotion, 10*, 601-626.

Penner, L.A., Dertkew, M.C., & Achenbach, C.J. (1973). The flash system: A field study of altruism. *Journal of Applied Social Psychology, 3*, 362-373.

Penner, L.A., Shiffman, S., Paty, J.A., & Fritzsche, B.A. (1994). Individual differences in intraperson variability in mood. *Journal of Personality and Social Psychology, 66*, 712-721.

Penton-Voak, I.S., Perrett, D.I., Castles, D., Kobayashi, T., Burt, M., Murray, L.K., & Minamisawa, R. (1999). Menstrual cycle alters face preference. *Nature, 399*, 741-742.

Perper, T. (1985). *Sex signals: The biology of love*. Philadelphia: ISI Press.

Perrett, D.I., Lee, K.J., Penton-Voak, I., Rowland, D., Yoshikawa, S., Burt, D.M., Henzi, S.P., Castles, D.L., & Akamatsu, S. (1998). Effects of sexual dimorphism on facial attractiveness. *Nature, 394*, 884-887.

Peters, L. H., Hartke, D. D., & Pohlmann, J. T. (1985). Fiedler's contingency theory of leadership: An application of the meta-analysis procedures of Schmidt and Hunter. *Psychological Bulletin, 97,* 274-285.

Petrie, K. J., Booth, R. J., & Pennebaker, J. W. (1998). The immunological effects of thought suppression. *Journal of Personality and Social Psychology, 75,* 1264-1272.

Pettigrew, T. F. (1979). The ultimate attribution error: Extending Allport's cognitive analysis of prejudice. *Personality and Social Psychology Bulletin, 5,* 461-476.

Pettigrew, T. F. (1997). Generalized intergroup contact effects on prejudice. *Personality and Social Psychology Bulletin, 23,* 173-185.

Pettigrew, T. F., & Meertens, R. W. (1995). Subtle and blatant prejudice in western Europe. *European Journal of Social Psychology, 25,* 57-75.

Pettigrew, T. F., & Tropp, L. R. (2006). A meta-analytic test of intergroup contact theory. *Journal of Personality and Social Psychology, 90,* 751-783.

Petty, R. E., & Cacioppo, J. T. (1986). The elaboration likelihood model of persuasion. In L. Berkowitz (Ed.), *Advances in experimental social psychology* (Vol. 19, pp. 123-205). New York: Academic Press.

Petty, R. E., Cacioppo, J. T., & Goldman, R. (1981). Personal involvement as a determinant of argument-based persuasion. *Journal of Personality and Social Psychology, 41,* 847-855.

Petty, R. E., & Wegener, D. T. (1998). Attitude change: Multiple roles for persuasion variables. In D. T. Gilbert, S. T. Fiske, & G. Lindzey (Eds.), *Handbook of social psychology* (4th ed., Vol. 1, pp. 323-390). New York: McGraw-Hill.

Petty, R. E., Wells, G. L., & Brock, T. C. (1976). Distraction can enhance or reduce yielding to propaganda: Thought disruption versus effort justification. *Journal of Personality and Social Psychology, 34,* 874-884.

Phares, E. J. (1976). *Locus of control in personality.* Morristown, NJ: General Learning Press.

Phelps, E. A., O'Connor, K. J., Cunningham, W. A., Funayama, E. S., Gatenby, J. C., Gore, J. C., & Banaji, M. R. (2000). Performance on indirect measures of race evaluation predicts amygdala activation. *Journal of Cognitive Neuroscience, 12,* 729-738.

Piaget, J. (1965). *The moral judgment of the child.* London: Kegan, Paul, Trench, Trubner, & Co. (Original work published 1932).

Piliavin, J. A., & Callero, P. L. (1991). *Giving blood: The development of an altruistic identity.* Baltimore: Johns Hopkins University Press.

Pinker, S. (1997). *How the mind works.* New York: W. W. Norton & Company.

Pinker, S. (2003). *The blank slate: The modern denial of human nature.* New York: Penguin.

Pinker, S. (2011). *The better angels of our nature: Why violence has declined.* New York: Penguin.

Plomin, R., DeFries, J. C., & Loehlin, J. C. (1977). Genotype-environment interaction and correlation in the analysis of human behavior. *Psychological Bulletin, 84,* 309-322.

Plomin, R., DeFries, J. C., McClearn, G. E., & McGuffin, P. (2008). *Behavioral genetics* (5th ed.). New York: Worth.

Plomin, R., & Rende, R. (1991). Human behavioral genetics. *Annual Review of Psychology, 42,* 161-190.

Plotnik, J., de Waal, F.B.M., & Reiss, D. (2006). Self-recognition in an Asian elephant. *Proceedings of the National Academy of Sciences of the USA, 103,* 17053-17057.

Pomazal, R. J., & Clore, G. L. (1973). Helping on the highway: The effects of dependency and sex. *Journal of Applied Social Psychology, 3,* 150-164.

Porges, S. P. (1995). Orienting in a defensive world: Mammalian modifications of our evolutionary heritage. A polyvagal theory. *Psychophysiology, 32,* 301-317.

Port, R. F., & Van Gelder, T. (Eds.). (1995). *Mind as motion: Explorations in the dynamics of cognition.* Cambridge, MA: MIT Press.

Powers, W. T. (1973). *Behavior: The control of perception.* Chicago: Aldine.

Pratkanis, A. R., Breckler, S. J., & Greenwald, A. G. (Eds.). (1989). *Attitude structure and function.* Hillsdale, NJ: Erlbaum.

Pratkanis, A. R., Greenwald, A. G., Leippe, M. R., & Baumgardner, M. H. (1988). In search of reliable persuasion effects: III. The sleeper effect is dead: Long live the sleeper effect. *Journal of Personality and Social Psychology, 54,* 203-218.

Premack, D. G., & Woodruff, G. (1978). Does the chimpanzee have a theory of mind? *Behavioral and Brain Sciences, 1,* 515-526.

Prior, H., Schwarz, A., & Gunturkun, O. (2008). Mirror-induced behavior in the magpie (Pica pica): Evidence of self-recognition. *PLoS Biol, 6*(8), e202. https://doi.org/10.1371/journal.pbio.0060202

Pronin, E., & Jacobs, E. (2008). Thought speed, mood, and the experience of mental motion. *Perspectives on Psychological Science, 3*(6), 461-485.

Pronin, E., Kruger, J., Savitsky, K., & Ross, L. (2001). You don't know me, but I know you: The illusion of asymmetric insight. *Journal of Personality and Social Psychology, 81,* 639-656.

Pronin, E., Lin, D. Y., & Ross, L. (2002). The bias blind spot: Perceptions of bias in self versus others. *Personality and Social Psychology Bulletin, 28,* 369-381.

Pruitt, D. G. (1971). Choice shifts in group discussion: An introductory review. *Journal of Personality and Social Psychology, 20*(3), 339-360.

Pruitt, D. G. (1997). Ripeness theory and the Oslo talks. *International Negotiation, 2,* 237-250.

Pruitt, D. G. (1998). Social conflict. In D. T. Gilbert, S. T. Fiske, & G. Lindzey (Eds.), *The handbook of social psychology* (4th ed., Vol. 2, pp. 470-503). New York: McGraw-Hill.

Pruitt, D. G., Kim, S. H., & Rubin, J. Z. (2004). *Social conflict: Escalation, stalemate, and settlement* (3rd ed.). Boston: McGraw-Hill.

Puts, D. (2005). Mating context and menstrual phase affect women's preferences for male voice pitch. *Evolution and Human Behavior, 26*, 388-397.

Quattrone, G. A., & Jones, E. E. (1980). The perception of variability within in-groups and out-groups: Implications for the law of small numbers. *Journal of Personality and Social Psychology, 38*, 141-152.

Queller, S. (2002). Stereotype change in a recurrent network. *Personality and Social Psychology Review, 6*, 295-303.

Queller, S., & Smith, E. R. (2002). Subtyping versus bookkeeping in stereotype learning and change: Connectionist simulations and empirical findings. *Journal of Personality and Social Psychology, 82*, 300-313.

Quoidbach, J., & Dunn, E. W. (2010). Personality neglect: The unforeseen impact of personal dispositions on emotional life. *Psychological Science, 21*, 1783-1786.

Quoidbach, J., Dunn, E. W., Petrides, K. V., & Mikolajczak, M. (2010). Money giveth, money taketh away: The dual effect of wealth on happiness. *Psychological Science, 21*, 759-763.

Radelet, M., & Akers, R. (1996). Deterrence and the death penalty: The views of the experts. *Journal of Criminal Law and Criminology, 87*, 1-16.

Rameson, L. T., Morelli, S. A., & Lieberman, M. D. (2011). The neural correlates of empathy: Experience, automaticity, and prosocial behavior. *Journal of Cognitive Neuroscience, 24*, 235-245.

Ratliff, K. A., & Nosek, B. A. (2010). Creating distinct implicit and explicit attitudes with an illusory correlation paradigm. *Journal of Experimental Social Psychology, 46*, 721-728.

Razran, G. H. S. (1940). Conditioned response changes in rating and appraising sociopolitical slogans. *Psychological Bulletin, 37*, 481-493.

Read, S. J., & Miller, L. C. (Eds.). (1998). *Connectionist models of social reasoning and social behavior*. Mahwah, NJ: Erlbaum.

Read, S. J., & Urada, S. I. (2003). A neural network simulation of the out-group homogeneity effect. *Personality and Social Psychology Review, 7*, 146-159.

Reber, R., Winkielman, P., & Schwarz, N. (1998). Effects of perceptual fluency on affective judgments. *Psychological Science, 9*, 45-48.

Reeve, J. (2006). Autonomy, volitional motivation, and wellness. *Motivation and Emotion, 30*, 257-258.

Regan, D. T. (1971). Effects of a favor and liking on compliance. *Journal of Experimental Social Psychology, 7*, 627-639.

Regan, D. T., & Totten, J. (1975). Empathy and attribution: Turning observers into actors. *Journal of Personality and Social Psychology, 32*, 850-856.

Reifman, A., Larrick, R. P., & Fein, S. (1991). Temper and temperature on the diamond: The heat-aggression relationship in major league baseball. *Personality and Social Psychology Bulletin, 17*, 580-585.

Reiss, D., & Marino, L. (2001). Mirror self-recognition in the bottlenose dolphin: A case of cognitive convergence. *Proceedings of the National Academy of Sciences, 98*, 5937-5942.

Requejo, R. J., & Camacho, J. (2011). Evolution of cooperation mediated by limiting resources: Connecting resource based models and evolutionary game theory. *Journal of Theoretical Biology, 272*, 35-41.

Rhodes, G., Proffitt, F., Grady, J. M., & Sumich, A. (1998). Facial symmetry and the perception of beauty. *Psychonomic Bulletin and Review, 5*, 659-669.

Rhodes, G., Sumich, A., & Byatt, G. (1999). Are average facial configurations attractive only because of their symmetry? *Psychological Science, 10*, 52-58.

Rhodes, G., Zebrowitz, L. A., Clark, A., Kalick, S. M., Hightower, A., & McKay, R. (2001). Do facial averageness and symmetry signal health? *Evolution and Human Behavior, 22*, 31-46.

Rhodewalt, F. (1994). Conceptions of ability, achievement goals, and individual differences in self-handicapping behavior: On the application of implicit theories. *Journal of Personality, 62*, 67-85.

Rhodewalt, F., & Hill, S. K. (1995). Self-handicapping in the classroom: The effects of claimed self-handicaps on responses to academic failure. *Basic and Applied Social Psychology, 16*, 397-416.

Rhodewalt, F., Saltzman, A. T., & Wittmer, J. (1984). Self-handicapping among competitive athletes: The role of practice in self-esteem protection. *Basic and Applied Social Psychology, 5*, 197-209.

Rholes, W. S., Simpson, J. A., & Orina, M. M. (1999). Attachment and anger in an anxiety-provoking situation. *Journal of Personality and Social Psychology, 76*, 940-957.

Richards, Z., & Hewstone, M. (2001). Subtyping and subgrouping: Processes for the prevention and promotion of stereotype change. *Personality and Social Psychology Review, 5*, 42-73.

Rideout, V. G., Foehr, U. G., & Roberts, D. F. (2010). *Generation M2: Media in the lives of 8-18 year olds*. Menlo Park, CA: Henry J. Kaiser Foundation.

Riess, M., Rosenfeld, P., Melburg, V., & Tedeschi, J. T. (1981). Self-serving attributions: Biased private perceptions and distorted public descriptions. *Journal of Personality and Social Psychology, 41,* 224-231.

Rilling, J. K., Gutman, D. A., Zeh, T. R., Pagnoni, G., Berns, G. S., & Kilts, C. D. (2002). A neural basis for cooperation. *Neuron, 35,* 395-405.

Ringelmann, M. (1913). Recherches sur les moteurs animés: Travail de l'homme [Research on driving forces: Human work]. *Annales de l'Institut National Agronomique,* series 2, *12,* 1-40.

Rippere, V. (1977). "What's the thing to do when you're feeling depressed?": A pilot study. *Behaviour Research and Therapy, 15,* 185-191.

Rizzolatti, G., & Craighero, L. (2004). The mirror neuron system. *Annual Review of Neuroscience, 27,* 169-192.

Robins, R. W., Spranca, M. D., & Mendelson, G. A. (1996). The actor-observer effect revisited: Effects of individual differences and repeated social interactions on actor and observer attributions. *Journal of Personality and Social Psychology, 71,* 375-389.

Robinson, M. (2000). The construction and reinforcement of myths of race and crime. *Journal of Contemporary Criminal Justice, 16,* 133-156.

Roccas, S., & Brewer, M. B. (2002). Social identity complexity. *Personality and Social Psychology Review, 6,* 88-106.

Rogers, R. (1983). Cognitive and physiological processes in fear appeals and attitude change: A revised theory of protection motivation. In J. T. Cacioppo & R. E. Petty (Eds.), *Social psychophysiology: A sourcebook* (pp. 153-176). New York: Guilford Press.

Rokeach, M. (1960). *The open and closed mind: Investigations into the nature of belief systems and personality systems.* New York: Basic Books.

Rokeach, M. (1973). *The nature of human values.* New York: Free Press.

Roney, J. R., Mahler, S. V., & Maestripieri, D. (2003). Behavioral and hormonal responses of men to brief interactions with women. *Evolution and Human Behavior, 24,* 365-375.

Rosenbaum, M. E. (1986). The repulsion hypothesis: On the nondevelopment of relationships. *Journal of Personality and Social Psychology, 51,* 1156-1166.

Rosenberg, M. (1965). *Society and the adolescent self-image.* Princeton, NJ: Princeton University Press.

Rosenberg, M. (1979). *Conceiving the self.* Malabar, FL: Robert E. Krieger.

Rosenberg, S., Nelson, C., & Vivekananthan, P. S. (1968). A multidimensional approach to the structure of personality impressions. *Journal of Personality and Social Psychology, 9*(4), 283-294.

Rosenberg, S., & Sedlak, A. (1972). Structural representations of implicit personality theory. In L. Berkowitz (Ed.), *Advances in experimental social psychology* (Vol. 6, pp. 235-297). New York: Academic Press.

Rosenblatt, A., Greenberg, J., Solomon, S., Pyszczynski, T., & Lyon, D. (1989). The effects of mortality salience on reactions to those who violate or uphold cultural values. *Journal of Personality and Social Psychology, 57*(4), 681-690.

Rosenblatt, P. C., & Cozby, P. C. (1972). Courtship patterns associated with freedom of choice of spouse. *Journal of Marriage and the Family, 34,* 689-695.

Rosenhan, D. L., Salovey, P., & Hargis, K. (1981). The joys of helping: Focus of attention mediates the impact of positive affect on altruism. *Journal of Personality and Social Psychology, 40,* 899-905.

Rosenthal, R., & Jacobson, L. (1968). *Pygmalion in the classroom: Teacher expectations and student intellectual development.* New York: Holt, Rinehart, & Winston.

Ross, L. (1977). The intuitive psychologist and his shortcomings: Distortions in the attribution process. In L. Berkowitz (Ed.), *Advances in experimental social psychology* (Vol. 10, pp. 174-221). New York: Academic Press.

Ross, L. D., Amabile, T. M., & Steinmetz, J. L. (1977). Social roles, social control, and biases in social-perception processes. *Journal of Personality and Social Psychology, 35,* 485-494.

Ross, L. D., Lepper, M. R., & Hubbard, M. (1975). Perseverance in self-perception and social perception: Biased attributional processes in the debriefing paradigm. *Journal of Personality and Social Psychology, 32,* 880-892.

Rotter, J. B. (1966). Generalized expectancies for internal versus external control of reinforcement. *Psychological Monographs, 80* (Whole No. 609).

Rotter, J. B. (1990). Internal versus external control of reinforcement: A case history of a variable. *American Psychologist, 45,* 489-493.

Rounding, K., Lee, A., Jacobson, J. A., & Ji, L. J. (2012). Religion replenishes self-control. *Psychological Science, 23,* 635-642.

Rowe, G., Hirsh, J. B., & Anderson, A. K. (2007). Positive affect increases the breadth of attentional selection. *Proceedings of the National Academy of Sciences of the United States of America, 104,* 383-388.

Rozin, P. (2010). Evolutionary and cultural psychology: Complementing each other in the study of culture and cultural evolution. In M. Schaller, A. Norenzayan, S. J. Heine, T. Yamagishi, & T. Kameda (Eds.), *Evolution, culture, and the human mind* (pp. 9-22). New York: Psychology Press.

Rozin, P., Lowery, L., Imada, S., & Haidt, J. (1999). The CAD triad hypothesis: A mapping between three moral emotions (contempt, anger, and disgust), and three moral codes (community, autonomy, divinity). *Journal of Personality and Social Psychology, 66*, 870-881.

Rozin, P., & Singh, L. (1999). The moralization of cigarette smoking in America. *Journal of Consumer Behavior, 8*, 321-337.

Rubin, Z., & Peplau, L. A. (1975). Who believes in a just world? *Journal of Social Issues, 31*, 65-89.

Ruder, M., & Bless, H. (2003). Mood and the reliance on the ease of retrieval heuristic. *Journal of Personality and Social Psychology, 85*, 20-32.

Rudich, E., & Vallacher, R. R. (1999). To belong or to self-enhance? The motivational bases for choosing interaction partners. *Personality and Social Psychology Bulletin, 25*, 1387-1404.

Rudman, L. A., & Ashmore, R. D. (2007). Discrimination and the IAT. *Group Processes and Intergroup Relations, 10*, 359-372.

Rudman, L. A., & Borgida, E. (1995). The afterglow of construct accessibility: The behavioral consequences of priming men to view women as sexual objects. *Journal of Experimental Social Psychology, 31*, 493-517.

Rudolf, U., Roesch, S. C., Greitemeyer, T., & Weiner, B. (2004). A meta-analytic review of help giving and aggression from an attributional perspective: Contributions to a general theory of motivation. *Cognition and Emotion, 18*, 815-848.

Ruelle, D. (1989). *Elements of differentiable dynamics and bifurcation theory*. New York: Academic Press.

Ruiter, R. A. C., Abraham, C., & Kok, G. (2001). Scary warnings and rational precautions: A review of the psychology of fear appeals. *Psychology and Health, 16*, 613-630.

Rusbult, C. E. (1983). A longitudinal test of the investment model: The development (and deterioration) of satisfaction and commitment in heterosexual involvements. *Journal of Personality and Social Psychology, 45*, 101-117.

Rushton, J. P., & Bons, T. A. (2005). Mate choice and friendship in twins: Evidence for genetic similarity. *Psychological Science, 16*, 555-559.

Rushton, J. P., Fulker, D. W., Neale, M. C., Nias, D.K.B., & Eysenck, H. J. (1986). Altruism and aggression: The heritability of individual differences. *Journal of Personality and Social Psychology, 50*, 1192-1198.

Russell, D. (1996). The UCLA Loneliness Scale (Version 3): Reliability, validity, and factor structure. *Journal of Personality Assessment, 66*, 20-40.

Russell, J. A. (1994). Is there universal recognition of emotion from facial expression? A review of cross-cultural studies. *Psychological Bulletin, 115*, 102-141.

Russell, J. A. (1995). Facial expression of emotion: What lies beyond minimal universality? *Psychological Bulletin, 118*, 379-391.

Ryan, R. M., & Deci, E. L. (2000). Self-determination theory and the facilitation of intrinsic motivation, social development, and well-being. *American Psychologist, 55*, 550-558.

Rydell, R. J., Rydell, M. T., & Boucher, K. L. (2010). The effect of negative performance stereotypes on learning. *Journal of Personality and Social Psychology, 99*, 883-896.

Saad, L. (2002, November 21). Most smokers wish they could quit. *Gallup News Service*. www.gallup.com/poll/releases/ pr021121.asp.

Sadalla, E. K., Kenrick, D. T., & Vershure, B. (1987). Dominance and heterosexual attraction. *Journal of Personality and Social Psychology, 52*, 730-738.

Sagar, H. A., & Schofield, J. W. (1980). Racial and behavioral cues in black and white children's perceptions of ambiguously aggressive acts. *Journal of Personality and Social Psychology, 39*, 590-598.

Salmivalli, C., & Nieminen, E. (2002). Proactive and reactive aggression among school bullies, victims, and bully-victims. *Aggressive Behavior, 28*, 30-44.

Salovey, P., & Mayer, J. D. (1990). Emotional intelligence. *Imagination, Cognition, and Personality, 9*, 185-211.

Salovey, P., & Rodin, J. (1989). Envy and jealousy in close relationships. *Review of Personality and Social Psychology, 10*, 221-246.

Sanchez-Burks, J., Bartel, C. A., & Bount, S. (2009). Performance in intercultural interactions at work: Cross-cultural differences in response to behavioral mirroring. *Journal of Applied Psychology, 94*, 216-223.

Sanday, P. R. (1997). The socio-cultural context of rape: A cross-cultural study. In L. L. O'Toole (Ed.), *Gender violence: Interdisciplinary perspectives*. New York: New York University Press.

Sanderson, C. A., & Cantor, N. (2001). The association of intimacy goals and marital satisfaction: A test of four meditational hypotheses. *Personality and Social Psychology Bulletin, 27*, 1567-1577.

Sapolsky, R. M. (1994). *Why zebras don't get ulcers*. New York: Freeman.

Saucier, D. A., Miller, C. T., & Doucet, N. (2005). Differences in helping whites and blacks: A meta-analysis. *Personality and Social Psychology Review, 9*, 2-16.

Savani, K., Stephens, N. M., & Markus, H. R. (2011). The unanticipated interpersonal and societal consequence of choice: Victim blaming and reduced support for the public good. *Psychological Science, 22*(6), 795-802.

Savin-Williams, R. C. (1990). *Gay and lesbian youth: Expressions of identity*. New York: Hemisphere.

Scarr, S. (1992). Developmental theories for the1990s: Development and individual differences. *Child Development, 63*, 1-19.

Scarr, S., & McCartney, K. (1983). How people make their own environments: A theory of genotype-to-environment effects. *Child Development, 54*, 424–435.

Schachter, S. (1951). Deviation, rejection, and communication. *The Journal of Abnormal and Social Psychology, 46*, 190–207.

Schachter, S. (1959). *The psychology of affiliation*. Stanford, CA: Stanford University Press.

Schachter, S., & Singer, J. (1962). Cognitive, social, and physiological determinants of emotional state. *Psychological Review, 69*, 379–399.

Schacter, D. I. (1996). *Searching for memory: The brain, the mind, and the past*. New York: Basic Books.

Schafer, M., Haun, D.B.M., & Tomasello, M. (2015). Fair is not fair everywhere. *Psychological Science, 26*, 1252–1260.

Schaller, M., Simpson, J. A., & Kenrick, D. T. (2006). *Evolution and social psychology*. New York: Psychology Press.

Scheier, M. F., & Carver, C. S. (1992). Effects of optimism on psychological and physical well-being: Theoretical overview and empirical update. *Cognitive Therapy and Research, 16*, 201–228.

Scheier, M. F., Fenigstein, A., & Buss, A. H. (1974). Self-awareness and physical aggression. *Journal of Experimental Social Psychology, 10*, 264–273.

Schein, E. (1956). The Chinese indoctrination program for prisoners of war: A study of attempted "brainwashing." *Psychiatry, 19*, 149–172.

Scherer, K. (1982). Methods of research on vocal communication: Paradigms and parameters. In K.R. Scherer & P. Ekman (Eds.), *Handbook of methods in nonverbal behavior research* (pp.136–198). New York: Cambridge University Press.

Scherer, K.R., & Wallbott, H.G. (1994). Evidence for universality and cultural variation of differential emotion response patterning. *Journal of Personality and Social Psychology, 66*, 310–328.

Schimmack, U., Oishi, S., & Diener, E. (2002). Cultural influences on the relation between pleasant emotions and unpleasant emotions: Asian dialectic philosophies or individualism-collectivism? *Cognition and Emotion, 16*, 705–719.

Schlenker, B. R. (1980). *Impression management: The self-concept, social identity, and interpersonal relations*. Monterey, CA: Brooks/Cole.

Schlenker, B.R., & Miller, R. S. (1977). Egocentrism in groups: Self-serving biases or logical information processing? *Journal of Personality and Social Psychology, 35*, 755–764.

Schmader, T., & Johns, M. (2003). Converging evidence that stereotype threat reduces working memory capacity. *Journal of Personality and Social Psychology, 85*, 440–452. doi:10.1037/0022-3514.85.3.440

Schmader, T., Johns, M., & Forbes, C. (2008). An integrated process model of stereotype threat on performance. *Psychological Review, 115*, 336–356. doi:10.1037/0033-295X.115.2.336

Schneider, D. J. (1973). Implicit personality theory: A review. *Psychological Bulletin, 79*, 294–309.

Schneider, W., & Shiffrin, R. M. (1977). Controlled versus automatic human information processing: I. Detection, search, and attention. *Psychological Review, 84*, 1–66.

Schooler, J. W. (1999). Seeking the core: The issues and evidence surrounding recovered accounts of sexual trauma. In I. M. Williams & V. I. Banyard (Eds.), *Trauma and memory* (pp.203–216). Thousand Oaks, CA: Sage.

Schooler, J. W., Fiore, S. M., & Brandimonte, M. A. (1997). At a loss from words: Verbal overshadowing of perceptual memories. *Psychology of Learning and Motivation, 37*, 291–340.

Schriesheim, C. A., Tepper, B. J., & Tetrault, L. A. (1994). Least preferred co-worker score, situational control, and leadership effectiveness: A meta-analysis of contingency model performance predictions. *Journal of Applied Psychology, 79*, 561–573.

Schultz, N. R., Jr., & Moore, D. (1984). Loneliness: Correlates, attributions, and coping among older adults. *Personality and Social Psychology Bulletin, 10*, 67–77.

Schuster, B., Forsterlung, F., & Weiner, B. (1989). Perceiving the causes of success and failure: A cross-cultural examination of attributional concepts. *Journal of Cross-Cultural Psychology, 20*, 191–213.

Schwartz, G. E., Weinberger, D. A., & Singer, J. A. (1981). Cardiovascular differentiation of happiness, sadness, anger, and fear following imagery and exercise. *Psychosomatic Medicine, 43*, 343–364.

Schwartz, S. H. (1975). The justice of need and the activation of humanitarian norms. *Journal of Social Issues, 31*, 111–136.

Schwartz, S.H., & Bilsky, W. (1990). Toward a theory of the universal content and structure of values: Extensions and cross-cultural replications. *Journal of Personality and Social Psychology, 58*, 878–891.

Schwarz, N. (1990). Feelings as information: Informational and motivational functions of affective states. In E. T. Higgins & R. M. Sorrentino (Eds.), *Handbook of motivation and cognition* (Vol. 2, pp.527–561). New York: Guilford Press.

Schwarz, N., & Clore, G. L. (1983). Mood, misattribution, and judgments of well-being: Informative and directive functions of affective states. *Journal of Personality and Social Psychology, 45*, 513–523.

Sears, D. O., & Henry, P. J. (2005). Over thirty years: A contemporary look at symbolic racism. In M. P. Zanna (Ed.), *Advances in experimental social psychology* (Vol. 37, pp.95–150). San Diego: Elsevier.

Sedikides, C. (1992). Mood as a determinant of attentional focus. *Cognition and Emotion, 6*, 129–148.

Sedikides, C., & Anderson, C. A. (1994). Casual perceptions of inter-trait relations: The glue that holds person types together. *Personality and Social Psychology Bulletin, 21*, 294–302.

Sedikides, C., Gaertner, L., & Yoshiyasu, T. (2003). Pancultural self-enhancement. *Journal of Personality and Social Psychology, 84,* 60–79.

Sedikides, C., & Skowronski, J. J. (1997). The symbolic self in evolutionary context. *Personality and Social Psychology Review, 1,* 80–102.

Seery, M. D. (2011). Resilience: A silver lining to experiencing adverse life events. *Current Directions in Psychological Science, 20,* 390–394.

Seery, M. D., Holman, E. A., & Silver, R. C. (2010). Whatever does not kill us: Cumulative lifetime adversity, vulnerability, and resilience. *Journal of Personality and Social Psychology, 99,* 1025–1041.

Seery, M. D., Leo, R. J., Lupien, S. P., Kondrak, C. L., & Almonte, J. L. (2013). An upside to adversity? Moderate cumulative lifetime stress adversity is associated with resilient responses in the face of controlled stressors. *Psychological Science, 24,* 1181–1189.

Segal, M. W. (1974). Alphabet and attraction: An unobtrusive measure of the effect of propinquity in a field setting. *Journal of Personality and Social Psychology, 30,* 654–657.

Seligman, C., Fazio, R. H., & Zanna, M. P. (1980). Effects of salience of extrinsic rewards on liking and loving. *Journal of Personality and Social Psychology, 38,* 453–460.

Seligman, M. E. P. (1975). *Helplessness: On depression, development, and death.* San Francisco: Freeman.

Seligman, M. E. P., & Csíkszentmihályi, M. (2000). Positive psychology: An introduction. *American Psychologist, 55,* 5–14.

Seta, C. E., & Seta, J. J. (1995). When audience presence is enjoyable: The influences of audience awareness of prior success on performance and task interest. *Basic and Applied Social Psychology, 16,* 95–108.

Shackelford, T. K., & Hansen, R. D. (Eds.). (2013). *Evolution of violence.* New York: Springer.

Shackelford, T. K., & Larsen, R. J. (1997). Facial asymmetry as an indicator of psychological, emotional, and physiological distress. *Journal of Personality and Social Psychology, 72,* 456–466.

Shah, J. (2003). Automatic for the people: How representations of significant others implicitly affect goal pursuit. *Journal of Personality and Social Psychology, 84,* 661–681.

Shapiro, P. N., & Penrod, S. D. (1986). Meta-analysis of facial identification studies. *Psychological Bulletin, 100,* 139–156.

Sharpe, D., Adair, J. G., & Roese, N. J. (1992). Twenty years of deception research: A decline in subjects' trust? *Personality and Social Psychology Bulletin, 18,* 585–599.

Shaver, P. R., & Brennan, K. A. (1992). Attachment style and the "big five" of personality traits: Their connections with each other and with romantic relationship outcomes. *Personality and Social Psychology Bulletin, 18,* 536–545.

Shea, C. T., Davisson, E. K., & Fitzsimons, G. M. (2013). Riding other people's coattails: Individuals with low self-control value self-control in other people. *Psychological Science, 24,* 1031–1036.

Shearn, D., Bergman, E., Hill, K., Abel, A., & Hinds, L. (1990). Facial coloration and temperature responses in blushing. *Psychophysiology, 27,* 687–693.

Sheldon, K. M., & Kasser, T. (1998). Pursuing personal goals: Skills enable progress but not all progress is beneficial. *Personality and Social Psychology Bulletin, 24,* 1319–1331.

Shepperd, J. A., & Arkin, R. M. (1991). Behavioral other-enhancement: Strategically obscuring the link between performance and evaluation. *Journal of Personality and Social Psychology, 60,* 79–88.

Sherif, M. (1936). *The psychology of social norms.* New York, NY: Harper & Brothers.

Sherif, M., Harvey, O. J., White, B. J., Hood, W. R., & Sherif, C. W. (1961/1988). *The Robbers Cave experiment: Intergroup conflict and cooperation.* Middletown, CT: Wesleyan University Press.

Shermer, M. (1997). *Why people believe weird things: Pseudoscience, superstition, and other confusions of our time.* New York: Freeman.

Shermer, M. (2011). *The believing brain.* New York: St. Martin's Press.

Shively, C. A., Register, T. C., & Clarkson, T. B. (2009). Social stress, visceral obesity, and coronary artery atherosclerosis in female primates. *Obesity, 17,* 1513–1520.

Showers, C. J. (1992). Compartmentalization of positive and negative self-knowledge: Keeping bad apples out of the bunch. *Journal of Personality and Social Psychology, 62,* 1036–1049.

Shrauger, J. S., & Shoeneman, T. J. (1979). Symbolic interactionist view of self-concept: Through the looking glass darkly. *Psychological Bulletin, 86,* 549–573.

Shweder, R. A. (1991). *Thinking through cultures: Expeditions in cultural psychology.* Cambridge, MA: Harvard University Press.

Shweder, R. A., Much, N. C., Hahapatra, M., & Park, L. (1997). The "big three" of morality (autonomy, community, divinity) and the "big three" explanations of suffering. In A. Brandt & P. Rozin (Eds.), *Morality and health.* New York: Routledge.

Sibley, C. G., & Duckitt, J. (2008). Personality and prejudice: A meta-analysis and theoretical review. *Personality and Social Psychology Review, 12,* 248–279.

Sicoly, F., & Ross, M. (1979). Facilitation of ego-biased attributions by means of self-serving observer feedback. *Journal of Personality and Social Psychology, 35,* 734–741.

Sidanius, J., & Pratto, F. (1999). *Social dominance: An intergroup theory of social hierarchy and oppression*. Cambridge: Cambridge University Press.

Silver, N. (2012). *The signal and the noise: Why so many predictions fail: But some don't*. New York: Penguin.

Simon, D., & Holyoak, K. J. (2002). Structural dynamics of cognition: From consistency theories to constraint satisfaction. *Personality and Social Psychology Review, 6*, 283-294.

Simpson, J. A., Rholes, W. S., & Phillips, D. (1996). Conflict in close relationships: An attachment perspective. *Journal of Personality and Social Psychology, 71*, 899-914.

Sinclair, L., & Kunda, Z. (2000). Motivated stereotyping of women: She's fine if she praised me but incompetent if she criticized me. *Personality and Social Psychology Bulletin, 26*, 1329-1342.

Singer, J. L., & Goldman, C. D. (1954). Experimentally contrasted social atmospheres in group psychotherapy with chronic schizophrenics. *Journal of Social Psychology, 40*, 23-37.

Singh, D. (1993). Adaptive significance of female physical attractiveness: Role of waist-to-hip ratio. *Journal of Personality and Social Psychology, 80*, 894-917.

Skinner, B. F. (1938). *The behavior of organisms*. Englewood Cliffs, NJ: Appleton-Century-Crofts.

Skinner, B. F. (1953). *Science and human behavior*. New York: Macmillan.

Skinner, B. F. (1971). *Beyond freedom and dignity*. New York: Knopf.

Skitka, L. J., & Tetlock, P. E. (1993). Providing public assistance: Cognitive and motivational processes underlying liberal and conservative policy preferences. *Journal of Personality and Social Psychology, 65*, 1205-1223.

Skov, R. B., & Sherman, S. J. (1986). Information-gathering processes: Diagnosticity, hypothesis-confirmatory strategies, and perceived hypothesis confirmation. *Journal of Experimental Social Psychology, 22*, 93-121.

Slovic, P., & Fischhoff, B. (1977). On the psychology of experimental surprises. *Journal of Experimental Psychology: Human Perception and Performance, 3*, 455-551.

Smaldino, P. E., Pickett, C. Sherman, J., & Schank, J. (2012). An agent-based model of social identity dynamics. *Journal of Artificial Societies and Social Simulation, 15*(4), 7. http://jasss.soc.surrey.ac.uk/15/4/7.html

Smaldino, P. E. (2013). Measures of individual uncertainty for ecological models: Variance and entropy. *Ecological Modelling, 254*, 50-53.

Smaldino, P. E., Schank, J. C., & McElreath, R. (2013). Increased costs of cooperation help cooperators in the long run. *The American Naturalist, 181*, 451-463.

Smith, A. E., Jussim, L., & Eccles, J. S. (1999). Do self-fulfilling prophecies accumulate, dissipate, or remain stable over time? *Journal of Personality and Social Psychology, 77*, 548-565.

Smith, D. M., Neuberg, S. L., Judice, T. N., & Biesanz, J. C. (1997). Target complicity in the confirmation and disconfirmation of erroneous perceiver expectations: Immediate and longer term implications. *Journal of Personality and Social Psychology, 73*, 974-991.

Smith, E. R., & Conrey, F. R. (2007). Agent-based modeling: A new approach for theory building in social psychology. *Personality and Social Psychology Review, 11*, 87-104.

Smith, E. R., & DeCoster, J. (1999). Associative and rule-based processing: A connectionist interpretation of dual-process models. In S. Chaiken & Y. Trope (Eds.), *Dual-process theories in social psychology* (pp. 323-336). New York: Guilford Press.

Smith, S. M., & Shaffer, D. R. (1995). Speed of speech and persuasion: Evidence for multiple effects. *Personality and Social Psychology Bulletin, 21*, 1051-1060.

Smith, S. S., & Richardson, D. (1983). Amelioration of deception and harm in psychological research: The important role of debriefing. *Journal of Personality and Social Psychology, 44*, 1075-1082.

Smith, V. L., Kassin, S. M., & Ellsworth, P. C. (1989). Eyewitness accuracy and confidence: Within versus between-subjects correlations. *Journal of Applied Psychology, 74*(2), 356-359.

Snijders, C., Matzat, U., & Reips, U. (2012). Big data: Big gaps of knowledge in the field of Internet. *International Journal of Internet Science, 7*, 1-5.

Snyder, C. R. (1978). The "illusion" of uniqueness. *Journal of Humanistic Psychology, 18*, 33-41.

Snyder, M. (1974). Self-monitoring of expressive behavior. *Journal of Personality and Social Psychology, 30*, 526-537.

Snyder, M., Grether, J., & Keller, K. (1974). Staring and compliance: A field experiment on hitchhiking. *Journal of Applied Social Psychology, 4*, 165-170.

Snyder, M., & Haugen, J. A. (1994). Why does behavioral confirmation occur? A functional perspective on the role of the perceiver. *Journal of Experimental Social Psychology, 30*, 218-246.

Snyder, M., & Swann, W. B., Jr. (1978a). Hypothesis testing processes in social interaction. *Journal of Personality and Social Psychology, 36*, 1202-1212.

Snyder, M., & Swann, W. B., Jr. (1978b). Behavioral confirmation in social interaction: From social perception to social reality. *Journal of Experimental Social Psychology, 14*, 148-162.

Sokolov, E. M. (1963). Higher nervous function: The orienting reflex. *Annual Review of Physiology, 25*, 545-580.

Sorensen, J., Wrinkle, R., Brewer, V., & Marquart, J. (1999). Capital punishment and deterrence: Examining the effect of executions on murder in Texas. *Crime and Delinquency, 45*, 481-493.

Spence, J. T., & Helmreich, R. L. (1972). The attitudes toward women scale: An objective instrument to measure attitudes toward the rights and roles of women in contemporary society. *Catalog of Selected Documents in Psychology, 2*, 66 (Ms. No. 153).

Spencer, C. M., Steele, C. M., & Quinn, D. M. (1999). Stereotype threat and women's math performance. *Journal of Experimental Social Psychology, 35*, 4-28.

Spencer, S. J., Fein, S., Wolfe, C. T., Fong, C., & Dunn, M. A. (1998). Automatic activation of stereotypes: The role of self-image threat. *Personality and Social Psychology Bulletin, 24*, 1139-1152.

Sporer, S. I., Koehnken, G., & Malpass, R. S. (Eds.). (1996). *Psychological issues in eyewitness identification*. Mahwah, NJ: Erlbaum.

Stallen, M., De Dreu, C.K.W., Shalvi, S., Smidts, A., & Sanfey, A. G. (2012). The herding hormone: Oxytocin stimulates in-group conformity. *Psychological Science, 23*, 1288-1292.

Stapel, D. A., & Koomen, W. (2000). How far do we go beyond the information given? The impact of knowledge activation on interpretation and inference. *Journal of Personality and Social Psychology, 78*, 19-37.

Steblay, N. H. (1987). Helping behavior in rural and urban environments: A meta-analysis. *Psychological Bulletin, 102*(3), 346-356.

Steele, C. M. (1997). A threat in the air: How stereotypes shape intellectual identity and performance. *American Psychologist, 52*, 613-629. doi:10.1037/0003-066X.52.6.613

Steele, C. M., & Aronson, J. (1995). Stereotype threat and the intellectual test performance of African Americans. *Journal of Personality and Social Psychology, 69*, 797-811.

Stel, M., Blascovich, J., McCall, C., Mastop, J., Van Baaren, R., & Vonk, R. (2010). Mimicking disliked others: Effects of a priori liking on the mimicry-liking link. *European Journal of Social Psychology, 40*, 867-880.

Stel, M., Van Baaren, R. B., & Vonk, R. (2008). Effects of mimicking: Acting prosocially by being emotionally moved. *European Journal of Social Psychology, 38*, 965-976.

Stel, M., & Vonk, R. (2010). Mimicry in social interaction: Benefits for mimickers, mimickees, and their interaction. *British Journal of Psychology, 101*, 311-323.

Stemmler, G. (1989). The autonomic differentiation of emotions revisited: Convergent and discriminant validation. *Psychophysiology, 26*, 617-632.

Stephan, C. W., Renfro, L., & Stephan, W. G. (2004). The evaluation of multicultural education programs: Techniques and meta-analysis. In W. G. Stephan & W. P. Vogt (Eds.), *Education programs for improving intergroup relations, theory, research, and practice* (pp. 227-242). New York: Teachers College Press.

Sternberg, R. I. (1986). A triangular theory of love. *Psychological Review, 93*, 119-135.

Stewart, J. E. (1980). Defendant's attractiveness as a factor in the outcome of criminal trials: An observational study. *Journal of Applied Psychology, 10*, 348-361.

Stipek, D. J. (1984). Young children's performance expectations: Logical analysis or wishful thinking? In J. Nicholls (Ed.), *Advances in motivation and achievement: The development of achievement motivation* (Vol. 3, pp. 33-56). Greenwich, CT: JAI Press.

Stokes, J., & Levin, I. (1986). Gender differences in predicting loneliness from social network characteristics. *Journal of Personality and Social Psychology, 51*, 1069-1074.

Stone, I. (1977). *The family, sex and marriage in England: 1500-1800*. London: Perennial.

Stone, J., Lynch, C. I., Sjomeling, M., & Darley, J. M. (1999). Stereotype threat effects on black and white athletic performance. *Journal of Personality and Social Psychology, 77*, 1213-1227.

Stone, J., Wiegand, A. W., Cooper, J., & Aronson, E. (1997). When exemplification fails: Hypocrisy and the motives for self-integrity. *Journal of Personality and Social Psychology, 72*, 54-65.

Stoner, J.A.F. (1961). *A comparison of individual and group decisions involving risk*. Unpublished master's thesis, MIT, Cambridge, MA.

Storey, A. E., Walsh, C. L., Quinton, R. L., & Wynne-Edward, K. E. (2000). Hormonal correlates of paternal responsiveness in new and expectant fathers. *Evolution and Human Behavior, 21*, 79-95.

Storms, M. D., & Nisbett, R. E. (1970). Insomnia and the attribution process. *Journal of Personality and Social Psychology, 16*, 319-328.

Strack, F., Martin, L. L., & Stepper, S. (1988). Inhibiting and facilitating conditions of the human smile: A nonobtrusive test of the facial feedback hypothesis. *Journal of Personality and Social Psychology, 54*, 768-777.

Street, R.L., Jr., Brady, R. M., & Putman, W. B. (1983). The influence of speech rate stereotypes and rate similarity on listeners' evaluations of speakers. *Journal of Language and Social Psychology, 2*, 37-56.

Strick, M., Dijksterhuis, A., Bos, M. W., Sjoerdsma, A., Van Baaren, R. B., & Nordgren, L. F. (2009). *A meta-analysis on unconscious thought effects*. Unpublished manuscript. www.unconsciouslab.com/publications/Paper_Meta.doc

Stroebe, W. (2012). The truth about Triplett (1898), but nobody seems to care. *Perspectives on Psychological Science, 7*, 54-57.

Stroebe, W., Diehl, M., & Abakoumkin, G. (1992). The illusion of group effectivity. *Personality and Social Psychology Bulletin, 18*, 643-650.

Stroebe, W., Stroebe, M., Abakoumkin, G., & Schut, H. (1996). The role of loneliness and social support in adjustment to loss: A test of attachment versus stress theory. *Journal of Personality and Social Psychology, 70*, 1241-1249.

Strogatz, S. (2003). *Sync: The emerging science of spontaneous order*. New York: Hyperion Books.

Stroufe, B., Chaikin, A., Cook, R., & Freeman, V. (1977). The effects of physical attractiveness on honesty: A socially desirable response. *Personality and Social Psychology, 3*, 59–62.

Struch, N., & Schwartz, S. H. (1989). Intergroup aggression: Its predictors and distinctness from in-group bias. *Journal of Personality and Social Psychology, 56*, 364–373.

Suls, J. M., & Fletcher, B. (1983). Social comparison in the social and physical sciences: An archival Study. *Journal of Personality and Social Psychology, 44*, 575–580.

Suls, J. M., & Wheeler, L. (Eds.). (2000). *Handbook of social comparison: Theory and research*. New York: Kluwer Academic/Plenum.

Surowiecki, J. (2004). *The wisdom of crowds*. New York: Random House.

Svenson, O. (1981). Are we all less risky and more skillful than our fellow drivers? *Acta Psychologica, 47*(2), 143–148. https://doi.org/10.1016/0001-6918(81)90005-6

Swaab, R. I., Maddux, W. W., & Sinaceur, M. (2011). Early words that work: When and how virtual linguistic mimicry facilitates negotiation outcomes. *Journal of Experimental Social Psychology, 47*, 616–621.

Swaminathan, N. (2008, April). Why does the brain need so much power? *Scientific American*.

Swann, W. B., Jr. (1990). To be adored or to be known: The interplay of self-enhancement and self-verification. In E. T. Higgins & R. M. Sorrentino (Eds.), *Handbook of motivation and cognition: Foundations of social behavior* (Vol. 2, pp. 408–448). New York: Guilford.

Swann, W. B., Jr. (1996). *Self-traps: The elusive quest for higher self-esteem*. New York: Freeman.

Swann, W. B., Jr., & Ely, R. J. (1984). A battle of wills: Self-verification versus behavioral confirmation. *Journal of Personality and Social Psychology, 46*, 1287–1302.

Swann, W. B., Jr., Griffin, J. R., Jr., Predmore, S. C., & Gaines, B. (1987). The cognitive-affective crossfire: When self-consistency confronts self-enhancement. *Journal of Personality and Social Psychology, 52*(5), 861–869.

Swann, W. B., Jr., Hixon, J. G., & De La Ronde, C. (1992). Embracing the bitter "truth": Negative self-conceptions and marital commitment. *Psychological Science, 3*, 118–121.

Swann, W. B., Jr., Hixon, J. G., Stein-Seroussi, A., & Gilbert, D. T. (1990). The fleeting glimpse of praise: Behavioral reactions to self-relevant feedback. *Journal of Personality and Social Psychology, 59*, 17–26.

Swann, W. B., Jr., & Predmore, S. C. (1985). Intimates as agents of social support: Sources of consolation or despair? *Journal of Personality and Social Psychology, 49*, 1609–1617.

Swann, W. B., Jr., Stein-Seroussi, A., & Giesler, B. (1992). Why people self-verify. *Journal of Personality and Social Psychology, 62*, 392–401.

Swartz, K. B., Sarauw, D., & Evans, S. (1999). Comparative aspects of mirror self-recognition in great apes. In S. T. Parker, R. W. Mitchell, & H. L. Miles (Eds.), *The mentalities of gorillas and orangutans: Comparative perspectives* (pp. 283–294). Cambridge: Cambridge University Press.

Sweller, J. (1988). Cognitive load during problem solving: Effects on learning. *Cognitive Science, 12*, 257–285.

Swim, J. K., Aikin, K. J., Hall, W. S., & Hunter, B. A. (1995). Sexism and racism: Old-fashioned and modern prejudices. *Journal of Personality and Social Psychology, 68*, 199–214.

Symons, D. (1979). *The evolution of human sexuality*. New York: Oxford University Press.

Tafarodi, R. W., Lo, C., Yamaguchi, S., Lee, W. W.-S., & Katsura, H. (2004). The inner self in the three countries. *Journal of Cross-Cultural Psychology, 35*, 97–117.

Tajfel, H. (1982). *Social identity and intergroup relations*. Cambridge: Cambridge University Press.

Tajfel, H., & Billig, M. G. (1974). Familiarity and categorization in intergroup behavior. *Journal of Experimental Social Psychology, 10*, 159–170.

Tamir, M. (2009). What do people want to feel and why? *Current Directions in Psychological Science, 18*, 101–105.

Tanford, S., & Penrod, S. (1984). Social influence model: A formal integration of research on majority and minority influence processes. *Psychological Bulletin, 95*, 189–225.

Tangney, J. P., Baumeister, R. F., & Boone, A. I. (2004). High self-control predicts good adjustment, less pathology, better grades, and interpersonal success. *Journal of Personality, 72*, 271–322.

Tangney, J. P., & Fischer, K. W. (Eds.). (1995). *Self-conscious emotions: The psychology of shame, guilt, embarrassment, and pride*. New York: Guilford Press.

Tangney, J. P., Miller, R. S., Flicker, L., & Barlow, D. H. (1996). Are shame, guilt, and embarrassment distinct emotions? *Journal of Personality and Social Psychology, 70*, 1256–1264.

Tapias, M. P., Glaser, J., Keltner, D., Vasquez, K., & Wickens, T. (2007). Emotion and prejudice: Specific emotions toward outgroups. *Group Processes and Intergroup Relations, 10*, 27–39.

Taylor, S. E. (2006). Tend and befriend: Biobehavioral bases of affiliation under stress. *Current Directions in Psychological Science, 15*, 273–277.

Taylor, S.E., & Brown, J.D. (1988). Illusion and well-being: A social psychological perspective on mental health. *Psychological Bulletin, 103*, 193-210.

Taylor, S.E., & Fiske, S.T. (1975). Point of view and perceptions of causality. *Journal of Personality and Social Psychology, 32*, 439-445.

Taylor, S.E., & Lobel, M. (1989). Social comparison activity under threat: Downward evaluation and upward contacts. *Psychological Review, 96*, 569-575.

Tellegen, A., Lykken, D.T., Bouchard, T.J., Jr., Wilcox, K.J., & Rich, S. (1988). Personality similarity in twins reared apart and together. *Journal of Personality and Social Psychology, 54*, 1031-1039.

Tesser, A. (1976). Attitude polarization as a function of thought and reality constraints. *Journal of Research in Personality, 10*, 183-194.

Tesser, A. (1978). Self-generated attitude change. In L. Berkowitz (Ed.), *Advances in experimental social psychology* (Vol. 11, pp.85-117). New York: Academic Press.

Tesser, A. (1988). Toward a self-evaluation maintenance model of social behavior. In L. Berkowitz (Ed.), *Advances in experimental social psychology* (Vol. 21, pp.181-227). Orlando, FL: Academic Press.

Tesser, A. (1993). The importance of heritability in psychological research: The case of attitudes. *Psychological Review, 100*, 129-142.

Tesser, A., Martin, L., & Cornell, D. (1996). On the substitutability of self-protective mechanisms. In P.M. Gollwitzer & J.A. Bargh (Eds.), *The psychology of action* (pp.48-68). New York: Guilford Publications.

Tetlock, P.E. (2007). Psychology and politics: The challenges of integrating levels of analysis in social science. In A.W. Kruglanski & E.T. Higgins (Eds.), *Social psychology: Handbook of basic principles* (pp.888-912). New York: Guilford.

Thagard, P., & Nerb, J. (2002). Emotional gestalts: Appraisal, change, and the dynamics of affect. *Personality and Social Psychology Review, 6*, 274-282.

Thaler, R.H. (1980). Towards a positive theory of consumer choice. *Journal of Economic Behavior and Organization, 1*, 39-60.

Thayer, R.E., Newman, R., & McClain, T.M. (1994). Self-regulation of mood: Strategies for changing a bad mood, raising energy, and reducing tension. *Journal of Personality and Social Psychology, 67*, 910-925.

Thibaut, J.W., & Kelley, H.H. (1959). *The social psychology of groups*. New York: John Wiley & Sons.

Thibaut, J.W., & Walker, L. (1975). *Procedural justice: A psychological analysis*. Hillsdale, NJ: Lawrence Erlbaum Associates.

Thorndike, E.L. (1920). A constant error in psychological ratings. *Journal of Applied Psychology, 4*, 25-29.

Thornhill, R., & Gangestad, S.W. (1994). Human fluctuating asymmetry and sexual behavior. *Psychological Science, 5*, 297-302.

Thornhill, R., & Gangestad, S.W. (1999). The scent of symmetry: A human sex pheromone that signals fitness? *Evolution and Human Behavior, 20*, 175-201.

Thornhill, R., Gangestad, S.W., Miller, R., Scheyd, G., McCollough, J.K., & Franklin, M. (2003). Major histocompatibility complex genes, symmetry, and body scent attractiveness in men and women. *Behavioral Ecology, 14*, 668-678.

Thornton, D., & Arrowood, A.J. (1966). Self-evaluation, self-enhancement, and the locus of social comparison. *Journal of Experimental Social Psychology, 1* (Suppl.), 40-48.

Tice, D.M. (1991). Esteem protection or enhancement? Self-handicapping motives and attributions differ by trait self-esteem. *Journal of Personality and Social Psychology, 60*, 711-725.

Tice, D.M., & Baumeister, R.F. (1990). Self-esteem, self-handicapping, and self-presentation: The strategy of inadequate practice. *Journal of Personality, 58*, 443-464.

Tice, D.M., Bratslavasky, E., & Baumeister, R.F. (2001). Emotional distress regulation takes precedence over impulse control: If you feel bad, do it! *Journal of Personality and Social Psychology, 80*, 53-67.

Todorov, A., & Bargh, J.A. (2002). Automatic sources of aggression. *Aggression and Violent Behavior, 7*, 53-68.

Todorov, A., Mandisodza, A.N., Goren, A., & Hall, C.C. (2005). Inferences of competence from faces predict election outcomes. *Science, 308*, 1623-1626.

Tolman, E.C. (1932). *Purposive behavior in animals and man*. New York: Century.

Tomkins, S.S. (1962). *Affect, imagery, consciousness: I: The positive affects*. New York: Springer.

Tomkins, S.S. (1963). *Affect, imagery, consciousness: II: The negative affects*. New York: Springer.

Tononi, G., & Edelman, G.M. (1998). Consciousness and complexity. *Science, 282*, 1846-1851.

Tooby, J., & Cosmides, L. (1992). The psychological foundations of culture. In J.H. Barkow, L. Cosmides, & J. Tooby (Eds.), *The adapted mind: Evolutionary psychology and the generation of culture* (pp.19-136). New York: Oxford University Press.

Tracy, J.L., & Robbins, R.W. (2003). "Death of a (narcissistic) salesman": An integrative model of fragile self-esteem. *Psychological Inquiry, 14*, 57-62.

Trafimow, D., & Finlay, K.A. (1996). The importance of subjective norms for a minority of people: Between-subjects and within-subject analyses. *Personality and Social Psychology Bulletin, 22*, 820-828.

Triandis, H.C. (1989). The self and social behavior in differing cultural contexts. *Psychological Review, 96*, 506-520.

Triandis, H.C. (1994). *Culture and social behavior*. New York: McGraw-Hill.

Triandis, H.C. (1995). *Individualism and collectivism*. Boulder, CO: Westview Press.

Triandis, H. C., Bontempo, R., Villareal, M. J., Asai, M., & Lucca, N. (1988). Individualism and collectivism: Cross-cultural perspectives on self-ingroup relationships. *Journal of Personality and Social Psychology, 54,* 323-338.

Triandis, H. C., Malpass, R. S., & Davidson, A. R. (1973). Psychology and culture. *Annual Review of Psychology, 24,* 355-378.

Triplett, N. (1898). The dynamogenic factors in pacemaking and competition. *American Journal of Psychology, 9,* 507-533.

Trivers, R. (1971). The evolution of reciprocal altruism. *Quarterly Review of Biology, 46,* 35-57.

Trope, Y., & Fishbach, A. (2000). Counter-active self-control in overcoming temptation. *Journal of Personality and Social Psychology, 79,* 493-506.

Trope, Y., & Gaunt, R. (2000). Processing alternative explanations of behavior: Correction or integration? *Journal of Personality and Social Psychology, 79,* 344-354.

Trope, Y., & Lieberman, N. (2003). Temporal construal. *Psychological Review, 110,* 403-421.

Tsai, J. L., Chentsova-Dutton, Y., Freire-Bebeau, L., & Przymus, D. E. (2002). Emotional expression and physiology in European Americans and Hmong Americans. *Emotion, 2,* 380-397.

Tugade, M., & Fredrickson, B. (2007). Regulation of positive emotions: Emotion regulation strategies that promote resilience. *Journal of Happiness Studies, 8,* 311-333.

Turner, M. E., & Pratkanis, A. R. (1993). Effects of preferential and meritorious selection on performance: An examination of intuitive and self-handicapping perspectives. *Personality and Social Psychology Bulletin, 19,* 47-58.

Turner, R. H., & Killian, L. M. (1957). *Collective behavior.* Englewood Cliffs, NJ: Prentice-Hall.

Tversky, A., & Khaneman, D. (1973). Availability: A heuristic for judging frequency and probability. *Cognitive Psychology, 5,* 207-232.

Tversky, A., & Khaneman, D. (1974). Judgment under uncertainty: Heuristics and biases. *Science, 185,* 1124-1131.

Twenge, J. M. (2017). *iGen.* New York: Simon & Schuster.

Twenge, J. M., Baumeister, R. F., Tice, D. M., & Stucke, T. S. (2001). If you can't join them, beat them: Effects of social exclusion on aggressive behavior. *Journal of Personality and Social Psychology, 81,* 1058-1069.

Twenge, J. M., Catanese, K. R., & Baumeister, R. F. (2002). Social exclusion causes self-defeating behavior. *Journal of Personality and Social Psychology, 83,* 606-615.

Ucros, C. G. (1989). Mood state-dependent memory: A meta-analysis. *Cognition and Emotion, 3,* 139-167.

Uleman, J. S. (1987). Consciousness and control: The case of spontaneous trait inferences. *Personality and Social Psychology Bulletin, 13,* 337-354.

Vaes, J., Paladino, M. P., Castelli, L., Leyens, J. P., & Giovanazzzi, A. (2003). On the behavioral consequences of infra-humanization: The implicit role of uniquely human emotions in intergroup relations. *Journal of Personality and Social Psychology, 85,* 1016-1034.

Valdesolo, P., & DeSteno, D. A. (2007). Moral hypocrisy: Social groups and the flexibility of virtue. *Psychological Science, 18,* 689-690.

Valdesolo, P., & DeSteno, D. A. (2008). The duality of virtue: Deconstructing the moral hypocrite. *Journal of Experimental Social Psychology, 44,* 1334-1338.

Vallacher, R. R. (2007). Local acts, global consequences: A dynamic systems perspective on torture. *Peace and Conflict: Journal of Peace Psychology, 34,* 445-450.

Vallacher, R. R. (2015). From choice to gridlock: Dynamic bases of constructive versus dysfunctional political process. In J. P. Forgas, K. Fiedler, & W. D. Crano (Eds.), *Social psychology and politics: 17th Sydney symposium of social psychology* (pp. 209-226). New York: Taylor & Francis.

Vallacher, R. R., Coleman, P. T., Nowak, A., & Bui-Wrzosinska, L. (2010). Rethinking intractable conflict: The perspective of dynamical systems. *American Psychologist, 65,* 262-278.

Vallacher, R. R., Coleman, P. T., Nowak, A., Bui-Wrzosinska, L., Liebovitch, L., Kugler, K., & Bartoli, A. (2013). *Attracted to conflict: Dynamic foundations of destructive social relations.* Berlin: Springer.

Vallacher, R. R., & Nowak, A. (Eds.). (1994). *Dynamical systems in social psychology.* San Diego: Academic Press.

Vallacher, R. R., & Nowak, A. (1997). The emergence of dynamical social psychology. *Psychological Inquiry, 4,* 73-99.

Vallacher, R. R., & Nowak, A. (2007). Dynamical social psychology: Finding order in the flow of human experience. In A. W. Kruglanski & E. T. Higgins (Eds.), *Social psychology: Handbook of basic principles* (2nd ed., pp. 734-758). New York: Guilford Press.

Vallacher, R. R., Nowak, A., Froehlich, M., & Rockloff, M. (2002). The dynamics of self-evaluation. *Personality and Social Psychology Review, 6,* 370-379.

Vallacher, R. R., Nowak, A., & Kaufman, J. (1994). Intrinsic dynamics of social judgment. *Journal of Personality and Social Psychology, 67,* 20-34.

Vallacher, R. R., Read, S. J., & Nowak, A. (Eds.). (2017). *Computational social psychology.* New York: Psychology Press.

Vallacher, R. R., & Selz, K. (1991). Who's to blame? Action identification in allocating responsibility for alleged rape. *Social Cognition, 9,* 194-219.

Vallacher, R. R., & Solodky, M. (1979). Objective self-awareness, standards of evaluation, and moral behavior. *Journal of Experimental Social Psychology, 15,* 254-262.

Vallacher, R. R., Van Geert, P., & Nowak, A. (2015). The intrinsic dynamics of psychological process. *Current Directions in Psychological Science, 24*, 58-64.

Vallacher, R. R., & Wegner, D. M. (1985). *A theory of action identification*. Hillsdale, NJ: Lawrence Erlbaum Associates.

Vallacher, R. R., & Wegner, D. M. (1987). What do people think they're doing? Action identification and human behavior. *Psychological Review, 94*, 3-15.

Vallacher, R. R., & Wegner, D. M. (1989). Levels of personal agency: Individual differences in action identification. *Journal of Personality and Social Psychology, 57*, 660-671.

Vallacher, R. R., & Wegner, D. M. (2012). Action identification theory. In P.A.M. Van Lange, A. W. Kruglanski, & E. T. Higgins (Eds.), *Handbook of theories of social psychology* (pp. 327-348). Thousand Oaks, CA: Sage.

Vallacher, R. R., Wegner, D. M., & Frederick, J. (1987). The presentation of self through action identification. *Social Cognition, 5*, 301-322.

Vallacher, R. R., Wegner, D. M., & Somoza, M. P. (1989). That's easy for you to say: Action identification and speech fluency. *Journal of Personality and Social Psychology, 56*, 199-208.

Van Baaren, R. B., Holland, R. W., Kawakami, K., & Van Knippenberg, A. (2004). Mimicry and prosocial behavior. *Psychological Science, 15*(1), 71-74.

Van Baaren, R. B., Holland, R. W., Steenaert, B., & Van Knippenberg, A. (2003). Mimicry for money: Behavioral consequences of imitation. *Journal of Experimental Social Psychology, 39*, 393-398.

Van Baaren, R. B., Horgan, T. G., Chartrand, T. L., & Dijkmans, M. (2004). The forest, the trees, and the chameleon: Context dependence and mimicry. *Journal of Personality and Social Psychology, 86*, 453-459.

Van Boven, L., & Gilovich, T. (2003). To do or to have? That is the question. *Journal of Personality and Social Psychology, 85*, 1193-1202.

Vandello, J. A., & Cohen, D. (1999). Patterns of individualism and collectivism across the United States. *Journal of Personality and Social Psychology, 77*, 279-292.

Van de Ven, P., Bornholt, L., & Bailey, M. (1996). Measuring cognitive, affective, and behavioral components of homophobic reaction. *Archives of Sexual Behavior, 25*, 155-179.

Van Goozen, S.H.M., & Frijda, N. H. (1993). Emotion words used in six European countries. *European Journal of Social Psychology, 23*, 89-95.

Van Lange, P.A.M. (Ed.). (2006). *Bridging social psychology: The benefits of transdisciplinary approaches*. Hillsdale, NJ: Lawrence Erlbaum.

Van Lange, P.A.M. (1991). Being better but not smarter than others: The Muhammad Ali effect at work in interpersonal situations. *Personality and Social Psychology Bulletin, 17*, 689-693.

Van Lange, P.A.M., Joireman, J., Parks, C. D., & Van Dijk, E. (2013). The psychology of social dilemmas: A review. *Organizational Behavior and Human Decision Processes, 120*, 125-141.

Van Lange, P.A.M., Otten, W., DeBruin, E.M.N., & Joireman, J. A. (1997). Development of prosocial, individualistic, and competitive orientations: Theory and preliminary evidence. *Journal of Personality and Social Psychology, 73*, 733-746.

Varshnay, W. (2002). *Ethnic conflict and civic life*. New Haven, CT: Yale University Press.

Vinokur, A., & Ajzen, I. (1982). Relative importance of immediate and prior events: A causal primacy effect. *Journal of Personality and Social Psychology, 42*, 820-829.

Vohs, K. D., Baumeister, R. F., & Ciarocco, N. (2005). Self-regulation and self-presentation: Regulatory resource depletion impairs impression management and effortful self-presentation depletes regulatory resources. *Journal of Personality and Social Psychology, 88*, 632-657.

Vohs, K. D., Baumeister, R. F., Schmeichel, B. J., Twenge, J. M., Nelson, N. M., & Tice, D. M. (2008). Making choices impairs subsequent self-control: A limited resource account of decision-making, self-regulation, and active initiative. *Journal of Personality and Social Psychology, 94*, 883-898.

Vohs, K. D., & Heatherton, T. F. (2000). Self-regulatory failure: A resource-depletion approach. *Psychological Science, 11*, 249-254.

Vohs, K. D., Meade, N. L., & Goode, M. R. (2006). The psychological consequences of money. *Science, 314*, 1154-1156.

Vohs, K. D., & Schooler, J. (2008). The value of believing in free will: Encouraging a belief in determinism increases cheating. *Psychological Science, 19*, 49-54.

Volpato, C., Maass, A., Mucchi-Faina, A., & Vitti, E. (1990). Minority influence and categorization. *European Journal of Social Psychology, 20*, 119-132.

Von Hippel, W., Sekaquaptewa, D., & Vargas, P. (1997). The linguistic intergroup bias as an implicit indicator of prejudice. *Journal of Experimental Social Psychology, 33*, 490-509.

Wade, M. J. (1977). An experimental study of group selection. *Evolution, 31*, 134-153.

Wagner, R. C. (1975). Complementary needs, role expectations, interpersonal attraction and the stability of work relationships. *Journal of Personality and Social Psychology, 32*, 116-124.

Waldrop, M. M. (1992). *Complexity: The emerging science at the edge of order and chaos*. New York: Simon & Schuster.

Walker, S., Richardson, D. S., & Green, L. R. (2000). Aggression among older adults: The relationship of interaction networks and gender role to direct and indirect responses. *Aggressive Behavior*, *26*, 145-154.

Wallach, M. A., Kogan, N., & Bem, D. J. (1962). Group influence on individual risk taking. *Journal of Abnormal Social Psychology*, *1*, 1-19.

Walster, E. B., Berscheid, E., & Walster, G. W. (1973). New directions in equity research. *Journal of Personality and Social Psychology*, *25*, 151-176.

Warneken, E., & Tomasello, M. (2008). Extrinsic rewards undermine altruistic tendencies in 20-month-olds. *Developmental Psychology*, *44*, 1785-1788.

Wason, P. C. (1966). Reasoning. In B. M. Foss (Ed.), *New horizons in psychology* (pp. 135-151). Harmondsworth: Penguin.

Watson, D. (1982). The actor and the observer: How are their perceptions and causality divergent? *Psychological Bulletin*, *92*, 682-700.

Watson, D., Clark, L. A., & Tellegen, A. (1988). Development and validation of brief measures of positive and negative affect: The PANAS scales. *Journal of Personality and Social Psychology*, *54*, 1063-1070.

Watson, D., & Tellegen, A. (1985). Toward a consensual structure of mood. *Psychological Bulletin*, *98*, 219-235.

Watts, D. (2003). *Six degrees: The science of a connected age*. New York: W. W. Norton & Company.

Waugh, C. E., & Fredrickson, B. L. (2006). Nice to know you: Positive emotions, self-other overlap, and complex understanding in the formation of a new relationship. *Journal of Positive Psychology*, *1*, 93-106.

Weary, G., & Williams, J. P. (1990). Depressive self-presentation: Beyond self-handicapping. *Journal of Personality and Social Psychology*, *58*, 892-898.

Weber, R., Ritterfeld, U., & Mathiak, K. (2006). Does playing violent video games induce aggression? Empirical evidence of a functional magnetic resonance imaging study. *Media Psychology*, *8*(1), 39-60.

Webster, D. M., & Kruglanski, A. W. (1994). Individual differences in need for cognitive closure. *Journal of Personality and Social Psychology*, *67*, 1049-1062.

Wedekind, C., Seebeck, T., Bettens, F., & Paepke, A. J. (1995). MHC-dependent mate preferences in humans. *Proceedings: Biological Sciences*, *260*, 245-249.

Wegener, D. T., & Petty, R. E. (1994). Mood management across affective states: The hedonic contingency hypothesis. *Journal of Personality and Social Psychology*, *66*, 1034-1048.

Wegner, D. M. (1994). Ironic processes of mental control. *Psychological Review*, *101*, 34-52.

Wegner, D. M. (2002). *The illusion of conscious will*. Cambridge, MA: MIT Press.

Wegner, D. M., Erber, R., & Bowman, R. (1993). On trying not to be a sexist. Unpublished manuscript. (Cited in Wegner, D. M. (1994). Ironic processes of mental control. *Psychological Review*, *101*, 34-52.)

Wegner, D. M., Erber, R., & Raymond, P. (1991). Transactive memory in close relationships. *Journal of Personality and Social Psychology*, *61*, 923-929.

Wegner, D. M., Erber, R., & Zanakos, S. (1993). Ironic processes in the mental control of mood and mood-related thought. *Journal of Personality and Social Psychology*, *65*, 1093-1104.

Wegner, D. M., Lane, J. D., & Dimitri, S. (1994). The allure of secret relationships. *Journal of Personality and Social Psychology*, *66*, 287-300.

Wegner, D. M., Quillian, F., & Houston, C. E. (1996). Memories out of order: Thought suppression and the disturbance of sequence memory. *Journal of Personality and Social Psychology*, *71*, 680-691.

Wegner, D. M., & Vallacher, R. R. (1977). *Implicit psychology: An introduction to social cognition*. New York: Oxford University Press.

Wegner, D. M., Vallacher, R. R., Kiersted, G. W., & Dizadji, D. M. (1986). Action identification in the emergence of social behavior. *Social Cognition*, *4*, 18-38.

Wegner, D. M., Vallacher, R. R., Macomber, G., Wood, R., & Arps, K. (1984). The emergence of action. *Journal of Personality and Social Psychology*, *46*, 269-279.

Wegner, D. M., & Wheatley, T. (1999). Apparent mental causation: Sources of the experience of will. *American Psychologist*, *54*, 480-491.

Weiner, B. (1980). A cognitive (attribution)-emotion model of motivated behavior: An analysis of judgments of help-giving. *Journal of Personality and Social Psychology*, *39*, 186-200.

Weiner, B., Graham, S., & Reyna, C. (1997). An attributional examination of retributive versus utilitarian philosophies of punishment. *Social Justice Research*, *10*, 431-452.

Weiner, N. (1948). *Cybernetics, or control and communication in the animal and the machine*. Cambridge, MA: MIT Press.

Weisfeld, G. (1994). Aggression and dominance in the social world of boys. In J. Archer (Ed.), *Male violence* (pp. 43-69). New York: Routledge.

Weiss, W. (1953). A "sleeper" effect in opinion change. *The Journal of Abnormal and Social Psychology*, *48*, 173-180.

Weldon, E., & Mustari, L. (1988). Felt dispensability in groups of coactors: The effects of shared responsibility and explicit anonymity on cognitive effort. *Organizational Behavior and Human Decision Processes, 41*, 330-351.

Wells, G. I., & Olson, E. A. (2003). Eyewitness testimony. *Annual Review of Psychology, 54*, 277-295.

Wells, G. I., Olson, E. A., & Charman, S. D. (2002). The confidence of eyewitnesses in their identifications from lineups. *Current Directions in Psychological Science, 11*, 151-154.

Wells, G. I., Small, M., Penrod, S. D., Malpass, R. S., Fulero, S. M., & Brimacombe, C.A.E. (1998). Eyewitness identification procedures: Recommendations for lineups and photospreads. *Law and Human Behavior, 22*, 603-645.

Wells, G. I., Wright, E. F., & Bradfield, A. I. (1999). Witnesses to crime: Social and cognitive factors governing the validity of people's reports. In R. Roesch, S. D. Hart, & J.R.P. Ogloff (Eds.), *Psychology and law: The state of the discipline* (pp. 53-88). New York: Kluwer.

Wells, G. L., & Petty, R. E. (1980). The effects of overt head movement on persuasion: Compatibility and incompatibility of responses. *Basic and Applied Social Psychology, 1*, 219-230.

West, S. G., & Brown, T. J. (1975). Physical attractiveness, the severity of emergency and helping: A field experiment and interpersonal simulation. *Journal of Experimental Social Psychology, 11*, 531-538.

West, S. G., Whitney, G., & Schnedler, R. (1975). Helping a motorist in distress: The effects of sex, race, and neighborhood. *Journal of Personality and Social Psychology, 31*, 691-698.

Westaby, J. D., Pfaff, D. L., & Redding, N. (2014). Psychology and social networks: A dynamic theory perspective. *American Psychologist, 69*, 269-284.

Weyant, J. (1978). Effects of mood states, costs, and benefits on helping. *Journal of Personality and Social Psychology, 10*, 1169-1176.

Wheatley, T., & Haidt, J. (2005). Hypnotic disgust makes moral judgments more severe. *Psychological Science, 16*, 780-785.

Wheeler, L., Koestner, R., & Driver, R. (1982). Related attributes in the choice of comparison others: It's there, but it isn't all there is. *Journal of Experimental Social Psychology, 18*, 489-500.

Wheeler, L., & Miyake, K. (1992). Social comparison in everyday life. *Journal of Personality and Social Psychology, 62*, 760-773.

Whisman, V. (1996). *Queer by choice.* New York: Routledge.

White, G. L., Fishbein, S., & Rutstein, J. (1981). Passionate love and the misattribution of arousal. *Journal of Personality and Social Psychology, 41*, 56-62.

White, R. W. (1959). Motivation reconsidered: The concept of competence. *Psychological Review, 66*, 297-333.

Wicker, A. W. (1969). Attitudes versus actions: The relationship of verbal and overt behavioral responses to attitude objects. *Journal of Social Issues, 25*, 41-78.

Wicklund, R. A., & Brehm, J. W. (1976). *Perspectives on cognitive dissonance.* Hillsdale, NJ: Erlbaum.

Wicklund, R. A., & Frey, D. (1980). Self-awareness theory: When the self makes a difference. In D. M. Wegner & R. R. Vallacher (Eds.), *The self in social psychology* (pp. 31-54). New York: Oxford University Press.

Wiederman, M. W. (1997). The truth must be in here somewhere: Examining the gender discrepancy in self-reported lifetime number of sex partners. *Journal of Sex Research, 34*, 375-386.

Wiegman, O., Kuttschreuter, M., & Baarda, B. (1992). A longitudinal study of the effects of television viewing on aggressive and prosocial behavior. *British Journal of Social Psychology, 31*, 147-164.

Wilkinson, R., & Pickett, K. (2009). *The spirit level: Why more equal societies almost always do better.* New York: Bloomsbury Press.

Willer, R. (2004). The effects of government-issued terror warnings on presidential approval ratings. *Current Research in Social Psychology, 10*, 1-12.

Williams, D. R., & Collins, C. (1995). U.S. socioeconomic and racial differences in health: Patterns and predictions. *Annual Review of Sociology, 21*, 349-386.

Williams, J. R., Insel, T. R., Harbaugh, C. R., & Carter, C. S. (1994). Oxytocin administered centrally facilitates formation of a partner preference in female prairie voles (*Microtus Ochrogaster*). *Journal of Neuroendocrinology, 6*, 247-250.

Williams, K. D. (2001). *Ostracism: The power of silence.* New York: Guilford.

Williams, K. D. (2007). Ostracism. *Annual Review of Psychology, 58*, 425-452.

Williams, K. D., Cheung, C.K.T., & Choi, W. (2000). Cyberostracism: Effects of being ignored over the Internet. *Journal of Personality and Social Psychology, 79*, 748-762.

Williams, K. D., Harkins, S., & Latané, B. (1981). Identifiably as a deterrent to social loafing: Two cheering experiments. *Journal of Personality and Social Psychology, 40*, 303-311.

Willis, J., & Todorov, A. (2006). First impressions: Making up your mind after a 100-ms exposure to a face. *Psychological Science, 17*, 592-598.

Wills, T. A. (1981). Downward comparison principles in social psychology. *Psychological Bulletin, 90*, 245-271.

Wilson, D. S., & Wilson, E. O. (2008). Evolution for the good of the group. *American Scientist, 96*, 380-389.

Wilson, E. O. (2012). *The social conquest of earth.* New York: Liveright Publishing Corporation.

Wilson, M.I., & Daly, M. (1996). Male sexual proprietariness and violence against wives. *Current Directions in Psychological Science,* *5,* 2-7.

Wilson, T.D. (2002). *Strangers to ourselves: Discovering the adaptive unconscious.* Cambridge, MA: Harvard University Press.

Wilson, T.D., Dunn, D.S., Bybee, J.A., Hyman, D.B., & Rotondo, J.A. (1984). Effects of analyzing reasons on attitude-behavior consistency. *Journal of Personality and Social Psychology, 47,* 5-16.

Wilson, T.D., Dunn, D.S., Kraft, D., & Lisle, D.J. (1989). Introspection, attitude change, and attitude-behavior consistency: The disruptive effects of explaining why we feel the way we do. In L. Berkowitz (Ed.), *Advances in experimental social psychology* (Vol. 19, pp.123-205). Orlando: Academic Press.

Wilson, T.D., Hodges, S.D., & LaFleur, S.J. (1995). Effects of introspecting about reasons: Inferring attitudes from accessible thoughts. *Journal of Personality and Social Psychology, 69,* 16-28.

Wilson, T.D., Lindsey, S., & Schooler, T.Y. (2000). A model of dual attitudes. *Psychological Review, 107,* 101-126.

Wilson, T.D., Lisle, D., Schooler, J.W., Hodges, S.D., Klaaren, K.J., & LaFleur, S.J. (1993). Introspecting about reasons can reduce postchoice satisfaction. *Personality and Social Psychology Bulletin, 19,* 331-339.

Wilson, T.D., & Schooler, J.W. (1991). Thinking too much: Introspection can reduce the quality of preferences and decisions. *Journal of Personality and Social Psychology, 60,* 181-192.

Wilson, T.D., & Stone, J.I. (1985). Limitations of self-knowledge: More on telling more than we can know. In P. Shaver (Ed.), *Review of personality and social psychology* (Vol. 6, pp.167-183). Beverly Hills, CA: Sage.

Wilson, T.D., Wheatley, T., Meyers, J.M., Gilbert, D.T., & Axson, D. (2000). Focalism: A source of durability bias in affective forecasting. *Journal of Personality and Social Psychology, 78,* 821-836.

Winch, R.F. (1955). The theory of complementarity needs in mate selection: A test of one kind of complementariness. *American Sociological Review, 20,* 52-56.

Winkielman, P., & Cacioppo, J.T. (2001). Mind at ease puts a smile on the face: Psychophysiological evidence that processing facilitation increases positive affect. *Journal of Personality and Social Psychology, 81,* 989-1000.

Winston, J., Strange, B., O'Doherty, J., & Dolan, R. (2002). Automatic and intentional brain responses during evaluation of trustworthiness of faces. *Nature Neuroscience, 5,* 277-283.

Winter, L., & Uleman, J.S. (1984). When are social judgments made? Evidence for the spontaneousness of trait inferences. *Journal of Personality and Social Psychology, 47,* 237-252.

Wisman, A., & Goldenberg, J.L. (2005). From the grave to the cradle: Evidence that mortality salience engenders a desire for offspring. *Journal of Personality and Social Psychology, 89,* 46-51.

Wittenbrink, B., & Schwarz, N. (Eds.). (2007). *Implicit measures of attitudes.* New York: Guilford Press.

Wixted, J.T., & Wells, G.L. (2017). The relationship between eyewitness confidence and identification accuracy: A new synthesis. *Psychological Science in the Public Interest, 18*(1), 10-65.

Wojnowicz, M.T., Ferguson, M.J., Dale, R., & Spivey, M.J. (2009). The self-organization of explicit attitudes. *Psychological Science, 20,* 1428-1435.

Wolf, S., & Latané, B. (1985). Conformity, innovation, and the psycho-social laws. In S. Moscovici, G. Mugny, & E. Van Avermaet (Eds.), *Perspectives on minority influence* (pp. 201-215). Cambridge: Cambridge University Press.

Wong, A.E., Vallacher, R.R., & Nowak, A. (2016). Intrinsic dynamics of self-evaluation: The role of self-concept clarity. *Personality and Individual Differences, 100,* 167-172.

Wood, J.V. (1996). What is social comparison and how would we study it? *Personality and Social Psychology Bulletin, 22,* 520-537.

Wood, W. (1987). Meta-analytic review of sex differences in group performance. *Psychological Bulletin, 102,* 53-71.

Wood, W., Wong, F.Y., & Chachere, J.G. (1991). Effects of media violence on viewer's aggression in unconstrained social interaction. *Psychological Bulletin, 109,* 371-383.

Wright, D.B., & Stroud, J.N. (2002). Age differences in lineup identification accuracy: People are better with their own age. *Law and Human Behavior, 26,* 641-654.

Wylie, R. (1979). *The self-concept* (Vol. 2). Lincoln: University of Nebraska.

Yerkes, R.M., & Dodson, J.D. (1908). The relation of strength of stimulus to rapidity of habit formation. *Journal of Comparative Neurology and Psychology, 18,* 459-482.

Youngson, N.A., & Whitelaw, E. (2008). Transgenerational epigenetic effects. *Annual Review of Genomics and Human Genetics, 9,* 233-257.

Zadro, L., Williams, K.D., & Richardson, R. (2004). How low can you go? Ostracism by a computer is sufficient to lower self-reported levels of belonging, control, self-esteem, and meaningful existence. *Journal of Experimental Social Psychology, 40,* 560-567.

Zajonc, R.B. (1965). Social facilitation. *Science, 149,* 269-274.

Zajonc, R.B. (1968). Attitudinal effects of mere exposure. *Journal of Personality and Social Psychology, 9* (Monograph Suppl. 2, pt. 2), 1-27.

Zajonc, R.B. (1980). Feeling and thinking: Preferences need no inferences. *American Psychologist, 35,* 151–176.

Zak, P.J. (2005). Trust: A temporary human attachment facilitated by oxytocin. *Behavioral and Brain Sciences, 28,* 368–369.

Zanna, M.P., & Cooper, J. (1974). Dissonance and the pill: An attribution approach to studying the arousal properties of dissonance. *Journal of Personality and Social Psychology, 29,* 703–709.

Zanna, M.P., & Cooper, J. (1976). Dissonance and the attribution process. In J.H. Harvey, W.J. Ickes, & R.F. Kidd (Eds.), *New directions in attribution research* (pp. 199–217). Hillsdale, NJ: Lawrence Erlbaum Associates.

Zanna, M.P., Goethals, G.R., & Hill, J. (1975). Evaluating a sex-related ability: Social comparison with similar others and standard setters. *Journal of Experimental Social Psychology, 11,* 86–93.

Zanna, M.P., Kiesler, C.A., & Pilkonis, P.A. (1970). Positive and negative attitudinal affect established by classical conditioning. *Journal of Personality and Social Psychology, 14,* 321–328.

Zebrowitz, L.A. (1999). *Reading faces: Window to the soul?* Boulder, CO: Westview Press.

Zebrowitz, L.A., & McDonald, S.M. (1991). The impact of litigants' babyfaceness and attractiveness on adjudications in small claims courts. *Law and Behavior, 15,* 603–623.

Zeigler-Hill, V. (2013). *Self-esteem.* New York: Psychology Press.

Zhong, C., & Leonardelli, G.J. (2008). Cold and lonely: Does social exclusion literally feel cold? *Psychological Science, 19*(9), 838–842.

Zietsch, B., Morley, K., Shekar, S., Verweij, K., Keller, M., Macgregor, S., et al. (2008). Genetic factors predisposing to homosexuality may increase mating success in heterosexuals. *Evolution and Human Behavior, 29,* 424–433.

Zillman, D. (1978). Attribution and misattribution of excitatory reactions. In J.H. Harvey, W.J. Ickes, & R.F. Kidd (Eds.), *New directions in attribution research* (Vol. 2, pp. 335–368). Hillsdale, NJ: Erlbaum.

Zillman, D. (1988). Cognitive excitation interdependencies in aggressive behavior. *Aggressive Behavior, 14,* 51–64.

Zillman, D. (1989). Effects of prolonged consumption of pornography. In D. Zillman & J. Bryant (Eds.), *Pornography: Research advances and early policy considerations* (pp. 127–157). Hillsdale, NJ: Lawrence Erlbaum Associates.

Zillmann, D., & Weaver, J.B., III. (1999). Effects of prolonged exposure to gratuitous violence on provoked and unprovoked hostile behavior. *Journal of Applied Social Psychology, 29,* 145–165.

Zimbardo, P.G. (1970). The human choice: Individuation, reason, and order versus deindividuation, impulse, and chaos. In W.J. Arnold & D. Levine (Eds.), *Nebraska Symposium on Motivation, 1969* (pp. 237–307). Lincoln: University of Nebraska Press.

Zuckerman, E.W., & Jost, J.T. (2001). What makes you think you're so popular? Self-evaluation maintenance and the subjective side of the "friendship paradox." *Social Psychology Quarterly, 64,* 207–223.

Zuckerman, M. (1979). Attribution of success and failure revisited: The motivational bias is alive and well in attribution theory. *Journal of Personality, 47,* 245–287.

Zuckerman, M., Kieffer, S.C., & Knee, C.R. (1998). Consequences of self-handicapping: Effects on coping, academic performance, and adjustment. *Journal of Personality and Social Psychology, 74,* 1619–1628.

Zuckerman, M., & Tsai, F.F. (2005). Costs of self-handicapping. *Journal of Personality, 73,* 411–442.

SUBJECT INDEX

Note: Page numbers in *italics* indicate figures and in **bold** indicate tables on the corresponding pages.

AUTHOR INDEX